# What Quart
# by Bobby Pe

"Playing quarterback for Coach Bobby Petrino was like a daily master class in offensive football. He taught us every detail of our position and explained why each technique and scheme would work, and it all fit together like a puzzle. It was fun playing in his exciting and creative system where a quarterback could develop all his skills—throw deep, short, move the pocket, run, audible, and surprise with the well-timed trick play.

"Coach would not only call the right play at the right time, but often it was the play that you would least expect. He set the standard on being daring and bold as a play-caller. With his attention to detail, our team always had the utmost confidence because we knew how well he had prepared us."

— Brian Brohm
University of Louisville Quarterback
NFL Quarterback, Green Bay Packers, Buffalo Bills
Offensive Coordinator, Purdue University

"Coach Petrino is an expert at designing plays and developing balanced offenses that can attack a defense both with the run and the pass. A master at the details of each position, Coach has a history of molding his offensive system to fit the talents of his players, especially the quarterback."

— Jeff Brohm
University of Louisville Quarterback
NFL Quarterback, San Fransisco 49ers, San Diego Chargers,
Washington Redskins
Head Football Coach, Purdue University

"It's been said that a good coach can take a player to a place that he can't get to on his own. That was Bob Petrino for me in Jacksonville. Bob was instrumental in my development and played a key role in our success as our offensive coordinator. Bob is regarded as having one of the brightest offensive minds in football and I'm thankful I was able to benefit from his coaching."

— Mark Brunell
Pro Bowl NFL Quarterback, Jacksonville Jaguars, Washington Redskins

"Coach Petrino is a perfectionist. He knows what he wants and how he wants it done and he will not settle for anything less. The attention to detail and the expectation he places on his coaches and players is why he is one of the best offensive minds in the game."

— Stefan LeFors
University of Louisville Quarterback
NFL Quarterback, Carolina Panthers

"With Coach Petrino, I always felt more prepared than the other team before every game and I never thought we were ever out of the game, as long as there was time on the clock. Simply stated, he was always the smartest guy on the field."

— Ryan Mallett
University of Arkansas Quarterback
NFL Quarterback, New England Patriots, Houston Texans, Baltimore Ravens

"Playing for Coach Petrino at Arizona State was amazing! My knowledge of the game was minimal when I first got to ASU and I quickly learned what he expected from his QBs during our first white board session: attention to detail, precise preparation, and thick skin. With his guidance and teaching I was ready when my opportunity to play came in my first game vs. WSU in Pullman. He coached the hell out of me and I never looked back."

— Jake Plummer
Pro Bowl NFL Quarterback, Arizona Cardinals, Denver Broncos

"There are only a few people in life who impact you forever. Coach P is someone I could say has done that for me. I have never walked to the line of scrimmage with more confidence as a quarterback, in knowing I was going to succeed."

— Chris Redman
University of Louisville Quarterback
NFL Quarterback, Baltimore Ravens, Atlanta Falcons

"I felt like Coach always had a grasp of what I did well as a player and the value I brought. Even though I might have been slightly different than his prototype, he found ways to utilize what I did really well and carve it into his system for success. ...11-2 and 29 school records later!

"What parents should want more than anything for their child is to have a chance to be successful. If their child is playing for Coach Petrino they will be pushed and challenged to an extreme level and there is no question Coach will put them in positions that give them the best chance to WIN!"

— Tyler Wilson
University of Arkansas Quarterback
NFL Quarterback, Oakland Raiders

# INSIDE THE POCKET

## An In-Depth Analysis of the Xs and Os

Bobby Petrino
with Joe Metzka, PhD

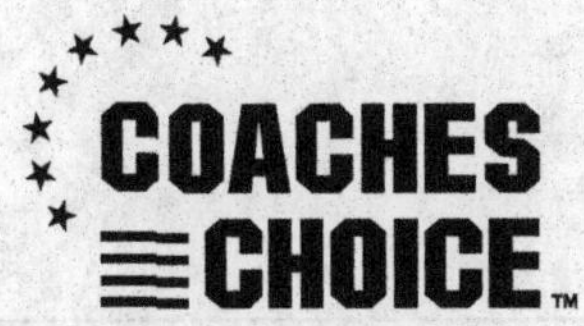

ISBN: 978-1-60679-486-9
Cover design: Cheery Sugabo
Book layout: Bean Creek Studio
Front cover photo: © Scott Kinser/CSM via ZUMA Wire
Back cover photo: © Brian Ciancio/ZUMA Wire

Coaches Choice
P.O. Box 1828
Monterey, CA 93942
www.coacheschoice.com

# Dedication

Coach Petrino dedicates this book to his late father, Coach Bob Petrino, Sr. with special thanks to his wonderful family.

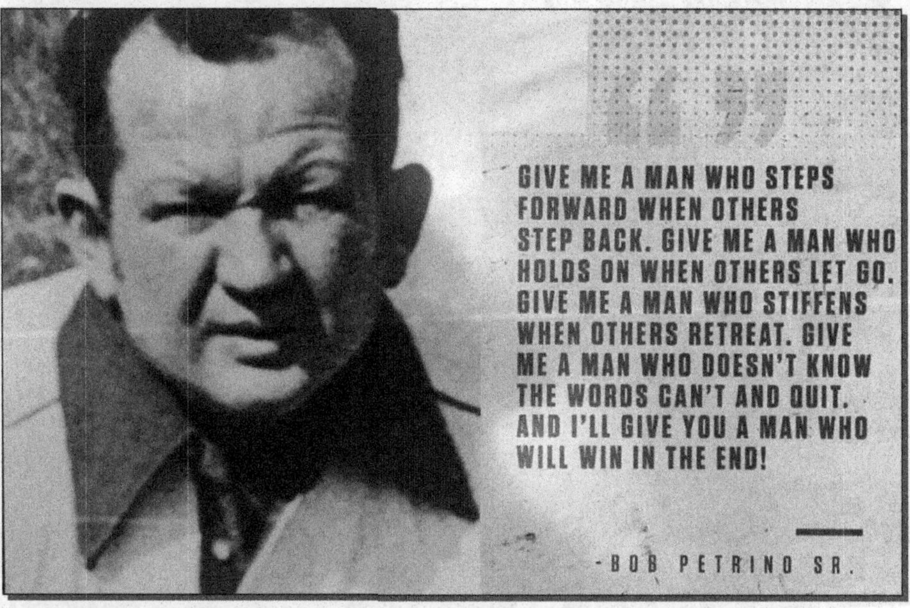


Joe dedicates this book to his late grandfather, Andrew Metzka, and to his late father-in-law, Jeff Moery.

# Contents

Dedication ....... 5
Foreword by Jeff Brohm ....... 8
Introduction by Joe Metzka ....... 9

**Chapter 1:** Philosophy of Offense ....... 13
**Chapter 2:** Passing Game Philosophy; Quarterback Play & Protections ....... 39
**Chapter 3:** Quick Game ....... 89
**Chapter 4:** Dropback Passing ....... 149
**Chapter 5:** Empty ....... 273
**Chapter 6:** Screens ....... 305
**Chapter 7:** Play-Action and Nakeds ....... 325
**Chapter 8:** The Age of RPO ....... 391
**Chapter 9:** Option to the Heisman ....... 417

**Appendix A:** Football Players and Psychology Concepts With Dr. Joe ....... 457
**Appendix B:** Summary of Dr. Joe's Dissertation ....... 473

About the Authors ....... 481

# Foreword

Coach Petrino is an expert at designing plays and developing balanced offenses that can attack a defense both with the run and the pass. A master at the details of each position, Coach has a history of molding his offensive system to fit the talents of his players, especially the quarterback–whether it be a prototypical dropback passer like Brian Brohm or a dual-threat, like Lamar Jackson. He has a unique ability to visualize how a play can exploit a weakness in a defense and knows how to get the ball to his best players in a position where they can be the most productive.

I remember once while game planning during the week, Coach Petrino said that on the first play of the game our opponent will come out in a certain defense and that the running play we will call would dissect that defense in just a way that it would go for a touchdown. When the game started, Coach called our running play and the opponent was in the defense he predicted. Once the ball snapped, the play developed just how he had envisioned and our running back exploded through a huge hole in the line for an 80-yard score.

His attention to detail in the game planning process is second to none, and our staff still follows many of the procedures and preparation philosophies that I learned from him as an assistant coach.

– Jeff Brohm
Head Football Coach, Purdue University
University of Louisville and NFL quarterback

# Introduction

My friendship with Coach Petrino began years ago, when I was a high school coach and he recruited my quarterback. When I left coaching to pursue a PhD in psychology, I kept in touch and maintained the ongoing offer to write a book with him whenever he was up for it. Obviously, I was excited when he agreed last spring to do so. We reached out to Coaches Choice, who immediately gave us the generous green light to write about whatever we wanted.

Coach Petrino visited me in St. Louis over the summer and—without a concrete plan for a book concept—we looked through his playbooks going all the way back to the 1980s and then audio-recorded a series of lectures and film study sessions, in order to capture some ideas. I was a good football player, I was an offensive-minded high school coach, and I hold a terminal academic degree, so I assumed I could explain ball pretty well. However, I joked with him throughout the sessions that it felt like I was taking guitar lessons with Eric Clapton or something. It was humbling and such a joy to really study the nuances of offensive football!

This was not a "ghost writing" project. Coach Petrino personally vetted every word of this book. We perused the audio recordings of about a dozen of these multi-hour sessions and transcribed them all to text. The project started with about 1300 pages of script and from that, we whittled the ideas down into this final product. We revised dozens of drafts of each chapter and he drew up literally hundreds of diagrams, in order to clarify precisely what he wanted to communicate about his offense.

Given coach Petrino's history with quarterbacks, it made sense to focus primarily on quarterback play and the passing game, within his offensive philosophy. We also thought it would be valuable to include some of his insights about "RPOs," as well as some of his recent innovations in the "read-option" game. Coach Petrino was also generous enough to have me include some sport psychology concepts as an appendix.

There's more material we stashed away. For example, we went through all kinds of his practice plans and game planning protocols. We documented several of his favorite runs, including his "down/stretch choice" scheme, as well as some concepts specific to various fronts, such as the 3-4 with "4I" techniques. We put together material on bunch formation plays, 2-point plays, and several other multiples of play packages beyond what's in this book. We went through all kinds of his play-calling ideas: various situational packages, tempo calls by personnel groupings, "2-play" calls, alerts, and kills. We do hope to share some of those ideas in another book.

For now, I hope you can find something in this book to take with you. If you're a ball player, take a coaching point with you to improve your own game. If you're a coach, hopefully, there are some ideas presented to help make your team a little better this season. And if you're a fan like me, I hope you enjoy reading about coach Petrino's offense and getting a sense of how his mind works. So, let's talk ball and take a look "Inside the Xs and Os"!

– Joe Metzka, PhD

## 10 KEYS TO EXCELLENCE

1. **The Power of Attitude.** The attitude you choose to assume toward life and everything it brings you will determine whether you realize your aspirations. What you are capable of achieving is determined by your talent and ability. What you attempt to do s determined by your motivation. How well you do something is determined by your attitude.

2. **Tackle Adversity.** You are going to be knocked down. I have been on top and I have been at the bottom. To achieve success, you are going to have to solve problems. If you react positively to them, you'll be stronger than ever. If you react to setbacks more quickly and positively, you gain a distinct advantage. I've never encountered a person who achieved anything worthwhile who didn't require overcoming obstacles.

3. **Have a Sense of Purpose.** Understand what you are trying to do. Stay completely focused on your primary purpose. Don't get sidetracked. Give a first-rate performance every day.

4. **Make Sacrifice Your Ally.** You can't be successful without making sacrifices. Most losing organizations are overpopulated with people who constantly complain about life's difficulties. They will drain your enthusiasm and energy. Take pride in making sacrifices and having self-discipline.

5. **Adapt or Die.** Things are always changing, so embrace the fact that your life and career are always in transition. Yes, you will achieve goals, but don't fall into the trap of thinking you don't need to go further. Even when you reach the top, remember to stay focused on the fundamentals.

6. **Chase your Dreams.** All great accomplishments start with a dream. Dreams fuel your enthusiasm and vision. They will give you a burning desire to get up and achieve.

7. **Nurture your Self-Image.** A positive self-image grows out of having strong character. To be trustworthy, committed to excellence and show you care for others are the underpinnings of a successful person.

8. **Foster Trust.** Relationships are based on trust. Many people have ruined tremendous opportunity because they didn't have the discipline and decency to do what's right. Continually ask yourself "is this the right thing to do?" Do what you feel is right, regardless of peer pressure or personal desires. Success and confidence will follow close behind.

9. **Commit to Excellence.** Do everything to the best of your ability. Everyone wants to be associated with people who set and maintain high standards. When you lower your standards, you only invite mediocrity.

10. **Handle with Care.** Treat others as you would like to be treated.

## KEY AREAS OF PLAYING QUARTERBACK

### Be a Football Junkie (The Great Ones Are)

- The QB, more than any other position, needs to love the game. The other players will feed off of his enthusiasm to play ball.
- Loves to throw. Like shooting baskets. "Let's go throw some." When you have free time, you are looking for someone to whom to throw.
- Always a positive demeanor. Whether it's about practice, workouts, games, or meetings. Don't be fake.

### Do Your Job

- You have the most responsibility on the offense, but for the team to be successful, just do your job.
- When you attempt to do more than your job, the team is in trouble.

### Completions

- Completions are the bottom line.
- The quarterback's job is to take positive yards on every pass play.
- It doesn't matter what the down and distance is. Take positive yards consistently and you will keep the chains moving.
- Throw catchable balls.

### Have Common Sense

- Know when to take calculated risks.
- Adjust to what is happening on the field.
- Be aware of game conditions/situations (score, weather, etc.).

### Take Care Of The Football

- Key aspect of successful offense.
- QB has biggest role in preventing turnovers.
- Know when to throw the ball away.
- Low turnover margin wins (proven).

# Chapter 1
## Offensive Philosophy

In order to be a great football team, it's critical to have a clearly defined philosophy of offense. Whatever you believe in, it's necessary that everyone in the program understands exactly what you're about. There are a lot of things you need to think through regarding offensive football, but if you want to be successful, you really need to define what you believe in and know why you're doing it.

We have a series of ideas we really believe in, which together form the foundation of our offensive philosophy. First and foremost, if you want to be an elite offense and a winning team, you *must* take care of the quarterback. Next, you have to get your best players the ball, which is what we refer to as "feed the studs." You must master the fundamentals and demand great effort from your team in order to win close games. We believe you must be able to run the football to win. Finally, we believe that you must have a tactical mastery of football strategy, so you can create mismatches and put your players in the best possible position to be successful. In this chapter, each of these ideas is introduced in detail. You'll see how they begin to build on each other, in order to create our offensive philosophy.

## Taking Care of the Quarterback

If your quarterback outplays the other team's quarterback, you have a great chance to win the game. If you want the quarterback to play well, the first priority is that you *must* know his strengths and his weaknesses. It's always about evaluating what he does well and what he needs to improve. That doesn't mean you throw out what he can't do; you continue to work at it, because he can get better at it as the year goes on. But you focus on what he does well!

We believe the most efficient way to get to know your quarterback is what is called a "three-step approach." You want to insert your teaching progression *three times*. Insert it for spring football, insert it for summer workouts, and then insert it in fall camp. So, you plan a 7- or 8-day installation, you repeat it and then you repeat it again a third time. At that point, your quarterback should get it and you should be able to identify his specific abilities. Psychologists claim you learn something three times and you're supposed to know it. That's how we operate, and the players would always understand the whole system at that point.

Throughout those three times through the installation, it's the staff's responsibility to document what you can do well as a team, what your quarterback does well and what you can execute. Then, when you know what the quarterback does best, you mold the playbook around those things. Maybe you don't throw out the other stuff, but now you know what he does best and when the game is on the line, you make *those* play calls. It's your job to play call for your quarterback's success—for his confidence, his energy and for what he gives to other people. You have to do a good job of taking care of the quarterback.

When there are times he's struggling, you have to find him completions. Some years, it was the hitch route, some years it was "Y delay" to the tight end, other seasons it was nakeds or screens. It's amazing how if a quarterback comes out and throws a hitch, a Y delay, and a screen, at that point he's going to feel great about throwing a deep post route for a touchdown, because he just completed three passes in a row, and all of them were as easy as it gets! On the other hand, you need to guide him toward building that confidence; the ability to stand in and throw it when he gets hit. It just changes his *mindset* when you can set those passes up. Throughout the season, you keep working on what he needs to improve on, because it may pay off later.

A great example of this is when I was the offensive coordinator at Auburn. We ran our empty game and we practiced it all year long, but we didn't run it a whole lot in games, because it wasn't really our thing. Our thing was running the ball with great running backs, but we still carried the empty package and worked on it all year long. Then, before the Alabama game, injuries forced us to start a true freshman running back. Since we had worked on the empty game all year, we did a good job with it during the game and made some big plays on it. We were able to find a way to win the game and that's because we stuck with it and the quarterback got better at executing it as the year went on.

Sometimes a quarterback is affected by past experience and you have to work through it with him. For example, you may know he can throw a particular route well, but maybe he fusses with you about it. As a rule, they all have a little bit of what I call "psycho" in them. Even the great lefty Mark Brunell, one of the best quarterbacks to ever play, was sometimes hesitant about things like throws out to his left and his drops to the right in the quick game (lefties often try to cheat their eyes over there to the right). Mark just didn't like outside throws to the field anymore, because he got intercepted for a touchdown once by a guy from Pittsburgh. (Baseball players call that a "yip." It was Steve Sax, right? The second baseman for the Dodgers who could no longer throw the ball to first base?) Mark, however, was willing to address it and work through it. Truly special players are willing to confront the little things like that!

I think one of the aspects of coaching quarterbacks is to be clear how you call them on it, and that goes for all of them at every level, from high school to even a Pro Bowler like Mark. I love grading the quarterbacks and filling out their grade sheet because I think that really makes it clear to them. Mark always laughed at it because he never had any coach in the NFL do a grade sheet. He was like "are you serious? I never got one of these before."

We grade the quarterback on *decision* and *execution*. Every play, I have a *decision* to make, whether it's in the run game, protection, who I'm keying, who I'm throwing the ball to, and so forth. There's a *decision* to make every play, and then I have to *execute it*. That might be the ability to throw the curl route accurately, check the ball down properly, or even just be on the proper track for the run game with good ball handling technique.

I've had quarterbacks who were great decision-makers but never got on the field, because they couldn't *execute*; they just couldn't throw the routes. We've also had the opposite, where they're never going to play if they can't make productive *decisions*. Although, with Lamar Jackson, he could sometimes scramble and convert a 3rd-&-10, rather than throw the route. Yeah, how do you grade that as a bad decision? Good *execution*. He probably got an extra plus for that!

Certainly though, with some guys you have to deliver the message differently than others. And it's about the *timing* of when you call them out. It might not be during the game, but when you're reviewing the video, maybe he's doing a 3-step drop and as it comes out, he always wants to cheat his head over there on his first step, trying to see it early instead of just trusting it. You have to be *honest* with them, they need to be *honest* with themselves. They're all different, and you need to understand what they react positively and negatively to, in order to handle them effectively in practice and during competition.

And to do that, it's okay to "push his buttons" at the right times. That's key for players to understand as well, that if they're going to be able to handle pressure situations in games, they need to first demonstrate that they can handle pressure during practice. That's kind of the brutal honesty of the whole deal is "don't act like you're mad at me, let's just get better!"

I've found that all quarterbacks (in fact, all people) have their unique "attention-getting mechanisms," when they get frustrated. Over the years, I've taken to calling that an "A.G.M." "You have these A.G.M.s and they're not making you a better football player. Just pay attention, fix it, and we'll get better together!" I think they accept it when you present it that way. Then, they begin to understand that you actually improve yourself by correcting mistakes, rather than "showing your A.G.M." Then, they'll start seeing the A.G.M.s from the other players on the team; there would be times in practice with the Jaguars where Mark Brunell would make a throw that didn't make sense, because his progression did not take him there. He'd turn around before I could point it out and say, "just feeding the pigeons, coach." He was just trying to keep the other players happy. He knew all their A.G.M.s. Pretty cool, actually!

Of course, it takes a lot of work with your quarterback to get to that point. For example, quarterbacks are the worst when the play clock is running out—where they completely screw it up, don't see it until the last second, and call timeout. Then he looks at the sideline and puts his hands up like we didn't get the play to him: "A.G.M." You know the quarterback is not going to put it on himself in the middle of the game, so you may not stop to address it. But in the meeting room? "Don't give me that! That was on you. You forgot to look at the play clock."

That's a truth about coaching is you must have the ability to *confront* your players and your other coaches and *demand* that they do things the right way! That's especially true with quarterbacks, if you want to see them fulfill their potential and play at their best. Now obviously, the way you demand things has changed tremendously over my time as a coach. In the old days, my dad used to rattle my cage; just grab my facemask and shake it. You have to demand it, but today you have to do it in a way that they accept and yet you still know it works. It has changed a lot and it continues to get harder. The players today—especially quarterbacks—want you to tell them "this is *why* we are doing this. This is *why* I'm calling you on the A.G.M."

Some of it is to work drills on it. When you're in the classroom coaching quarterbacks, you have the opportunity to point out "drill work," which is where you can see the drill from practice paying off when bullets are flying. You want to get to the point where you're watching the video of games (or scrimmages, or practices) and the quarterbacks can say, "that's drill work!" Whether it's about movement in the pocket or carrying the ball in the throwing position and making the throw for a touchdown, or even the proper track for a handoff, every skill should be reinforced in a drill. I think every coach on offense should also be able to do that, so the players can see the "drill work," and they understand that it carries over to the game. That's how our "drill tapes" are made, so there's video for the players to study of plays showing up in games of *that* drill. When you can get the players saying "drill work!", while they're watching video, and they're taking pride in those drills carrying over to the game, you have a chance to be pretty good. That's the case with the entire team, but that definitely applies to the quarterback.

Another key to coaching a quarterback is to understand his ability to picture what you're saying to him. You work on what psychologists call *mental imagery* by asking him to see it and then say it the same way you do. Your ability to make in-game adjustments with him on the sideline depends on your ability to communicate clearly and *say* the same things; picture it the *same way*. Then, when you're both on the sideline during a game and you say, "ok now, when we get a 2-high safety look and the boundary safety drops down," he gets the picture in his mind. Then, you can make precise, efficient adjustments. He can get to that point if you work together on *mental imagery* and understand how he pictures things in his mind.

On occasion you make the quarterbacks do that in the meetings, and even draw with their hands in the air, because, sometimes, critical adjustments that happen during the game you don't have time to draw up on a chalkboard. The players—and particularly the quarterback—just have to be able to get a mental picture of something like "this is a 6-1, double-dog defense." I always *see* the defense I'm talking about. So, everything that you teach the quarterbacks, you need to know they can picture it as well.

If you can't do *mental imagery* and build a picture of things in your mind, you're never going to be a great quarterback. For example, I got to coach John Friesz at the University of Idaho. He was the third ever Walter Payton Trophy winner, as the best player in 1-AA (what is now called the NCAA Football Championship Series or "FCS") and he went on to play in the NFL. He used to say to me "yeah, you know, that mental imaging really works. I actually learn a lot more when I'm driving from Spokane to Seattle than I really do watching video." People may not believe that, but it's a true story! If you can picture the play in your mind and learn even while you're driving, you're doing everything possible to find out how good you can be!

Those *mental reps* are critical when you're away from practice. In fact, the best backup quarterbacks have consistently great *mental* practices. He's got to be watching closely, and have the discipline to know the play, see the front & coverage of the defense, and take those *mental reps*. If he works at it, he will improve daily and then be fully prepared to succeed when he gets his chance in a game.

A lot of times what we'll do to start with is to come up after practice, have the quarterbacks pick up the "skelly" script (some teams call this "7-on-7") and say, "okay, everyone go home, draw up all the plays, and put your progressions in." Then, the next day, you do the same thing; pick up a skelly script and say, "okay, here's what I want you to do tonight." They can even be studying in bed: read the play, close their eyes, *see* the play, *see* the coverage, and go through the progression. I don't know how you can coach a game on the sideline, if the quarterback can't picture things in his mind!

We've always asked quarterbacks to quiz each other on our plays. Psychologists say they learn faster if they do that. Jake Plummer and his business partner designed a really good system called Ready List Pro (http://readylistsports.com/) where you can do this on a computer. Since all these kids today are growing up with technology, they can just pull it up online and it will test them. We installed it—hand signals and all—and our quarterbacks liked doing the weekly tests on the computer.

Quarterbacks must have the ability to confront their weaknesses and improve them. When I was at Auburn, Jason Campbell was our quarterback and he was always willing to work hard on his skills. When I first got him, he actually held the ball with his thumb above his index finger. I had him practice every night with a football down at a 45-degree angle and made him hold it there, to force his index finger above his thumb in his throwing grip. He'd pull it to his chest, then push the point out. My son, Nick, was a little kid at that time and Jason would practice it with him, just over and over. We just had them sit there for hours and work at it and Jason never once complained about it! We wanted to do every little thing possible to take care of our quarterback and he showed everyone he was willing to work hard at every detail!

You obviously make sure to take care of the quarterback during games as well. There was no question that Jason was going to be our starter, but we had two freshmen starting at tackles, a true freshman guard, three young receivers and I was like, "I think we should start the senior until these freshmen get better, and then bring Jason in." Later, he came in and won a game for us off the bench, and then once he started some games, the fans really got behind him. Jason's hard work paid off and he went on to a career in the NFL.

Taking care of the quarterback started the same way with Lamar Jackson as a true freshman in 2015 at Louisville. We had a very specific package for him against Auburn in the opener and he kept working and working at it. At first, we knew he couldn't learn the entire offense, so we just created a package which focused on what his strengths were at that point. We didn't put him under the center at all, we just put him in gun where he has a chance to be an athlete and make plays. We started him with an 80-play package of four formations, four runs, one draw or screen from each formation, and five each of quick game, dropback, and play-action. Then, as he kept growing, we'd add what we could add, and he kept getting better.

He came in after that first season and—this was his word choice—he said, "I want to be a *real* quarterback." So, for the bowl prep against Texas A&M, he came in every morning at 6:00 a.m. and went back through all the installation of the entire offense, so he could work at becoming what he called a "*real* quarterback." We all saw what happened for him the next year (winning the Heisman Trophy in 2016). You have to be honest with your quarterback and build a level of trust in order to help him confront his weaknesses, so he can accent his strengths. As a coach, it's your job to be able to help him identify and address whatever those are. Regardless of how unusual or unorthodox any issue may seem at first, you *must* take care of the quarterback.

## "F.T.S."

Our offensive philosophy, particularly with playcalling, always starts with "F.T.S.," which is "Feed the Studs." That basically means "get the ball to your best guys." It's always tough to watch a game where the best player on the team only touches the ball 10 times. Even when I was a kid growing up, I always thought, "what are you doing?" So, what we always try to do, first and foremost, is find a way to get the ball to our best players, so that they can go make plays.

That has always started with our opening script. The way we always did an opening script is we would come in on Wednesday morning and after watching the video of Tuesday's practice, I asked each coach to give me three plays (naturally the offensive line coach gave three runs and the receiver coach gave three passes). I'd then add what I liked, we listed all those up on the board by category—runs, quick game, dropback, play-action, screens/draws—and from that, we'd select the first series. We would just say, "okay, 1st-&-10 how do we want to open the game, run or pass?"

After we get those scripted plays up there, then we would go back through and say, "okay, who gets the ball here?" So, you'd say "okay, #8, or #9, or #23?" Then someone might say "hey man, we're not getting the ball to this guy at all." So, you might go back and change the play sequence to say "we've got to get him the ball early," because great players play better if you get them the ball early. Confidence and momentum really go together!

I never felt like it was bad for receivers or running back to be "selfish," as long as their actions didn't create an issue with the other players. Hell yeah, you want the ball! That's great! You *want* guys to want the ball, especially when the game is on the line. It's just key that they don't become a distraction with their attitude in a way that negatively affects other players. That is part of the "feed the studs" philosophy, not only because they would make plays for you, but because it helps their mentality as the game goes on, especially a guy that you get the ball to early. That's been the case with all the athletes I've coached at all levels, in every sport. The playmakers want the ball!

Another thing that you add to those first scripted plays that you sell to the offensive line is "hey, here's how we're going to run the ball on them," because all they want to know about is running. They want to feel like they can establish the line of scrimmage and run the football. When I was coaching at Idaho, we had beaten Boise State for 14 straight years, but this one year, there was no way we were supposed to beat them. They had this great defensive end. So, what we did in that first series is we gave every offensive lineman a shot at that defensive end, whether they were pulling and kicking him out, or double-teaming him or flipping the tight end so that they could leverage him; our back ended up rushing for a ton of yards and we beat the heck out of them. It's a *mental* game, and I believe the first part of it is about getting your players going. And of course, you want to score points! We've had teams where throughout the season, you scored on 10 out of 12 first drives. And they take pride in it!

I've always wanted players to memorize that first series, to *visualize* it. By Wednesday night, they know what our openers are. They should spend 10-to-15 minutes going through the first series: see the play, close their eyes, and picture themselves doing it. And you *always* visualize yourself making the play! You take those *mental reps* making the play, and then do it again Thursday and Friday. We do it again in our walkthrough and that's also the last thing you do in "clap" session, before you go to the game is to visualize the first series of plays, whether it's 8 or 12, or whatever you believe in.

We've mostly settled on the "first 8," but there are some years where it's been 12 openers. I think it's whatever you're most comfortable doing—though I don't think you need 20 or 25; that's excessive to me, because 3rd downs and certain places on the field take precedence over staying on the script. (In a game, you come off the script anytime it's 3rd down, or sometimes if you get in the red zone, you come off the script but then go back to it the next series.)

To make sure our "studs" get the ball, we also script the first series of the 3rd quarter. We go in at halftime and go through how to handle the pressures we've seen, what adjustments we need to make, and what we're going to do. Then we'll script the first six plays of the second half, which is always going to come back to "get the ball to our best guys," with a list of all the plays that worked in the first half. It comes down to the players: know who you're throwing the ball to, know who you're handing it to, and know how the quarterback is maintaining confidence. You've got to be able to get your quarterback to play well and you do that by "feeding the studs."

We always have a "get it to" section on our game plan and call sheet. So, let's say #9 is your best receiver, there's "get it to #9," which are plays where you know he's got a high chance to get the ball. In Jacksonville that was "get it to #82," Jimmy Smith. I knew what Jimmy was good at and how we were going to get him the ball. So, we'd "get it to" Fred Taylor and whoever your best players are. If you don't move the ball in a series, you go back and take a look at that: let's get our good players the ball and get them going.

The other thing that goes into "F.T.S." is matchups. Not only do I want to get the ball to these players, but I want to match up my best against their worst, whether it's through motion, shifting, or changing positions and alignments. That is something that's evolved over the years I've been coaching, being able to line up guys at different positions.

In some seasons, the X receiver was your #1 guy. Then, maybe the next year, the Z receiver was your #1 guy. So, what you did was you found ways to disguise their alignment: line them up in a 2x2 set into the tight end, or the other way from a 3x1, as either #2 to the 3-receiver side or solo over on the 1-on-1 side. Then, line him up in your "trips" formation as the #3 guy. You'd go into a game and say, "hey, we're not going to just let them bracket our best receiver and take him out of the game. We're going to be able to find a formation or motion or shift where he gets a 1-on-1."

Ideally, it's 1-on-1 vs. their worst corner or their #3 pass defender; what's always big to me is "how do I get him 1-on-1 with the safety?" At best, that safety is the #3 cover guy. They might even have a corner sitting on the sideline who is a better cover guy than that safety. Then, it's also about, "how do I get him matched up on a linebacker, or a nickel or dime defender?" Because again, the nickel or dime defender isn't going to be as good in coverage as those two starting corners.

Personnel and formation trends have changed over the years, but we have always tried to be as multiple as possible, in order to achieve our best matchups. We continue to work out of 21 or 20 personnel, 12 or 11 personnel. If you have tight ends with the ability to run wide receiver routes, you can line them up outside of the slot receivers and really dictate the matchups you want from the defenses you face.

Look at how the New England Patriots won the Super Bowl in 2019: they used their own personnel packages to get the Rams defense into base personnel, and then dispersed into empty formations to force them into a coverage mismatch. I really believe that's how they won the game. They got Edelman loose on the grass inside and then they threw the inside seam to Gronk along the college numbers. The Pats have done a really good job of being able to line up in various empty sets and yet also be able to run the ball out of those same personnel groupings. Then, at tempo, they won't allow the defense to substitute when they get caught playing base and they're stuck with a linebacker covering Edelman.

Sometimes, playcallers can get caught up in a "system," or worrying about whatever trendy play to call next, rather than focusing on matchups. I've always believed first and foremost in getting the ball to your best players, ideally against their worst. When we're game planning, we study the defensive schemes, but we really study personnel to determine what matchups we can get for our "studs" against their worst players. We work really hard at identifying the best matchups you can get in each game and finding ways to exploit them. To be a great offense, we believe you should always be thinking in terms of "Feed the Studs."

## Win With Fundamentals

I really believe that most people have the same plays, the same diagrams, and the same Xs and Os. It's really about how you coach *within* the Xs and Os. How do you get the plays to be executed precisely? Everyone in your organization needs to make a commitment to becoming an expert at what they do. Every man must understand the techniques and fundamentals of his position and be willing to work hard to perfect them.

As a team, you have to continue to work on technique and fundamentals throughout the entire season. The plays you call are certainly important, but you really win with your players and your technique. As you set up a practice plan, I always work to keep enough individual time in there so you could continue to improve and get better as the year went on. As you establish and emphasize the techniques, then you can really challenge the players to understand the details of their positions.

We always started in the offseason with written tests and verbiage, which really starts with your staff. What I really like to do at first is say, "ok, I've got five guys here on the offensive staff, let's send them to five different conventions and clinic everyone on our running game." You want everyone to understand the blocking schemes the same way, but you'd like all five guys to use exactly the same verbiage and draw the lines exactly the same way, so that everybody's on the same page. It's not okay to have a new guy come in and use the old verbiage that he had always used, in order to coach his position. He's got to "join the club" and become part of the team. That isn't always easy because coaches will say, "well, I've always called that something else." I think that's something that all has to fit together and the only way your players can do it is if the coaches do it together first. You have to be able to demand that they all use uniform language and draw plays the same way.

That's something Jake Plummer still jokes with me about: when I brought him in at Arizona State, I put him on the board in camp and said, "ok, draw up this first play." He was not great at drawing plays to start with and I would say, "that is the worst drawing I've ever seen! That route looks like it's about four yards!"

Jake is a free-living guy. He doesn't have a whole lot of things that worry him. He would look at me, then look at the board and just say, "coach, there's no lines on the board." So, I'd say "well, that doesn't look like a 12-yard out to me! Erase it and draw it again!" And I'd just get on him about the details and drawing things the right way. We worked hard at the techniques and fundamentals. Later that season when the starting quarterback got hurt, Jake went in there as a true freshman and did a good job. Obviously, he's had a great career, but it started with his willingness to get on the same page with us right away and establish a clear foundation in the fundamentals.

I really do think an important part of technique and fundamentals is that everybody verbalizes things and draws diagrams the exact same way. That's another thing that was always amazing about Mark Brunell in Jacksonville: at the end of the week, I would look at his game notes and he would be absolutely meticulous about the routes that he drew and the notes that he took down. It's a long season in the NFL. There are 20 games of preseason and regular season before you even get to the playoffs and within each game plan, there is maybe 60 or 70% of it that's the same each week. That didn't matter, he still took the exact same notes every week. He still drew the exact same plays and always did it perfectly. Mark was just a true professional, with regard to how well he studied in the classroom, how thorough he was, and how hard he worked on the details of his position. He understood the whole offense: the run game, pass game and protections. That's something you want all your players to work hard at understanding.

I believe strongly in using individual time in practice for technique and fundamentals. On occasion, teams can get hung up on new plays and neglect the practice of the fundamentals as the season goes along. I've visited practices and seen other coaches that don't value this as much, but I believe in using individual time to get better at technique and fundamentals. I believe the defensive unit should also be taking time to work fundamentals individually. Sometimes, when you put "individual" on the practice schedule for the defense coordinator, he'll make that a group period, where it's a walk-through of formations and motions and they're not really working their technique by each position. But if you work first at the techniques and fundamentals, you can really get better at them as the year goes on.

You know, another great example of that is when we started the 2014 season at Louisville, quarterback Kyle Bolin was interested in learning and practicing, even though he started camp as the 4th or 5th guy on the depth chart. He was very good about asking questions (though, sometimes he asked too many...). On Sunday nights in-season, we practice the guys who didn't play in the game. Kyle worked really hard and he kept improving as we worked those fundamentals. As the year went on, he still wasn't playing in games, but he got better and better. We're down one quarterback, two quarterbacks, and then three quarterbacks, and he was suddenly asked to come in when we're down 13 points to Kentucky in the season finale. Kyle led us to a comeback victory. That was fun to watch! But we knew what he was good at, because of those Sunday night practices and his willingness to continue to work hard at fundamentals. He ran the empty game really well, and he did a great job with run-checks at the line of scrimmage. We hit a couple screens and got a couple double-moves for touchdowns. All of that showed up because he continued to work on the details of his position and his understanding of the whole offense. Then, that allowed us to understand what he could do, and we didn't call the plays for him that he was not as great with. That also takes us back to the idea of taking care of the quarterback: understanding what he can and can't do and call your plays accordingly. Kyle was a tough kid. He did a good job. And like all successful football players, he understood the importance of winning with technique and fundamentals.

## Defeating the Blitz

Beating the blitz really starts with a *mindset*. The mindset of the coaches, the quarterback, and the rest of the players should be "bring it on, bring the blitz!" If we can establish that, then we will get big plays. It's not always that way, though. I remember some years, where guys were nervous about blitzes coming or were intimidated by certain blitzes. I think that can come with inexperience, just not being comfortable with it, and not growing up making big plays against it. But to be the best offense in the country, you have to *want* to see pressure.

We want to establish that *mindset* at the foundation of our offensive philosophy. If you're going to be the best, you have got to be able to *want* to see pressure and then defeat it for big plays. It's also about gaining experience in being able to communicate and rely on everyone together, so it becomes a well-coordinated team thing (which is, again, why we say everyone in our program needs to use the same language and draw the plays the same way).

We want to establish the *mindset* first. From there, we next define the tactical aspects of how we want to defeat pressure and for us that can include a variety of specific things, depending on our players, our matchups and any given game plan. We define our various "blitz beaters" by concepts categories: run-checks, run/pass options, quick game, and the dropback game.

For us, "dogs" are one man coming, "blitzes" are two guys or more coming and the combination of the two is "pressure." We define them as a "dog" or "blitz" and "pressure." The first thing I've always liked for defeating the blitz or pressure is *run-checks for big plays*. Great offenses can anticipate, recognize, and defeat pressure. But truly elite offenses can defeat it with the running game, regardless of down and distance.

The ability of the offense to stop or assume defensive movements destroys their gap integrity and creates seams for chunk plays in the running game. You need to have a way to defeat perimeter pressure, using run schemes that collect and stop the defensive movement, whether that's toward or away from the tight end. Against internal pressure, we like to use gap schemes to build walls, seal off movements, and isolate a single defender, where you can block him in space or target him for a quarterback read.

Your quarterback needs to have the ability to see the pressure coming, with the receivers and linemen pointing it out, so he can get you to the proper run-check. He needs to be able to do that in a way that everybody on the line understands what pressure is coming and what the defensive movement is going to be. Then you need to "code" something so that the line knows "when I hear this check, I know there's pressure coming." We believe you have to be able to use a *code* word, where the quarterback is telling the line, "I'm making this run check because this specific blitz is coming."

For example, a normal numbered play for us is "16," which is used when just calling the basic run play (Figure 1-1). But we add various *code names* around "16," where I'm also telling the o-line what specific movement is coming, so we can anticipate it and block it. The ability to do all of that creates big plays, because then, we anticipate the check and anticipate the defensive movement before they can execute it.

In practice, you obviously do a blitz-pickup period with the passing game, but you also need to do blitz work vs. the run at full speed, so that you're able to block those stunts and movements and the entire offensive unit develops proper timing and rhythm. Just walking through it won't work! Then, as you invest in the repetition needed to get good at it, you begin to create the *mindset* "here, this is what we do, you try to stop us." If you're going to run that pressure, you might even think you know what we're going to do—but try to stop it!

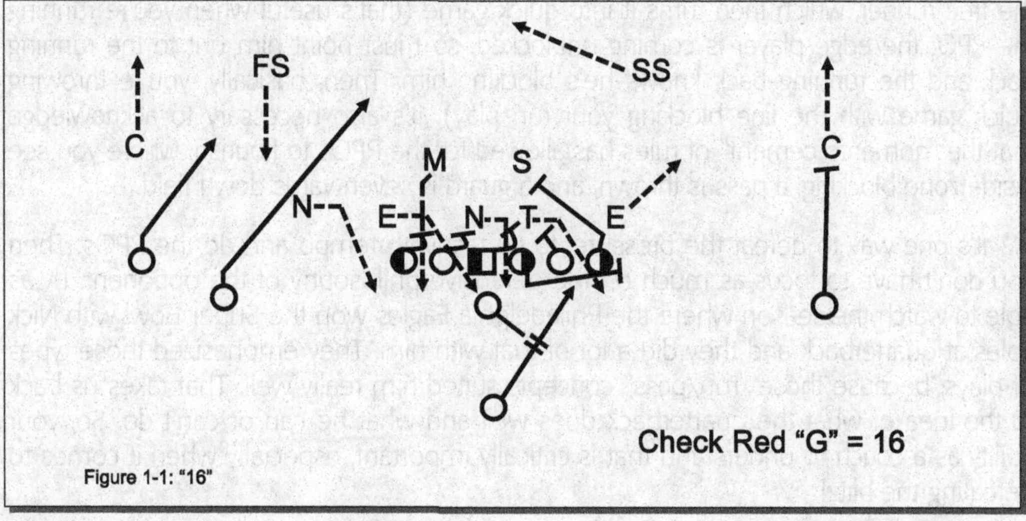

Figure 1-1: "16"

Over the years, we've seen every kind of pressure. It's been "all the above," where defensive coordinators have some of their own ideas and then add the new things that change with the times. In some years, it was the Buddy Ryan "46" stuff and sometimes it's the zone-blitz "field-scrapes" or what we call "field-sharks," with both the strong-safety and Sam coming. Often in the red zone, you get what we call the "6-1 double-dogs." You must have an answer for all of it, your quarterback must understand down & distance, and in my opinion, the truly elite teams are able to run the football against it.

A popular way nowadays to defeat pressures is the "RPOs"—the ability to execute "run/pass options," where "I'm going to run the ball but if they pressure us, I have a place to throw it" (Figure 1-2). Those can be effective, though sometimes a quarterback has to beat that free guy coming, which isn't fun. There, you can also just tell the back to block

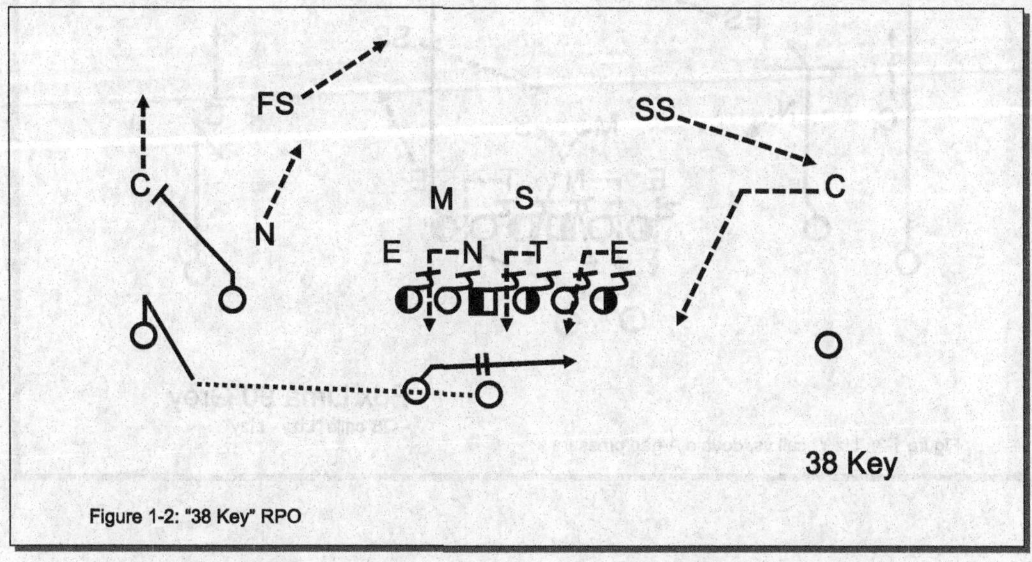

Figure 1-2: "38 Key" RPO

the free runner, which then turns it into quick game (that's useful when you're running the RPO: the edge player is coming unblocked, so I just point him out to the running back and the running back knows he's blocking him. Then, basically, you're throwing quick game with the line blocking your run play). It's also necessary to acknowledge that the "non-enforcement" of rules has allowed for the RPOs to flourish, where you see inside zone blocking, a pass is thrown, and a guard is seven yards down field.

It's one way to defeat the pressure, to go fast with tempo and do the RPOs. Then you don't have to focus as much on the defensive philosophy of the opponent. I was able to watch the season where the Philadelphia Eagles won the Super Bowl with Nick Foles at quarterback and they did a lot of that with him. They emphasized those types of plays, because those "run/pass" concepts suited him really well. That takes us back to the idea of what the quarterback does well and what he can or can't do. So, your ability as a coach to understand that is critically important, especially when it comes to defeating the blitz!

Next, you can defeat pressure with the passing game. You need to be able do it with quick game, but we also believe in beating the blitz with the dropback passing game. The quarterback must understand where the pressure is coming from. He may also be asked to make a "check" or a "call," and for us there's a difference between the two. A "check" is where he changes the entire play—the protection, the routes—everything. Situations arise throughout a game, where we need the quarterback to just get us out of the play against a bad look. On the other hand, a "call" is where he's just identifying the "Mike" linebacker in order to redirect the protection to a new point linebacker, but the route concept stays on. It's just a "call" to the line (and the running back, if he's involved,) so they know how to protect what's coming.

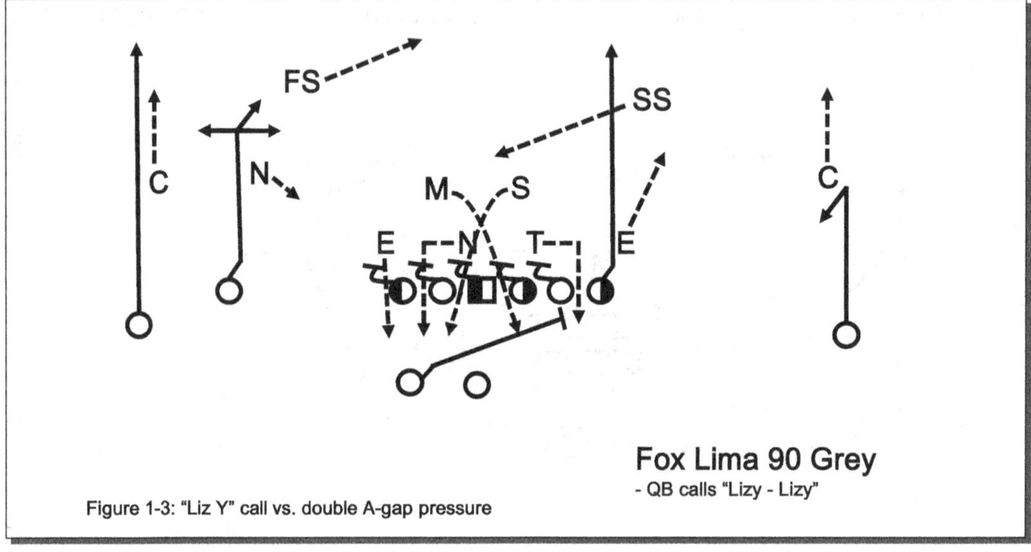

Figure 1-3: "Liz Y" call vs. double A-gap pressure

We use various terms to get that done; Liz/Rip, Lucky/Ringo, Louie/Roger, Sara/Sally, and so forth. When you re-identify the "Mike" linebacker and redirect the protection, what you're doing is changing the direction the uncovered lineman is going in order to pick up what's coming. Whether you beat the blitz with the quick or dropback game, you might have "calls" involved, so that you're able to full-slide the protection to pick up things like a "double a-gap" pressure (Figure 1-3). There's a lot to the communication involved in anticipating a "call" or a "check." Everyone must understand the defensive movement, so you can defeat the blitz.

If there is no "check" or "call" for a protection within a given pass play, you then have to utilize what we call "hots" and "sights" to defeat pressure. For us, a "hot" would be for a slot receiver, tight end or running back (Figure 1-4). He's *"hot, hot, hot!"* and you're yelling it out three times to alert the quarterback as you adjust the route. A "sight" adjustment (Figure 1-5) would be specifically by an outside receiver (running a hitch, a slant, or a "now" route) and he would yell out *"do it, do it, do it!"* We always make them say it *three times*, even though in a game—particularly on the road where it's noisy—the quarterback may not even hear him. But he hears it in practice, and you hear the coaches say it and emphasize it until it becomes a reflex action. Then, you have confidence that the receiver knows what he's doing, and the quarterback knows what he's doing. So even though there's 80,000 people at the game and we can't hear, you've worked on it and the receiver still should say it, so it just becomes a habit. Psychologists say that incorporating the other senses helps to burn the new information into memory. "I'm hearing it, I'm saying it, I'm seeing it"—no question all of that reinforces the learning and makes our reactions to dogs, blitzes, and pressure more consistently effective!

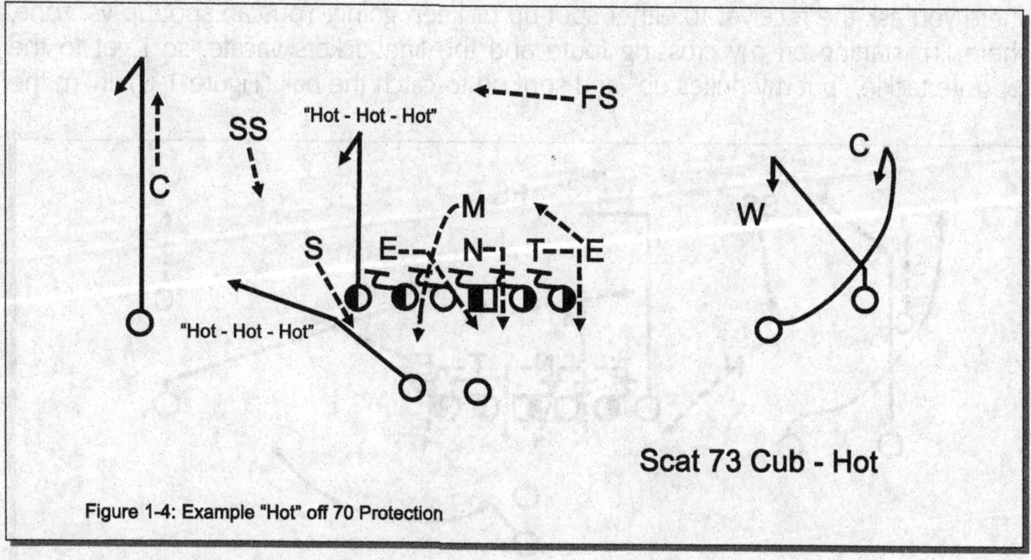

Figure 1-4: Example "Hot" off 70 Protection

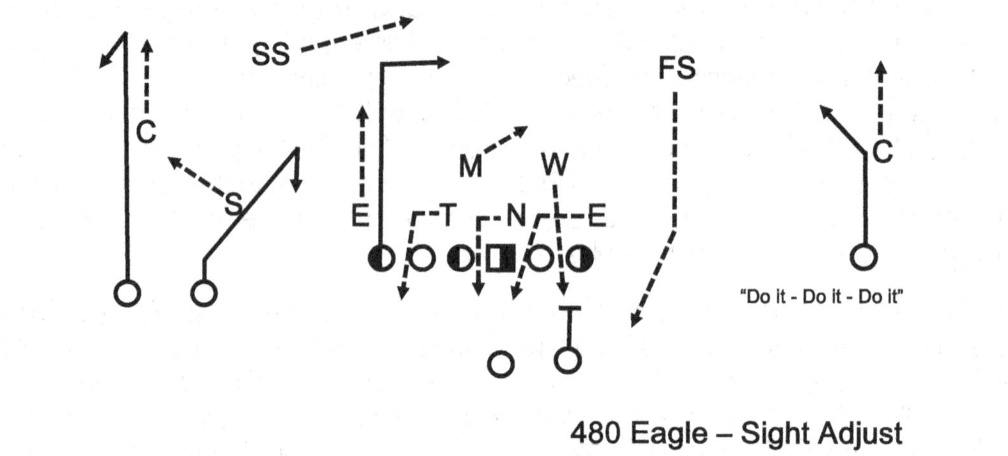

"Do it - Do it - Do it"

480 Eagle – Sight Adjust

Figure 1-5: Example "Sight Adjust"

We also carry certain routes where there are no hot or sight adjustments because it's automatically "built in." With some of our crossing or level routes, for example, there's already a built-in outlet, so the quarterback knows where to go if the pressure comes. As you put the offense together, you have certain plays where you can say to a quarterback, "hey look, we're good here, we are not changing anything." That's your 'built-in' outlet but you still have to know when it's coming. As a quarterback, I don't want to get hit in the back of the head or in the ear, so I need to understand that I have a "built-in," and I can just get my receiver involved.

When you talk about crossers and levels, for example, there are specific instances where you ask the receiver to either spot-up or keep going. You can spot-up vs. zone, where I'm starting on my crossing route and the linebackers vacate, so I get to the opposite tackle, "put my dukes up" and spot up to catch the ball (Figure 1-6). If I'm the

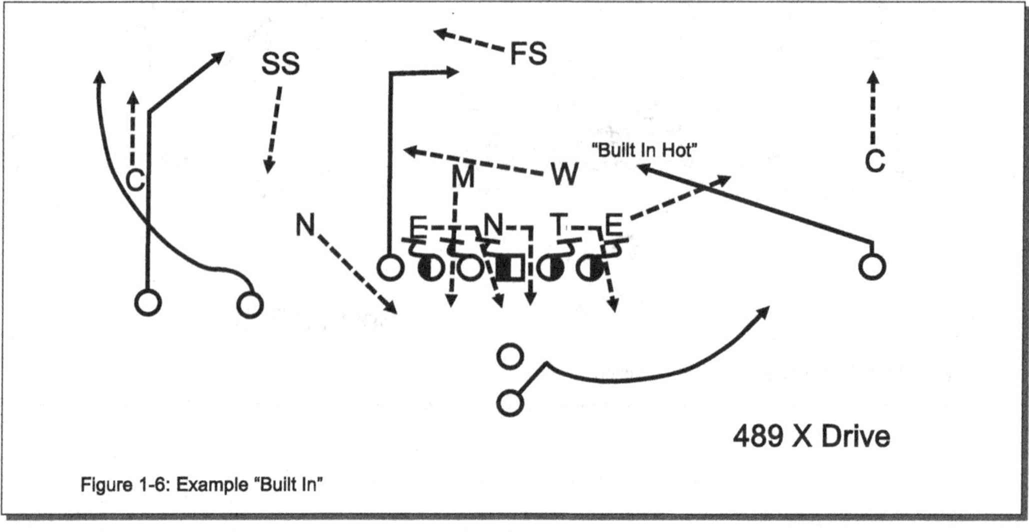


Figure 1-6: Example "Built In"

crossing receiver, it's a pressure situation and I see stuff coming, I might get eye contact and throttle down vs. blitz, but I don't necessarily spot up. (But I can't run in there blind either and not know enough to get eye contact with the quarterback. Then I get the ball bounced off my helmet!)

Quarterbacks need to work hard at every nuance of that in order to see it and understand it. There is a lot to work on, in order to defeat the blitz with the passing game. How much of that you do at any given time again depends on your quarterback's comfort level, the timing, and the situation. If you know you want to throw the dropback passing game, you better be able to redirect protection!

Then, there's times the quarterback gets hit. However, that's always been the way you test a quarterback's courage and competitive spirit is that he can stand in there, transfer his weight, follow through, and take a hit right in the chin. Is he tough enough to transfer his weight, follow through, take a hit right in the chin, and still make the completion? When you make the choice to be the quarterback, that part goes with it. As a coach, you need to acknowledge this aspect of beating the blitz and the quarterback needs to be able to understand when he's not getting it done.

It's a challenge to a quarterback, to be able to look in the mirror and say, "my eyes went down. I wasn't focusing. I wasn't being tough enough." There's a lot of what psychologists call *self-talk* involved for a quarterback to be able to admit when he didn't display courage and you have to display *courage* as a quarterback, or you have no chance of being a winner.

As far as a specific response you like to see from your guy, when he takes a hit? They're all different. Every quarterback's response is a little different but it needs to be authentic to his own personality. If the response is manufactured and outside of his personality, then it's affecting his concentration. For example, I used to say to Chris Redman, "you know, you can take off and run right there and just give me five or six yards, then 2nd & 4 is an easy call for me." And he would say, "yeah, I'm okay with getting hit. I can just stand in there, throw and get hit." He would rather get hit standing in the pocket while throwing the ball than while running. That was just his mindset, his personality, and his comfort zone. And even though there were times he took off and got us a first down, that wasn't as natural as his game was his arm and his accuracy. Each guy is a little bit different, but his understanding of himself and what he can do to be successful is as important to his success as anything.

The last—and maybe most important—part of defeating the blitz is that *all 11 players* are on the same page and execute their responsibilities effectively. You know as a coach that each player understands his own position. They all know why we made the run-check or why we made the pass-check or call. They all know what the defensive movement is going to be and what the other side of the ball is being taught. That understanding of *why* the defensive guys are doing certain things is as important as anything, to get all 11 men on the field coordinated together to defeat the blitz.

You have to understand what the defense is being taught in order to be a really good offensive player. You have to know your own position, know the entire offense, and also know how the defenders are being coached up. The idea of a "dumb" football player is ridiculous! It's just never been that way.

One of the really neat things about being an assistant coach in the NFL was seeing the minds and the hearts of the NFL players, the true professionals. They were really into it, the strategy and the mental part of it. And then their competitive spirit that came out was unbelievable! I have always stated to the college kids that there's a lot of guys walking the streets who have the talent to play in the NFL, but the difference is in their *mind* and their *heart*. And it's true, the guys who are in it are true professionals. They want to be involved in the game plan and they want to be involved in knowing "what can we do to beat this team? How do I get this matchup?" Really fun!

And you can't fake that, in my experience. All of the guys that I was ever around at that level put their hearts into it, and we knew it, because on a daily basis, we saw how hard they worked at it. I know how much it meant to them and how much pride they had as individuals and as part of a team. That's all a part of the offensive philosophy as well. When you can establish the right mindset, followed by the proper execution of the runs and passes, and then get everyone together onboard, you can consistently defeat the blitz!

## Effort and Finish

Your team must play with great effort and be able to finish. We believe coaches must always confront and demand *effort* and *finish*. We ended up calling it an "effort habit," because the ability to play hard and to finish everything you do needs to become a *habit*. Coaches need to set the standards in practice. It's really important that your running backs carry the ball 25 yards down the field, so they get used to making those long runs, keeping the ball tucked away. Receivers need to catch the ball and get 40 yards down the field after the catch, so they get used to making those plays and get used to playing with that kind of effort.

At Louisville, Lamar Jackson and Brandon Radcliffe took that to a different level; anytime they ran the ball, they would go all the way to the end zone. And to be honest with you, that's what made Brandon Radcliff get a position. In practice he's repeatedly giving great *effort* and it's like "we need to get this guy in the game!"

The first spring I came in, Brandon was a guy who got injured and couldn't participate, so we didn't know much about him. Then, you turn on the practice video and he is sprinting all the way to the end zone on every play! When a great example like that is set by your best players—your hardest working players—that's obviously great to the coach. Then what you do is you reward great effort during games, so they can sit and watch those great effort plays on video in front of their peers. I don't think there's anything better than that! We always did it on Friday night before the game. Part of the head coach's meeting was to play that video of great effort and great plays from the previous game.

Then you *grade* effort and every other player on the team gets after it! For example, the Atlanta Falcons gave out a competitive toughness grade the year they made a run to the Super Bowl. It was a big thing they thought helped their team. You can call it different things but it's really about how hard you play. How much *effort*! The NCAA cracked down on certain things years ago, but I think most high school coaches can still give out t-shirts as positive reinforcement. I know a high school coach who used to give his kids little "matchbox" trucks anytime there was a great block on film and the players would take great pride in carrying those little toy trucks around to class. Great effort allows you to finish off opponents and it needs to be both demanded and rewarded. We believe in effort and finish!

## Run to Win

You must be able to run the ball to win games, especially in the 4th quarter. You can say, "we will run first and set up our passing game off the run," and you can say, "we want to pass the heck out of the ball and set up our running game off that." We've done both throughout the years. Some years, our best running game was when we put four wide receivers out there, made teams defend the pass and leave a 5-man box (Figure 1-7). What more could you ask for? But whether you're a run-first or pass-first team, you must be able to run the ball to win.

I think it's simple to use what we call an advantage run. You know that the more *advantage runs* you can get, the better you're going to be running the ball. To do that, I think you need to utilize "direction runs," where you're able to run the ball either right or left based off the defense. We do that with a system we call "front, coverage, and personnel" that I learned from my dad. For example, the shade or 3-technique or our free-access tackle may tell the quarterback to run the ball to the right *(front)*. But then the pre-snap rotation of a drop-safety may tell him if that isn't going to work and if we need to run to the left instead *(coverage)*. I look at the *front*, which tells me I can run to the right, unless the *coverage* overrides that and tells me I should run the ball to the left instead. If the front is balanced, and the coverage is balanced, then I want to run behind my best guys against their worst *(personnel)*.

Our quarterbacks need to be able to tell me what this means. They should say the exact words "front, coverage, personnel." That system of "direction runs" also really does a lot for teaching quarterbacks how to identify and understand various fronts and coverages, even if you don't utilize it that often in game. The process of coaching it, working on it, preparing it. As a result, the quarterback is going to know fronts and he's going to know coverages, simply because he is constantly being forced to apply his understanding of the concepts. It's a great way to teach it.

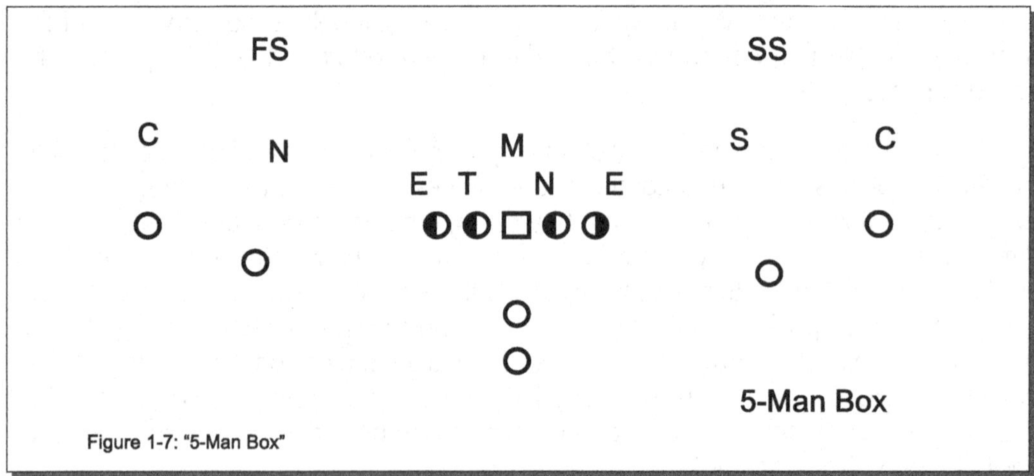

Figure 1-7: "5-Man Box"

That idea works well from 12 personnel. For example, the Colts in the early 2000s would get into what we call "thunder" formation (2x2 from 12 personnel) and they'd just check with Peyton Manning and run it with Edgerrin James (Figure 1-8). They got so good at it! That was a team I remember watching execute that system really well.

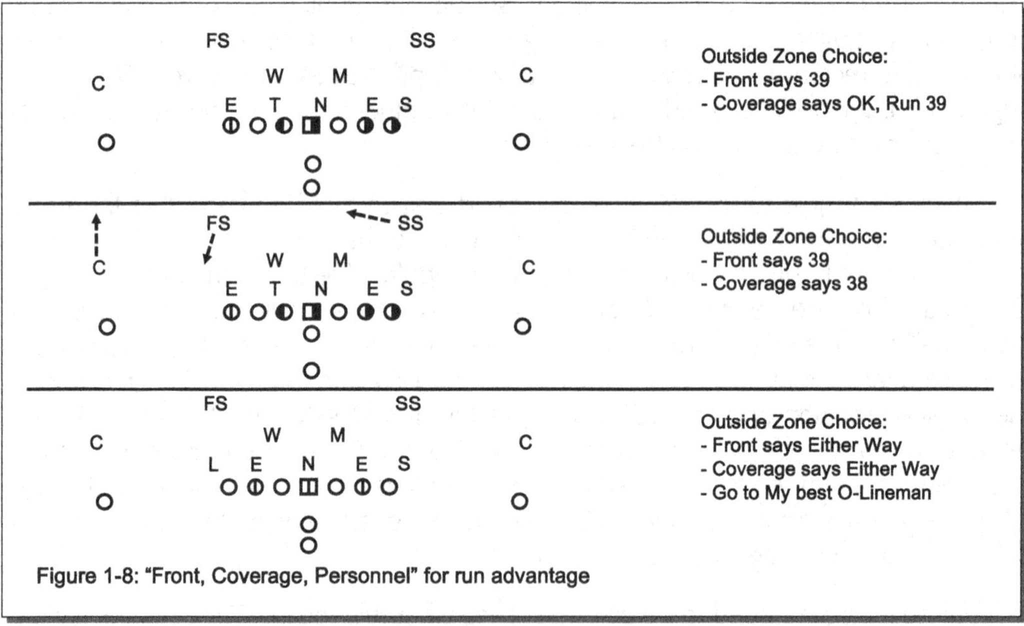

Figure 1-8: "Front, Coverage, Personnel" for run advantage

The other way to do it is with *packages*. We have the ability to carry "run-to-pass" or "pass-to-run" packages, which allow you to attack the specific look that you want. That's been labeled in the new era as "kill" packages, where if they're in a 2-high defense, I'm going to run the ball, but if it's a 1-high defense, I'm going to "kill" to the pass. It works well to gain an advantage and run the ball against the looks you want and then pass the ball vs. the looks and coverages that you want as well.

We took that into the red zone the last few years and it was great for us. In that situation, we would have a way to throw the ball vs. "blitz zero" coverage and yet run the ball when we got the look we wanted. A great example was that we wanted our tight end lined up outside of our Z receiver to motion him down inside. Double-edge pressure? We ran the crosser for a touchdown. The quarterback then knows he has to "beat the hugger" (unblocked defender in pressure). If they were in a 2-linelinebacker look, we'd run the "pitch crack" play and run for a touchdown (Figure 1-9).

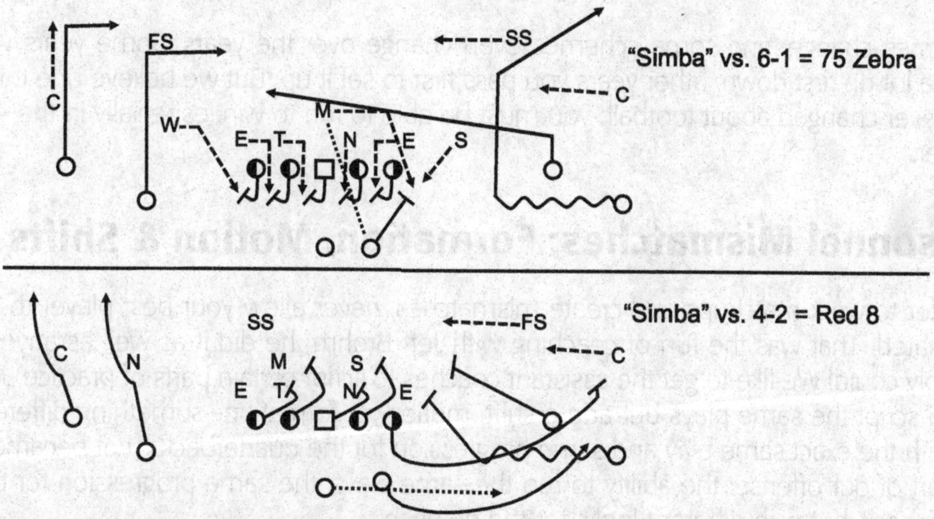

"Simba" vs. 6-1 = 75 Zebra

"Simba" vs. 4-2 = Red 8

Figure 1-9: Red Zone "2-Play" package example

It is also important to be able to do a good job with "reload." That's when you "kill" and they change defenses, so you "reload" to the original play called. We started this a long, long time ago, way back when I was at Utah State in the early 1990s. We had a junior college quarterback who could make a check in practice, but when he would get to a game, he wouldn't trust it. A lot of playing the position of quarterback is your ability to trust what you see and not hesitate. He was a first-year guy who would see it, then wouldn't trust it and make the call, so we just did it for him. We said "okay, vs. this look, we're running the ball, vs. that look, we're passing the ball." And at that time, we just made an "alert," where your play call is "90 alert." This was going to be your pass play for pressure and the "alert" was to get to "10 draw" or "16 down / stretch," so you know you have a way to run the football and beat man coverage. We taught him how to check by just making that call, so he would just holler "alert!" at the line when he saw it. The system was easy and that all started for us all the way back then as a way to put us in the best position to run the football and win games.

With the popularity of no-huddle today, the other way to do it is from the sideline, where you'll see something and then there's a "freeze cadence" to change the play from the sideline, instead of a quarterback audible. The issue with that is then the defense will check, because the defenses are better now. "They're checking, we're checking," so that they try not to let you call the play from the press box or the sideline.

For example, some really good teams anticipate that freeze count and just won't even line up. They'll refuse to show their hand and instead have a sort of "stare down" with the offensive line. You'll see d-linemen all just stand there, then get the signal, and line up really late. It's sometimes hard to declare the Mike and block people who aren't lined up! Against opponents like that, we had to go fast and utilize some other things in order to be able to create running opportunities.

Times change, and some schemes even change over the years. Some years you run it a lot on first down, other years you pass first to set it up. But we believe one thing has never changed about football: you must be able to run to win, especially in the 4th quarter.

## Personnel Mismatches; Formation, Motion & Shifts

In order to work matchups and create mismatches, *never* allow your best player to be eliminated. That was the fun of coaching with Jeff Brohm; he did it as well as anyone possibly could! We like to get the assistant coaches to script certain parts of practice. Jeff would script the same plays but add a shift, motion, or formation—something different but with the exact same play and same progression for the quarterback. That became a big part of our offense: the ability to run the same plays, the same progression for the quarterback, but with different looks for the defense.

For example, when we were at Arkansas, one of the ways we would get after teams with a sophisticated 3-4 package would be to change passing strength once or twice with a shift and motion. Then, they got screwed up on who the rush guy was, who the dropper was, and what the corner was doing. We could get the back wide open for a touchdown by understanding how defenses did things, based off passing strength with the rush and drop guy. In fact, on some of those films, you can see two of the defenders look at each other like "who's going and who's not?" For example, in one game, we "flipped to wing" and then motioned the wing outside the X, so we changed the passing strength three times. In that game, they both just kind of stood there, the corner stayed in press, and they let the back run right down the sideline for a touchdown. The next year, another way we did that to a 3-4 team was by lining the fullback up at tailback, and then putting him in motion outside of the widest receiver and sending him down boundary (Figure 1-10).

We were a "tempo huddle" team in those Arkansas years. Our ability to get out of the huddle, shift, and motion with *tempo* is something we were really good at. We became all no-huddle by 2016 at Louisville (and changed things up with various tempo packages within the no-huddle framework), but prior to that we still utilized tempo. In fact, that was one of the things that Manny Diaz said to me recently was "at

Arkansas, you guys were a really good 'tempo' team, not just all no-huddle. That made it hard to defend the way you came out of the huddle and then used shifting & motion to run and pass the ball so efficiently."

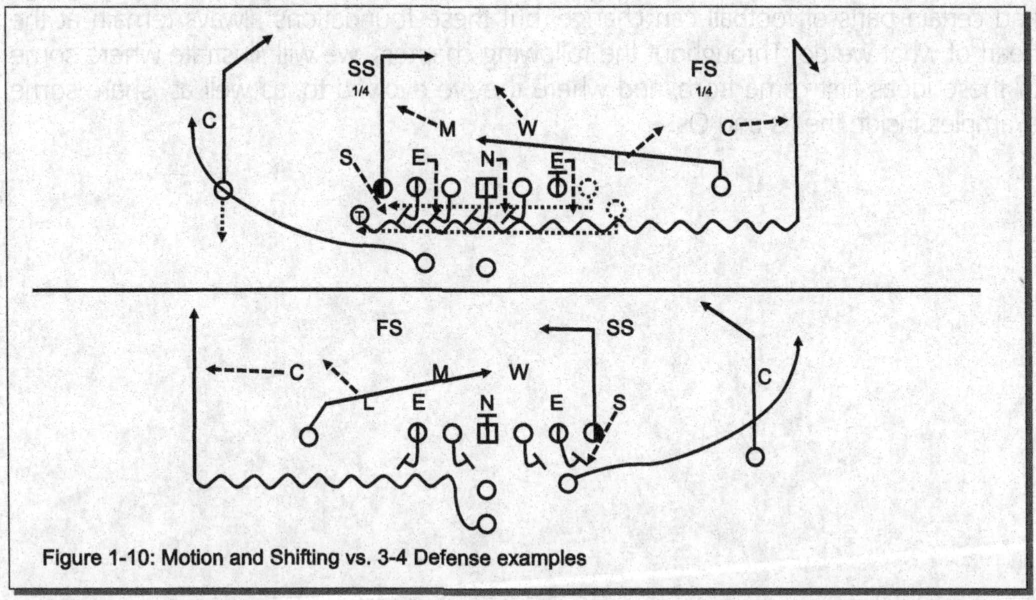


**Figure 1-10: Motion and Shifting vs. 3-4 Defense examples**

One of the things I learned as a head coach was to let your assistants handle certain parts of the script to see what input and creativity they could add to the offense; not change the offense, just add something new with a formation, shift, or a motion. Jeff Brohm was someone who excelled at it, along with my brother Paul Petrino, for sure. The three of us together, it was pretty good. We went 41-9 over four seasons together at Louisville. It was fun!

But that's something you always want to facilitate. I think it's a *must*, to be able to have everybody on staff want to give something creative to the offense. My son Nick is also really good at scripting. The last few years, he scripted both the "skelly" and "blitz" periods and I thought he really helped the scripted blitz period. Before that I did it with the running back coach, but Nick saw it more from a quarterback's standpoint. (Some of that depends on your other coaches. A lot of coaches don't want to give that up, so it does depend on the makeup of the staff each season.)

Like we said about how the quarterback and receivers "buy in" when you get them the ball early and they gain confidence. Something I think younger head coaches don't realize is how much of that you have to do with your offensive staff as well, in order to keep them happy. I've always tried to make sure they understand by the very first day that they're expected to give input. I just try to put myself in their shoes: you're sitting there seeing your input show up on the video, where *your* position guy makes a play on *your* play the first day. Then, you really see how all the motion, shifting, and formations work to create mismatches and why we believe in it!

These concepts form the foundations of our offensive philosophy. We believe in them and we've had a lot of success over the years as a result. I think you can see how they each flow and work together with each other as we develop the offense each season. There's always room for growth and adaptation, because times change and certain parts of football can change, but these foundations always remain at the heart of what we do. Throughout the following chapters, we will illustrate where some of these ideas first came from, and where they've evolved to, as well as, share some examples inside the Xs and Os.

# Louisville vs Clemson Oct. 1st 2016

## NORMAL DOWN & DISTANCE

| RUN: | PASS: |
|---|---|
| EVEN/ODD NINJA<br>ODD/EVEN – ODD/EVEN NOAH | HOUSTON – DALLAS 92 Y ARROW – RAIDER X HITCH |
| 3/12 CUT – 12/13 CUT /12 – 33/32 OPEN | 90 GREY – BLUE Y DBL SLANT<br>SAINT – OAKLAND SWIPE |
| 24/25 "O"<br>27/26 – ODD SKULL | SCAT 79 SNAPPER – HOUSTON LION<br>POPE – DICE 99 |
| 7 CROWN – 7/6 CROWN EVEN/ODD – ODD/EVEN DEVIL | DICE STAB – SEATTLE<br>9/8 DICE 94 – Z PATRIOT |
| EVEN/ODD DEMON EVEN/ODD – ODD/EVEN CRUISE | 80 – 480 MIDGET X SKINNY<br>70 WHEEL – 80 W WHEEL |
| PITCH 8/9 FORCE<br>PITCH 9/8 FORCE – 88/99 | 480 FALCON – EAGLE 71<br>MAYDAY – 81 "C" WASP-BLADE |
| 47/45<br>38/39 BOSS | 72 Z TOPPER – 82 X TOPPER<br>SCAT 73 MIAMI - CUB |
| MARS – TREY 10/11 | 73 POKER – 483 BILL<br>R 73 BILL |
| TANGO PEARL | 84 – 85 – 86 Z BINGO<br>75 ZEBRA – SCAT 485 ZEBRA |
| KANSAS NINJA CHOICE | CROSS<br>79 DOLPHIN – 79 ZOMBIE |
| DBLS Y FLY 39/38 | SCAT 77 WHALE<br>487 – SCAT 77 SHARK |
| OHIO (JUMP) 38/39 | SCAT 489 – 79 TUNA<br>SCAT 79 CHARGER |
| VG SLT T-FLY 24/25 PWR | JAPAN – 486 T BLADE<br>61 C Z SQUIRREL – W LEVEL POST |

| PLAY-ACTION PASS |
|---|
| 42 Z PACKER- Z BADGER – LOAD 2/3 Z PACKER<br>LOAD 2/3 DEEP CB – CADDY – GO |
| VG LOAD 2/3 Z "V" – X OVER – WG T FLY BLAZE 16 X SQUIRREL – 140-141<br>X DAGGER – WG T PEEL – PEPPER 41 X SQUIRREL |
| VG SLT FLASH RT/LT GREEN – BLAZE 23 RT "C"<br>ACT ¾ Z SQUIRREL – Z SAIL – T DAGGER |
| P LOAD 2/3 X "V" – Z OVER<br>ACT ¾ Z SQUIRREL – Z SAIL – T DAGGER |
| STORM LOAD 2/3 X PACKER- DEEP CB – CADDY – GO<br>STORM T MO KN 8/9 DEEP CB |
| BLAZE 33/32 RT Q – DWARF – SAIL<br>TANGO ACT 3 Z SQUIRREL – FLASH GREEN |

| OPENING SCRIPT |
|---|
| (TH) SHOT TH RT/LT CLOSE 81 "C" X BLADE |
| (POSSE) CARD RT/LT FLIP 4/5 DEVIL |
| (DEUCE) GUN 6/7 RT/LT RAM/LION OAKLAND SWIPE |
| (TH) SHOT WG SLT T FLY ODD NINJA "KEY" |
| (TH) SHOT WG RT/LT T ZIP 73 BILL |
| (ACE) SHOT POSSE Y HALF 12/13 CUT |
| (ACE) SHOT TAXI BOW 24/25 "O" KEY |

| SCREEN/DELAY PLAYS |
|---|
| WG 51/50 – WG SLT T FLOAT 50/51 |
| DIME W MO 51/50 – 9/8 TAXI BOW 51/50 |
| DIME W MO 51/50 – 9/8 TAXI BOW 51/50 |
| TREY 58/59 W LEVEL<br>TRIPS 58 Y DRIVE – ACT 3 SLOW SCREEN LT |

| "MUST" CALLS |
|---|
| TAXI ROSE/LIMA OAKLAND X HITCH<br>TAXI HOLLYWOOD – DBLS 483 BILL |
| TRIPS 89 STICK – TRAMP INTO LIQUOR<br>S WK STORM CLOSE PEPPER 41 X SQUIRREL |
| S STORM R 73 BILL – LIMO W SBACK X "V"<br>STORM T MO KN 8/9 DEEP CB |
| (ACE) DOT RT/LT 80 – DBLS 13/12<br>STR SLT RT 140/141 Y SHAKE |
| TOP RT/LT 13/12 – DBLS CLOSE 81 "C"<br>S TREY 70 W WHEEL – TRPS 71 "C" FALCON |
| S TOP RT/LT PAIR 69 TRIPLE – W SAIL<br>9/8 DICE LION Z PATRIOT (WHITE) |
| JACK RT/LT 27/26 BUBBLE – EVEN NINJA<br>TOP RT W FLY BURN 39 RT W TUBA |
| S KANSAS KN 8/9 F SAIL – TOP PAIR Y PEEL 140/141 X DAGGER – TRIPS LOUIE Z CAPTAIN |
| ROCK BAZOOKA 88/89 – TANGO WAGGLE LT TARZAN<br>Y MO SHOT STR RT EVEN NINJA |
| (TH) SHOT KING EVEN/ODD NINJA<br>SHOT POSSE FLASH LT/RT GREEN |

| 17/9 GET IT TO | 2 |
|---|---|
| LION/RAM POPE<br>LIMO SEATTLE | SAINT – SWIPE<br>RAIDER X SLANT – HITCH |
| POSSE GREY SWIPE<br>94 – 94Y – TRPS ORANGE | SCAT 79 SNAPPER<br>HOUSTON<br>HOUSTON – DALLAS |
| DICE STAB – 94 480 MIDGET – 70 W WHEEL | DICE WTAB – 94<br>LEE SINKER X JERK – SLOP |
| FAR WG FLANKER DRIVE<br>WG SLT 142 DUAL – ZOMBIE | TRPS CLOSE SEAHAWK<br>80 – 80 Y OPT |
| DOT CLOSE 81 "C"<br>72 Z TOPPER | 71 "C" – 480 FALCON<br>71 MAYDAY – 81 "C" X BLADE |
| POSSE RAM CROSS<br>DBLS 489 JAWS Z POST | 81 "C" WASP – X DIPPER<br>9/8 DICE LION Z PATRIOT |
| STORM KN 8/9 CB TRPS<br>79 DOLPHIN | PEPPER 41 X SQUIRREL<br>140 X DAGGER – LOAD CB |
| TRPS 89 STICK – CAT – Z CAPTAIN – SCAT 77 | SL LOAD 2/3 X "V"<br>KANSAS KN 8/9 F SAIL |

| TEX |
|---|
| (TEX) STR TEX T FLY BLAZE 39 RT T TUBE |
| (OHIO) STR TEX KN 8/9 FLOOD – BLAZE 13 NUDE |
| (OHIO) JUMP TO OHIO 38/39 –<br>KANSAS KN 8 F SAIL |
| KANSAS NINJA – NOAH – T FLY 12/13 – F MO 13/12 |
| KANSAS RT EVEN RAMBO |

| 2 TITE |
|---|
| TITE Z HALF 47/46 – 17/16 |
| TITE RT TOSS 39 TED – WK Y FLY 39/38 BOSS |

| 3RD & 1-3 12/19 63%<br>9/10 DIAMOND – AA VS CARD – WOLF V8 TH | |
|---|---|
| **RUN:** | **PASS:** |
| (OHIO) KANSAS E/O NINJA | (OHIO) STR TEX KN 8/9 FLOOD |
| (OHIO) JUMP TO KING 38/39 | (TEX) STR TEX T FLY BLAZE 39/38 T TUBE |
| (ACE) S JACK RT/LT PEARL BUBBLE | (OHIO) SHOT KANSAS RT/LT KN 8/9 F SAIL |
| (ROCK/POSSE) OVER/POSSE BOW DEVIL CHOICE | (ACE)(SHOT) DOT RT/LT CLOSE Y FLY KN 7/6<br>MOSES (TH) TH 75 ZEBRA (SOLO Y HALF)<br>TH SLT 488 Z MESH |

| 3RD & 4-6 4/7 57% | |
|---|---|
| **RUN:** | **PASS:** |
| (STRETCH) 8/9 TRPS BOW 5/4<br>DEVIL – 9/8 TAXI BOW 4/5 DEVIL | (TH) WG SLT SCAT 489 QR 79<br>TUNA – SCAT SNAPPER Z OPT |
| (TH) STORM T MO O/E NOAH –<br>EVEN NINJA – ODD NINJA<br>ROCK T FLY ODD NINJA | (TH/ACE) G ROCK T/W FLY<br>SCAT 73 CUB – T/W PEEL 489<br>CANNON |
| (ACE) 9/8 TAXI BOW<br>51/50 DIME W MO 51/50 | (POSSE) POSSE BOW RAM/LION GREY/OAKLAND SWIPE |
| | (STRETCH) 8/9 TRPS LION/RAM KENO – HOLSTER –SEATTLE – FALCON √ STAY – BOW 5/4 DEVIL |
| | (ACE) G TANGO Z MO LION/RAM MULE |
| | (TH) DICE FOX LIMA/ROSE 99 – STAB |

| 3RD & 7-10 10/20 50% | |
|---|---|
| **RUN:** | **PASS:** |
| (POSSE) G NR POSSE RL/LT ODD BLAST | (ACE) S DOT RT/LT (BOW) 80- 85-<br>66 Z BINGO- 89 SCOUT Z BINGO |
| S BOW DEVIL CHOICE | (POSSE/ROCKET) FOX LIMA/ROSE<br>– ROSE/LIMA 92 ALL – 94 (BLUE/GRIZ)- DBL HK – 489/79<br>LAKER – FOX ROSE Z<br>LAKER – LIMA X LAKER |
| | (POSSE/ACE) S POSSE(FLOOD) BOW 480 FALCON – 489 Y CAPTAIN –<br>RAM GREY SWIPE |
| | (ACE) GUN DOT RT/LT Y FLY<br>LION/RAM Z SNIPER |

| 3RD & 11+ |
|---|
| **PASS:** |
| (ACE) DICE RT CLOSE FOX ROSE JAPAN |
| (ACE) S TOP RT PAIR BOW 89 TRIPLE |
| DOT RT/LT 89 W SAIL – 81 "C" WASP |
| (ACE) G TRPS RT 79 WILDCAT |
| (ACE) G TAXI 483 ALL X ICE |

| 4th DOWN | |
|---|---|
| (1) MUSCLE DOWN CHOICE (TRAIN) TRAIN 13/12 CUT | (1) KANSAS EVEN RAMBO STR TEX KN 8 FLOOD |
| (4-6) TRPS CLOSE SEAHAWK<br>TH SLT 488 MESH | (4-10) (STRETCH) 8/9 TRPS CHICAGO – STAY WRAP – KENO – ZIPPER |

## QUARTERBACK CHECKLIST

**Game manager –** Pre-snap recognition situational awareness, adjustments pre and post snap decisions at the LOS

**Pocket awareness –** Feel for pressure, peripheral vision, courage/toughness, slide & avoid, maintain down field vision, extend play, ball security, avoids sacks

**Decision-making –** Intelligence, anticipation, ability to read coverage, understanding of where to go with the ball, knows when to throw the ball away

**Poise –** Calm, patient, under control, composed under pressure, courage/ toughness, body language

**Anticipation –** Delivering the ball on time, ability to throw WR open, understanding coverage/rotation, ability to put the ball in a spot before WR is open

**Arm strength –** Velocity, can make all throws, deep & sideline, throw off balance/under duress, throw from awkward positions, in all weather conditions

**Touch –** Pace, feel, loft, throw over defense with good location

**Accuracy short/med –** Catchable ball with few adjustments to keep WRs on routes. Can beat tight coverage, high percentage with short/med routes. Throws under 18 yards

**Accuracy long –** Catchable ball that can keep receivers on routes 18+ yards down field. Keeps ball away from DBs, doesn't hang ball too long

**Accuracy on the move –** Catchable ball with accuracy on move right or left. Good ball placement with timing. Boots, sprint outs, scrambles

**Run ability –** Speed, elusiveness, vision, instincts, designed run threat

**Delivery –** Consistent arm angle, release/spin ball, use of body in motion, release quickness

**Set up/feet –** Quickness to drop, proper footwork, smooth & relaxed in drop, base & set-up, ball carriage

**Escape –** Ability to extend plays, buy time, get out of trouble. Can be done by quickness, speed, or with strength

# Chapter 2
## Philosophy of the Passing Game
## (Quarterbacks & Protecting the Passer)

Throwing the football starts with you as a coach and the entire coaching staff making a *commitment* to it. You're going to win throwing the football. You have to make a commitment to it, and you have to be able to throw the ball when you *want* to, so that you can throw it to win games when you *have* to. A perfect example of that was in 2011 at Arkansas. We would throw the ball when we wanted to (which, if my mom had her way, would be every single play!). We had three games in a row, down double-digits at halftime and came back to win all three games, because we could throw it when we had to win. I don't know if we would have come back and won those games without our commitment to throwing the football.

That starts with the teaching of it, such as not being afraid to carry too many protections. The commitment also goes to recruiting and personnel, in identifying and getting the traits that you want at each position. Then, you develop all the different things that you have to do during practice in order to *execute*. If we start with personnel, everything starts at quarterback when you talk about throwing the ball. Let's talk about quarterbacks and about how to protect the passer, within our philosophy of the passing game.

## Quarterbacks

I think you can win with all kinds of different quarterbacks with different traits. However, there are specific things I think you look for. If you were to go out and pick a quarterback, it would start with leadership and his ability to direct and uplift other people. A great quarterback makes the players around him better and you need someone who's going to elevate his teammates. There are a lot of ways to do that, but I think it first starts with his leadership ability.

The second thing for me would be his intelligence and by that, I mean his ability to learn. The third thing is his ability to *want* to learn and his drive to put the time in. I really think you can teach guys like that when they're hard workers at it. Everyone learns differently, so as a coach you have to know the *way* he learns, so you can teach him how to execute what you want offensively. They don't all learn the same, but as long as he'll work hard at it and put in the time, you can understand how he learns. Then, you can accomplish great things together!

The next thing would be the physical skill of what I call a "natural passer." You need someone with the arm talent to be able to throw the ball when everything isn't perfect. You've got to be careful with that and see him throw the ball in person, because you can be tricked a little bit by a video. In a game, they're not always going to be able to set their feet right, they're not always going to be able to have the room in the pocket to step and transfer. There are some kids that if they can't set perfectly and transfer perfectly, they just can't make throws you need.

The guys who are natural throwers snap their wrist. I never like to say "arm strength." I think it's about snapping *wrists* and *fingers*. That's how you generate the spin and the velocity to throw the ball. Your quarterback needs to have that natural *snap* and the ability to throw with the wrist. Mike Price, who taught me a lot about quarterbacks, used to describe it like this:

> "You take three guys down to the river and they each pick up a rock. One guy throws and it goes out there about 20 yards and plops. The next guy throws, and it goes halfway over. The next guy picks it up and throws it clear across the entire river: that's the guy you want to be your quarterback."

I think the next thing is the ability to move, and there's different types: for example, there's the guy who can just move in the pocket, feel it, and get the ball out. I think that's a big thing, is the ability to *feel* the pressure and know what's going on around you (as opposed to not having a clue and getting hit in the back of the head...). There's the player who can take off a little bit and get you a first down with his legs and still move in the pocket and feel the pressure. And then there's the guy that can really run and can make plays with his legs; a guy who can run the option-type offense and who can make big plays by taking off when plays breakdown in the passing game. This person is the so called *dual-threat* quarterback.

You know that we had one of the greatest dual-threat quarterbacks before there was any such term in Stefan LeFors at Louisville. I believe he led the country in pass completion percentage and a lot of that was because if "1, 2, 3" wasn't there, he could take off and run instead of throwing an incomplete pass. Mark Brunell with the Jacksonville Jaguars had an unbelievable arm and yet could make all kinds of runs. I loved coaching him; he was one of the greatest runners ever at the position, in both the NFL and in college football.

It's really those abilities that you're looking for. To say "my quarterback is going to be 6'4", 220 pounds, and 4.7" (in the 40-yard dash)"—I don't think that that's how it needs to be. I think it's more about these other things: "my quarterback is going to be a tremendous competitor, a great leader, tough, and make the guys around him better. Then, he has to have the necessary skills and traits to be able to play the position." Those characteristics are more important than just his physical measurements and it doesn't have to be just one certain kind of guy. You know, they're all very, very different.

## Throwing Mechanics

We coach the ability to really *spin* the ball. That comes from my fingers, my grip, how I hold it and how I snap it. In bad weather games and outdoor games in the wind or cold, I know that if I can really *spin* the ball, it doesn't affect me as much as guys who haven't developed that ability. If a guy can't spin it as well, the wind and cold are a much bigger factor to him. While we know that's part of recruiting someone, you can work on it and get better at it just by how you hold the ball and how you push the point out; how you get on top of it and snap your wrist.

As far as grip, everyone's a little bit different. I prefer two fingers off the strings. If you can point the index finger up and get some of the seam, you're going to spin the ball a lot better. If you can get your index finger up on top of the seam and you snap it, it's going to come off spinning much better. While the hands of some guys are too big to do that, they're going to be able to spin it anyway, because they have great big hands.

That's another thing that you should do when you look at a quarterback is ask "how big are his hands?" I always get nervous about guys who have small hands. When I coached at Arizona State, I had a good job because I was free to go anywhere I wanted to find a quarterback, so I went up to Boise, Idaho to recruit Jake Plummer in the spring of his junior year. I spent the entire day watching every one of his games from his junior year. I loved him. I loved the way he made plays with his legs and ran around. He stood in the pocket and did just about everything well, but I really loved the way he *snapped* his wrist and how the ball came out of his hand. His coach said to me "would you like to meet him?" I said "yeah, I'd love to meet him!" (I always like to meet them.) He brought me up to the classroom, opened the door, and as I stood in the doorway, in walks this skinny, long haired kid who only weighted about a buck-sixty. And I thought to myself, "I just wasted my entire day."

Then, he came over and shook my hand—and when he did, he engulfed my hand all the way up to my wrist. Then I said to myself, "well, maybe I didn't waste my entire day after all!" He had these enormous hands; he could just snap his wrist and the ball would come spinning out. That's really what you saw on film was how *quickly* the ball came out of his hand and it certainly had something to do with his hand size, the ability to throw the ball with big hands. If the weather's bad, big hands are hugely important. I try to look at hand size, even when I go to shake a quarterback's hand. You know the ball is not going to fall out of his hand if it's sufficiently large.

If you have small hands, I think you can adjust how you grip it or get your coach to use the smallest regulation ball you can get, or underinflate the ball to the low end of regulation (Tom Brady is not the only one that ever did that, everybody did that!). I don't like to get too caught up in physical measurements, but I think when the quarterback's hands get above 9" or 9 1/4", you're in good shape. The bigger the hand size the better. If he's right at 9" and under, I think it can sometimes be a concern.

I really like *that* grip (Figure 2-1). There's also this "new" grip with the pinky off the seams. I don't know as much about it (Figure 2-2), but that could also be a hand size issue, if a guy's hands are just too big to hold it the other way. There are some guys who just can't hold the ball like I prefer, because their hands are so big. Then, they have to move the left hand down a little bit, as opposed to being parallel (Figure 2-3). You can see how his hands and fingers are down a little, because of how long his fingers are.

Figure 2-1

Figure 2-2

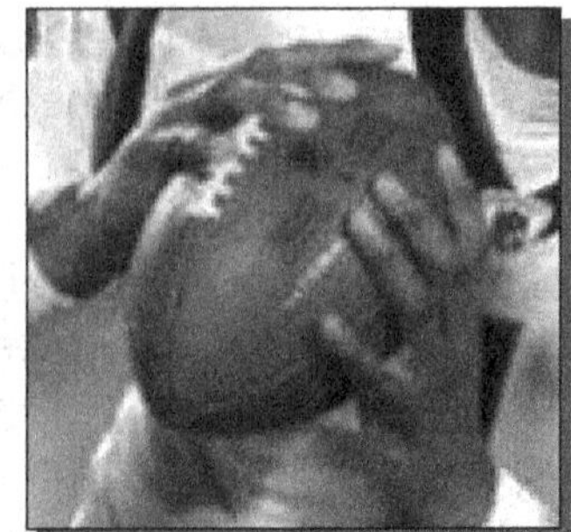

Figure 2-3

Again, the wrist snap and release concern me more than the throwing motion. I have a friend whose son is highly recruited going into his sophomore year of high school and everyone's giving him a bad time about how he kind of drops the ball down to throw. I said to him "I wouldn't worry too much about it. Pat Mahomes does it. The quarterback at Clemson (Trevor Lawrence) does it." People were saying that he held the ball too low on his chest and he drops it, as though that's an issue. It's more important that he can *spin* it and that he's a *natural thrower*.

## Touch Passing

I'm often asked if you can teach a guy to throw with "touch." I think you definitely can, and I think that happens as you talk about the different throws that you make. You teach him the different throws. Quarterbacks are of course going to have to be able to make what we call the "1 ball," which is on a line 12-to-15 yards, firing the fastball. Then we have a "2 ball," which is a seam throw, back shoulder fade throw, or fade throw inside the 20, where there is some air involved in it and some touch on it, but you need to get the ball to come down. You work *hard* on getting the ball to come down on that seam route between 18-to-22 yards.

A good way to do that is take some of those tackling dummies and put them out there at the linebacker areas, and have him get the ball over them, but come down. There's also throwing behind a goalpost, where you learn how to get your elbow and shoulder up to get the ball just over the goalpost. Then, you can back up and work on dropping it down over the goalpost. Those are two different drills to develop that. You can definitely work on that "2 ball" and getting better on "touch."

You can also do that with the "3 ball," which is the long ball. You get near the goalpost, tilt your left shoulder and release the ball over the goalpost to get air under it. Then, the more you back up, the more you're working on "touch," where you drop the ball in with less air on it. But you can certainly help quarterbacks develop those three kinds of throws ("1, 2 and 3 balls") with "touch" and then talk to them so they not only understand these differences, but they especially get a feel for *when* the ball comes out.

For example, a comeback is not a "1 ball." What you want to do on a comeback is get your feet set and throw the ball *before* the receiver is out of his break, to be able to make it a "2 ball" to the sideline. It's all about the *feel* of when the receiver is coming out of the break and getting the ball out before he's coming out of it. "Am I early? Am I late?" If I'm early, I throw it softer. If I'm late, I throw closer to a "1 ball." That anticipation just comes with the experience of doing it over and over and over again.

Screens, flares, and throws like that to the running back are often where the most touch is needed. That's a drill that you need to work at every day. On what we call our "fade drill," you "fade" back to your right, throw off your right foot, and then "fade" to your left, and throw off your left foot. You're working on getting your hips up and over and then snapping your wrist at the top to get the point of the ball to turn over. Then you, can fade to your right to throw off your *left* foot, and fade to your left and throw off your *right* foot. Again, working your hips up and over and getting the point to turn over.

You also need to do that on what we call "hots" and "built-ins," where I drift away from the blitz, I throw off either my right or left foot, snap my wrist, and get the ball out on time. That's what our quarterbacks call "drill work." In a game, it happens all the time like that; for example, there's all kinds of video out there of Lamar Jackson fading away from pressure in the red zone, and then hitting the crosser for touchdowns. He worked that every day during the special teams' portion of practice. Throwing with "touch" is really about developing the ability to have the drill show up, just like it does with every other position. If you're coaching it effectively, the drill shows up on the video. And you *certainly* can get better at that!

## Quarterbacks and Other Sports

It really is hard to change a guy's throwing motion. In that regard, I like a guy with a background in baseball, because they can often throw accurately from varying release points. In general, I like quarterbacks who play other sports besides football. You like guys who win at basketball, win at baseball; go play cards and win at poker. Some guys just win at everything–that's the guy you want! I think golfing is a good thing for quarterbacks (even though Lamar Jackson wasn't a golfer). I think a lot of really good quarterbacks are also really good golfers. Chris Redman was a scratch golfer. It's good for you because you develop the ability to concentrate and focus in order to make the shots. You put pressure on yourself as both a golfer and as a quarterback. One of the things you try to do is block the outside pressure out and just play within yourself. I think golf really helps that.

I don't like with young kids these days, where parents make them play one sport. Young athletes should get other experiences; that's what I told a friend of mine whose son didn't play high school baseball this year. Even though he could be the best baseball player in his state, he just wanted to work on being a quarterback. I said to him "oh, and by the way, let him play baseball. Being happy and winning–getting in the habit of winning every time he goes out on that mound–will help him be a better quarterback way more than going to all these camps you're sending him to." He's a great guy and was a little shocked by that. The other thing is, what if you burn him out at that age or he gets an overuse injury from just doing one sport? That whole concept of one sport is wrong. Go compete at everything, it all helps you!

We've had a lot of great football players who got drafted into the NFL, but who grew up thinking they were going to play in the NBA. Then 8th grade, freshman year, they're not growing anymore. Maybe you have to start earlier with basketball, because it's so much hand-eye coordination but if you've been competing in other sports, you can pick up football at a later age. Some of the best receivers we've ever had were that way. Play other sports, those are the good kids to go get!

## Quarterback Personality

Sometimes, you just have to beat the blitz and take a hit. That's when the quarterback needs to respond according to his personality. They're all going to act differently, but as long as it's consistent and within their personality, who really cares? It's when they step out of it, that their concentration is gone.

> Note: Psychologists call this *Persona*. It's this "front" that you put up, of how you want people to see you. The more of that *Persona* that you fight to put out there, the more poorly *integrated* you become. It begins to pull you apart from who you authentically are. People who do that—celebrities who manufacture a public image, for example—can get themselves out of balance, because everything in this *Persona* they've cultivated becomes less and less real, until they finally lose who they actually are. The words *integrated* and *integrity* are not a coincidence to psychologists. Be who you are!

That's important for a quarterback to understand; maybe I'm trying to act like this tough guy who can "talk trash," but if that's not what I naturally am, I can't maintain that "front" and still be zoned in to play at my best. Every quarterback needs to handle himself according to his own personality. For example, Stefan LeFors was one of the best quarterbacks I ever got to coach. Stefan was a ferocious competitor, but he was a quiet leader who led by example. But then Doug Nussmeier always wanted to act like a linebacker. Dave Raggone was a little like that as well and both of them are coaches now. Lamar Jackson didn't "yap," but he wanted to make sure that you knew "I'm better than you." He had some of that in him. If a quarterback is going to lead his team effectively, he has to do it in a way that's authentic to his own personality.

There are all different kinds of quarterbacks and many types of guys can help you win games. We obviously believe strongly in the specific skills and tangibles we've talked about. However, it's also necessary to help your quarterback establish the best version of who he truly is, in order to play at his highest level and lead your team. Passing the football starts with taking care of your quarterback. Next, let's talk about protecting the passer and our philosophy of various pass protections.

## Flipping Offensive Linemen

Our pass protections are set up as if we're flipping the line. We have a "strongside" line and a "weakside" line. The majority of the time, the strongside line goes *to* the call or *to* the tight end, and the weakside goes away (though we can also call certain things where they would just go line up left and right, such as our "tempo" packages).

The advantage of that is that you can put your best player at the weak tackle. He's generally going to be by himself, so he has to be able to handle speed rushes by defensive ends, and also blitzes by outside linebackers and safeties off that weakside edge. From there, you can help everybody else if you have issues, but the weak tackle has to be able to handle it himself. That's how the offense was first built.

You want a weak guard who's athletic, smart, and tough, who can really move. He's often asked to pull and trap. Center is always a crucial position. I've been fortunate enough to coach one of the best centers that was out there, a first-round draft pick in Eric Wood. He would be the perfect guy because he was athletic, he could bend, and he was tough; he had a little "nasty" in him. Your center needs the intelligence to make the right calls, but he also needs to have a bit of "sneaky nasty" in him, to do what he's asked to do, particularly in the run game to be able to get through to the linebackers.

Your strong guard should be your biggest, most physical guy (who can bend), because the majority of the time, he's going to have to block a 3-technique. Now, you can find ways to work the center to him or help him with the tackle or running back, but he's going to have to be able to handle a 3-technique. Then, your strong tackle ideally would be a young guy who has the ability to eventually play weak tackle, but he needs to grow and mature into it. He's going to be big and physical. He can get help with the tight end, chipping in protections and the run game, but you want him strong and physical. This way, we were able to say that you aren't necessarily required to have equal tackles. We were saying that a player is able to protect the open side and we're able to help everybody else.

Ideally, the strongside is the power-running side where they're able to do a great job on double-teams between either the strong guard/strong tackle or the tight end/strong tackle. Then, the "quickside" is where you're able to run the ball outside with quickness and speed. You can always get a tight end their way as well, so you can still run anything strong or weak, depending on who your best players are.

I think teams aren't doing that anymore because coaches like them in one stance, as opposed to two. The tempo stuff sometimes forces the issue of playing right and left as well. However, a lot of the NFL teams really liked it, because when they would come in, they got to watch a guy playing both in a left-handed and right-handed stance, which helped some of our linemen in their position flexibility to get into the NFL. I know we had more than one guy who stuck on in the NFL because of the ability to play in either stance and to be the backup right tackle, right guard and left guard.

We also like it, because we use it to get matchups; again, our philosophy always involves identifying and dictating matchups with whichever of our players we want on each of their defensive guys. We obviously do that with the backs and receivers but flipping linemen allows us to create mismatches up front as well. What's also interesting is that it can minimize various techniques, so we've actually been able to carry more plays by thinking of things as strong and weakside concepts.

It also makes pass protection easier for the running backs. For example, in our "70" protection, they just need to know to check to the side of the strong tackle and they can even just understand where to go by knowing who that player is. Also, I thought it was always an advantage for us, simply because nobody else was doing it.

## Pass Protections

Everything we will describe in this section will be set up terminology-wise as if you're in a "right" formation. I always like to have an overview of protections, so everybody *coaches* it that way, everybody *understands* it that way, and everybody knows exactly what it is (Figure 2-4). That starts with "what's the drop?" "What's the protection unit? "What does the tight end have?" "What does the o-line have?" "What's the running backs' responsibility?" "What's the quarterback's responsibility?" And if there are "sights" and "hots," what exactly are those? Let's look at the following protections, and address them each according to protection units:

**Rose/Lima Protection**
(1- or 2-Back Formations)
Combo Protections (½ Slide, ½ Man)

QUICK GAME
LIMA
6 MAN PROTECTION
- TE White Call
- OL 4 down to 1st (callside)(hot left)
- Back has 1 to 2 right from 0 pt (away callside)
- Vs 4 from side or gap pressure Lip/Rip Y Call

**360 Protection – 3 Step**
**60 Protection – 5 Step**
(2-Back Formations)

60 PROTECTION
DROPBACK
BASE 7 MAN PROTECTION/2 BACK
- TE White Call
- OL 4 Down to Mike
- Weak back Will to anything outside
- Strong back Sam to anything outside
- Vs 4 weak Lucky/Ringo Call (re-ID the Mike)

**Rip/Liz Protection**
(1- or 2-Back Formations)
Full Slide Protection

QUICK GAME NORMALLY
6 or 7-MAN PROTECTION
- TE White Call with Y call/if no Y call Black
- OL full slide gap protection to call side
- RB block opposite call off OT hip
- Vs 6-1 check Lima/Rose

**80 Protection**
(1-Back Formations)
Man-Based Protection

DROPBACK
7-MAN 1-BACK PROTECTION
- TE Grey Call
- OL 4 Down to 1st LB strong from TE Box – Picks up 4 Strong
- Back has 2 to 3 from pt LBer Weak
- Vs 4 Weak Lucky/Ringo Call

Figure 2-4. Protections Overview

**70 Protection**
(1- or 2-Back Formations)
Combo Protections (½ Slide, ½ Man)

DROPBACK
6-Man Protection
- TE White Call
- OL has 4 down to 1st LBer weak (hot left)
- Back has 1 to 2 strong from 0 pt
- Vs 4 from a side Lucky/Ringo Call

**142/143 Protection**
**140/141 Protection**
(2-Back Formations)
Combo Protections (½ Slide, ½ Man)

2-BACK PLAYACTION
142
7-MAN PROTECTION
- TE White Call
- OL has 4 down to Will (Hot Left)
- F has Mike, R has Sam to Anything outside
- Vs blitz check run

**Lucky/Ringo Protection**
(1- or 2-Back Formations)

DROP BACK
LUCKY
6-MAN PROTECTION
- TE White Call
- OL has 4 down to 1st LBer left (callside)
- Back has 4th rusher left (callside)
- Off 1 away from callside

**400 Protection**
(1- or 2-Back Formations)
Combo Protection (½ Slide, ½ Man)

DROPBACK
6-MAN PROTECTION
- TE White Call
- OL 4 Down to 1st LBer strong (hot right)
- Back has 1 to 2 weak from 0 pt
- Vs 4 from a side Ringo/Lucky Call

**Act 3/4 PROTECTION**
(1-Back Formations)
Man-Based Protection

1-BACK PLAYACTION
7-MAN PROTECTION
- TE Black Call
- OL has 4 down to the Mike + Sam
- RB fake 17 weak has Will to anything outside
- Vs blitz check run

**Ram/Lion Protection**
(No Back Protection)
Combo Protection (½ Slide, ½ Man)

5 MAN PROTECTION
- TE White Call
- OL down to 1st LBer callside (hot callside); alert sink backside
- Back free release
- Redirect w/ Ram-Ram/Lion-Lion Call

VS 30
- TE White Call
- OL double sort
- Back free release
- Redirect w/ Ram-Ram/Lion-Lion Call

Figure 2-4. Protections Overview (cont.)

7-Man Protections:

- 360, 60
- Solid, 80

6-Man Protections:

- Lima/Rose (Rose/Lima)
- Liz/Rip (Liz/Rip "Y")
- 70, 400

5-Man Protections:

- Lion/Ram (Ram/Lion)
- Scat 70, Scat 400
- Sara/Sally

## 360 and 60 (7-Man Protections)

When we're in 2-back offense (whether that's "regular" 21 personnel or "spread" 20 personnel), we have basic 7-man protections. We're able to use the same rules, whether it's a 3-step drop, a 5-step drop, or sometimes a 7-step drop. If we're going to run a 3-step drop, we call "360" (Figure 2-5). "60" protection would be a 5-step drop (Figure 2-6). If we wanted to go 7-step drop, then we would call "deep 60" protection, so the tackles understand where the quarterback's set is. For example, if you're going to call a comeback route, you would say "*deep* 63 comeback," in order to emphasize the depth of the dropback to the tackles.

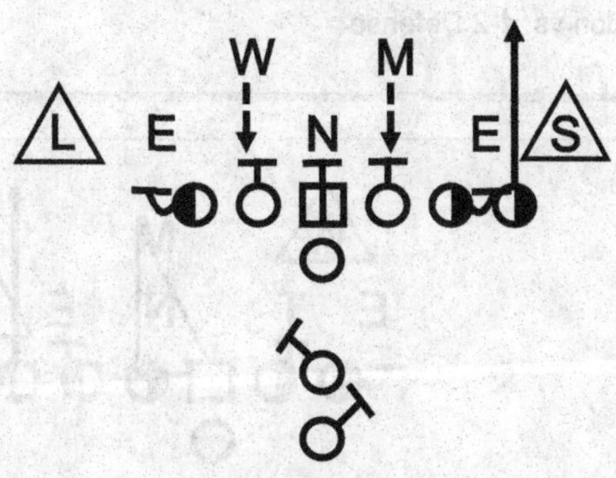


Figure 2-5a: 360 (3-step, 2-Back) Protection vs. 30 Defense

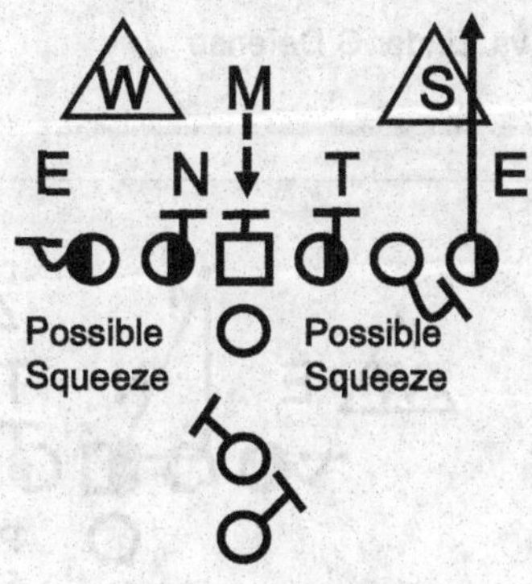


Figure 2-5b: 360 Protection vs. College 4-3 Defense

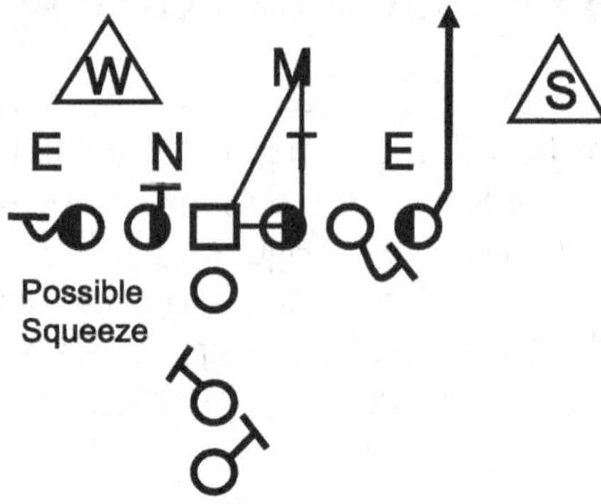


Figure 2-5c: 360 Protection vs. 4-2 Defense

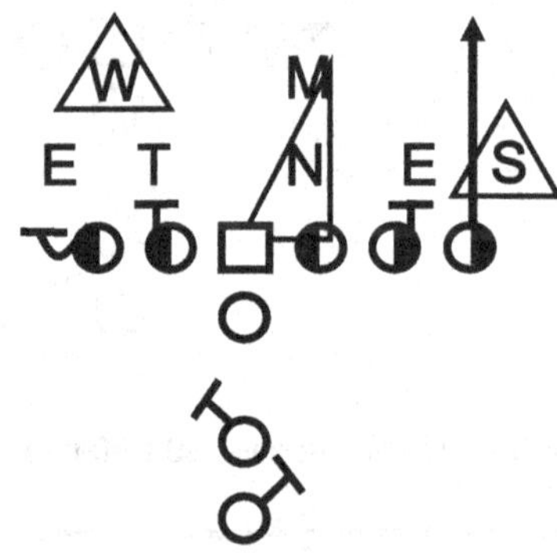


Figure 2-5d: 360 Protection vs. Under G Defense

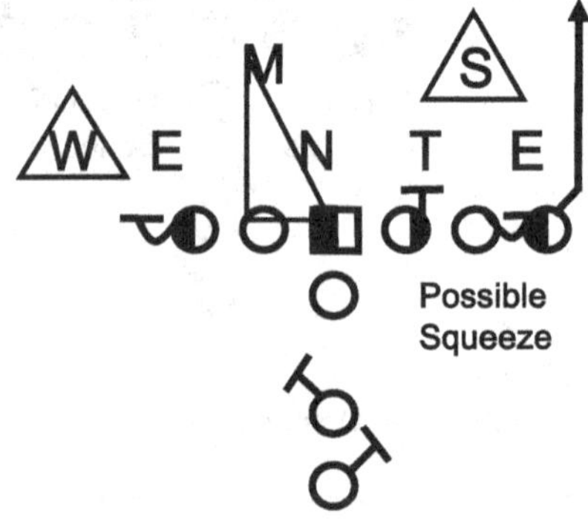


Figure 2-5e: 360 Protection vs. Over Defense

**360 Protection**

| Pos: | Rules: |
|---|---|
| Y | 1. Free release. Run route.<br>2. Max call: stay in. block Sam/DE. |
| ST | Man-on<br>1. Block first man-on or outside.<br>2. Alert squeeze call from RG. Signal to R. |
| SG | 1. vs. Uncovered: Make "talking" call. Possible Ray with center.<br>2. vs. covered: block man-on.<br>3. vs. non-point LB threat in A/B gap: Make "squeeze" call to RT. (When QB is under center |
| C | Base man-on, Declare MLB point (Middle of 3).<br>1. Make "Ray" or "Lou" call to guard<br>2. vs. 30 front: base<br>3. vs. 8-man front: point goes weak<br>4. Alert for Ringo/Lucky from QB to redirect the point |
| WG | 1. vs. Uncovered: Make "talking" call. Possible Lou with center.<br>2. vs. Covered: Block man-on.<br>3. vs. non-point LB threat in A/B Gap: Make "squeeze" call to LT (When QB is under center).<br>4. Alert for Ringo/Lucky from QB to redirect the point. |
| WT | Man-on<br>1. Block first man-on or outside.<br>2. Alert squeeze call from LG. Signal to R. |
| F | Must tell R which direction you are going.<br>1. Alert to point.<br>2. Block 1-2 LB away from point. Block 2-3 LB to point.<br>3. Alert to squeeze signal by tackle. Drive the hip.<br>4. Run 3-yd checkdown.<br>5. Alert for Ringo/Lucky from QB to redirect point. |
| R | Must know which direction F is going.<br>1. Alert to point.<br>2. Block 1-2 LB away from point. Block 2-3 to point.<br>3. Alert to squeeze signal by tackle. Drive the hip.<br>4. Run 3 yd checkdown.<br>5. Alert for Ringo/Lucky from QB to redirect point. |

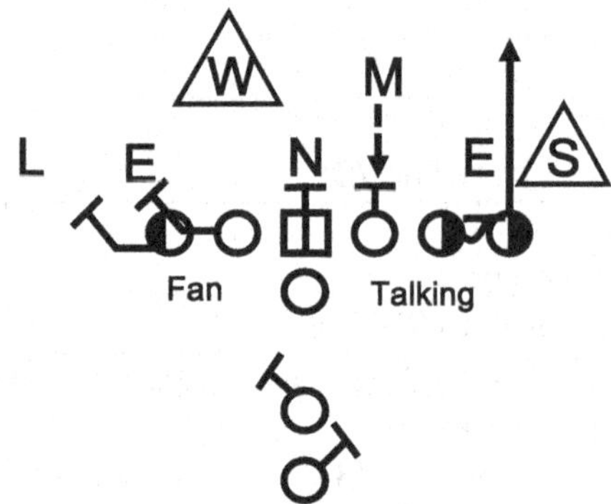


Figure 2-6a: 60 (5-step, 2-Back) Protection vs. 30 Defense

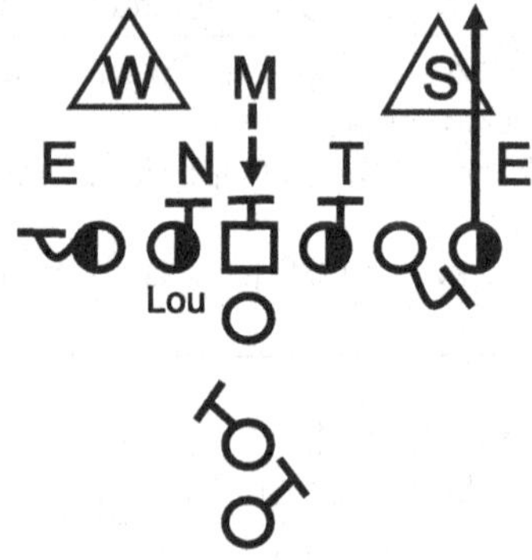


Figure 2-6b: 60 Protection vs. College 4-3 Defense

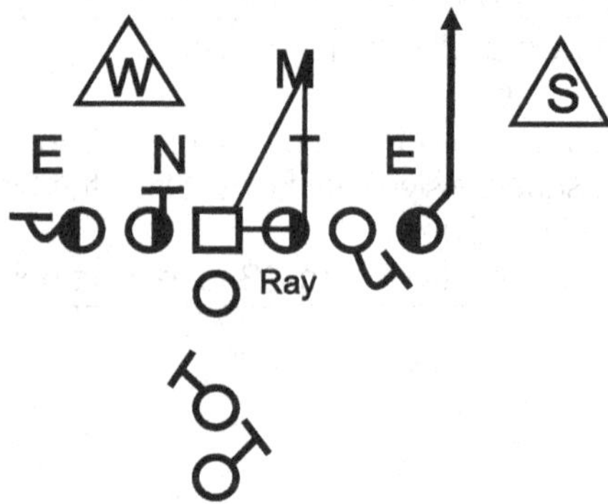


Figure 2-6c: 60 Protection vs. 4-2 Defense

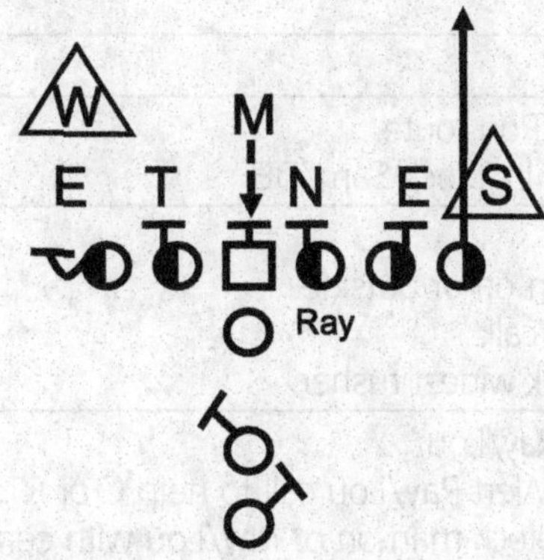

Figure 2-6d: 60 Protection vs. Under G Defense

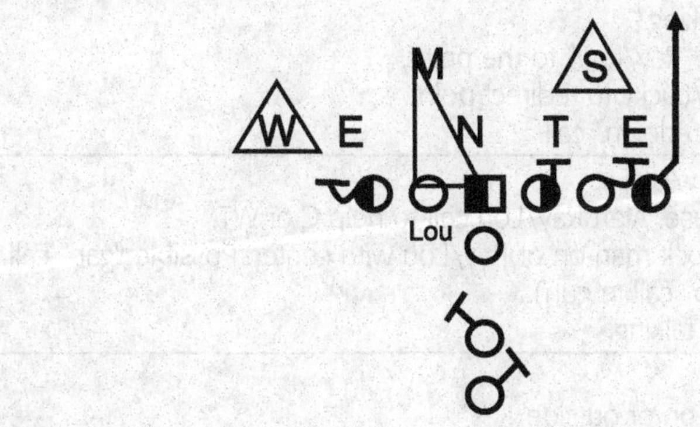

Figure 2-6e: 60 Protection vs. Over Defense

On our 360 and 60, it's a man-based protection, with a 7-man protection unit. The tight end has a free-release in the 2-back set, so he's what we call "white." The linemen have the "4-down linemen plus the middle linebacker," whom we refer to as the "middle of the 3." The backs have outside linebackers, depending on what formation we're in: if you're in a "strong" formation, the fullback would have the strong linebacker. In "weak" formation, the fullback would have the weak linebacker. In the "I" formation, the fullback will pat his hip to tell the tailback which way he's going, and the tailback goes opposite. The backs have the "first linebacker plus one past the point." That's something they need to understand.

Our sight adjustment in this instance is to the weakside. To that X receiver side, that means a secondary player (corner or free-safety) coming is "plus one" with a linebacker. If it's a "corner plus one," we're going to sight adjust to a hitch. If it's a "safety plus one," we "sight-adjust" to a slant. Then, X is going to have to "sight adjust" and say, "do it, do it, do it!" (Figure 2-7).

**"60" Protection**

| Pos: | Rules: |
|---|---|
| Y | 1. Free release. Run route.<br>2. Max call: stay in. block Sam/DE |
| ST | Man-on<br>1. Block 1st man-on or outside.<br>2. Alert 5-down call.<br>3. vs. Bear: Block widest rusher. |
| SG | Man-on, Base, Ray/Lou<br>1. vs. 30: base. Alert Ray/Lou call to help C or RT.<br>2. vs. covered: block man-on or Ray/Lou with center. Possible "gap" call away from Ray/Lou (no "gap" call in gun).<br>3. vs. uncovered: talking |
| C | Man-on, talking, Ray/Lou.<br>1. vs. covered: block man-on.<br>2. vs. 0 Mike: "talking."<br>3. vs. uncovered: "Ray/Lou" to the point.<br>4. Alert for Ringo/Lucky to redirect point.<br>5. vs. diamond: "5-down" call. |
| WG | Man-on, base, Ray/Lou.<br>1. vs. 30 front: base. Alert Ray/Lou call to help C or WT.<br>2. vs. covered: block man-on or Ray/Lou with center. Possible "gap" call away from Ray/Lou (no "gap" call in gun).<br>3. vs. uncovered: talking. |
| WT | Man-on.<br>1. Block 1st man-on or outside.<br>2. vs. 30: base/fan (gameplan). |
| F | Double-check, release on route.<br>1. vs. 30: base protection<br>2. Alert to point.<br>3. Block 1-2 LB away from point LB. Block 2-3 to point LB.<br>4. Alert gap call away from Ringo/Lucky. |
| R | Double-check, release on route.<br>1. vs. 30: base protection.<br>2. Alert to point.<br>3. Block 1-2 LB away from point LB. Block 2-3 to point LB.<br>4. Alert gap call away from Ringo/Lucky. |

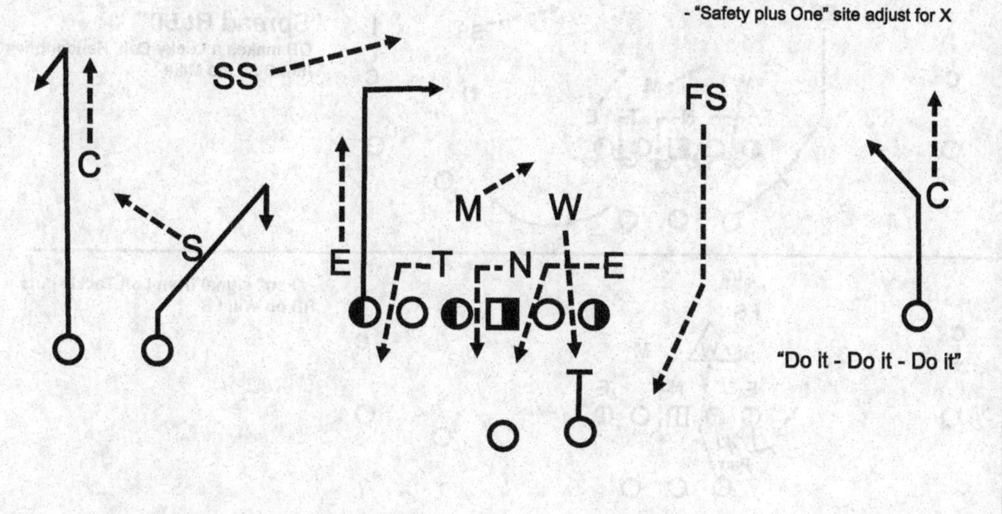

- "Safety plus One" site adjust for X

"Do it - Do it - Do it"

Figure 2-7: 480 Eagle – Sight Adjust

## Lucky/Ringo Call

We are able to redirect the point with a "Lucky/Ringo" (or "Ringo/Lucky") call. What we're doing in this instance is re-identifying the Mike linebacker. If the quarterback sees the Will/corner or Will/safety coming, he's going to redirect the point, make Will the "Mike," so the center and the line would then have "4-down plus the Will" (or "new Mike"). The back would have the first thing outside of the point (Figure 2-8). The back away from the slide would have the "first linebacker plus one" away from the new point. This is a way to redirect the protection or "re-ID" the Mike linebacker.

In a "30" front, we have 2 ways to block it. We can "base" it, where the back has the edge and the weak guard/weak tackle are "me/you" on the defensive end and Will linebacker. However, if we're getting a "30" defense, in which they like their rush guy to come from the weakside, we can signal that back a "fan" call and have the line "fan" to what we refer to as the "Liz" linebacker. At that point, the running back to that side would have the Will. We do this a lot and it's something that you have to carry, in order to be able to address those pressures (see Figure 2-8).

Against "diamond" (or "bear 46" defense), we make a "5-down" call and now the backs have to point to who their linebacker is "plus one to that side." It is a good protection vs. diamond, because you have the two backs in the backfield (Figure 2-9). The coaching point on 8-man front is "the point goes weak." If you get a true 8-man front like the old days, we have the point start weak. If it's a "4-2-5" defense, we usually start the point weak, so that the pressure side is picked up, and then you would "redirect" to the strong side.

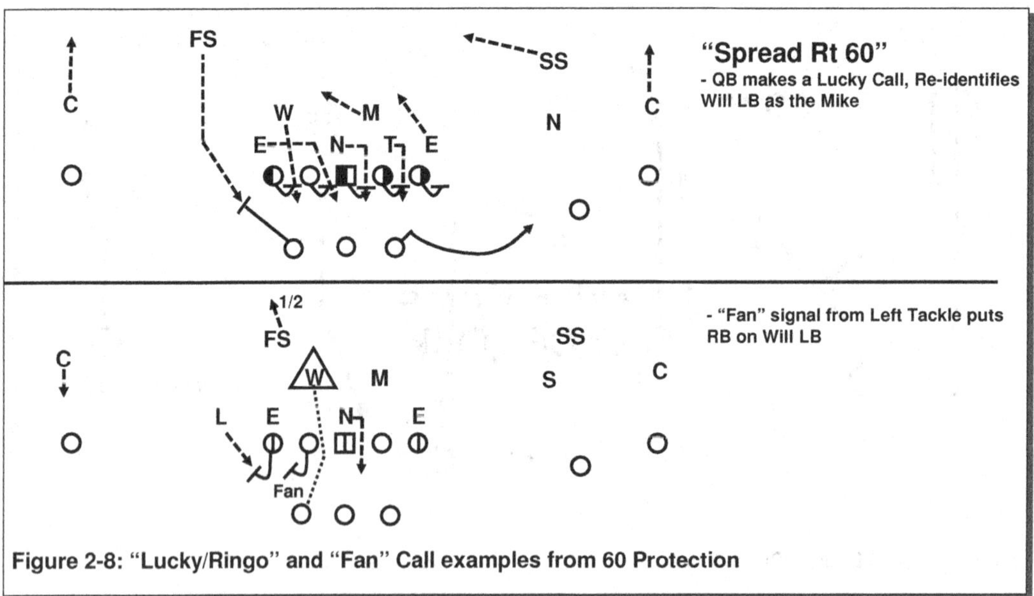

Figure 2-8: "Lucky/Ringo" and "Fan" Call examples from 60 Protection

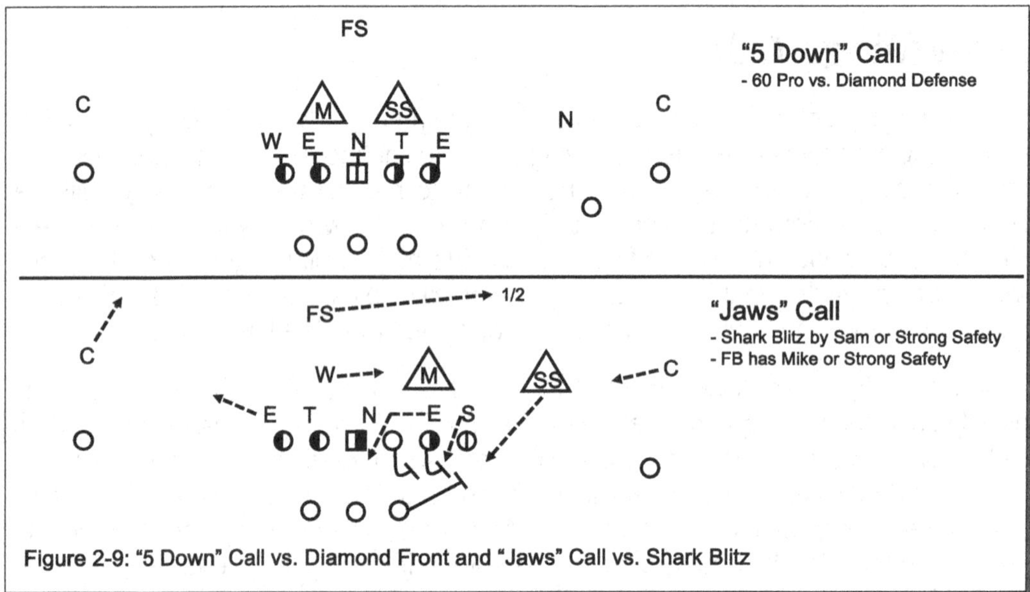

Figure 2-9: "5 Down" Call vs. Diamond Front and "Jaws" Call vs. Shark Blitz

## Gap, Squeeze, Jaws Calls

We carry certain *calls* in 60 protection. If we get A-gap pressure away from the point linebacker, and the quarterback is under the center, we may have to "gap" down with the guard and then the back takes the B-gap. This doesn't happen a whole lot (particularly since shotgun has become more popular), but the "gap" call means that the guard to that side would pick up the A-gap pressure and then the back to that side blocks the defensive lineman (see Figure 2-6). If it's a 3-step drop ("360"), we "squeeze" it, which means now the tackle comes down with the guard to pick up A and B-gap pressure, and the back blocks off the end (see Figure 2-5). Two things you always have to practice in this protection are "gap" and "squeeze."

We do have a "jaws" call, which is when we're getting Sam/strong-safety pressure (what we refer to as a "shark" blitz, thus "jaws"). Then, we're going to go ahead and "fan" the strong guard and tackle out to the Sam linebacker, and the running back would have responsibility for the strong-safety. In that look, we want to be able to block it up and still be able to get the tight end out (see Figure 2-9). This is a 2-back protection that picks up 4 to the side of the point and "3 out of 4" away from the point. It's very solid, sound protection, something that is good to show early in a game.

## Solid (7-Man Protection)

To get the equivalent of the 7-man protection out of 1-back, we call "solid" protection. What you're doing in this instance is your tight end is taking the responsibility of the second back. The rules in "solid" would be: if it's a 5-step drop back, the tight end is "black," which means he's now in the protection scheme. The o-line has the "4-down plus the Mike," the running back has the "Will plus one." The tight end's responsibility is the Sam linebacker, or to "scheme it" with the tackle to block the Sam linebacker. So, if the tackle is uncovered, the tight end has to be able to know where the Sam linebacker is; either the tackle and guard are responsible for Sam, or the tight end makes a "fan" call to the tackle and he and the tackle are responsible for Sam instead (Figure 2-10). It's something that's a very good "blitz check," especially against "blitz cover-zero."

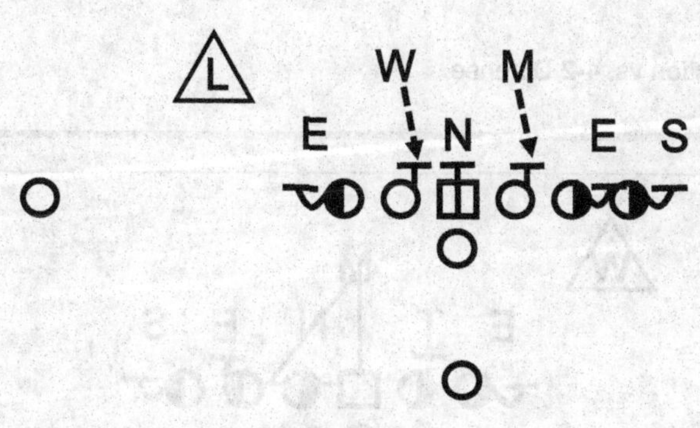


Figure 2-10a: Solid (5-step, 7-Man, Big-on-Big) Protection vs. 30 Defense

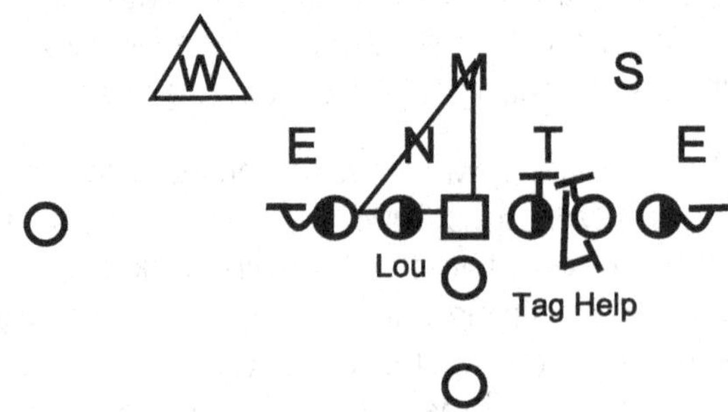

Figure 2-10b: Solid Protection vs. College 4-3 Defense

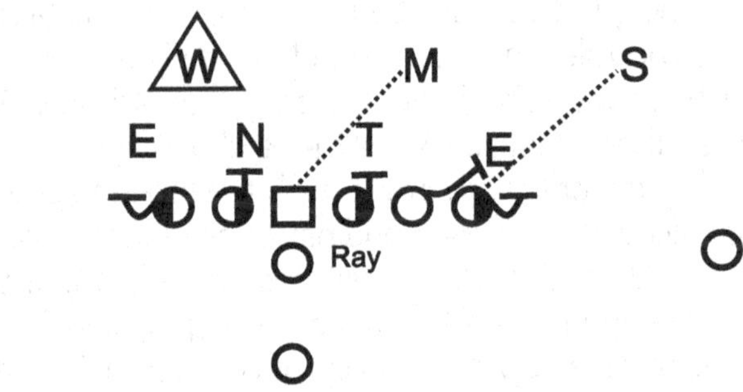

Figure 2-10c: Solid Protection vs. 4-2 Defense

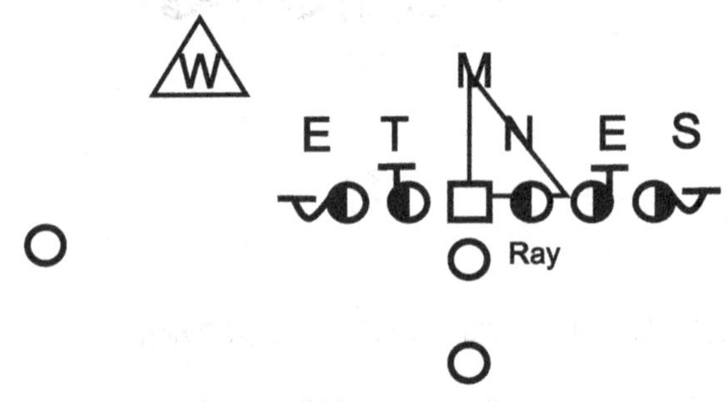

Figure 2-10d: Solid Protection vs. Under G Defense

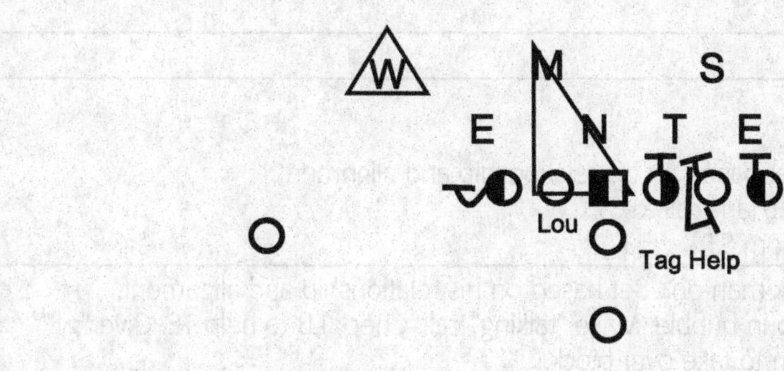

Figure 2-10e: Solid Protection vs. Over Defense

If it's a 3-4 defense, we usually "base" it. We're saying that we're in solid 7-man protection for pressure, so instead of "fan" to the weak side, we just make it an automatic "base" call. There's also a possibility you could "fan" it (as we previously described), if you wanted to use a lot of this protection.

## 80 (7-Man Protection)

We have "80" protection, which is kind of a unique protection; not a lot of teams carry this. It's another 5-step drop protection, with a 7-man protection unit. In this instance, the tight end can "check release," so the tight end is what we call "grey."

> (Note: our tight end rules are "white" he's free-release, "black" he's in, and "grey" he's checking his way out, so we can still get him involved in the route.)

On this protection, the o-linemen are going to have the "4-down linemen, plus the first linebacker from the strong tackle bubble weak." We have to understand where that linebacker is. Doing it this way, the quarterback understands that "I got 4-strong protected, I don't have to worry about my back, I just have to worry about making a 'Lucky/Ringo' call to the 4-weak." The running back has to check the "#2 to #3 linebacker from the strong tackle bubble weak." He's got to be able to count to three. He knows the center has that first linebacker in that bubble, so I have the next linebacker over "plus-one" (Figure 2-11).

**"Solid" Protection**

| Pos: | Rules: |
|---|---|
| Y | Man-on (black)<br>1. Make "black" call.<br>2. Block man-on. Set based on his relationship and alignment.<br>3. Alert to make "eat/fan" call to ST.<br>4. Alert for go call from ST. |
| ST | 1. vs. covered: block man-on. Set based on his relationship and alignment.<br>2. vs. uncovered: Lb in bubble. Make "talking" call. Check LB to help TE. Give "go" call when in position to take over block.<br>3. vs. LB stack: Make "tag/help" call to RB.<br>4. vs. 41: alert to make "eat/fan" call to TE. |
| SG | Man-on (or off ball)<br>1. vs. uncovered: make "talking" call. Check Mike to help.<br>2. vs. covered: block man-on. Alert for possible Ray from center.<br>3. No Ray call. Set based on his relationship and alignment.<br>4. vs. 42: must know where point LB is. |
| C | Man-on (or off ball). Set point LB to middle of 3.<br>1. vs. covered: block man-on.<br>2. vs. uncovered: make "talking" call. Check MLB to help.<br>3. Alert to make "Ray/Lou" call to guards.<br>4. Zone all line games and blitzes.<br>5. Alert for Ringo/Lucky call to redirect point.<br>6. vs. 42: declare point weak, alert fan call by TE. Move point strong. |
| WG | Man-on (or off ball)<br>1. vs. uncovered: make "talking" call. Check LB to help.<br>2. vs. covered: block man-on. Alert for possible Lou call from center.<br>3. Zone all line games and blitzes.<br>4. vs. KC left: fan. |
| WT | Man-on<br>1. Block man-on. Set based on his relationship and alignment.<br>2. Zone all line games.<br>3. vs. KC left: fan. |
| R | Check 1st LB weak from point<br>1. vs. under and KC weak: Check weak ILB<br>2. Key FS alignment to anticipate pressure.<br>3. Alert gap by LG to cut outside knee of 3 tech. |

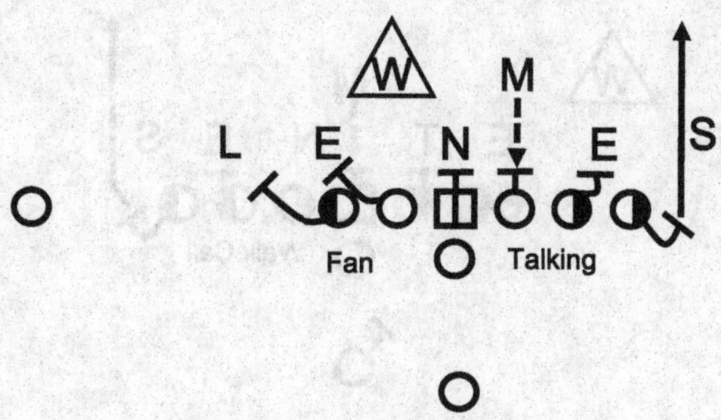


Figure 2-11a: 80 (5-step, Check Release by Tight End) Protection vs. 30 Defense

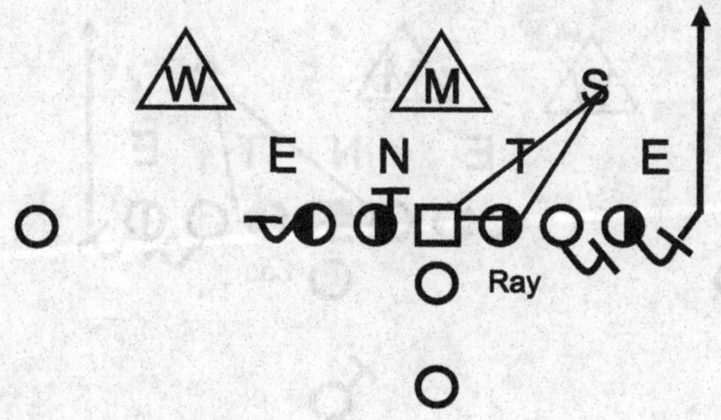


Figure 2-11b: 80 Protection vs. College 4-3 Defense

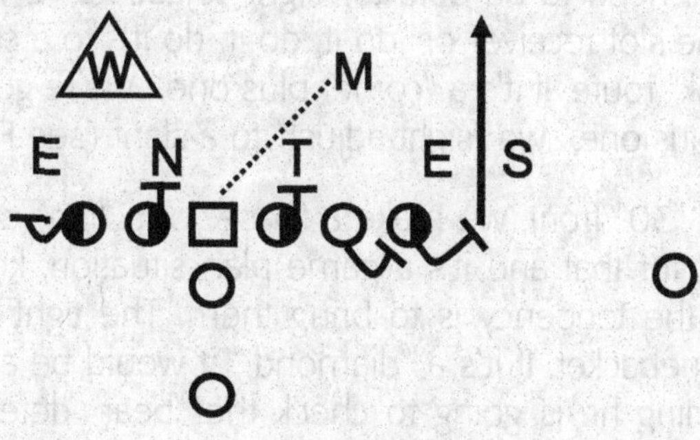


Figure 2-11c: 80 Protection vs. 4-2 Defense

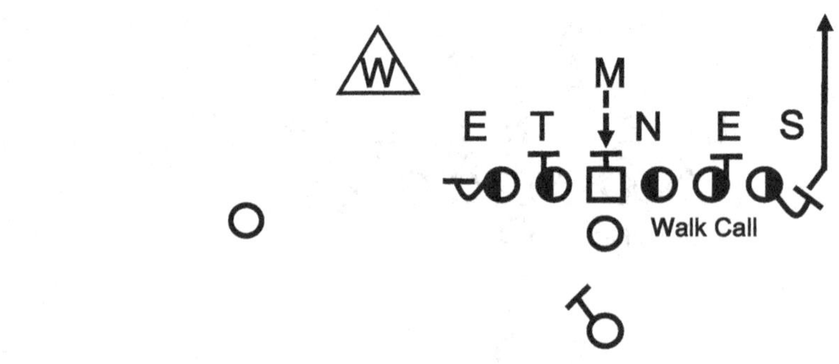


Figure 2-11d: 80 Protection vs. Under G Defense

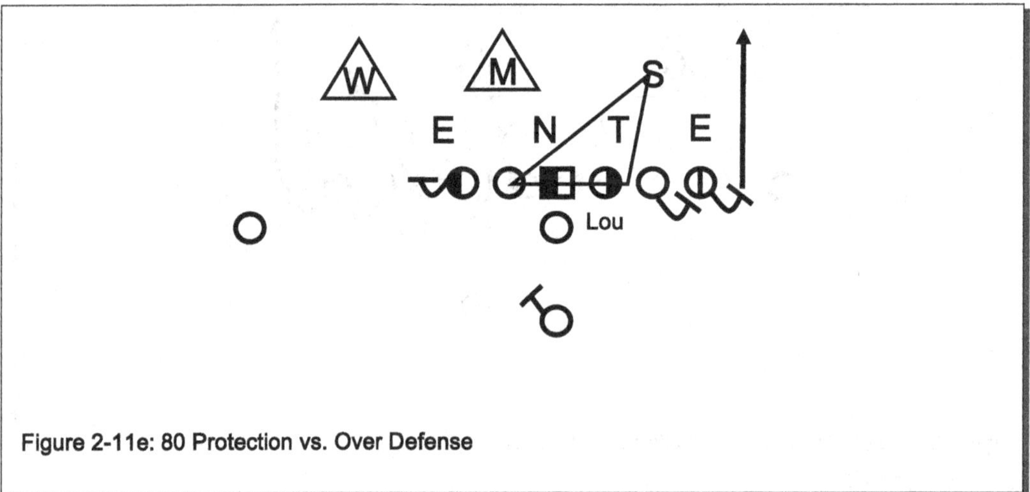


Figure 2-11e: 80 Protection vs. Over Defense

We still need to be able to "sight-adjust" to "2-weak," whether that's a "hot, hot, hot!" by the slot receiver or "do it, do it, do it!" to a single receiver. Our "hot" rule is to run a "hook" route. If it's a "corner plus one," we're going to sight adjust to a hitch. If it's a "safety plus one," we "sight-adjust" to a slant (see Figure 2-7).

With a "30" front, we make a "base" or a "fan" call weak, so the running back has to be alert for that and it's a game plan situation, knowing who the best rushers are and what the tendency is to bring them. The tight end is checking his way out, off the Sam linebacker. If it's a "diamond," it would be a "5-down" call with the tight end, understanding he is going to check the "bear" defender who is over him, and we'll "fan" the tackle past the "bear" defender for an outside guy coming. The running back is now in a "scan" (Figure 2-12). There are times we've mixed that up, so it's always a game plan-type of a deal.

**"80" Protection**

| Pos: | Rules: |
|---|---|
| Y | Check key to route called.<br>1. Make "grey" call to RT.<br>2. vs. covered and RT covered: check Sam. If he drops, run route.<br>3. vs. RT uncovered: key for pressure. Possible "out" call.<br>4. vs. Bear: check Bear and run route.<br>5. vs. no LB in box: make "walk" call. |
| ST | Man-on<br>1. vs. covered: block man-on. Set to his relationship and alignment.<br>2. vs. uncovered: block man-on or outside. Alert for possible out call from TE.<br>3. vs. no LB in box: make "walk" call to alert center. Set man-on.<br>4. vs. KC: fan with RG. |
| SG | Man-on or off ball (Talking)<br>1. vs. covered: block man-on. Alert for me/you (Ray) from center. You are protected inside.<br>2. vs. uncovered: talking. set, eyeball key to help (C/RT). Understand Ray/Lou call.<br>3. vs. KC: fan with RT. |
| C | Man-on to 1st LB in Strong Bubble<br>1. vs. covered (30 or under): block man-on. Set based on relationship and alignment.<br>2. vs. covered (over): make "Lou/Ray" call. Set strong A gap (borrow LG).<br>3. vs. uncovered: me-you/Ray with RG, DT to 1st LB strong.<br>4. vs. uncovered: 41 defense. Talking, with weak call, check key to help 1 technique first. |
| WG | Man-on or Off Ball<br>1. vs. covered: block man-on.<br>2. vs. uncovered (over): talking. Alert for Ray/Lou call. Set firm and block A gap defender alone.<br>3. vs. non-point LB in A gap: alert "gap" call (no "gap" call in gun) |
| WT | Man-on (No Help)<br>1. Block man-on. Set based on his relationship and alignment.<br>2. vs. 30: alert base/fan. |
| R | Check 1-2 LB from point LB working weak<br>1. Key LB 1-2 away from point LB.<br>2. Take check step.<br>3. Double-read inside-out.<br>4. vs. 30: alert base. |

# Walk, Stranger, Whale Calls

Some *calls* are involved in this protection. If there is no linebacker in the strong tackle bubble, we make a "walk" call, and now the center can go back inside to the next linebacker. That's something that happens a lot (see Figure 2-11). We also have a "stranger" call, which means if we're getting the "Mike/strong safety blitz," that we have

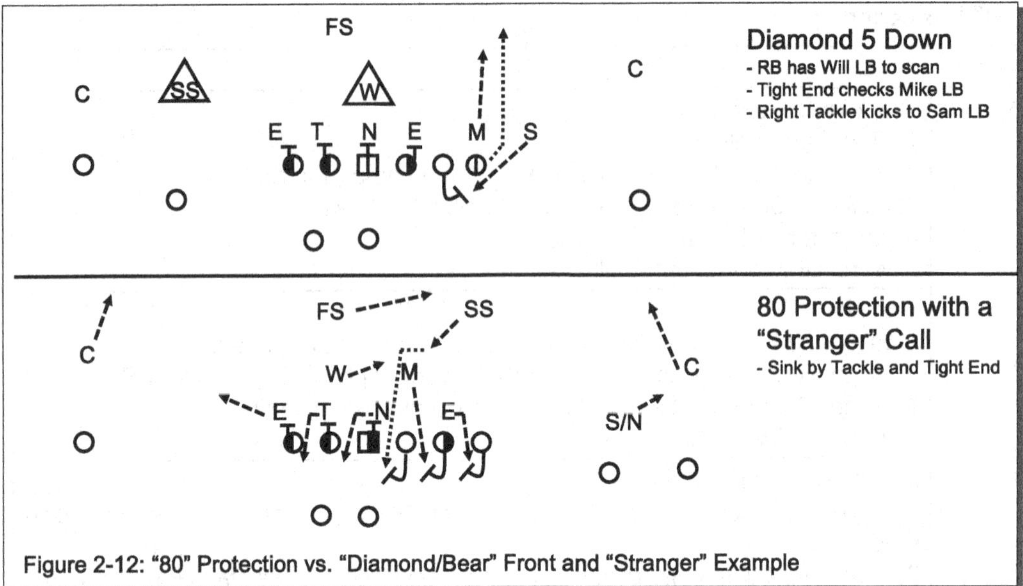

Figure 2-12: "80" Protection vs. "Diamond/Bear" Front and "Stranger" Example

a "stranger" in the box and now the tight end and strong tackle have to "sink" inside to pick up that "strong safety/defense end." That will happen every year at some point (see Figure 2-12).

We have a "whale" call, which is for a "Sam/strong safety" blitz (what we call a "shark" blitz, hence the call "whale"). That means that the tight end is going to "fan," the strong tackle is going to "fan," and the strong guard is going to "fan" out, to be able to block the strong safety, the Sam linebacker, and the defensive end, respectively (Figure 2-13). We want to make sure the quarterback understands that this protection can pick up "4-strong."

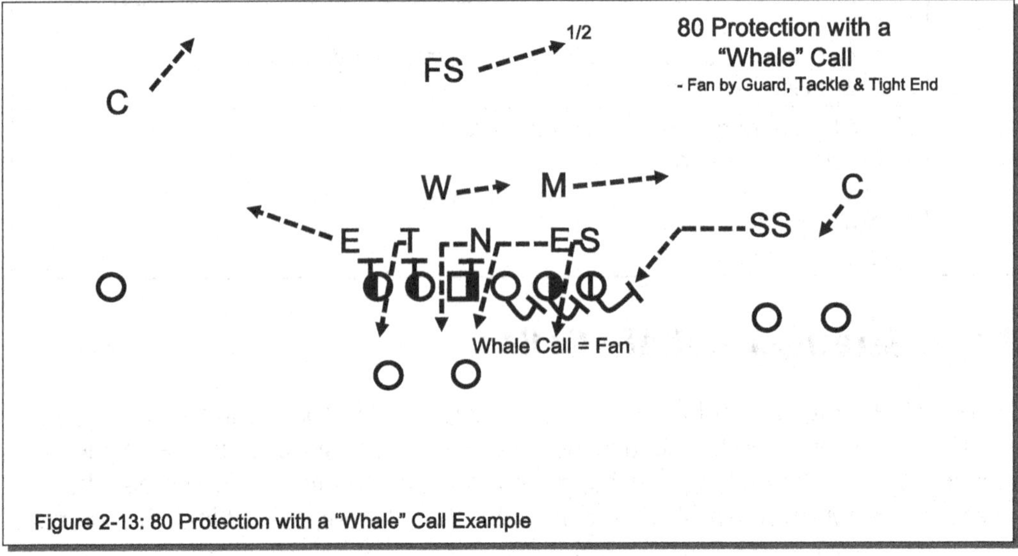

Figure 2-13: 80 Protection with a "Whale" Call Example

## Lima/Rose (6-Man Protection)

Our most used 3-step drop protection, we call either "Lima/Rose" or "Rose/Lima." This is a 3-step drop protection to a 6-man protection unit. The slide can go both weak *and* strong. Our tight end has no responsibility in this protection. He gets a free release and would make a "white" call, so the tackle knows he's out. The offensive line has the "4-down linemen first, plus the 1st linebacker to the slide call." Then, we call it "hot left" or "hot right," so they have to be able to pick up an inside linebacker to that side but also be able to "fan" to an edge blitzer (Figure 2-14).

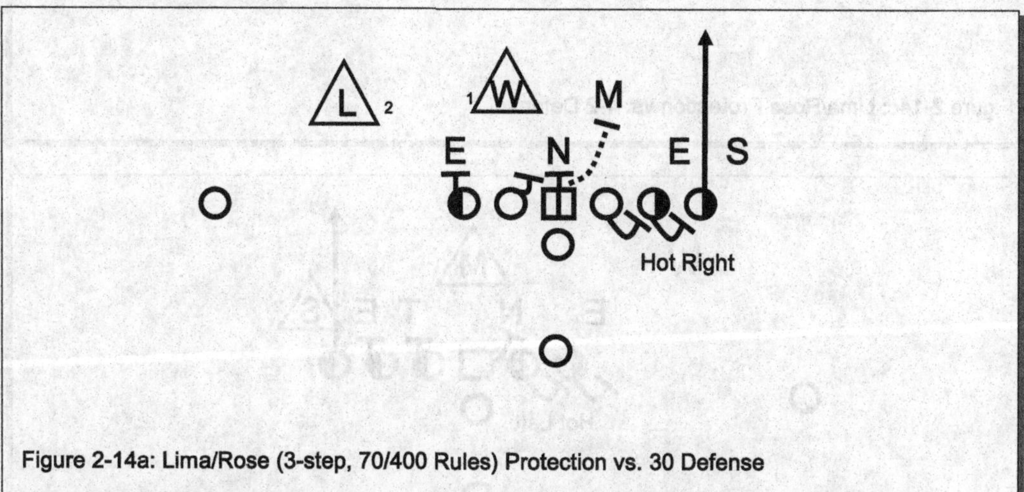

Figure 2-14a: Lima/Rose (3-step, 70/400 Rules) Protection vs. 30 Defense

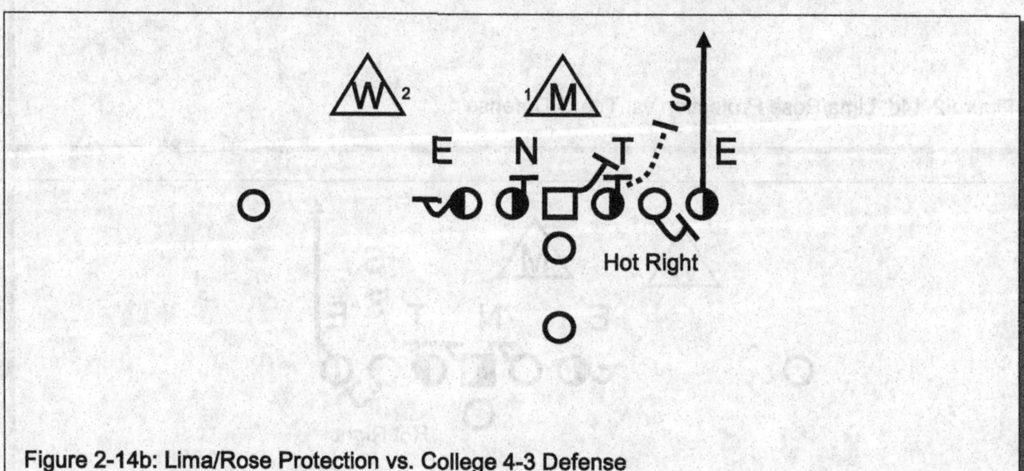

Figure 2-14b: Lima/Rose Protection vs. College 4-3 Defense

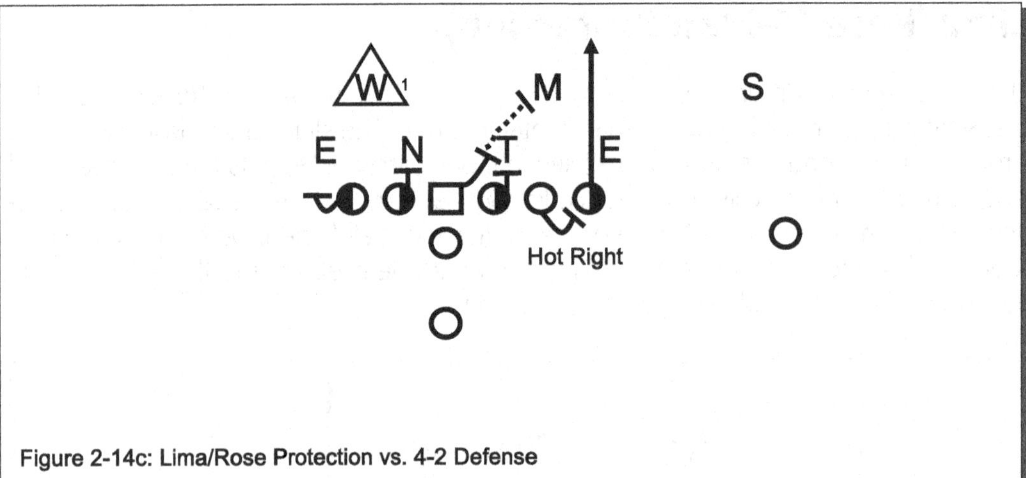

Figure 2-14c: Lima/Rose Protection vs. 4-2 Defense

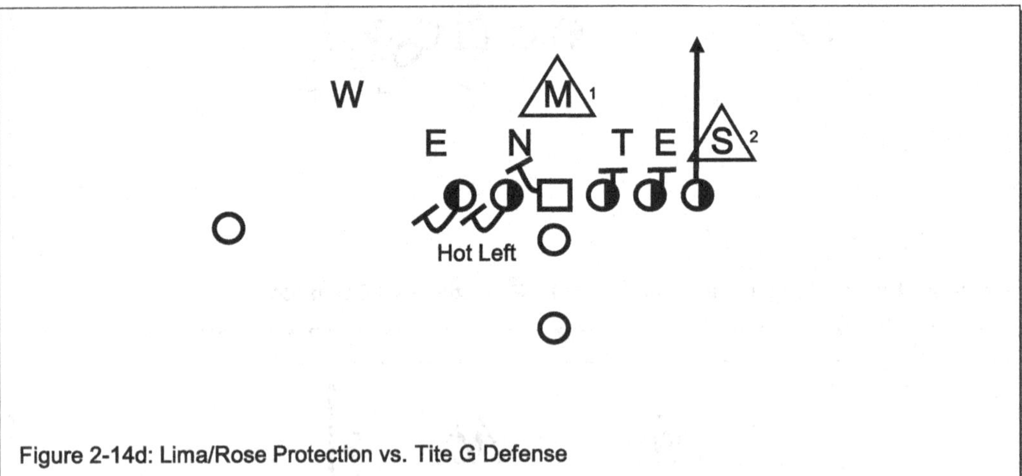

Figure 2-14d: Lima/Rose Protection vs. Tite G Defense

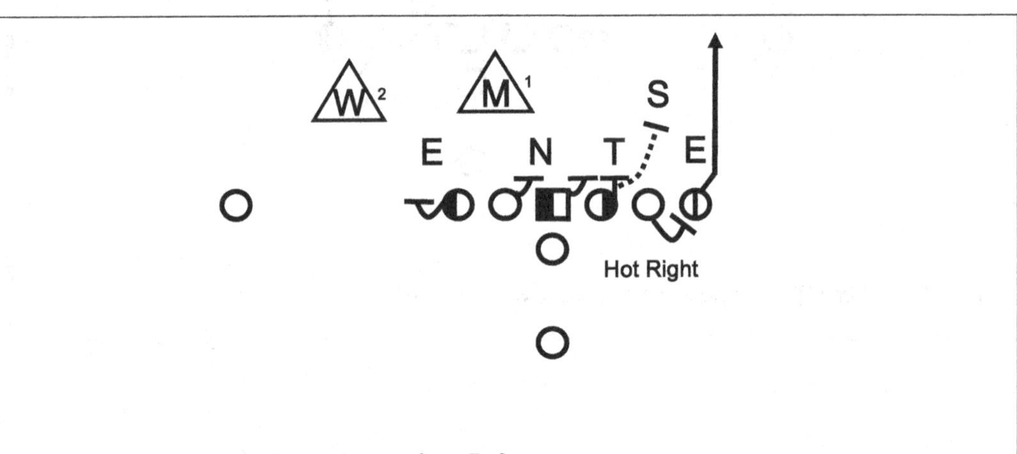

Figure 2-14e: Lima/Rose Protection vs. Over Defense

**"Lima/Rose" Protection**

| Pos: | Rules: |
|---|---|
| Y | Free release. Run route. |
| ST | 1. Listen for point LB and hot call.<br>2. Hot call to your side: check man-on, man-outside.<br>3. Communicate on call to RT<br>4. If the point is away from you, man-on. |
| SG | 1. Listen for point LB.<br>2. Me/You to the point: alert fan.<br>3. Man-on away from the point. Set firm, possible quick (cut technique). |
| C | ID the front. Declare point to the side of the call (Rose/Lima).<br>1. Make "hot" call to same side as the point LB.<br>2. vs. 30 front: borrow opposite guard. Set me/you to the point LB.<br>3. vs. Diamond: 5 down. Set firm, possible quick (cut technique). |
| WG | 1. Listen for point LB.<br>2. Me/you to the point. Alert fan.<br>3. Man-on away from the point. Set firm, possible quick (cut technique). |
| WT | 1. Listen for point LB and hot call.<br>2. Hot call to your side: check man-on, man-outside.<br>3. Communicate on call to LG.<br>4. If the point is away from you, man-on. Set firm, possible quick (cut technique). |
| R | 1-to-2, 2nd level from 0 LB away from the call (Rose/Lima). |

For example, on a "Lima" protection, the center would call "Lou to 52, hot left!" Then, if the tackle sees somebody coming, he would make an "on, on, on!" call and then the center would "fan" it. The running back has the "1 to 2" linebacker away from the point ("zero" linebacker). He always has to know where the *point* is, what the direction is, and then be able to understand who exactly he has.

The quarterback's responsibility is to be able to handle "A gap" pressure, or overload pressure (like a "scrape blitz"), by changing the protection to a full slide. If you're in the gun, some or two times you don't need to handle "A-gap" pressure with the full slide, but if you get an overload blitz to one side or the other, you have to be able to handle the protection by changing it to "Liz/Rip" or "Rip/Liz."

## Liz/Rip (& Liz/Rip "Y") Protection/Call

If the quarterback checks to "Liz/Rip" for a full slide, the tight end is automatically in. However, to get the tight end out and not have to change any routes, he says Liz or Rip "Y." At this point, we have a slide protection, but the tight end is still out in the route. Most of the time, to address A-gap pressures the quarterback would use Liz and Rip "Y," with the exception of some "cover-zero" checks, where it's true all-out pressure with no safety help. That's where we might use "Liz/Rip," keep the tight end in to generate a full-slide and maintain the ability to throw the ball down the field (Figure 2-15).

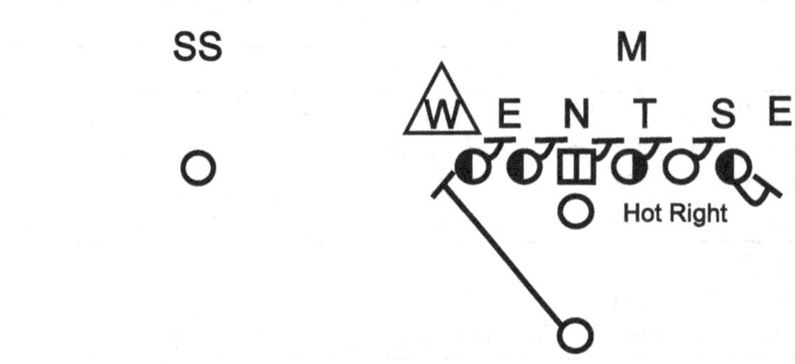


Figure 2-15a: Liz/Rip (3-step or quick 5-step Gap, Full Slide) Protection vs. Diamond/Bear Defense

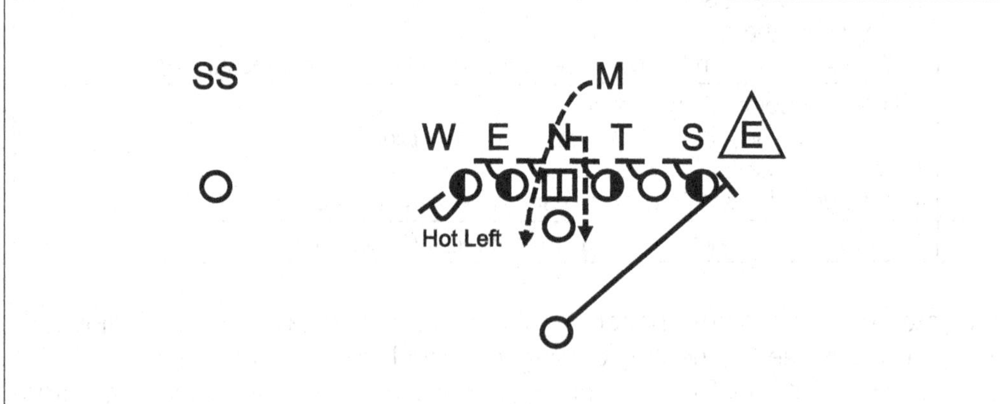


Figure 2-15b: Liz/Rip Protection vs. Diamond/Bear Defense

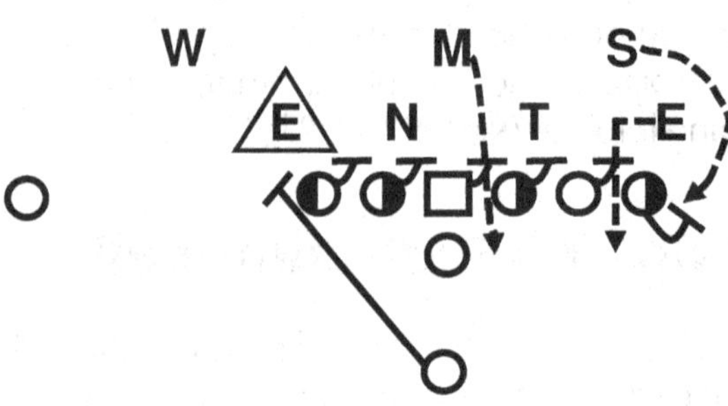


Figure 2-15c: Liz/Rip Protection vs. College 4-3 Defense

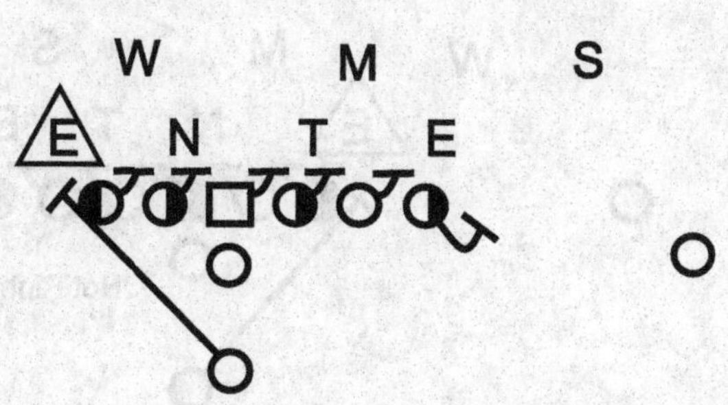


Figure 2-15d: Liz/Rip Protection vs. 4-2 Defense

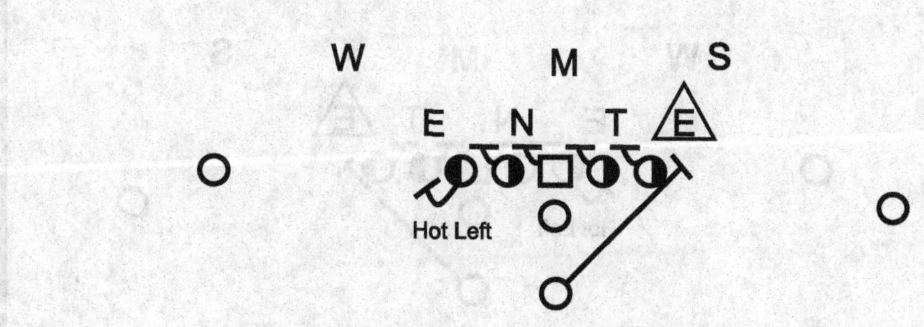


Figure 2-15e: Liz/Rip Protection vs. 4-2 Defense

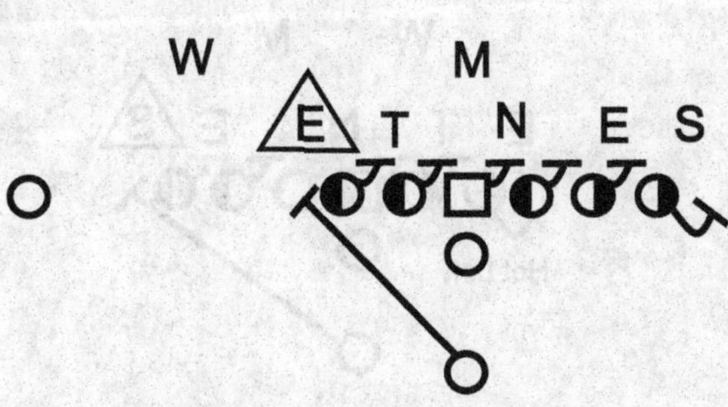


Figure 2-15f: Liz/Rip Protection vs. Under G Defense

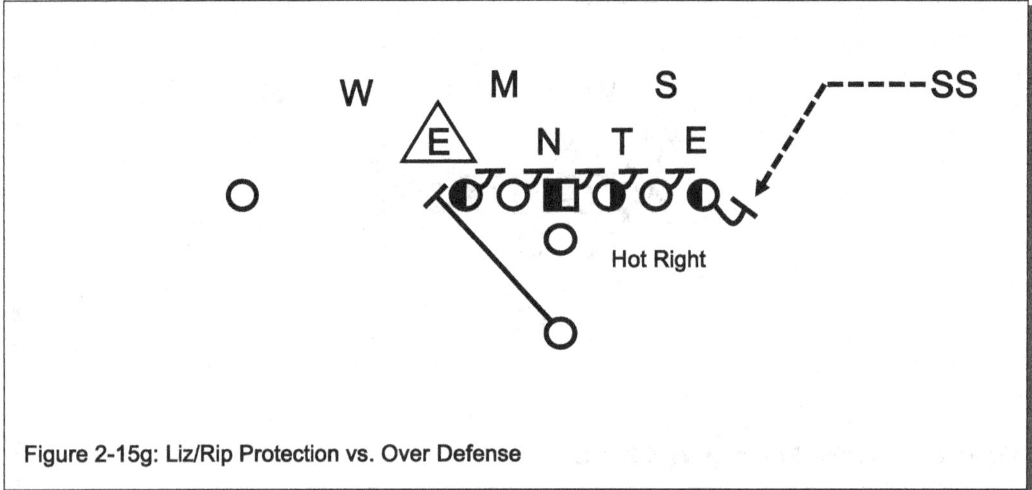

Figure 2-15g: Liz/Rip Protection vs. Over Defense

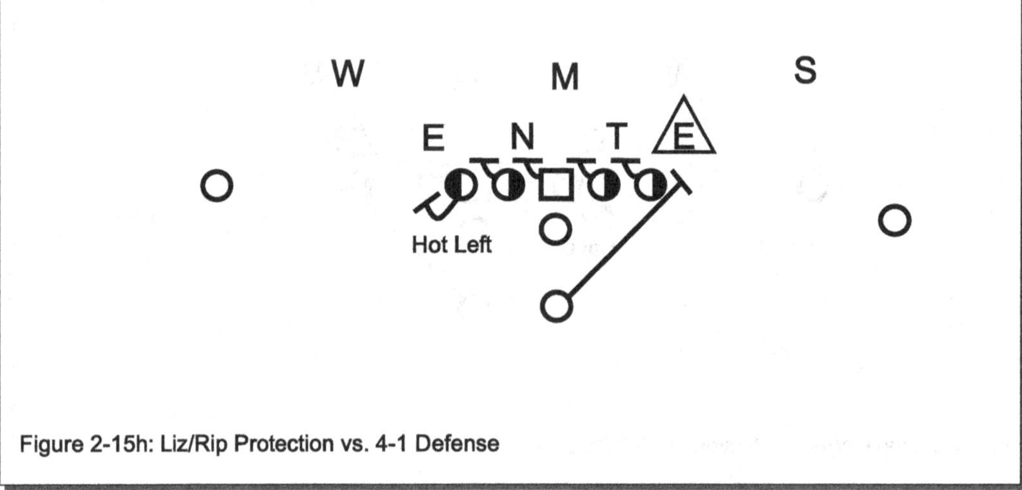

Figure 2-15h: Liz/Rip Protection vs. 4-1 Defense

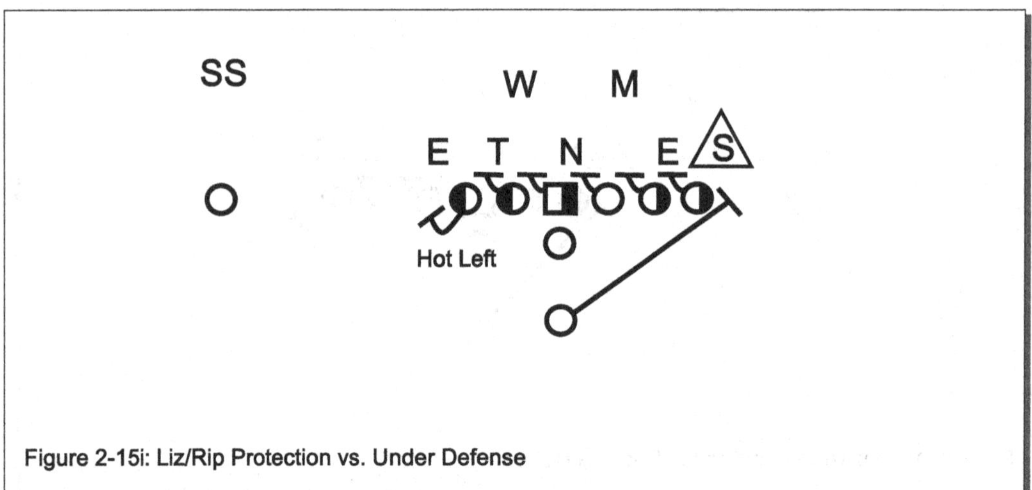

Figure 2-15i: Liz/Rip Protection vs. Under Defense

**"Liz/Rip" Full-Slide Protection**

| Pos: | Rules: |
|---|---|
| Y | Set inside block c gap:<br>1. Set inside, block most dangerous.<br>2. vs. bubble LB: set lateral, check, work outside to help F<br>3. vs. man on LOS (bear): block man-on, set inside.<br>4. Echo the call.<br>5. Y call: free release and run route. |
| ST | Step-replace block B gap:<br>1. Set lateral, protect B gap to help.<br>2. Keep shoulders square.<br>3. Echo the call.<br>4. Alert to defenders off the backside: slow tech. |
| SG | Step-replace, block A gap:<br>1. Set lateral, protect A gap to help.<br>2. Keep shoulders square.<br>3. Echo the call. |
| C | Step-replace, block left A gap:<br>1. Set lateral, protect left A gap to help.<br>2. Keep shoulders square.<br>3. Echo the call. |
| WG | Step-replace, block B gap:<br>1. Set protect B gap.<br>2. Keep shoulders square.<br>3. Echo the call. |
| WT | Kick set, block C gap:<br>1. PSL for most dangerous outside defender.<br>2. Keep shoulders square.<br>3. Echo the call. |
| R | 1. Block opposite the call.<br>2. Pivot off your outside foot. Drive TE's hip and block EMLOS.<br>3. Y call: drive outside hip of RT. |

"Liz/Rip Y" is often used as a "call," if we want to change the protection from "Lima" to "Liz Y" in quick game and leave the route on. For example, if the play is "Lima 90 Grey" and they "field scrape," we want to make a "Liz Y" call, slide everything, and pick that all up (Figure 2-16). Overload scrape blitz is where we need to slide to pick up the Mike and Nickel. "Lima" doesn't pick that up, so we need to full-slide it.

**"Liz/Rip" Full-Slide Protection (cont.)**

| Pos: | Rules: |
|---|---|
| Y | Kick set, block D gap:<br>1. PSL for most dangerous outside defender.<br>2. Keep shoulders square.<br>3. Echo the call.<br>4. Y call: free release and run route. |
| ST | Kick set, block C gap:<br>1. On Y call: PSL for most dangerous outside defender.<br>2. Keep shoulders square.<br>3. Echo the call. |
| SG | Step-replace, block B gap:<br>1. Set, protect B gap.<br>2. Keep shoulders square.<br>3. Echo the call. |
| C | Step-replace, block strong A gap:<br>1. Set lateral, protect right A gap to help.<br>2. Keep shoulders square.<br>3. Echo the call. |
| WG | Step-replace, block A gap:<br>1. Set lateral, protect A gap to help.<br>2. Keep shoulders square.<br>3. Echo the call. |
| WT | Step-replace, block B gap:<br>1. Set lateral, protect B gap to help.<br>2. Keep shoulders square.<br>3. Echo the call.<br>4. Alert defenders off the backside. Slow tech. |
| R | 1. Block opposite the call.<br>2. Pivot off your outside foot and drive outside leg of LT.<br>3. Block EMLOS. |

If we get "A/A" or "B/B" pressure from under center, we have to get to "Liz Y," because the back now can't get to his guy. Let's say we're under the center, the play is "strong right Lee: lima 90 grey," and they bring "A-gap" pressure. The quarterback will send the motion and then say, "Liz Y, Liz Y!," so the line can handle it (see Figure 2-16).

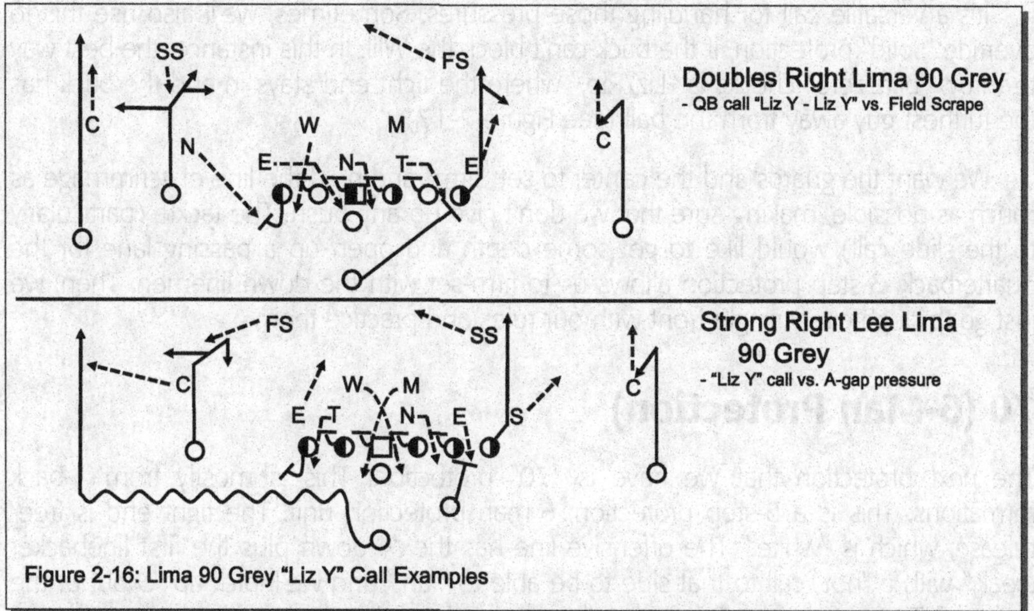

Figure 2-16: Lima 90 Grey "Liz Y" Call Examples

If we get "diamond," particularly if they're bringing "Mike linebacker A-gap pressure" with it, we again utilize the Liz and Rip "Y" call and slide the protection. For example, in the quick game if we are running "lima 92, Y arrow" and they come out in diamond, showing "Mike A," we can change "lima" to "Liz Y" and get it protected (Figure 2-17).

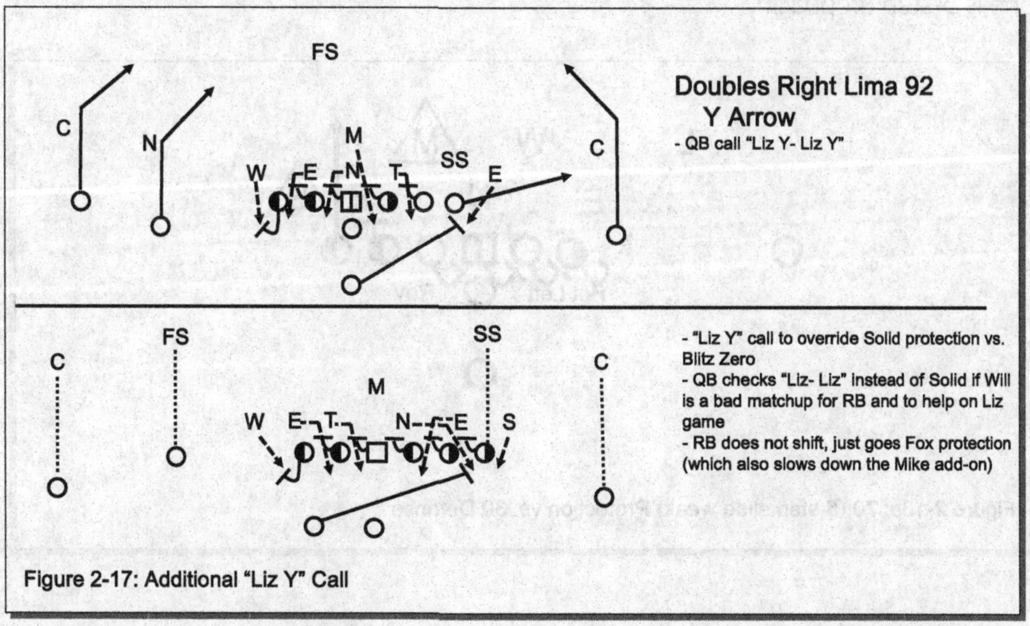

Figure 2-17: Additional "Liz Y" Call

It's a versatile call for handling those pressures. Sometimes, we'll also use this to override "solid" protection, if the back can't block the Will. In this instance, the best way to throw "blitz-zero" checks is "Liz/Rip," where the tight end stays in and the back has the furthest guy away from the ball (see Figure 2-17).

We want the guards and the center to set "firm" and hold the line of scrimmage as much as possible, making sure that we don't give up any push. The tackle (particularly to the slide call) would like to get some depth and open up a passing lane for the quarterback. 3-step protection allows us to firm-set with the down linemen. Then, we just go through every single front with our rules and practice them.

## 70 (6-Man Protection)

The next protection that we have is "70" protection. This is mostly from 1-back formations. This is a 5-step protection, 6-man protection unit. The tight end is free-release, which is "white." The offensive line has the "4-down plus the first linebacker weak," with a "hot" call to that side to be able to "fan," and we'll pick up "3 out of the 4 weak." The running back has the "first linebacker from the zero-linebacker, strong" (Figure 2-18). If you are in 2-backs, then the weakside back has a free-release, so we are able to run the same protection and many of the same-named routes out of our 2-back sets. (If you didn't want to carry the protection "Lima / Rose," you could also call this "370" to make it a 3-step drop with 70 protection rules. "Lima" and "70" are basically the same protection when you're in a right formation, only one is 3-step and one is 5-step dropback).

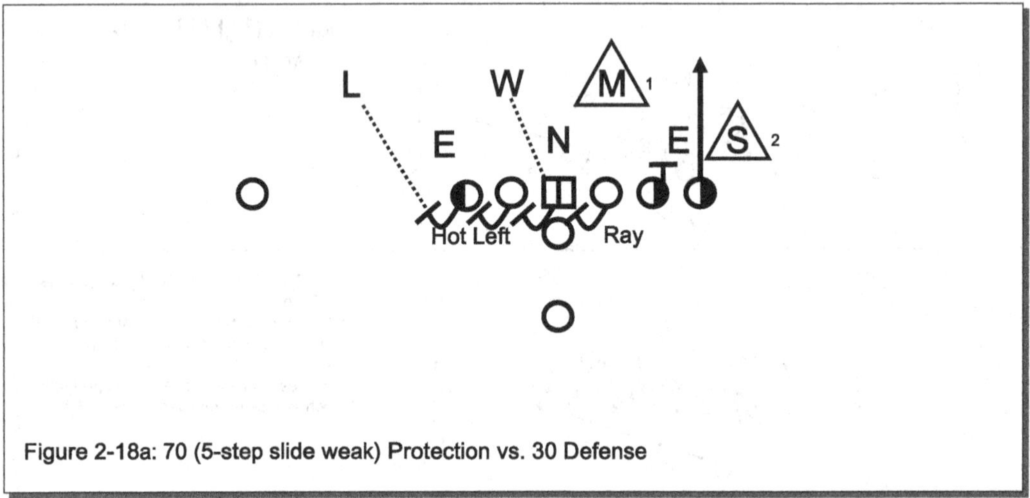


Figure 2-18a: 70 (5-step slide weak) Protection vs. 30 Defense

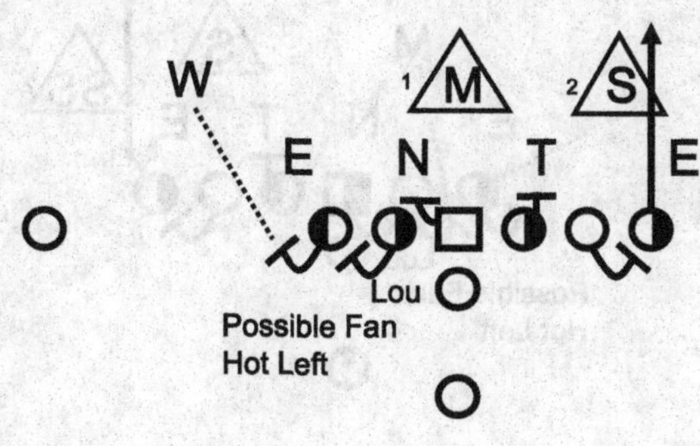


Figure 2-18b: 70 Protection vs. College 4-3 Defense

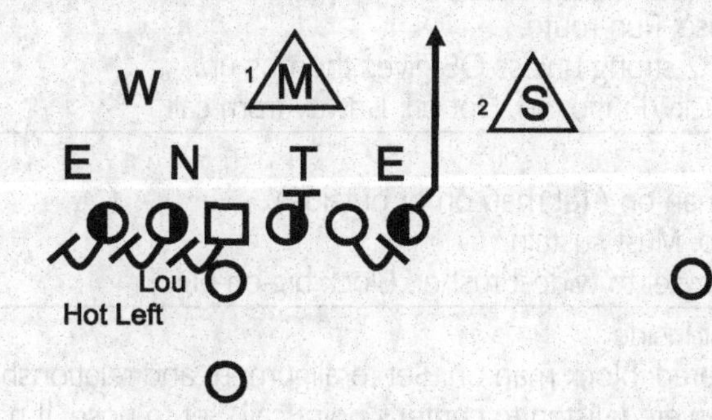


Figure 2-18c: 70 Protection vs. 4-2 Defense

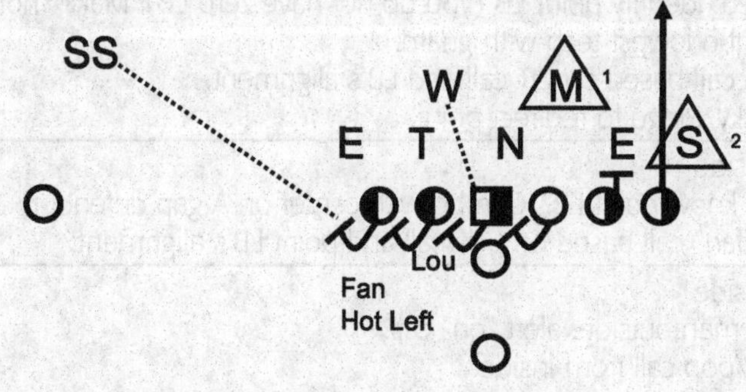


Figure 2-18d: 70 Protection vs. Under Defense

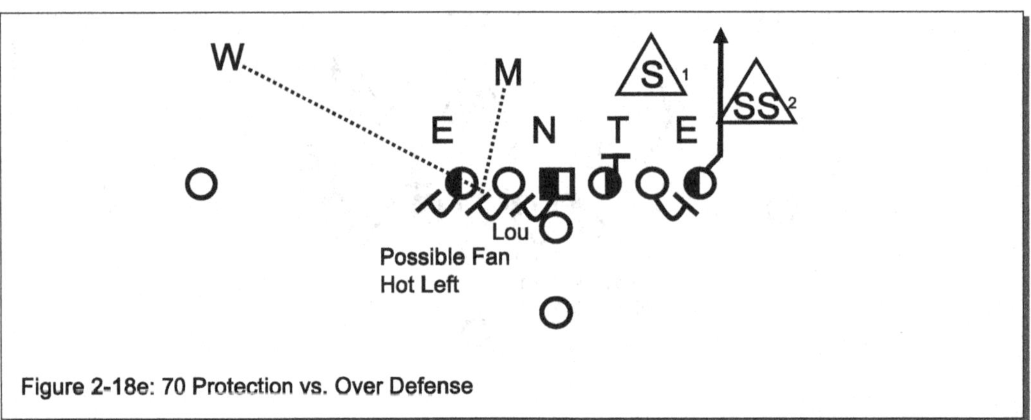

Figure 2-18e: 70 Protection vs. Over Defense

**"70" Protection**

| Pos: | Rules: |
|---|---|
| Y | Free release. Run route.<br>1. Hot off 2 strong unless QB gives thumbs up.<br>2. Alert Lucky/Ringo call. Hot off 1 away from call |
| ST | Man-on.<br>1. Block man-on (1st man on or outside).<br>2. No help. Must sustain.<br>3. vs. Bear: set to widest rusher. Block big-on-big. |
| SG | Man-on or inside<br>1. vs. covered: block man-on. Set to alignment and relationship.<br>2. vs. uncovered: listen to center's point call. Set to nose. If nose slants away, find point LB.<br>3. vs. LB threat in A gap: possible "gap" call.<br>4. Listen for weak fan call by center. |
| C | Weak A gap to LB<br>1. vs. 30: set nose to weak A gap. Combo nose to point LB with RG.<br>2. vs. uncovered: identify point LB (you do not have zero LB). Make "hot" call to weakside. Combo lowest tech with guard.<br>3. Possible fan call based on QT call and LB's alignment.<br>4. Alert for Lucky/Ringo to redirect point. |
| WG | Man-on or outside<br>1. vs. covered: know point LB. Combo with center on A gap defender.<br>2. Make "pop/fan" call based on LT's call and point LB's alignment. |
| WT | Man-on or outside<br>1. vs. man-on, man-outside: alert "on" call.<br>2. Alert for fan/pop call from inside.<br>3. Zone all line games. |
| R/F | Check 1-2 LB from 0 strong<br>1. Double-read inside LB to outside LB from center strong.<br>2. Protect inside-out. Alert for gap call by SG (no gap call in gun). |

We can redirect the point with the "Lucky/Ringo" call and then the quarterback gives a "thumbs up" to that side. If I'm the receiver and I'm thinking, "I'm going to have to sight-adjust," it is the quarterback's responsibility when he redirects the protection to give that receiver a "thumbs up," which means "you're good, run the route that you're supposed to run."

In the "30" front, you "borrow the backside guard" on the slide. On a "diamond" (or "bear," which we still consider five-down), there's a "five-down" call, which means there's no slide, the offensive line is blocking the five-down linemen, and the back now has a "scan," so you might not get your running back out (see Figure 2-12). We have "hots" and "sights" on this. The tight end knows that he is "hot off 2" to his side and he will yell, "hot, hot, hot!," if somebody comes like that (Figure 2-19). Then, if it's a 2x2, the slot receiver would be "hot off 2" from his side. If it's a 3x1, the outside receiver would "sight adjust." But this is saying that there's not a "built in"; sometimes we leave the routes on and understand there are no "hots" and "sights," because it's "built in." That's our "70," or "weakside slide" protection.

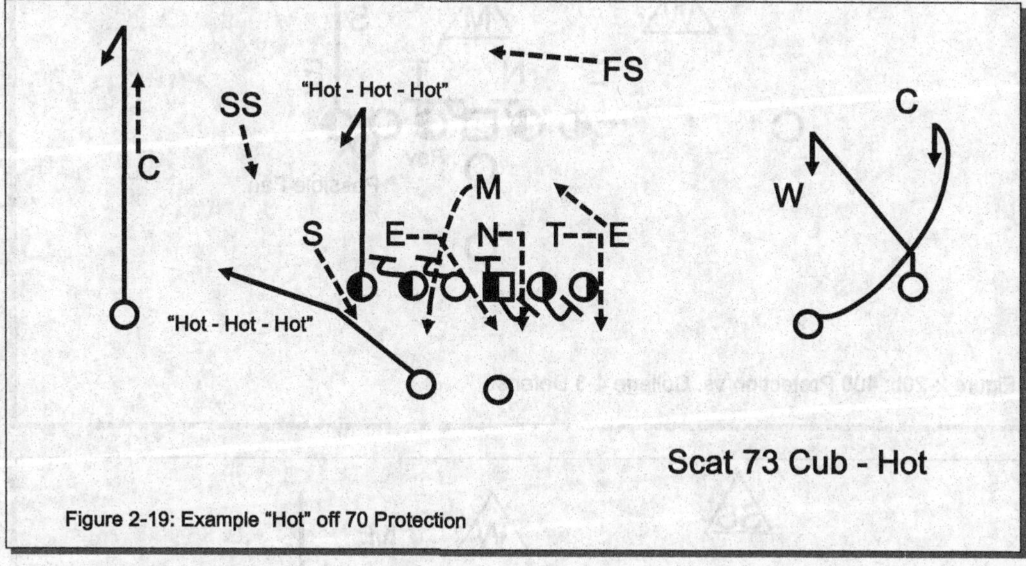

Figure 2-19: Example "Hot" off 70 Protection

## 400 (6-man)

To bring that running back to the other side, we call it 400 protection (Figure 2-20). Then, when you call the play, you would call it "480 or "481" or "482," whatever route concept is called with it (we will introduce this in the following chapters). The 400 protection is a 5-step drop protection, with a 6-man protection unit. The tight end is free-release (which is "white"), and he's "hot off of 2." The exception would be a "30" front, where we're bringing the backside guard and you know that you're good.

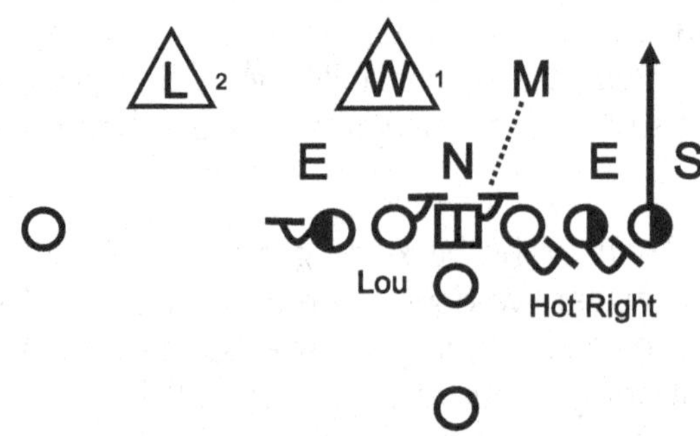


Figure 2-20a: 400 (5-step work strong, free release strong) Protection vs. 30 Defense

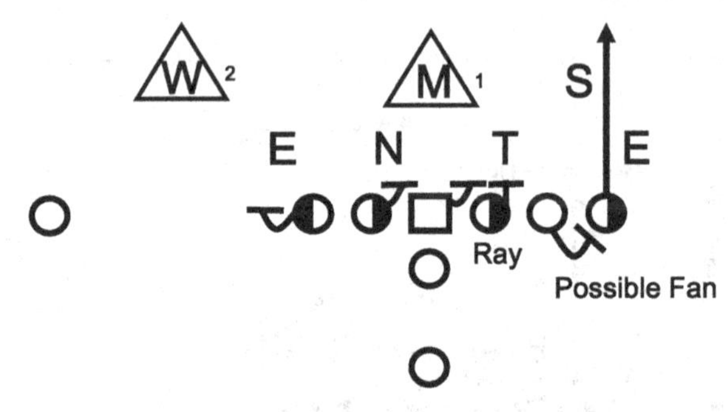


Figure 2-20b: 400 Protection vs. College 4-3 Defense

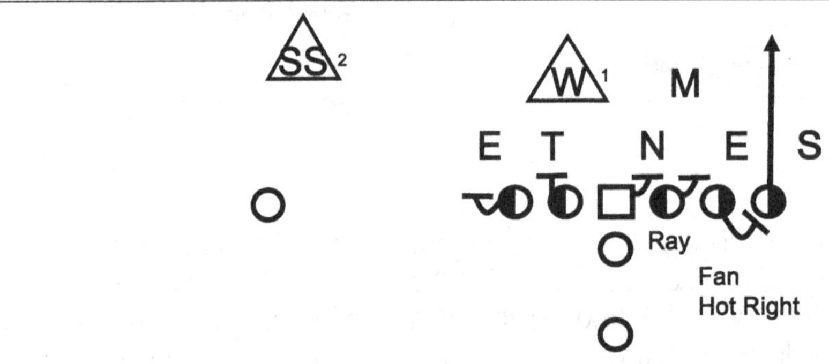


Figure 2-20c: 400 Protection vs. Under G Defense

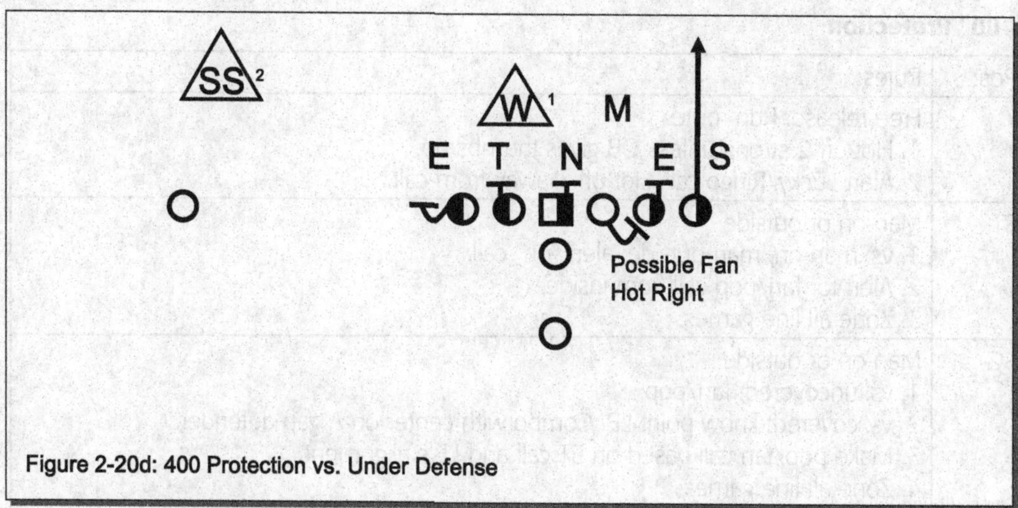

Figure 2-20d: 400 Protection vs. Under Defense

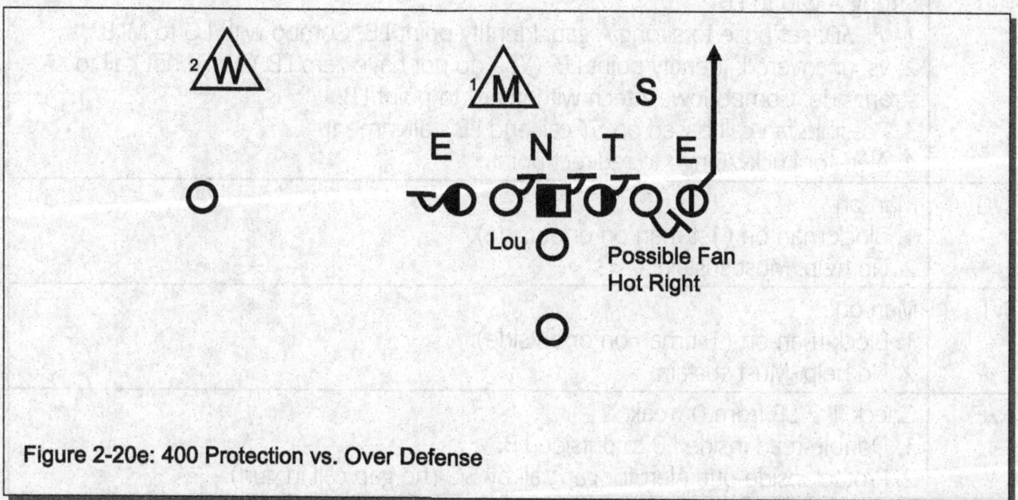

Figure 2-20e: 400 Protection vs. Over Defense

The o-line has the "4-down linemen plus the first linebacker strong" and makes a "hot" call to be able to "fan" to an outside pressure. The running back has "1 to 2 linebackers from the zero-linebacker weak," and if you're in a 2-back formation, the running back or tailback to the strong side has the free-release.

Again, you say it's a "sight" or "hot" off "2 from either side." The quarterback again can redirect the point by making a "Ringo/Lucky" or "Lucky/Ringo" call and giving a "thumbs up" to that receiver. (When he gives a "thumbs up" to one side, he has to give "1 finger" to the other, which means "we're good this side, but we're 'hot off 1' now to the other side.) The receivers *must* know when you redirect point, to be able to "sight" or "hot" off 1 to the opposite side. Against "diamond" front, we would "5-down" it and the back would again be in a "scan."

**"400" Protection**

| Pos: | Rules: |
|---|---|
| Y | Free release. Run route.<br>1. Hot off 2 strong unless QB gives thumbs up.<br>2. Alert Lucky/Ringo call. Hot off 1 away from call. |
| ST | Man-on or outside<br>1. vs. man-on, man-outside: alert "on" call.<br>2. Alert for fan/pop call from inside.<br>3. Zone all line games. |
| SG | Man-on or outside<br>1. vs. uncovered: fan/pop.<br>2. vs. covered: know point LB. Combo with center on A gap defender.<br>3. Make pop/fan call based on ST call and LB's alignment.<br>4. Zone all line games. |
| C | Strong A gap to LB<br>1. vs. 30: set nose to strong A gap. Identify point LB. Combo with LG to MLB.<br>2. vs. uncovered: identify point LB. (You do not have zero LB.) Make hot call to strongside. Combo lowest tech with guard to point LB.<br>3. Possible fan call based on ST call and LB's alignment.<br>4. Alert for Lucky/Ringo to redirect point. |
| WG | Man-on<br>1. Block man-on (1st man on or outside).<br>2. No help. Must sustain. |
| WT | Man-on<br>1. Block man-on (1st man on or outside).<br>2. No help. Must sustain. |
| R/F | Check 1-2 LB from 0 weak.<br>1. Double-read inside LB to outside LB.<br>2. Protect inside-out. Alert for gap call by SG (no gap call in gun). |

## Lion/Ram (5-Man)

The next protection can either be a 3-step or a 5-step drop out of empty or "no back" protection. It's a "combo" protection with "half-slide, half-man," in a 5-man protection unit. The tight end would have free-release "white," unless the quarterback brought him down and changed the protection, which is one of the ways to protect in empty against blitz. Offensive line has the "4 down linemen, plus the first linebacker from zero" to the call side. We call it "Lion/Ram" and "Ram/Lion." (On "Lion," the line is working to the left, on "Ram," the line is working to the right.) We make the "hot" call to the side of the point, so you have the ability to "fan" and you're always going to be able to pick up "three of the four" most dangerous rushers to the side of the call (Figure 2-21).

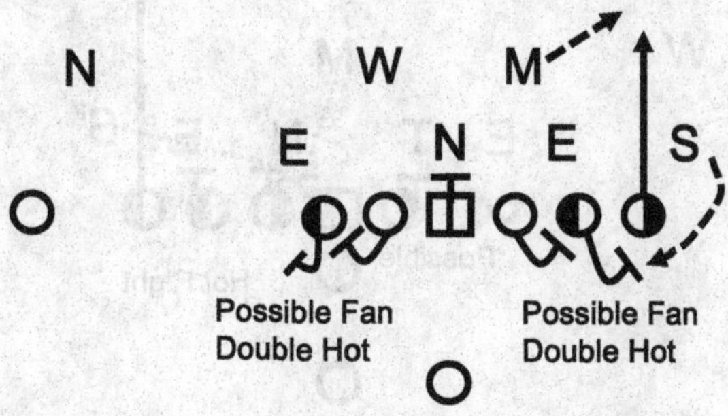


Figure 2-21a: Lion/Ram (3- to 5-step 5-man) Protection vs. 30 Defense

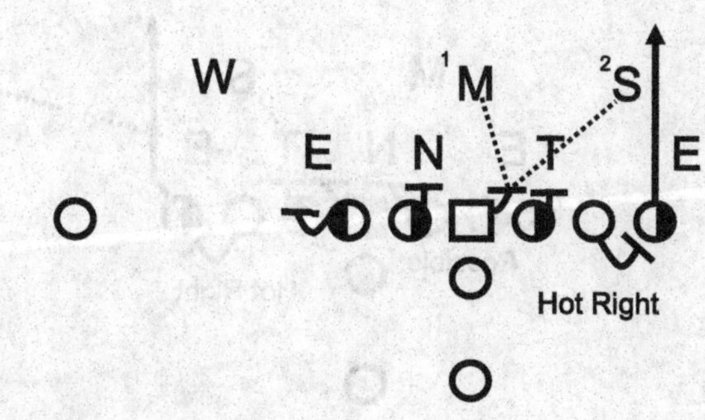


Figure 2-21b: Lion/Ram Protection vs. College 4-3 Defense

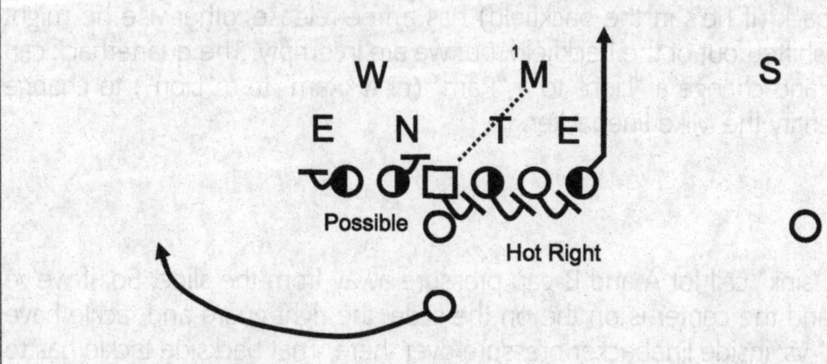


Figure 2-21c: Lion/Ram Protection vs. 4-2 Defense

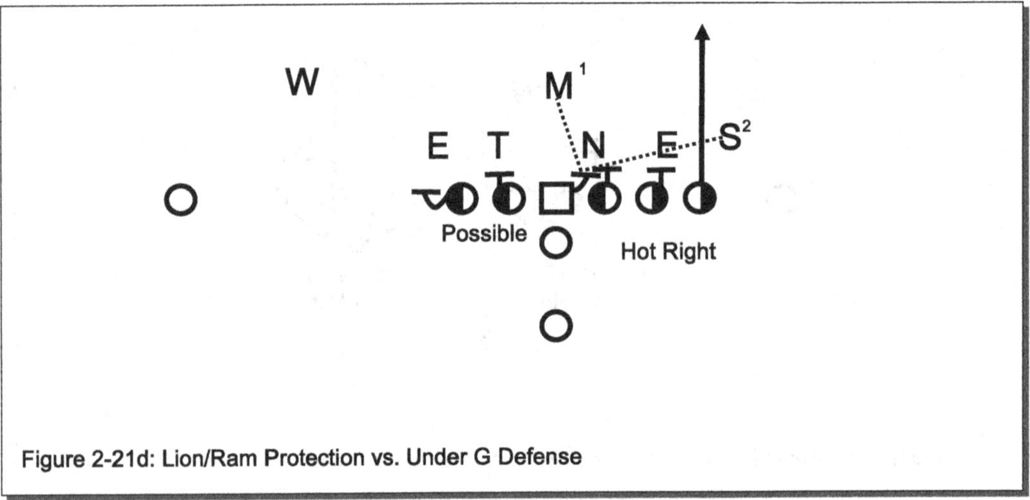

Figure 2-21d: Lion/Ram Protection vs. Under G Defense

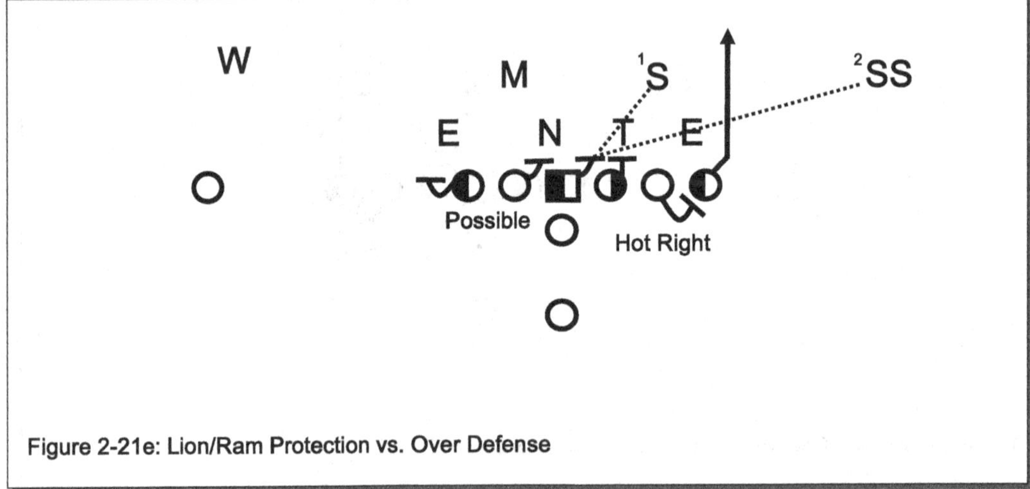

Figure 2-21e: Lion/Ram Protection vs. Over Defense

The running back (if he's in the backfield) has a free-release, otherwise he might motion out or be shifted out of the backfield, but we are in empty. The quarterback can redirect the point and change a "Lion" to a "Ram" (or a "Ram" to a "Lion") to change the point or re-identify the Mike linebacker.

## Sink Call

This does carry a "sink" call for A and B gap pressure away from the slide. So, if we've got "Lion" called and the center is on the on the slide, the right guard and tackle have the ability to "sink" vs. inside linebacker pressure over there. That backside tackle has to understand that "I'm not just responsible for the defensive end. If there's a linebacker or safety who's getting up in the B or A gap, we have to 'sink' and pick that up," so we block the most dangerous guys. It's something you really have to work at and give it

**"Lion/Ram" Protection**

| Pos: | Rules: |
|---|---|
| Y | Free release. Run route. |
| ST | Man-on or outside<br>1. vs. covered: block man-on.<br>2. vs. uncovered: block EMLOS<br>3. Alert to hot side: possible fan/pop.<br>4. Alert to man side: possible sink. |
| SG | Man-on or over<br>1. vs. covered: block man-on. Know hot side. Make pop/fan call if necessary. Man side possible sink.<br>2. vs. uncovered: listen to center's point and hot side.<br>3. Sort: set deep, read NG |
| C | Man-on or over<br>1. ID front, set point to 1st LB 0 to callside. Hot call to Ram or Lion.<br>2. vs. 30: make "sort" call. Set deep – read NG.<br>3. Alert Ram/Lion call from QB to redirect point.<br>4. Alert Ram/Lion Lion call to borrow guard and slide to the call. |
| WG | Man-on or over<br>1. vs. covered: block man-on. Know hot side. Make pop/fan call if necessary. Man side possible "sink".<br>2. vs. uncovered: listen to center's point and hot side.<br>3. Sort: set deep, read NG. |
| WT | Man-on or outside<br>1. vs. covered: block man-on.<br>2. vs. uncovered: block EMLOS.<br>3. Alert to hot side: possible fan/pop.<br>4. Alert to man side: possible sink. |
| R | Free release. Run route. |

enough reps in in practice, because it's certainly going to happen in a game on "scat" protection (which is a code for 5-man protection). We want to pick up the five most dangerous rushers.

## Scat (5-Man Protection)

On the 70 and 400 protections, if we want to free-release the back, we can make a "scat" call. Sometimes, this is better than calling "Ram/Lion," because it's easier to call the play and the line understands it. So, you could say "scat 70" or "scat 400," and all that does is tell the back he has a free-release. We like to carry the "scat" term, so we have the ability to get the precise reaction we want out of the players in any given situation. The word choice really matters as a teaching tool, in order to get players to create the mental image we are after. We take extra time to teach these details, instead of just lumping it all together. A good example is how we do this within our crosser series, which we will introduce within the dropback chapter.

This does give us some "hot" rules for the back and the tight ends. If we were to go "Scat 70," then the back has a free-release and the tight end and the running back know they're "hot off 1," and there is no protector to that side. If we go "scat 400," we're "hot off 1" to the weak side (Figure 2-22).

**Scat 70/400/80 Protection**
(1- or 2-Back Formations)
Combo Protection (½ Slide, ½ Man)

5-Step Drop

5-Man Protection Unit

TE – Free release (white) (Scat 80 – Check release grey)

OL – 4 down lineman + normal point LB in 70/400/80 protection

RB – Free release into route. Hot off 1 from your side

QB – Off 1 away from the point (RB side)
Off 2 tot eh side of the point(OL side)

30 Front – sort

C.P. – same protection calls as normal 70/400/80

C.P. – guard and tackle away from point LB must "sink" any A or B gap pressure. We will block the most dangerous 2 out of 3 rushers away from the point.

Normal protection rules. Scat allows the back to free-release and tells the backside blockers to block the most dangerous two rushers away from the point with a "sink" call.

Figure 2-22 ("Scat" Protections)

(Note: we sometimes also use "scat" with 80 protection, which gives the back a weakside free-release and then makes it a 6-man protection scheme.)

## Sara/Sally

We recently added a new 5-man protection we call "Sara/Sally." If we call that, it means the line is sliding to the *same direction* the back is free-releasing. This means they are now all going the same way. We had to do that, because, against things like "scat

73 Miami," people were dogging the back and then clicking people out and playing zone. So, we had to call "Sara Miami" or "Sally Miami," where you set the protection to the same side that the back is free-releasing. Now, the line has to be aware to the possibility of a "sink" call the other side (Figure 2-23). That's going back to Lavell Edwards and his "scat" protection; they would've called it "scat right Miami."

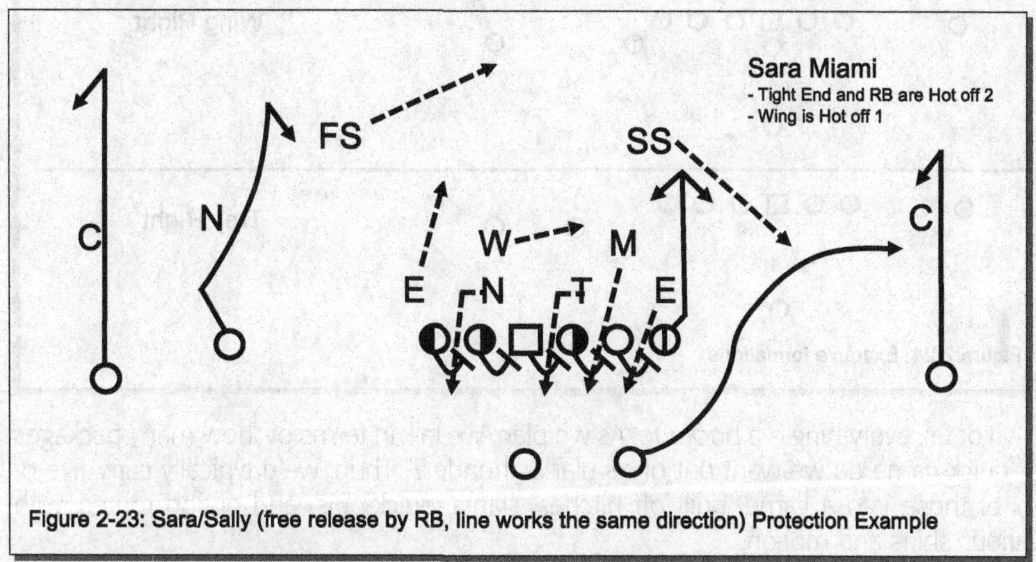

Figure 2-23: Sara/Sally (free release by RB, line works the same direction) Protection Example

## Formations, Personnel and Concepts

I'd like to add one final idea about our passing game philosophy before we go on to look at some routes. In order to build our pass routes on top of these protections, it's important that coaches are able to see our formations and personnel grouping as *concepts*. To begin with, we call our base receivers "X and Z," with "Y" as the tight end and "R" as the running back. A fullback would be called "F," a third wide receiver would be called "W," and a second tight end is called "T," in order to clarify who we have on the field. Anything we run out of 21 personnel, we want to be able to run out of 12 personnel, using the extra tight end ("T") in place of the fullback. We want to dictate personnel and matchups and we don't want to be forced out of part of the offense, because one guy gets hurt. We really *package* the idea that "12 equals 21" and so forth. This is important: "12 equals 21" in the run game and play-action game. "12 equals 11" in the pass game, quick game, and dropback.

We want assistants to echo back that "12 equals 21." The offensive coaches will talk in terms of our code names, such as "thunder equals ace in dropback." For example, "wing right" and "right" are exactly the same thing in run game and play-action. Then, "wing right" and "trey" are the same thing for quick game and dropback (Figure 2-24). That way, we're never forced out of any particular package, it categorizes our concepts more clearly for the quarterback, and it really helps you to practice them as well.

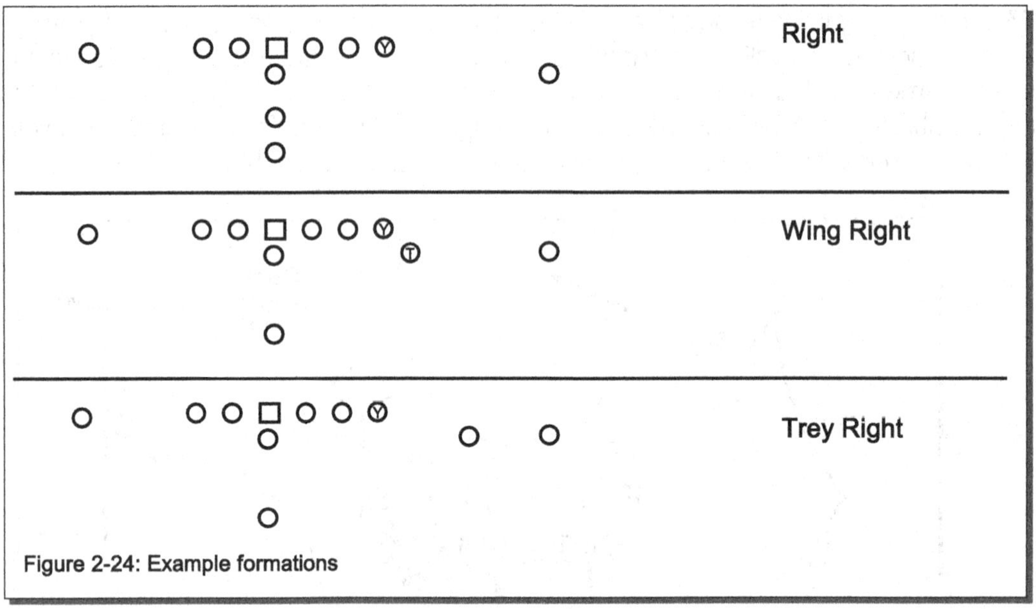

Right

Wing Right

Trey Right

Figure 2-24: Example formations

For us, everything is a *package*. As we plan, we talk in terms of "how many packages of quick game do we want out of regular & thunder?" Then, we'd typically carry five or six of those into a game, built off hitches, slants, quick-outs, and option routes, with various shifts and motion.

We then build up more advanced packages of passing concepts from "12 to 11 personnel" by thinking in terms of "thunder-slot *is* trips" (Figure 2-25) and "wing-slot *is* doubles snug" (Figure 2-26). From there, we can still keep the same packages and concepts when we add shifts and motion. This way any single concept (such as our "Miami" play) can be *packaged* from a variety of formations and it's all similar for the quarterback, backs, receivers, and offensive line. Most importantly, as the play caller, this kind of "concept thinking" helps you to "feed the studs," as we will see in the chapters to follow!

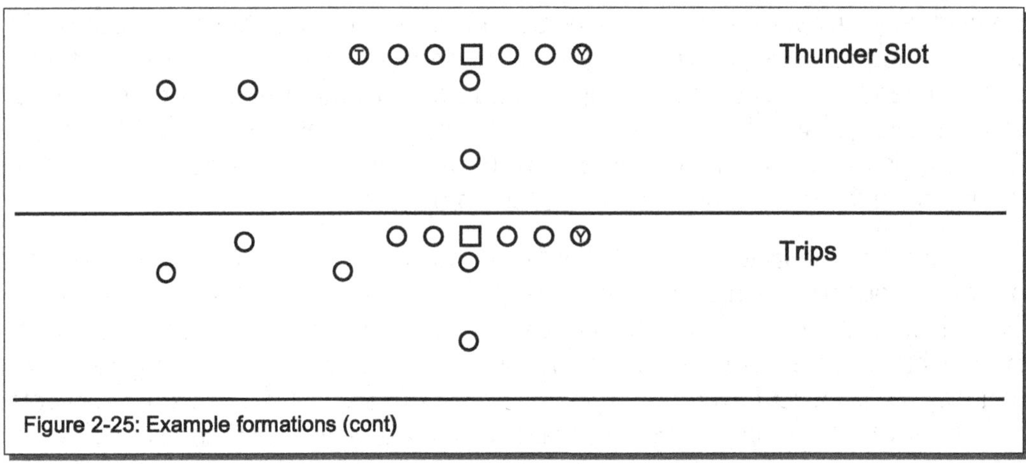


Figure 2-25: Example formations (cont)

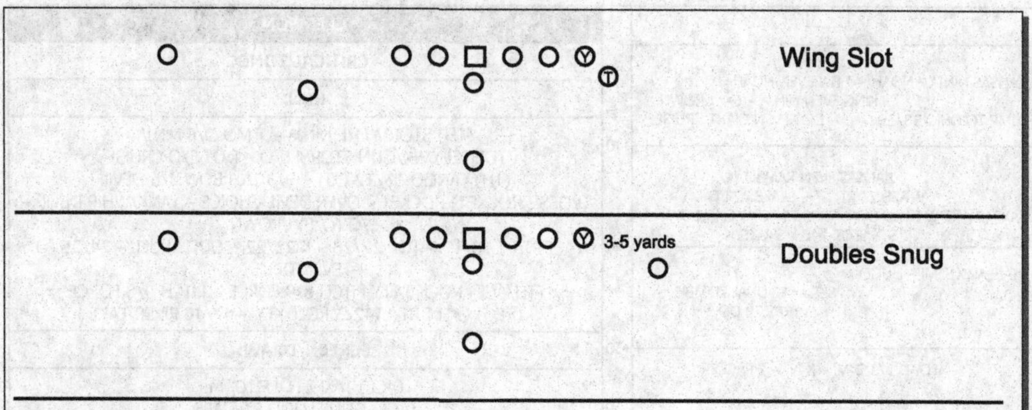

Wing Slot

3-5 yards

Doubles Snug

Figure 2-26: Example formations (cont)

KANSAS NINJA – NOAH – T FLY EVEN NOAH
KING EVEN NINJA – 6/7 CROWN
JUMP TO OHIO 38/39 DOT EVEN GIANT CRUISE

+10

KANSAS EVEN RAMBO
BLAZE 23 RT "C" – BLAZE 22 LT
TAXI 481 "C" W SHALLOW – TRPS 71 "C" W SHALLOW
STR SLOT 140 Y SHAKE

+20

79 BEAR X SEMI – HUGO
WG SLT 1432 DUAL ZOMBIE
TRPS 79 DOLPHIN

+30

LOAD 2/3 Z "V" – X "V" – Z PACKER

BLAZE 33 RT DWARF – Q – W SAIL

+40

50

-40

RUN:
(TH) KING RT/LT EVEN NINJA - ODD NOAH – ODD NINJA – 13/12
(OUT/DIESEL) G SLT RT/LT 5/4 ~~DEVIL~~

-30

(POSSE/ROCKET) POSSE/OVER DEVIL CHOICE
(REG) KING FT/LT 35/39 BOSS
(ACE) JACK EVEN NINJA – OCD NOAH – 27/25 – ODD SKULL – Y

-20

FLY ODD GIANT
(TH) ROCK INTO BAZOOKA 83/89
DBLS EVEN BLAST ALERT??

-10

## PASS +10

SIX PACK HALF SIX PACK
(STRETCH) 7/6 TAXI RAM GATOR
(ACE) G TRPS 71 "C" HAWK
(ACE) G DBLS CLOSE 79 VIKING PASS
(ACE) X BNCH RT/LT 489 DENVER

## SCORING PLAYS

(+4) 2 P.P.
(+6) SIX PACK RT HALF SIX PACK (X BUNCH 489 DENVER)
TRIPS X HALF 489 W DRIVE
(+8) 9/8 TRAMP RAM JAPAN W JERK (GATOR)
(+12) (ACE) G DBLS 485 JAGUAR
(+16) (ACE) GUN TREY 480 FALCON
(+20) (STAR) 9 TRAMP RT RAM DAYTONA X INN

# CLEMSON

## CRITICAL ZONE

### RUN:

(TH) STORM O/E NINJA – T MO O/E NINJA
(DEUCE) WK/GUN STORM E/O – DOT E/O CRUISE
(TH) TANGO 13/12 CUT – 9/8 TAXI BOW 4/5 DEVIL
(POSSE/ROCKET) ROCKET – OVER DEVIL CHOICE – YANK/WHIP DEVIL – E/O (O/E) CROWN
(ACE) TAXI 18/17 – TOP 27/28 – K 23/22 – ODD SKULL – 24/25 "O" – EVEN DEVIL
(TH/ACE) ROCK T FLY PITCH 8/9 FORCE – PITCH 9/8 FORCE
(REG) G SLT RT/LT42/3 ROLL KEY – 47/46 RIVER/LAKE

### SCREEN/DRAW:

(ACE) TAXI Z HALF 10/11
(ACE) GUN FLOOD RT MARS
(ACE) S DIME W MO 51/50 – (BAMA) CARD 50/51

### PLAY ACTION:

(REG/TH) RT/LT (Z HALF) 143/142 Z PACKER – Z BADGER
(ACE) G DBLS STRIKE ROSE/LIMA CRUSH
(TH) TH Z FLY BLAZE 39/38 Z TUNNEL
(TH) ROCKET FLY BURN 39/8 TUBE
(ACE) TOP RT/LT CLOSE W FLY BURN 39/38 RT/LT TUBA
(ACE) DOT BLAZE 23/2 RT Z DRAGON – (TH) WG T FLY BLAZE 16/17 Z DRAGON
(ACE) TOP BOW BLAZE 33/32 RT W SAIL – Q
(ACE/TH) DOS W/T HALF BLAZE 38/39 LT/RT BOAT
(ACE) DOT RT/LT CLOSE Y FLY KN 7/6 MOSES

### PASS:

(TH) WG 73 BILL – (ACE) TOP BOW EVEN DART – CHINA
(TH) TH 75 ZEBRA – 487 SHARK – 78 – WG SLT FOX 79 ZOMBIE
(ROCKET) ROCKET WHIP/YANK SARA/SALLY CROSS
(ACE) G TRPS 79 DOLPHIN
(ACE) SHOT/GUN TRPS X HALF 489 DRIVE – EVEN DART X SNG – 79 Y SHOOTER
(ACE) DBLS INTO 71 MAYBE (X POST) – 72 Z TOPPER – 489 JAWS (Z POST)
DOT 80 – TAXI 480 MIDGET X SKINNY
(TH) DICE CLOSE FOX ROSE/LIMA JAPAN – (STRETCH) 9/8 TRAMP/ FLOOD RAM JAPAN W/Y JERK
(ACE) TRPS SCAT 79 CHARGER – TAXI 79 BEAR X SEMI – X HITCH
(ACE) FLOOD – TAXI 481 "C" – TRPS 71 "C" W SHALLOW
(ACE/POSSE) FOX LIMA/ROSE DALLAS
(POSSE) ROSE/LIMA OAKLAND – GREY SWIPE
(STRETCH) 9/8 TAXI RAW/LION SINKER X JERK – ORLANDO/OAKLAND X SLOP – SEATTLE STAB
(CHECK STAY)

## RUN: GOAL LINE PASS:

| RUN | PASS |
|---|---|
| (TRAIN) TRAIN RT/LT 13/12 CUT – EVEN NINJA 16/17<br>(MUSCLE) MUSCLE JUMP 38/39 – SKIP 39/38 DOWN CHOICE | (OHIO) KANSAS F MO KN 8 T SNG<br>(MUSCLE) T MOVE INDIAN RT BLAZE 23 RT "C"<br>(TEX) STR TEX T FLY BLAZE 39/8 RT LT T TUBE<br>(OHIO) S WK TEX BLAZE 13 RT NUDE RT<br>(UNDER) KANSAS RT EVEN RAMBO |

## RUN: (LH) 2 POINT CALLS (LH) PASS:

| RUN | PASS |
|---|---|
| | (STRETCH) 9 TANGO LT RAM RAVEN<br>(STRETCH) 7 TAXI RT RAM GATOR |

# Chapter 3
# Quick Game

A discussion of our passing game installation begins with the quick game. I'd like to share with you the design of our quick game, some concept foundations, and some specific coaching points. We include an option route package within our quick game that has been very good for us over the years. I'd also like to show you some example packages for the quick game that we've designed in an effort to create matchups for our receivers. I'd like to conclude the chapter by sharing some recent developments in our quick game package. Let's look at the design of the quick game first.

## Quick Passing Game

The quick passing game is designed for the quarterback to (a) have a comfort level with knowing "I can take 3-steps (or 2 in the gun) and get the ball out of my hands;" (b) take advantage of run formations (off of run looks) to throw 1-on-1 matchups; (c) be very confident with our *combo* philosophy of "1-high, I go to this side, 2-high I go to the other;" (d) try to isolate an outside linebacker/inside linebacker in coverage and take advantage of the mismatch.

The quarterback should always have a comfort zone where he knows "I can beat the pressure coming. I can get to a better protection vs. A-gap or overload pressures but I still should have the ability to beat anything they want to bring." The quarterbacks I've coached have all been very comfortable with and have excelled in the quick game.

The quarterback is taught to identify pre-snap coverage in order to get an idea of what the defense is doing. His ability to see post-snap coverage is really what's important. The safety rotation will tell us 2-high or single-high and the linebackers will tell us "man, zone or pressure." When we face a true 3-4 team, the boundary outside linebacker becomes a concern and can cause us to override some things, if he buzzes the flat.

## Quarterback 3-Step Drop

There are a few variations of 3-step drops from under center that quarterbacks need to be able to do. There are certain throws with the 3-step drop where the quarterback needs to "hit his 3rd step, break his hands, and throw the ball." If I'm throwing a hitch, I go "1, 2, 3, break my hands, throw the hitch," and read it "outside-in." If I'm throwing a hook route or an option route, the 3-steps are "right, left, right, looking past zero," I pivot "sit" on that 3rd step. If I'm throwing a slant, I go "1, 2, 3 'sit on it' and locate the receiver." I have a "rhythm throw," where I hit on my 3rd step, break my hands and throw the ball. Then, I have a "sit throw," where I have to sit on the 3rd step and be in position, balanced, and ready to break my hands and throw the ball.

When I say three steps from under the center, that's two steps out of gun (which always reminds me of Mark Brunell and how meticulously he worked at the correlation of footwork from under the center to gun). The 2-step in gun for a hitch is "left, right, break my hands, throw the hitch." If I'm right-handed, throwing a hook route or an option route from gun, I go 2-steps: "left, right, looking past zero," and I "sit" on that 2nd step. It's similar with a slant from gun: left, right, and I've got to "sit" on it, because sometimes the receiver needs time to win on a slant.

We have a clearly defined system of footwork, but you also need to pay attention to your quarterback and once he begins to understand the footwork, adapt to what makes him play at his best. As we say, you need to *take care of your quarterback*. For example, Ryan Mallett didn't like the 2-step drop from gun for our option routes, so he took a quick 3-step drop instead. I said "fine, as long as you get the ball out on time." With Lamar Jackson, we allowed him to set his feet with a narrower base, because when we'd coach him to "sit" with a standard base, he'd drop his elbow down. If you look closely, you can see on his Louisville film that he's "sitting" on that right foot, but he's just moving his left foot a little closer, instead of keeping it to the ground. But the *timing* was really good. Those are good examples of how we define our teaching progression for the 3-step drop but still always take care of the quarterback.

## Thoughts on the Quick Game

You'll want to clearly define the quick game. The first idea is to line up in run personnel and run the quick game off of quick play-action (or a quick 3-step drop, with some cut protection). We go *get* the d-linemen, and take advantage of the "drop-safety defense," where I'm getting 1-on-1s with my outside receivers. Quick game for us starts there, where we work from run looks, where it's primarily designed to get 1-on-1 matchups with your outside receivers vs. "drop safety, single-high coverage." We evolve the package from there to build our combo concepts and then add multiples of spread sets and motions, in order to get our matchups with receivers on linebackers.

## "Flash" Hitch-Fade-Slant

The first part of the package in the quick game is to make it look like run. You have your "flash" protection, which is a quick play-action protection where the quarterback takes a 3-step drop from under the center. The line understands that this is a run-blocking play-action with "low hats." We want to come off the ball, with the exception of a tackle to the open side with a wide end. He can't come off the ball; he needs to make sure he doesn't get the quarterback hit in the back of the head, but inside you want to push. We call it based on the corresponding run play, such as "flash 42/43" or "flash 30/31," and the first route you call is usually a hitch. We might call "right: flash 42 hitch," with a "streak-read" for the tight end, or just keep him home in protection (Figure 3-1).

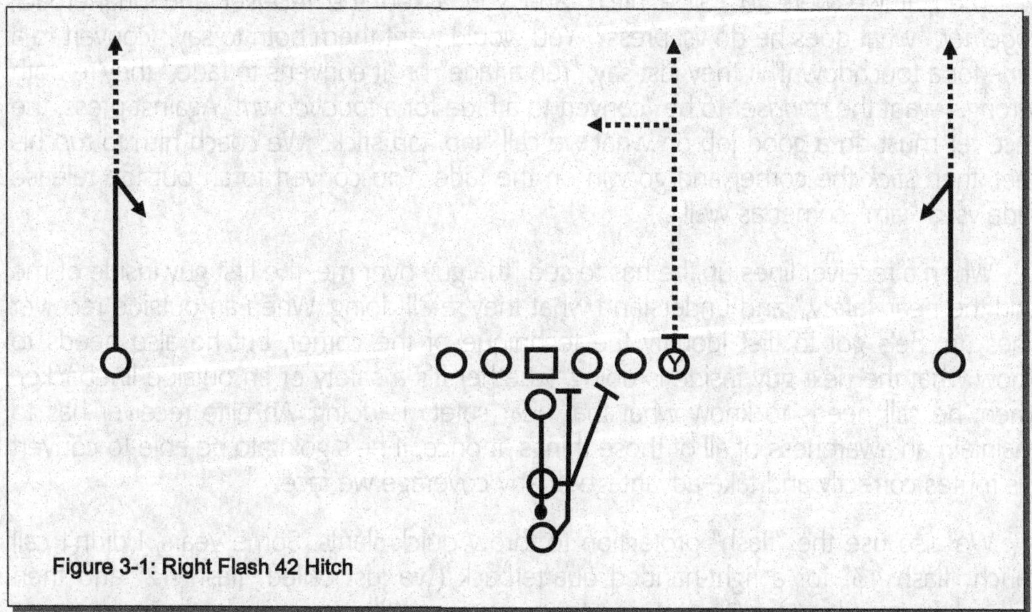


Figure 3-1: Right Flash 42 Hitch

You really want to be specific when you run the hitch route. With the *outside* foot back in your stance, it's a 5-step hitch route, "3 long, 2 short," which gets you six yards off the ball—not from your alignment, but from the *ball*. Our best hitch runners were the long-striders. Some guys cut it short, but the long striders always get to the right depth. Then, you want *at least 10 yards* on a hitch: five from the route and at least five after the catch.

**Play: Flash 42 Hitch**

| Pos: | Assignment: |
|---|---|
| QB | Coaching points: Quick 3-step play-action. Set point is behind the center.<br>Progression: 1. Z   2. X (away from rotation) |
| F | Cheat your alignment up. Block flash. 42 protection. |
| R | Cheat your alignment up. Run play fake. Block flash. 42 protection. |
| X | Run hitch (normal conversion). |
| Y | Block flash. 42 protection. |
| Z | Run hitch (normal conversion). |

Once you catch the ball, in order to beat that corner, you need to "know where you left him." As a receiver, you "tight turn" inside or outside, away from where you left that corner and you've got to work *hard* on the tight turns to get the yards you want after the catch. Some guys have a really good knack of "dipping" and then tight-turning. That's what Coby Hamilton was so good at: he would "know where he left" the corner, and then he would "dip" the way he left the corner and "tight turn" opposite and go for 60 yards.

Then, if we were to call a hitch, and you asked the receiver and quarterback *together*, "what does he do vs. press?" You would want them both to say, "convert to a fade for a touchdown!" If they just say, "run a fade" or "it converts to fade," they're both wrong. I want the *mindset* to be "convert to a fade for a *touchdown*!" Against press, the receiver must do a good job on what we call "tap, tap stick." We coach him to *tap* his feet, then *stick* the corner and go win on the fade. You convert to an outside release fade vs. a "jam" corner as well.

When a receiver lines up, he has to see "the guy over me, the first guy inside of me and the near safety," and understand what they're all doing. When an outside receiver lines up, he's got to first identify the technique of the corner, but he also needs to know what the next guy inside is doing, whether it's a safety or an outside linebacker. Then, he still needs to know what that near safety is doing. An elite receiver has to maintain an awareness of all of those things at once, if he's going to be able to convert his routes correctly and take advantage of any coverage we face.

We also use the "flash" protection to throw quick slants. Some years, I didn't call much "flash 43" for a right-handed quarterback (we just called "flash 42" and then with a lefty you do more "flash 43"). However, one of the most productive quick game routes for us is, "right, pepper 43 brown," which is a form of a 5-step slant. We're faking it weak and the tight end is responsible for #4, and then checks his way out to an arrow route, with the 5-step slants on the outside (Figure 3-2). The throw is off safety rotation: if the safety comes down, we throw to the opposite side. It's still a "3-long" drop for the quarterback.

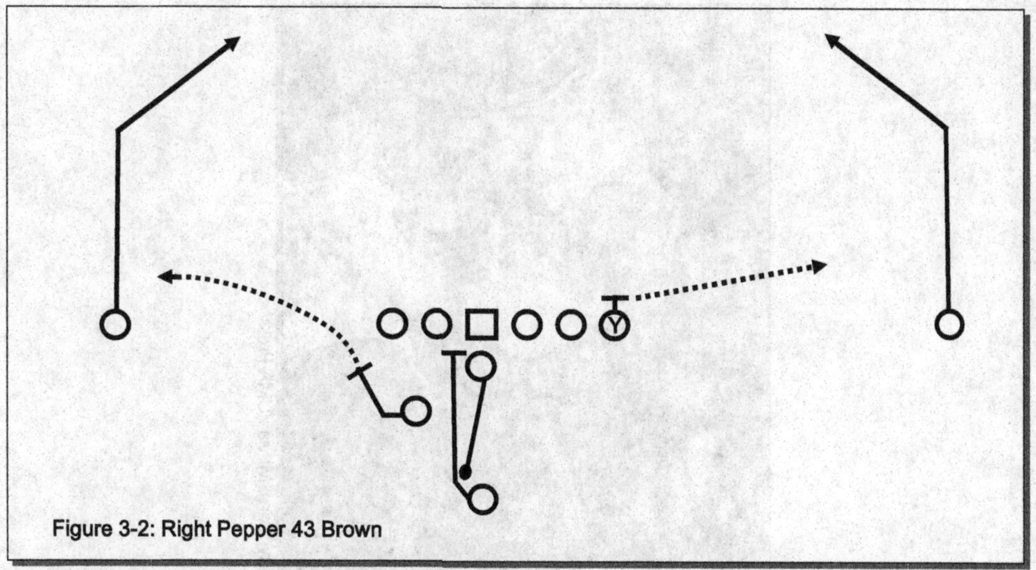

Figure 3-2: Right Pepper 43 Brown

**Play: Right Pepper 43 Brown**

| Pos: | Assignment: |
|---|---|
| QB | Coaching points: quick 3-step play-action. Set point is behind the center.<br>Progression: 1. Z 2. X (away from rotation) |
| F | Cheat your alignment up. Block pepper protection. |
| R | Cheat your alignment up. Run play fake. Block pepper protection. |
| X | 5-step slant. |
| Y | Run block pepper protection. |
| Z | 5-step slant. |

This 5-step slant route is really still a part of quick game (Figure 3-3). You can throw it off the "quickest five steps in the world" or a "long 3." Our quarterbacks tend to be better about being on time with a long 3, rather than the quickest 5, though Mark Brunell could do the "quickest 5" drop, because his feet were so good. This is also a route that's used heavily in the modern RPO packages ("run/pass options"), which we will talk about in Chapter 8.

## Y Hook With Hitch or Slant

We like to package the hitch with two-tight end sets, though we won't call "flash hitch" from something like "thunder right, T mo." Instead from 12 personnel, we like to package the hitch with a tight end hook route: "wing right: rose Orlando, X hitch" (Figure 3-4). "Rose" is the protection and "Orlando" is a code word for the "Y hook" concept. We also like to throw the 3-step slant route with the tight end hook route: "wing right: lima Orlando, X slant" (Figure 3-5). This is where the quarterback needs

Figure 3-3. The 5-step slant route is a part of quick game.

to "sit on it" and give the receiver a chance to get open on the slant. When a backside slant is involved, the quarterback really reads the Will linebacker to determine where to go with the ball. We often like to script this particular play early in the game and then when the quarterback comes to the sidelines, I'll ask "did the Will flow?" in order to determine how we may want to set up more slant throws as the game unfolds.

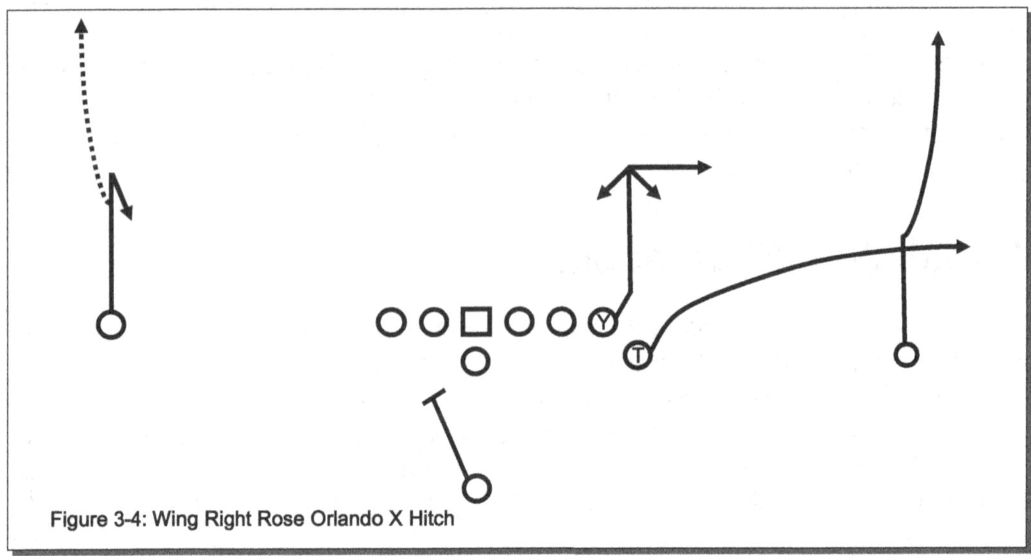


Figure 3-4: Wing Right Rose Orlando X Hitch

**Play: Wing Right: Rose Orlando, X Hitch**

| Pos: | Assignment: |
|---|---|
| T | Arrow |
| R | Block Lima protection. |
| Y | 5-yd hook route |
| X | 5-step hitch (normal conversion) |
| Z | Fade (outside release) |
| QB | Progression:<br>1. X<br>2. Y<br>3. T |

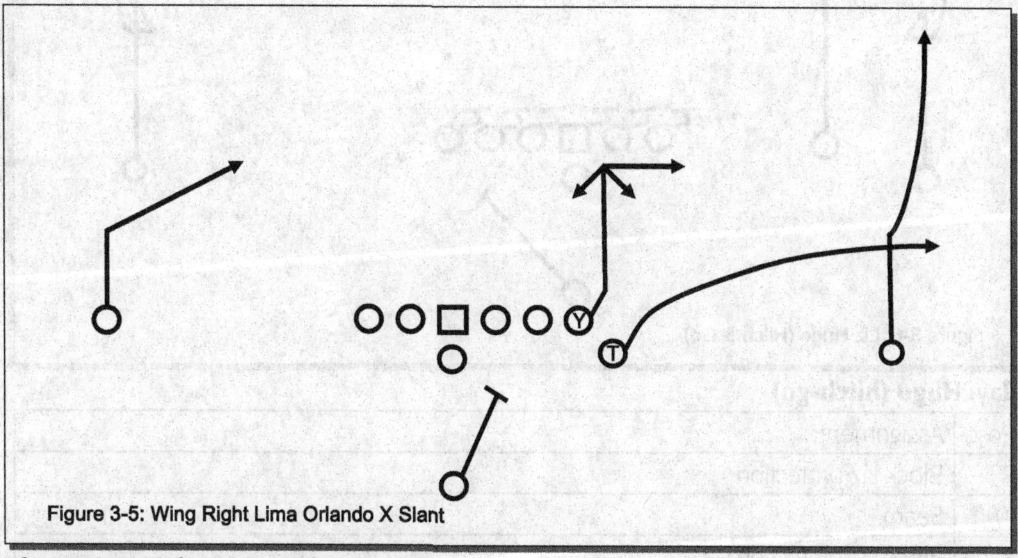


Figure 3-5: Wing Right Lima Orlando X Slant

**Play: Wing Right: Lima Orlando, X Slant**

| Pos: | Assignment: |
|---|---|
| R | Block Lima protection. |
| Y | 5-yd hook route |
| T | Arrow |
| X | 3-step slant |
| Z | Fade (outside release) |
| QB | Progression:<br>1. X<br>2. Y<br>3. T |

## Double-Moves

We also package forms of "double-moves" off quick hitches and slants, such as a basic "hitch-and-go" concept. Once again, it's important to coach the routes clearly. On our "Hugo," for example, the hitch runner wants to sell the hitch and go, but if the corner bails out, we "re-hitch" at 10 yards (Figure 3-6). If you're good at slants, you'll want to include forms of "sluggo" or "sluggo-seam" in your quick game package as well (Figure 3-7).

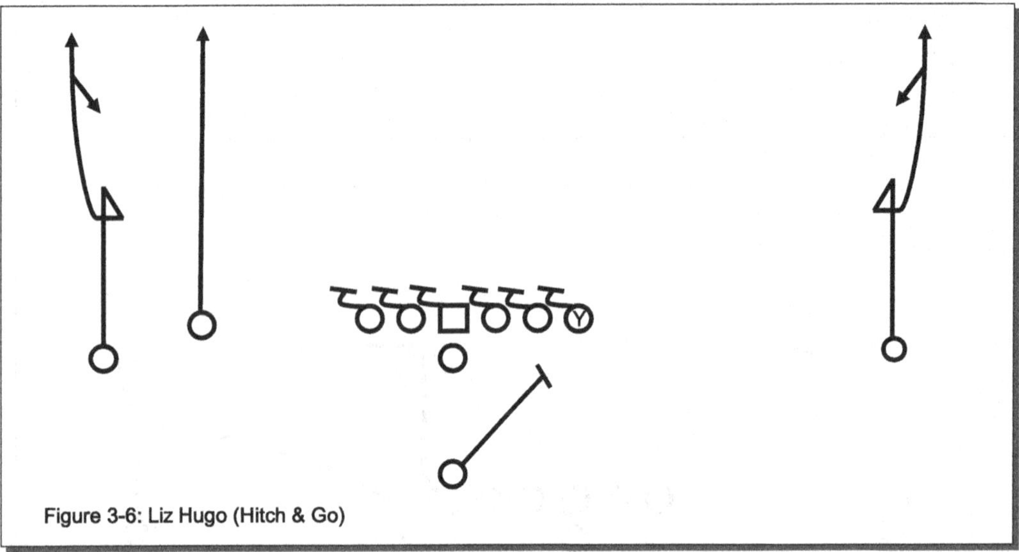


Figure 3-6: Liz Hugo (Hitch & Go)

**Play: Hugo (hitch-go)**

| Pos: | Assignment: |
|---|---|
| R | Block Liz protection |
| W | Seam |
| Y | Block Liz protection |
| X | Hitch go (re-hitch 10) |
| Z | Hitch go (re-hitch 10) |
| QB | Progression:<br>1. Z or X<br>2. W |

## Blue (Quick Out)

"Blue" is our code for an outside fade and 6-yard out from the slot. We typically install this first from a 2x2 set. It's paired again with the "Lima/Rose" quick game protection (Figure 3-8). When we started out, we'd call this "Lima/Rose 97" but the one-word code "blue" has replaced it over the years.

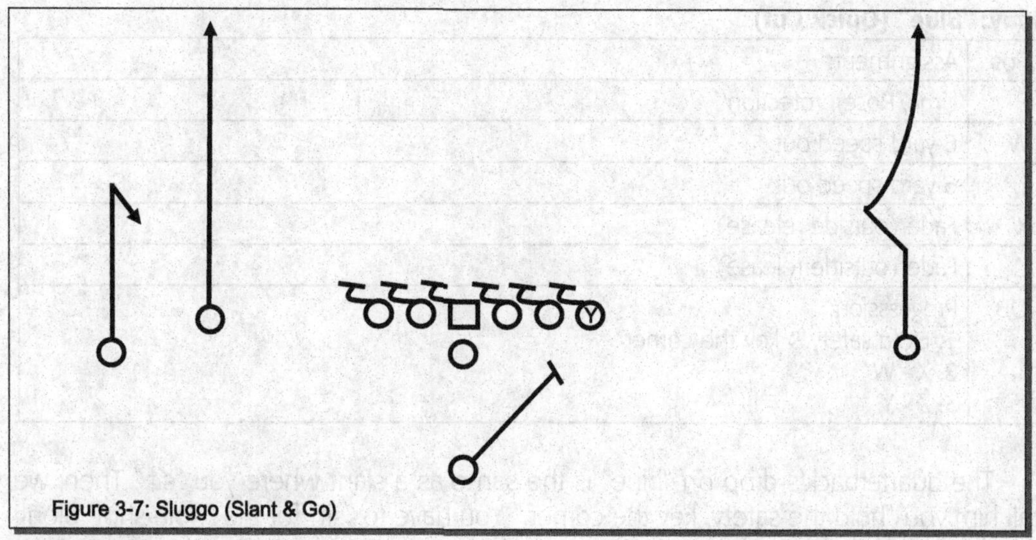
Figure 3-7: Sluggo (Slant & Go)

**Play: Sluggo (slant-go)**

| Pos: | Assignment: |
|---|---|
| R | Block Liz protection |
| W | Seam |
| Y | Block Liz protection |
| X | 5-step hitch |
| Z | Slant go |
| QB | Progression:<br>1. Z<br>2. W<br>3. X |

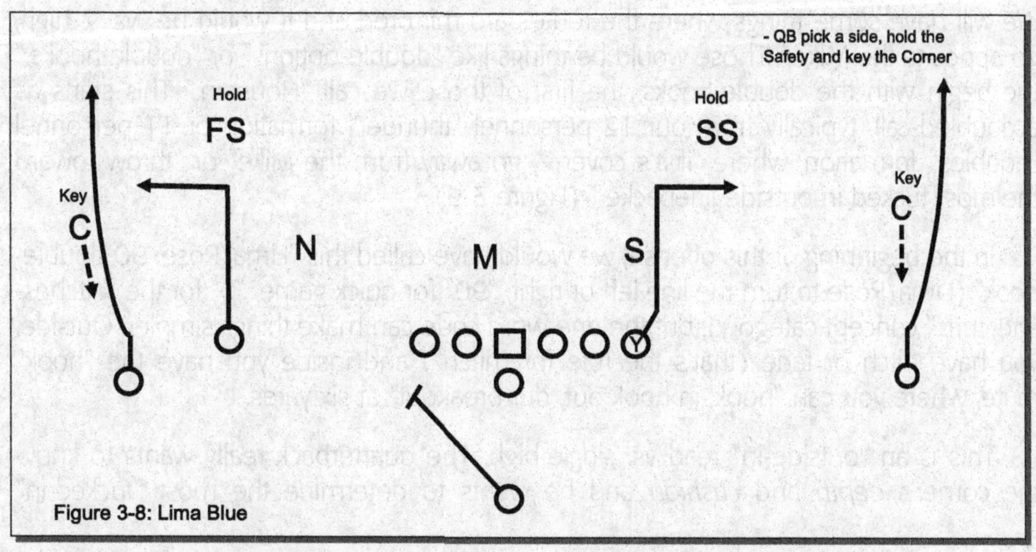

Figure 3-8: Lima Blue

**Play: "Blue" (Quick Cut)**

| Pos: | Assignment: |
|---|---|
| R | Lima/Rose protection |
| W | 6-yard speed out |
| Y | 6-yard speed out |
| X | Fade (outside release) |
| Z | Fade (outside release) |
| QB | Progression:<br>1. Hold safety & key the corner<br>2. X - W<br>3. Z - Y |

The quarterback's drop on "blue" is the same as a slant where you "sit." Then, we tell him you "hold the safety, key the corner." You have to "sit" for the "hole shot" along the sideline or the 6-yard out. It's a 2-step drop from gun, but again you may need to work with your quarterback and help him to find what he does best, such as how we said Ryan Mallett could do a quick-3 from gun. However, the quarterback should always say the exact words, "hold the safety, key the corner," so his reaction becomes a habit.

We have had great success with this concept over the years, particularly against cover 2. We also like to *package* it as a "cover 2 beater" with various other concepts on the other side, in our *combo* plays (which we will explore in a bit). This is also a good 2-minute call because the quarterbacks understand that the fade is #1. We have won a lot of games with this play in 2-minute situations.

## Double-Hooks

We will have some things where the routes are mirrored and it would be "vs. 2 high, go opposite the Mike." Those would be things like "double-options" or "double-hooks." We begin with the double-hooks, the first of those we call "Houston." This starts as a doubled-call, typically from our 12 personnel "thunder" formation or 11 personnel "doubles" formation, where "if it's cover-2, go away from the Mike" or "throw toward the most tucked in outside linebacker" (Figure 3-9).

In the beginning of this offense, we would have called this "Lima/Rose: 90 double-hook" (Lima/Rose to turn the line left or right, "90" for quick game, "0" for the "hitches-and-curls" concept category), but the one-word code can make things simpler. Outside, you have hitch or fade (that's the rule for "hitch") and inside you have the "hook" route, where you can "hook, in hook out, our breakout" at six yards.

This is an "outside-in" read vs. single-high. The quarterback really wants to know the corner's *depth* and *cushion* and he wants to determine the most "tucked-in"

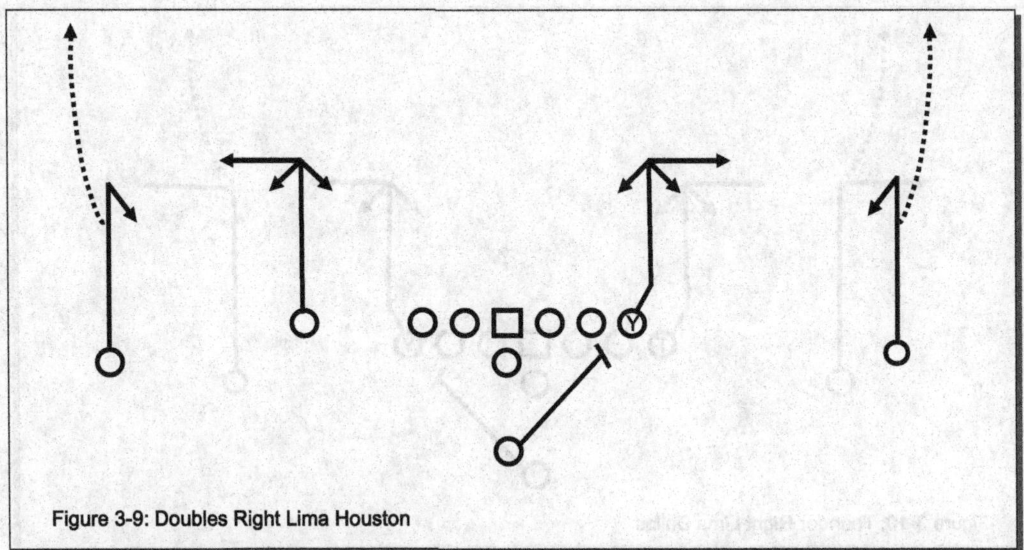

Figure 3-9: Doubles Right Lima Houston

**Play: Doubles Right: Lima Houston**

| Pos: | Assignment: |
|---|---|
| R | Block Lima protection. |
| X | 5-step hitch |
| Y | 6-yd hook route |
| W | 6-yd hook route |
| Z | 5-step hitch (normal conversion) |
| QB | Progression:<br>1. Away from Rotation – outside in<br>2. vs. cover 2: to tucked-in LB |

linebacker. If he's throwing the hitch, he wants to understand which corner leaves the biggest cushion, where we're going to get the most yards and what the best matchups are. If he feels like the hitch is being taken away, he needs to know where the most "tucked-in" linebacker is for the easiest hook. If we get true cover 2, he and the slot receivers have to understand that it should just become a "blue" read after the route conversions, where the quarterback "holds the safety, keys to corner, and looks "fade to a 6-yard out."

"Dallas" is next, which is quick-outs that convert (instead of the hitch), with the hooks inside (Figure 3-10). When this offense started out, we called this "Lima/Rose: 91 double-hook" ("1" is the "outs-and-corners" concept category). Sometimes, you get more yards on "Dallas," especially vs. teams that are really reading the 3-step drop of the quarterback and the corners are breaking straight ahead. That's when you throw the out and he runs down the sideline after the catch (which is also why these are really good tempo calls).

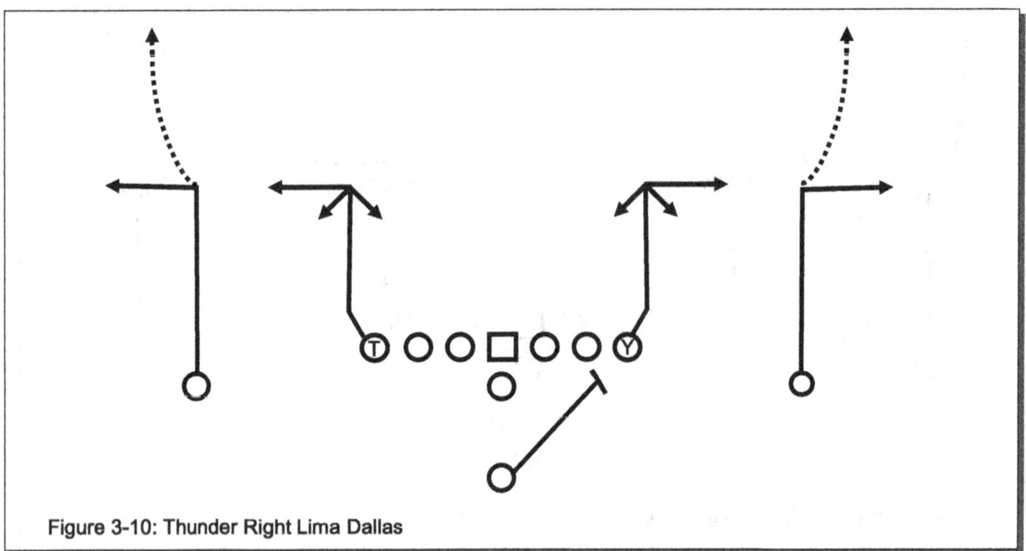


Figure 3-10: Thunder Right Lima Dallas

**Play: Thunder Right: Lima Dallas**

| Pos: | Assignment: |
|---|---|
| R | Block Lima protection. |
| T | 6-yd hook route |
| X | 6-yd quick out (normal conversion) |
| Y | 6-yd hook route |
| Z | 6-yd quick out (normal conversion) |
| QB | Progression:<br>1. Away from rotation – outside in<br>2. vs. cover 2: to tucked-in LB |

This outside route is a 4-step speed out, where we're rounding it from 6-to-8 yards. Not everyone can run it; you have to have a good stride and you've got to turn your outside foot at a 45-degree angle and roll the route. So, that I start at six yards and I catch it at eight. The quarterback is taught to "throw it through his inside number." If I run the route right, I'm "1, 2, 3, I turn my foot 45 degrees, and I'm rolling out of the route." Then, if the quarterback throws it properly at my inside jersey number, I will have to gain depth upfield to make the catch at eight yards. If I square it out instead, then it's a pivot catch behind me and I get no run-after-catch yardage. I've usually only ever had maybe two guys a year that can run it right. It's very hard to do. On the other hand, you get more yards on it than a hitch, if you can execute it correctly. Then, you still have the same "hook in, hook out or breakout" from the inside receivers.

On occasion, we call these with our "fox" protection from gun. That would be "fox, lima: Dallas" (Figure 3-11). We don't ball fake on "fox," although Stefan LeFors could do it and still be on time with the throw. (We felt like if you wanted the ball fake, call it "wolf" and then you're throwing the ball deeper downfield, trying to affect safeties.) We carry the "fox" tag with the quick game, to be able to set the back on the other side. When you package it like this, you can handle teams that like to set pressure to the running back. As with all our base concepts, we also like to *package* these within *combo* routes, which we will discuss ahead.

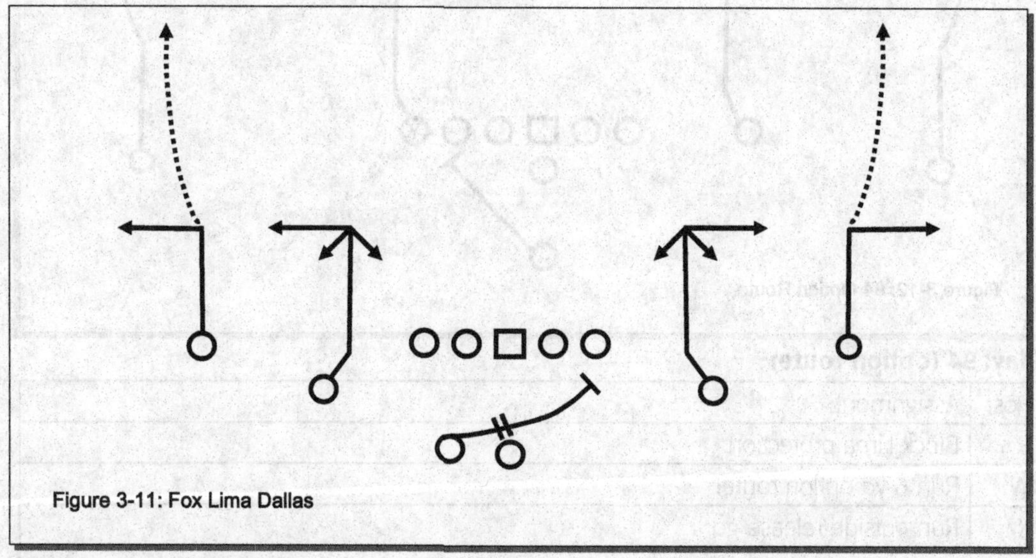

Figure 3-11: Fox Lima Dallas

## Option Routes

The inside option route series has been consistently really effective for us. Our option routes fall under the "4" concept category, and in the quick game, and if we want to call our option routes to both inside receivers rather than the hook routes, we call that "94." We have what we call a "protect fade" outside of the option route, where you have to outside release in order to "protect" the inside receiver, if he's breaking out. We often just use the one-word code name "grey" for this concept (especially within our *combo* packages).

The slot receiver has an option route at 6-to-8 yards. (I eventually started telling the receivers eight yards on an option so they would get to six, because they always seem to cut it too short). On an option route, I can go *in* (vs. zone I can break in and sit down), I can break *out*, or I can go over the top for a touchdown. We say: "in, out, or over the top" (Figure 3-12). How do I run the option route? I want to have great get-off, I want to threaten the nearest defender's leverage, and then I break "in, out, over the top."

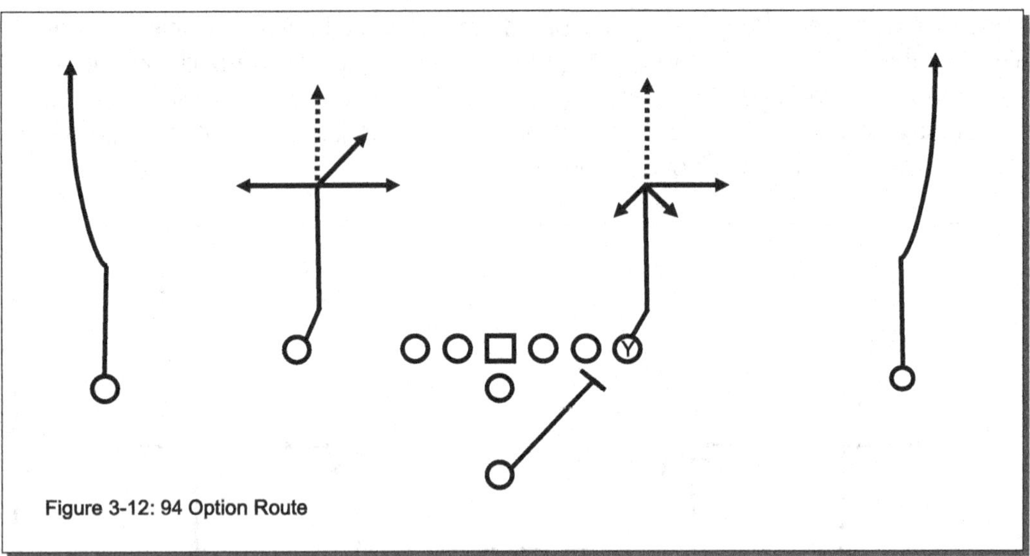

Figure 3-12: 94 Option Route

**Play: 94 (option route)**

| Pos: | Assignment: |
|---|---|
| R | Block Lima protection. |
| W | Run 6-yd option route. |
| X | Run outside release go. |
| Y | Run 6-yd option route. |
| Z | Run outside release go. |
| QB | Progression:<br>1. W (alert to Pop backside)<br>2. Y |

One of the things that you do have to coach about the route is to get the receiver to run at the defender first, because sometimes he needs to stem in to attack those "apex" players. To do that, you can use a garbage can to simulate the defender, move it two yards inside him and then the receiver has to "stem in and square it up" first. Then, you tip the garbage can in or out and he reacts to you as he runs the route.

In a 2x2 set, both of the slots line up and look "man over me, first guy inside" and both of them should know right away, if the middle is open. Initially when you see a linebacker or apex player inside with his inside foot forward, I'd like the option runner to think, "if I get inside, I've got a touchdown." All he has to do is "break that hip" and the defender can't recover, and then we get tons of yardage after the catch. If the defender works away from him, he just breaks out instead. In a 2x2, you usually can't take it over the top against cover 2, because there's no other threat to that safety (Figure 3-13). However, if you're in a 2x2 set from the hash, the boundary slot has an opportunity to take it over the top on a seam, if that safety works away from him (Figure 3-14). (Incidentally, I figured out that we didn't practice that enough. We practiced it to the field guy all the time and not enough to the boundary guy.) If we get cover 2 in a 3x1 to the field, now my first thought is "take it over the top" (Figure 3-15). That's also the case for our #3 in empty, such as "shift right: 94" (Figure 3-16), because that safety also has to worry about #1 and #2.

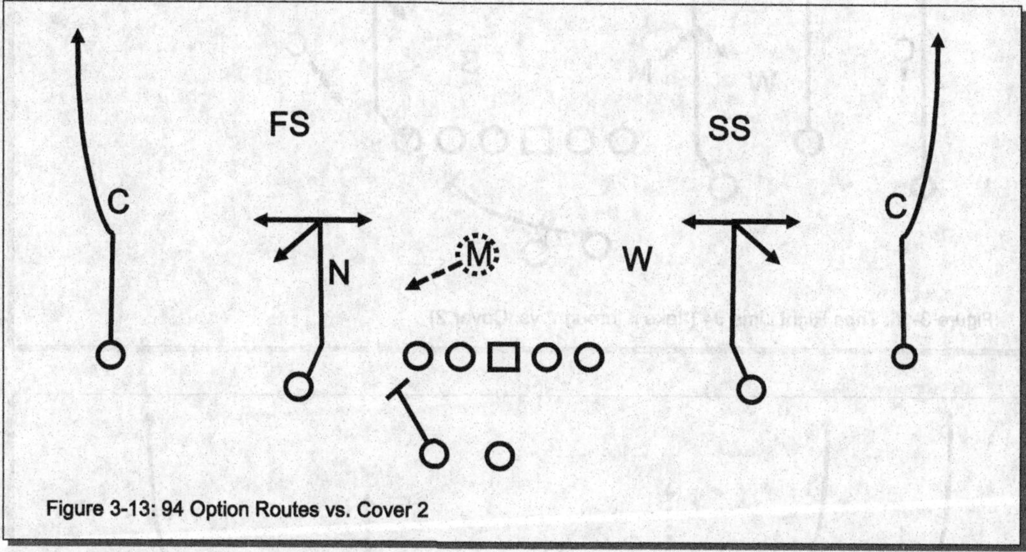


Figure 3-13: 94 Option Routes vs. Cover 2

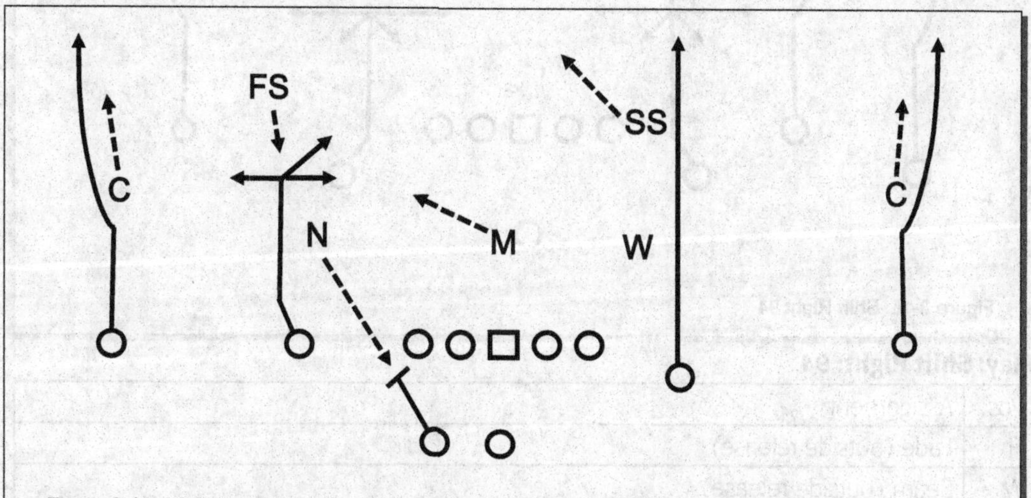

Figure 3-14: 94 Option Routes vs. rotation away (chance to "take it through")

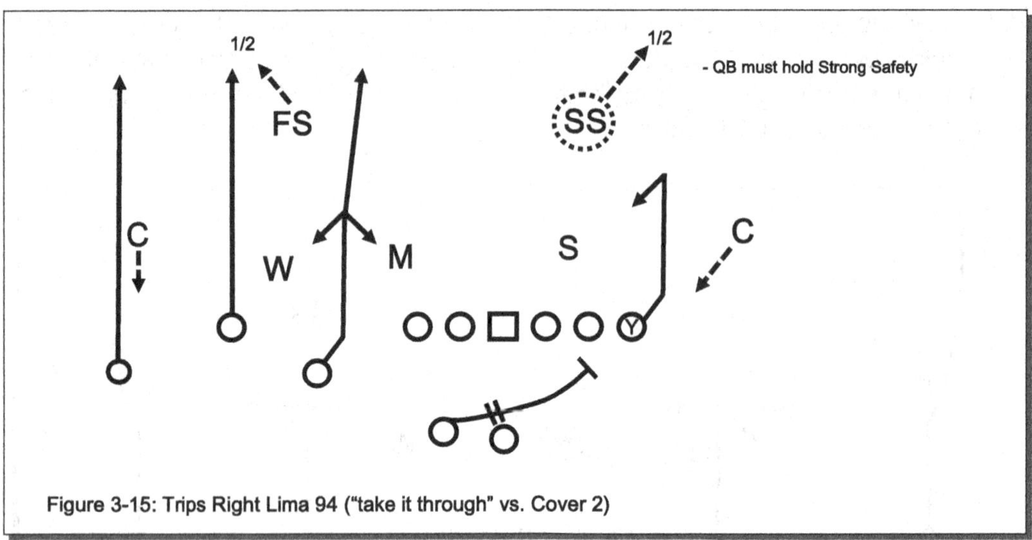

Figure 3-15: Trips Right Lima 94 ("take it through" vs. Cover 2)

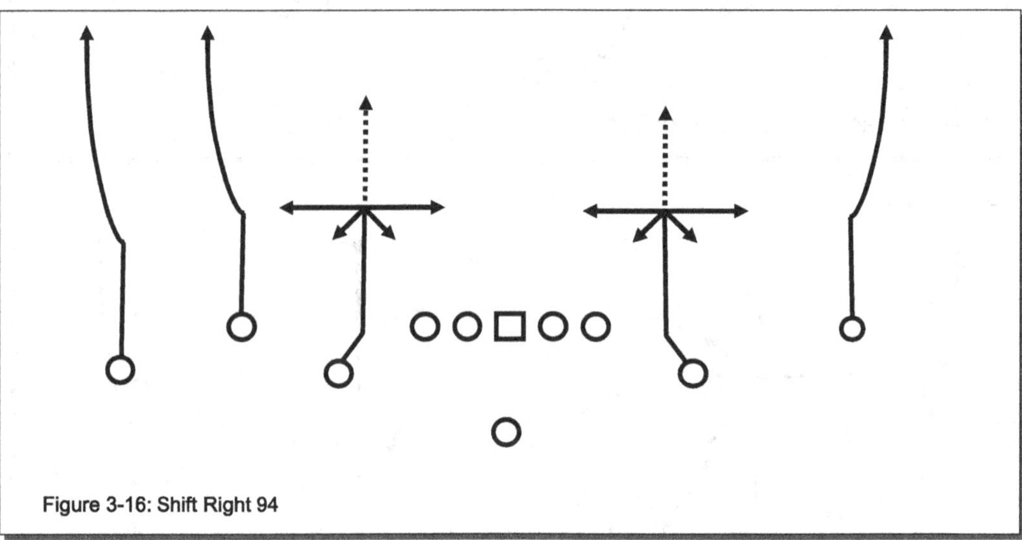
Figure 3-16: Shift Right 94

**Play: Shift Right: 94**

| Pos: | Assignment: |
|---|---|
| H | Fade (outside release) |
| W | Seam (outside release) |
| X | Fade |
| Y | 6-yd option route |
| Z | 6-yd option route |
| QB | Progression:<br>1. Z<br>2. Y<br>3. Alert W on seam or H on fade |

Great "get-off" is the key to the option route. However, when you're coaching it, you'll find that some guys really just kind of get a feel for it and some guys struggle with it. We use all of these coaching points to help them, but if a guy can do a good job of reading the defenders and getting over the top, we give him the freedom. I don't overcoach it, if you get a guy who is a special option-route runner. If he has a great *feel* for it, you can really see that he's always ready to take it through for a touchdown. On film, you can actually see that receiver thinking, "I see that safety, I widen the apex defender, I blow by the linebacker, and it's six points."

Another thing you can watch for is that the guys who are good at the option route can catch the football without seeing the ball come out of the quarterback's hands. Some guys can't do that. If a guy always has to see the ball thrown, he needs to play outside receiver. You don't put him inside. The inside option route guys have to just be able to locate the ball at the catch point and stick their hands up to make the catch.

When the quarterback makes his read, sometimes you may have to live with the quarterback's decision to take the short completion, even though you might see on film that he had the home run available on the other side. Because it's the same thing, don't overcoach it. We just always ask them "why?" "Why did you do that? Okay, good." All I want players to do is have an answer for me: "tell me why you did it, what you were thinking, what you saw. If you were wrong, I need to be able to tell you how to fix it." On film, you can always see when the receiver and the quarterback are on the same page. When that's happening, let them play!

## Tight End Option Route

If the tight end is in-line and we call "94." He can hook over his alignment but the tight end cannot break inside on this. He can go over the top on what we call "bear" or what some people call "vice," which is the Buddy Ryan "46" look, with the strong safety or linebacker aligned on him (Figure 3-17). If you can get a free release, you can take that over the top for a touchdown. In fact, that used to be one of our checks for it: go over the top or 6-yard out, depending on the release. There's a drill where you take the tight ends and Mike or Sam linebackers (whoever they use as their "vice" guy on our own team) and work that for 5-to-10 minutes a day during camp.

## Choke Option

Some of the NFL teams run an option route, but they want the quarterback on a 5-step drop. We can do that with a "choke-option," where he doesn't come off the ball full speed, he chokes his release, and then accelerates and runs it. Sometimes, you'll set that up with a combo, where the guy's reading something else on the other side. There, it's "5-off-the-plant" throw from under center and "3-quick" from gun.

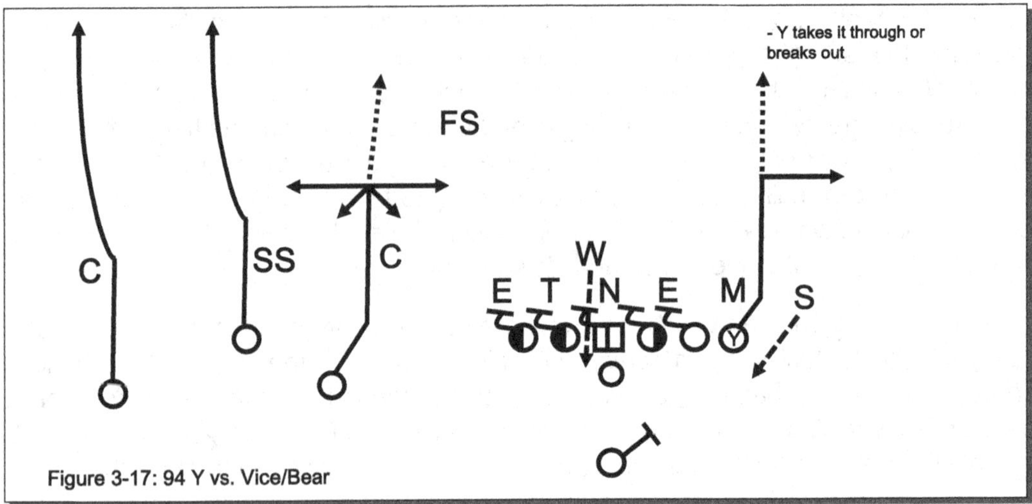


Figure 3-17: 94 Y vs. Vice/Bear

**Play: 94Y (Y "takes it through" vs. "Vice/Bear")**

| Pos: | Assignment: |
|---|---|
| R | Block Lima protection. |
| W | Seam (outside release) |
| X | Fade (outside release) |
| Y | 6-yd option route |
| Z | 6-yd option route |
| QB | Progression:<br>1. Z-Y |

# Trips: Silver, Gold, 94 Y, Seattle

One of the things people like to do is play "trio" coverage to our "trips" formation. That means they're going to man-up the outside receiver, try to cheat the Mike linebacker to help with run, and then "in & out" the #2 and #3 receivers with the safety over the top. (We named that "in-and-out" type of coverage "trio" because it was "3-on-2.") So, our first "trio beater" is what we called "fox lima (rose): 99 Y drag" (Figure 3-18). Then we gave it a one-word code: "silver."

We ran a 5-step post with the outside receiver, a wheel route by #2, a 6-yard out by #3, and a drag by the tight end. The quarterback's *key* is the guy over #2. If he goes with the wheel, I look to throw the "6-yard out, to the drag." If he doesn't go with the wheel, then I'm looking to throw "post-to-wheel." Simple as that. Again, it's a "trio beater."

The thing we like best for cover 3 or "blitz 3" is what we call "97 Y drag." We named this one "gold." This is also one of the best checks for the quarterback vs. "field scrape" cover 3 pressure. Against that, we prefer to change the protection from "Lima" to "Liz Y," so we'd call this "trips right, Liz Y: gold" (Figure 3-19).

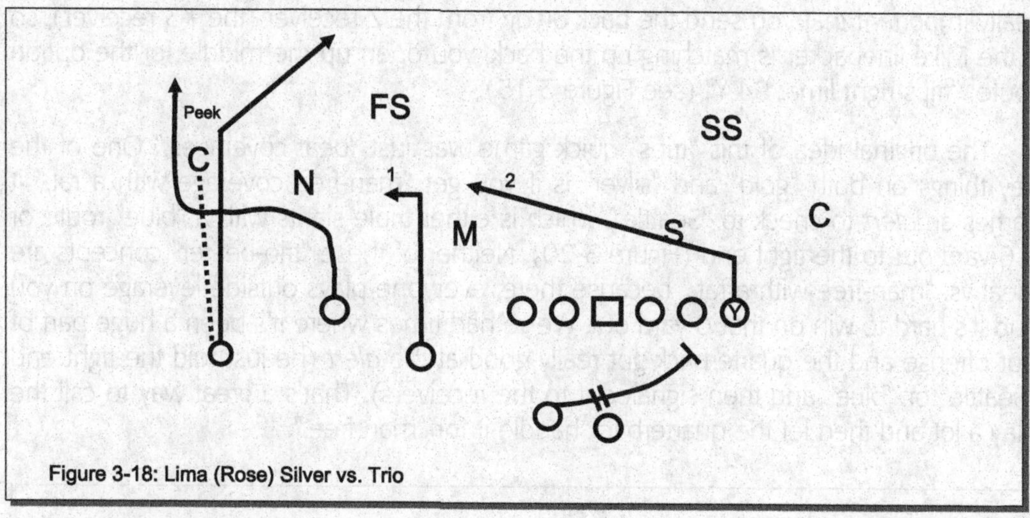

Figure 3-18: Lima (Rose) Silver vs. Trio

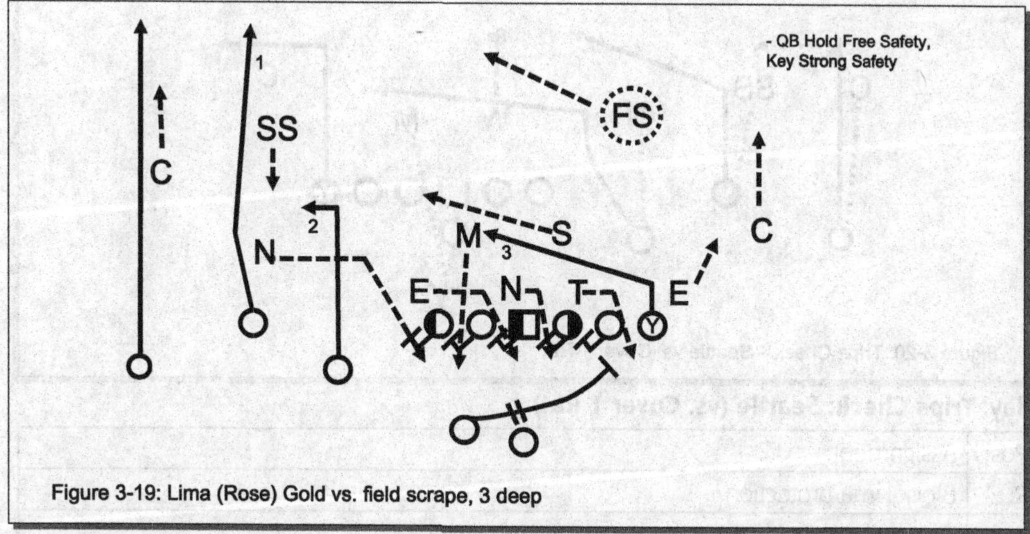

Figure 3-19: Lima (Rose) Gold vs. field scrape, 3 deep

What you're doing now is running a "protect go" route by #1 and a "protect-seam" route by #2 (it's an outside-release and he needs to get outside of the single-high strong safety). It's then the 6-yard out by #3 and the tight end drag route coming after it. We practice the "blue" route where we "hold the safety, key the corner," and we're doing the same thing in this instance vs. single-high. I'm "holding the free safety, keying the strong safety," going "1, 2, 3" (seam, out, drag). Simple as that. If you get cover 2, you're in an *alert* to check to "94 Y," which is the next play I like in this package.

When I see cover 2, I would get to "94 Y," which is our option route to the inside receiver again. We have the protect-fade, protect-seam and now the 6 to 8-yard option route ("in, out, or over the top"). The tight end has the 6-yard option route which is "hook or out" (again, he can go "over the top," if he has a "vice" or "bear"). As such, it's really important that you send the back *away* from the Z receiver (the #3 receiver), so if the Mike linebacker is matching up the back, you open up the middle for the option route: "trips right lima: 94 Y" (see Figure 3-15).

The original idea of this "trips" quick game was just "beat coverages." One of the key things on both "gold" and "silver" is if you get "man-free coverage with a rat," it carries an *alert* to check to "Seattle," which is either triple slants with a "blue" route or a 6-yard out to the tight end (Figure 3-20). Neither of these "trio-beater" concepts are ideal vs. "man-free with a rat," because there, everyone plays outside leverage on you and it's hard to win on that 6-yard out. We've had times where it's been a huge part of our offense and the quarterback got really good at the *alert* (he just told the tight end "Seattle" or "blue" and then signaled it to the receivers). That's a great way to call the play a lot and then let the quarterback handle it for "man-free."

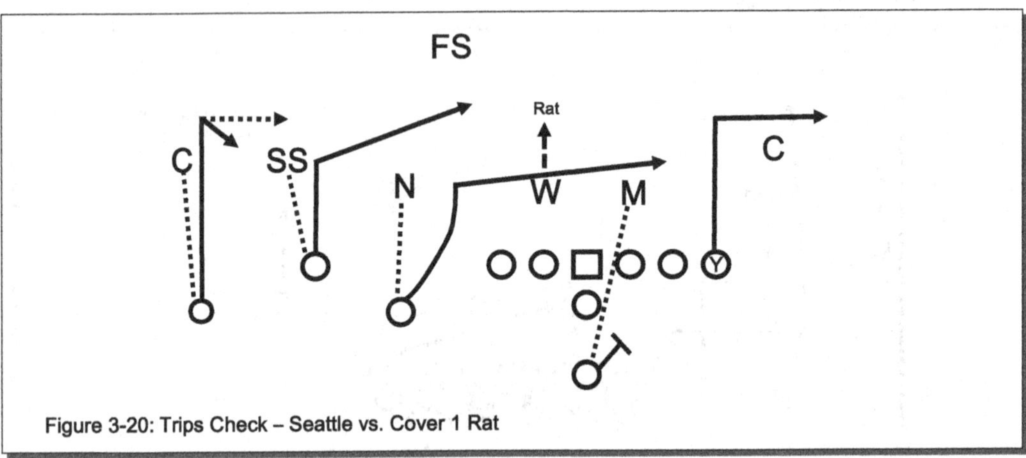

Figure 3-20: Trips Check – Seattle vs. Cover 1 Rat

**Play: Trips Check: Seattle (vs. Cover 1 Rat)**

| Pos: | Assignment: |
|---|---|
| R | Block Lima protection. |
| W | 3-step slant |
| X | 5-yd smash |
| Y | 6-yd speed out |
| Z | Collision drag through inside shoulder |
| QB | Progression:<br>1. Z-W<br>2. X |

# Quick Game Package Examples

When we develop our offense in any given season, we always want to think in terms of *packages*. For example, with the "Orlando, X hitch (X slant)" 3x1 concept we first talked about, you can also cut the d-linemen with a "quick" tag: "wing rt. *quick* Orlando, X hitch/X slant." This gives you another way to get into the heads of the pass rushers and slow them down. Another question is "do you want to be under center or shot (pistol) or gun?" I don't want to be under center all the time, especially if the quarterback can run the read-option game from shot and gun.

You'll also want to add motion. A great way to run that same type of play is "thunder right, T mo: rose Orlando, X hitch" (Figure 3-21). Another way to do it is "wing right, T fly: Lima Houston" (Figure 3-22). You'll want the *package* to include all of these.

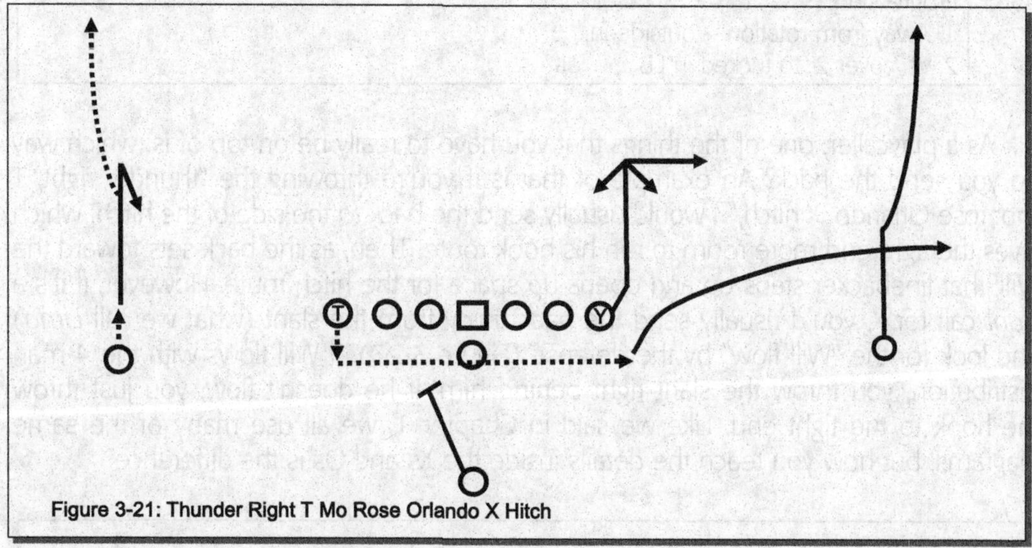

Figure 3-21: Thunder Right T Mo Rose Orlando X Hitch

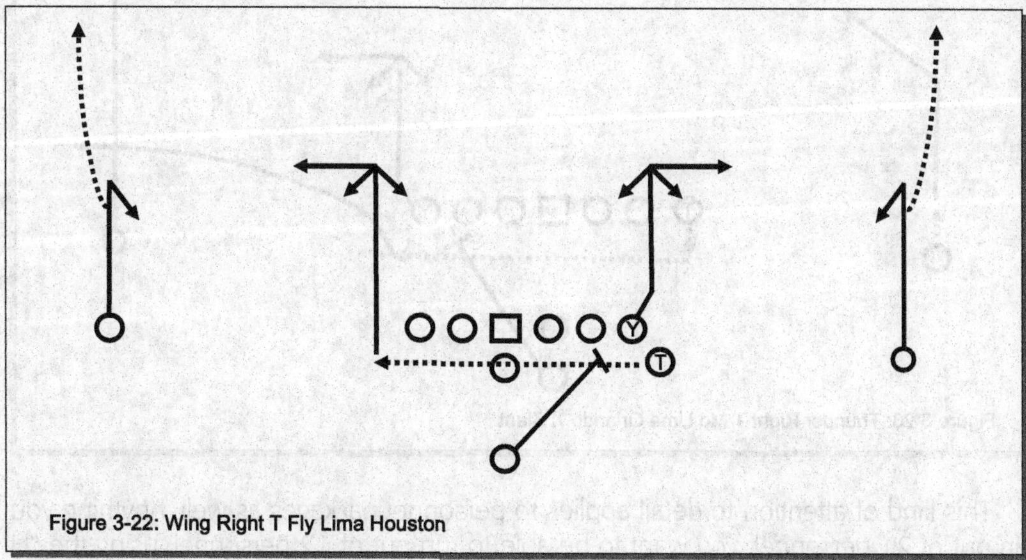

Figure 3-22: Wing Right T Fly Lima Houston

**Play: Wing Right, T Fly: Lima Houston**

| Pos: | Assignment: |
|---|---|
| R | Block Lima protection. |
| T | 6-yd hook route |
| Y | 6-yd hook route |
| X | 5-step hitch (normal conversion) |
| Z | 5-step hitch (normal conversion) |
| QB | Progression:<br>1. Away from rotation – outside-in.<br>2. vs. cover 2; to tucked in LB |

As a playcaller, one of the things that you have to really be on top of is: which way do you send the back? An example of that is if you're throwing the "thunder right, T mo: rose Orlando, X hitch," I would usually send the back *to* the side of the hitch, which gives the tight end more room to run his hook route. Then, as the back sets toward the Will, that linebacker steps up and opens up space for the hitch route. However, if it's a *slant* call for X, you'd usually send the back *away* from the slant (what we call *Lima*) and look for the "Will flow" by the defense (Figure 3-23). If Will flows with the 4-man distribution, you throw the slant right behind him. If he doesn't flow, you just throw the hook to the tight end. Like we said in Chapter 1, we all use many of the same diagrams, but how you teach the details inside the Xs and Os is the difference.

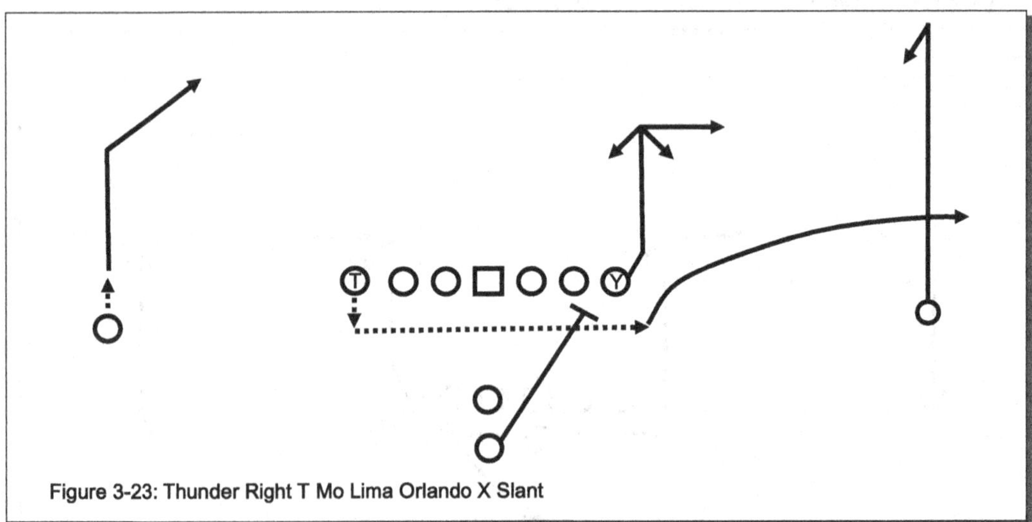

Figure 3-23: Thunder Right T Mo Lima Orlando X Slant

This kind of attention to detail applies to personnel packages as well. Anything you run out of 21 personnel, you want to be able to run out of 12 personnel, using the "H back" (extra tight end) to replace the fullback. As we've stated, we want to control the matchups and I never want to be forced out of any of this offense. This is important: "12 equals 21" in the run game and play-action game. "12 equals 11" in the pass game (quick game and dropback). For us, everything is a *package*. As we plan, we talk in terms of "how many packages of quick game do you want out of 'regular' (21 personnel) & 'thunder' (12 personnel)?" Then, we'd typically carry five or six of those into each game, built off the hitches, hooks, slants, quick-outs and option routes, with various shifts and motions.

I'm big on *packages*. For example, my little brother asked me the other day about "T fly" motion out of bunch (Figure 3-24). I said to him "I want to carry like, 10 plays," because I don't think you can line up in that formation and only have two or three plays. I think, in any given formation, you need to have at least one run play, you need to have quick game, you need dropback and you need to have play-action and quarterback movement. Then, you package those plays with shifts and motions, so it's not like every time you line up in a given formation, the opponent can predict what you're doing. There's always a *package*.

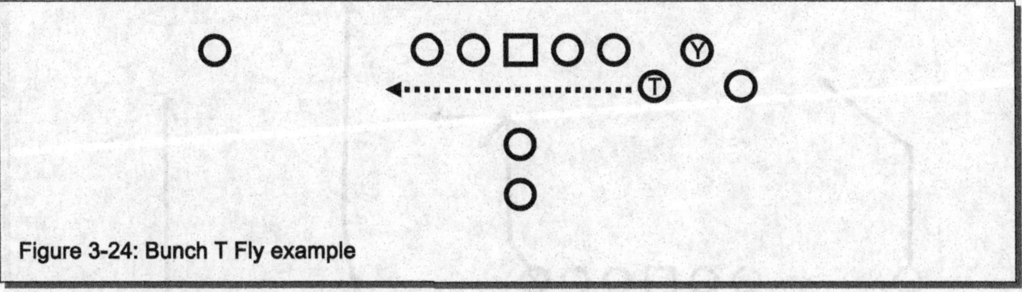

Figure 3-24: Bunch T Fly example

## Quick Game Package Example

The following is an example of how we might build up a series of concepts into a package of "fox Rose/Lima" from a "trey" set. One of the things on that is you get the defense into a 4x1 look, with the back set "near," toward the 3-receiver side. That's where most defenses will say, "that's 65-70% run." So, the back comes across your protection, you get him away from the tight end and your protection goes to the right in the call: "trey right: fox Rose, Oakland, Z halt" (Figure 3-25). Again, in this instance, we'd send the back *away* from the hook route, toward the backside hitch. "Oakland" is a hitch to the field (to take advantage of the high percentage of "off corner" to the field), a seam, and a hook. If you call "halt," instead of "hitch," that's a locked hitch, so if you're in 3rd-&-5, you're going to probably call "halt" to get the 1st down.

The next thing to do is go, "trey right: fox Lima, Oakland, Z slant" (Figure 3-26). Now, you're sending the back away from the slant and seeing what that Will linebacker is going to do: go with "flow" and open up the slant, or sit and give me the "Oakland" side? (Or "Orlando," if you prefer that concept.) Again, we're talking about understanding what to do with your running back to open up what inside routes you're wanting to run.

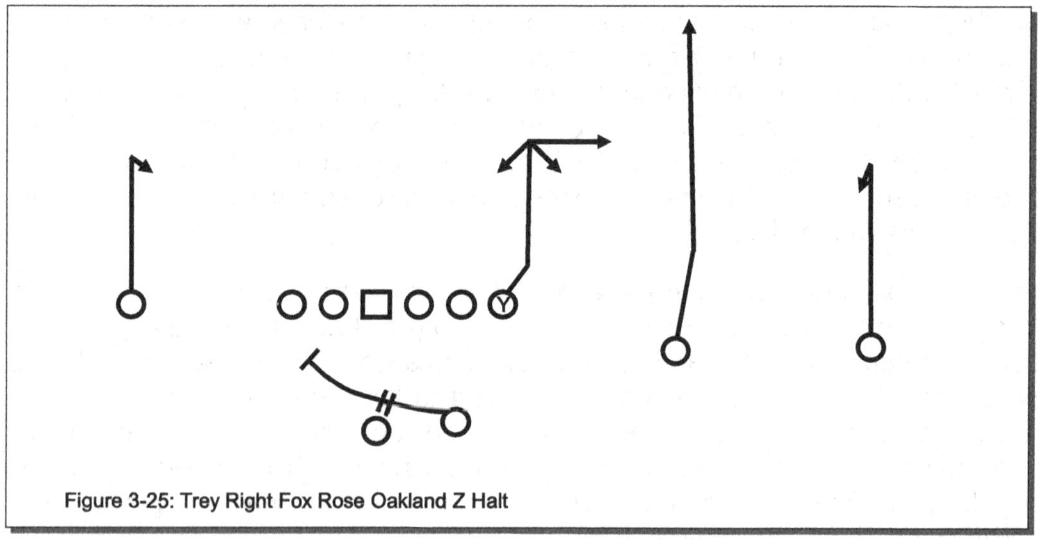

Figure 3-25: Trey Right Fox Rose Oakland Z Halt

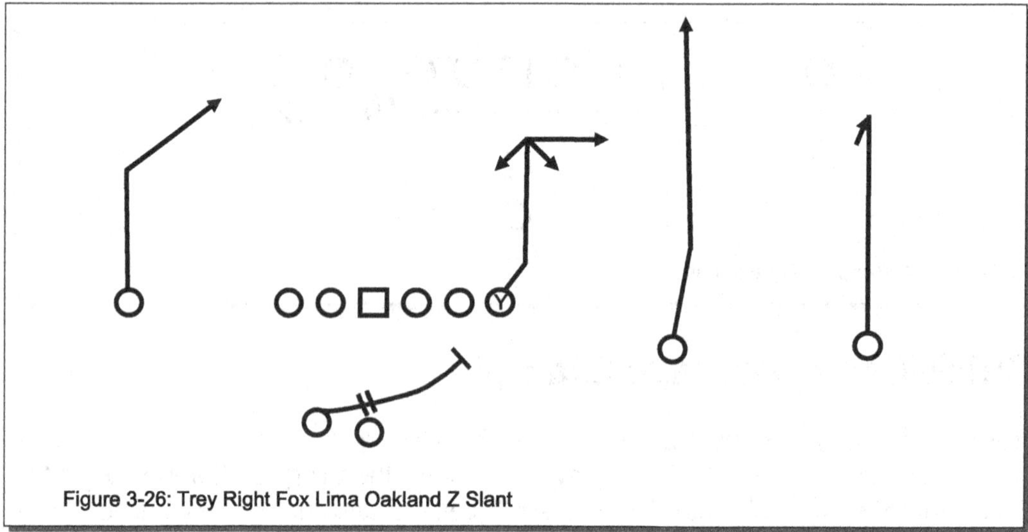

Figure 3-26: Trey Right Fox Lima Oakland Z Slant

You can then package that in "wing" and call the same things. The difference in "wing" with "Orlando" is if you're attached at #2, you run an arrow route (Figure 3-27). If you're off the ball detached, as in the previous examples, you run a 5-yard out. An attached wing runs an arrow instead to stretch it *right now.* I also prefer to do this from under center in "wing" sets, because from under the center, it's harder for the Mike linebacker to get under the tight end's hook route. Like we first said, that's often a run look and then Mike is intent on playing the run. From my experience, I don't think it affects his mindset the same way from a gun or pistol alignment.

So, there's a little example of two basic "hook" concepts ("Orlando" or "Oakland") with three backside routes (hitch, halt, slant) in a 3x1 look. When you begin to package these basic concepts together, the quarterback's alignment, the back's alignment, the protection and the personnel grouping all need to be considered, if you want to put your guys in the best position to be successful. As you can see, there's a lot there to think about already, even before we begin to multiply the formations and start to realign our guys through various shifts and motions.

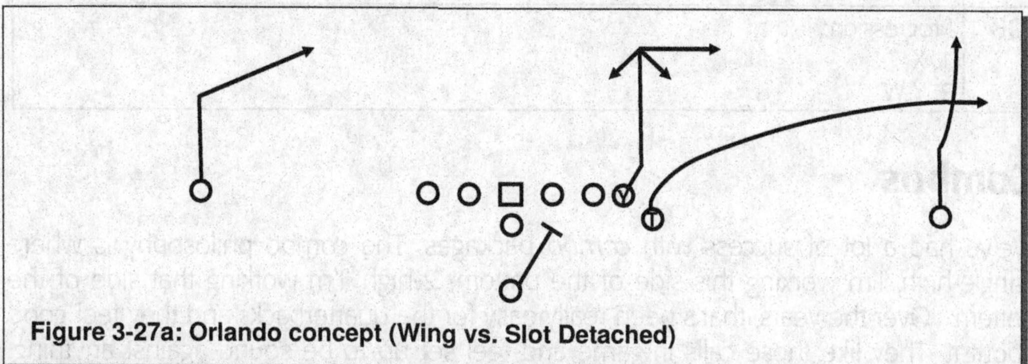

**Figure 3-27a: Orlando concept (Wing vs. Slot Detached)**

**Play: Figure 3-27a**

| Pos: | Assignment: |
|---|---|
| R | Block Lima protection. |
| Y | 6-yd hook route |
| T | Arrow |
| X | 3-step slant |
| Z | Fade (outside release) |
| QB | Progression:<br>1. X<br>2. Y<br>3. T |

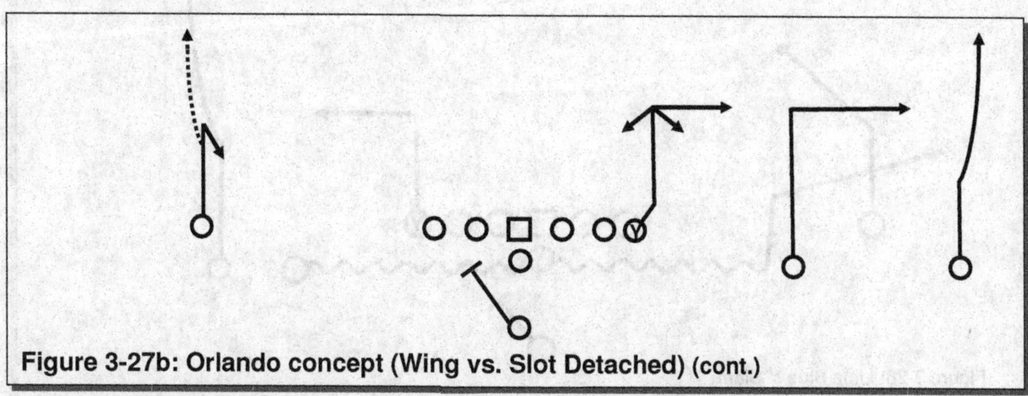

**Figure 3-27b: Orlando concept (Wing vs. Slot Detached) (cont.)**

**Play: Figure 3-27b**

| Pos: | Assignment: |
|---|---|
| R | Block rose protection. |
| W | 6-yd speed out |
| X | 5-step hitch (normal conversion) |
| Y | 6-yd hook route |
| Z | Fade (outside release) |
| QB | Progression:<br>1. X<br>2. Y-W |

# Combos

We've had a lot of success with *combo* packages. The combo philosophy is where "single-high, I'm working this side of the pattern, 2-high, I'm working that side of the pattern." Over the years, that's been really easy for the quarterbacks and they feel good about it. They like those calls in-game and feel set up to be sound against anything. Quarterbacks like the combo package.

# Blue Y / Slam

If you want to draw a combo package for the tight ends, you could go, "wing right, T fly: Lima blue Y/ slam." If it's cover 2, I'm going to "hold the safety, key the corner" to the tight-end side. "Slam" is a diagonal/slant on the other side, which is the "single-high" side. When thinking in concepts, this is the same play as "taxi right, W fly: Lima blue Y/ slam" (Figure 3-28).

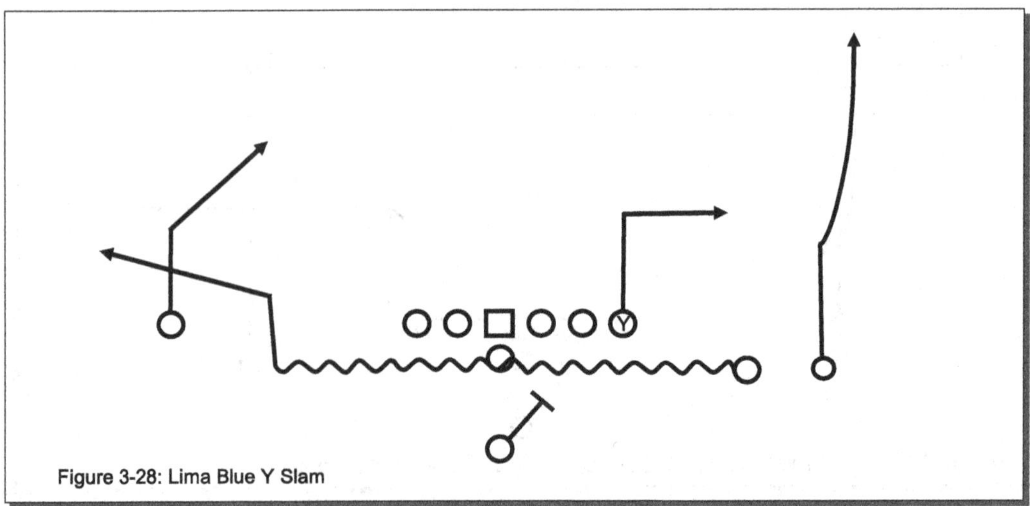


Figure 3-28: Lima Blue Y Slam

**Play: Lima Blue Y/ Slam**

| Pos: | Assignment: |
|---|---|
| R | Block Lima protection. |
| W | Arrow |
| X | 3-step slant |
| Y | 6-yd speed out |
| Z | Fade (outside release) |
| QB | Progression:<br>1. Hold safety, key corner.<br>2. Z-Y<br>3. Single High: X-W |

# Y Slider

"Doubles right: rose, Y slider" was a good quick game combo for us when we had a tight end like DJ Williams. You'd run the "Y slider" and he would run the arrow with the 8-yard, "point-to-point" curl right on the numbers. On the backside, you'd run "blue" (Figure 3-29). That was another one of those things that was really good against field pressure. You're a man short—you can't block it all—but you have the 8-yard route, so you can beat it with the throw. The defensive end either has to go with the tight end or drop vertical, so there's no way he can cover it all.

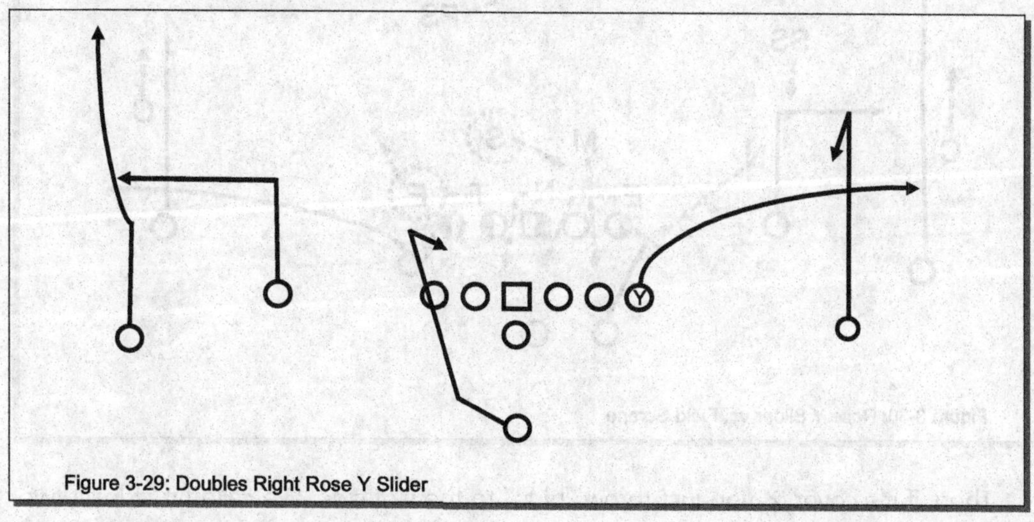


Figure 3-29: Doubles Right Rose Y Slider

**Play: Doubles right: Rose, Y slider**

| Pos: | Assignment: |
|---|---|
| R | Block rose protection. |
| W | 6-yd speed out |
| X | Fade (outside release) |
| Y | Arrow |
| Z | 8-yd stop route |
| QB | Progression:<br>1. vs. 2 high: X-W<br>2. vs. 1 high: Z-Y |

We set the back *to* the blue, because this was really called for zone blitz. It was good off "solo, Y half," to disguise the split of Z. So, let's say they're bringing a "field scrape" where Will has to relate to #3. "Slider" is a "field scrape beater" (Figure 3-30). Z aligns and runs a "point-to-point" curl right on the numbers and Y runs the arrow. You know you can't block one of those two guys (unless you changed the protection and made a "Lucky" call), but we really just said to the quarterback "get the ball snapped and you have to beat him with the throw."

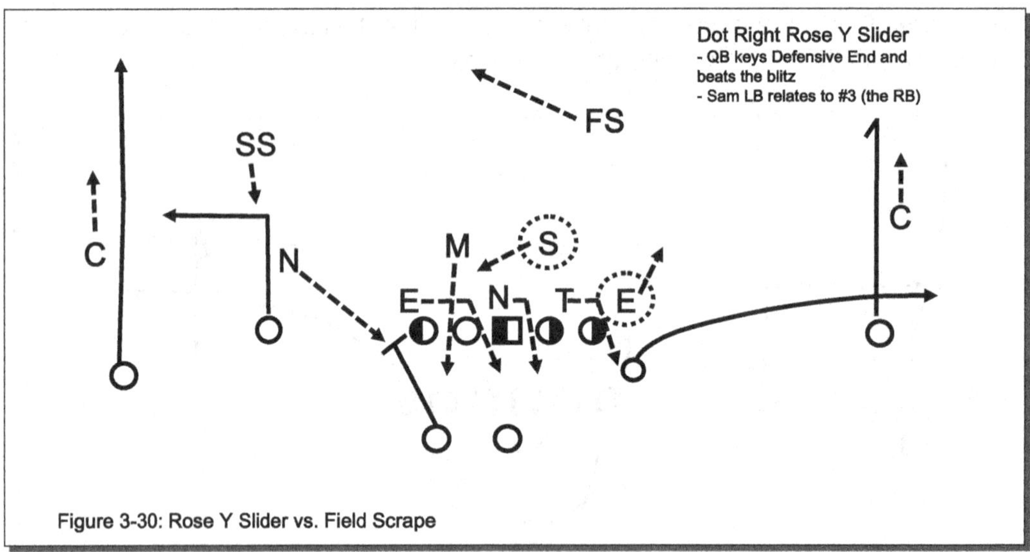


Figure 3-30: Rose Y Slider vs. Field Scrape

Then, if it's cover 2, you just throw "blue" to the slot side. We called it at least two, maybe three times a game with DJ Williams. Thinking of the protection scheme again, the Will has to relate to #3, so you don't want to send the back that way, because then he's standing right there. Get the ball snapped and read him, don't worry about protection calls, which also makes this is another good tempo play.

## 90 Grey

A good combo call for us in the quick game has been "90 grey." "90 protection" is quick game and the "0" concept category is hitches and curls. "Grey" is the code for the option route on the other side. The first way to call it would be "doubles right: Lima 90 grey" (Figure 3-31). On your hitch side, what we say is, "if they give you the hitch, take it." The tight end knows "I'm running the seam-hook as tight as I can over my alignment." When you run the seam route and the guy sits on you, you want to go through his inside shoulder, so you take his body away from the hitch and we get more yards after the catch on the hitch. It's a *drill* you need to work with your tight ends. If someone buzzes the flat, then he's "hot to a hook" at 5-to-6 yards (Figure 3-32). The quarterback is reading every hitch "outside-in," so he's reading the hitch first and then coming back to the inside (if you try to read it inside-out, you're always late on that hitch, but you also don't want to throw a pick for a touchdown, so you have to see the "buzz" linebacker).

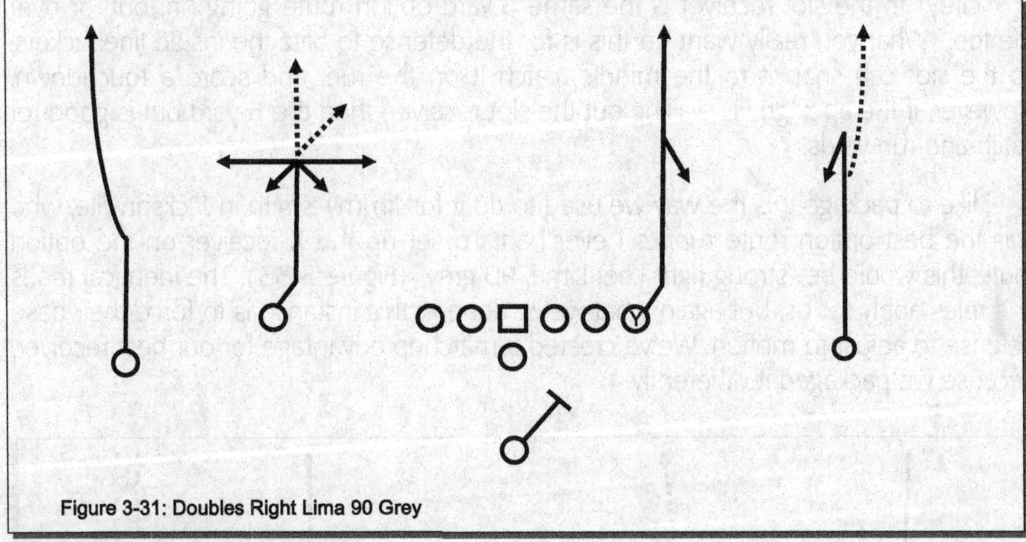

Figure 3-31: Doubles Right Lima 90 Grey

**Play: Doubles Right: Lima 90 Grey**

| Pos: | Assignment: |
|---|---|
| R | Block Lima protection. |
| W | 6-yd option route |
| X | Outside release go |
| Y | Seam-hitch |
| Z | 5-step hitch (normal conversion) |
| QB | Progression:<br>1. Z<br>2. W |

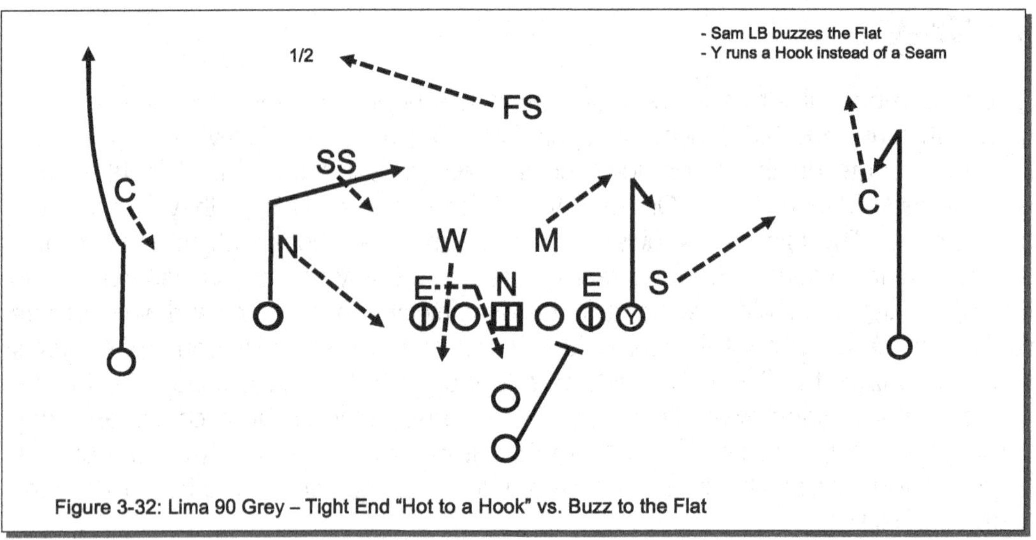

Figure 3-32: Lima 90 Grey – Tight End "Hot to a Hook" vs. Buzz to the Flat

"Grey" to the slot receiver is the same 6-yard option route going "in, out, or over the top." What you really want on this is for the defense to blitz the inside linebackers, so the slot can snap it to the middle, catch it on the run, and score a touchdown. However, if the apex guy is walling out the slot receiver, then the 6-yard out is good for catch-and-run yards.

I like to package this the way we used to do it for Jimmy Smith in Jacksonville, who was the best option route runner I ever had. To set up the X receiver on the option route, this would be "strong right Lee: Lima, 90 grey" (Figure 3-33). The identical reads and rules apply for us, but again what we've done in this instance is to force their base defense to adjust to motion. We've created a matchup advantage for our best receiver, because we packaged it differently.

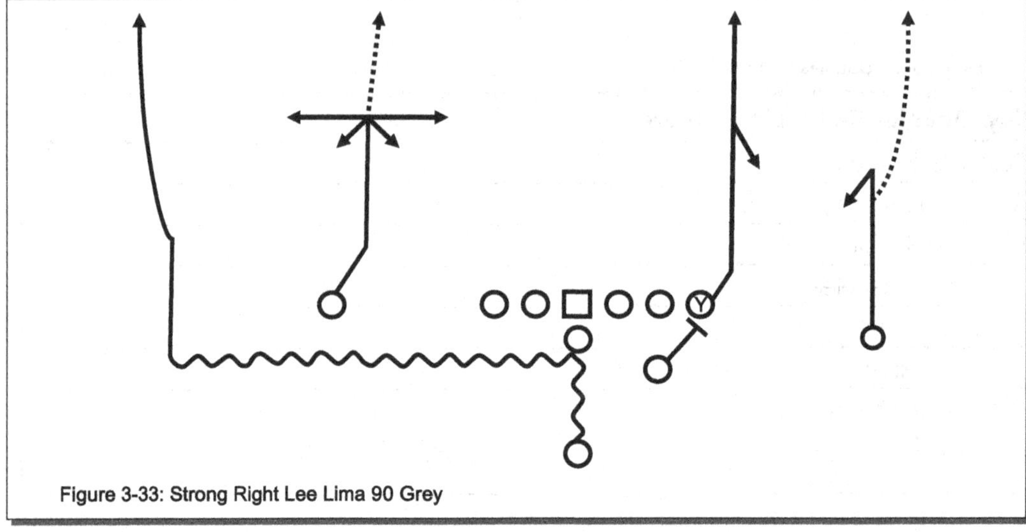

Figure 3-33: Strong Right Lee Lima 90 Grey

**Play: Strong Right Lee: Lima, 90 Grey**

| Pos: | Assignment: |
|---|---|
| F | Block Lima protection. |
| R | Fade (outside release) |
| Y | Seam-hitch |
| X | 6-yd option route |
| Z | 5-step hitch (normal conversion) |
| QB | Progression:<br>1. vs. off corner: Z/Y<br>2. vs. Jam: X |

If we do it like this though, the quarterback needs to really understand protections. The issue you get into with the "strong" formation is that people like to run that "field scrape." So, for example a "Liz Y" call, in this instance, can be safer, because "Lima" can be vulnerable to some issues with that "field scrape" (Figure 3-34).

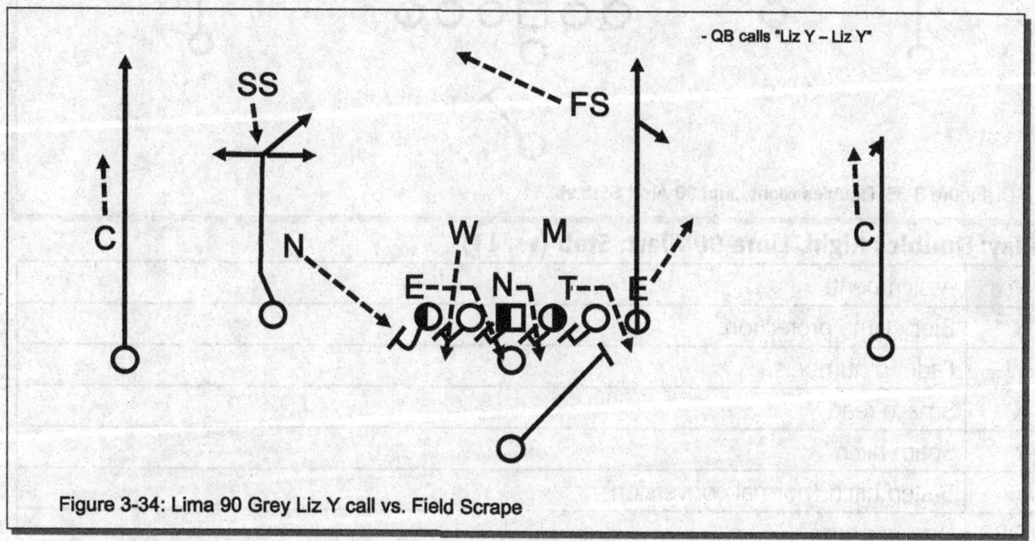

Figure 3-34: Lima 90 Grey Liz Y call vs. Field Scrape

(Note: again "Liz Y" is a full slide and the back blocks off the tackle's hip. "Lima" is just regular slide-weak protection, where the back has Mike-to-Sam.)

## 90 Grey, Alert: Stab

If we prefer to just call the play from 11 personnel (which can simplify some of that protection responsibility for the quarterback), I like to put an *alert* on it: "doubles right, Lima 90 grey, alert: stab." In this instance you still have the hitch/fade to Z, with the seam-read but this way, we can beat cover 11 with the boundary safety rotation in press coverage, if we signal the alert to the "stab" concept (Figure 3-35). Again, that's another *combo* call, so really what we're saying is "it's hard to call enough hitches in a game." As such, you're saying, "okay, I'm calling the hitch. If that's there, we're taking it." If it's not there, we're going to our best option route receiver on the other side. But if you get "cover 4 sky press," or that "cover 11," you give him a "stab" signal instead. The quarterback and slot receiver are responsible for giving it to the outside receiver. Brian Brohm threw a ton of touchdowns and won us a lot of games on this play.

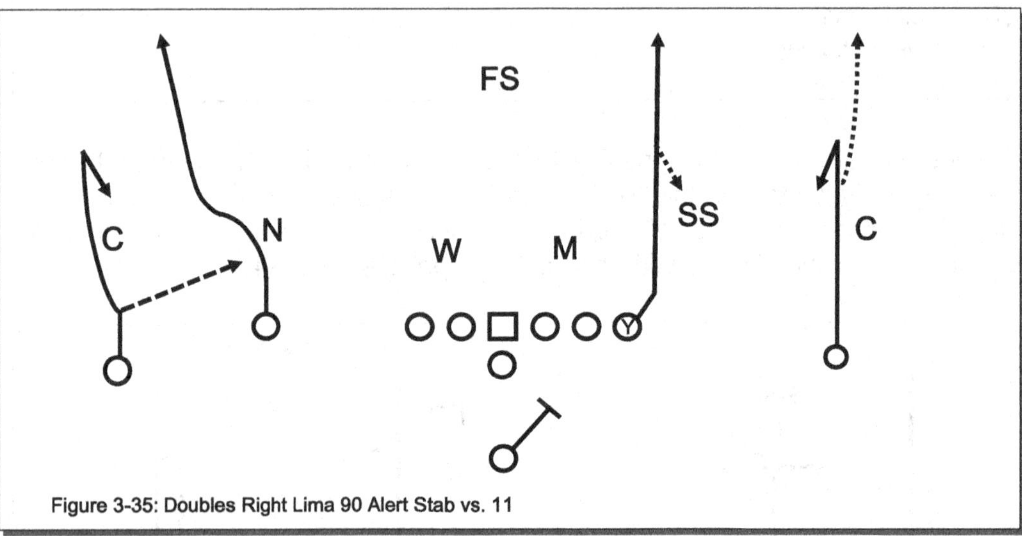

Figure 3-35: Doubles Right Lima 90 Alert Stab vs. 11

**Play: Doubles Right, Lima 90 Alert: Stab (vs. 11)**

| Pos: | Assignment: |
|---|---|
| R | Block Lima protection. |
| W | Fade to numbers. |
| X | Smash read |
| Y | Seam hitch |
| Z | 5-step hitch (normal conversion) |
| QB | Progression:<br>1. Combo call<br>2. vs. 2 high: X-W; vs. MF: signal stab<br>3. vs. 1 high: Y-Z<br>4. vs. man: work match-up |

The quarterback could alert the slot to "stab" against man coverage, but sometimes he just already knows he is going to throw the fade to Z for a touchdown and can just let it rip. That's again why I say when you got a hitch and you get pressed, the receiver says, "run the fade for a touchdown!" I want those words coming out of his mouth. Then, the quarterback will do his job: hold the safety, go "1, 2, 3 - sit on it," and throw the fade for a touchdown.

## Steamer

This is a version of a famous Jon Gruden play: "wing right, Z float: rose (Lima) Orlando, X steamer." You're trying to get them to go single-high and hit the seam to X, so we like to package it from this formation and motion. Z has an 8-yard hitch here, because to throw the seam to X, you're going to pump to the right first and it needs to time up (Figure 3-36). The quarterback would come out "1, 2, 3 pump fake" and then look "seam to 8-yard hitch." The 8-yard hitch (instead of six) allows you to look inside-out, for the timing. This concept is best from the middle of the field, which is why you tend to see it more in the NFL than college, with their narrower hash marks.

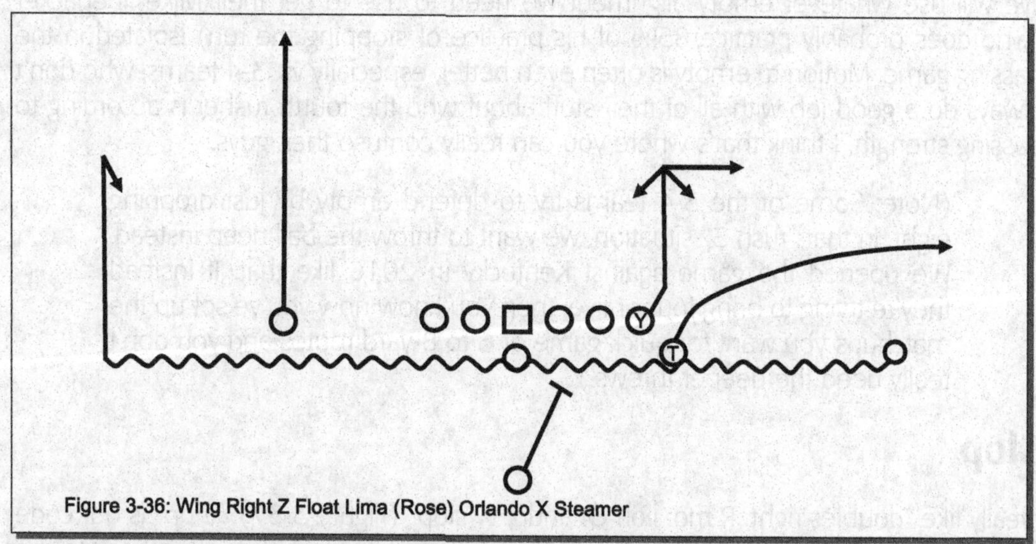


Figure 3-36: Wing Right Z Float Lima (Rose) Orlando X Steamer

**Play: Wing Right, Z Float: Lima (Rose) Orlando, X Steamer**

| Pos: | Assignment: |
|---|---|
| R | Block Lima protection. |
| T | Arrow |
| X | Seam |
| Y | 6-yd hook |
| Z | 8-yd stop |
| QB | Progression:<br>1. X-Z<br>2. Y-T |

## "Pop Back" Drill for Combo Reads

Something that's good for your quarterbacks on these is to work a "pop back" drill. So, he's looking to one side and if it's not there, "I pop backside." That's a drill that you do with the quarterbacks and you try to do it every day. (You don't always get to do it every day, but you try.) So, you put a coach here and a coach there; he goes "left, right—throw to his right." If you put your hand up, he hits the hand with the ball. If you clap your hands, he "pops back" and throws to the other side.

## Isolating a Linebacker in Quick Game

The next thing with the quick game is to isolate an outside linebacker or an inside linebacker mismatch. This is achieved with motion, personnel groupings and formations (getting your best guy in the slot or aligning your tight ends outside). That's also where empty comes in, so they have to cover down with a linebacker against a great receiver. We will use whatever empty alignment we need to use to get their Mike linebacker (who does probably practice 85% of his practice of stopping the run) isolated in the passing game. Motion to empty is often even better, especially vs. 3-4 teams, who don't always do a good job with all of their stuff about who the fourth rusher is according to passing strength. I think that's where you can really confuse their guys.

> (Note: Some of the 3-4 teams try to defend empty by just dropping eight. In that "rush 3" situation, we want to throw the ball deep instead. We opened the game against Kentucky in 2016 like that. If instead they're trying to bring four or five, then you know now you've set up the matchups you want for quick game or 6 to 8-yard routes and you don't really need the deeper throws.)

## Slop

I really like "doubles right, R mo: lion Orlando, W slop" (Figure 3-37). "Slop" is our code for "slant-option." If you get cut off on the slant, then you pivot and return back to the outside. #1 has to run a "protect fade" outside. You can also package this concept for X or Z, depending on who you want on the slot option route (Figures 3-38 and 3-39).

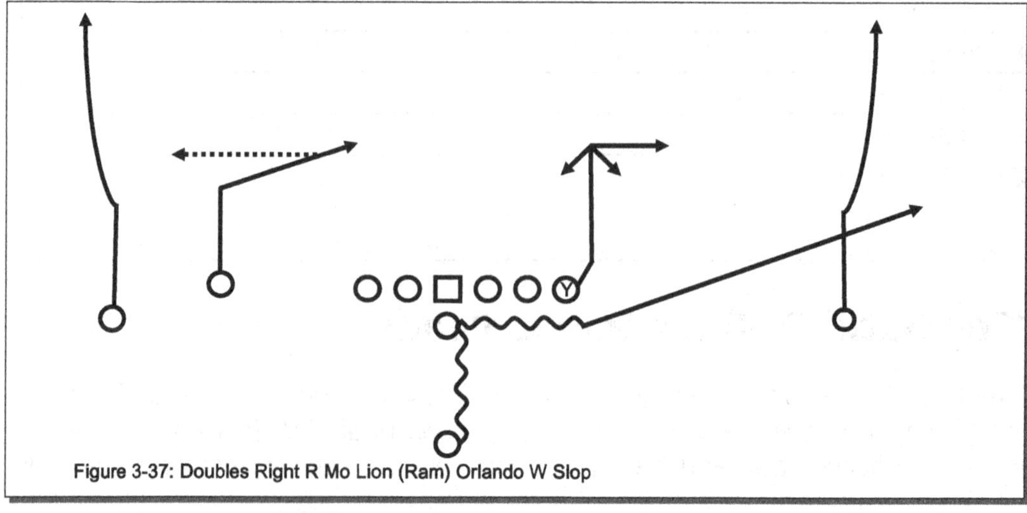

Figure 3-37: Doubles Right R Mo Lion (Ram) Orlando W Slop

**Play: Doubles Right, R Mo: Lion (Ram) Orlando, W Slop**

| Pos: | Assignment: |
|---|---|
| R | R-mo. Run arrow. |
| W | Run slop route (slant option). |
| X | Outside release go |
| Y | 6-yd hook route |
| Z | Outside release go |
| QB | Progression:<br>1. Read away from MLB<br>2. Y or R<br>3. W |

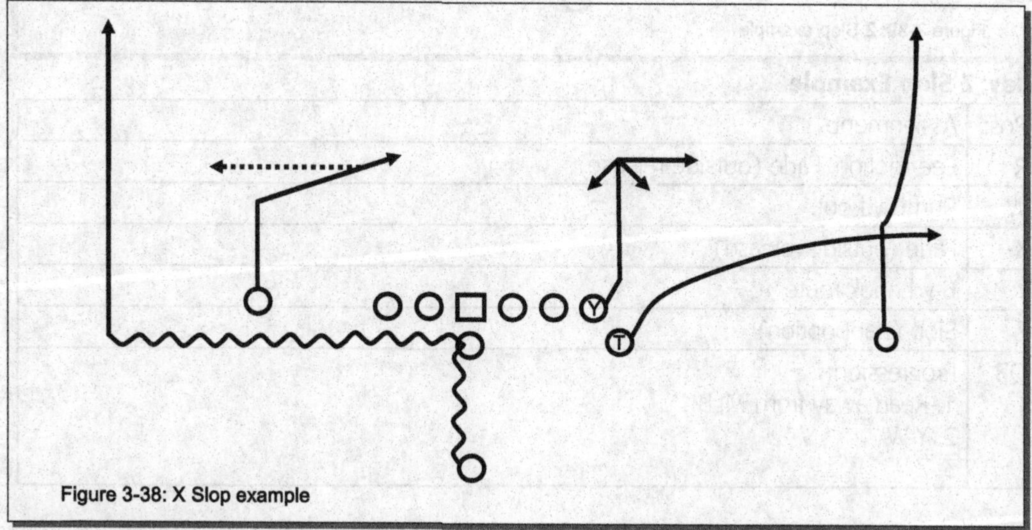

Figure 3-38: X Slop example

**Play: X Slop Example**

| Pos: | Assignment: |
|---|---|
| R | Lee motion<br>Outside release go |
| T | Arrow |
| X | Cut split<br>Slop route |
| Y | 6-yd hook route |
| Z | Fade (outside release) |
| QB | Progression:<br>1. Read away from MLB<br>2. Y or T<br>3. X |

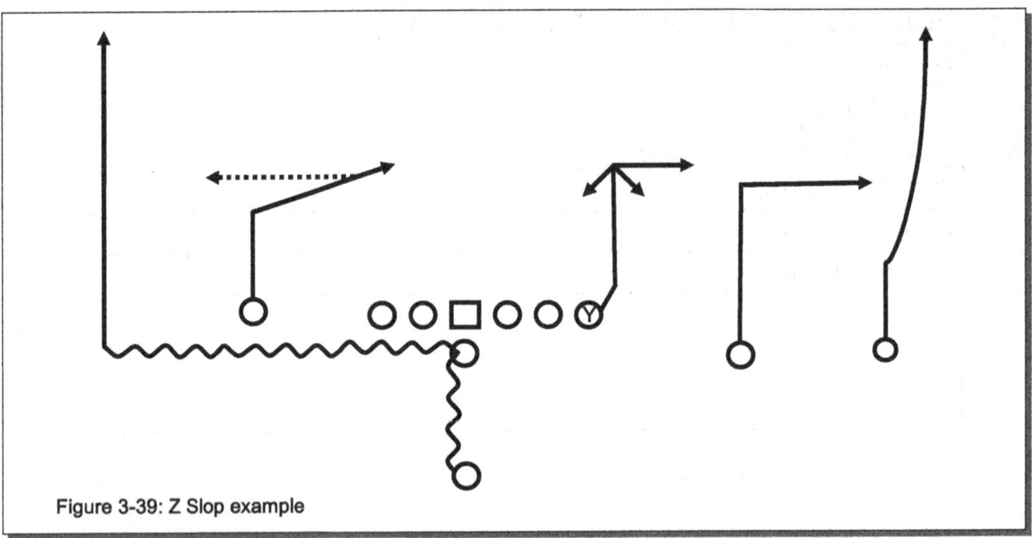

Figure 3-39: Z Slop example

**Play: Z Slop Example**

| Pos: | Assignment: |
|---|---|
| R | Lee motion. Fade (outside release) |
| W | Run 6-yd out. |
| X | Fade (outside release) |
| Y | 6-yd hook route |
| Z | Slop (slant option) |
| QB | Progression:<br>1. Read away from MLB<br>2. Y-W<br>3. Z |

What you do, is make the Mike linebacker cover the "Orlando" to open up the middle and then you get a mismatch on the Will linebacker. It's a really good play vs. any "2-high" type of coverage. Jerry Rice is the guy who really made this famous. They used to tear up quarters coverage with it; motion the back out and he'd beat that Will linebacker on a slant.

You're then trying to isolate the Will linebacker. The quarterback needs to think "make the Mike linebacker run over there and cover that tight end hook route." (If he doesn't, then just give the tight end the ball.) Once the Mike linebacker is committed to undercutting or playing the hook route, the entire middle opens up for the slot receiver. The quarterback's timing to come back to it is "bring your eyes first, and then your feet," so that you can see whether he's winning on the slant or if he returns on the option part of the route. And again, he will have to "sit" on that third step (or second step out of the gun).

## Seattle

Another one I really like is "gun doubles right Lee: lion Seattle" (which makes it automatic "blue Y" as a "built-in"). "Seattle" is triple-slant. Again, it's really important for the receivers to understand to "split for success" and to set their splits for the play we call. The two receivers over here have to understand to adjust their split *correctly* and the X receiver now is just one yard outside the hash (Figure 3-40). The running back motions out and has a "smash read," which means "off corner, I run a hitch; if I get any squat or press, I run a 5-yard in." You get your fade and 6-yard out on the tight end side, in case you get a "cloud" look there. Then the inside receiver on Seattle has a "1- to 3-step slant," and the middle receiver has a "3-step slant."

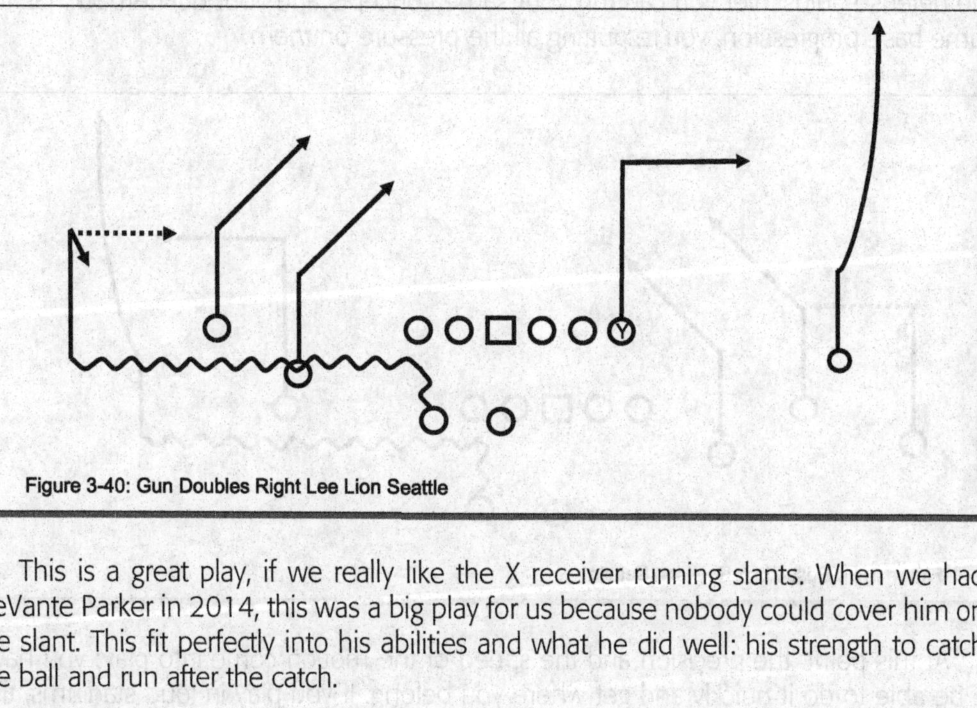

Figure 3-40: Gun Doubles Right Lee Lion Seattle

This is a great play, if we really like the X receiver running slants. When we had DeVante Parker in 2014, this was a big play for us because nobody could cover him on the slant. This fit perfectly into his abilities and what he did well: his strength to catch the ball and run after the catch.

The quarterback wants to read the adjustment to motion. Understand that if the "blue" to Y is a "gimme" with a "tucked-in linebacker" to that side, we want to go ahead and "hold the safety, and key the corner" to that side. When people are adjusting to "single-high, man-free," the inside slant handles the "rat" and X wins the 1-on-1. So, this is another *combo* read: the 2-high with a tucked linebacker would go to the "blue" side and any single-high would go the triple-slant side. You have a "built-in" hot to the inside slant vs. pressure. That's when #3 gets the ball (or if they just screw up their adjustment to motion).

The spacing is also really important between X and W; they can't be too close together. That's why we say "1-3 step slant," so that the slot understands, "if I've got press and there's people fighting, I take 1 step and get out of the way." That really makes it a "collision drag," where I "take 2"—I take the guy over me plus I take the inside linebacker to open up that area for X. If I've got "off-man" coverage, I run a "3-step slant to win."

We're starting that from 2x2, but if you have a back who can win on a fade, another way to package the same play is from "posse left Roy," where the "blue" is on the singled wide-receiver instead of the tight end (Figure 3-41). We did a lot of that when we had backs like Michael Bush and Reggie Bonnafon. This is another example of winning with personnel matchups, because when you motion to empty and make the defense adjust, yet you can run your same concepts and your quarterback has the same base progression, you're putting all the pressure on *them*.

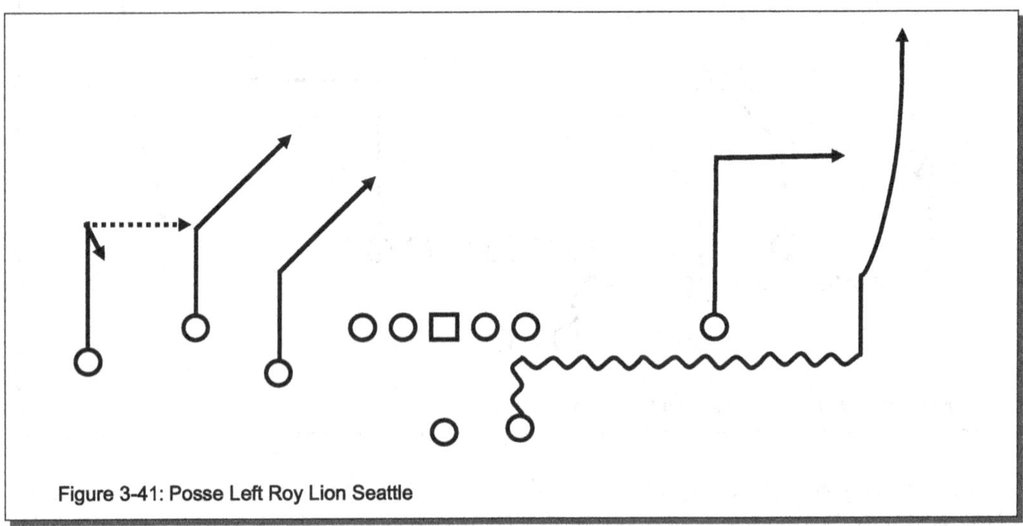

**Figure 3-41: Posse Left Roy Lion Seattle**

At this point, the precision and the speed of the motion come into play; you have to be able to do it quickly and get where you belong. If you play in loud stadiums, the motion guy has to *look at the feet* of the receiver inside of him to know when to go, because you're not gonna hear the cadence. So, as he shuffles, he looks at the feet of the receiver inside of him which tells him when to be able to get off and go. That can make it sometimes harder to run "fades to win." It just has to be a special player to do that. He has to get to his landmark and the quarterback has to allow him to do that. Then, as he shuffles, he looks at the feet of the inside receiver—the first guy inside of him.

## Sinker

This one would be "trey right Lee: ram sinker, Z jerk" (Figure 3-42). We can also package the concept as "posse left Roy: lion sinker, Z jerk" (Figure 3-43). "Posse" is a

3x1 set from 4-wide receiver personnel. You have a "hook-go," which gives you a "stab" outside and then X (or Z) on the slop. Again, you need to have the flexibility to put your best receiver on the 1-on-1 side (or whoever is best at running that particular route), so it can always be a part of the game plan. If we wanted the X over there in 10 personnel, then we could call "cab" formation ("taxi" and then "cab" to single up the X instead).

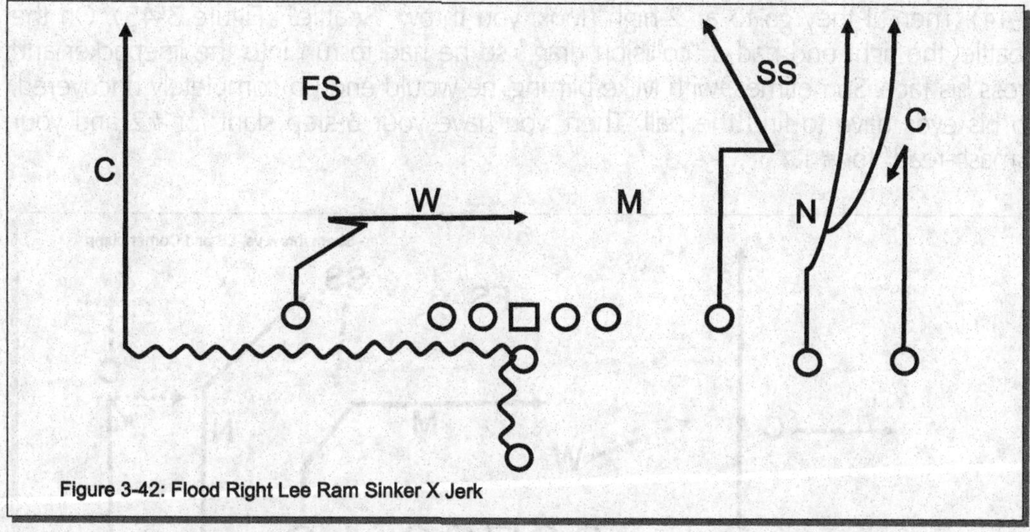

Figure 3-42: Flood Right Lee Ram Sinker X Jerk

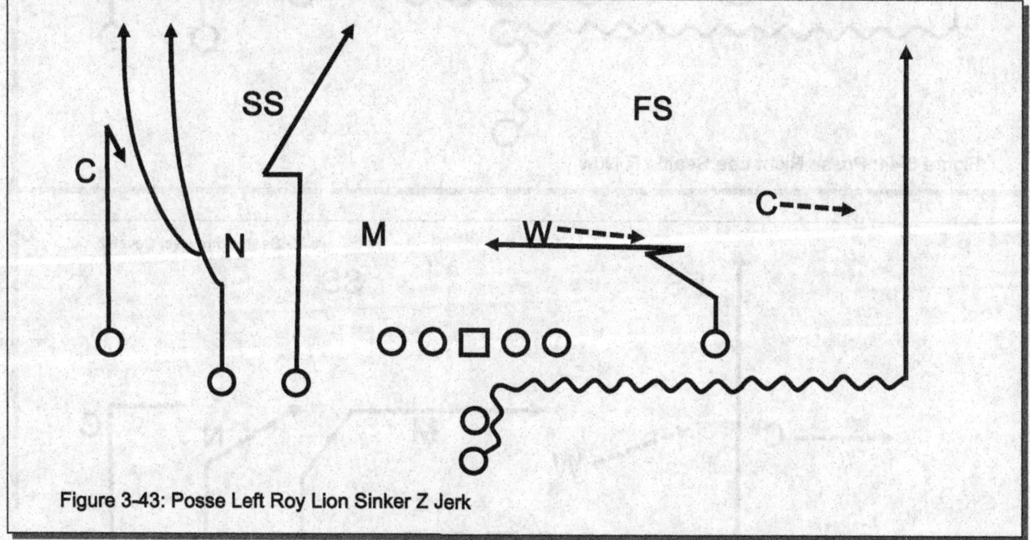

Figure 3-43: Posse Left Roy Lion Sinker Z Jerk

This is a really good "red zone" play between the 12-and-20 yard area. You can't hit it when you're in there too tight, but we've scored a lot of touchdowns over the years in that 12-to-20 area. You can get to that from just lining up in empty, and we've done that as well, but I think it's harder on the defense when you motion to it, because they have to adjust to it and again, you can get a wide receiver really mismatched on a linebacker.

## Lee, R Now

One of the plays we talked about earlier that's really good out of 3x1 is to run what we call "Lee, R now," which gives you a seam to the single-receiver side. If we call "taxi right Lee: Seattle, R now," and they were going strong rotation and bumped the linebacker and corner out, you could throw the seam for a touchdown, similar to "steamer" (Figure 3-44). Then, if they go to a "2-high" look, you throw "Seattle" (Figure 3-45). On the Seattle, the tight end had a "collision drag," so he had to run into the linebacker and cross his face. Sometimes, with Mike blitzing, he would end up completely uncovered, so his eyes have to find the ball. Then, you have your 3-step slant for #2 and your "smash-read" for #1.

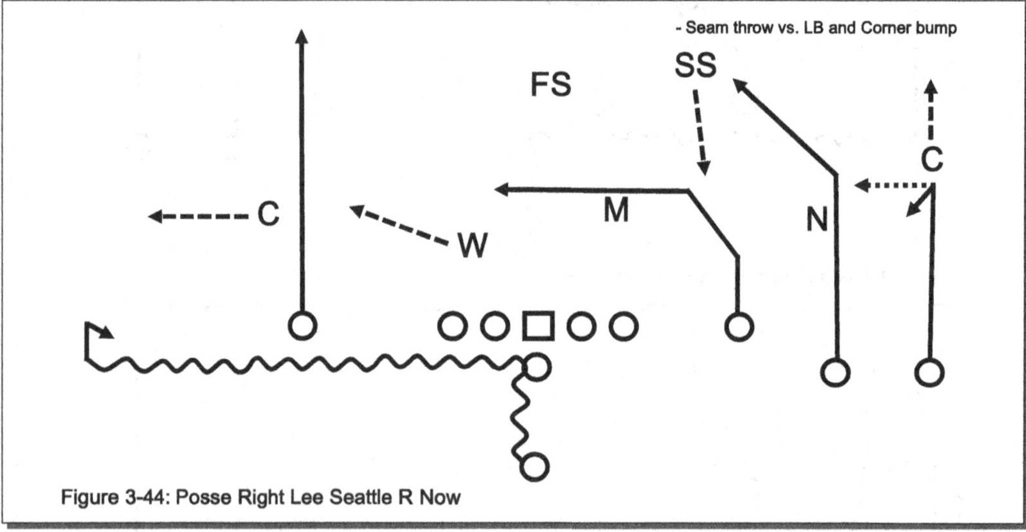

Figure 3-44: Posse Right Lee Seattle R Now

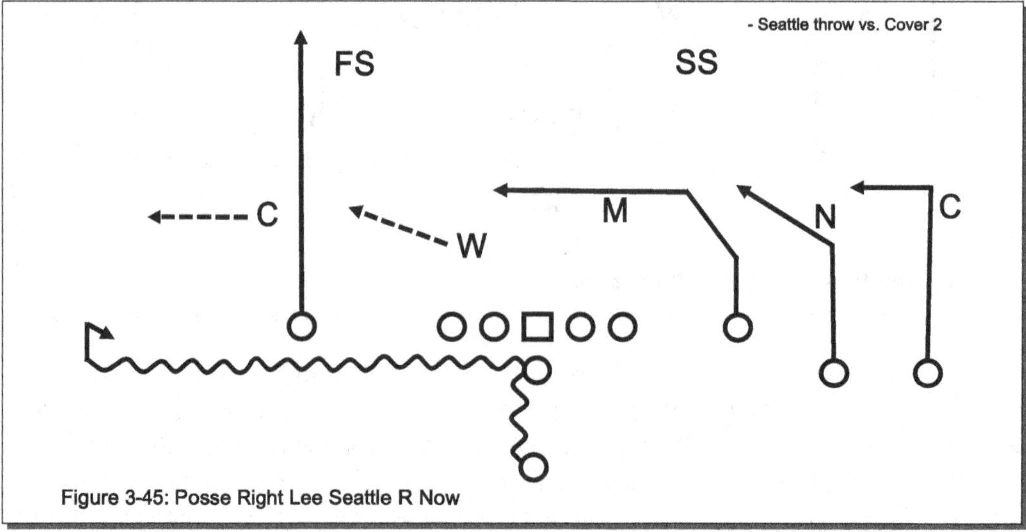

Figure 3-45: Posse Right Lee Seattle R Now

(Note: This used to be true triple-slant. The reason we changed this to a "smash-read" is because sometimes in true cover 3, the strong safety would start to squeeze with the inside slant and then come back outside and pick the outside one off. So, we went to just "smash-read" at five yards for the sake of spacing and timing.)

## Option Route Mismatches

If we want to match an inside option route on a linebacker, we can package "94" in any 2x2, 3x1, or 3x2 sets and also get there with all kinds of motion. Once you understand what the other team's linebackers are being taught, you want to build your packages off that, while keeping the reads the same for your quarterback and receivers. "Trips right: lima 94 Y" (see Figure 3-20) is the same play as "strong slot right Roy: Lima 94 Y" (Figure 3-46) or "wing slot right, T float: Lima 94 Y" (Figure 3-47). With the motion, we can really get the linebackers to have to defend receivers.

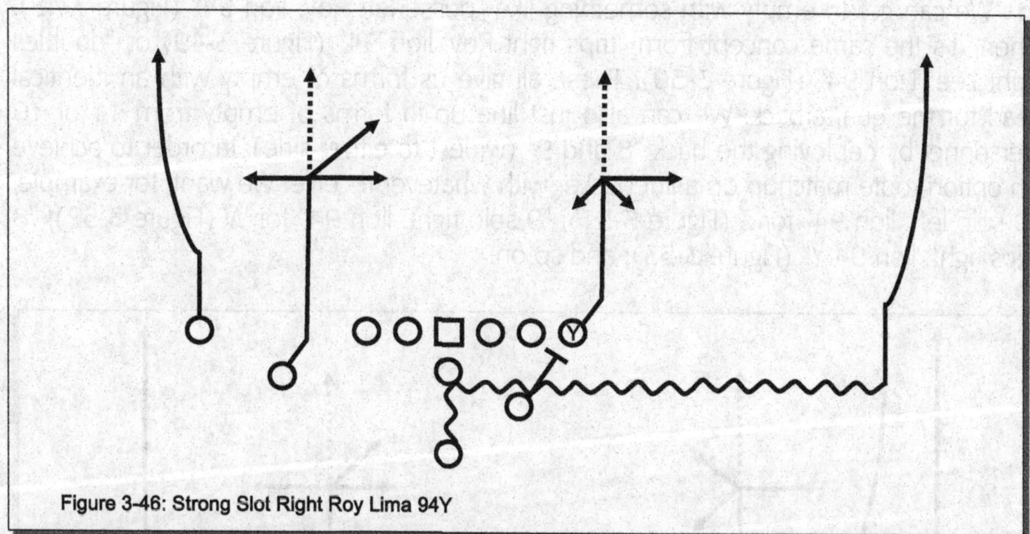

Figure 3-46: Strong Slot Right Roy Lima 94Y

**Play: Strong Slot Right Roy: Lima 94 Y**

| Pos: | Assignment: |
|---|---|
| R | Roy motion: fade (outside release) |
| F | Block Lima protection. |
| X | Fade (outside release) |
| Y | 6-yd option route |
| Z | 6-yd option route |
| QB | Progression:<br>1. Z<br>2. Y |

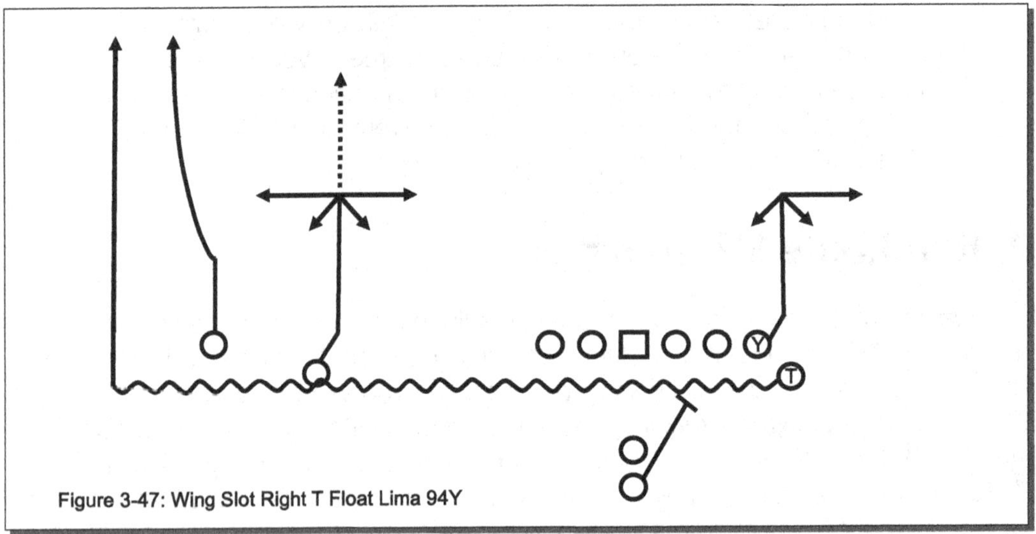

Figure 3-47: Wing Slot Right T Float Lima 94Y

We can get to empty with something like "posse left Roy: lion 94" (Figure 3-48). Then, it's the same concept from "trips right Roy, lion 94" (Figure 3-49) or "doubles right Lee: Lion 94" (Figure 3-50). These all give us forms of empty with an identical read for the quarterback. We can also just line up in forms of empty from 11 or 10 personnel by deploying the back "8 and 9" (widest to either side), in order to achieve an option route matchup on a linebacker with whatever receiver we want, for example, "9 solo left: lion 94" for Z (Figure 3-51); "9 solo right: lion 94" for W (Figure 3-52); "8 trips right: lion 94 Y" (Figure 3-53); and so on.

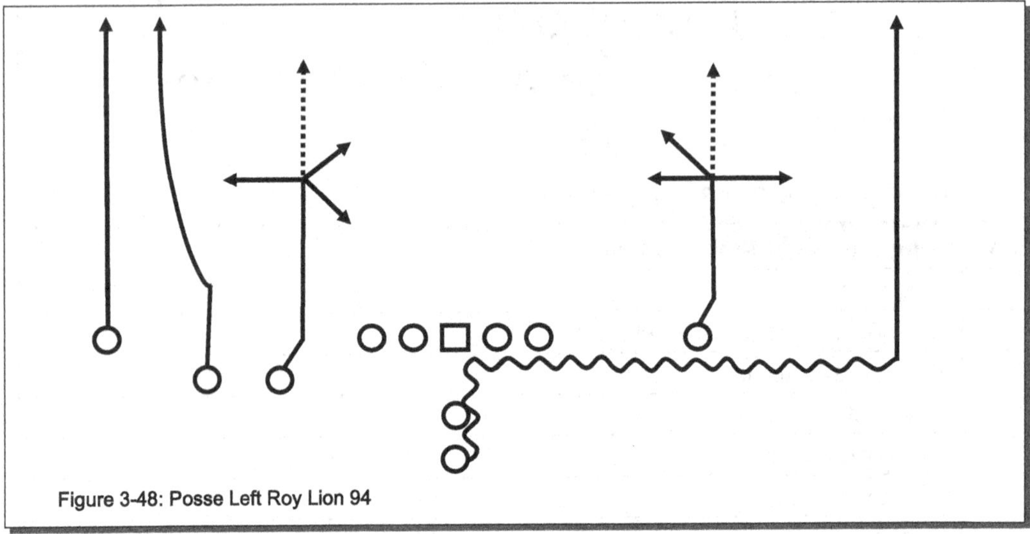
Figure 3-48: Posse Left Roy Lion 94

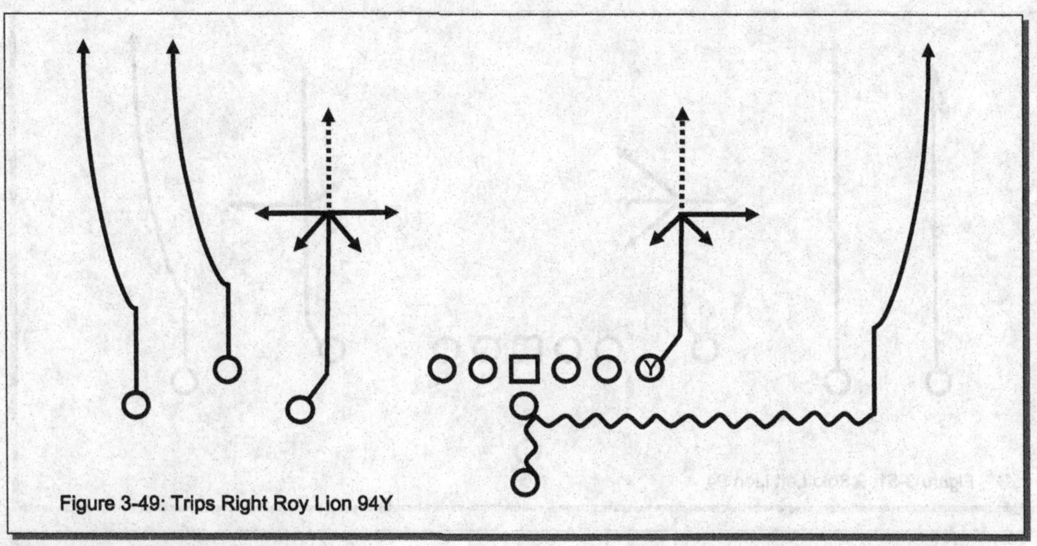

Figure 3-49: Trips Right Roy Lion 94Y

**Play: Trips Right Roy, Lion 94 Y**

| Pos: | Assignment: |
|---|---|
| R | Roy motion: run outside release go |
| W | Seam (outside release) |
| X | Fade (outside release) |
| Y | 6-yd option route |
| Z | 6-yd option route |
| QB | Progression:<br>1. Z-Y |

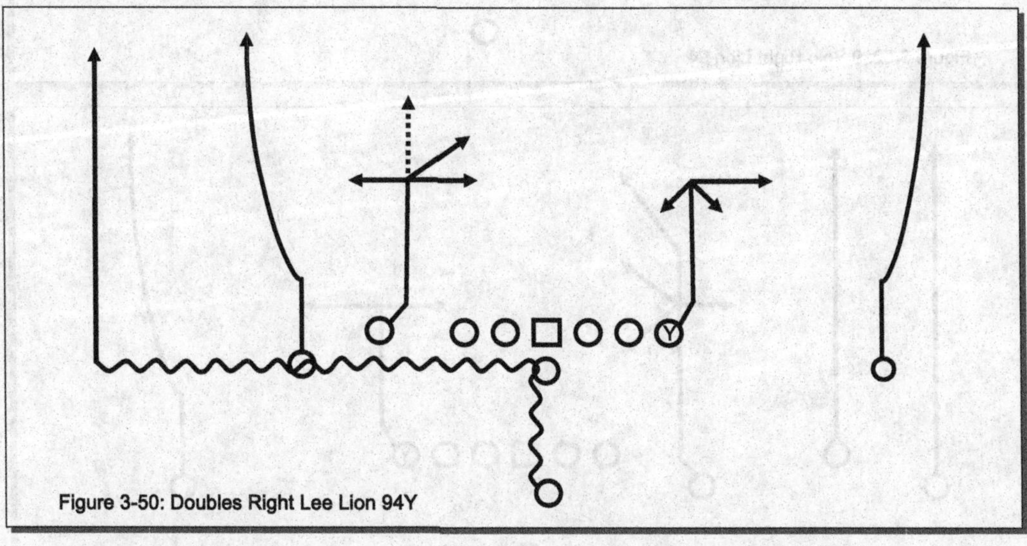

Figure 3-50: Doubles Right Lee Lion 94Y

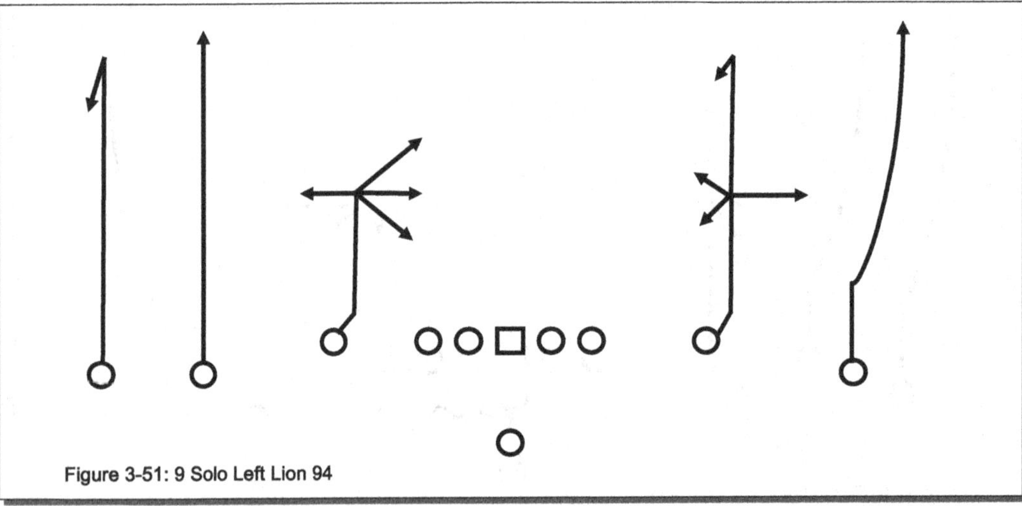
Figure 3-51: 9 Solo Left Lion 94

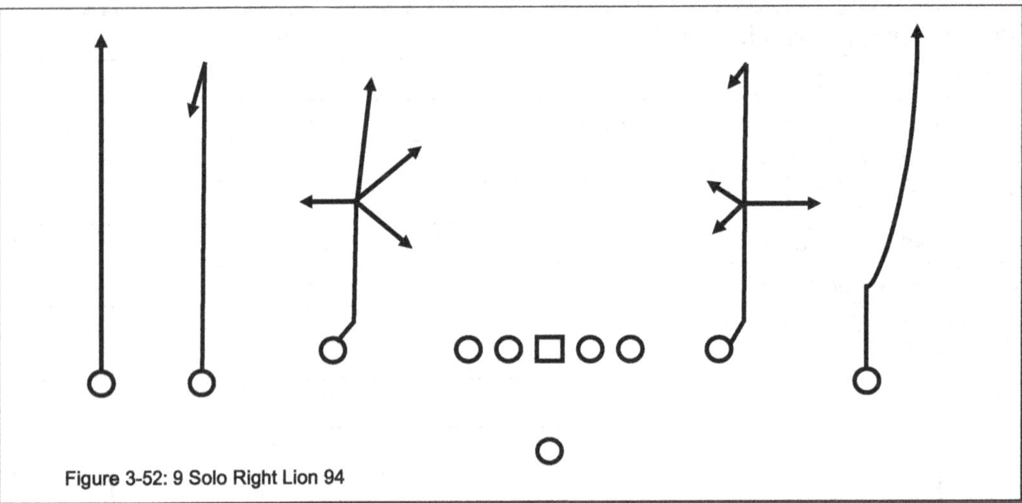
Figure 3-52: 9 Solo Right Lion 94

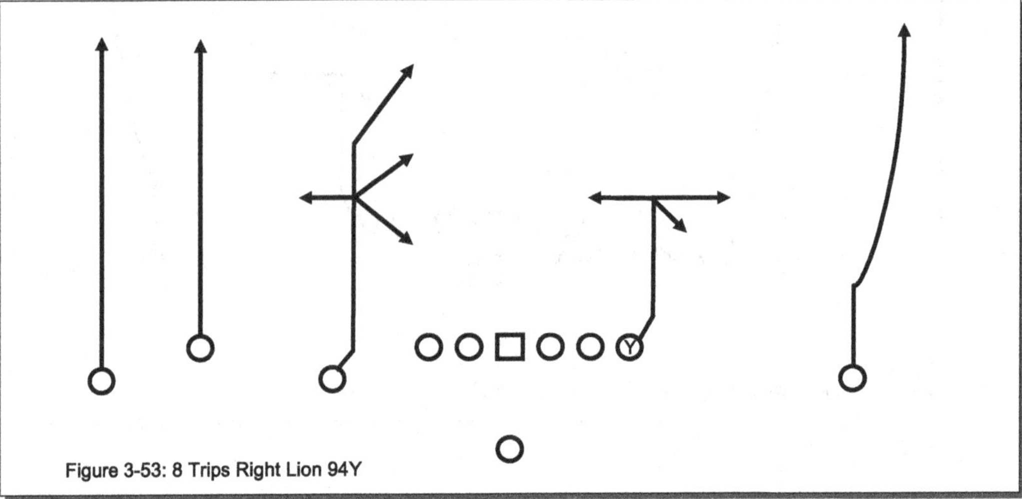

Figure 3-53: 8 Trips Right Lion 94Y

## Recent Developments: Scat Package, Tempo, One-Word Playcalls

We evolved into a no-huddle team at Louisville and because our quarterback felt comfortable in spread-out sets, we evolved to using several "one-word" codes for a lot of our quick game concepts. We could either code each side of the field or simply code a whole play with a single syllable. We also used more "scat" releases with the back, to compliment the zone-read type runs at which Lamar Jackson excelled.

We did this a lot out of 3x1, with what we call "scat" (which is the same as our "ram/lion") for a 5-man protection. We like to detach #3 on these (whether it's a tight end or receiver), because that always causes more problems for the Mike linebacker. Again, this is also where we tried to give some of the plays "one word" names, so you could go faster. I'd like to conclude the quick game presentation with some of the following recent developments.

❑ Saint

The first one would be "saint" (Figure 3-54). You're running "Orlando" out to the field. There's your hook route ("hook in, hook out, or break out"), your 5-yard out, and your fade. On the backside, you're running a 3-step slant (or "defeat-press" slant) and a free-release stretch with the back (very important that he sprints for three steps laterally before he looks for the ball). That's a "one word" call at tempo for the whole play. What we had first described as "rose Orlando, X slant," with a free release stretch by the running back, subsequently became just "saint."

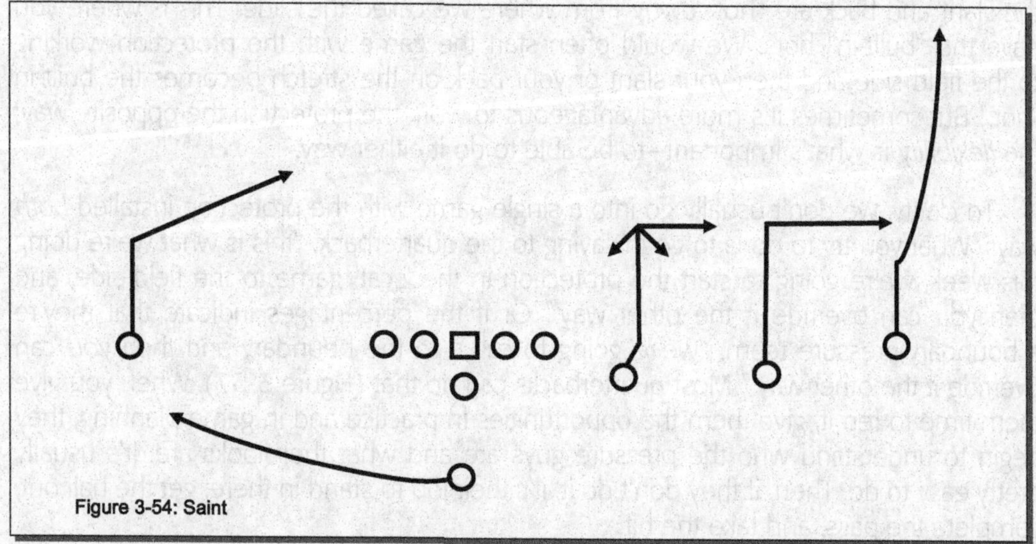

Figure 3-54: Saint

**Play: Saint**

| Pos: | Assignment: |
|---|---|
| W | 6-yd out |
| R | Free release stretch |
| Y | 6-yd hook route |
| X | 3-step slant |
| Z | Fade (outside release) |
| QB | Progression:<br>1. X-R<br>2. Y-W |

You have to work that free-release stretch throw to the back with the quarterback; it's not the easiest throw in the world. The quarterback is taking a 2-step drop from gun and he has to reset his feet to make the throw to the running back. And you don't want it to be a lateral. It's something that you take time during individual drills with the running back and quarterback to work on it. Again, the quarterback should say "if it's 2-high, make the Mike linebacker cover the hook." If he covers the hook, you've isolated the Will linebacker on the backside "stretch / slant."

If they drop the safety weak, then you key the Will linebacker. If he's in a "skate" coverage (which means both Will and Mike are working to the field), just key the drop safety: if he's going straight back down the hash, then I'm throwing the "Orlando" side, making the Mike linebacker cover it (Figure 3-55). If I get rotation strong, I'm working 1-on-1 back to the "slant / stretch" (Figure 3-56). On any pressure, the quarterback has to know that it's picked up *to the side of the slide*, and then either the tight end or the slant and back are "hot" *away* from where we called the slide. This is where you have the "built-in" hots. We would often start the game with the protection working to the field side and then your slant or your back on the stretch becomes the built-in "hot." But sometimes it's more advantageous to work the protection the opposite way; the *flexibility* is what's important—to be able to do it either way.

To clarify, we don't usually go into a single game with the protection installed *both* ways. What you try to do is to go in saying to the quarterback, "this is what we're doing this week, we're going to start the protection in the 'scat' game *to* the field side, and then *you* can override it the other way." Or if the percentages indicate that they're a boundary-pressure team, "we're going to call it *to* the boundary and then *you* can override it the other way." Most quarterbacks can do that (Figure 3-57). When you give them time to rep it, give them the opportunities in practice and in game planning, they begin to understand who the pressure guys are and what their looks are. It's usually pretty easy to do. Then, if they don't do it, it's their job to stand in there, get the ball out, complete the pass, and take the hit.

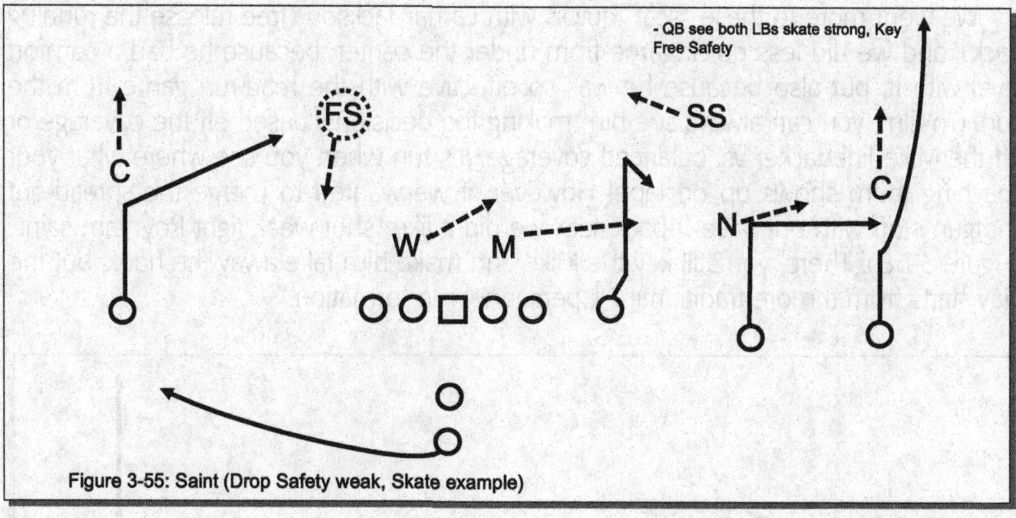

Figure 3-55: Saint (Drop Safety weak, Skate example)

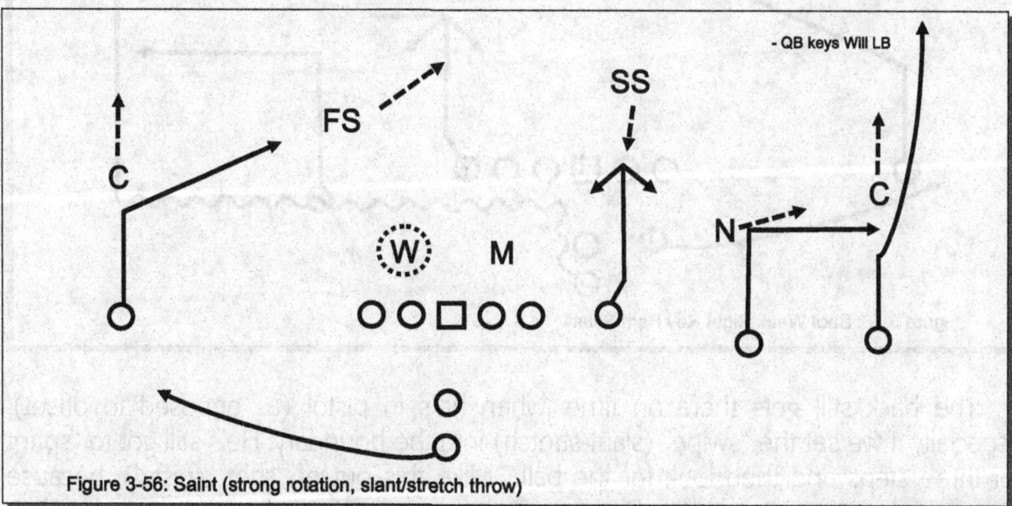

Figure 3-56: Saint (strong rotation, slant/stretch throw)

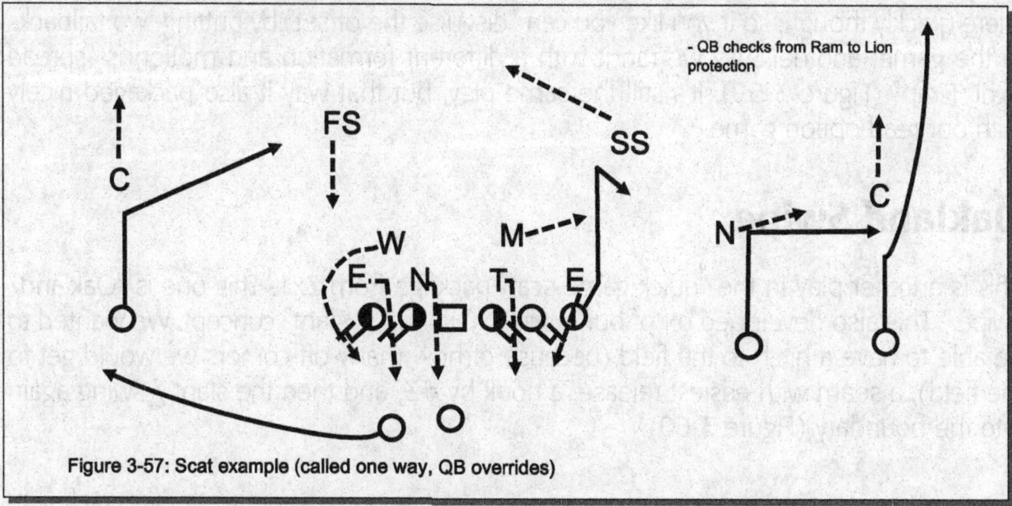

Figure 3-57: Scat example (called one way, QB overrides)

We went more to these "scat" quicks with Lamar Jackson (free release the running back), and we did less quick game from under the center, because he had a comfort level with it, but also because he was so effective with the read-run game from the gun. On film, you can always see him making the decisions, based off the coverage or off the Mike linebacker vs. balanced coverage. It's fun when you see where what your coaching them shows up on tape! However, if we wanted to merge the spread-out shotgun stuff with our base 2-back sets, we did it like "shot weak right Roy: ram saint" (Figure 3-58). There, you still key the Mike and make him take away the hook, but the play starts from a more traditional 21 personnel run formation.

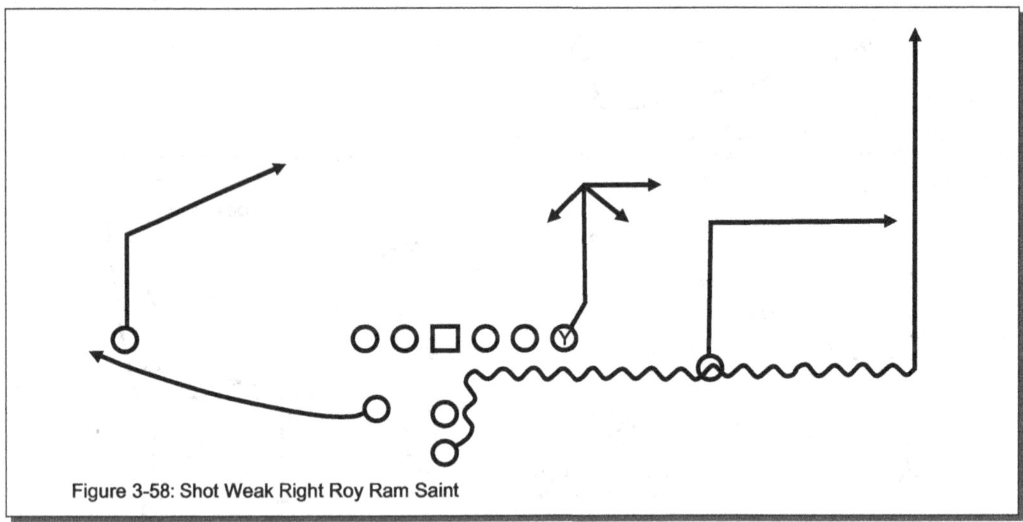

Figure 3-58: Shot Weak Right Roy Ram Saint

The back still gets there on time, when he's in pistol (as opposed to offset), especially if we set the "swipe" (slant-stretch) into the boundary. He's still got to "sprint for three steps and then look for the ball." I like this out of "shot" (pistol), because teams don't set pressure to the back as often that way. Offset does open up the slant more quickly though, so if you like you can "disguise the offset" by putting two tailbacks in the game; another way we ran it with a different formation and motion is "spread right, F zip" (Figure 3-59). It's still the same play, but that way it also packaged nicely with our read-option game.

## Oakland Swipe

This is another play in the "quick game scat" package from 3x1. This one is "Oakland/ swipe." This also developed off of our original "Orlando, X slant" concept. We wanted to be able to have a hitch to the field (because of how many off-corners we would get to the field), a seam with easiest release, a hook by #3, and then the slant / swing again into the boundary (Figure 3-60).

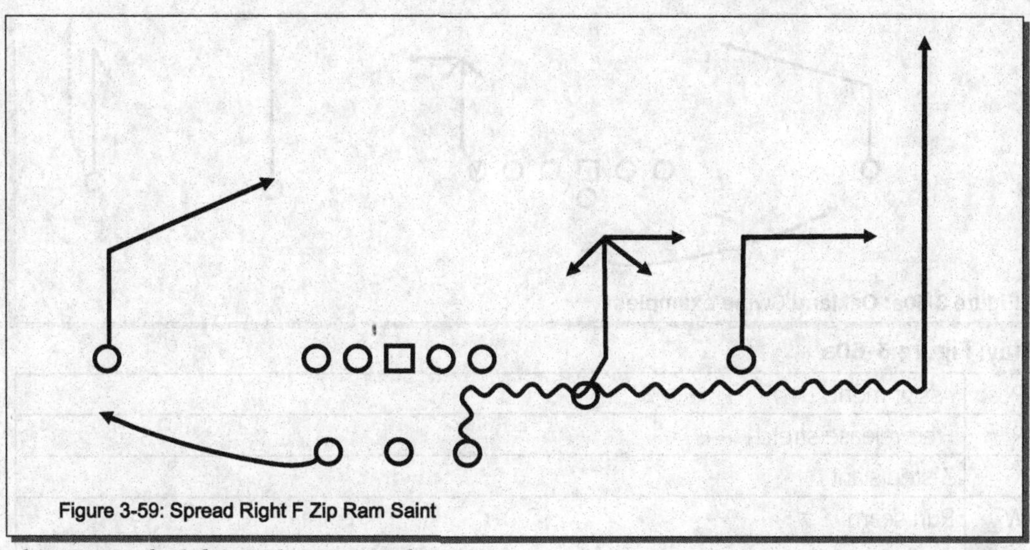
Figure 3-59: Spread Right F Zip Ram Saint

**Play: Spread Right, F Zip: Ram Saint**

| Pos: | Assignment: |
|---|---|
| F | Zip motion. Run go |
| R | Run stretch. |
| W | Run 6-yd hook. |
| X | Run 3-step slant. |
| Z | Run 6-yd out. |
| QB | Progression:<br>1. X-R<br>2. W-Z |

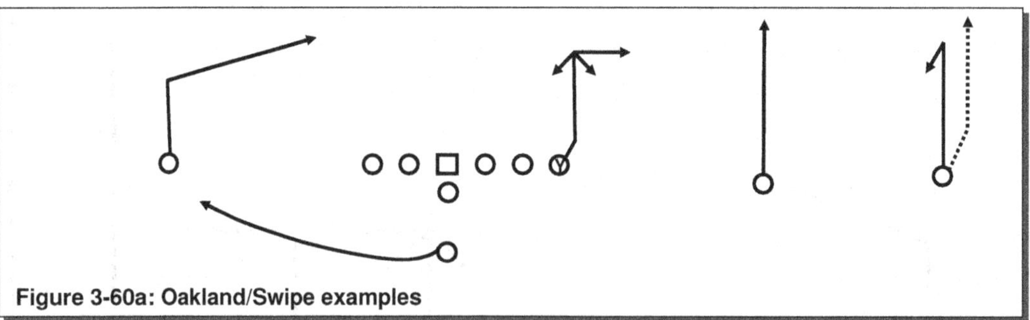
Figure 3-60a: Oakland/Swipe examples

**Play: Figure 3-60a**

| Pos: | Assignment: |
|---|---|
| R | Free release stretch |
| X | 3-step slant |
| W | Run seam. |
| Y | 6-yd hook route |
| Z | 5-yd hitch. Convert to fade vs. press/jam. |
| QB | Progression:<br>1. Cushion on z<br>2. X-R<br>3. Y |

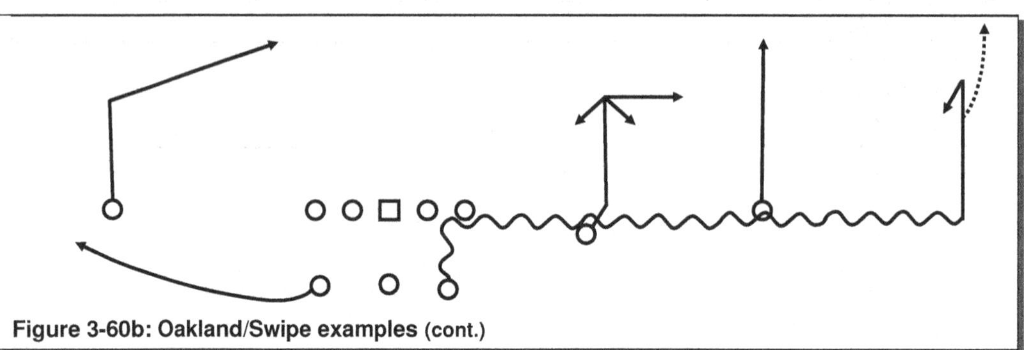
Figure 3-60b: Oakland/Swipe examples (cont.)

**Play: Spread Right, F Zip: Ram Saint**

| Pos: | Assignment: |
|---|---|
| F | Zip motion. Run hitch. Normal conversion |
| R | Run stretch. |
| W | Run 6-yd hook. |
| X | Run 3-step slant. |
| Z | Run inside release seam. |
| QB | Progression:<br>1. Key cushion (match-up)<br>2. F or X to R |

I also like this play out of "wing," because I think it defines the hitch more clearly and then teams also gave us a little more strongside rotation, so the backside slant/swing was really good (Figure 3-61). The quarterback should take the hitch to the field, if they're playing it loose. That field hitch is a long throw, now. The quarterback must be able to really *snap it*, so it gets there and it's not dropping off the end of the earth. He also needs to really *spin it*, so it's catchable when it gets there. Not everyone can make that throw.

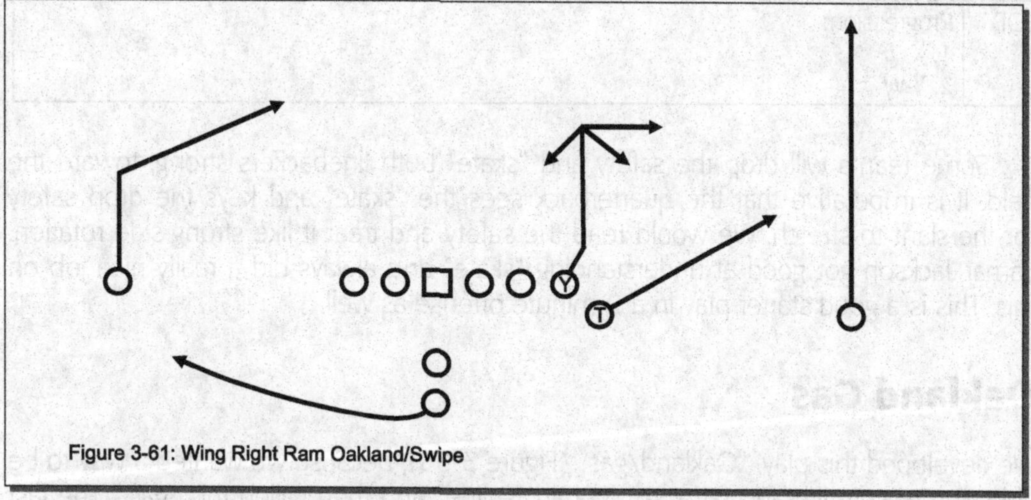

Figure 3-61: Wing Right Ram Oakland/Swipe

(Note: We didn't hit that seam to the field that often on this, but if we saw more man coverage and we wanted #2, we did have a play we called "pink," where #2 ran a stab route (Figure 3-62).

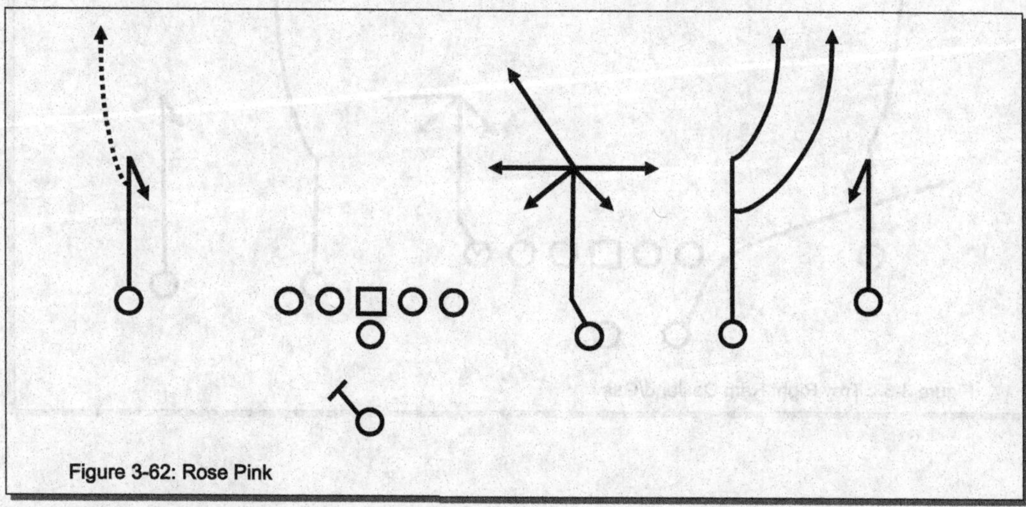
Figure 3-62: Rose Pink

**Play: Pink (stab route to #2)**

| Pos: | Assignment: |
|---|---|
| R | Block rose protection. |
| W | Run seam or stab route. |
| X | 5-step hitch |
| Y | 6-yd option route |
| Z | 5-step hitch (normal conversion) |
| QB | Progression:<br>1. X<br>2. Y-W |

Some teams will drop the safety and "skate" both linebackers strong, toward the field. It is imperative that the quarterback sees the "skate" and keys the drop safety for the slant to stretch. We would read the safety and treat it like strong-side rotation. Lamar Jackson got good at understanding "skate" and always did a really nice job on this. This is a good starter play in a 2-minute offense as well.

## Oakland Gas

We developed this play, "Oakland/gas" (Figure 3-63), because we wanted a way to be able to run a stretch and fade, so we had "swipe" and then called this "gas." The last three weeks of the 2017 season, we completed several fades on the "gas" concept.

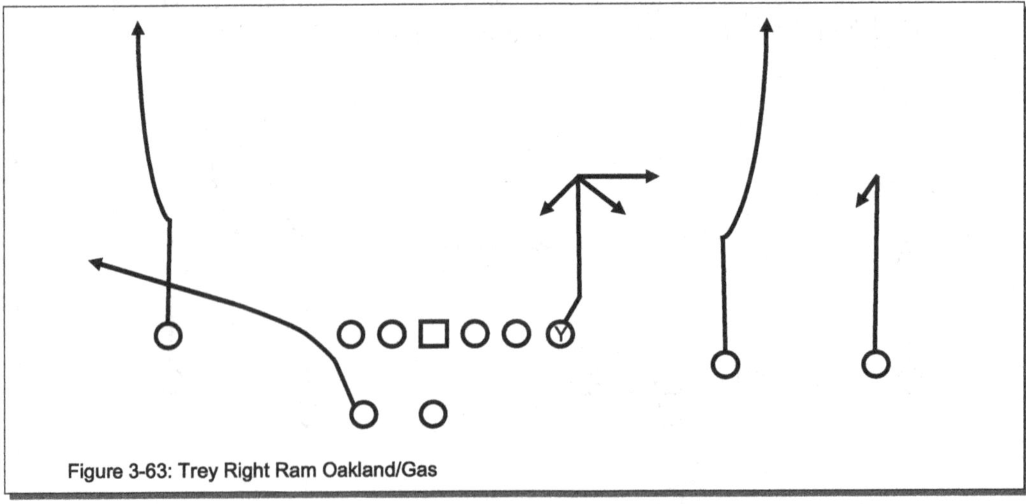


Figure 3-63: Trey Right Ram Oakland/Gas

## Grey/Swipe, Gas

The one in this package that I like the best is "grey/swipe," because it gives you an option route. So, now it's the option route, with the protect seams outside it, with the slant-stretch backside (Figure 3-64). We also liked it out of that spread look with two tailbacks, such as "spread right, F zip" (Figure 3-65). Then, if you want to have the ability to throw the fade 1-on-1, you can call "gas" instead of "swipe" (Figure 3-66).

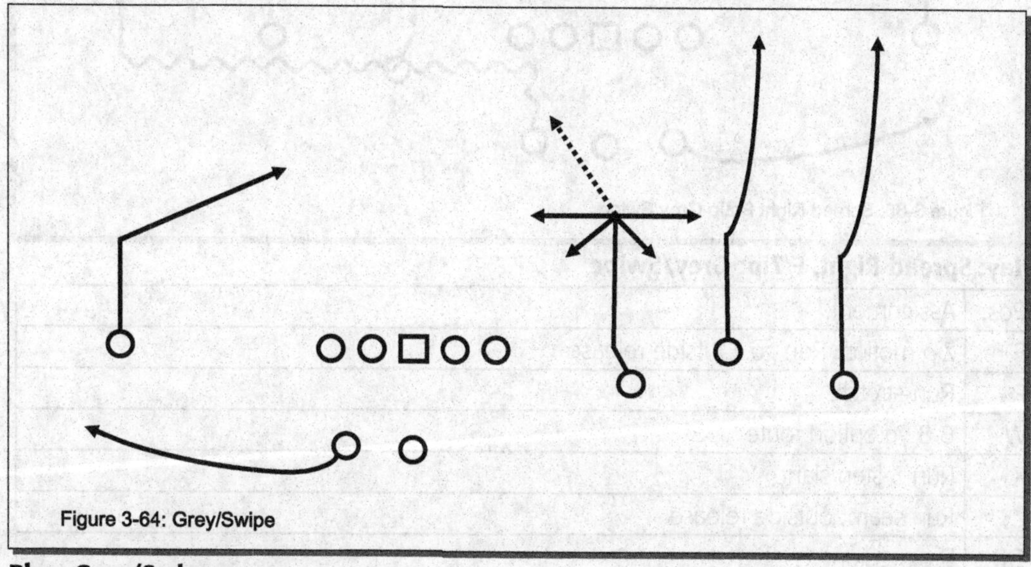

Figure 3-64: Grey/Swipe

**Play: Grey/Swipe**

| Pos: | Assignment: |
|---|---|
| R | Free release stretch |
| W | 6-yd option route |
| X | Outside release go |
| Y | Seam (must outside release) |
| Z | Run 3-step slant. |
| QB | Progression:<br>1. X to R<br>2. W |

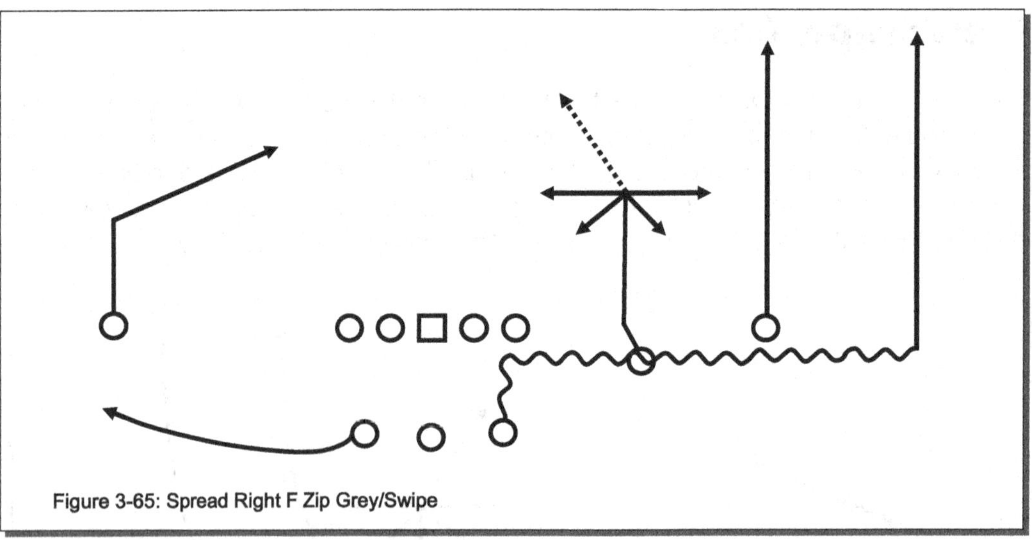
Figure 3-65: Spread Right F Zip Grey/Swipe

**Play: Spread Right, F Zip: Grey/Swipe**

| Pos: | Assignment: |
|---|---|
| F | Zip motion. Run go. Outside release |
| R | Run stretch. |
| W | 6-8 yd option route |
| X | Run 3-step slant. |
| Z | Run seam; outside release. |
| QB | Progression:<br>1. X to R<br>2. W |

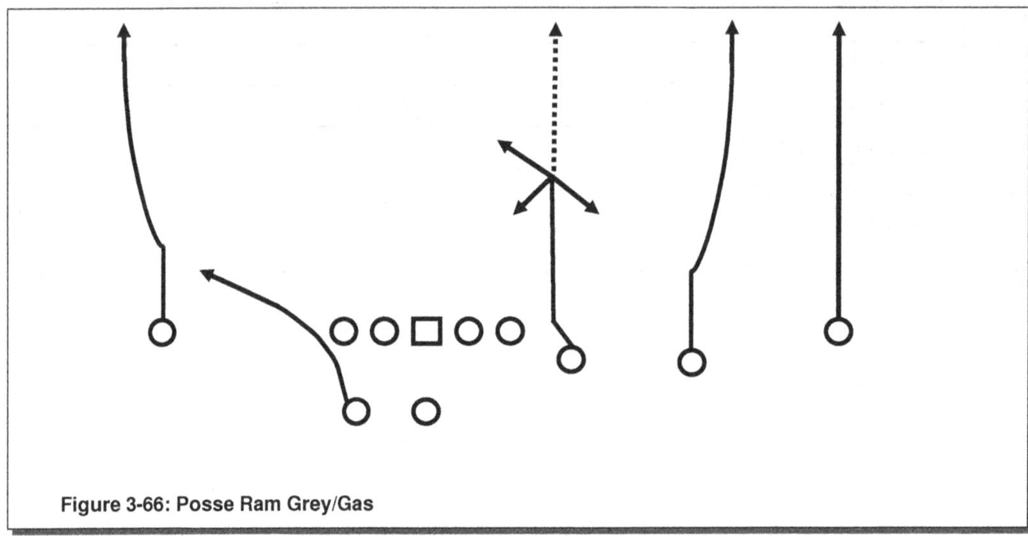
Figure 3-66: Posse Ram Grey/Gas

## Swag (Swipe/Snag)

Snag is a fieldside quick game concept, which we run from 2x2, 3x1, and 2x1 that we called "jet" (that's 20 personnel with two tailbacks in the game, for when we wanted to rest our tight end). The most productive play for us out of "jet" was "gun spread right: ram swag." So, you ran "swipe" to the boundary and "snag" to the field. It's a "snag/swipe," free-releasing both backs (Figure 3-67). That was really good for us in 2017, so we gave it the one-word code name. We sometimes game-planned to put the strongside back on a diagonal route, so we could throw something out there quick to the flat, instead of letting linebackers sit back on mirrored stretch routes and try to break on them (Figure 3-68). On that, the running back should catch the ball by opening his hips and not turning around.

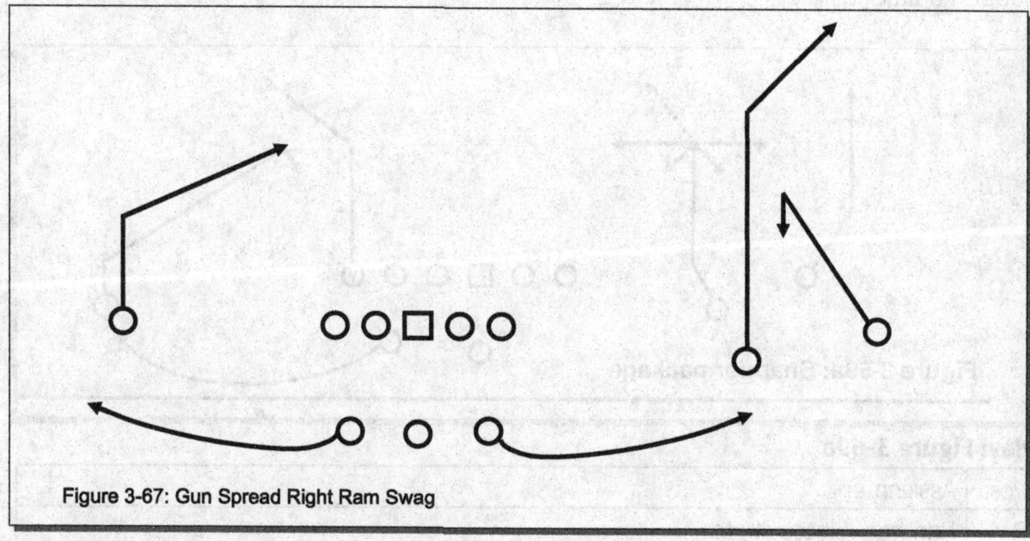

Figure 3-67: Gun Spread Right Ram Swag

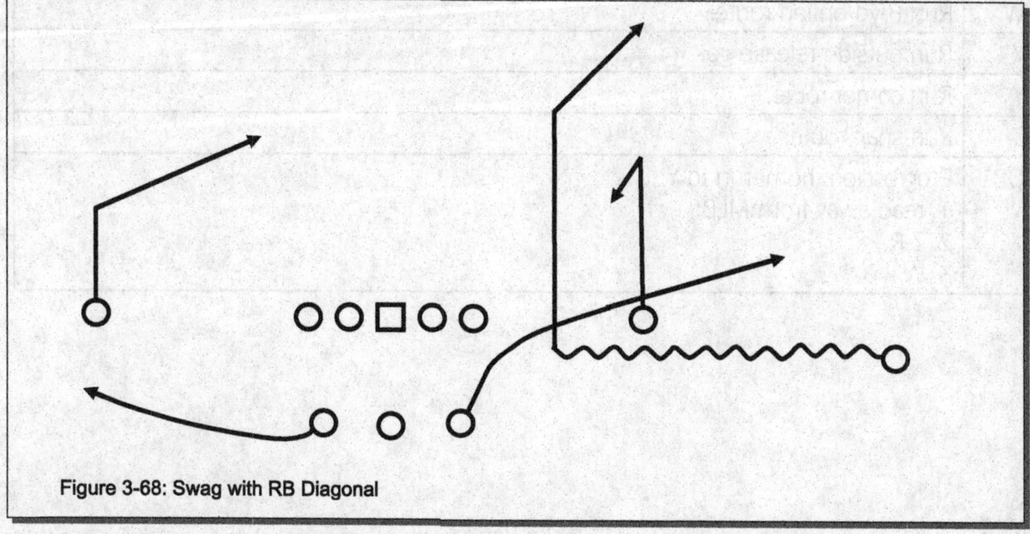

Figure 3-68: Swag with RB Diagonal

You really only look at the corner route on this, if the corner is in press (we did complete it to the tight ends on "snapper" into the boundary, though). It's a very high percentage completion play but not huge yards: 1st-&-10 play to get us to 2nd-&-short. This is definitely a good tempo play; snag and snapper were two of our best "tempo" plays.

## Snapper

"Snapper" is a boundary call (which equals "snag" to the field). With this, we ran different combinations to the wide side of the field, such as "double slant, Houston, or the option routes (grey, slop)" (Figure 3-69). Snapper times up fine with the back behind the quarterback in "shot" (pistol) or "near," where like we said, the stretch can happen a little faster.

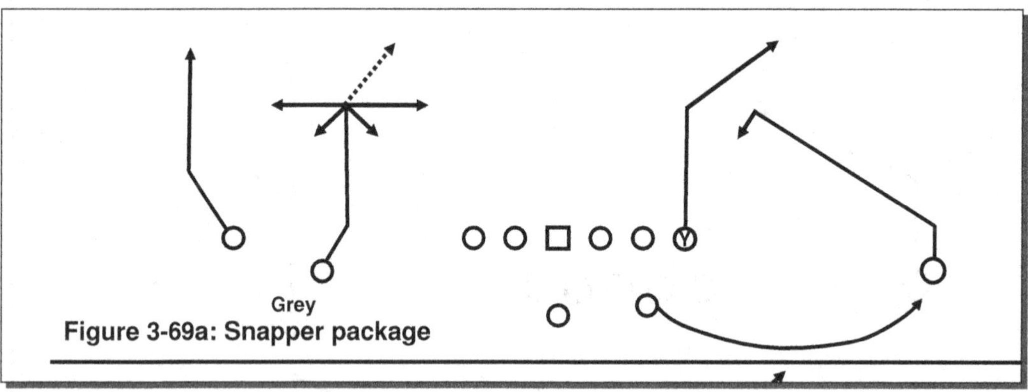

Figure 3-69a: Snapper package

**Play: Figure 3-69a**

| Pos: | Assignment: |
|---|---|
| R | Run free release stretch. |
| W | Run 6-yd option route. |
| X | Run outside release go. |
| Y | Run corner route. |
| Z | Run snag route. |
| QB | Progression: homerun to Y<br>1. read away from MLB:<br>2. Z-R<br>3. W |

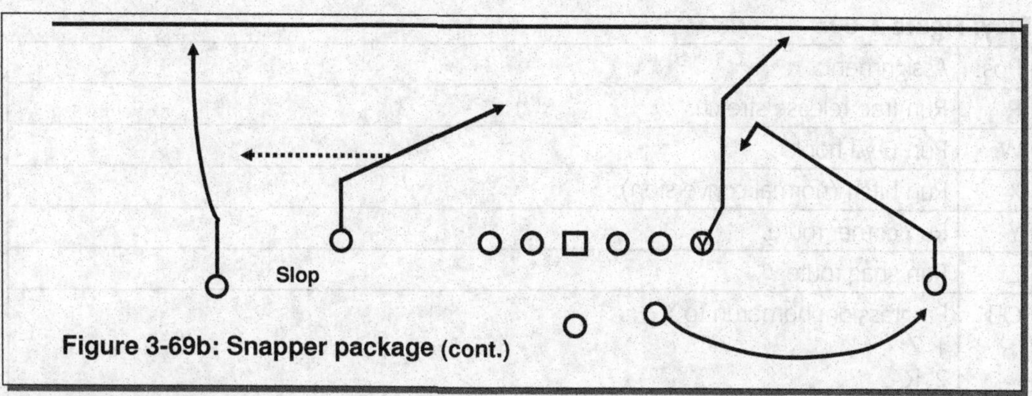

Figure 3-69b: Snapper package (cont.)

**Play: Figure 3-69b**

| Pos: | Assignment: |
|---|---|
| R | Run free release stretch. |
| W | Run slop route (slant option). |
| X | Run outside release go. |
| Y | Run corner route. |
| Z | Run snag route. |
| QB | Progression: homerun to Y<br>1. Read away from Mike:<br>2. Z-R<br>3. W |

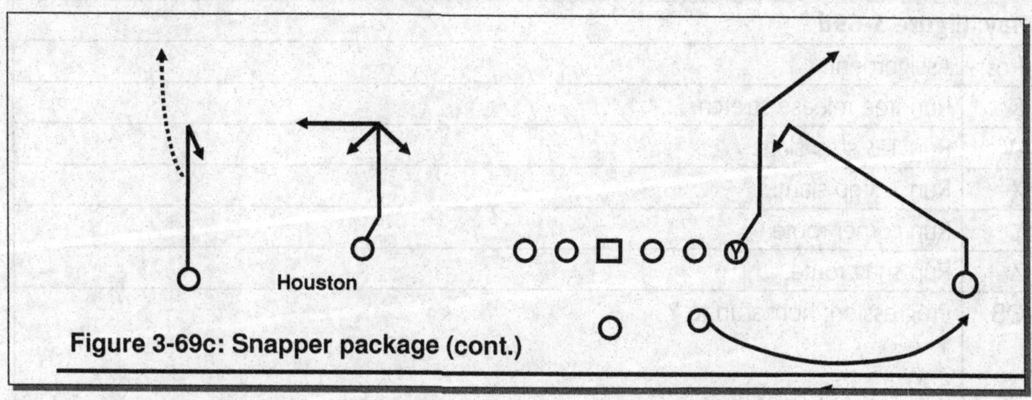

Figure 3-69c: Snapper package (cont.)

**Play: Figure 3-69c**

| Pos: | Assignment: |
|---|---|
| R | Run free release stretch. |
| W | Run 6-yd hook. |
| X | Run hitch (normal conversion). |
| Y | Run corner route. |
| Z | Run snag route. |
| QB | Progression: homerun to Y<br>1. Z<br>2. R<br>3. vs. off corner to field alert Houston |

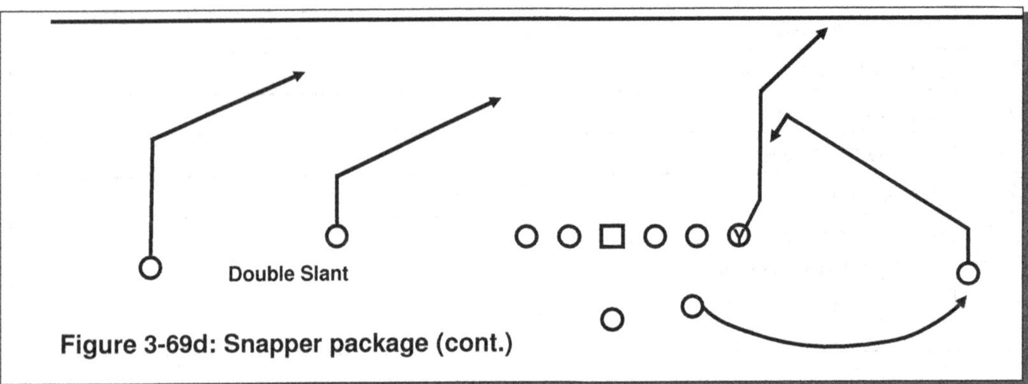


Figure 3-69d: Snapper package (cont.)

**Play: Figure 3-69d**

| Pos: | Assignment: |
|---|---|
| R | Run free release stretch. |
| W | Run 1-3 step slant. |
| X | Run 3-step slant. |
| Y | Run corner route. |
| Z | Run snag route. |
| QB | Progression: homerun to Y<br>1. Z-R<br>2. W-X<br>3. vs. Man alert Dbl slant |

This becomes a "combo-drop" for the quarterback from the gun: 3-step for "snapper" side and 2-step to the field side. With the QB in gun, Houston and hitch are the same 2-step footwork. If it's the slant, I "take two and sit." Because it's only a 2-step throw from gun, he's got to get it out, so his eyes drifting over there are less of an issue (which is why we don't run this from under center). "Snapper" from gun is the "quickest three you can take."

Typically, quarterbacks have liked to combo "double-slant" or "option" with that. Sometimes, they get nervous about throwing that hitch all the way to the field on "Houston," even though that's usually when you get the most cushion. That can also depend on what receiver he has confidence in, or where Mike is taking him. Sometimes, he just makes a pre-snap decision to go hitch all the way and lives with it.

A great way to run this is "wing right Z float: lion snapper, Houston" (Figure 3-70). The difference, in this instance, is that #1, as a tight end, is running a 5-yard "stop" route (it's a "snag" route if I'm split out, where my angle would be coming in). The back still has a free-release "stretch." This is another great "sound play on sound" to use with tempo out of our "wing slot" package.

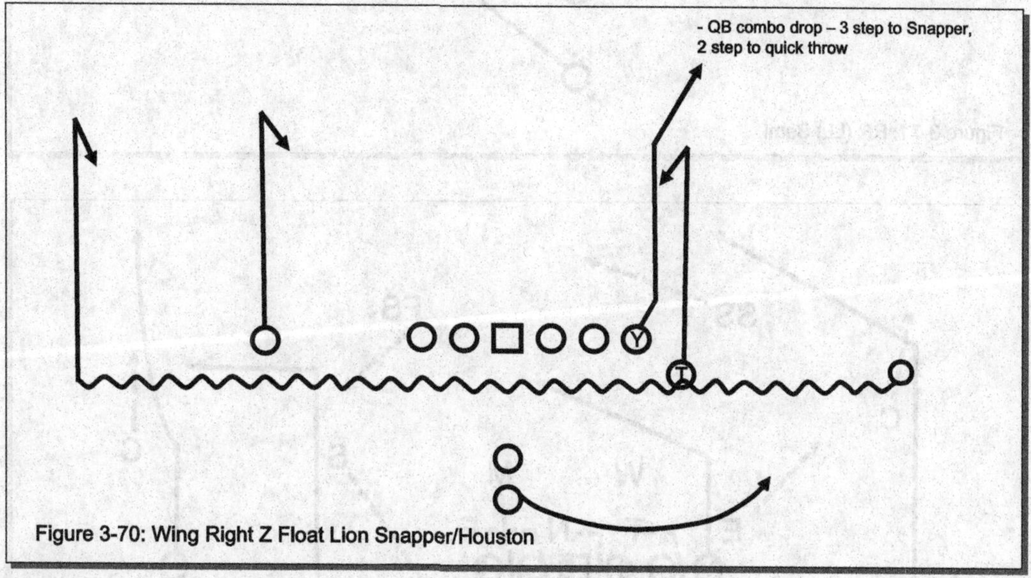

Figure 3-70: Wing Right Z Float Lion Snapper/Houston

## Pope

"Pope" became a pressure check with the "RR (LL) semi" for field scrape. The ball is on the left hash. Say we're getting pressure and he's relating to the back, so we carry "RR (LL) semi" (Figure 3-71). Then, we also went with "RR Pope." As such, we ran a drag with a slant, and then we offset the back and he ran the stretch route (Figure 3-72). So, that defender had to match the drag and you're able to throw the slant vs. the off-corner and a defensive end. We just ran "blue" on the other side. It ended up being good for us at times.

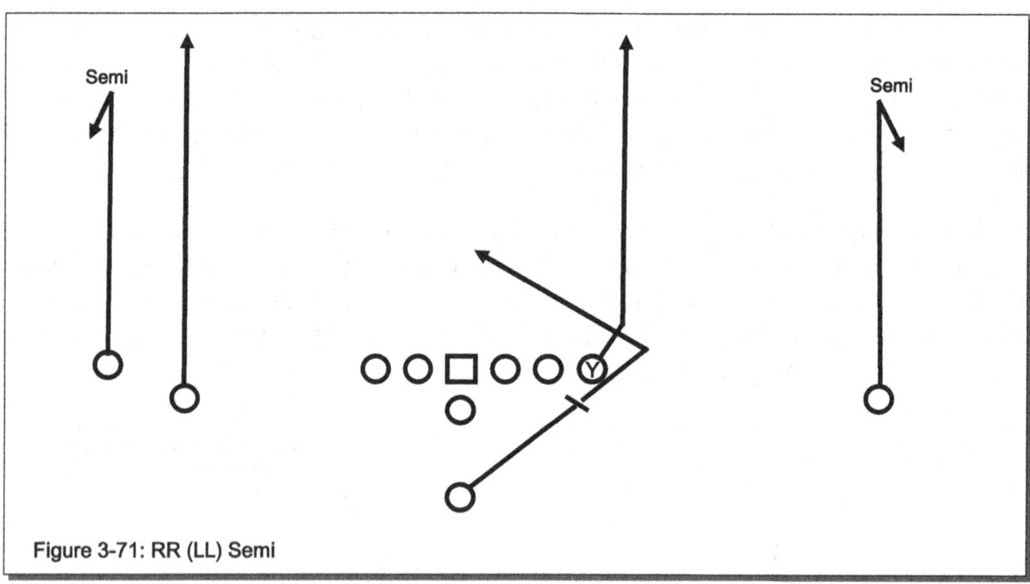

Figure 3-71: RR (LL) Semi

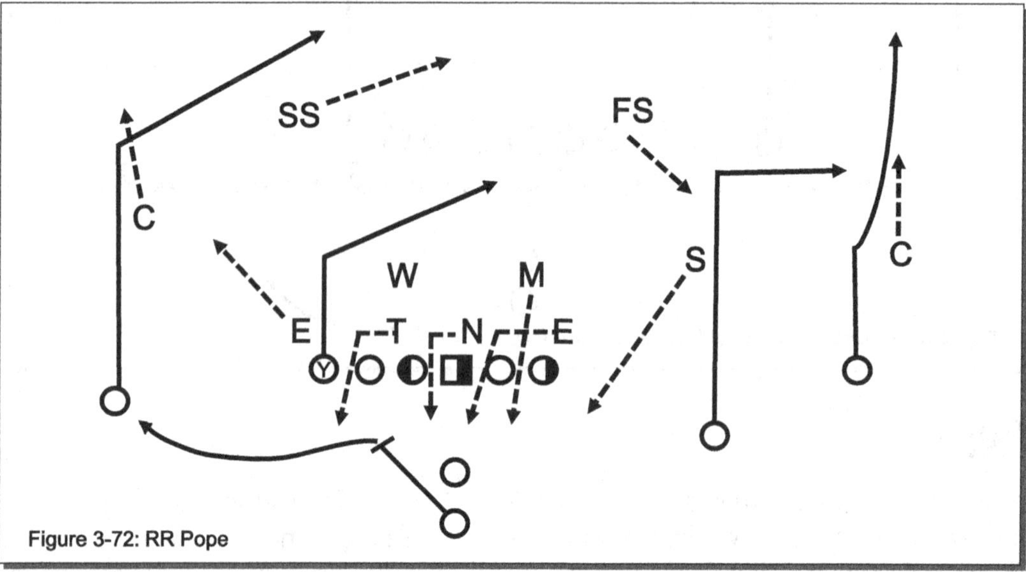

Figure 3-72: RR Pope

## Final Thoughts on Quick Game

This chapter has addressed our philosophy of the quick game, our base routes, how we construct our packages, what we do to create matchup advantages and some recent developments in this particular phase of the offense. The chapter has also pointed out the attention to detail which we believe is necessary, in order to get the most out of the quick passing game. Next, let's move forward and take a look at dropback passing.

# Chapter 4
## Dropback Passing

I really believe in the dropback passing game. We like to say that if we can throw the dropback game when we *want* to, then we will be able to throw when we *need* to! In our offense, we use a numbered system along with certain code words to establish our routes and pass protections. In the dropback game, the numbered system (0-9) represents the routes, but these really refer to "concept categories," rather than specific routes. So, the way it's organized, we have our base concepts and then we also have code names for several additional packages as well. While we believe we have established a comprehensive passing system with answers for everything we will face, we also strive to keep all the verbiage as simple as is reasonably possible. It takes a tremendous commitment and a lot of hard work in order to be a great dropback passing team, but we've found the payoff to be worth it! This chapter shows you the foundation of our dropback passing game and also shares some ideas from our experiences over the years that we think will be helpful to your team.

## Concept Categories

The dropback passing game is based off a series of numbers that each indicate the route that's going to be run but also the *concept* within that. Everybody on the team has to learn *concepts*. If you can learn concepts, then you're able to play different positions and we have more freedom to substitute guys in, line people up in different places across all the formations, and really get the matchups we want.

The basic concept number can change; for example, our curls are "zero." Our outs and outside corners are "1." Our posts and "toppers" are "2." Our go routes and seams are "3." Our inside option route at 8-yards is "4." Our "high-low" with the read route on top to our slot receiver is a "5." Our corner route/smash/China/return is "6." The "7" is some type of "high-low," with the tight end on top on the read route (and "tags" to get who you want as the underneath crosser route). The "8" category is a "mesh," with an in-cut and a post over the top. Although we don't use it as much anymore, we still employ it, on occasion, in the red zone out of our "trips" formation. Then, "9" is a "catch-all" category. That's where you can put new things in and utilize tags. The players just understand that the "9" doesn't have a specific meaning (Figure 4-1).

**ROUTE TREE SHEET**

| OUTSIDE WR | QUICK GAME 90s | DROPBACK 60/70/80/480 |
|---|---|---|
| 0 | HITCH (GREEN) | CURL |
| 1 | QUICK OUT | SEMI |
| 2 | SLANT (RED) | POST |
| 3 | FADE | GO |
| INSIDE WR | | |
| 4 | 6-YD OPTION (GREY) | 8-YD INSIDE OPTION |
| 5 | RUB SERIES | HI-LOW (W) |
| 6 | STAB | SMASH |
| 7 | FADE – 6-YD OUT (BLUE) | HI-LOW (Y) |
| 8 | BUBBLE | MESH |
| 9 | SEAM, STAB – 5YD UNDER | SPECIAL |

Figure 4-1.

Something we do to help package our personnel groupings in the dropback passing game is package ideas by formations. For example, we say our "regular" and our "spread" (in other words 21 and 20 personnel) "equal each other." Our "thunder" (which is a 2x2 set out of 12 personnel) and our "doubles" (a 2x2 set out of 11 personnel) "equal each other." Our "wing" and our "trey" (3x1 sets) "equal each other." The "trips" formation equals "thunder-slot." Our "wing-slot" is a great *packaged* formation for runs, quick game, dropback game, and really good play-action and movement. There you'd say, "wing slot" equals "doubles-snug," where you just tighten the Z's split up, or call "trips, Z mo," where Z motions over to it (Figure 4-2). We establish those packages and then from there, we build up the empty game.

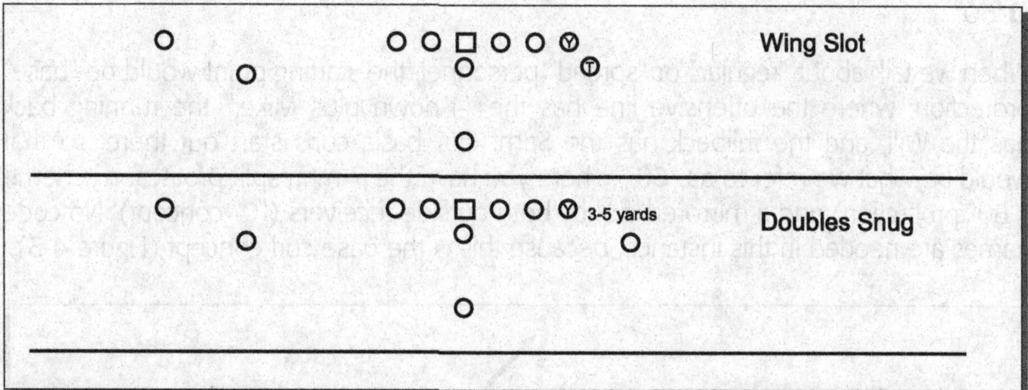

Figure 4-2.

We want to be able to *package* all the concepts exactly like we did with the quick game. Again, this means we all need to learn the protections and the concepts, then everything can go together in those groupings and we can keep it all organized. If the entire staff can think in terms of those *concept categories*, then as you get to studying with your coaches, their input and their creativity can really show up each week in game planning!

I do think that in order to be a complete offense, you have to be a good dropback team. It is a lot of work, you need to make a commitment to it, and you've got to practice the heck out of it! You must be able to utilize the protections, and you have got to be able to "override" the protections. You have to be able to utilize "hots" and "sights." Then, you also have to be able to utilize "built-ins," where the "hots" and "sights" are already available within the play, and everyone knows we're good. "Thumbs up, we're running the play called. I'm the quarterback, I'm going to handle it!"

I think you need to have the dropback game available for 3rd-&-medium or 3rd-&-long situations. However, I like to throw it on both 1st-&-10 and 2nd down, because I feel like the more you throw your 3rd-down passes on 1st-&-10, the better you're going to be with them. Then, the more you carry those plays over to 3rd down, the better you're going to be about 3rd-down conversions. So, the idea that "I just have these 3rd-down calls" really doesn't exist for me. We say, "we will throw when we *want* to, so we can throw when we *need* to." And I think our quarterbacks have all really liked it that way as well.

## Curls

We begin our dropback game installation with the curl route. We believe in throwing curls and we practice the heck out of them! Again, the "zero" concept category represents our hitches, when we're in the quick game, and it represents our curls in the dropback game. Players all need to understand the nuances of the routes themselves, the various associated code words, and the corresponding protections in order to execute the concepts correctly.

❑ 60

When we talk about "regular" or "spread" personnel, the starting point would be "base" protection, where the offensive line has the "4-down plus Mike," the running back has the Will, and the fullback has the Sam. Our basic curls start out there, so that would be what we refer to as "60," where you have the 7-man split protection scheme ("60" protection) and a mirrored curl by both outside receivers ("0" concept). No code names are needed in this instance, because this is the base curl concept (Figure 4-3).

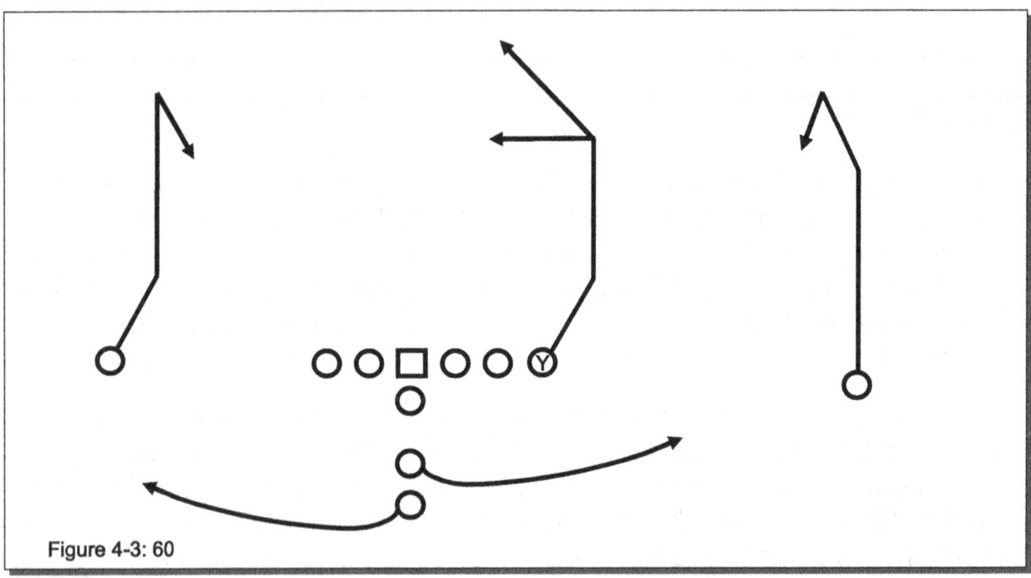


Figure 4-3: 60

**Play: 60**

| Pos: | Assignment: | Coaching Points: |
|---|---|---|
| F | Check 60 protection. Run stretch route. | Catch ball 2-3 yds from LOS. |
| R | Check 60 protection. Run stretch route. | Catch ball 2-3 yds from LOS. |
| X | Run 5-4 or 4-5 curl route. | Eyes inside to LB on 2nd stem. |
| Y | Run streak read at 2nd-level depth. | vs. cover 2: take the middle. |
| Z | Run 5-4 or 4-5 curl route. | Eyes inside to LB on 2nd stem. |
| QB | Homerun: Key: Read away from secondary rotation.<br>Progression: 1. X-Z<br>2. R-F vs. 2 high: Work control side<br>3. Y<br><br>Outlet: | |

The receivers need to count their strides on a curl route, but there are specific coaching points a receiver needs to understand. This is a base 9-step route, but the coverage scheme may require either a "5-4" or "4-5" curl route. If we get a jam corner, we like to run a "4-5" stem. For the receiver, my first four steps are going to be an inside stem on a slight angle (it can't be a big angle). I'm going to "dip and rip" with my outside arm for the *contact point* with the corner, and then push vertical for five steps and beat the underneath linebacker to get open. If I get "free access" or an "off corner," I like to run a "5-4" stem, so I'm going to push vertical for five steps, then I'm going to stem at the post for four and then beat the underneath linebacker to get open. If they show press-man coverage, I need to burst outside to 14 yards, throw the corner by, come back hard to the ball in the open space, and expect the ball right out of the break (Figure 4-4). Then, there may be other play calls that require a "point-to-point" curl route, where I stay on my vertical stem, in order to accommodate spacing with the other routes.

The tight end (or W receiver in a "spread" set) runs what we refer to as a "streak-read." What that means is "if the middle is open, I'm going to take it." If it's cover 2 and the safeties get width as I come off the ball, I'm going to try to "take it through for a touchdown." If, instead, there's a single-high safety (or there's a quarters safety there), then that's considered "closed." If the "middle is closed," I'm going to "snap it at second-level depth," which means behind the Mike linebacker—unless he overruns me, then I'm going to slip inside of him, turn, and "get my dukes up" to the quarterback. We really feel like the "streak-read" is the most effective way to hold the Mike linebacker within a curl concept, so the quarterback can then read the outside linebacker or strong safety to go "curl to back."

When you mirror the route and you have curls on both sides, then it's strictly an "off-of-coverage" read for the quarterback, in terms of which side to go to. If it's a "2 high" safety, then I'm going to the "control side," which means I'm going to where I'm "controlling the safety with the streak-read." In that case, I would be going to the tight-end side, because he's the "streak-read" (or to the W receiver in "spread," because he's the streak-read"). I want to *"hold* the linebacker and *key* the flat defender." I never talk to the quarterback about "looking off," I always talk to him about "who do I *hold*, who do I *key*?" For the quarterback, it's a "5-step rhythm throw" (or "3-step rhythm throw" out of the gun). What I mean by that is I need to be able to take a 5-step drop in rhythm with one hitch-step, turn, and be prepared to throw the ball to the curl. The second hitch-step would be to the back on a "stretch" route. You've got to be "in rhythm" with it, on balance, and get the ball out on time.

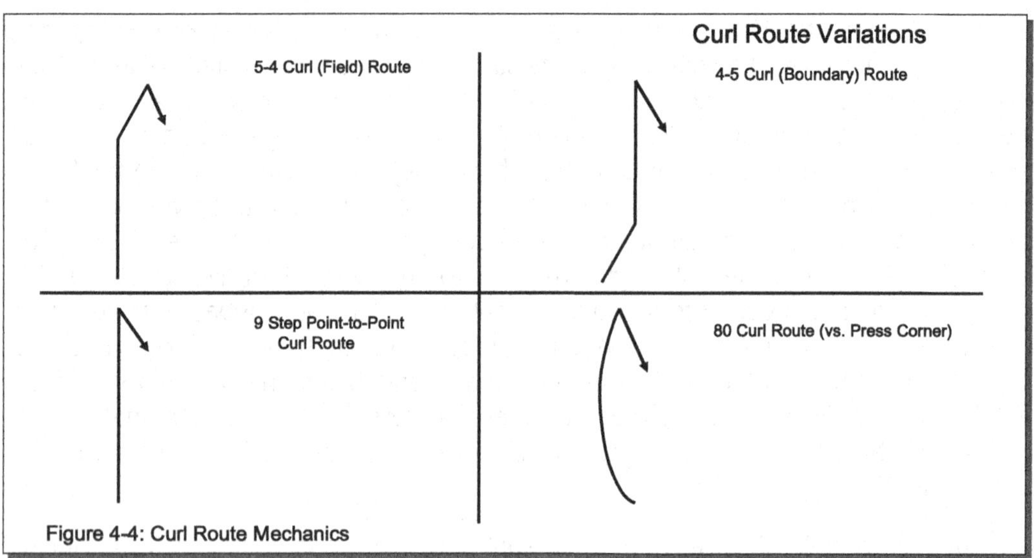

Figure 4-4: Curl Route Mechanics

**5-4 Curl (Field) Route:**
Sprint off the ball with great arm drive. 5-4 steps on curl. Route depth is 14 yards. 5 steps, stick and burst to the post. 4 steps, and plant, point and drive back to the quarterback. Eyes, quick tuck and tight turn.

**4-5 Curl (Boundary) Route:**
Sprint off the ball with great arm drive. 4-5 steps on curl. Route depth is 14 yards. Stem release using the width of the numbers. 4 steps and stick, rip inside arm and push vertical for 5 steps. Plant point and drive back to the quarterback. Eyes, quick tuck and tight turn.

**9-Step Point-to-Point Curl Route:**
Sprint off the ball with great arm drive. Vertical stem on 14-yard depth curl route. 9 steps on vertical release then plant, point and drive back to the quarterback. Eyes, quick tuck and tight turn.

**80 Curl Route (vs. Press Corner)**
1. Outside release and accelerate hand up field to 14-yeards – get on top of defender
2. Sit your hips down and pull defender past you with your inside arm
3. Come hard back to the ball in the open hole
4. Be ready for ball right out of your break

❑ 480 Midget

We can also shorten all that down and make it an "off-the-plant" throw for the quarterback, timed up with slightly shorter routes by the outside receivers. We call that "midget," which means the receivers are going to tighten their splits (they're going to take more of a "post-split") and it's going to be a "point-to-point" 12-yard curl, instead of the deeper "5-4" or "4-5" curl. To make that work, you have to change the protection and free-release a back to one side so that you create the stretch right away. We call this "400 protection," which would be a weakside check-release, where the running back either runs a "diagonal" or a "stretch" depending on what formation he lines up in. A strongside back (if we are in a 2-back set) would have a free-release. We now call the play "480 midget," whether that's from "regular" or "spread" sets (Figure 4-5). Again, the quarterback has to now take a 5-step drop and make the throw "off the plant" to get it there on time. If he tries to take a hitch-step, the timing is lost.

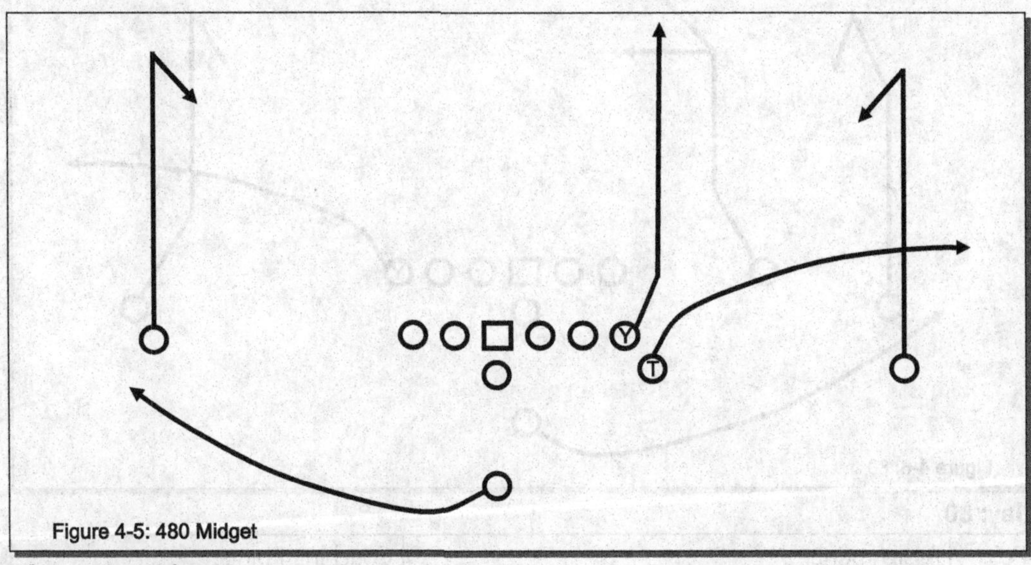

Figure 4-5: 480 Midget

**Play: 480 Midget**

| Pos: | Assignment: | Coaching Points: |
|---|---|---|
| R | Check 400 protection. Run stretch route | |
| T | Run diagonal. | |
| X | Run 12-yd P.P. curl. | |
| Y | Run seam route. | vs. cover 2: take the middle. |
| Z | Run 12-yd P.P. curl | Take midget split. Fld + 3 hash, Bdry -2 top #'s, MF divide split. |
| QB | Homerun: Y Key: pie snap: FS<br>Progression: vs. fld rotation: 1. X 2. R; vs. 2 high: 1. Z 2. T<br>Outlet: R | |

❑ 80 / 480

When we get into the 2x2 sets, whether that's "doubles" or "thunder," we have the ability to get the "streak-read" on either side. I think that's important, simply because then you aren't allowing the defense to take your best receiver out of running a curl route. In the 2x2 set, we could call "80" or "480," which would give us the "streak-read" by the slot receiver, the tight end would run a "diagonal" (he checks his way out on "80" and has a free-release on "480"), the back would be going towards the slot receiver on a "check-stretch" route, and you mirror the outside curls (Figure 4-6).

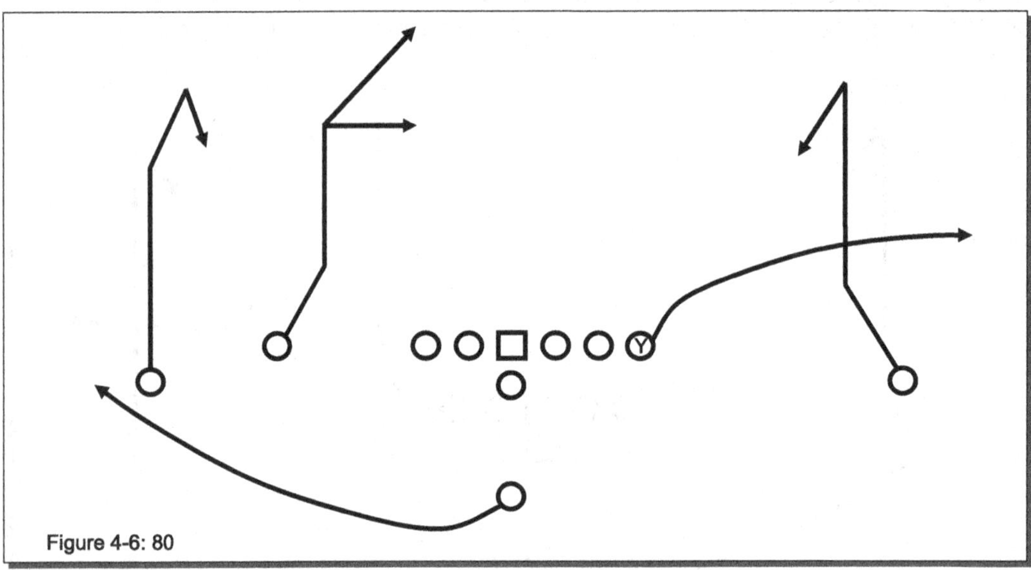

Figure 4-6: 80

**Play: 80**

| Pos: | Assignment: | Coaching Points: |
|---|---|---|
| R | Check 80 protection. Run stretch route. | Catch ball 2-3 yds from LOS. |
| W | Run streak read. | vs. 1 high: snap off. vs 2 high: take through |
| X | Run 5-4 or 4-5 curl route at 14 yds back to 12. | Eyes inside to LB on 2nd stem. |
| Y | Check 80 protection. Run diagonal. | vs. cover 2: take the middle. |
| Z | Run 5-4 or 4-5 curl route at 14 yds back to 12 | Eyes inside to LB on 2nd stem. |
| QB | Homerun: W Key: pre-snap. FS.<br>Progression: 1. X-R-W<br>2. Z-Y-W post-snap: curl/flat player<br><br>Outlet: | vs. 2 high: think control side.<br>vs. 1 high: think strongside. |

This is still a "coverage-progression" read: if you get 2 high, your base progression is to the "streak-read" side. If you get single high, your base progression is away from the rotation; if the rotation is to the tight end, then I read it to the weakside. If the rotation is to the slot, then we read the tight end and Z receiver. I'm going to "*hold* that inside linebacker and *key* the flat defender." (By "rotation," we mean a safety on one side or the other comes down toward the line of scrimmage and the other safety goes to the middle. We want to throw *away* from the drop safety.)

Some people say, "well, what do you do if it's man coverage?" The quarterback has to know (whether the play is 60, 80, 480, whatever) that "as I drop, I want to hold the linebacker." *Hold* the linebacker. I also need to know as I drop that if linebacker works downhill at a 45-degree angle, that that clues me in that it's man-coverage. So then, the quarterback needs to know what the best matchup is. "Who is my best curl runner against their worst corner?" And the receiver *has* to win. I get back in rhythm, "pull the string" and throw the curl. If the receiver can't win, then we need to get a different receiver in there. You have to have a receiver who can win on the curl and we work it hard enough that he should be able to do so.

As we said, that receiver has a lot of responsibility, because he's got to run a curl vs. free-access (off technique), he's got to be able to run a curl against press technique, and he's got to be able to run a curl against "jam," which is a cover 2 corner. There's a lot of different techniques he has to work just to get open on his curl route.

❑ 70

If we want the streak-read to be to the tight-end side, then we simply flip the protection, slide the protection weak, and work the running back strong instead. So, the line would have the "4-down plus the Will," the back will have "Mike, Sam, release to his route," to the strongside. "Y" (tight end) would have the "streak-read" and then the slot receiver would now have a diagonal route. You're just flipping the route the other way, so that would now be called "70" in our terminology ("70" protection and "0" curl concept). The quarterback again needs to understand where the streak-read is (for his 2-high side), and where his diagonal /curl side is (Figure 4-7).

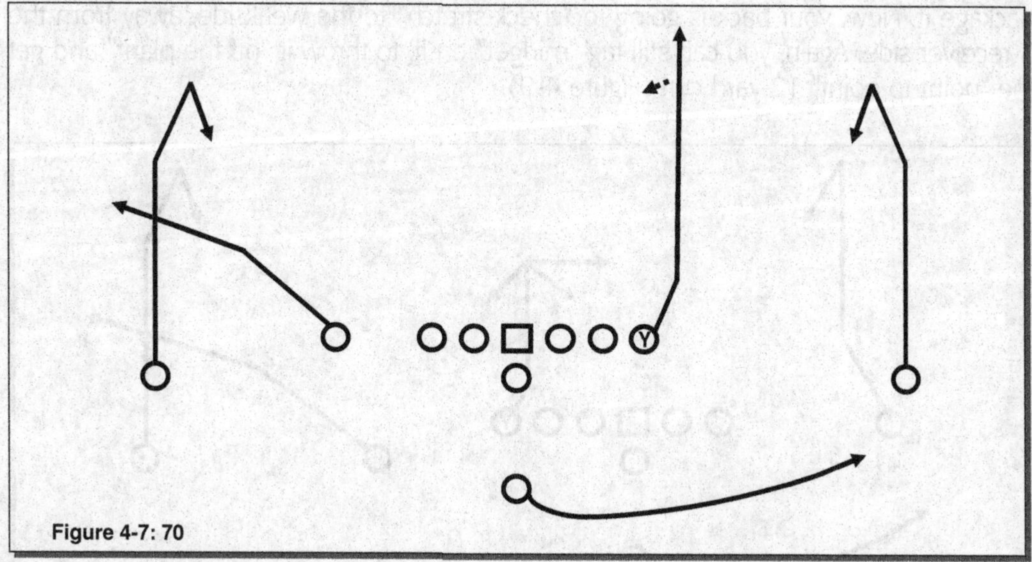


Figure 4-7: 70

**Play: 70**

| Pos: | Assignment: | Coaching Points: |
|---|---|---|
| R | Check 70 protection. Run stretch route. | Catch ball 2-3 yds from LOS. |
| W | Run diagonal. | |
| X | Run 5-4 or 4-5 curl route at 14 yds back to 12. | Eyes inside to LB on 2nd stem. |
| Y | Run streak read. | |
| Z | Run 5-4 or 4-5 curl route at 14 yds back to 12. | Eyes inside to LB on 2nd stem. |
| QB | Homerun: Key: pre-snap: FS<br>Progression: 1. Z to R<br>2. X to W post-snap: curl/flat player<br><br>Outlet: | vs. cover 2: Think strongside – control side.<br>vs. cover 3: think weakside.<br>vs. pressure: alert check. Built-in hot to W. |

❑ Y Option

When we get into 3x1 (which would be the "wing" set in 12 personnel, or "trey" if we are detached), most of the time we're going to tag an option route to the #3 receiver. In that situation, one of our favorite calls would be "480 Y option." So now, I've got the mirrored curls outside, and the #2 receiver has a diagonal. If that route is "attached" in "wing right: 480 Y option," the T (wing) runs hard to the sideline at a target of four yards. However, if we run that diagonal route from "trey right" with a W (wide receiver), he runs at what we call "golf cart" speed, so he doesn't sprint to the flat and get out there way too soon (Figure 4-8). He takes a little bit off of his speed to get out there, so it times up right with the quarterback and the curl route, regardless of how we package it. Now, your back is going to "check-stretch" to the weakside, away from the 3-receiver side. Again, you can still tag "midget" on it, to throw it "off the plant" and get the "point-to-point" 12-yard curl (Figure 4-9).

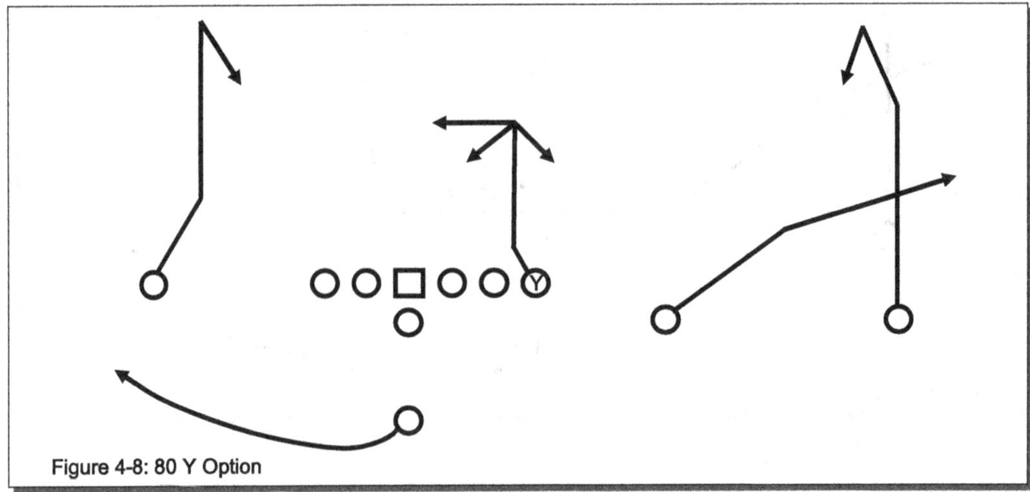

Figure 4-8: 80 Y Option

**Play: 80 Y Option**

| Pos: | Assignment: | Coaching Points: |
|---|---|---|
| R | Check 80 protection. Run stretch route. | |
| W | Run diagonal route. | |
| X | Run 5-4 or 4-5 curl route at 14 yds back to 12. | Eyes inside to LB on 2nd stem. |
| Y | Check 80 protection. Run 10-yd inside option route. | Work over my alignment inside. |
| Z | Run 5-4 or 4-5 curl route at 14 yds back to 12. | Eyes inside to LB on 2nd stem. |
| QB | Homerun: Key: pre-snap: FS<br>Progression: 1. Z-R-Y<br>or post-snap: curl/flat player<br>2. X-W-Y<br><br>Outlet: | |

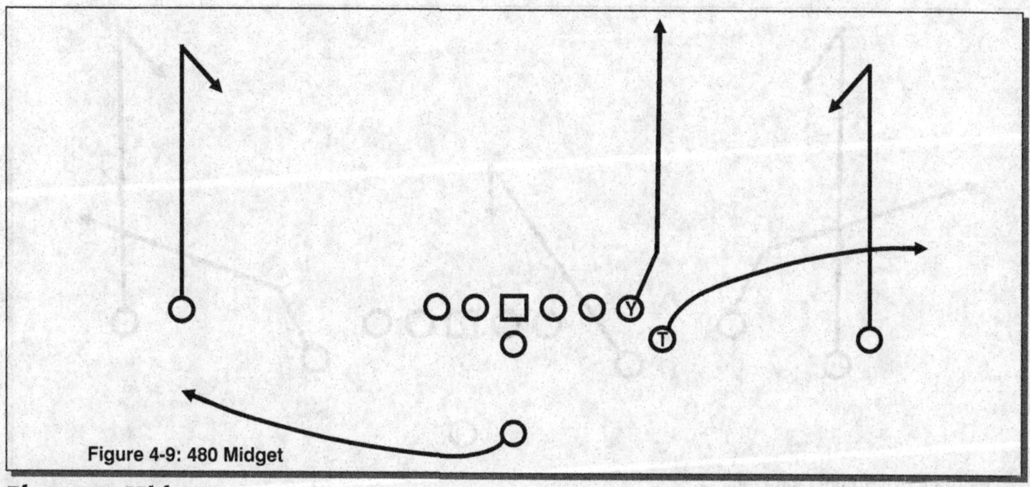

Figure 4-9: 480 Midget

**Play: 480 Midget**

| Pos: | Assignment: | Coaching Points: |
|---|---|---|
| R | Check 400 protection. Run stretch route. | |
| T | Run diagonal. | |
| X | Run 12-yd P.P. curl. | Eyes inside to LB on 2nd stem. |
| Y | Run seam route. | |
| Z | Run 12-yd P.P. curl. | Take midget split fld: +3 hash, bdry: -2 top #'s. MF: divide split. |
| QB | Homerun: Y Key: pre-snap:<br>FS<br>Progression: vs. fld rotation vs. 2 high<br>1. X 1. Z<br>2. R 2. T<br>Outlet: R | |

(Note: the more "point-to-point" curls you throw, the better chance you're going to have for the "topper" or deep post over the top for a touchdown, so "midget" is also a way of setting up the post throw for a touchdown).

❑ Empty Hank

Those are the base curls that we throw. You don't throw a lot of base-curls out of the "trips" formation, but we will do it when we get into empty, especially when people line up in "man-free with a rat." "Lion/ram:" is 5-man protection (lion or ram), with a "look" route by #3, and "diagonal / curls" outside on both sides (Figure 4-10). The idea of "Hank" is that whatever linebacker squeezes that "look" route, the quarterback goes "curl/flat" to *that* side. You'll remember that when we run "90 double-hook" ("Houston") in the quick game, the quarterback locates the most "tucked-in" linebacker and throws to that side. The teaching for the quarterback carries over to this concept in the dropback game.

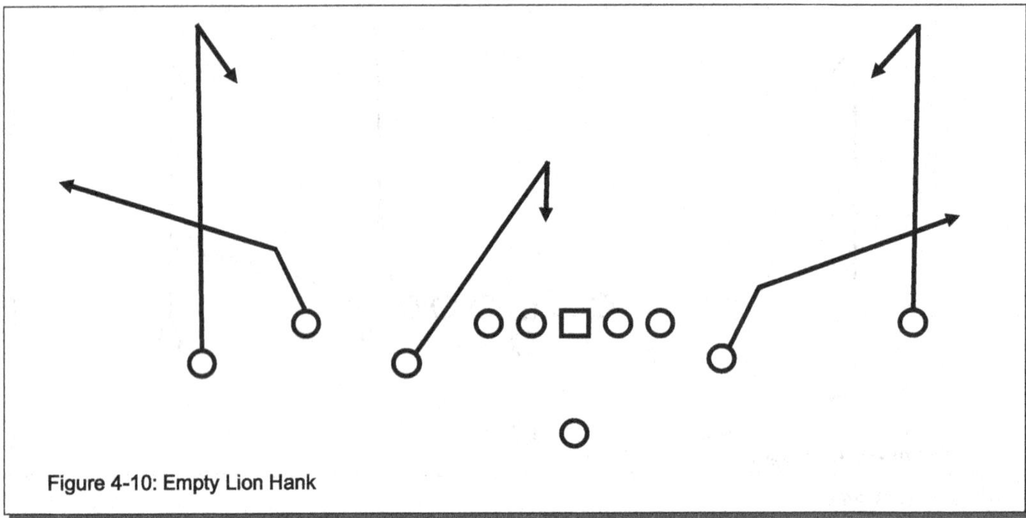

Figure 4-10: Empty Lion Hank

**Play: Empty Hank**

| Pos: | Assignment: |
|---|---|
| H | 12-yd PP curl |
| W | Run golf-cart speed diagonal. |
| X | 12-yd PP curl |
| Y | Diagonal route |
| Z | Run look route over ball. |
| QB | Progression:<br>1. Z 1. Z<br>2. H 2. X<br>3. Y 3. W<br>Key: secondary rotation |

We carry that in empty for that particular coverage, because we work curls *every single day* vs. press corners. So, if you're in empty and they're going to play "press man-free," I believe we will win on the curl and we'll throw him open, and the receiver will make a contested catch. As you can see, you want to package your best routes out of your best formations and allow the concepts to carry over.

❑ Curl Combos

One of the things that I really like, and I know our quarterbacks have always liked, is what we call "combo" plays. This carries over from the quick game as well. The number one way we like to run them in dropback (not the only way, but our number one way) is off of curls. "Combo" means that I have a curl to one side (normally to the "seam-read" or "control" side) and then on the backside of it, I have a "2 beater" or "cloud beater," something that's going to isolate the linebacker. One of the examples of that is called "480 Z grab."

❑ 480 Z Grab

This would be "doubles right: 480 Z grab" (Figure 4-11). Remember, 400 protection takes the back to the open side, so to that slot receiver side, we're going to have a "seam-read" by the W, a curl route by the X, and then the "check-stretch" by the running back. Then, on the backside, we're going to have a "grab" route, which means the tight end runs a "2nd-level read route," where he gets behind the Sam linebacker and snaps it, in order to work the middle. The Z receiver is going to adjust his split a little bit and come down and try to "grab" the Sam linebacker; he's going to spot up at 5-yards depth at the outside shoulder of where that Sam linebacker originally started. If he gets walled off or cut off (even by the corner), then he'll return back outside, similar to the "slop" or slot-option in the quick game. For the quarterback it's simple: if I get single-high, I'm working the curl side; if I get cover 2, I work the "grab" side.

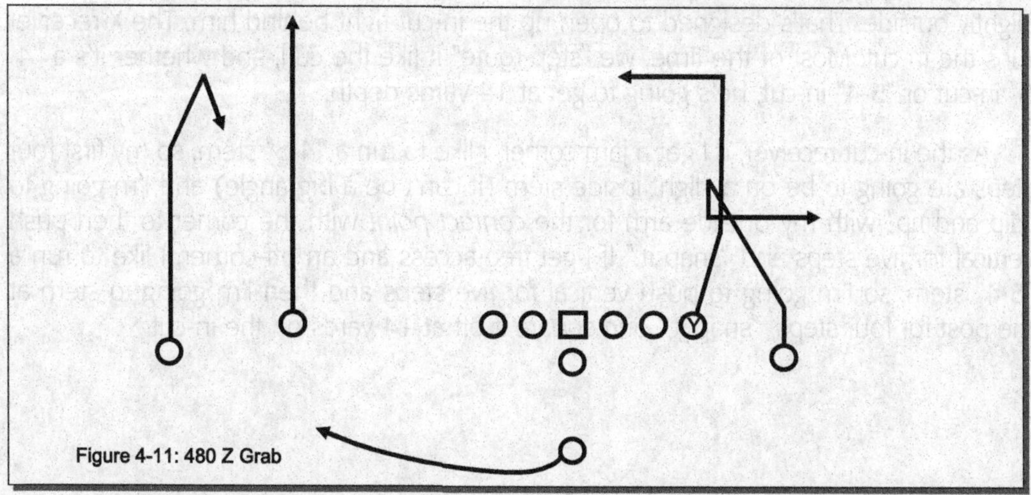

Figure 4-11: 480 Z Grab

**Play: 480 Z Grab**

| Pos: | Assignment: | Coaching Points: |
|---|---|---|
| R | Check 400 protection: run stretch route | |
| W | Run seam. | |
| X | Run 5-4 or 4-5 curl route at 14 yds back to 12. | Eyes inside to LB on 2nd stem. |
| Y | Run read route at 2nd-level depth. | |
| Z | Run grab route. | |
| QB | Homerun: W  Key: FS<br>Progression: vs. 1 high  vs. 2 high<br>1. X  1. Y<br>2. R  2. Z<br><br>Outlet: R | vs. cover 2: think strong (grab side) |

If I get "quarter-quarter-half," I can't be wrong at quarterback, because both sides should win against that coverage. One thing that I have to understand that if it's *true quarters* coverage, then I need to work the curl side, because that safety can be sitting right down on top of the tight-end's read route.

❑ 70 X Laker

You can do this same thing to the other side and call "double right: 70 X grab" (Figure 4-12). You could also call "70 X Laker" (Figure 4-13). That would give your tight end the "seam-read," your Z the curl route and your running back the "check-stretch," where 70 protection takes the back strongside. If you think in concepts, you can see that is still that same combination that we like to work. On the backside, "X Laker," is where the W (slot receiver) would try to work a "pivot" route on that outside linebacker. He takes a little bit of time with his release—he doesn't want to do it too soon—works at him, looks him in the eyes, sits down "with his dukes up," and if he doesn't get the ball, he slides slightly outside. That's designed to open up the in-cut right behind him. The X receiver runs the in-cut. Most of the time, we "step-route" it like the curl, and whether it's a "4-5" in-cut or "5-4" in-cut, he's going to get at 14 yards depth.

As the in-cut receiver, if I get a jam corner, I like to run a "4-5" stem, so my first four steps are going to be on a slight inside stem (it can't be a big angle) and I'm going to "dip and rip" with my outside arm for the *contact point* with the corner to then push vertical for five steps and "snap it." If I get free-access and an off-corner, I like to run a "5-4" stem, so I'm going to push vertical for five steps and then I'm going to stem at the post for four steps, "snap it," and square it off at 14 yards on the in-cut.

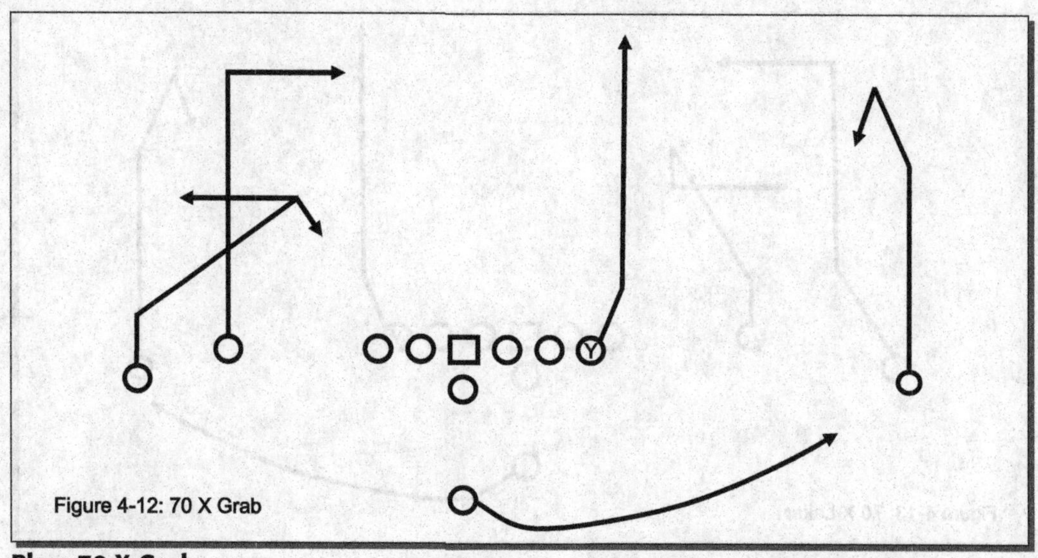


Figure 4-12: 70 X Grab

**Play: 70 X Grab**

| Pos: | Assignment: | Coaching Points: |
|---|---|---|
| R | Check 70 protection. Run stretch route. | |
| W | Run read route at 2nd-level depth. | |
| X | Run grab route. | |
| Y | Run seam route. | |
| Z | Run 5-4 or 4-5 curl route at 14 yds back to 12. | Eyes inside to LB on 2nd stem. |
| | Homerun: Y Key: pre-snap: FS<br>Progression: vs. 1 high vs. 2 high<br>1. Y 1. W<br>2. Z 2. X<br>3. R post-snap: str flat defender or Will<br>Outlet: R | |

Ideally, you'd like to say you're "coming downhill at 89 degrees." If you get "2 man" or you get "press-man," the most important aspect is that you push vertical and you *get out* of that break. You can now *roll* out of it and get across the field, and beat that coverage across the field. There, you don't want to be coming to a stop and snapping it, you want to be rolling out of it and running vs. press man-to-man.

The timing between X and W is really important, so that we're able to try to "grab" that linebacker and open the in-cut up right behind him. Again, it's the same progression, whether I'm reading the "curl side" or the "Laker side." That's a good example of some of the base combinations off 2x2.

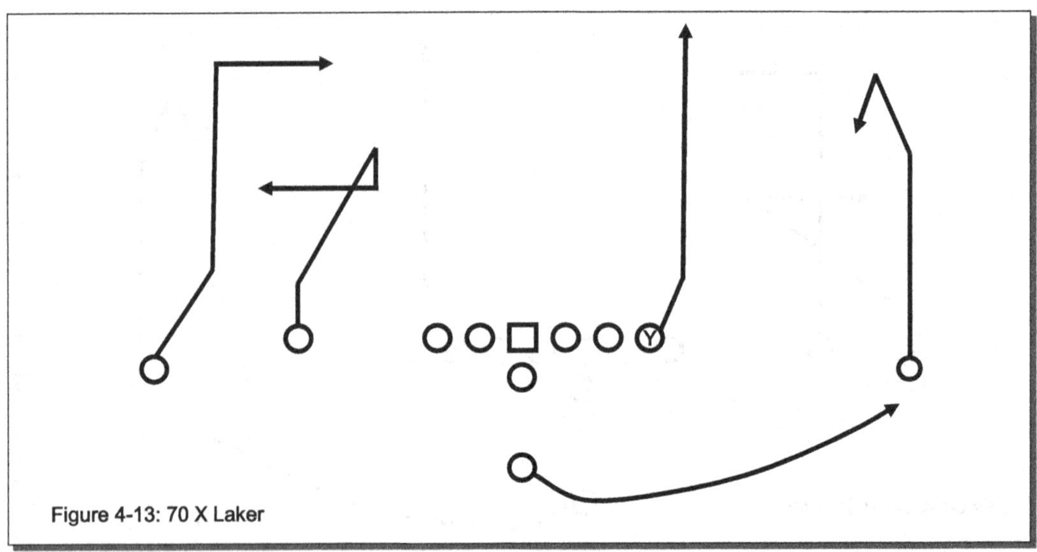


Figure 4-13: 70 X Laker

**Play: 70 X Laker**

| Pos: | Assignment: | Coaching Points: |
|---|---|---|
| R | Check 70 Protection. Run stretch route. | |
| W | Run pivot route. | |
| X | Run 14-yd in. | |
| Y | Run seam route. | |
| Z | Run 5-4 or 4-5 curl at 14 yds back to 12. | Eyes inside to LB on 2nd stem. |
| QB | Homerun: Y Key: pre-snap: FS<br>Progression: vs. 1 high vs. 2 high<br>1. Y 1. X<br>2. Z 2. W<br>3. R post-snap: str flat defender<br>Outlet: R | vs. cover 2: think weak (Laker). |

# In-Cuts

We don't devote a numbered concept category to in-cuts, but we add them as "combos" to all our various core plays. There are some important coaching points we found that we needed to emphasize to get good at them. For example, we don't ever go out and throw in-cuts on air. I always put an outside linebacker and an inside linebacker out there and you throw the in-cut into the open hole, when the receiver is behind the first linebacker. Because if you just go out with the receiver and a quarterback and throw in-cuts on air, you're going to have 50% incompletions. If you go with the receiver and a quarterback and throw in-cuts with those two linebackers standing there, you're going to be up at 80% completions. It's *unbelievable*. The difference is just unbelievable.

We've evolved to where we want to throw in-cuts *between* the linebackers, rather than throw *over* them, for a couple reasons. First, I think that it depends on the *depth* of the cut. If you're running the 14-yard in-cut, then you really have to throw in the open hole. In the NFL, we were good at running the 18-yard in-cut (or deeper), so we could throw it early and over the top of the linebackers. In Jacksonville, Mark Brunell liked taking a 5-step drop out of the gun, so he could see them set up and he could really throw them. But that also creates the second reason we don't throw over linebackers, in that we throw fewer of those deep 7-step drops (5-step in shotgun) and the depth of the route needs to time up with the drop of the quarterback. Those deep 7-step drops make the job of the tackles harder. Our great tackle Tony Boselli would come back and tell us about it, because he didn't want Mark that deep. So, the conflict was if I tell the tackles the quarterback is going to be at that depth, and then the tackle comes back and gets on you about it. It was the same with Lamar Jackson: I *know* he can throw them—he's an excellent deep in-cut thrower—but we didn't throw the 18+ in-cuts, because the 14-yard route with a 5-step drop is simply more consistent, both for the protection and in terms of the throw itself. So, I would say that we "get whatever we coach" with those throws and we've had nice success with them over the years.

❑ Y Chop, Z Ice

We have numerous other tags we can add. We like to add a "combo" to the fieldside of our base "Y option" play. We call this "trey right: 480 Y chop" (Figure 4-14). In this instance, we can throw the seam route to the field for a "home run," if the safety gives us an advantageous look. If we get a strongside rotation (the strong safety dropping down toward the slot), the progression takes us to the "curl/stretch" on the single-receiver side.

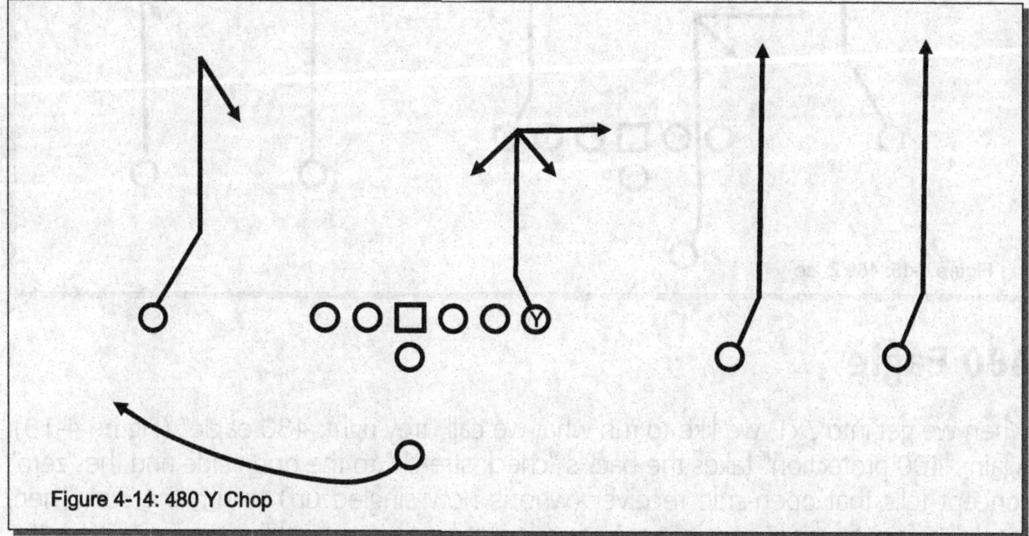


Figure 4-14: 480 Y Chop

**Play: 480 Y Chop**

| Pos: | Assignment: | Coaching Points: |
|---|---|---|
| R | Check 400 protection. Run stretch route. | |
| W | Seam. | Outside release |
| X | Outside release go. | Max split |
| Y | Run 10-yd streak route. Break out. Get open! | |
| Z | | |
| QB | Homerun:<br>Progression: 1. W vs. Strongside rotation: 1. Z<br>2. Y 2. R<br><br>Outlet: R | |

We can also tag this "Z ice" to give the singled receiver the in-cut. We can do this, if he's a better in-cut runner than X (X Laker, falcon, etc.). In this case, we would introduce it as a "9" concept, since we're now worked away from a base curl. If we call "trey right: 489 Z ice" (Figure 4-15), you can still understand the foundation of the play, if you know the basic concept. Once again, the idea is to think in *concepts*, and then think about building them into *packages*.

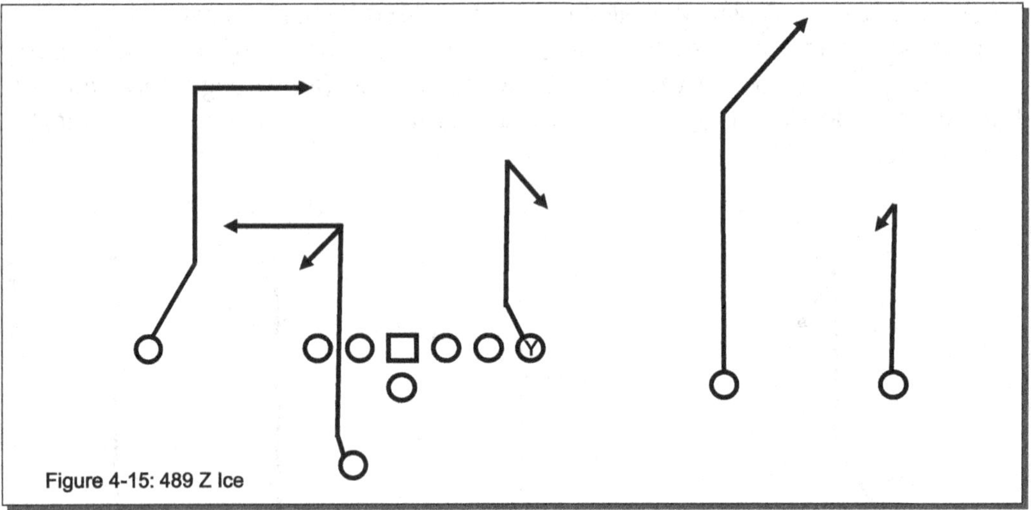

Figure 4-15: 489 Z Ice

## 480 Eagle

When we get into 3x1, we like to run what we call "trey right: 480 eagle" (Figure 4-16). Again, "400 protection" takes the back's "check-stretch" to the open side and the "zero" concept tells that open-side receiver (who is now singled up) to run the curl. Then, "eagle" refers to the 3-receiver side and is similar to our "grab" concept, but for the

**Play: 489 Z Ice**

| Pos: | Assignment: | Coaching Points: |
|---|---|---|
| R | Check 400 protection. Run 5-yd outside option route. | |
| W | Run corner route at 12 yds. | Must outside release. |
| X | Run 6-yd gain hitch. | |
| Y | Run 10-yd stick route. | |
| Z | Run 12-14 yd in route. | |
| QB | Homerun: Y<br>Progression: 1. Z<br>2. R<br>vs. weakside rotation: 1. Y<br>2. X | vs. pressure: alert check |

inside receivers. To that side, the tight end (or whoever is #3) is going to have "the streak-read." If the middle is open, he wants to "take it through for a touchdown" and with the middle-closed, he's going to "snap it" at 2nd-level depth. The #2 receiver is going to run what we call a "snag-option." He wants to take a little bit of time, and then start in on a "snag" route and read the Mike linebacker. If the Mike linebacker walls the tight end, he's going to stay on the move, catch the ball from the quarterback, and get north and south. (Though he has to be aware of the far linebacker, he can't just run in there and get whacked by the Will!) If the Mike linebacker is in "nowhere land," where he just kind of hesitates and stops, then the slot receiver will run a snag route, "put his dukes up," and catch the ball in space. If he gets walled off, then he's going to return back outside. The #1 receiver outside of that is running a comeback route, which is there if the quarterback has to move or come out late (we can also throw that comeback, if for some reason they're trying to work the corner to the inside, but it would be an "alert" to do it).

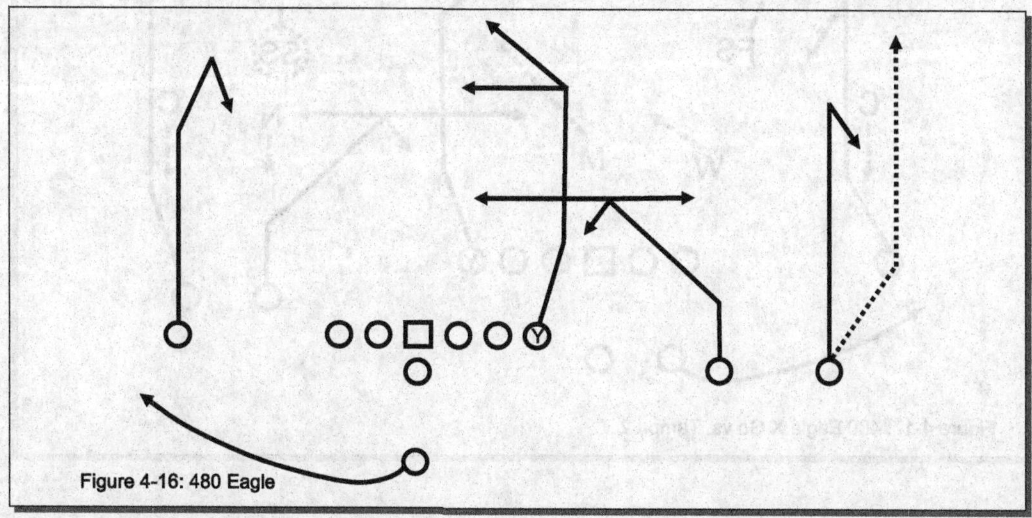

Figure 4-16: 480 Eagle

**Play: 480 Eagle**

| Pos: | Assignment: | Coaching Points: |
|---|---|---|
| R | Check 400 protection. Run stretch route. | |
| W | Run 6-yd snag option route. | Key man over Y. If cut-off, return outside. |
| X | Run 15-yd caddy. | vs. cover 2: convert fade. |
| Y | Run streak read at 2nd-level depth. | vs. cover 2: take the middle. |
| Z | Run 5-4 or 4-5 curl route at 14 yds back to 12. | |
| QB | Homerun:<br>Progression: 1. Y-W<br>vs. field rotation: Z-R<br><br>Outlet: R | vs. cover 2: work 2-on-1 ball Y-X to W. |

❑ 480 Eagle, X Go (vs. Tampa 2)

There have been times when teams have run "2 Tampa" against us, the Mike is running down the middle and the safety to the field is not getting any width at all. There, we want to be able to call "trey right: 480 eagle, X/Z go" (Figure 4-17). That tells the quarterback to read the "2 on 1" ball between the Y and the X, and it's an *alert* that the safety's not getting any width, he's just backpedaling straight back down the hash. (My belief in "2 Tampa" is that safety should be getting width, because it's basically a "3-deep" type of coverage. You need to have something to go after him when he's not doing that. We've made this work and have gotten some big plays throughout the years doing it.)

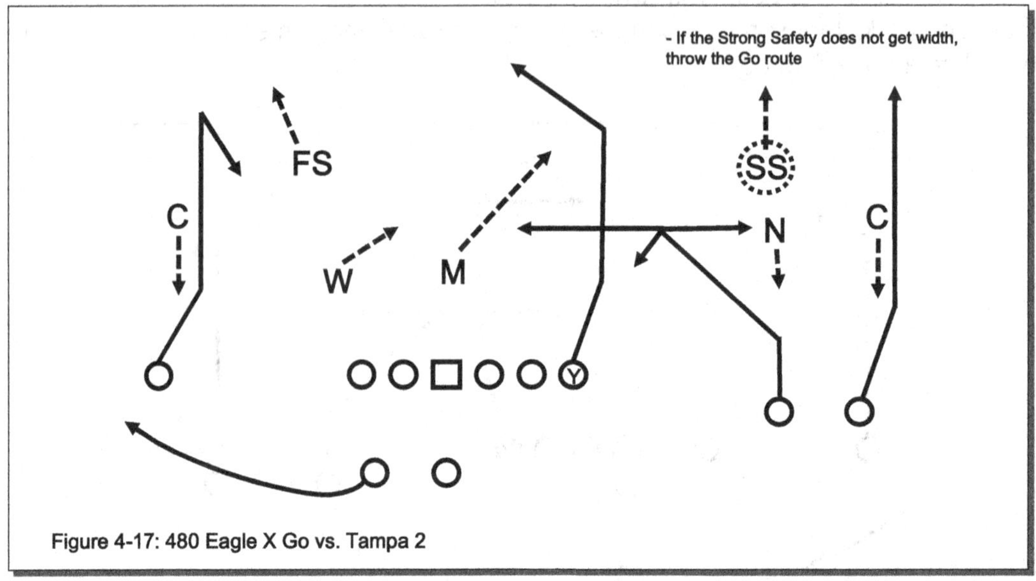

Figure 4-17: 480 Eagle X Go vs. Tampa 2

❑ 480 Falcon

The next thing that we like to run off 3x1 is what we call "480 falcon." In this case, you've again got the "curl / stretch" into the boundary ("480"), but the "falcon" tag is a way for us to work an in-cut on the 3-receiver side (Figure 4-18). You've now got the tight end running a seam route tight over his alignment, so we still have the ability to get the ball down the middle vs. cover 2. He wants to make sure he gets vertical, but he can't get wide. He wants to stay as "tight over his alignment" as he can to maintain spacing from the in-cut outside of him. (If we need to, we can flex him a little bit at times to get the release we need. We call that formation "flood.")

The W (#2 receiver) is basically running the same thing he runs on "Laker," only this time he stays right on the hash. He wants to come off the ball at a controlled speed, accelerate a little bit to six yards, turn to show his numbers, and "put his dukes

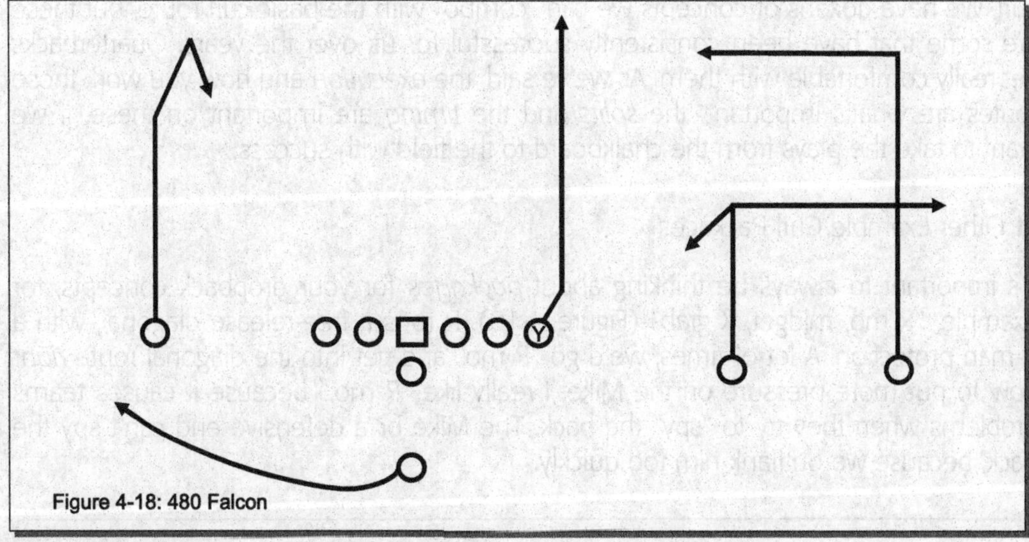

Figure 4-18: 480 Falcon

**Play: 480 Falcon**

| Pos: | Assignment: | Coaching Points: |
|---|---|---|
| R | Check 400 protection run stretch | |
| W | Run 6 yd block route. Then slide to sideline | Hook based on defender's leverage |
| X | Run 14 yd in-out | |
| Y | Run seam | |
| Z | Run 5-4 or 4-5 curl route at 14 yds back to 12 | |
| QB | Homerun: Y<br>Progression: 1 X<br>2 W<br>Vs. strong side rotation Z-R | Vs cov 2 alert Y |

up" to the quarterback. Then if he doesn't get the ball, he slides back outside. The #1 receiver has to adjust his split properly (he cuts it down a little bit to what we call a "divide" split). In this instance, you would like to run a "point-to-point" 14-yard in-cut and time it out between him and the W on that "nickel" defender, so he can get into that open seam. If the Mike carries the tight end down the seam and the nickel latches down on the W, then the in-cut comes open right behind them. It's been a very good play for us for 1st-and-10 but it's also been a really good play on 3rd-&-long.

The *timing* for the quarterback and where he throws the ball is really what's important. I always try to have that *strike point* on that in-cut to be the receiver's *helmet*. Then, all he has to do is reach his hands up and catch the football. Receivers like to catch balls thrown at their *helmet*. It's easy for them. The quarterback has to understand that the *strike point* is really important.

The aforementioned are just some examples of the *combo* routes that we like off a curl. We have dozens of concepts we can "combo" with the basic curl route, but these are some that have been consistently successful for us over the years. Quarterbacks get really comfortable with them. As we've said, the *execution* and how you work those routes are what's important: the *splits* and the *timing* are important on these, if we want to take the plays from the chalkboard to the field with success.

❑ Other Example Curl Packages

It's important to always be thinking about *packages* for your dropback concepts, for example, "R mo, midget, X grab" (Figure 4-19). R runs a free-release diagonal, with a 5-man protection. A lot of times, we'd go "R mo" and get into the diagonal route *right now* to put more pressure on the Mike. I really like "R mo," because it causes teams problems when they try to "spy" the back. The Mike or a defensive end can't spy the back, because we outflank him too quickly.

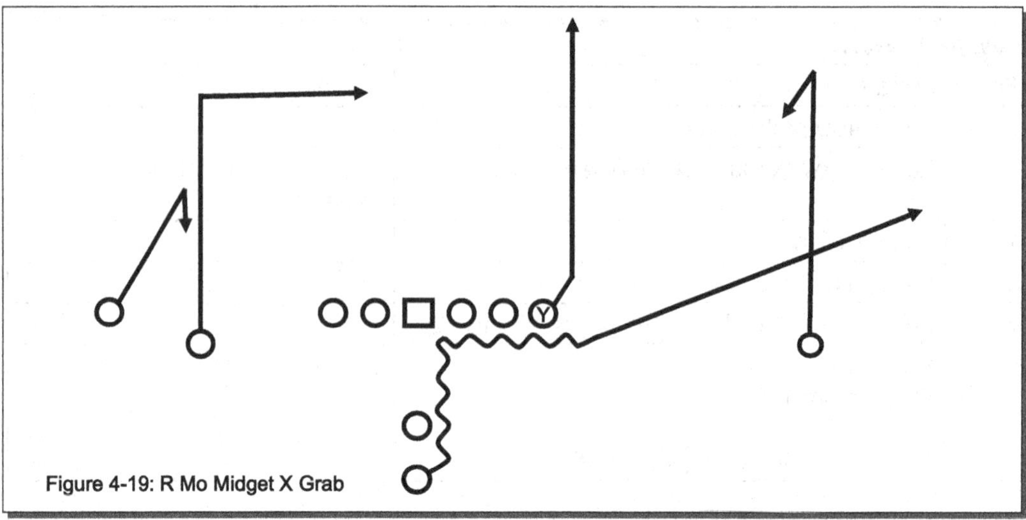

Figure 4-19: R Mo Midget X Grab

"480 Dakota" also became really good for us as part of the package. The quarterback wants to read the Will. If he follows the slot on the crosser, you know it's man coverage, so the quarterback reads "curl to back." If he stays or sits, then you "high-low" from Y to W (Figure 4-20). The tight end thinks to "spot up" over the ball at 10 yards and then if you don't get it right away, you work back down your stem. We caught a lot of those as well, especially if the quarterback has to flush up or moves and it pops open late.

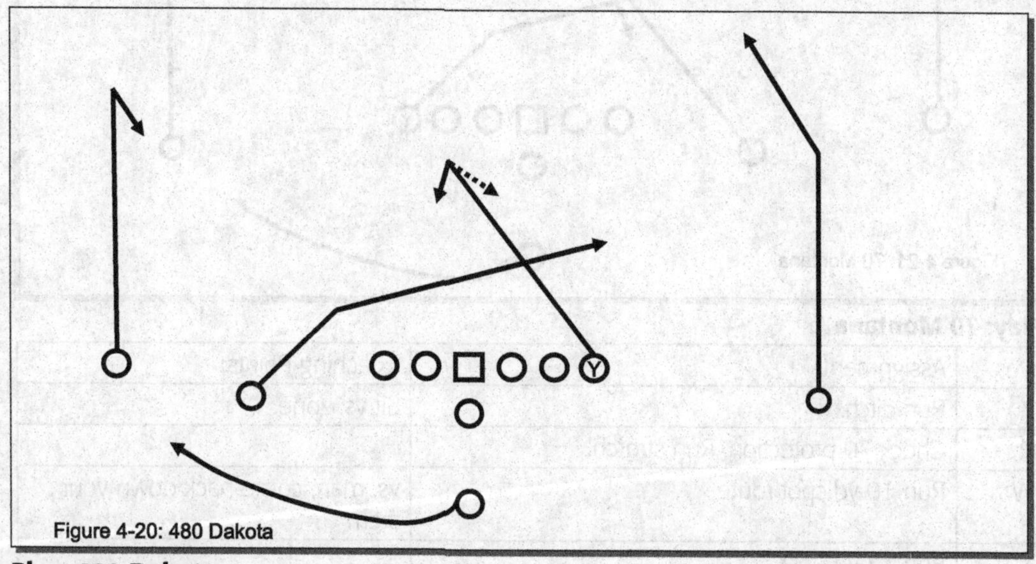

Figure 4-20: 480 Dakota

**Play: 480 Dakota**

| Pos: | Assignment: | Coaching Points: |
|---|---|---|
| Y | Run 10-yd spot route. | vs. man come back down your stem |
| R | Check 400 protection. Run stretch. | |
| W | Run ditch. | Sit vs. zone. |
| X | 14-yd point to point curl. | |
| Z | Run 12-yd post. | |

"70 Montana" is the same concept but inverted (Figure 4-21). The quarterback still reads the defender over the crosser (here, it's the tight end) to determine if it's a "curl-flat" or a "high-low" read. It really screws up "match" coverage; there's times where the outside linebacker would turn the spot runner loose to pick up the drag, but Mike is also covering him too and the middle of the field ends up completely uncovered.

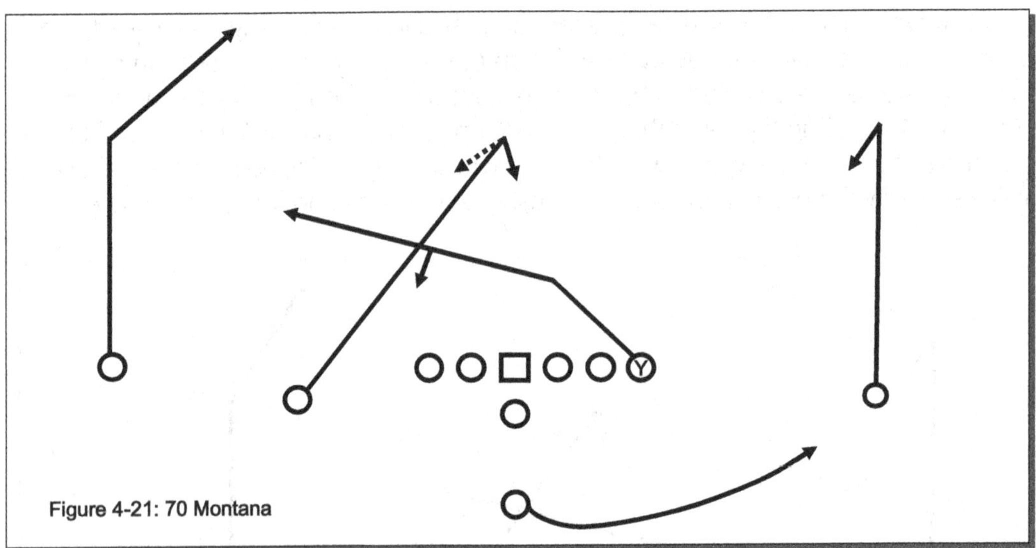

Figure 4-21: 70 Montana

**Play: 70 Montana**

| Pos: | Assignment: | Coaching Points: |
|---|---|---|
| Y | Run ditch. | Sit vs. zone. |
| R | Check 70 protection. Run stretch. | |
| W | Run 10-yd spot route. | vs. man, come back down your stem |
| X | Run 12-yd post. | |
| Z | Run 14-yd point-to-point curl. | |

Those are also good examples of how we use code words off our base numbered system to indicate additional concepts. You might not technically consider this a curl-combo or a crosser-combo since it's not a pure "2 beater/1 beater" read, but it's definitely a "coverage progression" type of play. It's a form of the curl package and it's been very good for us.

## Outs and Corners

The next concept that we talked about and arguably utilize more in the NFL than college football is our "outs/corners." In the dropback game, there's basically three different type of outs for an outside receiver: one would be the "6-step speed out" where you've got a great stride and you're able to roll out of it and run it from 10-to-12 yards ending up at 12 yards, much like that "Dallas" route off of the quick game. The ability to bend and roll and come out of it takes great get off; it's better against zone coverage and "off" man, which you see more in the NFL than you do in college. It's also easier in the NFL than in college, because a lot of times in college, you're getting press corner into the boundary (no free access) and an off-corner to the field, which is a long way to throw it from the wider college hash marks.

Receivers have to adjust the route. If you get press, it becomes what we call a "trace" route, where I'm going to come off the ball and get vertical like running a fade, throw the hip of the corner by me, and "retrace" back down my stem. The quarterback will then take a hitch and throw the ball to my outside hip.

If he is throwing the speed-out, the key for a quarterback is to be able to dropback and keep his eyes *straight ahead* at least for three steps, then throw it 5-steps "off the plant" *before* the receiver breaks. If you try to hitch up and throw a speed-out, you increase your chances of seeing it go the other way for a touchdown.

Sometimes, in the college game, we throw what I call a "semi" or a "poor man's out," which is basically a "mini" comeback at 12-yards. On this route, you break on an angle to the sideline at 12 yards and allow the quarterback to take the hitch to throw it, as opposed to throwing off the plant. Hence, a "poor man's" route. A quarterback really does have to have a strong arm and great sense of timing to throw a true speed-out. And like I said it's something that's a lot easier to do in NFL football than in college football.

Then, there's also a 15-yard comeback, which we call a "caddy." Some years we were much more effective with that than with the speed-out or semi. In this situation, the quarterback can take a "long 5-step drop," one hitch, and throw the ball to the outside on that 15-yard comeback.

Those are the three different types of outside out-routes we run in the dropback game. With any of these, we merge the routes with the protections the same as we did the curl concepts. In the 2-back sets off the 7-man protection, you start with "61" for your mirrored-out routes on the outside. The tight end has a "streak-read," and both backs have "check-stops" (Figure 4-22). Then, we can tag it "61 semi" (Figure 4-23) or "61 caddy" for a deeper route, using the code word with the numbered concept to get the specific route we want. It really comes down to what your quarterback does best and if you have a real speed-threat receiver who can stride out and roll out of that speed-out.

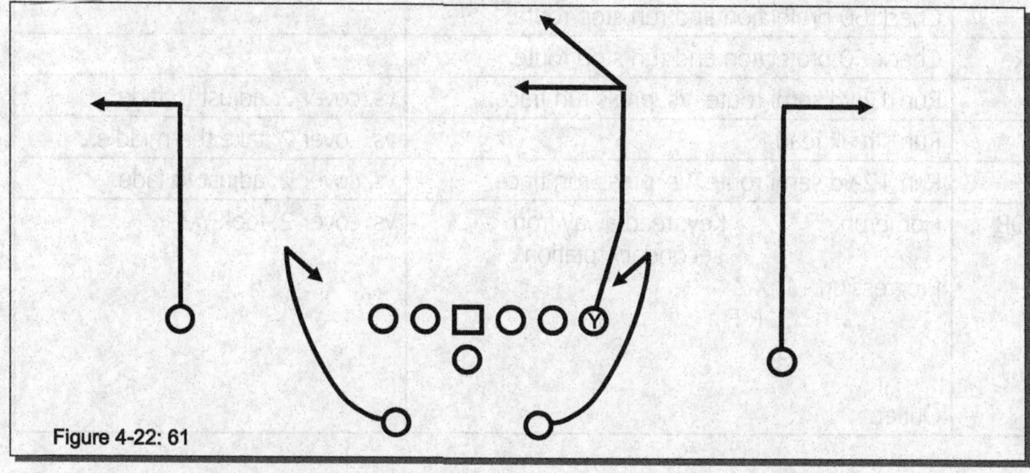

Figure 4-22: 61

**Play: 61**

| Pos: | Assignment: | Coaching Points: |
|---|---|---|
| F | Check 60 protection. Run stop route. | |
| R | Check 60 protection. Run stop route. | |
| X | Run 10-yd speed out vs. press run trace. | vs. cover 2: fade. |
| Y | Run streak read at 2nd-level depth. | vs. cover 2: take the middle. |
| Z | Run 10-yd speed vs. press run trace. | vs. cover 2: fade. |
| QB | Homerun: Key: read away from secondary rotation.<br>Progression: 1. X-Z<br>2. R-F<br>3. Y<br>Outlet: | vs. cover 2: Y-Z-F. 2-on-1 ball. |

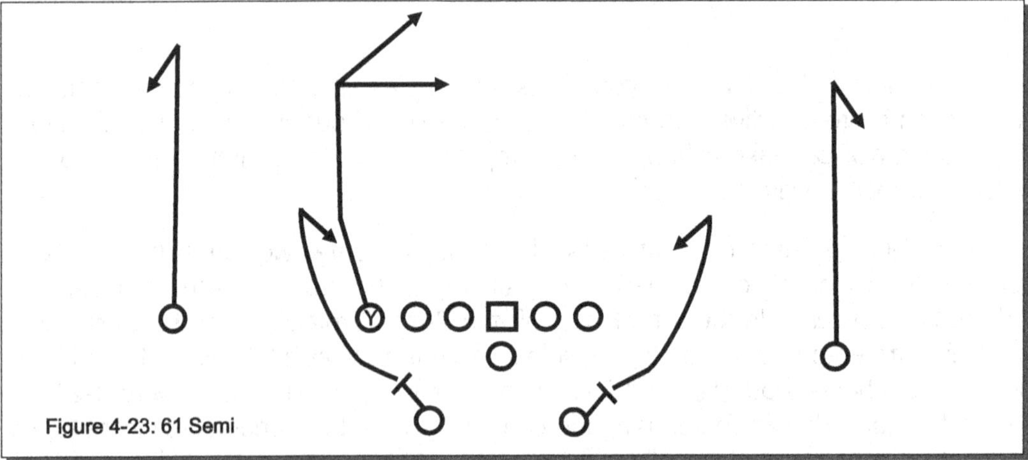

Figure 4-23: 61 Semi

**Play: 61 Semi**

| Pos: | Assignment: | Coaching Points: |
|---|---|---|
| F | Check 60 protection and run stop route. | |
| R | Check 60 protection and run stop route. | |
| X | Run 12-yd semi route. Vs. press run trace. | vs. cover 2: adjust to fade. |
| Y | Run streak read. | vs. cover 2: take the middle. |
| Z | Run 12-yd semi route. Vs. press run trace. | vs. cover 2: adjust to fade. |
| QB | Homerun: Key: read away from secondary rotation.<br>Progression: 1. X-Z<br>2. R-F<br>3. Y<br>Outlet: | vs. cover 2: look Y-Z-F |

❑ Combos and Packages for Out-Routes

There are times we want to "combo" the outs with something inside, such as a "high/low" between the slot receiver and the tight end. The outside-out routes are effective against free-access, 3-deep type coverages and just as we did with quicks and curls. It's useful to be able to "combo" the out-cut with something to handle cover 2. For example, we could call "doubles right 81" or "81 semi" to get a solid protection with the outs on the outside, along with the ability to get the "streak-read" on the inside for cover 2 (Figure 4-24).

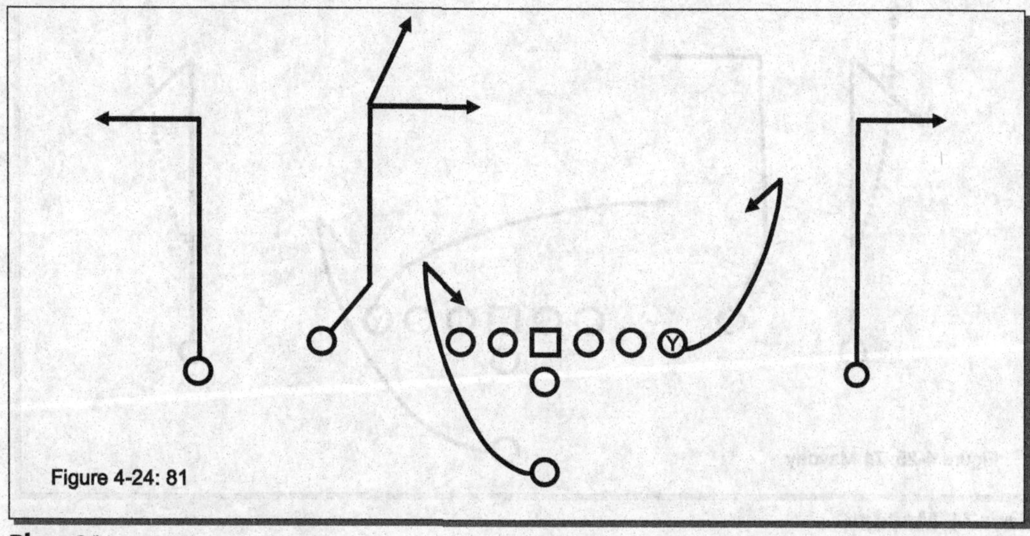

Figure 4-24: 81

**Play: 81**

| Pos: | Assignment: | Coaching Points: |
|---|---|---|
| R | Check 80 protection. Run stop route. | Bdry: 3x1; field 3x3; MOF 3x2. |
| W | Run streak read at 2nd-level depth. | vs. man: snap-post for a TD. |
| X | Run 10-yd speed out. | vs. cover 2: convert fade; vs. press trace. |
| Y | Check 80 protection. Run stop route. | Bdry: 5x1; field 5x3; MOF 5x2. |
| Z | Run 10-yd speed out. | vs. cover 2: convert fade; vs. press trace. |
| QB | Homerun: W Key: pre-snap: FS<br>Progression: 1. X 1. Z post-snap: curl/flat player<br>2. R 2. Y<br>3. W 3. W<br>Outlet: R | vs. cover 2: 2-on-1 ball. W-X-R<br>Alert 1-on-1 to Z. |

Another way you can do it is what we call "71 mayday" (Figure 4-25). This actually started as a 2-minute play, where if I get free-access, I can throw the out, catch the ball, and get out of bounds. If they go cover 2, the W receiver runs a read route, the tight end runs a drag underneath, and the running back checks down three yards outside of the tight end's alignment, three yards past the line of scrimmage. If you're getting cover 2, the quarterback reads the "high-low" inside. If the quarterback checks it down, the back wants to catch it and get vertical. It was a good 2-minute play that carried over. Quarterbacks can execute it and they really like it.

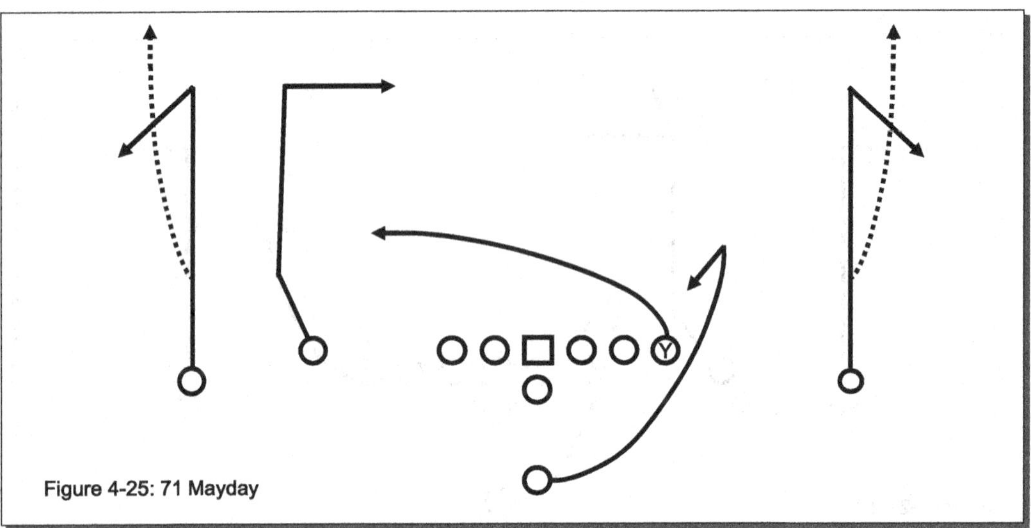

Figure 4-25: 71 Mayday

**Play: 71 Mayday**

| Pos: | Assignment: | Coaching Points: |
|---|---|---|
| R | Check 70 protection. Run stop route. | |
| W | Run read route at 2nd-level depth. | Must get over the top of WLB |
| X | Run 12-yd semi. | vs. cover 2: cover fade vs. press: run trace. |
| Y | Run drag route. | Be at 6 yds over opposite tackle. |
| Z | Run 12-yd semi. | vs. cover 2: convert fade vs. press: run trace. |
| QB | Homerun: Key: pre-snap: FS<br>Progression: 1. Z/X post-snap: curl/flat player or<br>2. W weakside LB<br>3. Y<br>Outlet: R | vs. off corner: throw Z or X<br>vs. cover 2: work W-Y-R<br>vs. LB plug: Y |

And of course, as with the previous packages, you might also add a "run / pass" or "alert" check, where "I'm going to run the ball vs. 2-high and I'm going to throw the ball vs. 1." You can build these off your best runs, as well as from your best personnel groupings and formations, the same as we talked about with the quick game packages, such as "doubles right 71 mayday, *alert*: 24 O" (Figure 4-26). A lot of times, quarterbacks have a clear preference from among all of these.

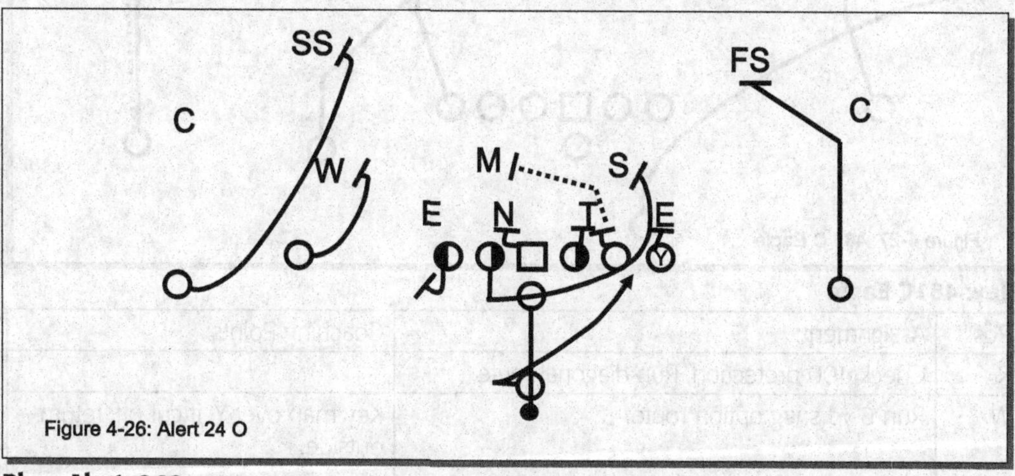

Figure 4-26: Alert 24 O

**Play: Alert: 240**

| Pos: | Assignment: |
|---|---|
| QB | Reverse out. Step at 6 o'clock. Get the ball to R as quickly and as deep as possible. |
| W | Crossfield technique |
| X | Crossfield technique |
| Z | Push crack. |

❑ 481

If you're better at throwing the outs and corners than the curls, you can utilize the combinations we already talked about on the backside of 3x1 sets. So, as opposed to calling "480 Y option, Y chop, falcon or eagle," you could call them "481 falcon" or "481C eagle" (Figure 4-27). In this instance, the only difference is we want to coach the running back a little bit more in conjunction with the outs. When the single receiver has the out-cut instead of a curl, the running back now has what we call a "rule" route, so he needs to really understand the coverage. If it's any single-high, he would run a "check-stop" three yards outside that tackle's alignment, in order to occupy the underneath coverage (we used to run a "medium" route, but sometimes a linebacker would get in the way of the out-cut). The "rule" comes into place against cover 2, where now he adjusts it to a "stretch" route, trying to affect the Will linebacker, so the slot is able to run his route on something like "eagle," catch the ball and go. This way we can take whatever basic outside route we're best at (curl or out) and "combo" it with those "named" concepts on the backside.

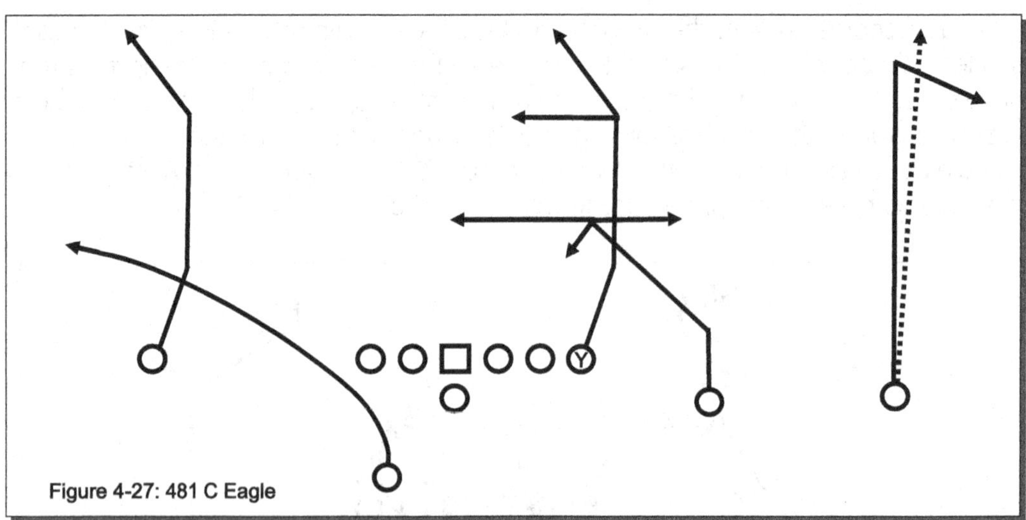

Figure 4-27: 481 C Eagle

**Play: 481C Eagle**

| Pos: | Assignment: | Coaching Points: |
|---|---|---|
| R | Check 400 protection. Run diagonal route. | |
| W | Run 6-yd snag option route. | Key man over Y, if cut off, return outside. |
| X | Run 18-yd comeback. | vs. cover 2: convert to fade. |
| Y | Run streak read at 2nd-level depth. | vs. cover 2: take the middle. |
| Z | Run 4-6 corner route. | |
| QB | Homerun:<br>Progression: vs. 1-on-1: Z-R<br>vs. cover 2: Y-W<br>Outlet: R | vs. cover 2: work 2-on-1 ball Y-X to W. |

❑ Corners (1 "C")

From there, we advance to the corner route concept. What you do is you call "61 C," where "C" means "corner" (Figure 4-28). The way you do that with the college football hash marks is the outside receiver to the field runs a "post-corner," so he's running seven steps, three steps to the post, and then out of it to the corner. The key is that he "sprints three steps out of it," before he looks for the ball, or you end up with a lot of misses right off his fingertips. And he has to know where that "catch point" is, where he can locate the ball. "Sprint three steps out of your break, and then look at the catch point to locate the ball." That route is generally good vs. defenses, where they like the "field corner" to play "middle-inside" leverage or even man coverage.

The boundary receiver runs what we call a "4-5-1" corner route. So, he buys himself some "green" by stemming inside, pushing vertical for five steps, then giving the quarterback an *indicator* with his inside step (that's where the "1" comes into play) and then back out to the corner. Both of them set the angle high, with the regular distance of 25 yards on the sideline (but once you get inside the 30-yard line, you're setting them to the back flag). Then, the quarterback has the responsibility to flatten the receiver out. So, if there's a middle safety back there, he can flatten the receiver out to the sideline to get him the ball on the sideline.

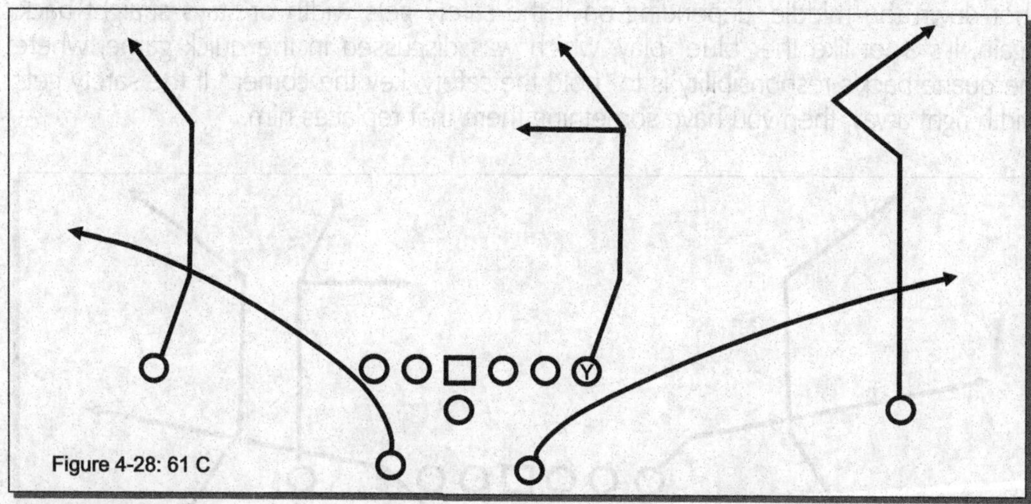

Figure 4-28: 61 C

**Play: 61 "C"**

| Pos: | Assignment: | | Coaching Points: |
|---|---|---|---|
| F | Check 60 protection. Run diagonal route. | | |
| R | Check 60 protection. Run diagonal route. | | |
| X | Run 4-6 corner route. | | |
| Y | Run streak read at 2nd-level depth. | | vs. cover 2: take the middle. |
| Z | Run 7-3 corner route. | | |
| QB | Homerun: Y<br><br>Progression: 1. X-Z<br>2. R-F<br>3. Y<br><br>Outlet: | Key: Read away from secondary rotation. | |

What I really like to do in this instance is get the flat responsibility covered. Whether you do that with a diagonal, a 6-yard out, or whatever fits best into your offense, you have to have somebody who affects the corner, in case it's a "cloud" corner (cover 2 corner), which is what this is really good against. Then, you typically add a "streak-read," and you have diagonals with the backs to both sides, where you may even game plan to have them chip the defensive ends on their way out.

❑ 81 C

In a "doubles" formation, the first call would be "doubles right: 81C," where the running back has the diagonal, the W has the "streak-read," both outside receivers have "corner routes," and the tight end has a "check-diagonal" (Figure 4-29). Your flat responsibility is occupied, and the middle has a chance. If you get true cover 2, you can take a shot down the middle, depending on if the safety gets width or stays straight back. Again, it's a lot like the "blue" play, which was discussed in the quick game, where the quarterback's responsibility is to "hold the safety, key the corner." If the safety gets width right away, then you have something there that replaces him.

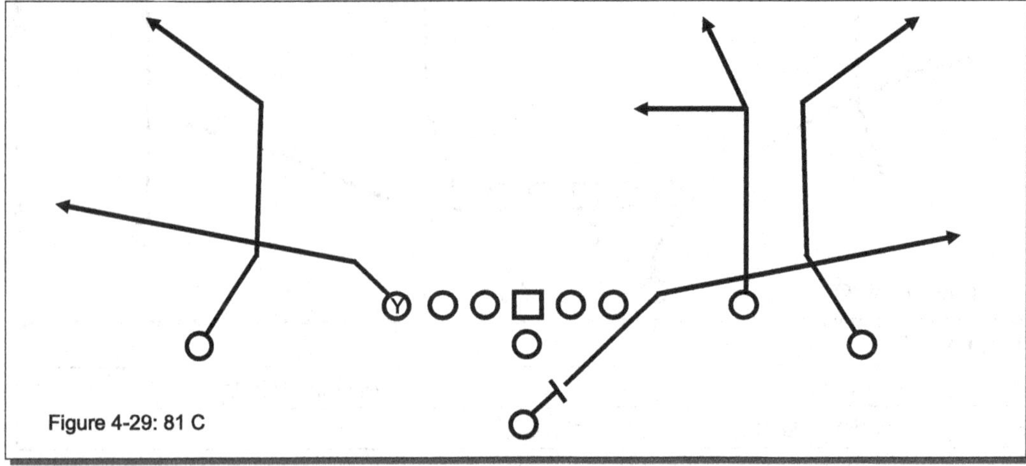


Figure 4-29: 81 C

**Play: 81C**

| Pos: | Assignment: | | Coaching Points: |
|---|---|---|---|
| R | Check 80 protection and run diagonal route. | | |
| W | Run streak read. | | |
| X | Run corner sell the post at 12 yards. Run 25-yd corner route. | | |
| Y | Check 80 protection and run diagonal. | | |
| Z | Run corner sell the post at 12 yards. Run 25-yd corner route. | | |
| QB | Homerun: W<br><br>Progression:<br>1. Z/W or X/W<br>2. Y or R<br><br>Outlet: R | Key: pre-snap: FS<br>post-snap:<br>safety to<br>corner | Cover 2 look: must hold the safety and key the corner. |

❑ 81 C Wasp

You can add other combos to the "outs and corners" category, and we've used dozens of them over the years, especially from 2x2. "81C wasp" is one that has always been good for us. This is also an example of the "11 equals 12 personnel in the passing game" package of "doubles snug" (where the Z reduces this split) and "wing slot" (Figure 4-30). We used a "W" name for the concept, to be a buzz word for the "W" receiver, but I think by now you can see how the concept is compatible with the "wing slot" formation as well.

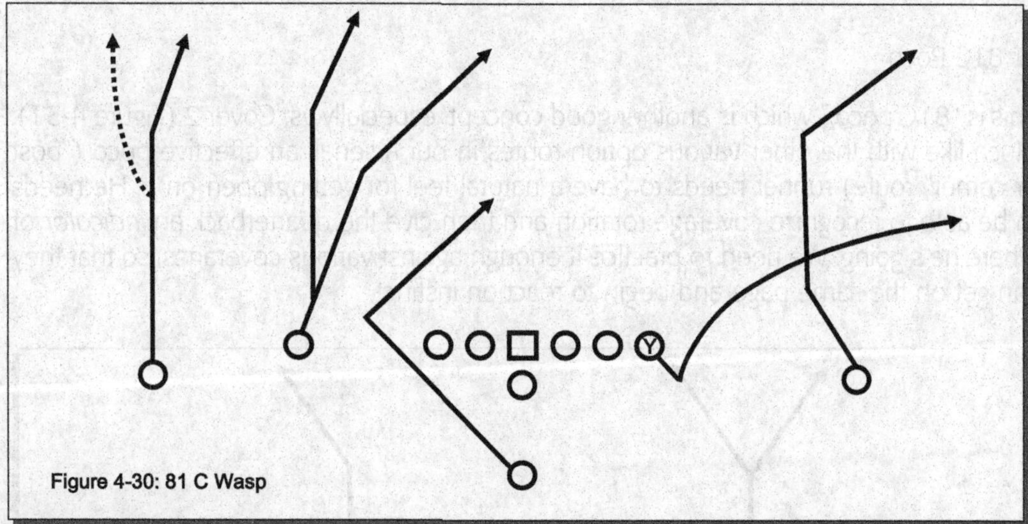

Figure 4-30: 81 C Wasp

**Play: 81C Wasp**

| Pos: | Assignment: | Coaching Points: |
|---|---|---|
| R | Check 80 protection. Run angle route. | |
| W | Run fence post route. | vs. 2 high: thin post, vs. 1 high: fence |
| X | Run 9-step post. 12-14 yds. | Convert vs. cover 2 |
| Y | Check 80 protection. Run diagonal route. | |
| Z | Run corner route. | Field: 7-3 corner. Boundary 4-6 corner |
| QB | Homerun:<br>Progression: <u>1 High:</u><br>1. Z<br>2. Y<br><u>2 High:</u><br>1. W<br>2. X<br><br>Outlet: R | |

In this instance, we've got the same corner route by the Z (or the T if we like it from "wing slot") and the Y on the "check-diagonal." The "wasp" concept is a double-post that converts. In other words, if we get single-high or quarters, we're running double-post. If you get cover 2, we adjust to a go route on the outside and w takes the middle, so you get a 2-on-1 ball on the backside safety.

To give the quarterback a passing lane, we like to have the running back run an angle route. If the quarterback picks the "wasp" side and he doesn't like it, he has the running back coming right into his vision on an angle route for a check-down. This is a very good combo route for us, from either personnel grouping or formation.

❑ 81C Poco

This is "81C poco," which is another good concept, especially vs. Cover 2 (Figure 4-31). Much like with the other various option routes in our arsenal, an effective poco ("post or corner" route) runner needs to have a natural feel for getting open on it. He needs to be able to recognize coverage rotation and then give the quarterback an *indicator* of where he's going. We need to practice it enough against various coverages, so that they can get on the same page and begin to react on instinct.

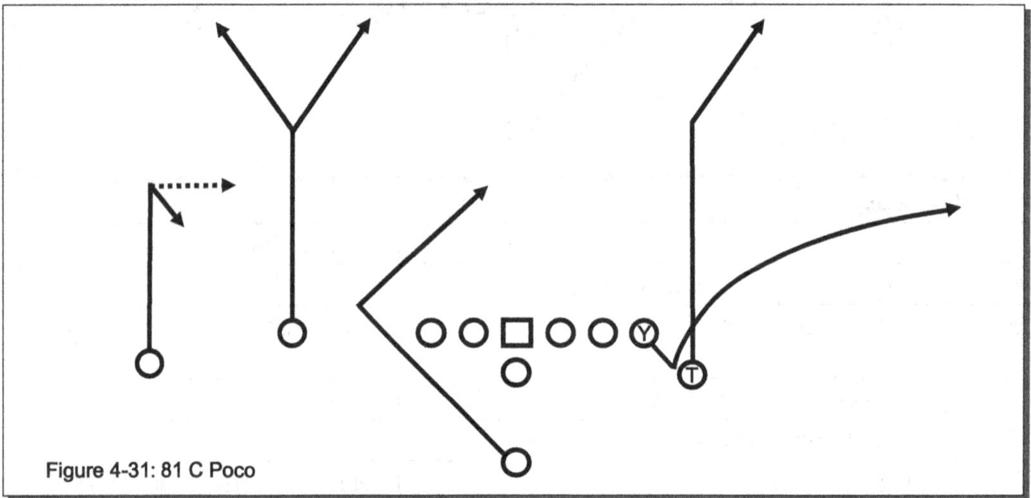

Figure 4-31: 81 C Poco

❑ 81C, X Blade

This is called "81C, X blade" (Figure 4-32). When we first put it in, the "blade" runner (in this case X) used to fall down and then get up to trail behind W. Now, W runs a corner route and X needs to trail four yards behind him, and then break to the post. You're affecting that weak safety; it's a *chunk* play, good in 2-minute situations or in plus territory.

**Play: 81C Poco**

| Pos: | Assignment: | Coaching Points: |
|---|---|---|
| R | Check 80 protection. Run angle route. | |
| T | Run corner | |
| X | Smash read. | |
| Y | Check 80 protection. Run diagonal route. | |
| Z | Run post or corner route. | Run route off safety. |
| QB | Homerun: Z Key: pre-snap: SS<br>Progression: 1. Z-X-R post-snap: curl/flat player<br>2. T-Y<br>Outlet: | |

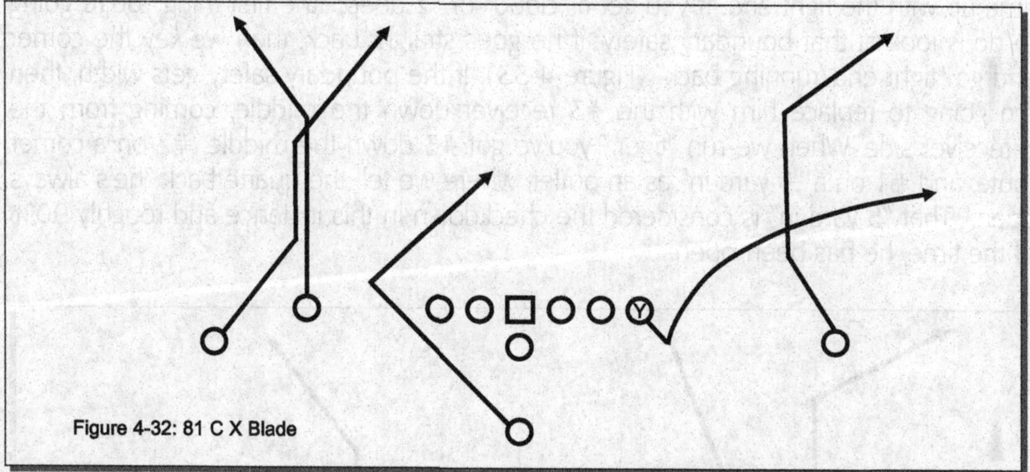

Figure 4-32: 81 C X Blade

**Play: 4-32**

| Pos: | Assignment: | Coaching Points: |
|---|---|---|
| R | Check 80 protection. Run angle route. | |
| W | Run corner route. | |
| X | Stem in & run post. | Get 2 yds outside & behind W before snapping post. |
| Y | Check 80 protection. Run diagonal route. | |
| Z | Run corner route. | Field: 7-3 corner. Boundary 4-6 corner |
| QB | Homerun:<br>Progression: 1 High:<br>1. Z<br>2. Y<br>2 High:<br>1. W<br>2. X<br>Outlet: R | |

The back checks "80 protection" and runs an angle route to open up a passing lane to X on post. Some weeks, we game plan for the back to "chip" the defensive end on his way out as well. "81C" puts the same corner route to the callside. We can also tag this "blade" concept to our smash category, if we want to package it differently for a given game plan. We can illustrate that in context, when we get to the "6" concept category.

❑ Trips 71 C Tiger

We can also build combo calls out of our "trips" formation and involve the tight end on the primary corner route. On "trips right: scat 71C tiger," the tight end (who is now the singled receiver to the callside) is running the corner route, with the running back in the flat. The back has a "scat" or free-release and runs a "bend" route, in order to time up with the tight end. If you get a "cloud" or "2 deep," the first thing you're going to do is look at that boundary safety; if he goes straight back, then we *key* the corner and go "tight end/running back" (Figure 4-33). If the boundary safety gets width, then I'm going to replace him with the #3 receiver down the middle, coming from the 3-receiver side. When we run "tiger," you've got #3 down the middle, #2 on a corner route, and #1 on a "5-yard in" as an outlet, where we tell the quarterback "he's always open." That "5-yard in" is considered the checkdown in this instance and roughly 90% of the time, he has been open.

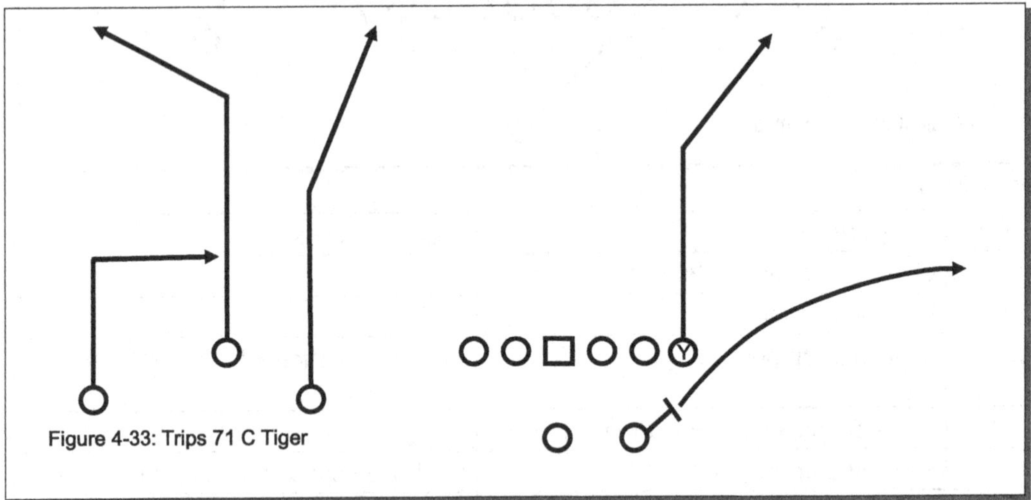

Figure 4-33: Trips 71 C Tiger

(Note: this is a good example of using the term "scat," instead of calling the play "lion tiger," which we also could do since it's a 5-man protection. By calling it "scat 71C," we are emphasizing the corner route to both the tight end and quarterback, in order to generate that specific mental image.)

**Play: 4-33**

| Pos: | Assignment: | Coaching Points: |
|---|---|---|
| X | 5-yd under | |
| W | 12-yd corner | |
| R | Check 70 protection. Run diagonal | |
| Y | 12-yd corner | |
| Z | Run post down middle of field. | |
| QB | Homerun: Z Key: pre-snap:<br>FS<br>Progression: vs. 1 high: vs. <u>2 high:</u><br>1. Y 1. Y or Z<br>2. R 2. X<br>3. X<br><br>Outlet: | |

From "trips" you have to be able to live with (and get the quarterback comfortable with) "if I get single-high, I can hit Z on the 'fence post,' or my '5-yard in' is going to be good for me." There, the receiver is going to catch the ball and get yards; he understands "against zone, I get north and south, against man I run away from the guy trying to cover me." The "catch-and-run" element has to come into play there.

When we throw these types of corner routes at the college and pro level, it can be a different type of throw to a tight end, as opposed to a receiver. In general, when you throw a corner route to tight ends, you put the ball on a line, put the ball right on him, and "make him wear it." You usually don't want to be relying on tight ends and running backs to run balls down for you. You need to put the ball on them: on their *body*, on their *helmet,* or on whatever that "strike point" is. By contrast, when you throw corner routes to wide receivers, you can "throw them open" and they'll run the ball down for you.

Depending on your players, you sometimes need to be careful and keep this *in the quarterback room*, between the coach and the quarterbacks. As a quarterback, you have to understand there's certain things you're going to talk about with the head coach, coordinator, and the quarterback coach regarding other players on the team, their strengths and weaknesses and what they can do. There has to be a trust issue, where all that information stays *in the room. It does not leave the room!* That's the decision you made to be a quarterback. Nothing can hurt a team worse than bringing out confidential information that was said in the meeting room and telling another player about it. If you let that kind of thing out, it means you really haven't accepted the responsibility to be a leader and that you don't really want to be a quarterback.

❑ Trips 71C Falcon

You can call the "falcon" concept we talked about before: "trips right: 71C falcon" (Figure 4-34). We still start with that boundary safety vs. "2 I." If the boundary safety (hash defender) goes straight back, I'm again going to read the tight end to the back. If he gets width, I'm then going from Z down the middle, to X on the in-cut, and finally to W on the little "pivot-option" as a checkdown. It's a good, easy, sound progression that is effective against any coverages that we've faced. It works as nicely with the tight end corner route in trips as it does to the singled wide receiver in trey that we previously discussed.

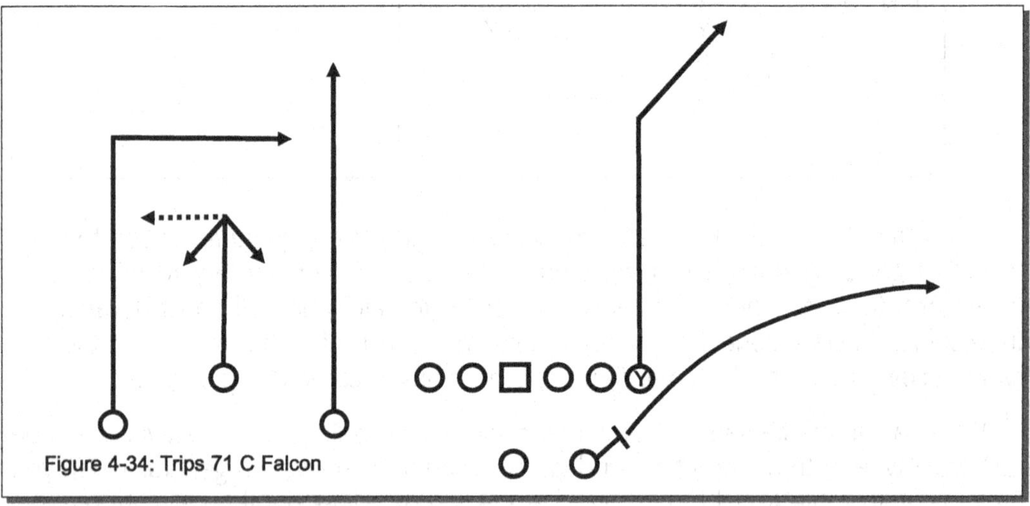

Figure 4-34: Trips 71 C Falcon

**Play: 4-34**

| Pos: | Assignment: | Coaching Points: |
|---|---|---|
| R | Check 70 protection. Run diagonal. | |
| W | Run 6-yd pivot-option. | |
| X | Run 14-yd in-cut. | Divide split. |
| Y | Run corner route. | |
| Z | Run seam. | |
| QB | Homerun: Z<br>Progression: 1. X<br>2. W<br>vs. strongside rotation, can work corner to diagonal<br><br>Outlet: | vs. 2 alert Z |

❑ 481 C, W Shallow

The "W shallow" concept is also great from "trey." One of the things that we got to vs. "quarters" teams, is "trey right: 481C, W shallow" (Figure 4-35). We did that, because a lot of teams were coaching the Will linebacker in quarters "if the back runs a stretch route, hold it and then break to tackle the ball as they to throw it to the back." When the back runs a diagonal route, though, he has to buy it." The key is to understand what they're coaching the Will to do.

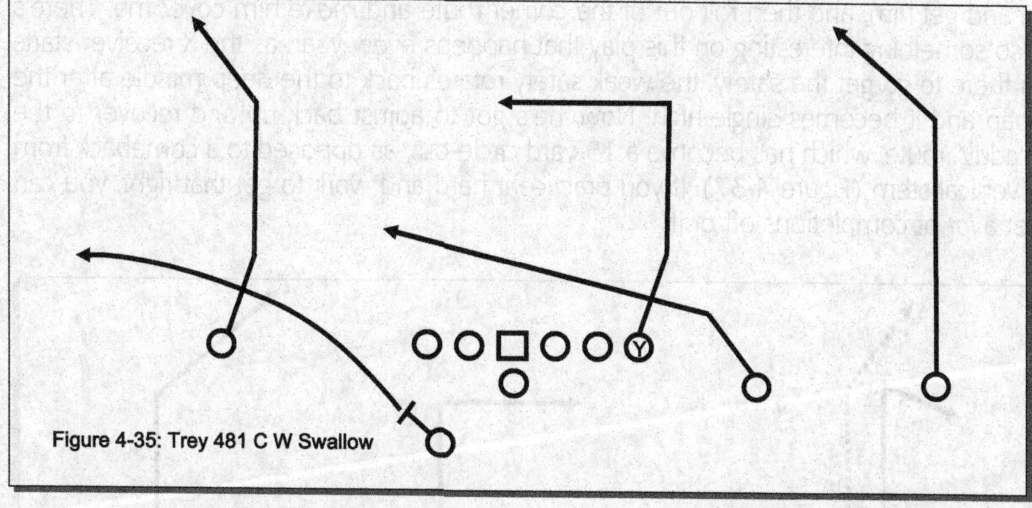


Figure 4-35: Trey 481 C W Swallow

If you get a cloud look, then you've got the corner with the back in the flat, the Y on a "streak read," with W stepping on a 45-degree angle and bringing it. In quarters, the Will has to buy the back and the Mike has a hard time defending both Y to W. So, it's a really good play, especially to get it to a slot receiver who can really catch and run. We also sometimes give Z a comeback route out there, in case of a scramble.

## Posts and Toppers

The "2" concept category in the dropback game is based on the post route and what we call our "topper" concept, which is a post route over the top of a read-route or in-cut. Again, players need to understand the pass protection that is called with each play, in order to be able to picture the entire pass route. We can add code words, the same as we do for the curl and out concept categories. What we begin to see at this stage is that several of our "combo" passes could technically fit into multiple categories (similar play, different name), so the players' understanding of the *concepts* becomes critical as these ideas continue to multiply.

### ❑ 62 Z Topper

In college football, because of the hashes, one of the best ways we've found to run a post is to the field vs. quarters coverage. One of the ways we do that from "regular" (21) personnel is to call "gun right, 62 Z topper" (Figure 4-36). The first thing that comes into play is actually the X receiver, running what we call a "circus" route. X is going to line up, read the coverage, and either run that 15 yard "caddy" against free-access 1-high, or convert to a "corner-out" (that ends up more of a "banana corner") against 2-high. The underlying idea is to occupy a backside quarters safety; I have to go in and get him, and then roll out of the corner route and *make* him cover me. There's also something interesting on this play that happens every year: as the X receiver starts in there to go get the safety, the weak safety rotates back to the deep middle after the snap and it becomes single-high. Now, he's got to adjust back up and recover to the "caddy" route, which has become a 15-yard circle-out, as opposed to a comeback from a vertical stem (Figure 4-37). If you practice it hard and work to get that right, you can get a *lot* of completions off of it!

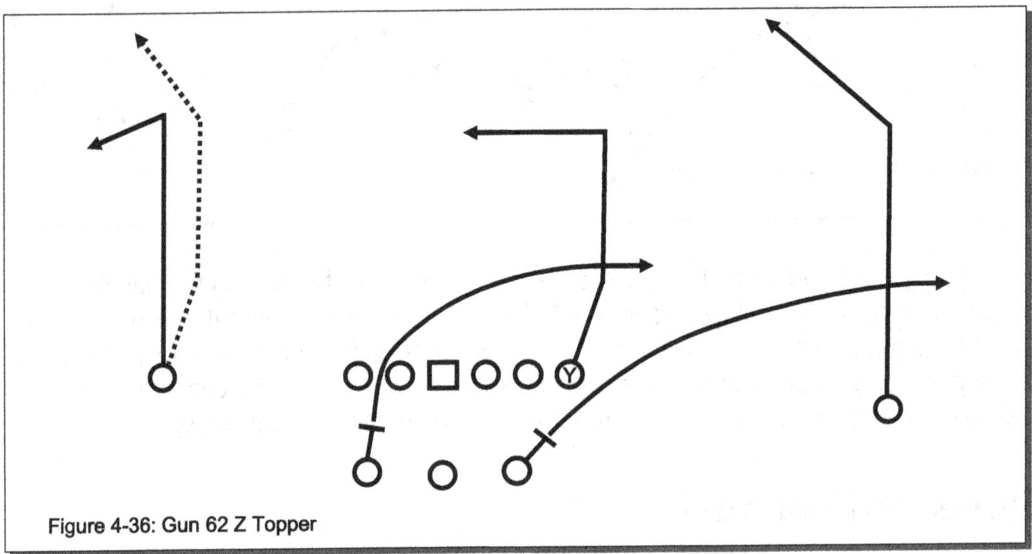


Figure 4-36: Gun 62 Z Topper

The "topper" concept (what we call a post over the "top" of an in-cut) is between the Y and Z to the callside. The Y is going to run a second-level, in-cut route, which means "I get behind the Mike linebacker." That is usually at 12 yards depth with a tight end, and closer to 14 yards if we run this with a flexed third wide receiver in "spread" (20) personnel. Either way, he's going to come off the ball with great get-off, *snap it* inside, and read the middle. Then, the Z receiver is going to run the post and blow the top off the coverage.

We actually used to call it "62 Z topper, backs right," which meant the fullback was running a diagonal, and the running back is running the "away" route, where he goes "A or B gap insertion," pushes to five yards and runs away to the same direction as the

**Play: Gun 62 Z Topper**

| Pos: | Assignment: | Coaching Points: |
|---|---|---|
| F | Check 60 protection. Run diagonal route. | |
| R | Check 60 protection. Run cross route. | |
| X | Run circus. | vs. cover 2: run 4-5-1 corner. |
| Y | Run read route at 2nd-level depth. | |
| Z | Run 9-step post. | vs. cover 2: convert fade. |
| QB | Homerun: Z Key: SS<br>Progression: 1. Y<br>2. Z<br>3. R<br><br>Outlet: R | Alert 1-on-1 to X.<br>Hand signal route to X. |

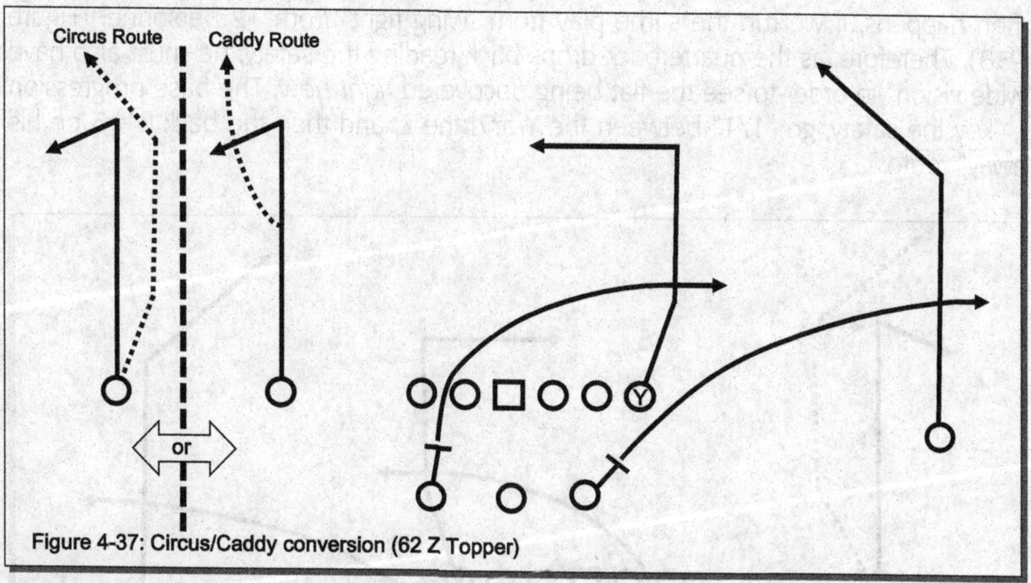

Figure 4-37: Circus/Caddy conversion (62 Z Topper)

**Play: Circus/Caddy Conversion**

**Circus Route:**

vs. 1 high: sprint off the ball with great arm drive. At 15 yards depth, plant, point, and drive. Hard angle return to the sideline.

vs. 2 high: run 4-5-1 corner route. Sprint off the ball with great arm drive. Stem release 4 steps, using the width of the numbers. Stick an drip inside arm. Push vertical for 5 steps, stick 1 to post and back to corner. Eyes, quick tuck. Eyes on the safety.

**Caddy Route:**

Sprint off the ball with great arm drive. At 15 yards, plant, point, and drive. Hard angle return towards sideline. vs. jam coverage convert.

fullback. However, as players began to understand the *concept*, we were able to just abbreviate the play call.

> (Note: We also used to sometimes tag it "62 Z topper, backs cross" in order to defeat "cover 2 man," but teams threw that coverage out the door with the increased threat of a running quarterback.)

For a quarterback, the progression is, "if I get 2-high or quarters, I'm going to drop back and read that field safety. If the safety jumps the tight end, I'm going to throw the ball to the post over the top. If he gets depth, I'm going right now to Y. If that's not there, then I've got my running back coming across as a check-down." And as we say, "the running back is always open."

The quarterback needs to be aware that there are times when the corner gets very deep, and he needs to throw the post short. Another thing that happens a lot is the fullback out in the flat ends up wide open, completely uncovered. The same thing often happens, if we run the same play from "wing right" from 12 personnel (Figure 4-38). Therefore, as the quarterback drops back reading the safety, he must also have "wide vision" in order to see the flat being uncovered *right now*. The base progression is, "key the safety, go "1/1" between the Y and the Z, and then the back is #3 on his "away" route.

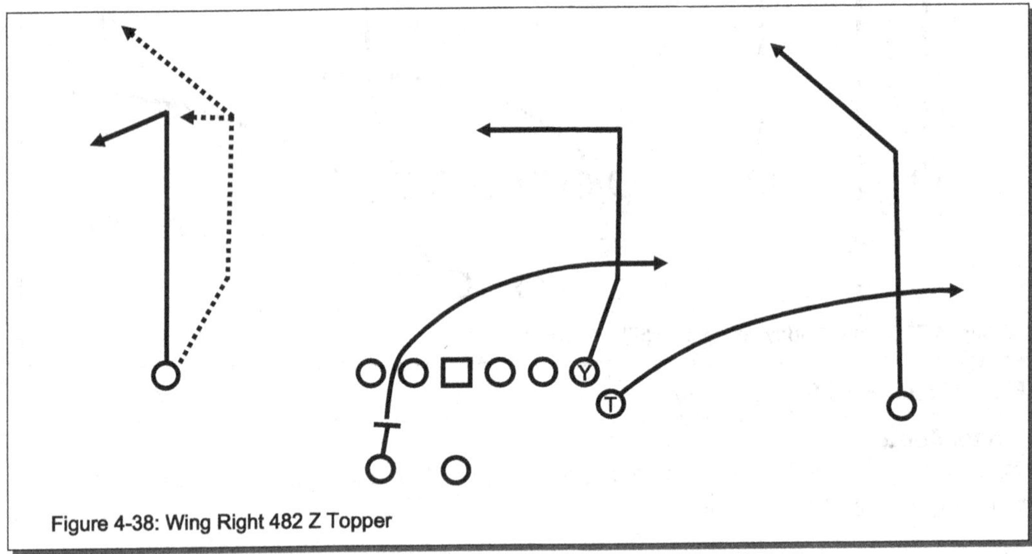


Figure 4-38: Wing Right 482 Z Topper

❑ 72 Z Topper

In a 2x2 set, we can call "72 Z topper." This is a situation in which the back should be offset, "near" the tight end side, in order to check his protection responsibility and attack the flat more quickly (Figure 4-39). However, we also like to run this version with 5-man protection, where we put the running back in motion to the point just outside the tight end. We'd call it "shot doubles right, R mo: scat 72, Z topper" (Figure 4-40). Y has the read route, Z has the post. Where "70" protection tells the running back to run a "check-diagonal" to the tight end side, now the "scat" tag allows him a free release. The slot has what we call a "ditch" route; he should take some time on the route and let the timing of the whole pattern set itself up. With a ditch route, he starts inside for three steps, pushes vertical for two steps and then brings it across at 5-yards depth over the opposite tight end area. Then, because of the "topper" call, the X has the "circus" route. To picture this concept with the original version of the play from "regular" (21) personnel, you can think of it as W replacing the running back's route and the running back replacing the fullback's, in the same distribution as the "backs right." Same progression for the quarterback, same read.

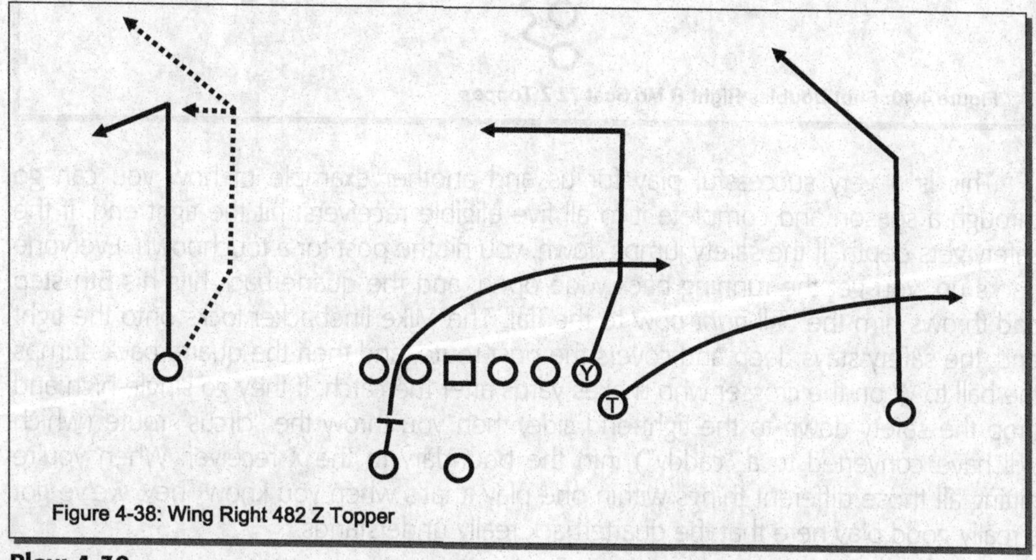

Figure 4-38: Wing Right 482 Z Topper

**Play: 4-39**

| Pos: | Assignment: | Coaching Points: |
|---|---|---|
| R | Check 70 protection. Run diagonal. | |
| W | Run ditch route. | |
| X | Run circus. | vs. 2 high: run corner route. |
| Y | Run read route at 2nd-level depth. | |
| Z | Run 9-step post (12-14 yds). | |
| QB | Homerun: Z Key: pre-snap: FS<br>Progression: 1. Z post-snap: SS<br>2. Y<br>3. W<br>4. R | Alert 1-on-1 to X vs. 1 high. |

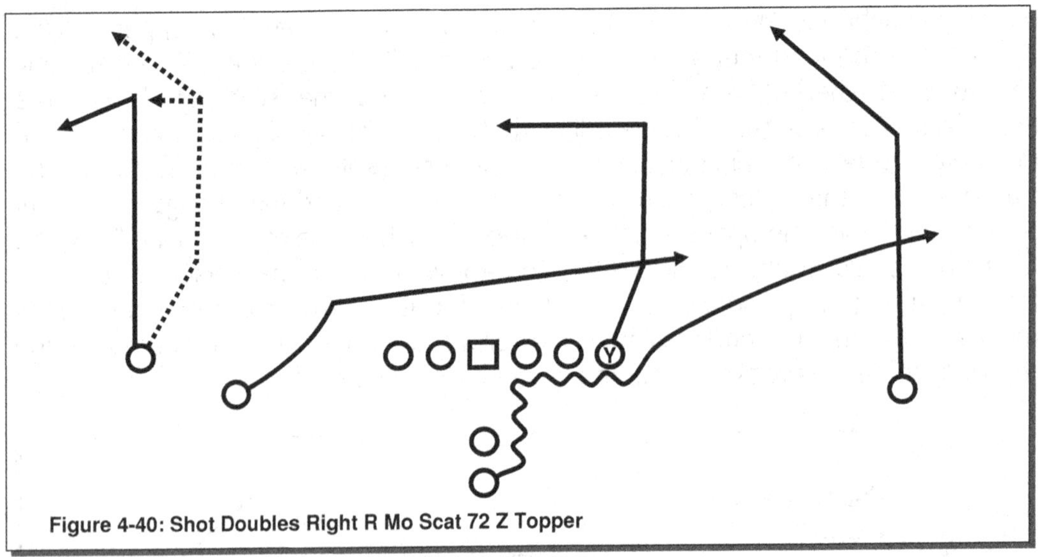

Figure 4-40: Shot Doubles Right R Mo Scat 72 Z Topper

This is a very successful play for us and another example of how you can go through a season and complete it to all five eligible receivers: hit the tight end, if the safety gets depth. If the safety jumps down, you hit the post for a touchdown. Everyone backs up, you get the running back wide open, and the quarterback hits his 5th step and throws him the ball *right now* to the flat. The Mike linebacker locks onto the tight end, the safety stays deep and covers the post route, and then the quarterback dumps the ball to W on the crosser who makes yards after the catch. If they go single-high and drop the safety down to the tight-end side, then you throw the "circus" route (which will have converted to a "caddy") into the boundary to the X receiver. When you're hitting all those different things within one play, that's when you know "hey, we've got a really good play here that the quarterback really understands."

## 82 X Topper

To give X a chance to blow the top off, we mirror the concept to the other side and call "doubles right: 82 X topper" (Figure 4-41). This puts Z on the "circus" route, with the same reads and conversion rules. In "80" protection, the tight end checks his blocking responsibility to that side and on this play, he knows to run a drag. The back understands that on "80" protection, he checks away from the tight end. W has the same read route, now from the other side, with X on the post. So in this instance, the "topper" concept occurs between W and X. This is a good "formation into" playcall, from the right college hashmark, in order to create more space for the routes to develop. It's also useful to call "Z half" and allow him to motion halfway down, in order to gain leverage for his 15-yard out route.

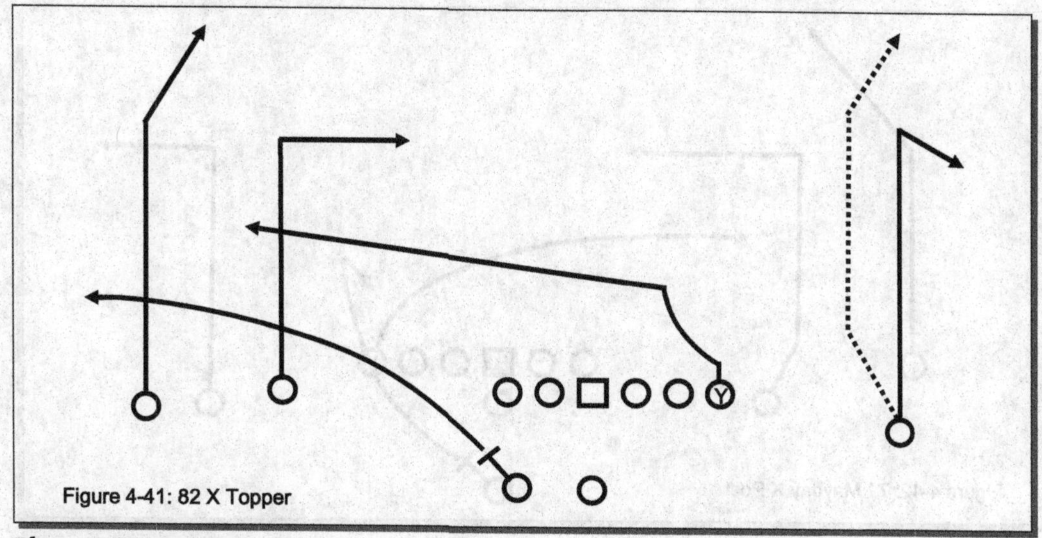

Figure 4-41: 82 X Topper

**Play: 82 X Topper**

| Pos: | Assignment: | Coaching Points: |
|---|---|---|
| R | Check 80 protection. Run diagonal. | |
| W | Run read route at 2nd-level depth. | |
| X | Run 9-step post. | vs. cover 2: convert fade. |
| Y | Run ditch route. | |
| Z | Run circus. | vs. 2 high: run corner route. |
| QB | Homerun: X Key: pre-snap FS<br>Progression: 1. X-W post-snap: FS<br>2. R<br>3. Y | Alert 1-on-1 to Z. |

# 71 Mayday, X Post

Even though we packaged "82 X topper" to simply mirror the "62" play, what we found was this didn't actually work as well for the players as calling "71 mayday, X post" (Figure 4-42). It's virtually the same play, but the name affected their *mindset* differently. Sometimes, it's one of those things where "well, this just works, and this doesn't," so you stop agonizing over it and just do it the other way. This is also a good example of why we want to maintain the verbiage flexibility in the system, so we always have a chance to make it work better for the players.

The only change this way is that rather than the circus route, Z runs the speed-out (or the "semi"), with the ability to convert to fade vs. a jam corner. The tight end still has the drag, the running back still has the "check-stop," and the W receiver still has the "read" route. Then, because you've been getting the safety cheating down on that "read" route, you add the "post" call to "mayday," especially against quarters to that

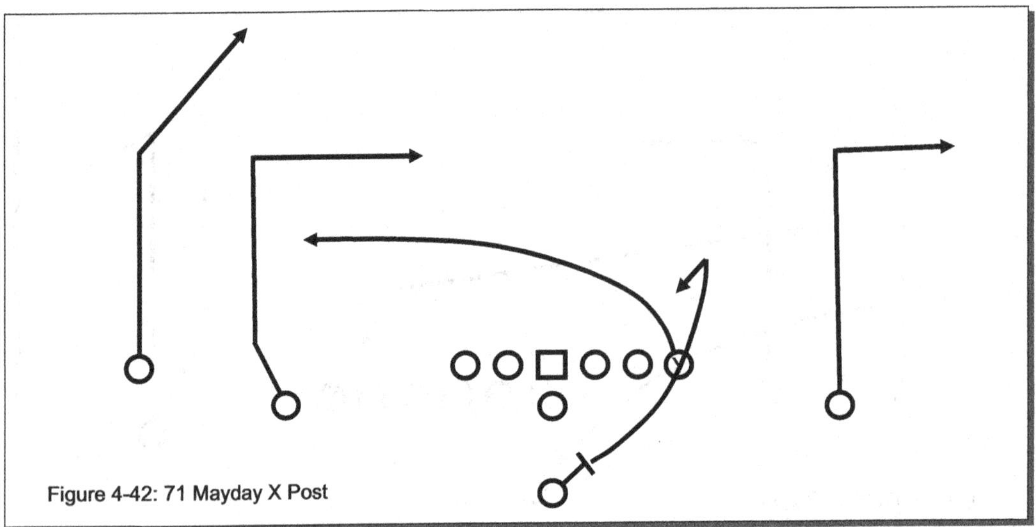
Figure 4-42: 71 Mayday X Post

**Play: 71 Mayday, X Post**

| Pos: | Assignment: | Coaching Points: |
|---|---|---|
| R | Check 70 protection. Run stop route. | |
| W | Run read route at 2nd-level depth. | Must get over the top of WLB. |
| X | Run post route. | |
| Y | Run drag route. | Be at 6 yds over OT. |
| Z | Run 10-yd speed out. | vs. cover 2: convert fade. vs. press: trace. |
| QB | Homerun: Key: pre-snap: FS<br>Progression: 1. Z/X<br>2. W<br>3. Y<br>Outlet: R | vs. off-corner: throw Z or X.<br>vs. cover 2: work W-Y-R<br>vs. LB plug: Y |

side of the field. The quarterback can think of it as running "mayday," but adding a chance for a touchdown, if you get that specific coverage. It's a good "into" play too, where you put the slot *into* the boundary and run that topper into the short side. Our history has been that this really affects quarters coverage and gives you a chance for an easy touchdown throw.

## 79 T Level, Z Post

As we said, we have multiple packages for running our post route, and there could be more than one way to call a given play, depending on what mental image we want from the players. For example, another great way to run the concept is from 12 personnel: "wing right: 79 T level, Z post" (Figure 4-43). It becomes a "full flow" or "four-man distribution" play this way.

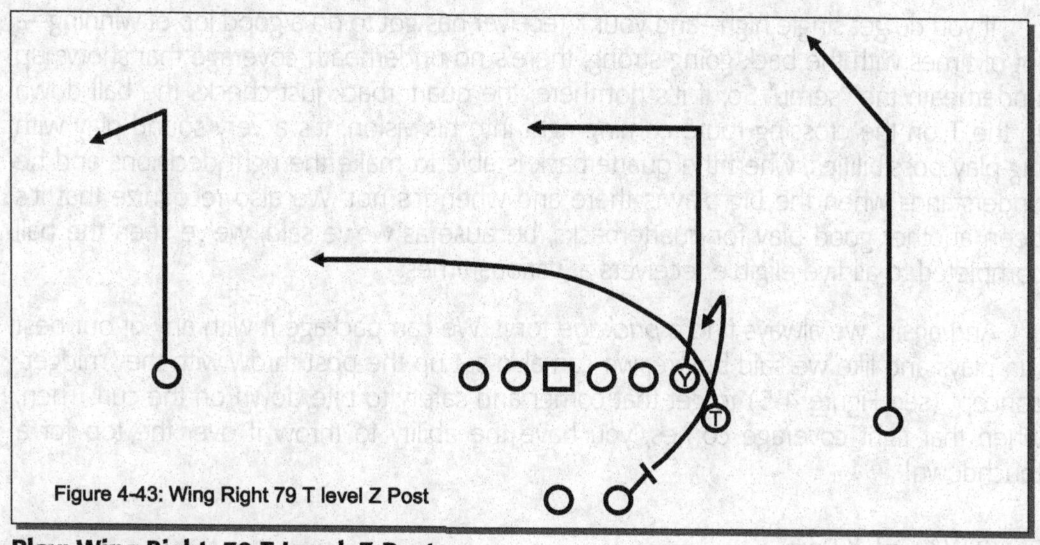

Figure 4-43: Wing Right 79 T level Z Post

**Play: Wing Right: 79 T Level, Z Post**

| Pos: | Assignment: | Coaching Points: |
|---|---|---|
| R | Check 70 protection. Run check stop. | |
| X | Run semi. | vs. cover 2: convert fade. |
| T | Run level route. | |
| Y | Run read route at 2nd-level depth. | |
| Z | Run post. | |
| QB | Y-Z-R | |

The singled receiver on the "circus" route still has to understand the coverage and convert his route accordingly. The running back runs a "check-stop" to the tight-end side, where his responsibility is to find a window in there for the quarterback to check the ball down to him. It's another "topper" concept, even though we don't actually say "topper" within the playcall. In this case, we found that players really got the *mental image we wanted when we called this from "70 protection"* and the "9" category, so we built the play this way and then we could install it within the "topper" package.

The Y receiver is running the same "read" route: get a great release, get to second-level depth, and *snap it*. The play name obviously tells Z to run the post and blow the top off and he understands to take a "post-split," so it looks the same as "midget" as he comes off the ball (we may also package it as "Z half," if we want him in motion for a particular package or game plan). In this instance, the T receiver (second tight end) is going to run a "drive" route, but because he's attached to the formation, he's going to start at a 45-degree angle outside for three-steps, plant his outside foot in the ground, and then come underneath and "level" it out on his cross route. That way, he buys some time, he doesn't get there too soon, and it allows the quarterback the opportunity to see the entire pattern open up.

If you do get single high—and your X receiver has got to do a good job of winning—a lot of times with the back going strong, there's no underneath coverage that shows up underneath the "semi." So, if it's not there, the quarterback just checks the ball down to the T on the crossing route coming right into his vision. It's a very sound play with big-play possibilities, when the quarterback is able to make the right decisions and he understands when the big play is there and when it's not. We also recognize that it's been another good play for quarterbacks, because as we've said, we've seen the ball completed to all five eligible receivers at various times.

And again, we always find a *package* for it. We can package it with any of our best run plays and like we said before, we can also set up the post throw with the "midget" concept (see Figure 4-5) to get that corner and safety to bite down on the curl. Then, when that tight coverage comes, you have the ability to throw it over the top for a touchdown!

❑ 79 W Level, X Post

We like to run that same play with 11 personnel and maybe add a little motion to it. So, you can start in "limo right," which means the W lines up widest, outside of Z in 3x1. This way, Z can take his "post-split to win." Or from "trey right," have W motion down inside ("W half") and we now call it "trey right: 79 W level, X post" (Figure 4-44). It's the exact same concept as "wing right: 71 T level," only we added the motion to it and you have a chance for a big play off of it, with the compressed split from Z. In this instance, players understand that the "9" concept category (79) means it's got special rules that break from the base system.

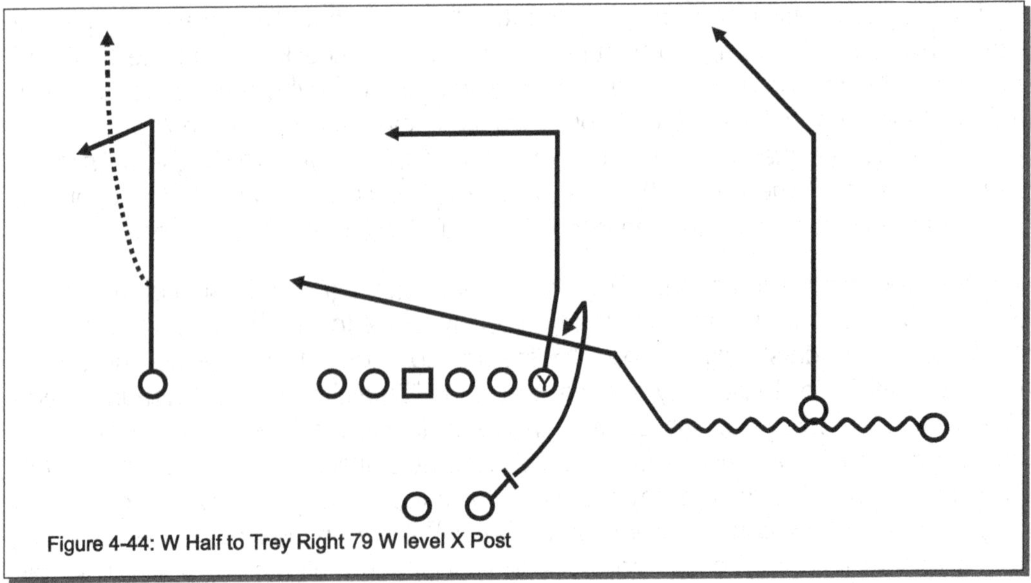

Figure 4-44: W Half to Trey Right 79 W level X Post

**Play: 4-44**

| Pos: | Assignment: | Coaching Points: |
|---|---|---|
| R | Check 70 protection. Run stop route. | |
| W | Run ditch route. | |
| X | Run 12-yd post. | |
| Y | Run read route at 2nd-level depth. | |
| Z | Run semi. | vs. cover 2: convert fade. |
| QB | Homerun: Z Key: pre-snap: FS<br>Progression: 1. W<br>2. Y<br><br>Outlet: R | |

❑ 489 Double-Hook, Z Post

We use that "9" category to build the post route into other concepts. This is an example from a game plan against one of the best defenses in the country: "489 double-hook, Z post" (Figure 4-45). We also think of this as a "palms-beater" concept. You can see how this looks similar to our "91 double-hook" ("Dallas") concept from quick game, except in this instance in the dropback game, those hook routes are pushed up to 8-10 yards and we have a comeback for X on the outside. However, for the quarterback, this isn't a pure "outside-in" read, like it was in the quick game.

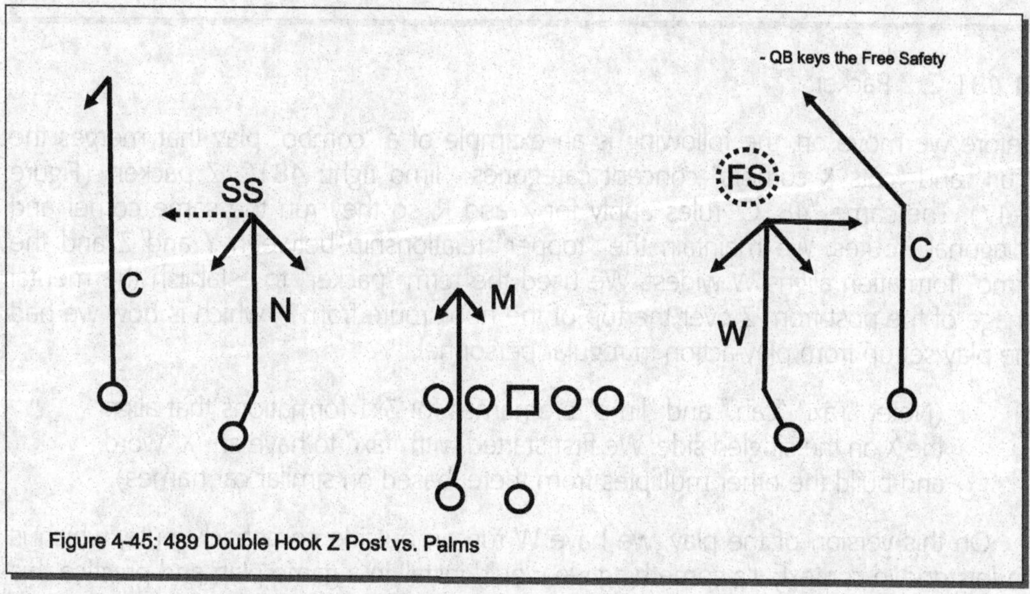

Figure 4-45: 489 Double Hook Z Post vs. Palms

The quarterback keys that safety to determine whether to throw "hook to back." If the safety jumps down, then he reads "post to back." We set the formation left-handed and sent the back to the field that week, because they had shown some "2 Tampa" coverage and we wanted to dictate to the Mike to open away from the post route (Figure 4-46). In the game plan, we said, "when they're in single-high, the safety tries to play shallow on the option routes." We used the code word to create the *mental image* for the players and we were able to hit the post over the top for big plays.

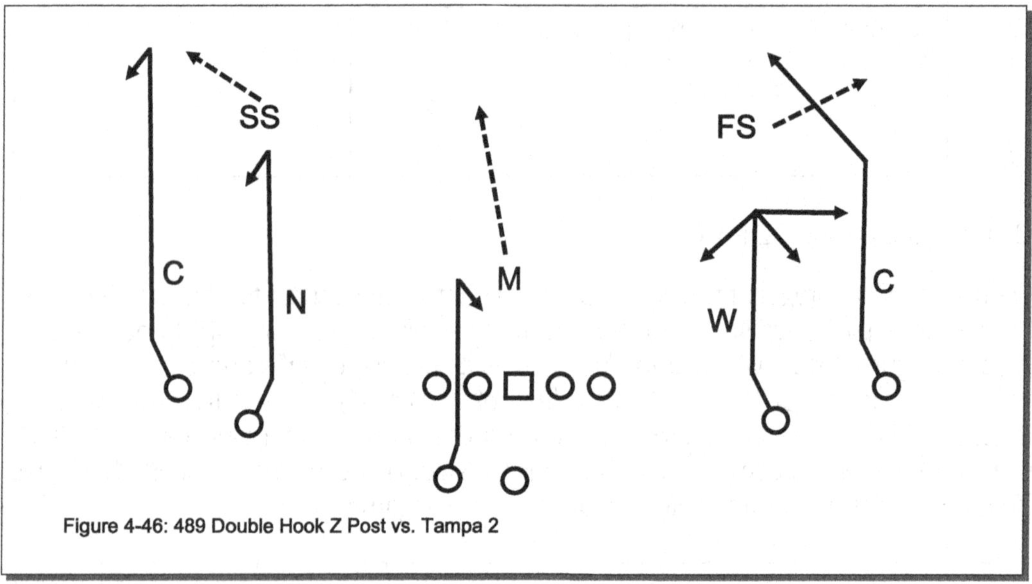


**Figure 4-46: 489 Double Hook Z Post vs. Tampa 2**

❑ 481 C, Z Packer

Before we move on, the following is an example of a "combo" play that merges the "curl" and "cuts & corners" concept categories: "limo right: 481C, Z packer" (Figure 4-47). The same "481C" rules apply for X and R, so they run the same corner and "diagonal" routes. We maintain the "topper" relationship between Y and Z and the "limo" formation aligns W widest. We used the term "packer" to establish the mental image of the post from Z over the top of the hook route from Y, which is how we had the play set up from play-action in regular personnel.

> (Note: "Taxi" "cab," and "limo" are names for 3x1 formations that align the X on the singled side. We first started with "taxi" to have an "X" word and build the other multiples from there, based on similar car names).

On this version of the play, we have W run an outside comeback route, which is understood in context; it's something we would install in a game plan and practice this way all week. You can see how this is another way to use the post route to the field to attack a quarters safety, just like the basic version of "62" with which we started. However, we also use this version of the play to attack the "trio" (3 over 2) types of "in

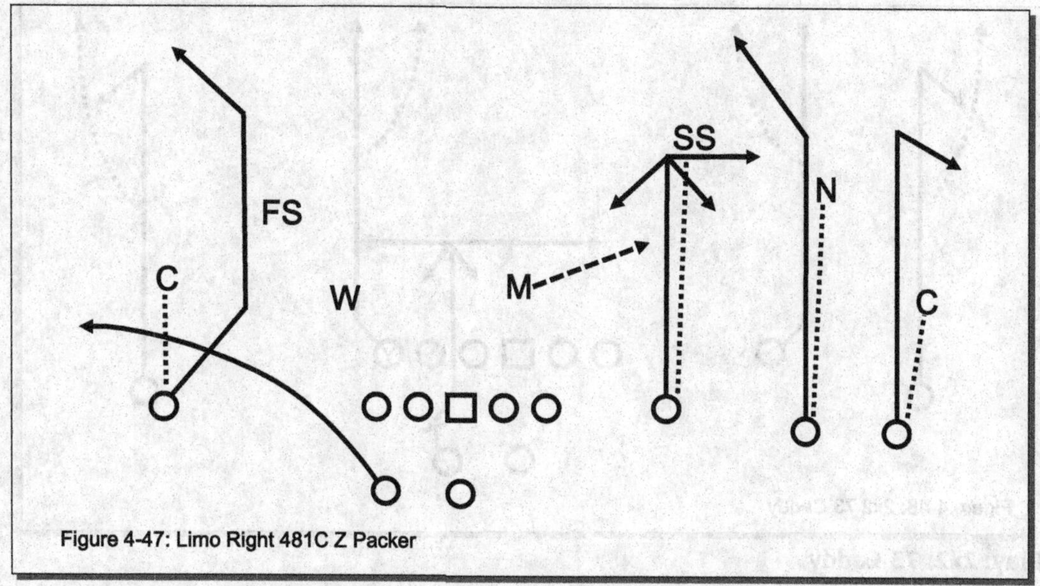

Figure 4-47: Limo Right 481C Z Packer

and out" coverage that teams often use to the three-receiver side. This is a way we can do that with a little bit different combination that includes both the "1" and "2" concept categories.

## Verticals

Our "3" concept category is verticals, which includes go routes and seams. This started life as the "four verticals" play. Some of the individual routes have changed over the years. We don't see a lot of true cover 3 anymore in the leagues in which I've been, so the "seams" become a little different. A number of teams are "carrying" verticals, in what's called "pattern-match" or "pattern reading." So, what starts as cover 3 ends up being more like a "man-free" as the defenders match the inside seams and "carry" or turn and run with them. Despite that, we certainly use our base vertical passes, including what we call a "control" concept within them. Let's take a look at them.

❑ 2x2 Verticals

We don't really run a true 4-verticals (or 5-verticals) anymore, because of the popularity of the aforementioned pattern-match coverage. We went to running the 15-yard caddy route with the outside receivers (or even a drop-off route, where if the corners get high, the outside go routes "drop off" and fall back to the sideline at 15 yards). This way, you're no longer worried about throwing a go route vs. a deep corner who is bailing out. Against 1-high teams, we'd call this "73 caddy" (Figure 4-48), which we can package with four wides, or from "ace" (11) personnel, if we have a tight end who can really run.

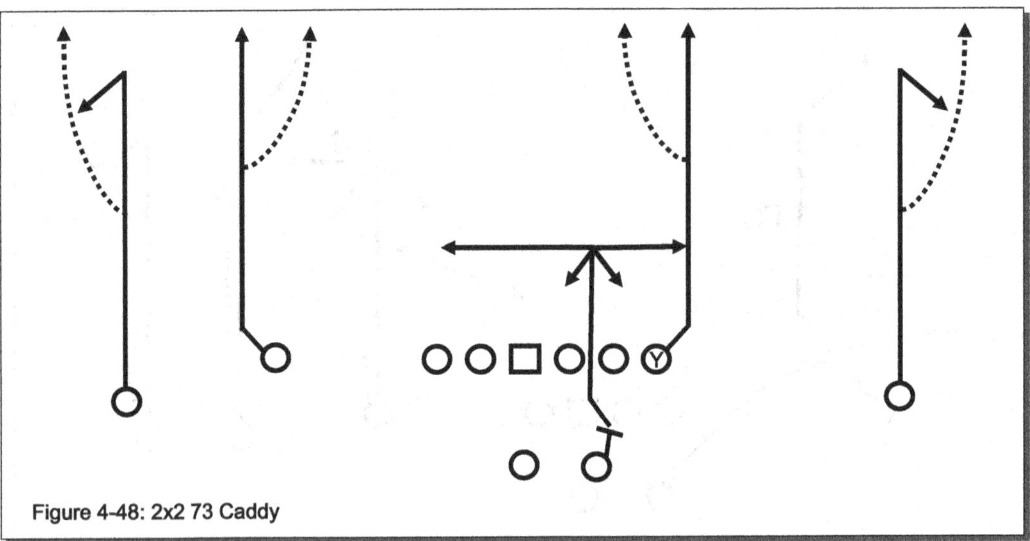

Figure 4-48: 2x2 73 Caddy

**Play: 2x2: 73 Caddy**

| Pos: | Assignment: | Coaching Points: |
|---|---|---|
| R | Check 70 protection. Run 5-yd option route. | |
| W | Run seam 2 yds outside the hash. | vs. cover 2: bend to the middle. |
| X | Run caddy. | vs. cover 2: convert fade. |
| Y | Run seam 2 yds outside the hash. | into the boundary run over my alignment |
| Z | Run caddy. | vs. cover 2: convert fade. |
| QB | Homerun: All Key:FS<br>Progression: 1. W to Y<br>or<br>2. W to X, Y to Z<br>Outlet: R | |

The technique of the respective inside seams is important. The slot receiver into the boundary wants to be able to get the cleanest release he possibly can, "run the seam over his alignment," and only let the quarterback bend him, if it's 2-high. The slot to the field wants to try to run his seam "two yards outside the college hash." It's important that he understands what split to use. If he's getting an outside-leverage strong safety, he can split on the hash, widen him, slip him, and get back on his landmark. If he's getting an "apex" linebacker who is trying to run out there and get his hands on him, he can take a little narrower split, angle *to it*, then beat him over the top. Either way, his landmark needs to be *two yards outside the hash*. If we get a cover 2 look, the field-side slot is the automatic "bender" that's able to get second level, put his outside foot in the ground and snap it to the middle.

The running back is usually going to run an option route (though you can certainly give him other routes, depending on what team you're facing and what his specific skill set is). The quarterback has to be able to rely on him, if we're going to have consistent success with this play. He can get an "A or B gap release," he then pushes it to five yards *past the line of scrimmage*. I think that's the biggest thing you have to coach in this instance, is that he gets 5 yards *past* the line of scrimmage, so that the timing is correct when the quarterback is ready to check it down. If the back only goes two or three yards past the line of scrimmage, he's open before the quarterback is ready to throw him the ball, the under-coverage can rally to tackle him, and we don't get as many yards after the catch.

For the quarterback, if it's single-high, he's going to key the free safety. He needs to look at depth *and* width; some teams play the free safety so deep that it really doesn't matter what his width is, and you can just hit either seam. But if he's favoring one side or the other, you know that's when you want to work the other side. This is an "inside-out" read. If the free safety tells me to go to the seam to my right and it's not open, because the alley guy carried it, I go from seam, to caddy, to the running back underneath. But again, there are certainly times where the free safety plays so deep that you can take either seam.

I think it's important that the quarterback understands the *depth* of the seam route. The *worst* thing you can do is throw the seam too deep; you'll get the receiver killed and probably get intercepted as well. It's a "2 ball," which means the quarterback drops three steps out of the gun and takes a hitch, and then the ball comes out in rhythm, with a little air under it. He gets it to the inside seam, somewhere between 18 and 22 yards, and strikes the receiver *on the helmet*. It's also fine if you have to sometimes slow him down; if he's getting a quick release, getting a little bit deep and you have to slow him down and have him throw it to the receiver's back shoulder, that's fine. It's a good throw, a good *completion*. The commentators can say "well, the ball was a little bit behind him," but the quarterback and receiver know that's the only place the ball could go: a little bit behind, to get the completion and protect the receiver from being hit.

If we get cover 2, the quarterback needs to understand "I have a 2-on-1 ball," which means I've got two verticals on a half-field safety. The outside receiver understands that vs. cover 2, he gets to use a "slip release" vertical, which means that he picks a spot five yards outside the corner and he's going to come off the ball as *hard* as he possibly can. If the corner doesn't get there, he's going to "dip and rip," get through, and get vertical down the field. If he gets width and shuffles high, he can slip inside of him, as long as he stays on his track. He's getting the easiest release to get vertical as quickly as he possibly can.

The quarterback is going to *hold* the backside safety; he's going to look right at him, take a hitch-step, and then *key* the other safety to identify his "width and depth" (everything is "width and depth," when you're throwing off of a safety). Both verticals are "1/1" and the check down to the back is "3." (A lot of times I don't say "1, 2, 3" in progression reads, I say "1/1, 3." Both guys are #1, and then you go to 3.)

The quarterback needs to be alert to "quarter-quarter-half" coverage. What's important on "quarter-quarter-half" is that the quarterback identifies and eliminates the quarters-side, and instead throws the "2-on-1" ball to the "half" side, so he has room to stretch the safety and put pressure on him. If the quarterback makes a mistake, which happens sometimes, then he needs to take five steps, hitch-up, and throw the ball to the outside receiver.

I personally don't like trying to throw a seam route vs. a quarters-safety. I think you're "hoping," when you say, "he's running a bender, so you need to throw it in there." I've never seen that work consistently, so we prefer not to force the issue and instead do some other things against that particular coverage.

❑ 3x1 Verticals

In the 3x1 set, the #3 receiver needs to know that he's working to the opposite side of the field. What's most important for him is a great "get-off," so he can beat the inside linebacker over the top and then *bend* to that opposite hash. It doesn't matter if #3 is a tight end, such as "trey right: 73 all" (Figure 4-49), or a wide receiver. If he gets cut off or knocked inside the linebacker, then I tell the quarterback to eliminate him from the read.

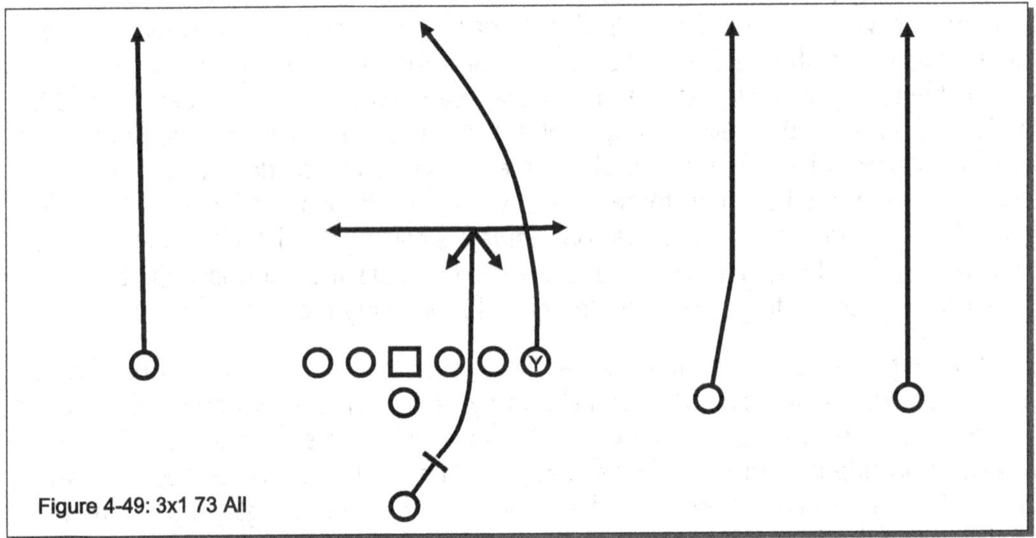

Figure 4-49: 3x1 73 All

If it's single-high, the read is "1/1" with the seams, just like we did before. If it's 2-high, then I now understand if I'm keying the boundary safety. I've got the #3 receiver coming from the other side. So again, that's "1/1, 3" with the checkdown to the back. With the width of the college hashmarks, we generally want to read the *boundary safety*, unless there's some specific reason to take me to the fieldside; we might have a specific game plan or situational alert that takes the read over there. The field safety might not get width. For example, if it becomes "2 Tampa," then the progression becomes "seam-to-#2 to the outside receiver," because a lot of times, the Mike linebacker runner will jump on that over seam and then *bang*, that second seam comes wide open.

**Play: 3x1: 73 All**

| Pos: | Assignment: | | Coaching Points: |
|---|---|---|---|
| R | Check 70 protection. Run 5-yd option route. | | |
| W | Run seam 2 yds outside the hash. | | Take best release. |
| X | Run go at bottom of #'s to the field. | | vs. cover 2: use slip release |
| Y | Run over route to opposite hash. | | Get over MLB, don't cross hash. |
| Z | Run go between #'s and sideline. | | vs. cover 2: use slip release. |
| QB | Homerun: All<br>Progression: vs. cover 3<br>1. Y to W<br><br>Outlet: R | Key: FS<br>vs. cover 2<br>1. Z to Y | vs. 2-man: remember R on option route.<br><br>vs. pressure: alert check |

❑ Verticals vs. 2 Tampa

Cover "2 Tampa" always changes the progression for a quarterback. When you face a team that majors in "2 Tampa"—and this is really important—you want to be able to send your back to the field. We don't want to get locked into always calling it "73." If you set the tight end into the boundary, you'll want to call "doubles right: 483 caddy" (Figure 4-50), so the back can chase the Mike to the field-side, turn around, catch the ball, and get the first down. This way we're reading that boundary seam to the tight end, since the back is now releasing away from him. If you face a "2 Tampa" team, you need to know what they're teaching the Mike linebacker (most of them will coach the Mike to open up to the field or the faster inside receiver against a 2x2 set). Therefore, the quarterback has to know what they're being taught in order to identify the coverages correctly, execute the reads correctly, manipulate their defenders, and get accurate, consistent completions.

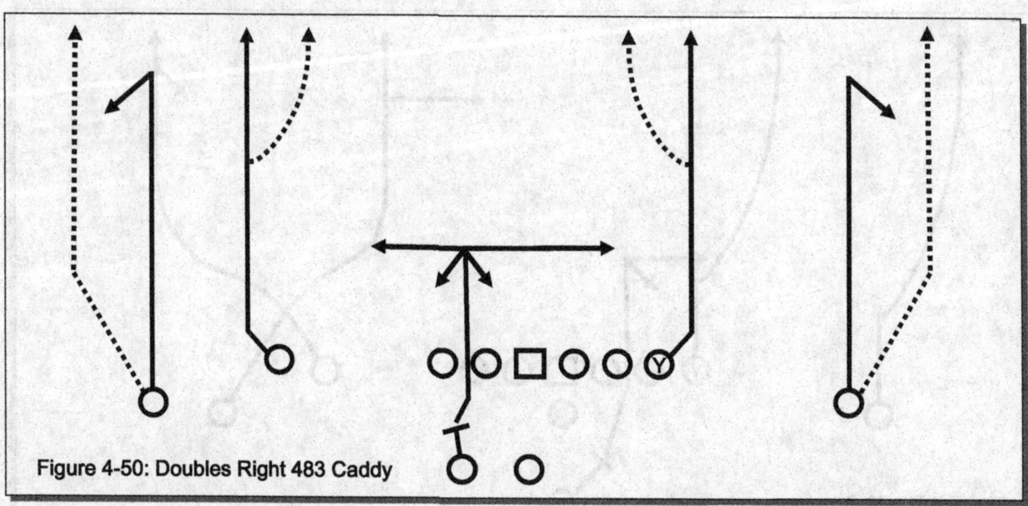

Figure 4-50: Doubles Right 483 Caddy

**Play: 4-50**

| Pos: | Assignment: | Coaching Points: |
|---|---|---|
| R | Check 400 protection. Run 5-yd option route. | |
| W | Run seam 2 yds outside the hash. | vs. cover 2: bend to the middle. |
| X | Run caddy. | vs. cover 2: convert fade |
| Y | Run seam 2 yds outside the hash. | into the boundary run over my alignment |
| Z | Run caddy. | vs. cover 2: convert fade. |
| QB | Homerun: Z Key: FS<br>Progression: 1. W to Y<br>or<br>2. W to X. Y to Z<br>Outlet: R | vs. 2 man: remember R on option route.<br><br>vs. pressure: alert check |

❑ 3 Combos

We used to run a combo we call "73 Cougar" (Figure 4-51). I always liked the "switch" and really liked all the various options that could occur off of it. However, if you're going to emphasize it and do it well, it takes work and the players need to practice it enough to experience all those different options. It takes time and repetitions to get a feel for keeping spacing after the switch against zone, where you can work the levels after the switch, or closing down splits and getting vertical quickly against man, to create that natural pick as the switch works up the field. But that's the question of, "how much time do you have to practice and what do you want to prioritize?" It's sometimes an issue of time and distance and what your players can do. For us, it also became a function of facing more quarters and more match-coverage coming from #2, so we just kind of got away from the play and prioritized other things.

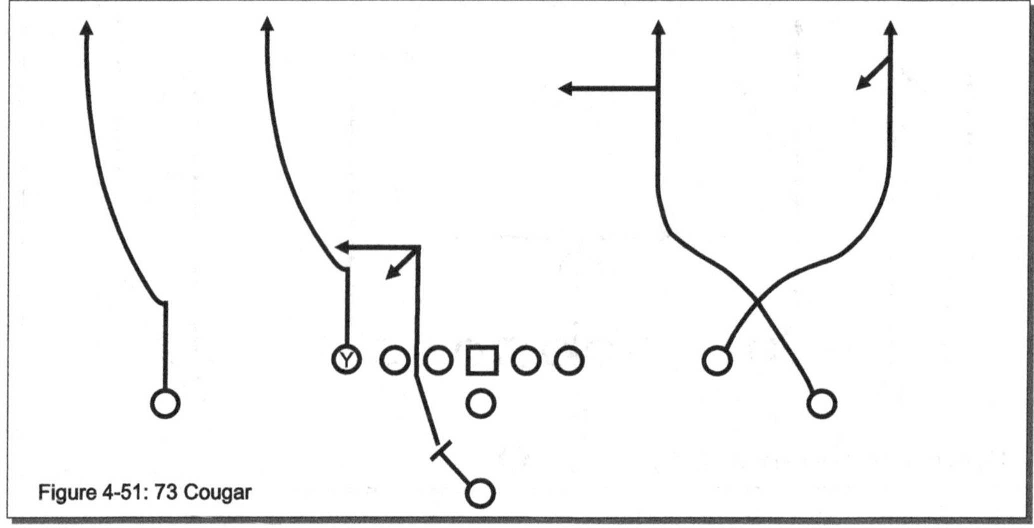

Figure 4-51: 73 Cougar

**Play: 4-51**

| Pos: | Assignment: | Coaching Points: |
|---|---|---|
| R | Check 70 protection and run 5 yd outside option. | |
| W | Run wheel route. vs. deep 1/3 defender, stop at 10 yds. | |
| X | Run seam vs. 1 high. | Run 12-yd in vs. middle field open |
| Y | Run seam 2 yards outside hash. | |
| Z | Run go between #'s and sideline. | vs. cover 2: use slip release. |
| QB | Homerun: X or Y Key: FS<br>Progression: 1. X to Y<br>2. X to W. Y to Z<br>Outlet: R | Look off: move the FS to where you want him.<br>vs. cover 2-man: remember R on the outside option. |

❑ Controls and Option-Routes

The next thing we do off the "3s" is to throw our "controls." It's something we've always been really good at, something that our players like a lot, and something our quarterbacks consistently feel comfortable with. We chose to include some of these under "3" (instead of "4," which is technically the option-route concept category), because the outside receivers still have "go" routes, and players seemed to just get the *mental image* of the play this way. It's like we keep saying that we will adjust the system, in order to do what works best for our guys. It still correlates to the system this way, where the "3" concept category is "go routes," so we've just lived with it ever since.

❑ 73 Miami

The first one we start with is what we call "doubles right: scat 73 Miami" (Figure 4-52). The receiver into the boundary has to do a great job on his outside release and expect the football, because a lot of times into the boundary, if we're sending the back that way, the "hole shot" to Z becomes "in play." A boundary corner will often come off that receiver, when the back bends to the flat. When that happens, we've had some huge plays, especially in "2-minute."

On this play, our tight end gets the middle. He has a 10-yard option route. He wants to be able to attack the leverage of the Mike linebacker, when the Sam gets width and goes to the running back. The tight end needs to push it and then either hook in, break in, hook out, or break out. One of the things that we really coach on the stick route, when he breaks outside, is the concept of "89 degrees." He's not breaking flat and letting the Mike linebacker undercut him. Rather, he's coming "downhill one degree" when he breaks, so that the Mike can't recover. There is some physicality to

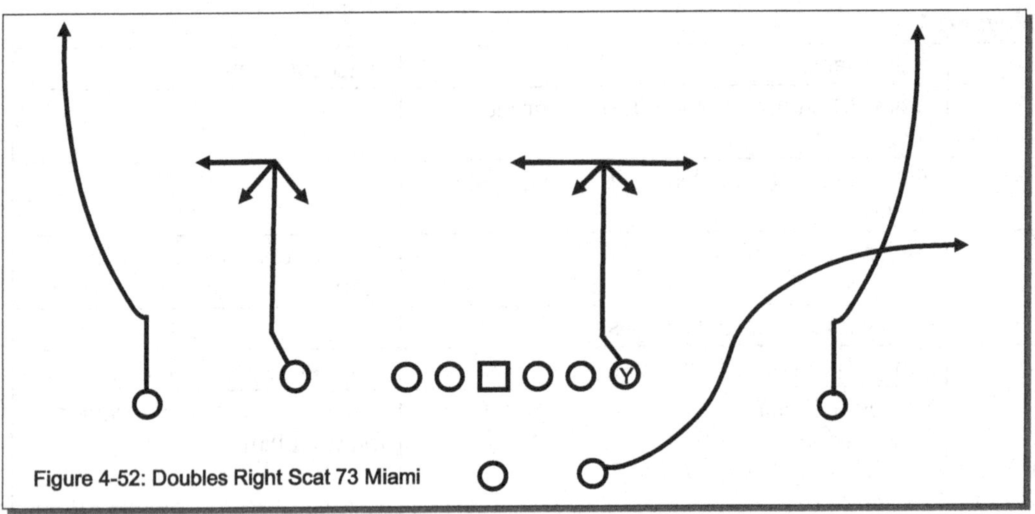

Figure 4-52: Doubles Right Scat 73 Miami

**Play: 4-52**

| Pos: | Assignment: | Coaching Points: |
|---|---|---|
| R | Free release. Run bend route. | vs. strong pressure: 1-yd hot. |
| W | Run 8-10 yds outside option route. | Work over my alignment–outside. |
| X | Run go. | Must outside release. |
| Y | Run 10-yd option route. Get open! | Stem inside. You get the middle.<br>Alert: hot off 1 strong. |
| Z | Run go. | Must outside release. |
| QB | Homerun: X/Z Key: pre-snap: FS<br>Progression: 1. Y<br>2. R post-snap: strong ILB<br>3. W<br>Outlet: | vs. strong pressure: hit R hot in flat. |

it; he needs to be able to headbutt, collision, and be physical with the Mike linebacker. He needs to get enough experience and reps at it so that when he feels the Mike linebacker undercutting him, he can "wrap" him and win back to the inside. It's another one of those things that when you get a guy that's good at it, don't over coach him: give him the freedom to get himself open. For example, we've even had tight ends who "took it through" for touchdowns, even though they weren't coached that way. If a guy can demonstrate in practice that he is good at it, we give him a little more freedom with his route depth and technique.

The slot receiver on the other side has what we call an "outside-option," which means he can run the 10-yard option route "over his alignment," hook out, or break outside. He's got to give the middle to the tight end. As he comes off the ball, if people drop away from him, he can hook up inside but *over his alignment*. Most of the time though, he will be stemming inside, pushing up and then running a "stick" route outside. Again, the concept of "89 degrees" downhill helps him to get open and stay open.

The quarterback needs to understand the coverage, so he knows when the "hole shot" comes into play and he can "peek" at it. Then he's got a "1/1, 3" read: "1/1" between the running back and tight end, with the W on the other side as #3 in the progression. The running back's route is called a "bend" route; it's not a diagonal, it's a *bend*. What he wants to do is get an arc release—one step, lateral crossover, 3rd step with width—and then get up the field to two yards, and "bend" the route to five yards. If he runs a diagonal, he gets to the sideline too soon and he's not going to get anything after the catch. If he runs a really good bend route though, he will create room for himself to catch the ball and then be able to use his skills in space.

He has to be able to let the quarterback throw the ball to him at the inside jersey number; the *strike point* for the running back is the *inside number*. He's got to have the mobility to be able to "open his hips, catch the ball, dip his shoulder, and run down the sideline." You don't want him to pivot inside with that catch. We want him to open his hips, catch the ball on his inside chest, dip his shoulder, and then be able to run down the sideline and make a play.

❑ 73 Cub

Something we incorporated into this that I really liked was what we call "cub." The play is now called "doubles right: scat 73 cub" (Figure 4-53) and we want to set it into the other hash mark. To the tight-end side, it's still "Miami" and into the boundary. We now have the "cub" route, where X is going to start inside and "replace W's alignment" at five yards and W is going to run a swing route and "replace X's alignment" at five yards, turning inside to the quarterback (there have also been times where we've let him take this down the sideline on a "rail" or "fade" route, if it pops wide open). This creates a "built-in" hot so, against teams that set up the "field scrapes" and "field sharks," the quarterback understands that he has a "built in" hot into the boundary, because there's only one defender dropping that way. If the protection is called away from them, the tight end and running back are also "hot off of one."

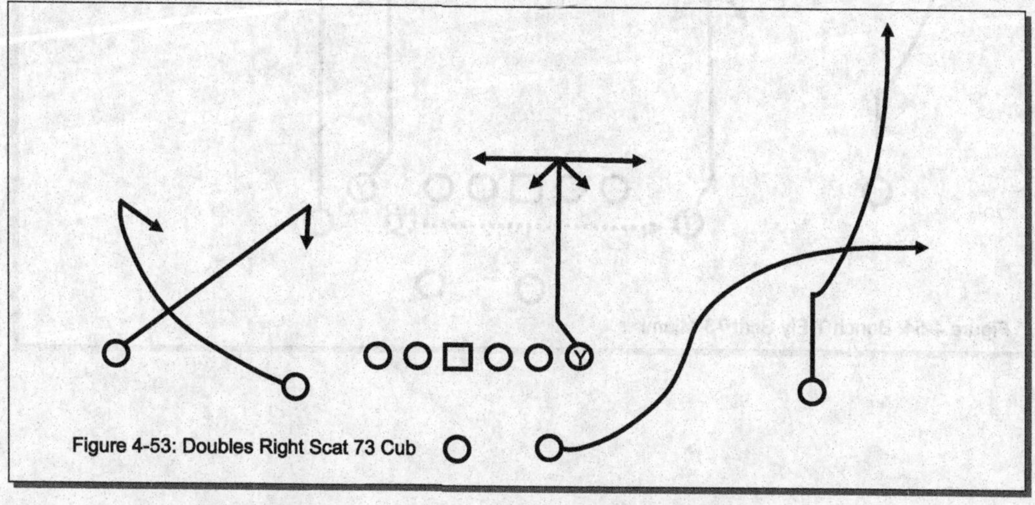

Figure 4-53: Doubles Right Scat 73 Cub

**Play: 4-53**

| Pos: | Assignment: | Coaching Points: |
|---|---|---|
| R | Free release. Run bend route. | vs. strong pressure: 1 yd hot. |
| W | Run cub route. | Catch ball outside the #'s. |
| X | Run 5-yd snag route. | Sit down. Don't work out. |
| Y | Run 10-yd option route. Get open! | Stem inside. Get the middle. |
| Z | Run go. | Must outside release. |
| QB | Homerun: Z<br>Progression: 1. R<br>2. Y<br>3. X<br><br>Outlet:<br>Key: pre-snap: FS<br>post-snap: Strong ILB | vs. strong pressure: hit R hot in flat.<br>vs. weak pressure: W-X |

❑ Control Packages

We run "Miami" out of a lot of different formations. It's good out of "bunch" (Figure 4-54) and what we call "close" sets. In a close formation, what we teach the outside receivers is anytime you have a go route and we tighten you up in a "snug" or "close" alignment, your "go" turns to a "corner" route. So, if you call "doubles right close: scat 73 Miami" (Figure 4-55) in which both Z and X are in close alignments, both of them would run corner routes and there have been times where Z has popped wide open, because the back's free-release threatens the corner.

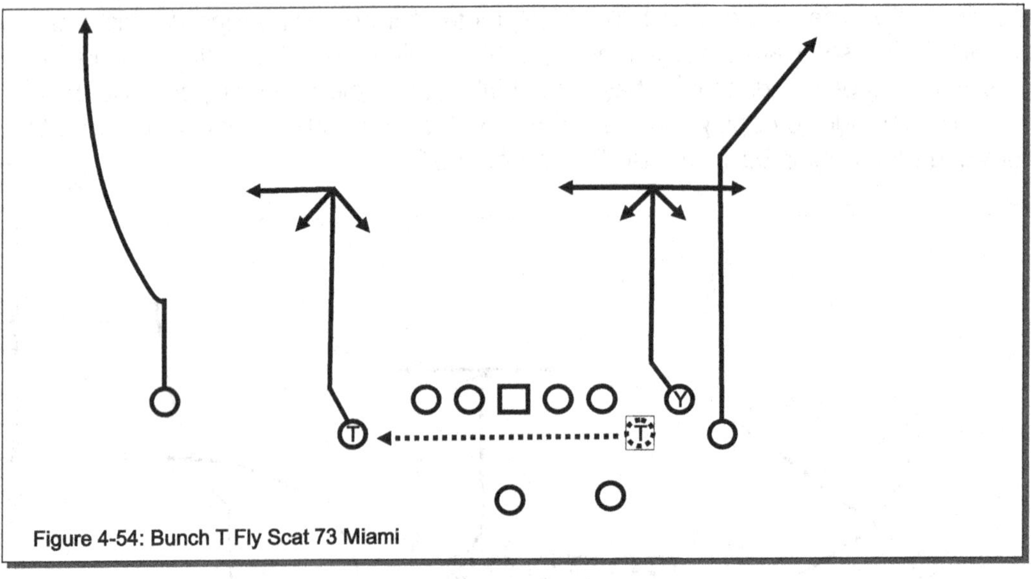

Figure 4-54: Bunch T Fly Scat 73 Miami

**Play: 4-54**

| Pos: | Assignment: | Coaching Points: |
|---|---|---|
| R | Free release. Run bend route. | vs. strong pressure: 1 yd hot. |
| W | Run 8-10 yd outside option route. | Work over my alignment—outside. |
| X | Run go. | Must outside release. |
| Y | Run 10-yd option route. Get open! | Stem inside. Get the middle. Alert: hot off 1 strong. |
| Z | Run corner route. | |
| QB | Homerun: Z Key: pre-snap: FS<br>Progression: 1. Y<br>2. R post-snap: strong ILB<br>3. W Alert rolled corner for Z.<br><br>Outlet: R | vs. strong pressure: hit R hot in flat. |

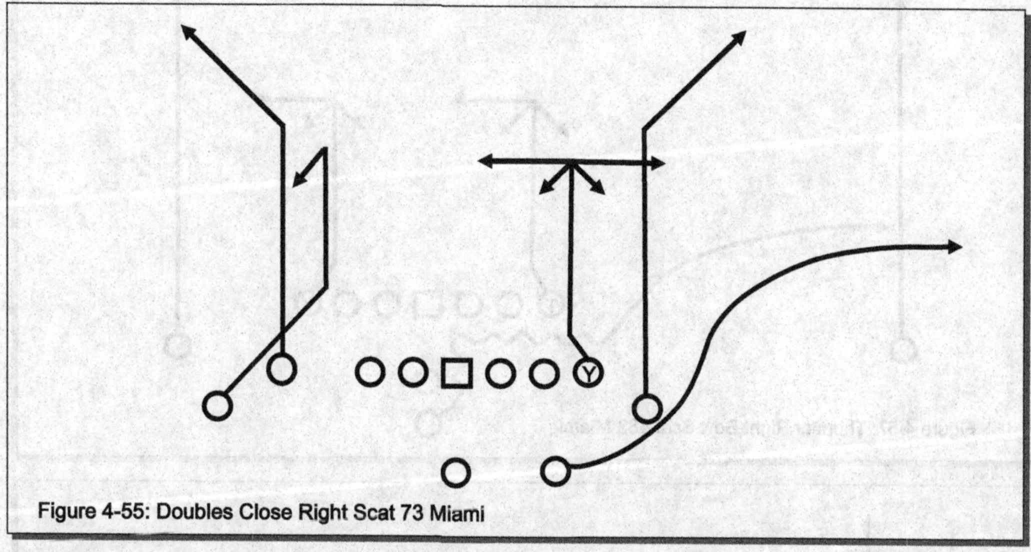

Figure 4-55: Doubles Close Right Scat 73 Miami

When we run it out of 2-tight end sets, we can set the option route either way, depending on where we send the back. We can still send the running back to the Y by calling "thunder right: scat 73 Miami" (Figure 4-56) or instead toward the T by calling "thunder right: scat 483 Miami" (Figure 4-57). We might also "bow" the back from "shot" to "gun" alignment (he understands where to go in motion, based on his assignment). There, the tight ends have to understand who gets the middle and who has the outside-option. We can run it out of "trips" alignment, which has always been good for us. If we call "trips right: scat 73 Miami" (Figure 4-58), you still have the running back bending toward the tight end into the boundary. Then, the #3 receiver on the opposite side (Z) runs the outside-option and W knows he needs to run a "protect seam," so it's a forced outside release.

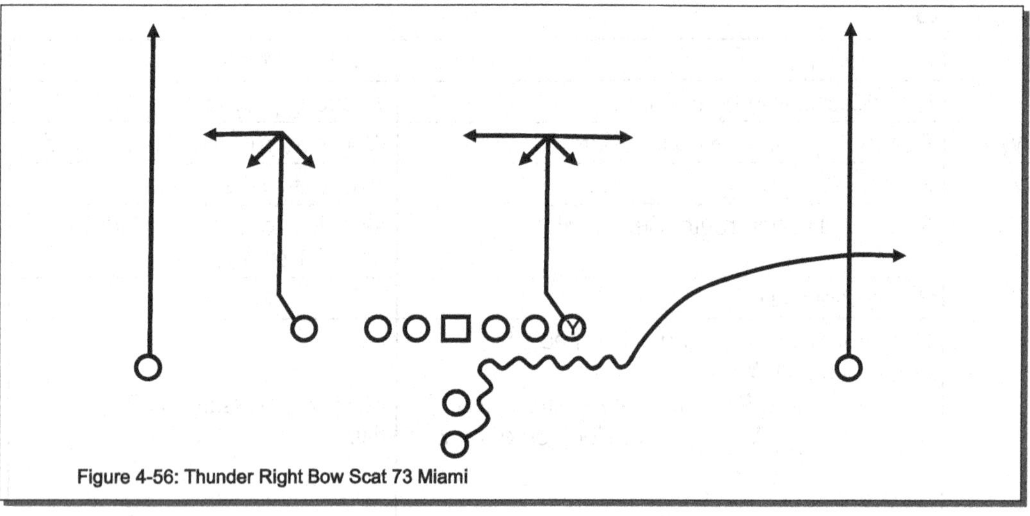

Figure 4-56: Thunder Right Bow Scat 73 Miami

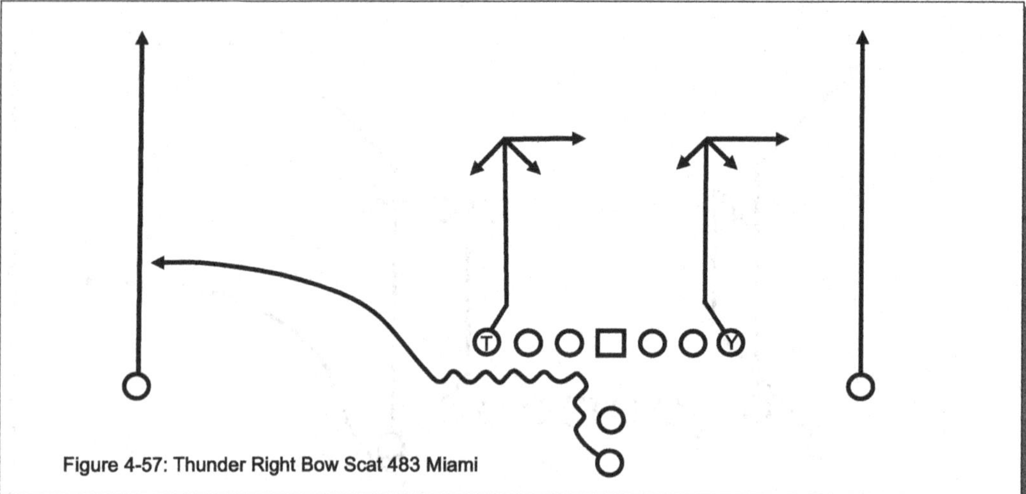

Figure 4-57: Thunder Right Bow Scat 483 Miami

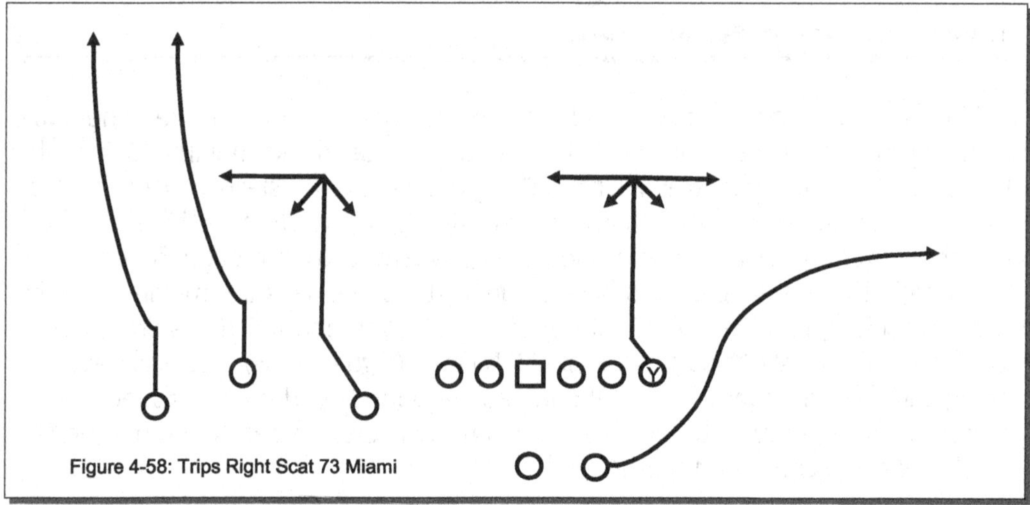

Figure 4-58: Trips Right Scat 73 Miami

**Play: Trips Right: Scat 73 Miami**

| Pos: | Assignment: | Coaching Points: |
|---|---|---|
| R | Free release. Run bend route. | vs. strong pressure: 1-yd hot. |
| W | Run seam. | Must outside release. |
| X | Run go. | Must outside release. |
| Y | Run 10-yd option route. Get open! | Stem inside. Get the middle. Alert: hot off 1 strong. |
| Z | Run 8-10 yd outside option route. | Work over my alignment—outside. |
| QB | Homerun: X/W<br>Progression: 1. Y<br>2. R<br>3. Z | vs. strong pressure: hit R hot in flat. |

A great way to package this a step farther is to go "mix to doubles right, scat 73 Cub" which includes both a tight end shift to the right, and then the W motion back into the boundary (Figure 4-59). The back is already set with the "free-release" split and the quarterback is comfortable with the play, because we've maintained the integrity of the concept for the offense but changed the passing strength twice for the defense.

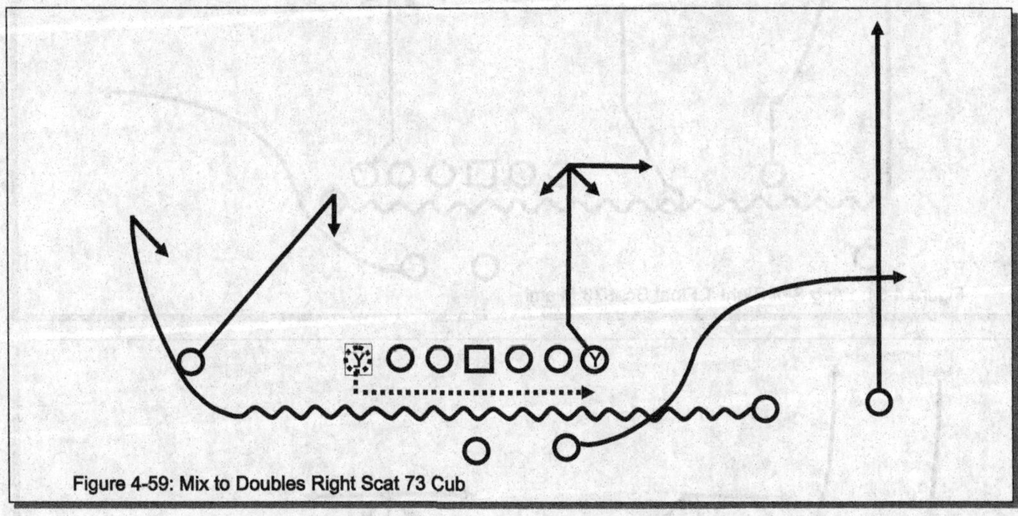

Figure 4-59: Mix to Doubles Right Scat 73 Cub

"Thunder slot right: scat 73 Miami" from 12 personnel is the same play (Figure 4-60), because we say "thunder slot *is* trips" as we plan our dropback passing game concepts. "Wing slot right, T float: scat 73 Miami" (Figure 4-61) and "shot strong slot right Lee: scat 73 Miami" (Figure 4-62) are exactly the same play. We can go "wing slot Lee: scat 73 Miami" (Figure 4-63) by game plan and just tag something that week for T, so he knows to replace the back and run the bend route.

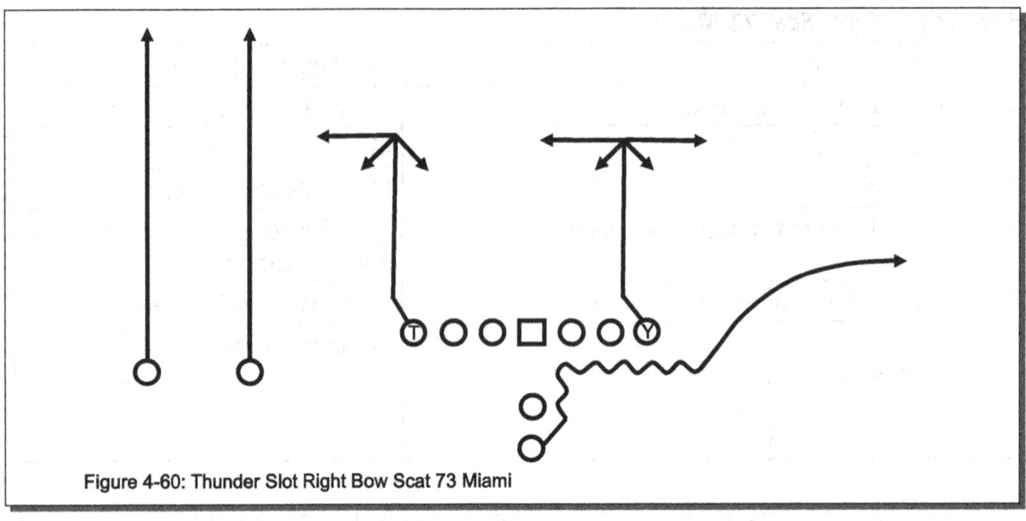

Figure 4-60: Thunder Slot Right Bow Scat 73 Miami

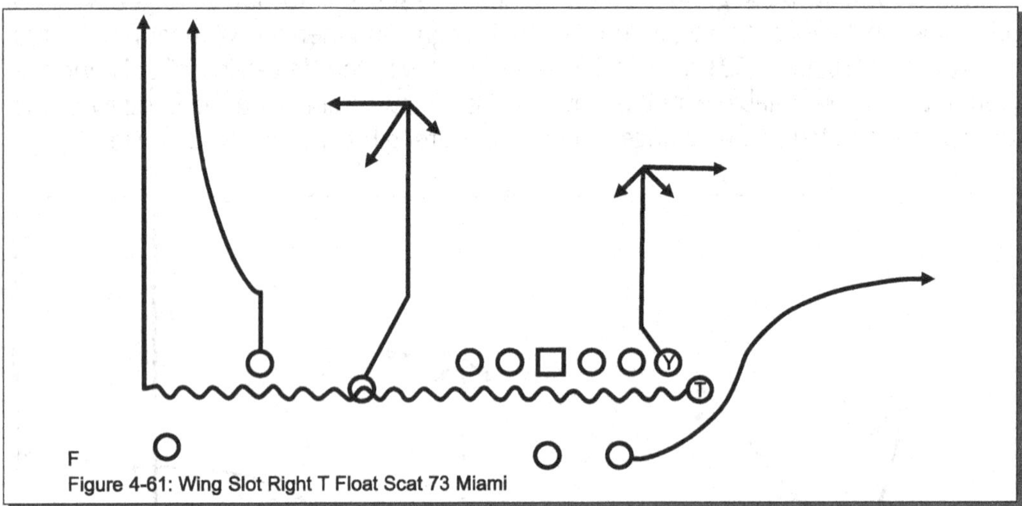

Figure 4-61: Wing Slot Right T Float Scat 73 Miami

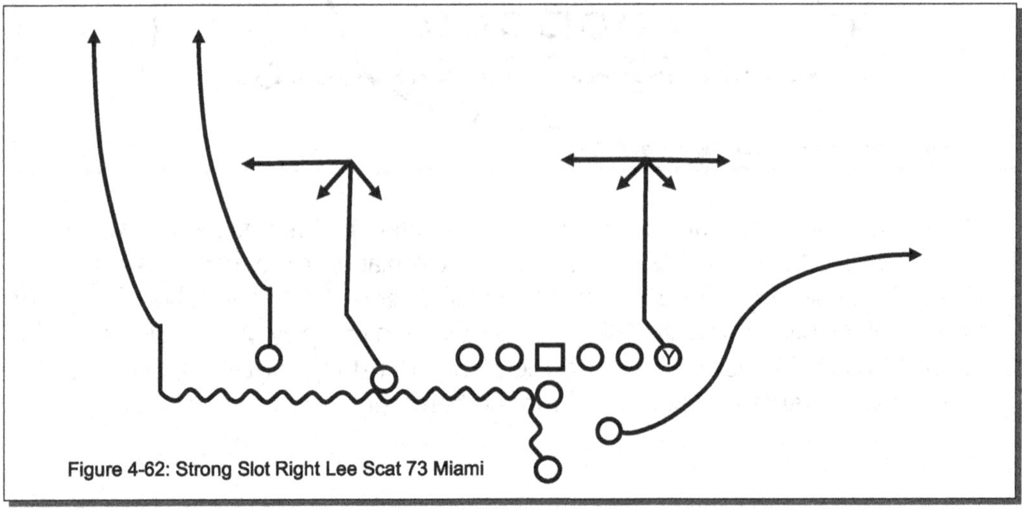

Figure 4-62: Strong Slot Right Lee Scat 73 Miami

**Play: 4-62**

| Pos: | Assignment: | Coaching Points: |
|---|---|---|
| R | Run go. | Must outside release. |
| F | Free release. Run bend route. | vs. strong pressure: 1 yd hot. |
| X | Run seam. | Must outside release. |
| Y | Run 10-yd option route. Get open! | Stem inside. Get the middle. Alert hot off 1 strong. |
| Z | Run 8-10 yd outside option route. | Work over my alignment–outside. |
| QB | Homerun:<br>Progression: 1. Y<br>2. F<br>3. Z<br><br>Outlet: R | vs. strong pressure: hit R hot in flat. |

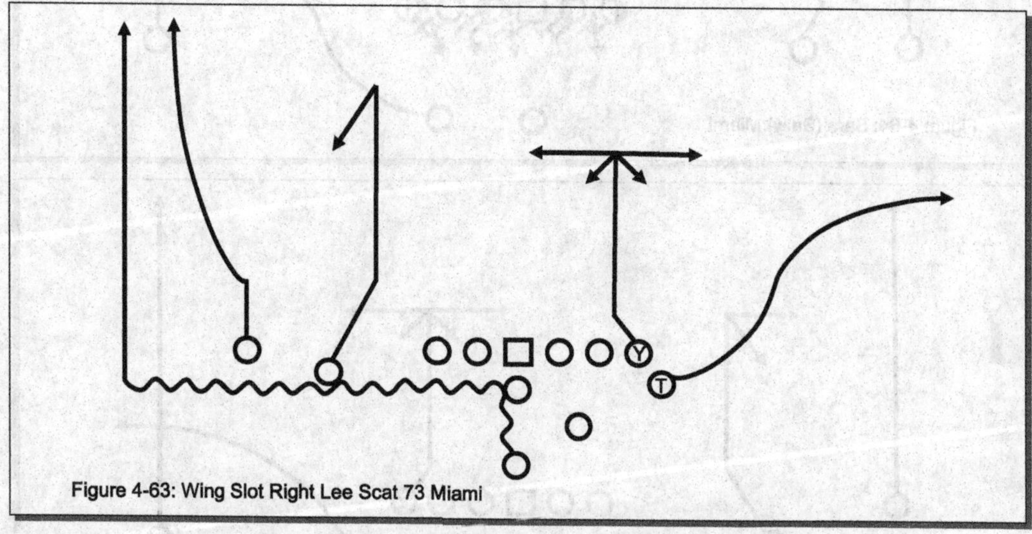

Figure 4-63: Wing Slot Right Lee Scat 73 Miami

When teams started blitzing the back, bringing guys, and then dropping a bunch of other guys out in various "zone-replace" schemes, we added "Sara/Sally Miami" (Figure 4-64). I also really like "R mo" against some of those schemes, because then they can't spy the back and the defensive end can't keep leverage to peel off with him. If teams bring inside pressure and ask that defensive end to "green dog" the back, we just motion the back outside of the tight end by calling "doubles right, R mo: scat 73 Miami" (Figure 4-65).

Again, we want our coaches and players to be able to visualize the *concepts*. Once you can visualize each of these pass plays as a concept first, it then becomes pretty easy to see how each concept is compatible with any number of personnel groupings, formations, motions and shifts. You begin to understand how "Miami" and "94" ("grey" from the quick game) are similar *concepts*. This really frees up a playcaller to be able to dictate things to the defense, so that they can't take you out of best plays. For a quarterback, if he can start to picture these mental images this way, he can really begin to take command of the offense and play with a contagious level of confidence. When the playcaller and quarterback can then get themselves in tune with each other, that's when the passing attack can truly become special!

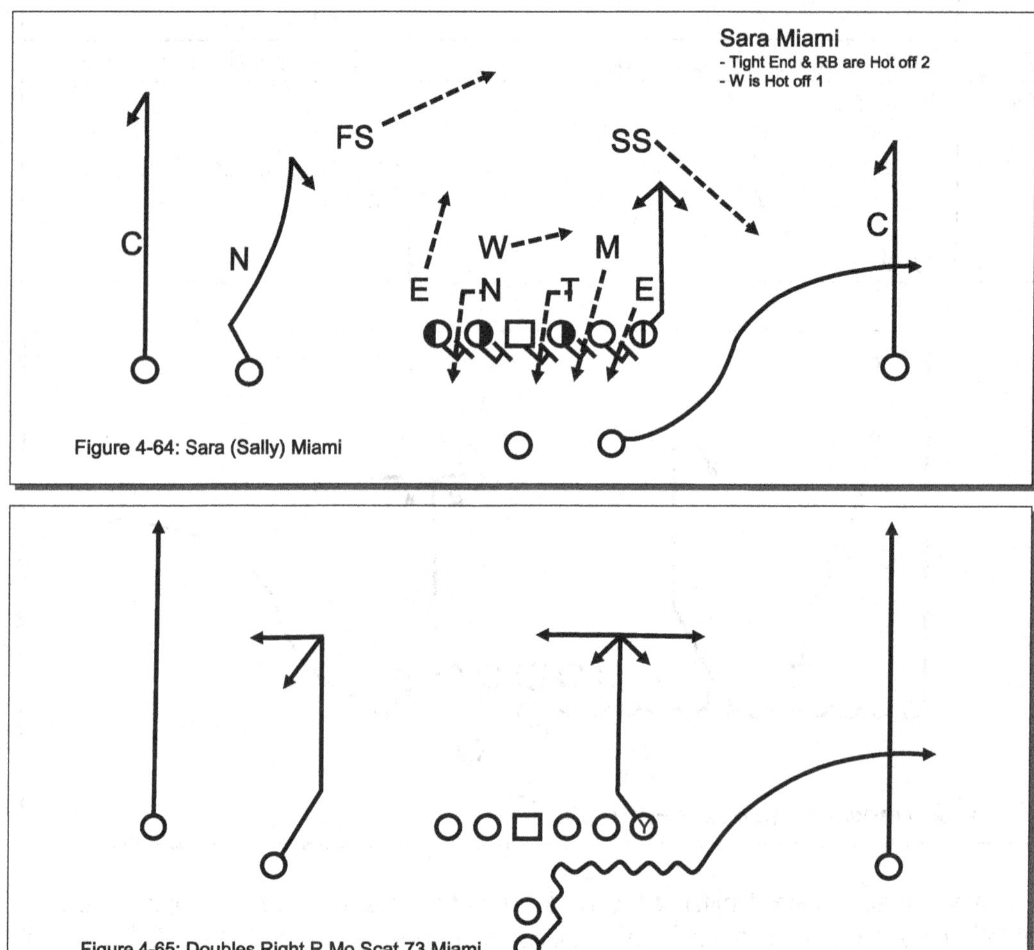


Figure 4-64: Sara (Sally) Miami

Figure 4-65: Doubles Right R Mo Scat 73 Miami

❑ Option Routes

This category began life as our option route series, but like we said, it has since sort of merged with the "Miami" concept that we install with the "controls" category. There are several ways to package option routes in the dropback passing game and this is just what we did to maintain a sense of continuity for our players. Again, when we talk about a "control" concept, we aren't necessarily trying to hit the home run. Rather, we want to get a clean completion, move the chains, and build offensive momentum into the next playcall.

❑ 84

The option route for W becomes another "control" concept that has been consistently very good for us. It's really best from "trips" formation; you don't really need to carry it from too many formations. "Trips: 84" (Figure 4-66) is a good "3rd-&-6 we need a 1st-down" play and also a great "1st-&-10" play, because like we've said, we also believe in throwing our favorite passes on 1st down, not just when we *have* to throw. Z has a "collision-drag." He's got to come off the ball and try to collision that inside linebacker and drag across his face, which has always been a hard thing to coach. Sometimes, we just say, "run a 5-step post to the other side," because wide receivers don't always like to go down in there like the tight ends do. The tight end checks 80 protection and runs a 10-yard out route. The back runs a "check-stretch" to the slot-receiver side. The outside receiver (X) has a post over the top. The coaching point for X is if he gets a jam corner, he must outside release it, so if the running back catches the ball on a stretch route, the X doesn't bring the corner's eyes there.

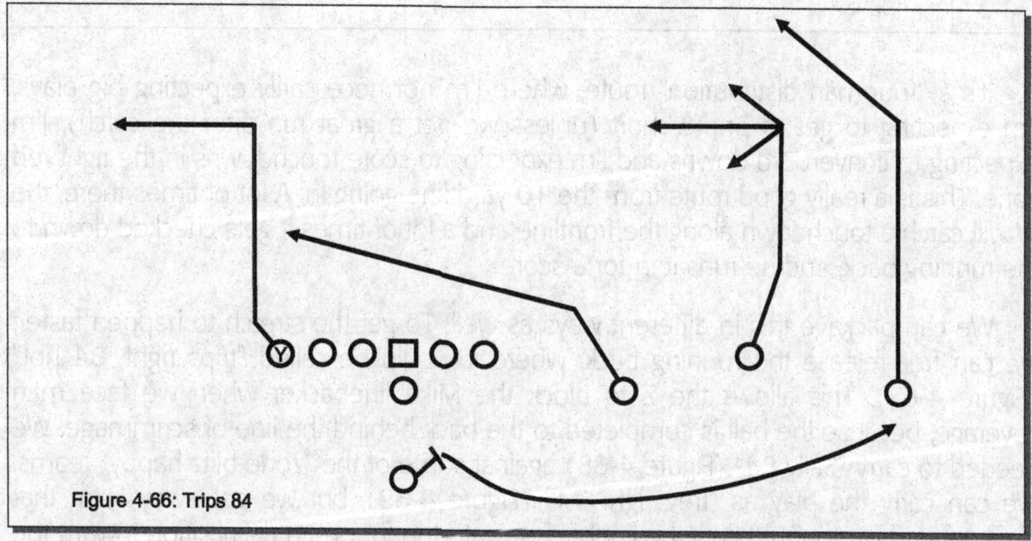


Figure 4-66: Trips 84

The W receiver has the option-route from the #2 position. He wants to get an arc release, push vertical to eight yards, and then understand "man or zone." If it's zone coverage, he's going to snap it inside and settle, and the quarterback needs to "throw him open" to his inside hand. If it's man coverage, he's going to *snap it* and stay on the move. The quarterback needs to keep him open and throw him open on the move. The quarterback takes a 5-step drop from under the center, throwing the option route "off the plant" (or 3-steps off the plant in the gun). He's got to throw the ball *before* the W breaks, so he has to understand by reading the inside linebackers whether it's man or zone. If it's not there, he resets his feet to throw an accurate, catchable ball to the back on the stretch route, so we can get yards after the catch.

**Play: 4-66**

| Pos: | Assignment: | Coaching Points: |
|---|---|---|
| R | Check 80 protection and run stretch route. | Check step. Gain width. Catch ball 2-3 yards from LOS. |
| W | Run 8-10 yard inside option route. Get open! | vs. man coverage snap post for a TD |
| X | Square corner up and run post route. | vs. cover 2: run fade route and outside release. |
| Y | Check 80 protection and run 10-yard out route. | |
| Z | Run collision drag. | |
| QB | Homerun: W Key: pre-snap: FS<br>Progression: 1. W<br>2. R post-snap: weak inside LB<br>3. Y<br><br>Outlet: R | Be aware of no player at strongside for Y. |

It's a "four-man distribution" route, where I'm not necessarily expecting big plays, I'm expecting to get to 2nd-&-short (unless we get a great run after the catch), I'm expecting to convert 3rd downs and I'm expecting to score touchdowns in the tight red zone. This is a really good route from the 10-yard line going in. A lot of times there, the W will catch a touchdown along the frontline and a lot of times it gets checked down to the running back, and he runs it in for a score.

We can package this in different ways as well. To get the stretch to happen faster, we can free-release the running back, where it would be called "trips right, 84 hot" (Figure 4-67). This allows the Z to block the Mike linebacker when we face man coverage, because the ball is completed to the back behind the line of scrimmage. We needed to carry "Sally 84" (Figure 4-68) against some of the "zone-blitz happy" teams. We can carry the play as "trey right 74" (Figure 4-69), but we got away from that because defenses would flow the linebackers with the four-man distribution toward the tight end and the Mike linebacker would get underneath the read. I also think that in general, a Sam linebacker doesn't work a flow call against "trips" formation as much or as well as a Will does against "trey" formation, so we prefer to just carry the play from "trips" instead.

❑ R Burst: Sally 84 Z Grab

The following is an example of how we packaged this concept. We called this "doubles right, R burst: Sally 84, Z grab" (Figure 4-70). "Burst" motion, where the back leaves the backfield but maintains his depth, can be useful for various types of curl and spot routes, in order to get the stretch to happen faster. We'd set the option route right on the hash at eight yards, and on the backside, would run "grab." If Mike goes with the

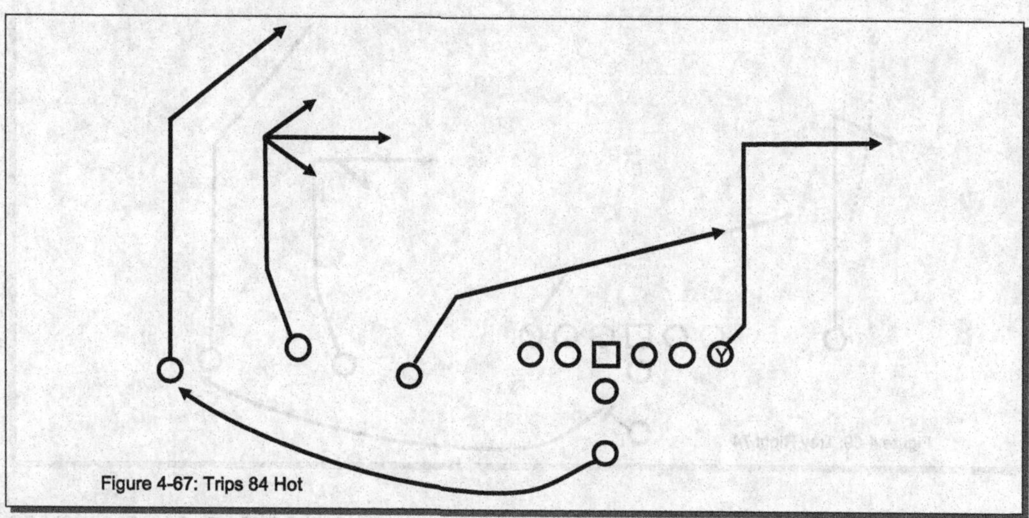
Figure 4-67: Trips 84 Hot

**Play: 4-67**

| Pos: | Assignment: | Coaching Points: |
|---|---|---|
| R | Free release. Run stretch route. | Catch the ball 2-3 yds from LOS. |
| W | Run 8-10 yd inside option. Get open! | vs. man: snap post for TD. |
| X | Square corner up and run 12-yd post. | vs. cover 2: convert fade. |
| Y | Stay call black<br>84 grey. Check 10-yd out. | |
| Z | Run collision drag. | Bang 1st LB inside. |
| QB | Homerun: X Key: pre-snap – FS<br>Progression: 1. W<br>2. R post-snap – Weak ILB<br>3. Y<br>Outlet: | Be alert to no flat player to strongside for Y. |

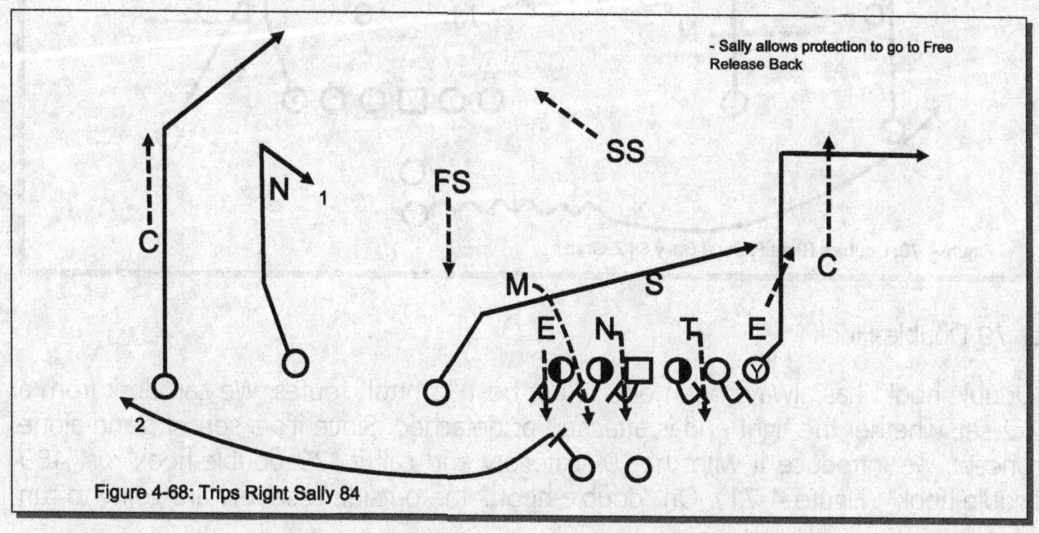

Figure 4-68: Trips Right Sally 84

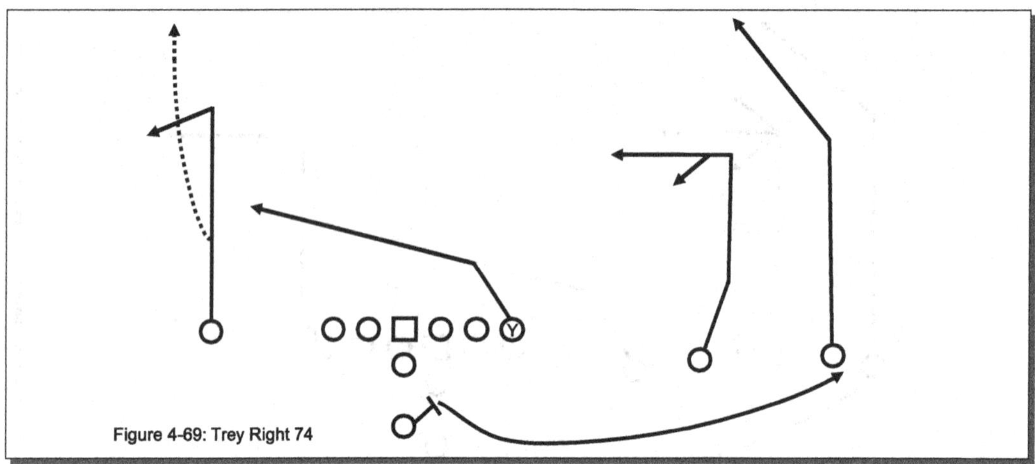

Figure 4-69: Trey Right 74

motion, then Sam is isolated "high-low" with the grab. We liked it vs. cloud coverage into the boundary, but if they show a quarters-look, it wasn't as good and we didn't want to get into coaching "grab," where #2 just "runs through" a quarters safety. We didn't "burst" the back that much from 11 personnel, because we wanted to maintain the threat of zone-read runs from our 1-back sets, though we did like to package it out of that "spread" look and then "burst" to get into 3x1 sets. (Our "scat" examples in the quick game chapter were a good illustration of that kind of idea.)

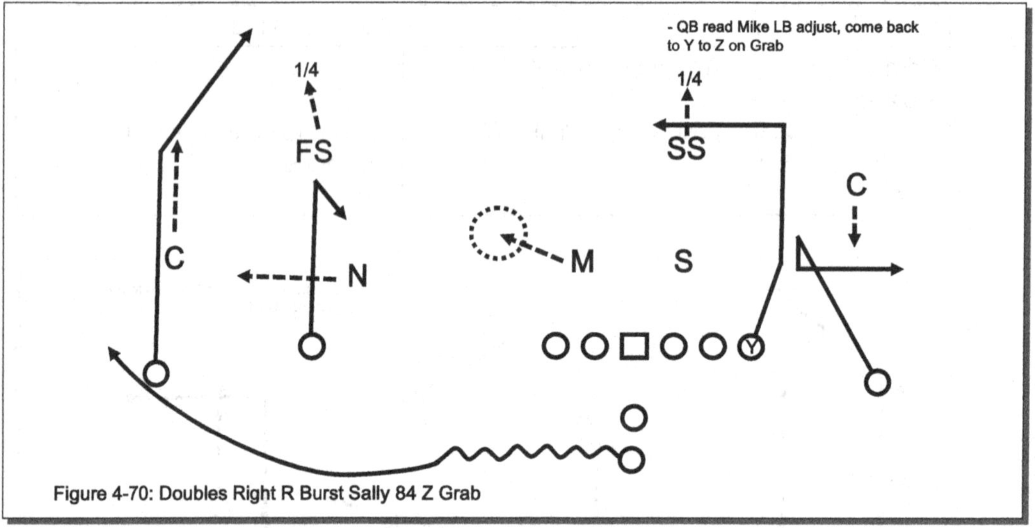

Figure 4-70: Doubles Right R Burst Sally 84 Z Grab

❑ 79 Double-Hook

"Double-hook" has always been one of our best "control" routes. We can do it from a 2x2 set, whether the tight end is attached or detached. Since it's a sort of stand-alone concept, we introduce it with the "9" category and call it "79 double-hook" or "489 double-hook" (Figure 4-71). On "double-hook," the outside receivers are going to run

16-yard comebacks, which they convert vs. jam corners. Both inside receivers have 8-to-10-yard "hook" routes, where "I get to the nearest defender, drive my depth, and 'hook in, hook out, or break out.'" If we break out, we want to think of the idea of coming downhill at "89 degrees," and not getting undercut. I understand how to "wrap" the guy, if he is undercutting me, and I need to understand vs. press how to "dive inside, push vertical, throw him by, and break back outside." There's a lot to a "hook" route.

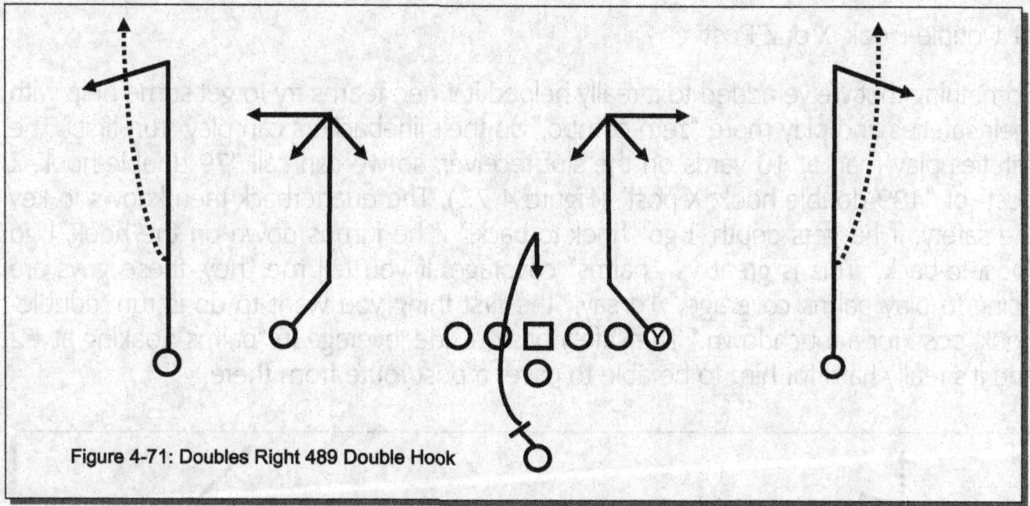


Figure 4-71: Doubles Right 489 Double Hook

**Play: Doubles Right: 489 Double-Hook**

| Pos: | Assignment: | Coaching Points: |
|---|---|---|
| R | Check 400 protection. Run checkdown over the ball. | |
| W | Run 10-yd hook route. | |
| X | Run 15 yd caddy. | vs. cover 2: convert fade. |
| Y | Run 10-yd hook route. | |
| Z | Run 15 yd caddy. | vs. cover 2: convert fade. |
| QB | Progression: 1. X-W-R<br>2. Z-Y-R<br><br>Outlet: | vs. cover 2: key away from the Mike linebacker<br>vs. single high: read outside-in |

With 2-high, the quarterback wants to key the Mike linebacker, so wherever the Mike linebacker goes, he wants to go "opposite the Mike," from the hook-receiver on that side, down to the running back on the "check-through." (We call it a "check-through" route, where he wants to be able to get open over the ball, but in the "A or B gap window," so the quarterback can see him). You need to know where you want to send your back. If you get "2 Tampa," send your back to the field or to the "speed receiver," so he can chase the Mike, turn around, catch the ball, and get the 1st down. That's again when we can also call it "489" to be able to send the back in either direction.

If you get single-high, the whole play changes. Now, I'm going from an "outside-in" read. So, the quarterback pictures "I got two linebackers and two drop safeties, with a single-high safety." I'm going to drop back thinking, "outside-in," so I want to throw the comeback. If the guy over my slot receiver gets underneath the comeback, I'm going to throw the hook. If the linebacker gets underneath the hook, I'm going to throw the back on the check-through. It's a simple progression "outside-in, 1, 2, 3."

❑ Double-Hook, X or Z Post

Something that we've added to it really helped it when teams try to get some help with their safeties and play more "zero-combo," so their linebackers can play "run-first." The safeties play man at 10 yards on the slot receiver, so we can call "79 double-hook, Z post" or "489 double-hook, X post" (Figure 4-72). The quarterback then knows to key the safety: if he gets depth, I go "hook-to-back," if he jumps down on the hook, I go "post-to-back." This is great vs. "palms" coverage. If you tell me "hey, these guys are going to play palms coverage," I'd say, "the first thing you want to do is run 'double-hook, post' for a touchdown." The safety has outside leverage in "palms" looking at #2 and it's really hard for him to be able to cover a post route from there.

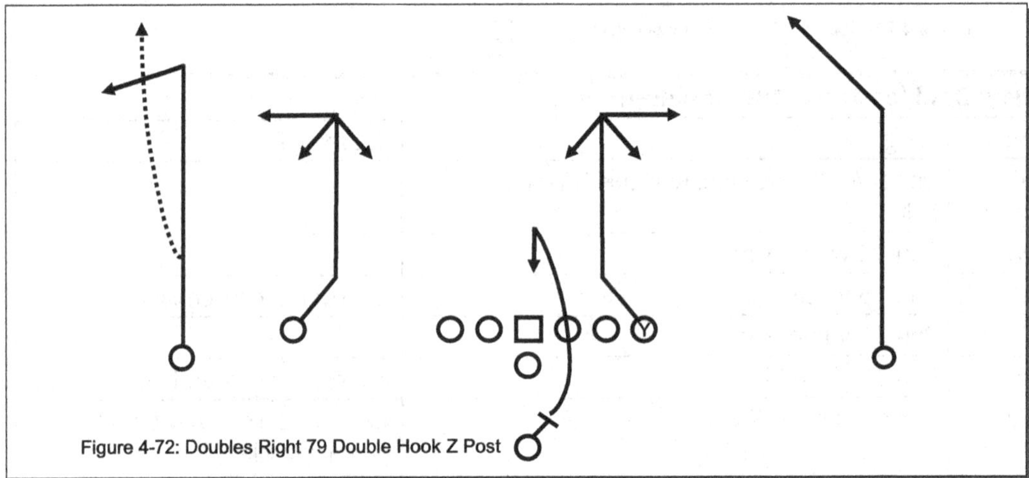
Figure 4-72: Doubles Right 79 Double Hook Z Post

**Play: Doubles Right: 79 Double-Hook, Z Post**

| Pos: | Assignment: | Coaching Points: |
|---|---|---|
| R | Check 70 protection. Run checkdown over the ball. | |
| W | Run 10-yd hook route. | |
| X | Run 15-yd caddy. | vs. cover 2: convert fade. |
| Y | Run 10-yd hook route. | |
| Z | Run 12-yd post. | |
| QB | Progression: 1. X-W-R vs. single high<br>2. Z-Y-R vs. 2 high<br>Outlet: | |

❑ Smash (6)

At this point, I'd like to introduce our "6" or "smash" series. Just like we said about the control and option-route plays, the learning curve for our crossers was faster and seemed to stick with players better when we began to introduce them all together. Our "5s" involve the W on the read route over the top of Z or Y on the shallow cross and the "7s" take the tight end over the top of W or X on the shallow crosser instead. "8" is the mesh series and we also use "9" for some miscellaneous crosser concepts. So, at this point, let's take a look at our "6" category, and then finish the dropback presentation with all of those crossers together.

We have three basic ways we like to run our base smash. Within our "6" concept, we basically have three things we run: "smash," "China," and "return." We install and teach those first, then begin to introduce the various combos from there. As with the other packages, let's take a look at the basics first, then some combos, and finally some newer developments, so you can get a sense of how we build up and put together the various packages.

❑ Smash

The "smash" tag for us means that the outside receiver reads it and is either going to run a basic hitch against free-access or "bring it" on a 5-yard in, if he's pressed. If it converts, he needs to gain depth on that as he brings it; he starts inside, pushes vertical, and then separates away from coverage (Figure 4-73). Our slot receiver (#2) is going to run the corner route. With a wide receiver, we teach it as a 12-yard breaking point to 25 yards on the sideline. Then if you're inside the 30, you need to run it to the back pylon. We tell tight ends "you must run past two lines before you break to the corner," because a lot of times tight ends shorten that route up and end up at eight yards. (If they're used to running receiver routes, they can use the yardage at 12, but if they can't, you have to "at least go by two lines." At most it could end up 14-yards deep before he breaks, but that's better than eight yards, in order to maintain proper spacing.)

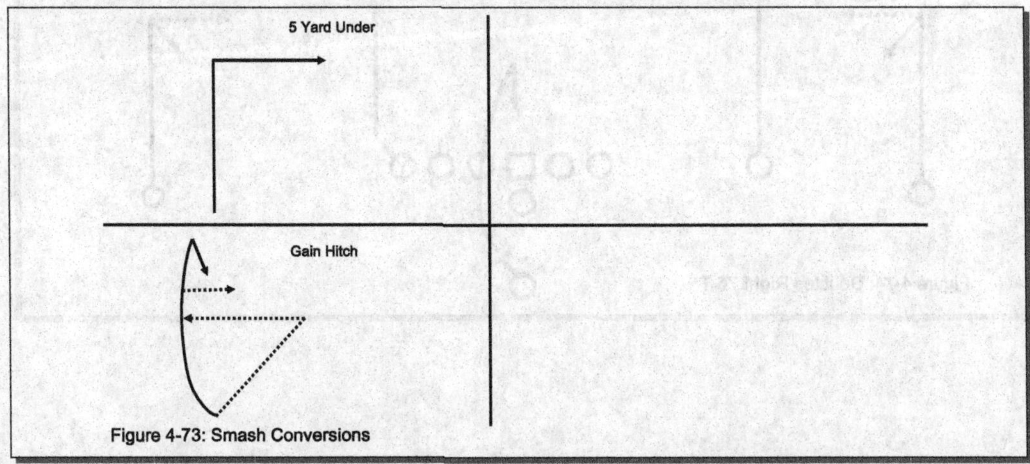

Figure 4-73: Smash Conversions

**Play: Smash Conversions**

**5-Yard Under Route:**
Proper split (max) come off the ball under control. Good footwork and run 5-yard under route. "Bring it."

**Gain Hitch Route:**
vs off, sprint off the ball, gaining width. 5 steps, 3 big, 2 little. Sit down with your dukes up.

vs press, run return route. Work up the field, stick at 45 degrees, sink hips, and return towards sideline.

vs jam, run 5-yard under, "bring it".

On vertical-stemming routes, like a corner, the most important part of that is that "I'm going to sprint three-steps out of my break," before I look up. Nothing bothers me more than when a corner route is open and "aw, shoot! It's right off his fingertips," because he didn't *sprint* three-steps out of his break before he looked back. (That makes quarterbacks mad too, when they think they threw a perfect pass and we don't get to it.)

The inside receiver also needs to understand coverages, because if he gets cover 3, it's very important for him to inside-release the strong safety (not outside-release him), so the strong safety squeezes and his body turns away from our hitch. If you get true cover 3, the quarterback needs to "bang the hitch" and get the ball out there. It's a way to throw a hitch and get a little bit more cushion for the run after the catch off of a 5-step drop (but if W doesn't run it right, it doesn't work). You can "mirror" this to both sides as a starting point. We started using a "T" tag to tell the tight end to mirror it, such as "76T" (Figure 4-74).

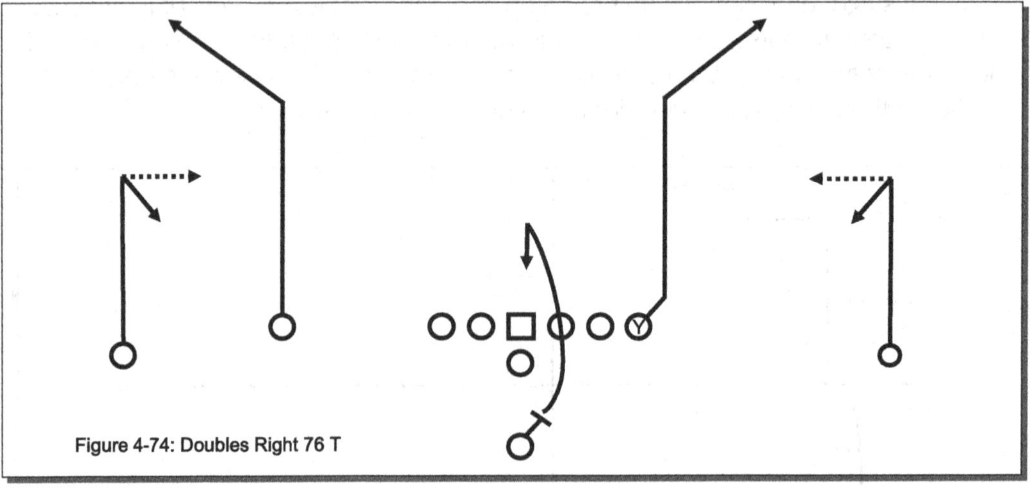


Figure 4-74: Doubles Right 76 T

**Play: Doubles Right: 76 "T"**

| Pos: | Assignment: | Coaching Points: |
|---|---|---|
| R | Check 70 protection. Run checkdown. | |
| W | Run corner route at 12 yds. | |
| X | Run 6-yd smash read. Sit vs. zone at 6 yds. | vs. press: outside release to 6 yds and bring it. |
| Y | Run corner route at 12 yds. | |
| Z | Run 6-yd smash read. Sit vs. zone at 6 yds. | vs. press: outside release to 6 yds and bring it. |
| QB | Homerun: Key: pre-snap: FS: 1. W<br>Progression: 1. Y 2. X<br>2. Z post-snap: Corner<br><br>Outlet: R | vs. pressure: alert check |

❑ China

"China" gives us different conversions for the outside receiver. In this instance, if I have an off-corner, I still run the hitch, sit and wait, and expect the ball. The quarterback is going to "bang it," or check it down to you, so you just sit there and be patient. If I get a jam corner (cover 2), I want to act like I'm trying to run a fade. I let him think he's beating me, getting his hands on me, and kicking my butt, so he doesn't pivot inside, read #2, and run back out of there. If I get pressed, I run a "return" route, which means I'm going to dive down inside, get to five yards, plant my inside foot in the ground, come out of it, and "return" back to the sideline. It's important on my return route that I *sprint* to the sideline with my shoulders to the sideline, and only turn my *head* back to the quarterback. If I open my shoulders to run a return, we're not going to complete many passes.

❑ Return

Sometimes, we'll just call "return," where it's now a "locked" return. Some quarterbacks really like us to call "return" as a check vs. "blitz zero," because it forces the corner to declare what he's doing. If he starts down in there, we have the corner route for a touchdown. If he hangs back, then we throw the "return" route. Normally in that coverage, the guy playing the slot receiver takes inside leverage, so quarterbacks like this down in the red zone, to be able to take advantage of man coverage and throw touchdowns on the corner route.

❑ 6 Combos

We don't call the 2x2 mirrored smash play that much, but we've had a lot of success with "6" as a combo. We tag it like that: "86T return" or "486 smash," so you have different ways to be able to combine the smash concept with other ideas. We have dozens of these available, but I'll share some of our favorites.

❑ 86 Z Bingo

We carry a lot of different combinations off this basic concept. We typically introduce it within our installation with what we call "doubles right: 86 Z bingo" (Figure 4-75). This means that we're running the "China" route to the field, but in this case, the back's rules are overridden by the "bingo" call, which tells Z to run the 14-yard in-cut and both the tight end and the running back to run outside-option routes, after they check their respective "80 protection" responsibilities. It's important for the running back to push it to five yards past the line of scrimmage and it's a great play for the tight end to chip the defensive end, "get some ribs," and also get to five yards, running an outside-option route. If you get cover 2, you're opening up that big in-cut for the solo receiver. We've already introduced the mechanics of those particular routes and those skills carry over to this play.

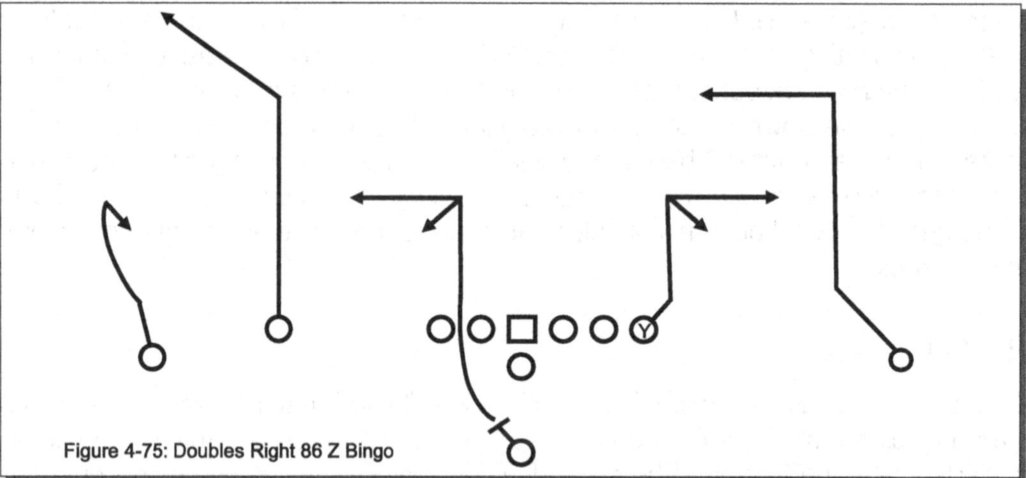


Figure 4-75: Doubles Right 86 Z Bingo

It's been very good to us over the years. There are times where you carry it as a formation "into," so you get that China route into the boundary. As a quarterback, I understand that I might have to "bang the hitch" and I might have to throw those checkdowns on the option routes. I don't see this as a 3rd-down play as much as I do a 1st-&-10 "chunk" play. It's very good vs. the "4Q" coverage, because basically that ends up "cover 2 to the Z receiver side," which still allows you to throw the in-cut.

**Play: Doubles Right: 86 Z Bingo**

| Pos: | Assignment: | Coaching Points: |
|---|---|---|
| R | Check 80 protection. Run outside option. | |
| W | Run corner route at 12 yds. | |
| X | Run 6-yd China route. | |
| Y | Check 80 protection. Run outside option. | |
| Z | Run in-cut at 14 yards. | |
| QB | Progression: 1. Z 1. W<br>2. Y 2. X<br><br>Outlet: R | |

❑ Z Squirrel

As that Z is releasing inside, pushing up, and snapping it, some coaches will teach that safety to start sitting down on an inside release of Z to cheat the big in-cuts. This brings us to our next play in the series: "doubles right: 86 Z squirrel" (Figure 4-76). It's still "86" to the X and W, nothing's changed there. The running back will still run the outside-option. On this play, our tight end is going to "chip" and run a diagonal route, so he occupies the corner to the side of the Z. A lot of times we might call "snug" on this, so z tightens his split (or we'll just make him tighten his split by game plan). Now, he's going to run a "corner-post" on that safety. If he doesn't tighten his split, he's going to stem down inside, push vertical, sell the corner for a step, and then come back to the post. If he runs it from a tightened-down split, it's a "point-to-point" route, as opposed to an inside stem.

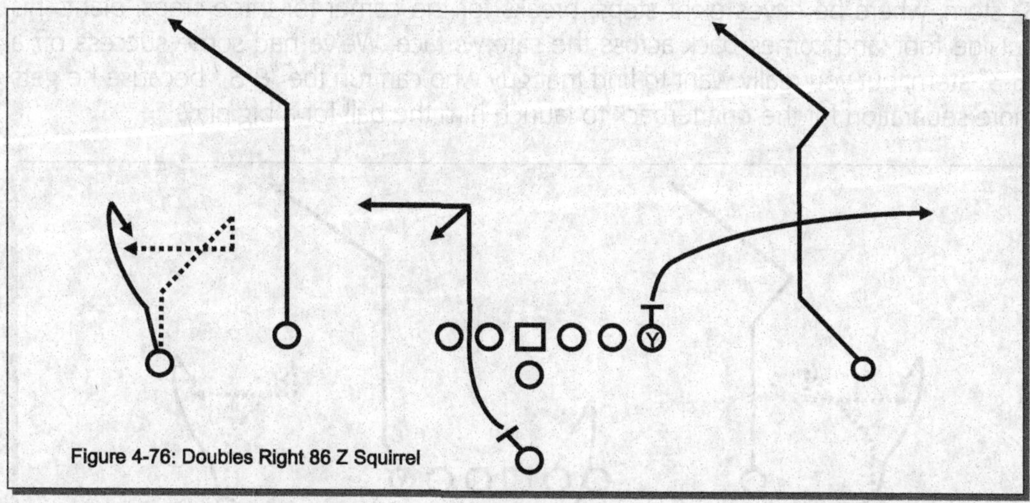

Figure 4-76: Doubles Right 86 Z Squirrel

**Play: 4-76**

| Pos: | Assignment: | Coaching Points: |
|---|---|---|
| R | Check 80 protection. Run outside option. | |
| W | Run corner route at 12 yds. | |
| X | Run 6-yd halt.<br>vs. press: return. | |
| Y | Check 80 protection. Run diagonal route. | |
| Z | Run squirrel route. | |
| QB | Progression: 1. Z 1. W<br>2. Y 2. X<br><br>Outlet: R | |

This is a way to get a double-move on a safety and get you a chance for another "chunk" play. You have a place for a "win" and places to go with the ball if it isn't there. A lot of years, this has been a productive 1st & 10 opener in 2-minute situations as well.

❑ W Squirrel

We can set the "squirrel route" up for the slot receiver by calling "486T, W squirrel" (Figure 4-77). Now your W receiver gets a chance to run that corner-post against a safety, which is really good vs. a "quarters" safety. This is good as a 1st-down "shot" playcall, especially when you know they're playing more "zero-combo" than quarters coverage, where the linebackers are playing the run and the safety is alone on the slot with straight-man coverage. The best guys that we've had can run this off an "8-3" stem, where he drives eight steps, breaks for the corner for three steps, plants his outside foot, and comes back across the safety's face. We've had some success off a "6-3" stem, but you really want to find that guy who can run the "8-3," because he gets more separation for the quarterback to launch him the ball for a big play.

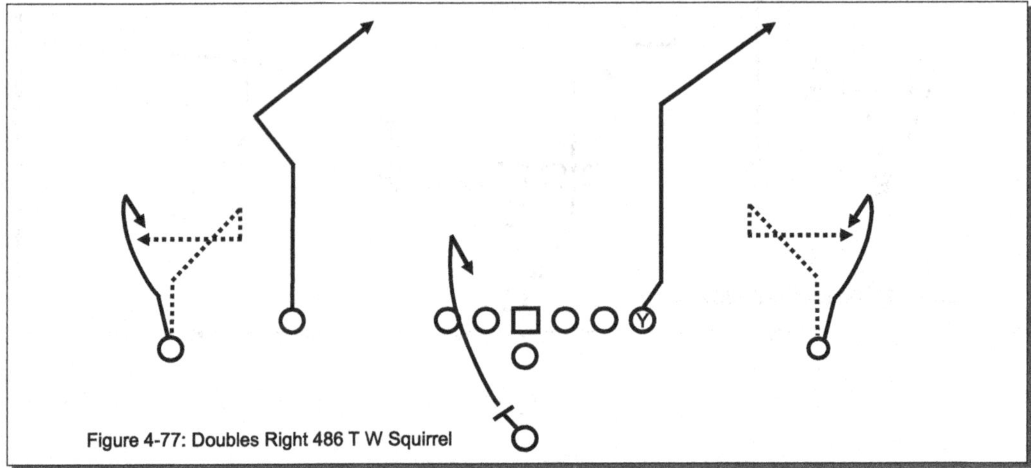


Figure 4-77: Doubles Right 486 T W Squirrel

**Play: 4-77**

| Pos: | Assignment: | Coaching Points: |
|---|---|---|
| R | Check 400 protection. Run checkdown. | |
| W | Run squirrel route. | |
| X | Run 6-yd halt.<br>vs. press: return. | |
| Y | Run corner route at 12 yds. | |
| Z | Run 6-yd halt.<br>vs. press: return. | |
| QB | Homerun: Key: pre-snap: FS<br>Progression: 1. Y 1. W<br>2. Z 2. X<br><br>Outlet: R | vs. pressure: alert check |

❑ R Option

We like to mirror the concept, if we have an explosive running back, where we can call "486T return, R option" (Figure 4-78). Again, the "T" for the tight end means we're running it on both sides. Both receivers have locked "return" routes, so they don't "bring it" inside and get in the way of the back. Then, you have "R option," in order to give the back the freedom to get open. We gave this the one-word code "rat." We're trying to isolate the running back on a Mike linebacker in "2-deep" and you still have the ability to "hold a safety, key a corner," or bang the return route vs. cover 3.

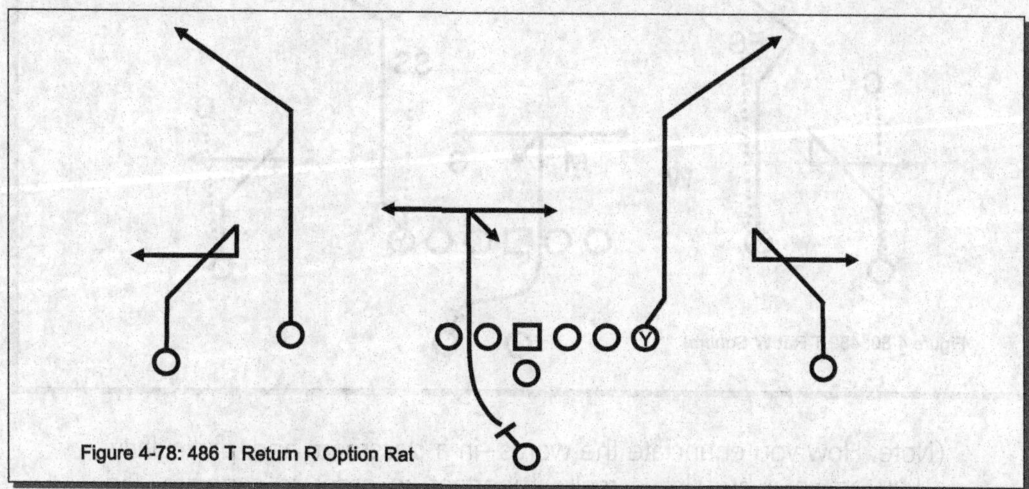

Figure 4-78: 486 T Return R Option Rat

It's really good to set this up from 10 personnel in 2x2, where you get free-releases. It's also nice to get the tight end flexed out and package the 2x2 formation from various 11 and 12 personnel groupings. When they try to match personnel, you can really get the Mike linebacker isolated and get a lot of yards after the catch. "Solo right: rat" (Figure

4-79) is an example, where you have your faster wide receivers aligned in the slots for the vertical routes on safeties and your tight end (or tight ends) aligned outside.

We can also package these two concepts and call: "486T rat, W squirrel" (Figure 4-80), which we like with "fox" action by the back. The "rat" call locks the outside receivers into return routes. You have the chance for the big play, the back on his option route and places to go outside with the football.

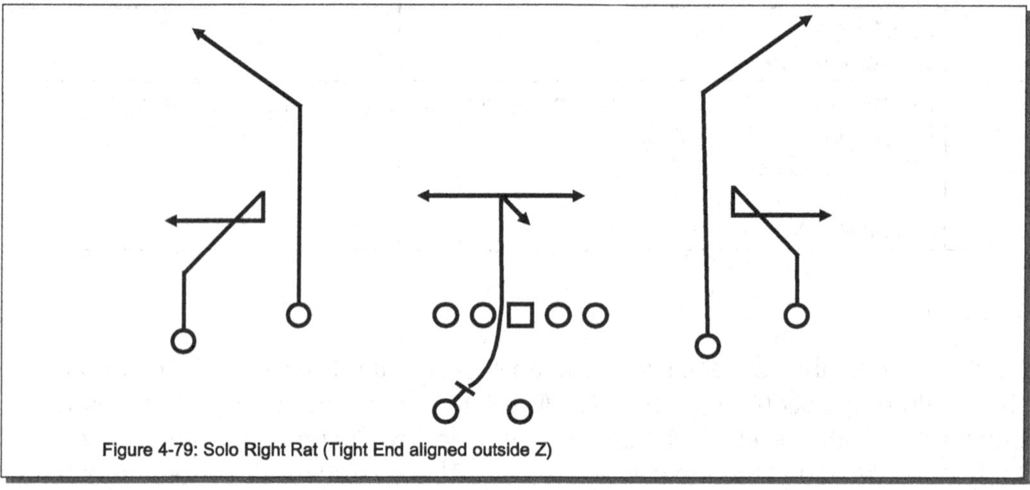

Figure 4-79: Solo Right Rat (Tight End aligned outside Z)

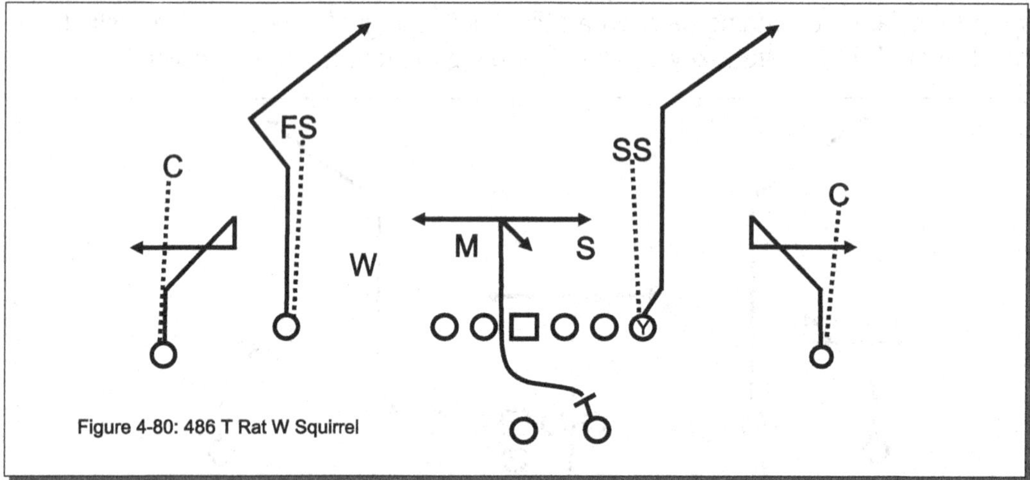


Figure 4-80: 486 T Rat W Squirrel

(Note: How you enunciate the words—in a classroom and, particularly, if you are in a huddle—is really important, in order to separate and emphasize certain things you want for the players: "486T rat, W squirrel.")

❑ Z Dream

We call this "doubles right: 486T, Z dream" (Figure 4-81). This is a newer concept, a way we added to both the "smash" and "shallow cross" packages, and something that has worked really well for us. You're running "486T" to the field. The "Z dream" would give you a return route by that X receiver, the corner routes, and on this, an outside-option route by the running back from a "far" alignment, after his "400 protection" responsibility.

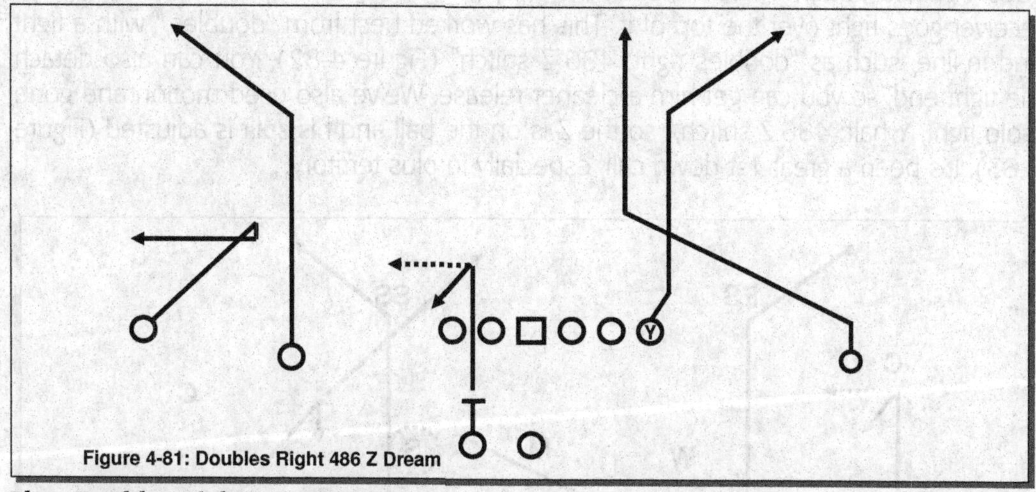
Figure 4-81: Doubles Right 486 Z Dream

**Play: Doubles Right: 486, Z Dream**

| Pos: | Assignment: | Coaching Points: |
|---|---|---|
| R | 400 protection. Outside option | |
| X | Run return route. | |
| W | Run corner route 12 yds. | |
| Y | Run corner route 12 yds. | |
| Z | Run dream route 1 yd O/S hash. | |
| QB | Progression: 1. Z<br>2. W to X<br>3. R | |

Z wants to start on a "drive" route, like he's coming down and running the shallow cross or drive route. He "sets" the corner with his footwork; he starts down like he's running a drive route and then plants his inside foot in the ground at Y's alignment and runs straight up the seam. He can't get too far inside or it's a really hard throw for the quarterback. This is a "drive-seam" route, that's similar to a double-move.

We remind the tight end again to cross two yard lines, to make sure he pushes his corner route sufficiently down the field. A lot of times what happens is that boundary safety has to cover the tight end, the linebacker thinks he's going to wall off the shallow crosser, and then the Z goes vertical and is wide open for a huge play. At worst, you throw the outside option to the running back on the other side. It's a recent development and has been a good play for us.

❑ Snitch

This is another way we protect our smash package. On "dream," the designated receiver runs a drive and then goes; on "snitch," the receiver instead runs a "snag" and then goes. Against "pattern-match" teams, the alley player turns to wall it off, and then the receiver goes right over the top of it. This has worked best from "doubles," with a tight end in-line, such as "doubles right: 486 Z snitch" (Figure 4-82). You can also detach the tight end, so you can get him a cleaner release. We've also used motion and gone "solo right, Y half: 486 Z snitch," so the Z is on the ball and his split is adjusted (Figure 4-83). It's been a great 1st-down call, especially in plus territory.

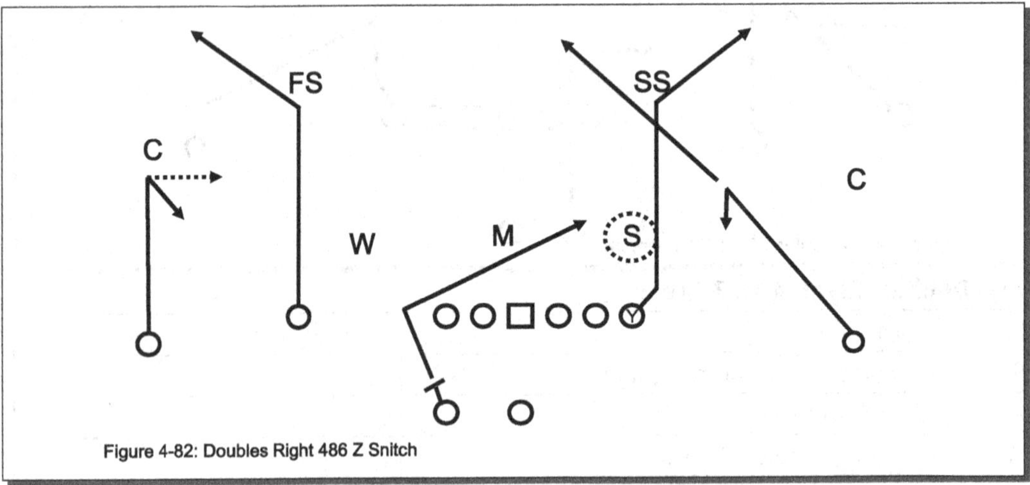

Figure 4-82: Doubles Right 486 Z Snitch

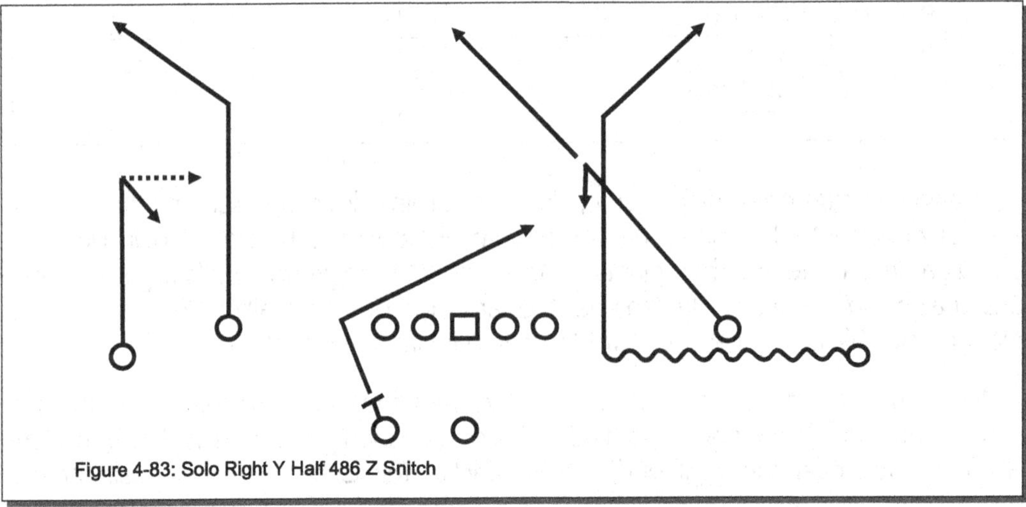
Figure 4-83: Solo Right Y Half 486 Z Snitch

❑ Cat (Cop)

From 3x1, we can use a "cat" tag. Once again, we may break from the "6" category for the playcall itself, but it's still certainly a smash concept. "Thunder slot right: 71C cat" (Figure 4-84) and "trey right: cat" have both been good for us. In any 3x1 formation with #3 detached ("trey, taxi, cab, posse," etc.), you can call it "480 cat" for a curl (Figure 4-85), "481 cat" for the out (Figure 4-86) or whatever route you want on the single-receiver side.

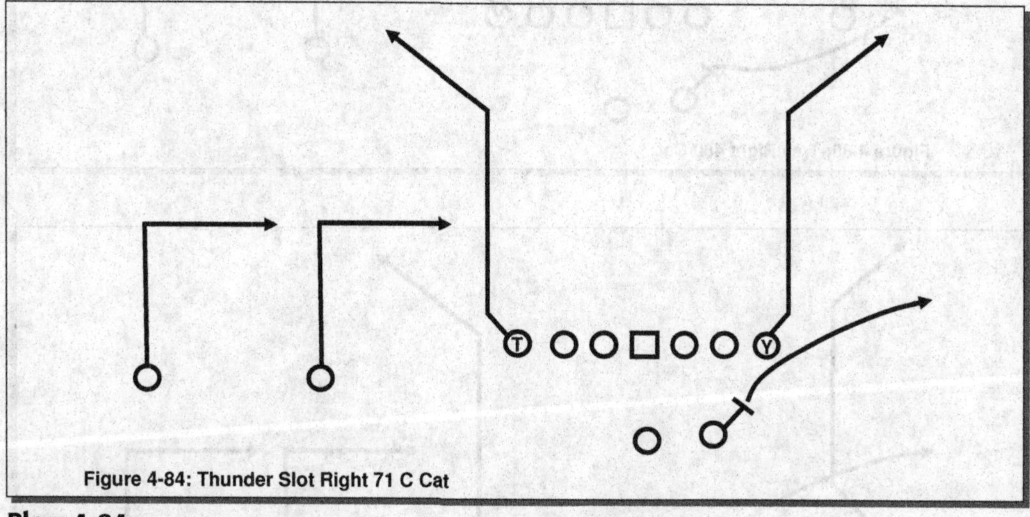


Figure 4-84: Thunder Slot Right 71 C Cat

**Play: 4-84**

| Pos: | Assignment: | Coaching Points: |
|---|---|---|
| R | Check 70 protection. Run diagonal route. | |
| T | Run 12-yd corner route. | Sprint 3 steps out of your break. |
| X | Run 5-yd under route. | |
| Y | Run 12-yd corner route. | Sprint 3 steps out of your break. |
| Z | Run 5-yd under route. | |
| QB | Homerun: Key: pre-snap: FS<br>Progression: 1. T or 1. Y<br>2. Z 2. R<br>3. X<br><br>Outlet: R | |

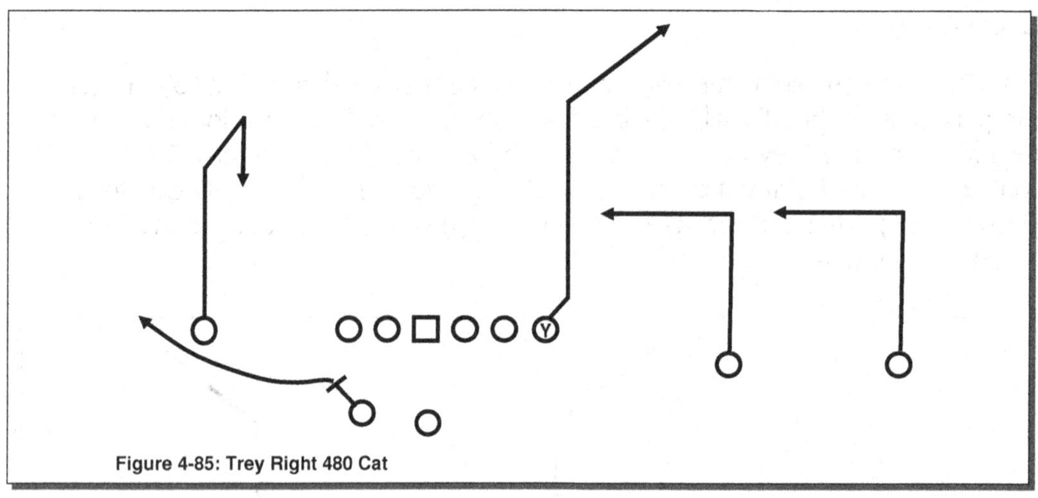

Figure 4-85: Trey Right 480 Cat

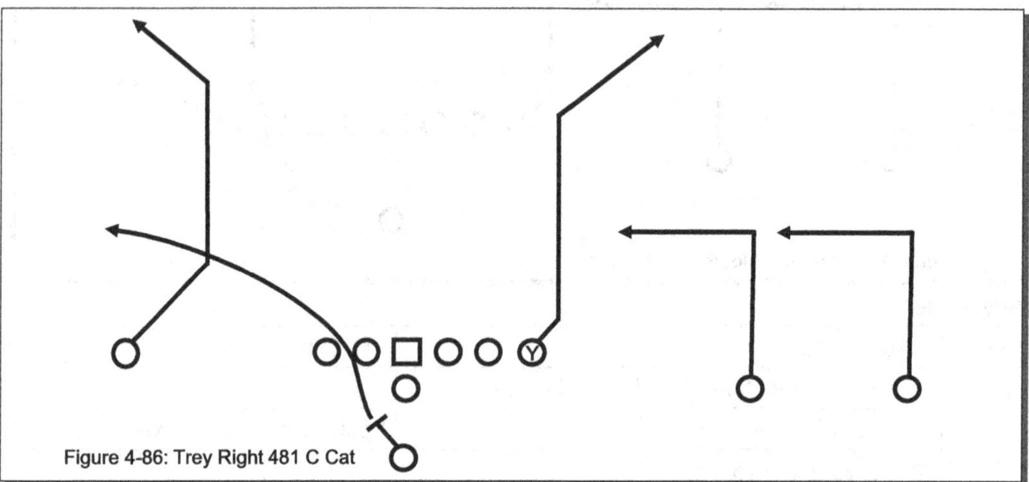

Figure 4-86: Trey Right 481 C Cat

**Play: 4-86**

| Pos: | Assignment: | Coaching Points: |
|---|---|---|
| R | Check 400 protection. Run diagonal route. | |
| W | Run 5-yd under route. | |
| X | Run 5-yd under route. | |
| Y | Run 12-yd corner route. | Sprint three steps out of your break. |
| Z | Run 4-5-1 corner. | |
| QB | Homerun Key: Pre-snap FS<br>Progression: 1.Y or 1. Z<br>2. W 2. R<br>3. X | |

The idea of "cat" is #3 runs the corner route, and the other two receivers run 5-yard ins. At one time, it was a really good check out of "trips" vs. "blitz-zero" in the red zone, where we would call "solid: cat" to get 7-man protection (Figure 4-87) and then run the "cat" route for a touchdown. If we have a receiver who has a natural ability to do it, we might also tag that as "cop" for "corner or post" (Figure 4-88), where he wants the corner route but has the option to break to the post, if he's walled off.

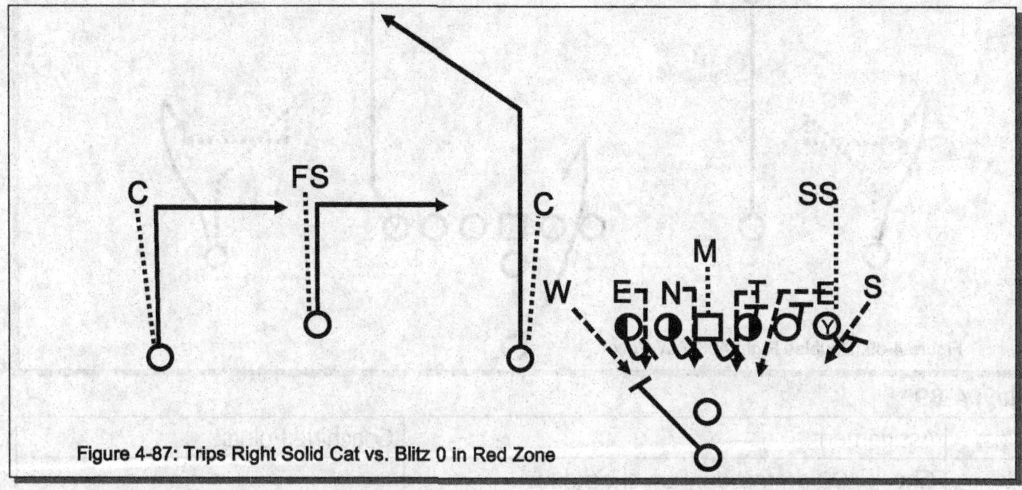

Figure 4-87: Trips Right Solid Cat vs. Blitz 0 in Red Zone

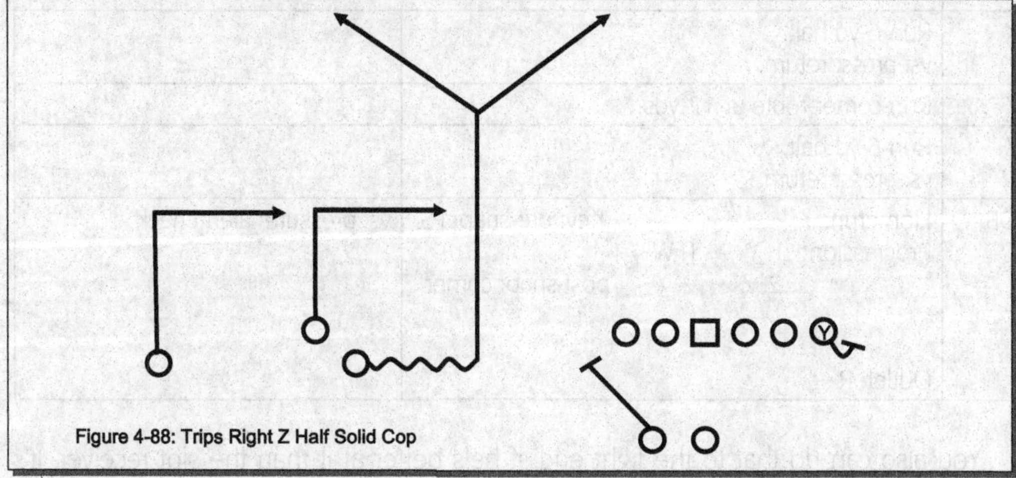

Figure 4-88: Trips Right Z Half Solid Cop

❑ Poco

We call the basic option route a "poco" for "post or corner." We've done this out of a 2x2, where you call "486T, W poco" (Figure 4-89). As with all our arsenal of option routes, he and the quarterback have to be on the same page. But this it's a good concept that we've had a lot of success with when we have a receiver who can run it. You have to have a quarterback who really understands coverage and he stays aware of the field corner; the only time you hesitate to install this is if the quarterback forgets about what the corner is doing on the outside, the receiver runs to the outside, and you throw a pick right to the corner.

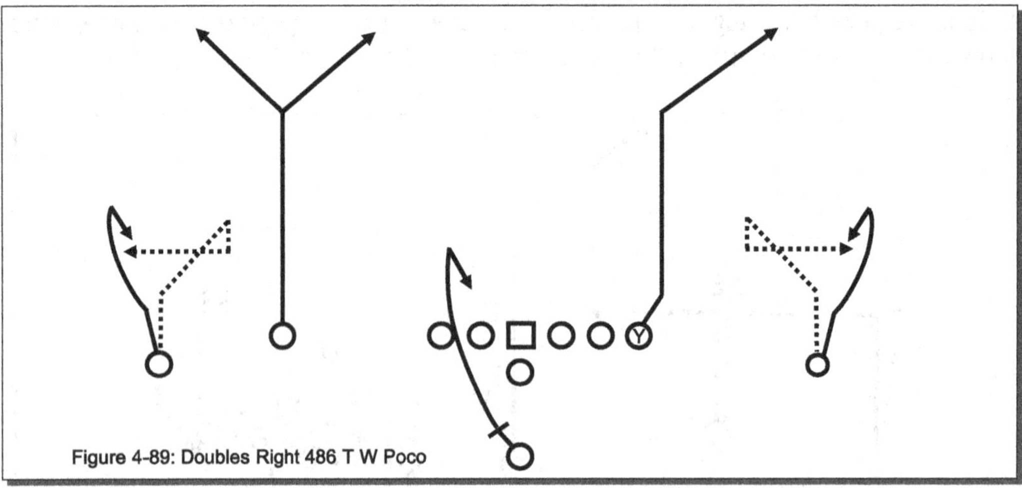

Figure 4-89: Doubles Right 486 T W Poco

**Play: 4-89**

| Pos: | Assignment: | Coaching Points: |
|---|---|---|
| R | Check 400 protection. Run checkdown. | |
| W | Run post or corner route. | Run route off safety. |
| X | Run 6-yd halt.<br>vs. press: return. | |
| Y | Run corner route at 12 yds. | |
| Z | Run 6-yd halt.<br>vs. press: return. | |
| QB | Homerun: Key: pre-snap: FS<br>Progression: 1. Y 1. W<br>2. Z 2. X post-snap: corner<br><br>Outlet: R | vs. pressure: alert check |

You also can do that to the tight end, if he's better at it than the slot receiver. It's really good off "strong slot right: 140 China, Y poco" (Figure 4-90). In this situation, Y runs either a post or corner route and you have a fullback in the flat. So if it's cover 2, the tight end is running it off that safety. If the safety stays inside, he runs a corner. If the safety gets width, he runs a post. As we build our packages, it's always based on "what can I coach? What can I teach? What can he do?"

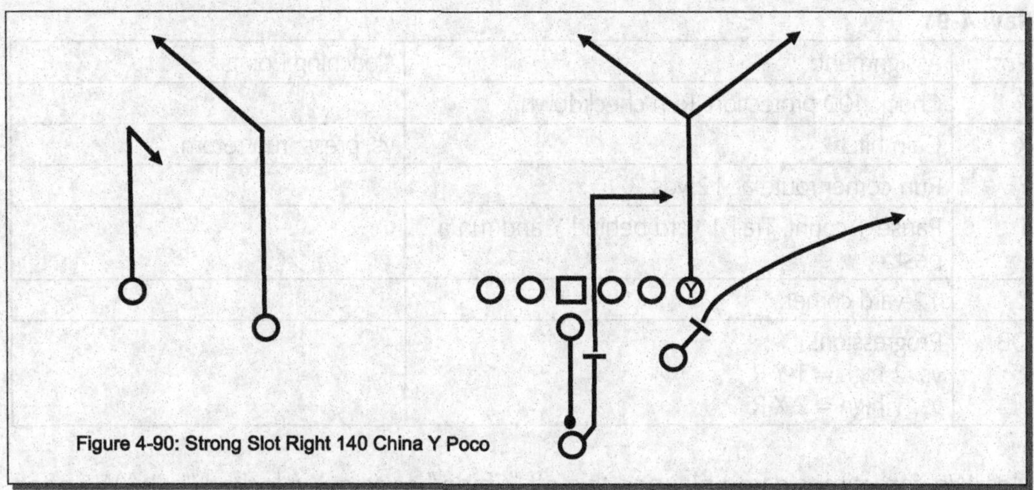

Figure 4-90: Strong Slot Right 140 China Y Poco

Some guys are really natural at it. Cole Hikutini could naturally run a poco route without much coaching whatsoever, so it was simple to build packages for him. He had great "get-off, great depth, and a great understanding of leverage. He understood "sprint out of my break three steps before I look for the ball." And he took those ball skills with him to the NFL.

❑ 486 T Blade

Remember our "blade" concept that we introduced in the "outs and corners" category as "81C blade"? This is another "blade" call within the "6" category: "wing slot right: 486T blade" (Figure 4-91). What we liked to do in this instance is we'd switch and put the fastest tight end at Y to run the corner route. T should hesitate—pause—follow him, and then break to the post. You always want to give the quarterback an "indicator" when you make your move. It's "486" so the split-end and slot understand their respective

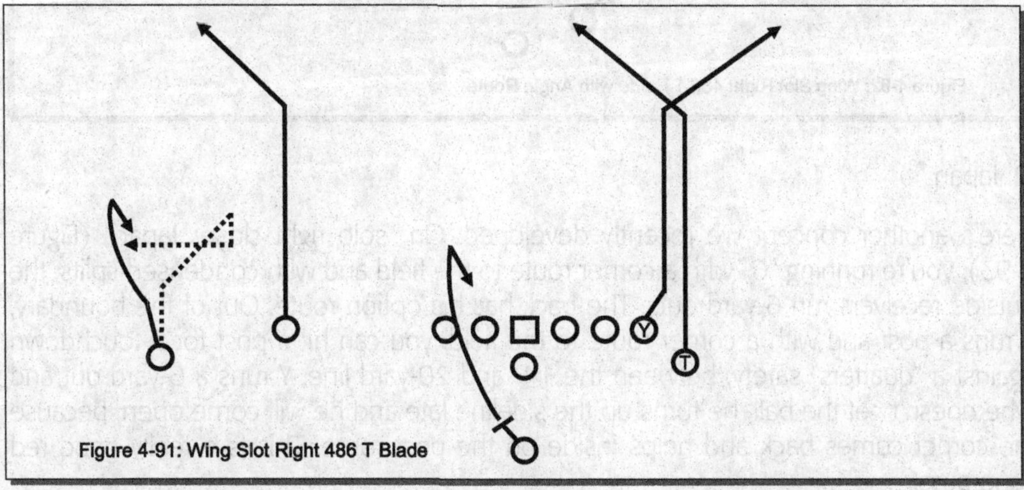

Figure 4-91: Wing Slot Right 486 T Blade

**Play: 4-91**

| Pos: | Assignment: | Coaching Points: |
|---|---|---|
| R | Check 400 protection. Run checkdown. | |
| X | Gain hitch. | vs. press: run return. |
| Y | Run corner route at 12 yds. | |
| T | Pause 1 count. Trail 1 yard behind Y and run a post. | |
| Z | 12-yard corner. | |
| QB | Progression:<br>vs. 2 high = T-Y-R<br>vs. 1 high = Z-X-R | |

rules. We sometimes game-planned this off "China," or gave X a locked "halt." We often did this off a "fox," so the back crossed the formation in order to hold that linebacker, though sometimes the quarterback liked the running back's "angle route" as an outlet coming into his field of vision, so we could tag that as well (Figure 4-92).

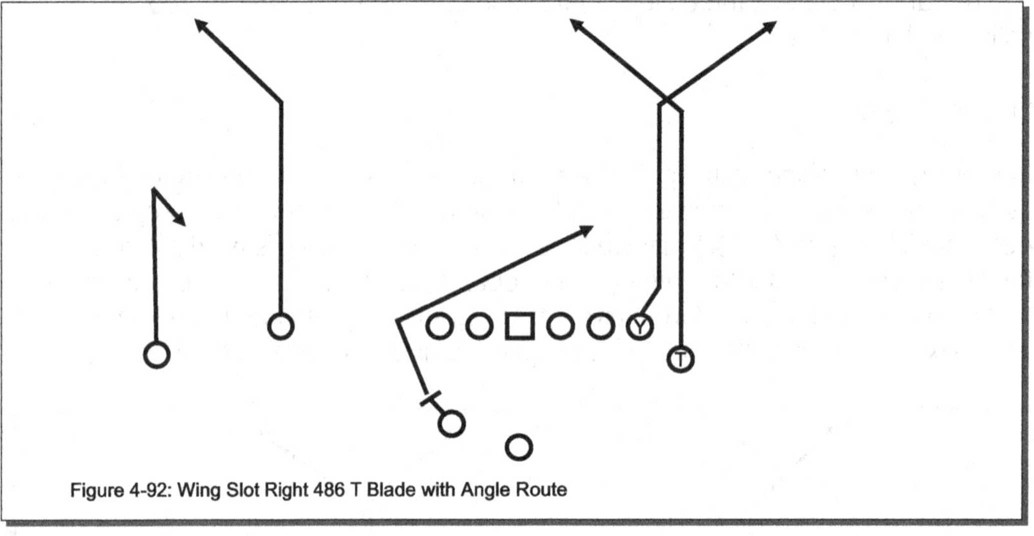

Figure 4-92: Wing Slot Right 486 T Blade with Angle Route

❑ Japan

Here's another concept we recently developed. On "solo right close: Japan" (Figure 4-93), you're running "6" with a corner route to the field and with condensed splits, the outside receivers run 6-yard outs. The back has his option route. Out of the boundary, Z runs a post and with a corner route to the field, you can hit a post for a touchdown against a "quarters" safety, between the 14- and 20-yard line. Y runs a 6-yard out and if he doesn't get the ball, he turns up the sideline late and he will come open, because the corner comes back and helps inside on the post route. This is a really good red zone pass.

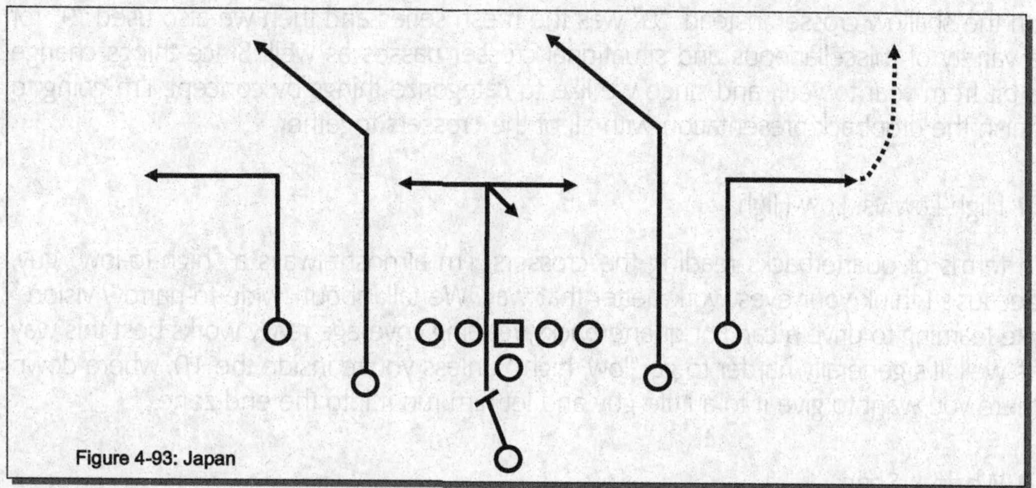
Figure 4-93: Japan

**Play: 4-93**

| Pos: | Assignment: | | Coaching Points: |
|---|---|---|---|
| R | Check rose protection. Run checkdown. | | |
| W | Run corner route at 12 yds. | | Into bdry: run post. |
| X | Run 6-yd out. | | |
| Y | Run post route. | | To the field: run corner route. |
| Z | Run 6-yd out. | | Turn upfield if ball not thrown to you. |
| QB | Homerun:<br>Progression: 1. Y 1. W<br>2. Z 2. X<br><br>Outlet: R | Key: pre-snap: FS<br><br>post-snap: corner | vs. pressure: alert check |

It's important to constantly look for new ideas and we really pay attention to what our players are doing, in order to try to find some new things. For example, we actually added this late-sideline route to the basic condensed smash play after the Clemson game in 2015. Our guy ran the out, looked at the quarterback, didn't get the ball, and then delayed and turned down the sidelines. We studied it on film to determine how it got open and why it happened, and then we decided to just install it that way.

## Crossers (5, 7, 8, 9)

When we get questions about our passing game, the crossers seem to generate the most interest from other coaches. We've had a great deal of success with them over the years and have a lot of ways to set them up. In the origins of the system, our "5s" involved a shallow crosser, with the W on the read route over the top of Z or Y underneath. The "7s" told the tight end to run the read route over the top of W or X on the shallow crosser instead. "8" was the mesh series and then we also used "9" for a variety of miscellaneous and situational crosser passes as well. Since things change a bit from year to year, and since we like to categorize things by concept, I'm going to finish the dropback presentation with all of the crossers together.

❑ High-Low vs. Low-High

In terms of quarterbacks reading the crossers, I'm almost always a "high-to-low" guy, because I think your eyes work better that way. We talk about "wide-to-narrow vision," like learning to drive a car. For quarterbacks, reading coverage really works best this way as well. It's generally harder to go "low, high," unless you're inside the 10, where down there you want to give it to a little guy and let him run it into the end zone.

❑ Whale & Shark

We want the progression for the quarterback on these to be the same, regardless of how we package things and we first try to get a 5-man protection scheme, with the back on a free-release, to clear out the box for the crosser. We usually start with "whale," which is the code word for the shallow cross to W. On "doubles right: scat 77 whale" (Figure 4-94), the "7" tells the tight end he has the 2nd-level read route. Z knows when there's a tag from the other side, he runs a post. The running back now has a free-release "rail" route. He runs it to the outside of the numbers or between the numbers and the sideline, depending on whether the ball is snapped from the hash or the middle of the field. For the play to be sound in protection, he has to understand to break his route off to the flat and holler "hot! hot! hot!", if we get pressure from his edge.

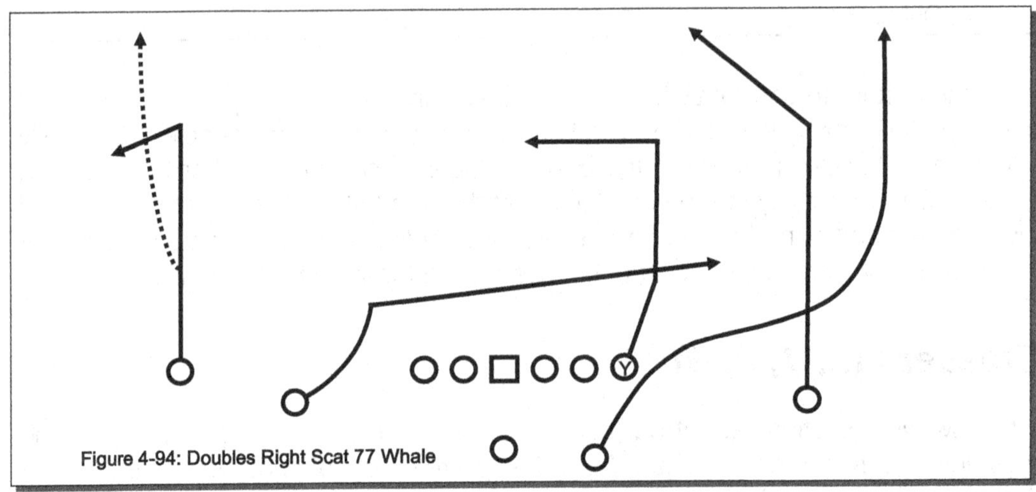

Figure 4-94: Doubles Right Scat 77 Whale

**Play: 4-94**

| Pos: | Assignment: | Coaching Points: |
|---|---|---|
| R | Free release and run wheel route. | |
| W | Run ditch route. | Use nod to beat man coverage or a rat. |
| X | Run 12-yd semi. | vs. press: trace. |
| Y | Run read route at 2nd-level depth. | |
| Z | Run post route (12-14 yds). | |
| QB | Homerun: Z/R<br>Progression: 1. Y<br>2. W<br><br>Outlet: | |

From the #2 position, W runs a "ditch" route in which he's going to start in, push up, buy a little time, and then run that route (the teaching here carries over from "72 Z topper"). He understands that he's the "built-in" hot and has to be aware of how to adjust and find open grass, when the pressure comes. On the backside, we game plan the route for X, based on what coverages we expect. In the early years we had him run a "semi that converts," because we faced more free-access, middle-field covered teams. We have him run a "circus" against cover 2 teams, because we want him to handle that backside safety. The base progression for the quarterback is "peek at the rail, key the safety: 1/1, 3" where "3" catches a bunch of these on the crosser.

Then, we like to add shifts and motions. It's really good off of "mix," which is a "Y flip" and then a "W motion." If we call "mix to doubles right: scat 77 whale" (Figure 4-95) or if we package it like "doubles right, R mo: scat 77 whale" (Figure 4-96), the read is identical for the quarterback.

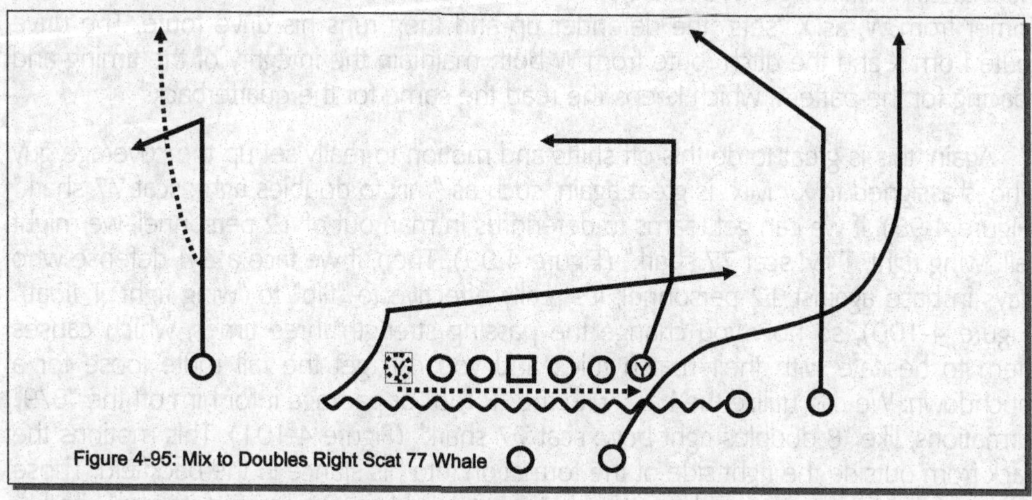

Figure 4-95: Mix to Doubles Right Scat 77 Whale

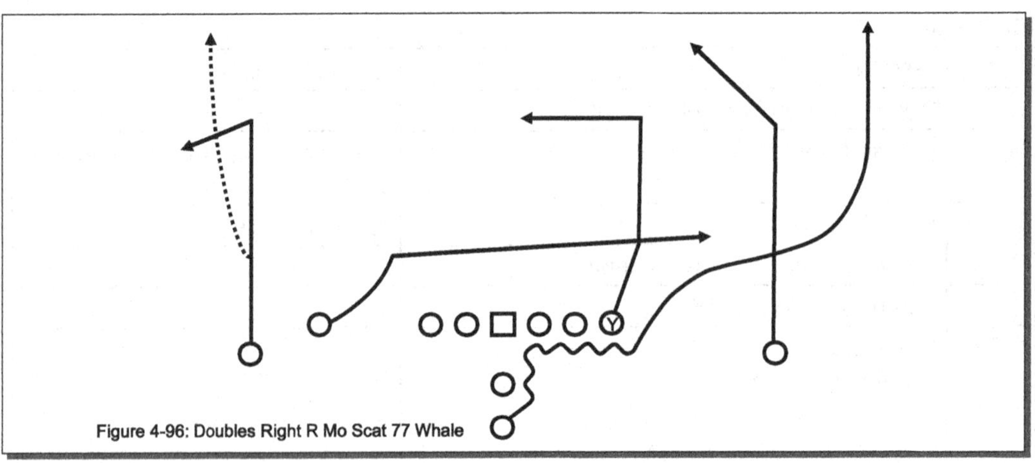

Figure 4-96: Doubles Right R Mo Scat 77 Whale

**Play: 4-96**

| Pos: | Assignment: | Coaching Points: |
|---|---|---|
| R | Free-release, run wheel route. | |
| W | Run 5-yd under route. | |
| X | Run 5-yd under route. | |
| Y | Run 12-yd corner route. | Sprint 3 steps out of your break. |
| Z | Run 4-5-1 corner. | |
| QB | Homerun: Key: pre-snap: FS<br>Progression: 1. Y-Z<br>2. W<br>3.<br>Outlet: | Alert 1-on-1 to X |

To get X on the shallow cross instead, we call it "shark." It's the same concept but in this instance, X runs a "drag" route and W runs a corner route (Figure 4-97). You really want to call "shark" against some type of man coverage, where you get a "rub" on the corner from W, as X "sets" the defender up and then runs his drive route. The drive route from X and the ditch route from W both maintain the integrity of the timing and spacing for the pattern, which keeps the read the same for the quarterback.

Again, this is great to do this off shifts and motion to really set up the coverage guy who is assigned to X. "Mix" is great again, such as "mix to doubles right: scat 77 shark" (Figure 4-98). If we can get teams to defend us in man out of 12 personnel, we might call "wing right, T fly: scat 77 shark" (Figure 4-99). Then, if we face a 3-4 defense who stays in base against 12 personnel, it's really effective to "flip" to "wing right, T float," (Figure 4-100), so now you change the passing strength three times, which causes them to hesitate with their match rules and you can get the rail route loose for a touchdown. We can utilize the back with the "R mo" or package it for him off the "8/9" formations, like "8 doubles right bow: scat 77 shark" (Figure 4-101). This motions the back from outside the right side of the formation into his stance in the backfield. Those are just some examples of where the old timers would say we "manufactured" shark.

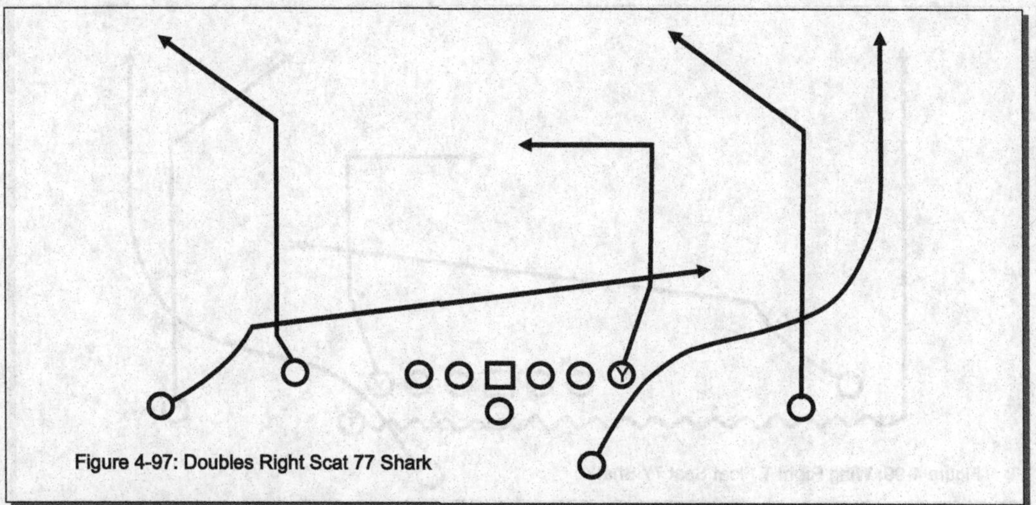

Figure 4-97: Doubles Right Scat 77 Shark

**Play: Doubles Right: Scat 77 Shark**

| Pos: | Assignment: | Coaching Points: |
|---|---|---|
| R | Free release. Run wheel route. | Alert: hot off 1 |
| W | Arc release for rub with X. Run corner route. | |
| X | Run drive route. Work for mesh off W. | You are responsible for the mesh. |
| Y | Run read route at 2nd-level depth. | vs. zone: settle; vs. man: run away |
| Z | Run 12-yd post. | |
| QB | Homerun: Z/R Key: SS depth to MLB<br>Progression: 1. R/Z<br>2. Y<br>3. X<br>Outlet: | vs. inside leverage man: alert corner route. |

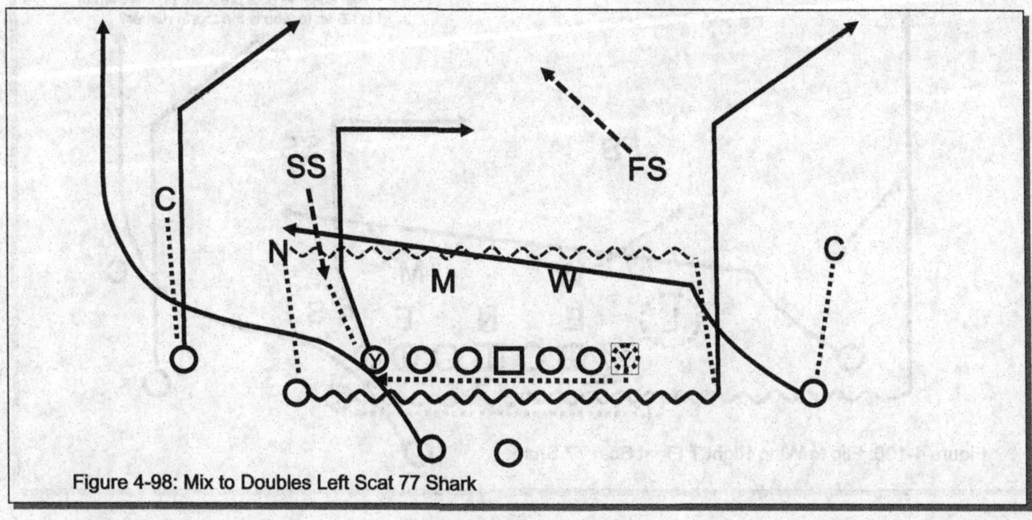

Figure 4-98: Mix to Doubles Left Scat 77 Shark

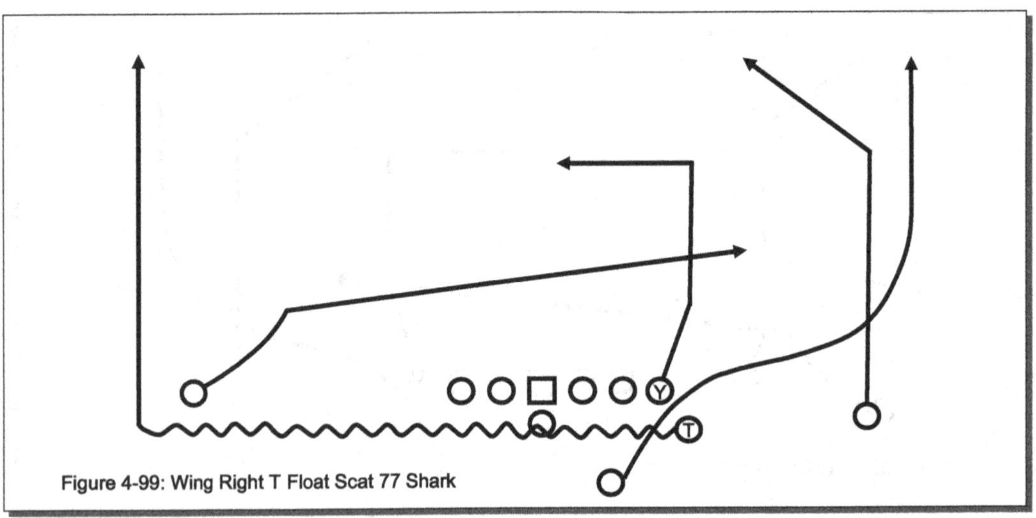

Figure 4-99: Wing Right T Float Scat 77 Shark

**Play: 4-99**

| Pos: | Assignment: | Coaching Points: |
|---|---|---|
| R | Free release and run wheel route. | |
| T | Execute float motion. Run go route. | |
| X | Run drive route. | |
| Y | Run read route at 2nd-level depth. | |
| Z | Run 12-yd post. | |
| QB | Homerun: Z/R Key: SS depth to MLB<br>Progression: 1. R/Z<br>2. Y<br>3. X | |

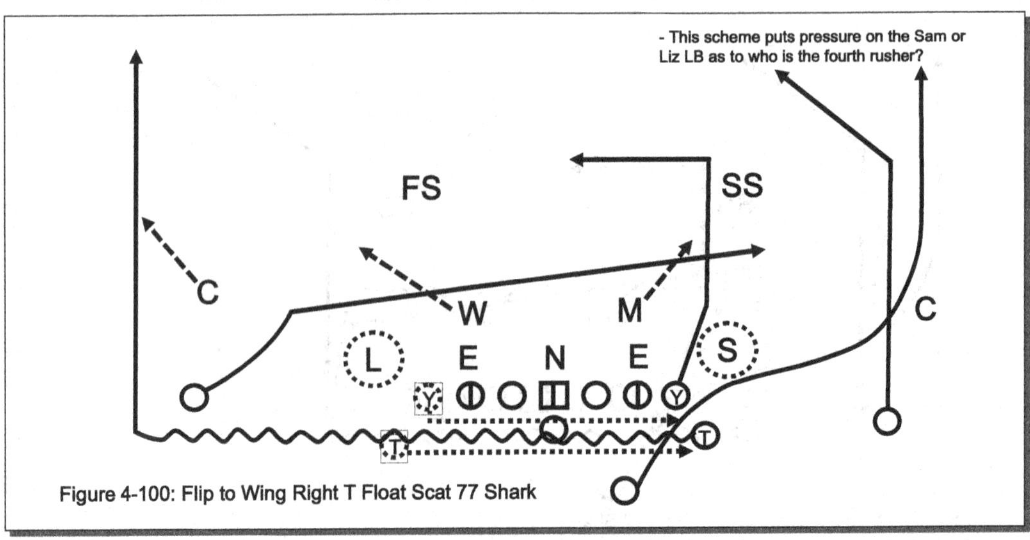

Figure 4-100: Flip to Wing Right T Float Scat 77 Shark

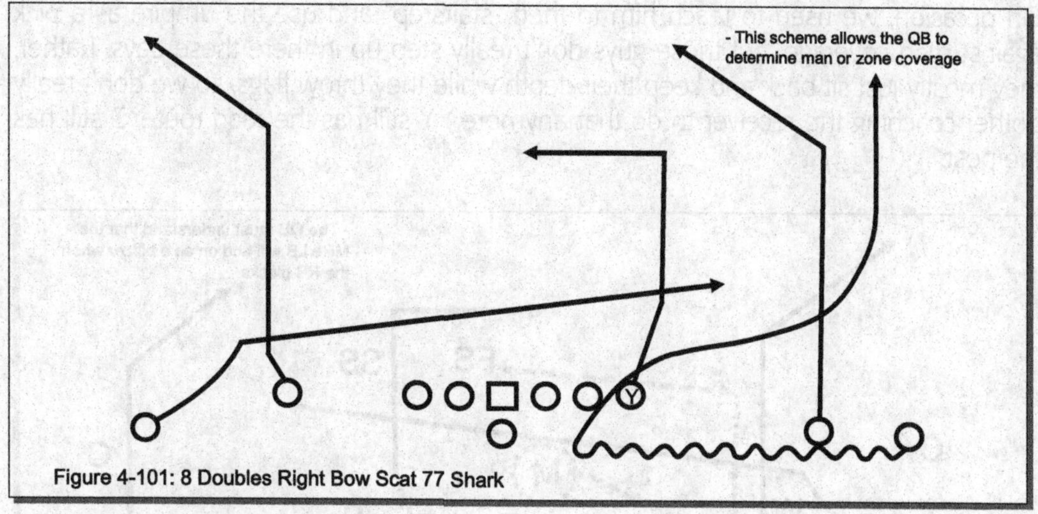

Figure 4-101: 8 Doubles Right Bow Scat 77 Shark

❑ Notes on Shifting and Motion

As you build up your packages, it's important to pay attention to which plays are conducive to pre-snap shifting and motion and which ones maybe aren't as good. You really want to build up your shifting and motion packages from your best plays, ones that you really believe in, and we've found that our crossers are definitely good for that. We like to try to disguise who's coming from where and get the focus off the running back, while keeping the read the same for the quarterback. If we script our practices carefully, we can accumulate a ton of repetitions on this base concept, while building multiple looks for defenses to have to scout for and deal with.

For us, our crosser package has always been a great place to utilize shifting and motion. We know it's been one of our best dropback passes year-in and year-out, because we've hit every different eligible receiver on the play, in just about every conceivable game situation. We are confident with all the "window dressing," because we understand how to keep the routes and reads consistent, no matter how we decide to package the play in any given season, for any particular game plan, in any type of situation.

❑ Crossers vs. Pressure

You still want to be able to run the "7" series for touchdowns in the red zone. The difference down there is we want to have a way to pick up "blitz-zero" without re-structuring the entire play, so what works best for us is to change from 5-man protection to a 6-man scheme the other direction and have the quarterback "handle the hugger" (extra rusher). If we get into 12 personnel, we could call "wing right, T fly: 487 shark" (Figure 4-102). T is now going in motion to "rub" the corner. X is going to "set" the corner. I always tell him "on a on a drag or drive route, you need to *set* the corner." So, if he's pressed, you do it by planting your outside foot in the ground, using the rub, and running away from him. If he's off, you need to *set*, then come underneath.

On occasion, we used to teach him to then "stairstep" and use the umpire as a pick against man coverage, but those guys don't really step up in there these days. Rather, they mostly just sit back and keep their depth while they throw flags, so we don't really bother coaching the receiver to do that anymore.) Y still has the read route, Z still has the post.

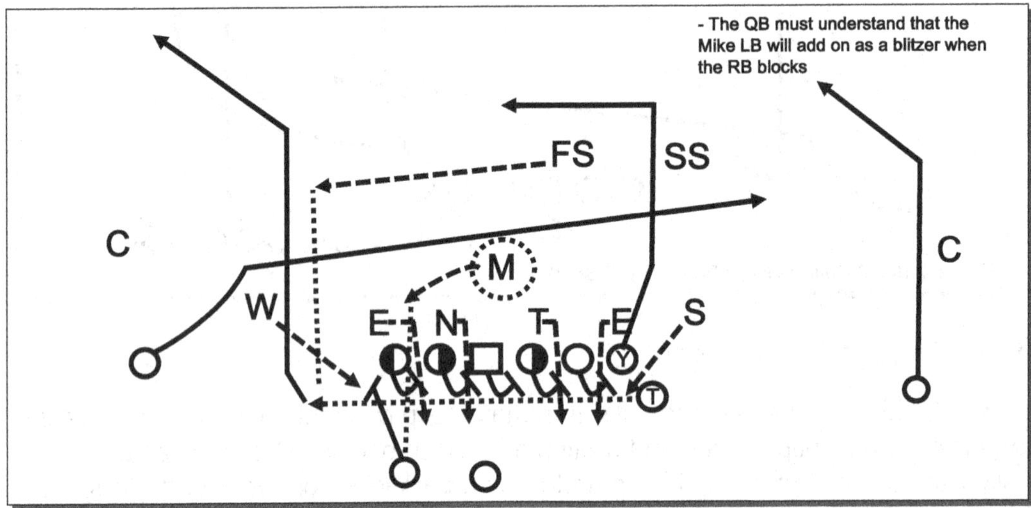


In this situation, when we call the protection this way, we expect the running back to be used up in protection, but if he's not, he would run a stretch route. Again, we're doing this for "blitz zero," where it's mathematically impossible to block them all. Therefore, against something like a "6-1 double dog," the quarterback has to beat the "hugger," which is what we call that extra unblocked defender. When we get all that done, it's a touchdown!

All else being equal, we prefer to free-release the back and send him on that "rail" route. The idea is to get the running back and whatever linebacker is asked to cover him out of there (or else just throw it to him for a touchdown if they blow the coverage), so we can get more yards after the catch on the shallow cross. But if you feel like you're getting "blitz-zero" in the red zone or man coverage on "3rd and 4," then you send the back *to* the crosser, so that when he pass-blocks, the linebacker guarding him comes that way and then your crosser can run past him and pop open on the other side. For the quarterback, you have to work a "drift drill," where the quarterback has to be able to drift away from the pressure and get his hips up in the air to complete the crosser in traffic.

❑ Zebra and Yankee

Then, we flip the protection and do the exact same thing the other way by calling "doubles right: scat 485 zebra" (Figure 4-103). The "5" means the in-cut now belongs to the slot receiver. He has the read route, X now has the post, Y now has the "rub" corner route, and Z is going to be your crosser on his drag route. We call "doubles right: scat 485 yankee" (Figure 4-104) to run the crosser for Y and have him run that "ditch" route instead. If we call it that way, Z would then run the "circus" route.

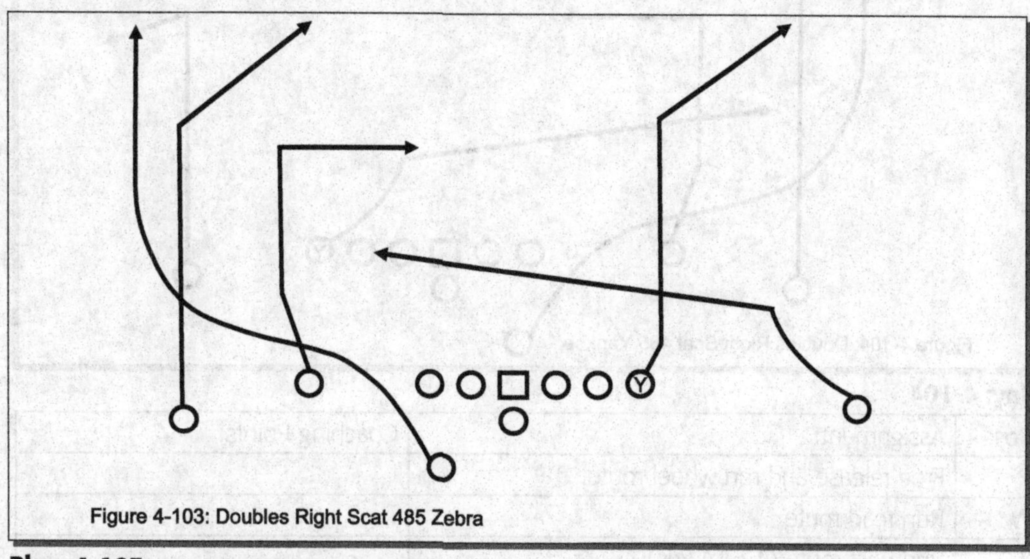


Figure 4-103: Doubles Right Scat 485 Zebra

**Play: 4-103**

| Pos: | Assignment: | Coaching Points: |
|---|---|---|
| R | Free release and run wheel route. | Alert: hot off 1 |
| W | Run read route at 2nd-level depth. | |
| X | Run 12-yd post. | |
| Y | Arc release for rub with Z. Run corner route. | Sprint 3 steps out of your break. |
| Z | Run drive route. Work for rub off Y. | You are responsible for the rub. |
| QB | Homerun: X/R Key: FS depth to weak LB<br>Progression: 1. R/X<br>2. W<br>3. Z<br>Outlet: | vs. single high with press on Z: alert Y.<br><br>Alert: possible Liz Y |

If you want the base 5-man protection scheme, you send the back down the rail *away* from the crosser ("scat 485"). If you expect pressure and want 6-man protection, you send the back *to* the crosser ("75"). And we still want to think it terms of packaging the play, such as "doubles right Z half: scat 485 zebra" (Figure 4-105) or "solo right, Y half: scat 485 zebra" (Figure 4-106). So, our one-word code names for our four base crosser calls are: zebra, yankee, whale, and shark. ("Shark" became the code for X, because no one could agree on an animal name with an X, so we said "why don't we just call it a shark? Sure.")

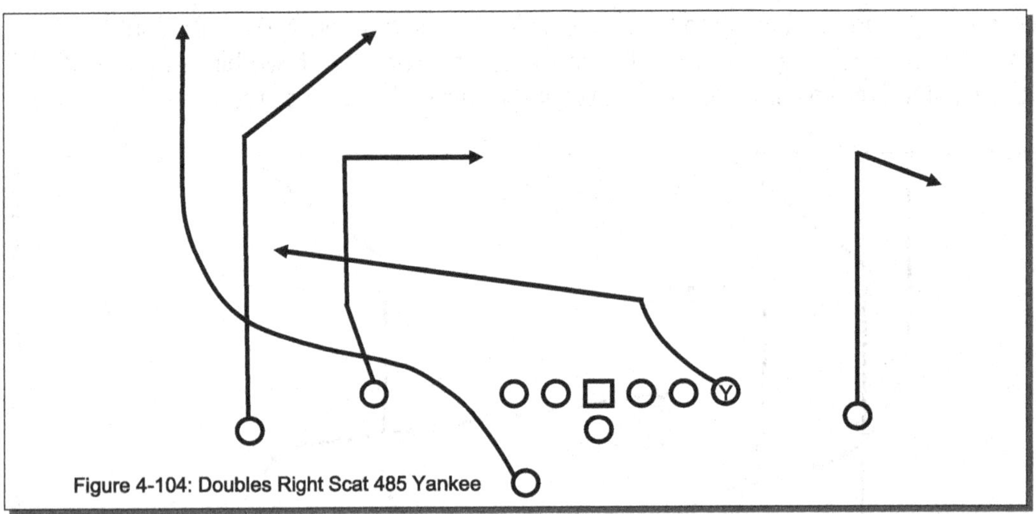

Figure 4-104: Doubles Right Scat 485 Yankee

**Play: 4-104**

| Pos: | Assignment: | Coaching Points: |
|---|---|---|
| R | Free release and run wheel route. | |
| W | Run read route. | |
| X | Run post route (12-14 yds). | |
| Y | Run ditch route. | |
| Z | Run 12-yd semi. | vs. press: trace |
| QB | Homerun: post/wheel (X-R)<br>Progression: 1. R/X<br>2. W<br>3. Y<br>Outlet: R | vs. Q4: throw semi to Z. |

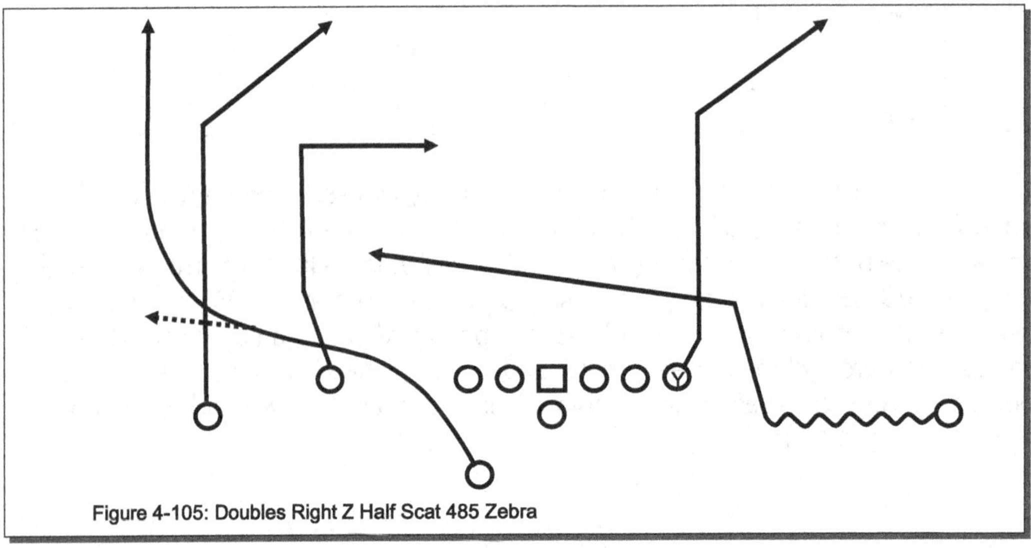

Figure 4-105: Doubles Right Z Half Scat 485 Zebra

**Play: Doubles Right Z Half: Scat 485 Zebra**

| Pos: | Assignment: | Coaching Points: |
|---|---|---|
| R | Free release. Run wheel route. | Alert: hot off 1. |
| W | Run read route at 2nd-level depth. | vs. zone: settle; vs. man: run away |
| X | Run 12-yd post. | |
| Y | Arc release for rub with Z. Run corner route. | Sprint 3 steps out of your break. |
| Z | Run drive route. Work for mesh off Y. | You are responsible for the mesh. |
| QB | Homerun: X/R Key: FS depth to weak LB<br>Progression: 1. R/X<br>2. W<br>3. Z<br>Outlet: | vs. single high with press on Z: Alert Y.<br>Alert possible Liz Y. |

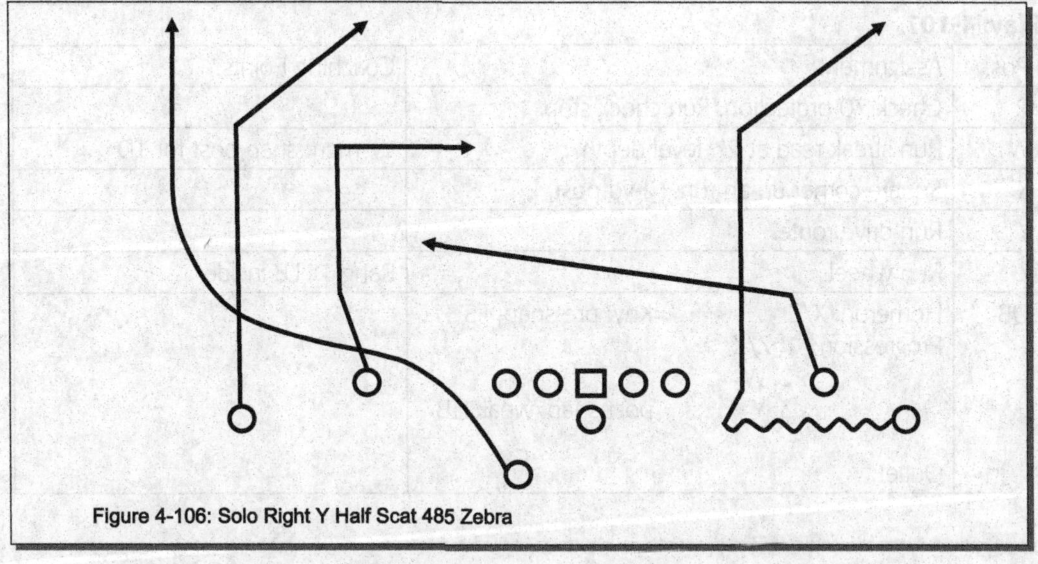

Figure 4-106: Solo Right Y Half Scat 485 Zebra

From there, we can build up numerous other ideas off the base crosser concept. Over the years, we've constructed things like "trips right: 75 yankee, Z wheel" to create more room for a great tight end (Figure 4-107), or "trips right, X mo: scat 485 Exxon" to mirror the "zebra" concept for X, in the years where he's been the best matchup guy (Figure 4-108). Once you have built a foundation of the basic concept and you pay attention to "feeding the studs," the possibilities are really only limited by the creativity of you and your staff.

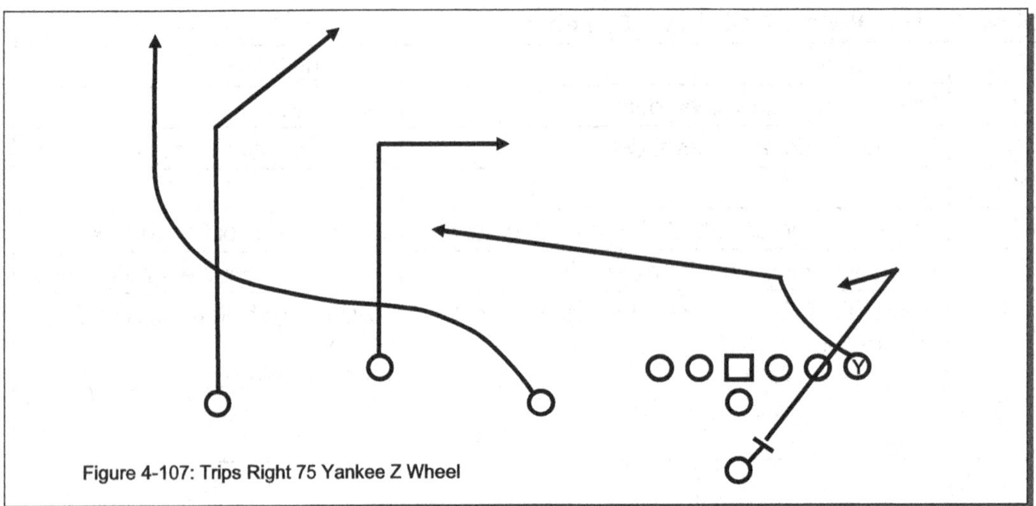

Figure 4-107: Trips Right 75 Yankee Z Wheel

**Play: 4-107**

| Pos: | Assignment: | Coaching Points: |
|---|---|---|
| R | Check 70 protection. Run check stop. | |
| W | Run streak read at 2nd-level depth. | vs. man: snap post for TD |
| X | Square corner up an run 12-yd post. | |
| Y | Run drive route. | |
| Z | Run wheel | Bang 1st LB inside |
| QB | Homerun: X/Z Key: pre-snap: FS<br>Progression: 1. Z/X<br>2. W<br>3. Y post-snap: weak ILB<br><br>Outlet: | |

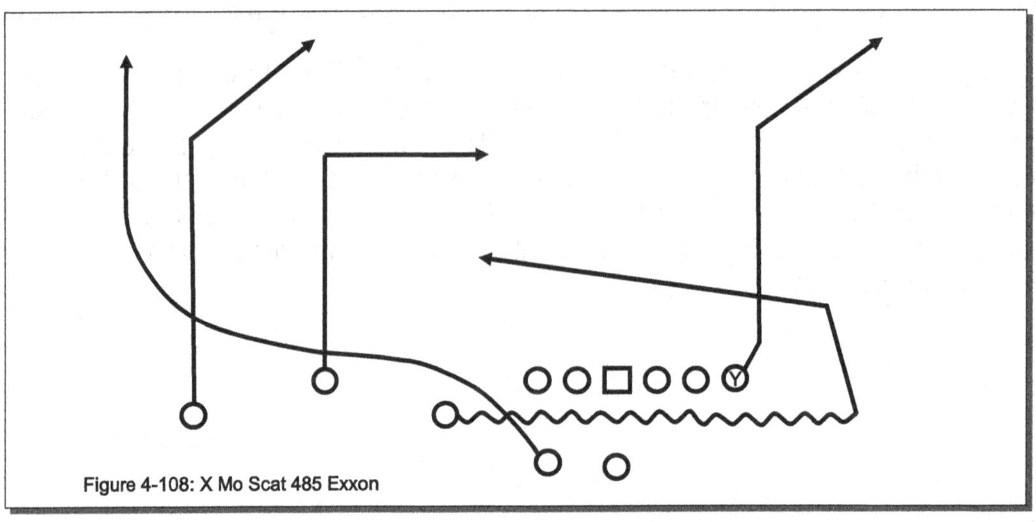

Figure 4-108: X Mo Scat 485 Exxon

**Play: 4-108**

| Pos: | Assignment: | Coaching Points: |
|---|---|---|
| R | Free release and run wheel route. | vs. weak pressure: 1-yd hot |
| W | Run read route at 2nd-level depth. | |
| X | Run drive route. | |
| Y | Run rub corner for X. | |
| Z | Run post. | |
| QB | Homerun: Z/R<br>Progression: 1. Z/R<br>2. W<br>3. X<br>Outlet: | vs. weak pressure: hit R hot in flat. |

## Red Zone "2-Play Calls"

If we want the crosser in the red zone, we can certainly dial one up with the 6-man protection scheme, when we anticipate blitz. However, if we think the defense might check out of their all-out pressure, we may want to use a "2-play call" to give us a better way to attack a 2-linebacker box. A good one for us has been where we called "solo right, Y half; 75 zebra," which you could picture as the tight end motioning down to "doubles right" (Figure 4-109). We want the *mindset* to be "zero equals zebra," so the tight end motions down and runs his "rub corner" for Z on the drag route. On the other side, we have the read route from W and post route from X, which in that area of the field may end up bending across the backline of the end zone. Again, in this situation against pressure, we're expecting the back to end up in the protection.

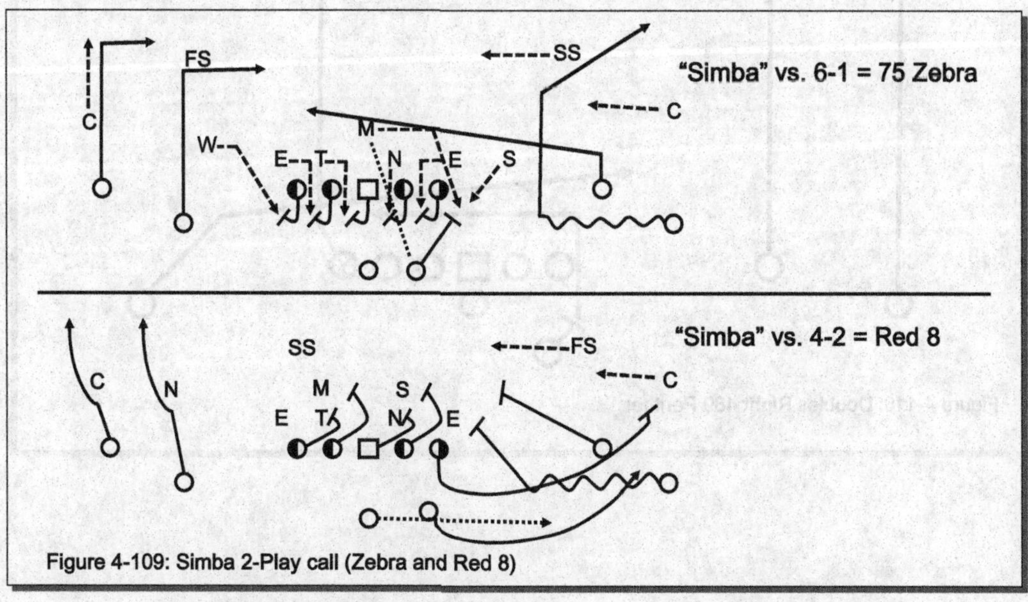

Figure 4-109: Simba 2-Play call (Zebra and Red 8)

However, if it's not blitz-zero and we get two linebackers in the box, we may want to change the play to something that's better to out-flank the defense, such as our toss-crack run (see Figure 4-109). We plan on running "zebra," but if the quarterback identifies the 2-linebacker box, he makes the call and the tight end motions down and cracks the end instead. This particular "2-play" call was originally part of a game plan against Florida State in 2016. They called timeout and we just said, "if it's '6-1 double-dog,' go 'zebra,' but if it's zone, go 'red 8.'" When we saw them line up for the blitz after the timeout, we knew it would be the shallow cross for the touchdown.

Then, the next week, we said, "let's just give it a one-word *code name,* so it's a quick call." We ended up with the name "Simba," because the kids liked the "Lion King" movie. "Zebra," "Simba" - sometimes it doesn't even matter, because they'll understand the call if you practice it well enough.

❑ Panther

This became a good play for us, built off that base "zebra" concept. We called it "doubles right: 489 panther" (Figure 4-110), and gave it the "9" category, since it breaks from the system. This is a way we can combo an in-cut with the crosser package. Z and Y ran the same zebra and corner routes, now in a combo with a "pin" concept for X and W. On this, the back knows to run a cross route, underneath. This was a productive part of the crosser package in those years, especially because Lamar Jackson could throw in-cuts so well.

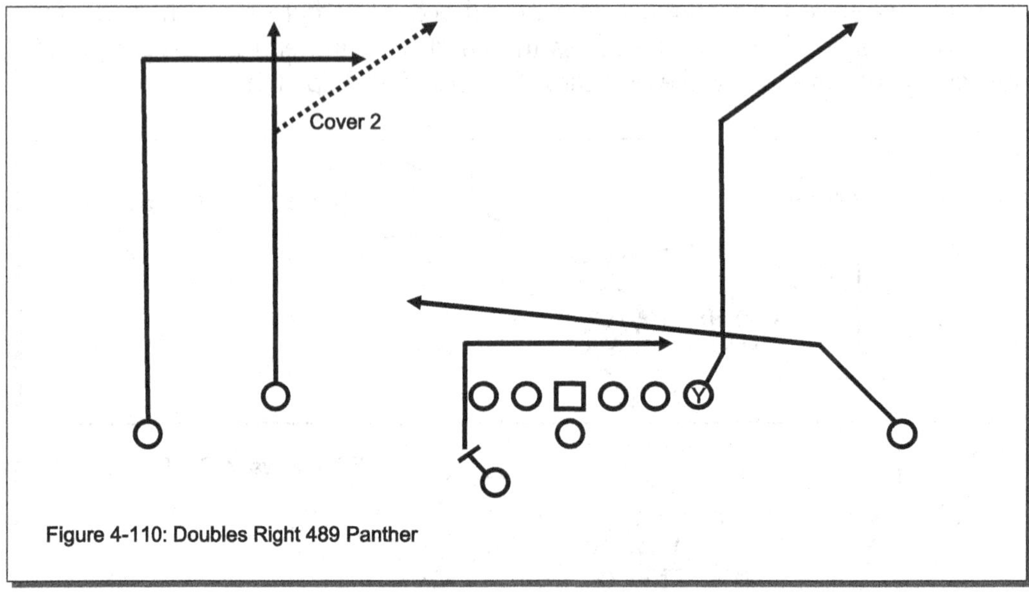


Figure 4-110: Doubles Right 489 Panther

**Play: 4-110**

| Pos: | Assignment: | Coaching Points: |
|---|---|---|
| R | Check 480 protection. Run away route. | |
| W | Run seam. | vs. cov 2: take middle |
| X | Run 16-yd in-cut. | |
| Y | Run rub corner. | |
| Z | Run drive. | |
| QB | Homerun: W — Key: pre-snap FS<br>Progression: vs. 1 High — vs. 2 High<br>1. W-X — 1. W<br>2. Z — 2. X-Z<br>Outlet: R — post-snap: Weak ILB | |

❑ Packages and Mental Images

While you were reading about crossers, you might have noticed that on paper, "doubles right: 77 whale" looks really similar to "doubles right: 72 Z topper"? It is. It's the exact same play (Figure 4-111). It's just that when you *say* "Z topper," the quarterback will focus on throwing the post. During the week as you practice the game plan, you try to gain a sense of when you think you can hit the Z post, so that's when you'll call "Z topper." But if you're anticipating hitting the catch and run to the shallow cross, you'll want to call it "whale" instead. You're calling the game, you've gotten a feel for how they're going to defend you, and you want to dial up the play, so you call it one way or the other, based on what you want your quarterback to be thinking about. If we've got the ball back with six seconds until half, what are we doing? Throwing the post for a touchdown! The *mental image* is always critical, and the words matter.

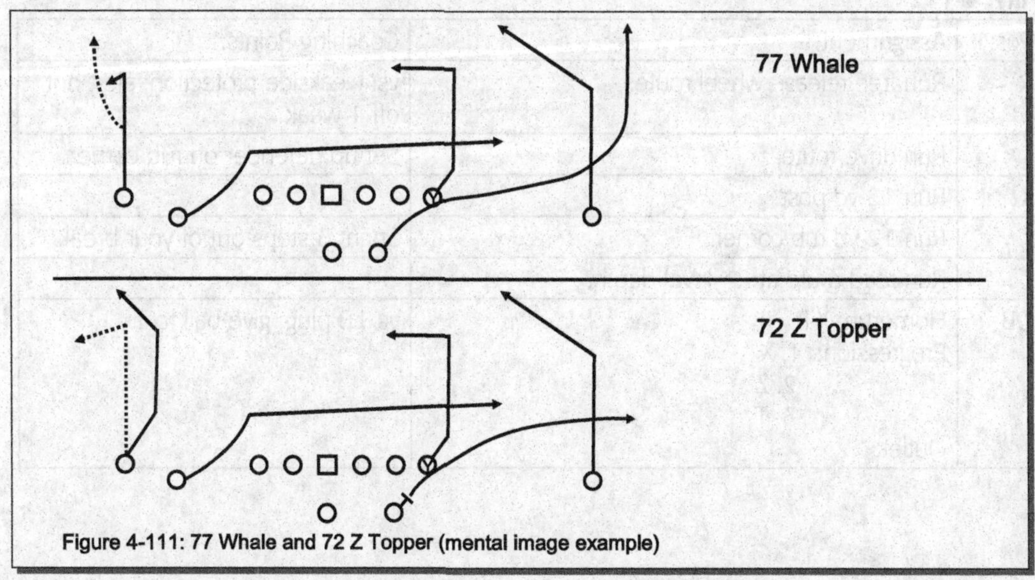

Figure 4-111: 77 Whale and 72 Z Topper (mental image example)

❑ Tuna

Our "wing slot" package has always been good for us, so we also added versions of the crosser for the second tight end, such as "wing slot right, scat 489 tuna" (Figure 4-112). The code word "tuna" lets T know he has the crosser. T is going to take three steps out, at a 45-degree angle before he comes in on his drag route, which allows him to see what the boundary corner is doing and also keeps the timing and spacing of the pattern the same as the other crosser concepts in the package. Y has a corner route; we don't tell him anything about a rub, because T is so close to him. X runs the post and Z has the read route. We call it "scat 489" or "79" (rather than 485 or 75), because "5 belongs to W" in 11 personnel, so we listed this play within the "9" category instead.

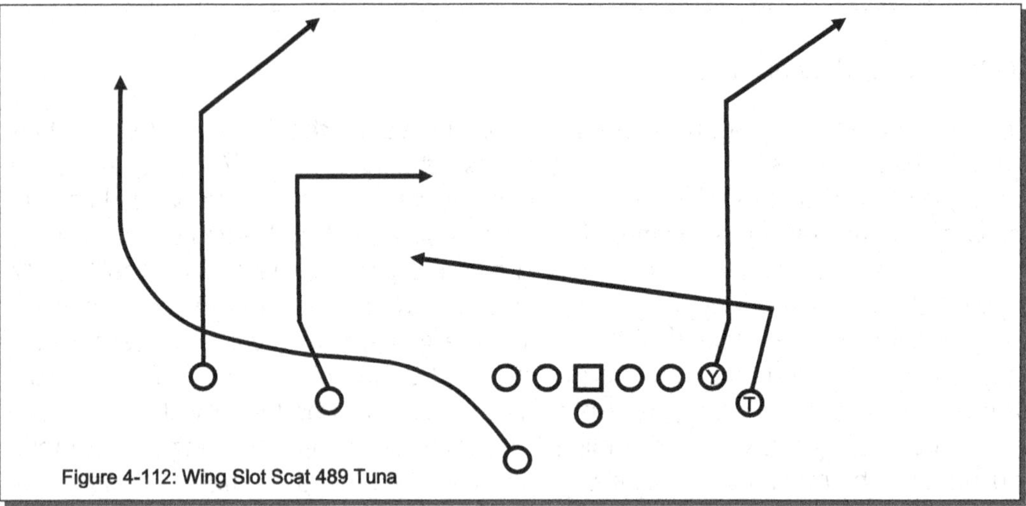

Figure 4-112: Wing Slot Scat 489 Tuna

**Play: 4-112**

| Pos: | Assignment: | Coaching Points: |
|---|---|---|
| R | Run free release wheel route. | vs. weakside protection: alert hot off 1 weak |
| T | Run drive route. | Set up defender on rub corner. |
| X | Run 12-yd post. | |
| Y | Run 12-yd rub corner. | Sprint 3 steps out of your break. |
| Z | Run read route at 2nd-level depth. | |
| QB | Homerun: X-R<br>Progression: 1. X<br>2. Z<br>3. T<br>Outlet: | vs. LB plug: give ball to T. |

We could technically make it a "hot off 2" or a "hot off 1," because it's "scat," but it was simplest to keep the crosser as the "built-in," if the corner or Sam comes, so the package remains consistent. T just needs to take three steps outside and set up the timing of the route, this way the teaching and the spacing, as well as the read for the quarterback, remain as similar as possible to the base crossers. It's been good for us to run crossers off run formations like this. We used to do it with Michael Bush and called the same thing "79 A drive," because he was the "A" back. So, then in 2-back personnel, he just knew to line up as a wing to run the drive route.

❑ 79 Scout, T Shallow

What turned out better than that though, especially in the red zone, was to call "wing slot right: 79 scout, T Shallow" (Figure 4-113). Y runs the read route, and T runs the same drag. In this instance, however, you get the "scout" concept between Z and X, which is a go route, with a 10-yard out (square-out, "scout"). We describe it to the quarterbacks as a "deeper blue read," which allows the coaching to carry over from our quick game.

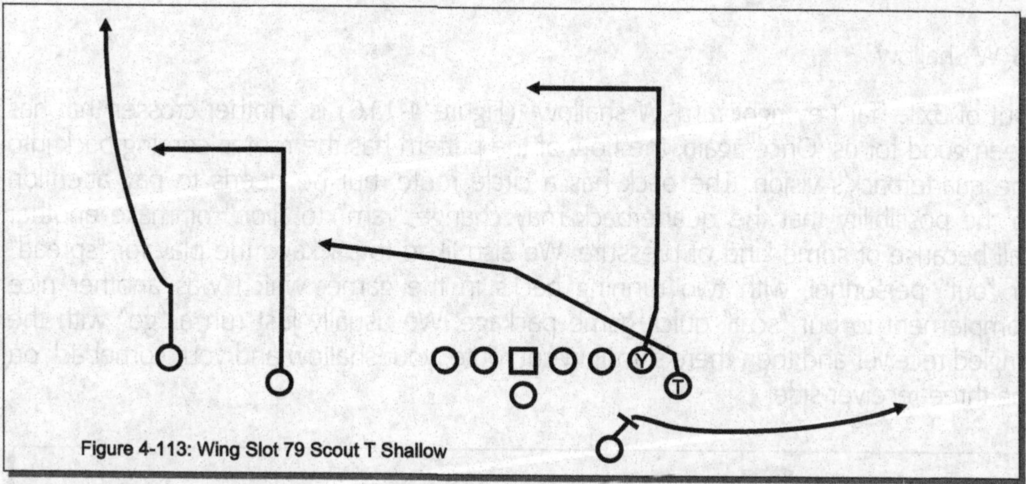

Figure 4-113: Wing Slot 79 Scout T Shallow

**Play: 4-113**

| Pos: | Assignment: | Coaching Points: |
|---|---|---|
| R | Check 70 pro. Run stretch | |
| T | Run drive. | Expand 3 steps. |
| X | Outside release go. | |
| Y | Run read route at 2nd-level depth. | |
| Z | Run 10-yd out. | |
| QB | Homerun: X<br>Progression: 1. Z<br>2. T-Y<br>3. R<br>Outlet: | |

The quarterback is taught to first read the "scout" against 2-high: "hold the safety, key the corner." Then, everything else (Y, T, R) is working back to you, "1, 2, 3, 4, checkdown." If everything gets clogged up inside as you drop, you know that the running back will catch the stretch route and run it into the end zone. It's another good play to use in the package, because the quarterbacks like to hear "scout is just a deeper 'blue' read for you." They *know* "blue." That's the underlying idea behind teaching in *packages*. Then, players don't have any panic hearing another new play. "Oh, yeah. Okay, gotcha." Lamar Jackson said that the very first day we put it in. "I like that, it's all coming back *to* the progression."

That kind of concept reminds me of Peyton Manning's first years in the NFL; that's the kind of thing the Colts did right away, in order to accent his talents. For example, they'd run what we call "wing slot right: 489 Z sail, T drive," and then they had the outlets coming the same direction (Figure 4-114). Or they would run what we call "doubles right: 89 W sail, Z shallow" (Figure 4-115). Those kinds of ideas (with the routes flowing into the quarterback's field of vision) are things I really like. It's a very natural progression and a great way to "take care of your quarterback."

❑ W Shallow

Out of 3x1, "far trey right ram, W shallow" (Figure 4-116) is another crosser that has been good for us. Once again, the flow of the pattern has the routes coming back into the quarterback's vision. The back has a circle route, but he needs to pay attention to the possibility that the quarterback may change "ram" to "lion" or make another call because of some kind of pressure. We also liked to package the play for "spread" or "out" personnel, with two running backs in the game, which was another nice complement to our "scat" quick game package. We usually just run a "go" with the singled receiver and then there's your in-cut route, your shallow and your comeback on the three-receiver side.

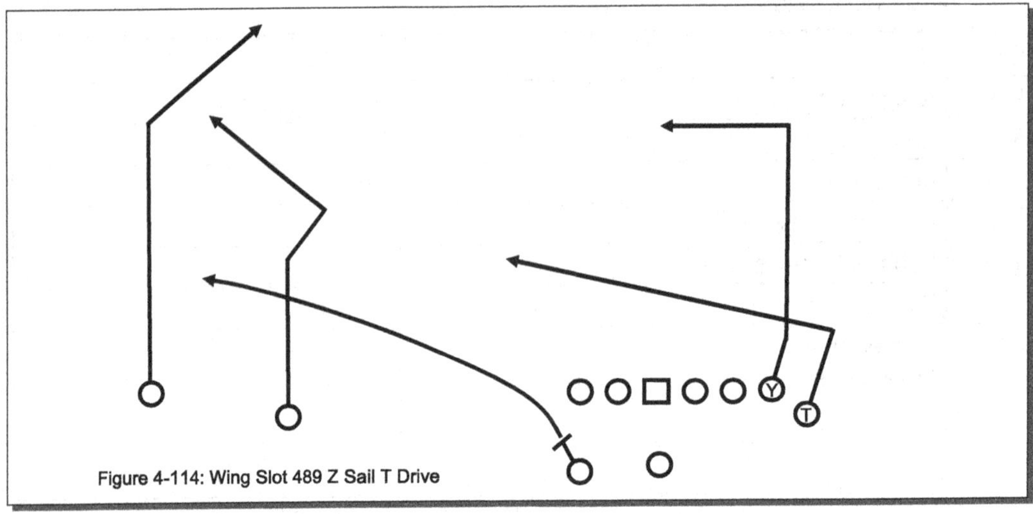

Figure 4-114: Wing Slot 489 Z Sail T Drive

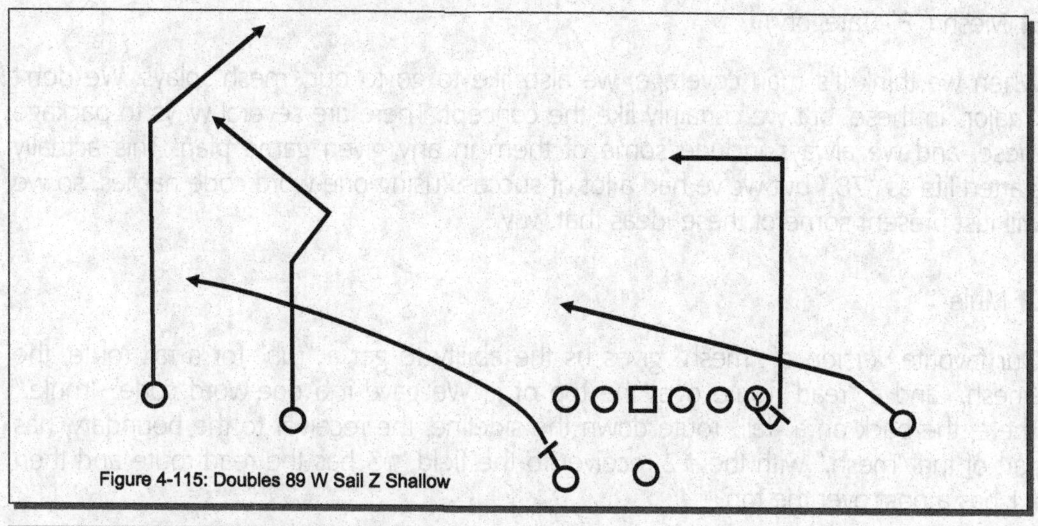

Figure 4-115: Doubles 89 W Sail Z Shallow

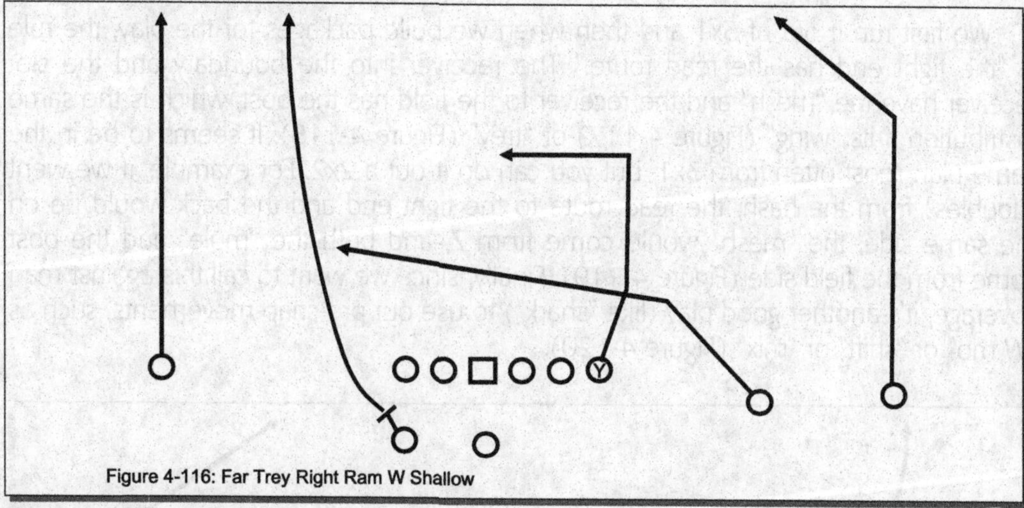

Figure 4-116: Far Trey Right Ram W Shallow

**Play: 4-116**

| Pos: | Assignment: | Coaching Points: |
|---|---|---|
| R | Free release, run circle route. | Alert: hot off 1 weak |
| W | Run shallow crossing route. | |
| X | Run 12-yd post. | |
| Y | Run read route at 2nd-level depth. | vs. zone: settle. vs. man: run away |
| Z | Run go. | Must outside release. |
| QB | Homerun: X<br>Progression: 1. R<br>2. W<br>3. Y<br>Outlet: | |

❑ Mesh ("8" Category)

When we think it's man coverage, we also like to go to our "mesh" plays. We don't "major" in these, but we certainly like the concept. There are several ways to package these, and we always include some of them in any given game plan. This actually started life as "78," but we've had a lot of success using one-word code names, so we will just present some of these ideas that way.

❑ Mule

Our favorite version of "mesh" gives us the ability to get a "rub" for a rail route, the "mesh," and a "read" route over the top of it. We gave it a one-word code: "mule." There, the back on a "rail" route down the sideline, the receiver to the boundary, has part of the "mesh," with the #2 receiver to the field, #3 has the read route and then #1 has a post over the top.

We first run it out of 3x1 and then when we build packages for the play, the rule is "the tight end has the read route." The receiver into the boundary and the slot receiver have the "mesh" and the receiver to the field has the post, which is the same distribution if its "wing" (Figure 4-117) or "trey" (Figure 4-118). It seems to be in the game plan most often from 3x1, but you can do it out a 2x2. For example, if we went "doubles" from the hash, the read route to the tight end and the back would be on the same side, the "mesh" would come from Z, and both the "mule" and the post come from the field side (Figure 4-119). Finally, since we want to call this against man coverage, it's another good play (like "shark") to use our pre-snap movements, such as "W mo" or "shift" or "mix" (Figure 4-120).

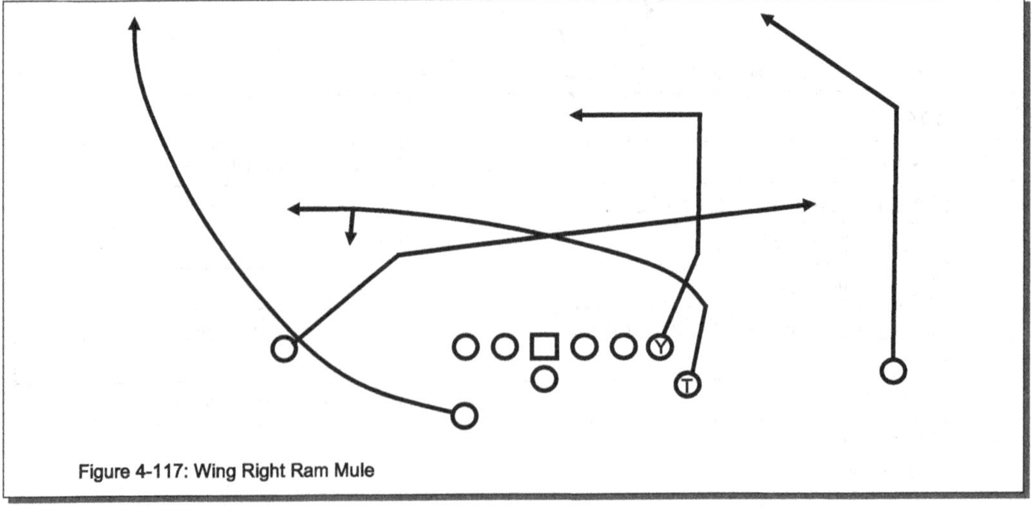

Figure 4-117: Wing Right Ram Mule

**Play: 4-117**

| Pos: | Assignment: | Coaching Points: |
|---|---|---|
| R | Free release rail. | |
| X | Run drive route. | You are responsible for the mesh.<br>vs. zone: sit down. |
| T | Run drag route over the top of X. | vs. zone: sit down. |
| Y | Run react route. | |
| Z | Square corner up and run 12-yd post. | |
| QB | Homerun: R Key: pre-snap: FS<br>Progression: 1. Y<br>2. X/T<br><br>Outlet: | |

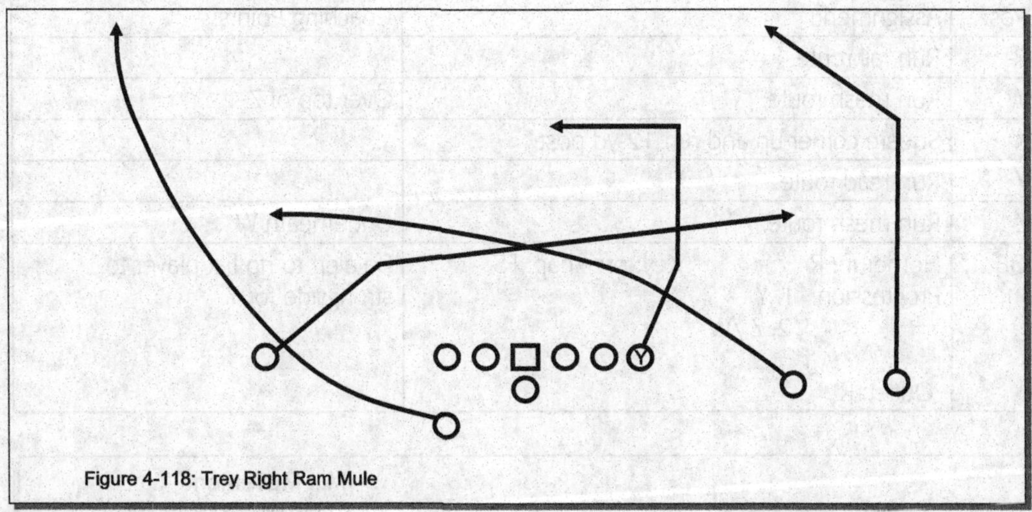

Figure 4-118: Trey Right Ram Mule

**Play: 4-118**

| Pos: | Assignment: | Coaching Points: |
|---|---|---|
| R | Free release rail | |
| W | Run drag route. | Over top Z |
| X | Square corner up and run 12-yd post. | |
| Y | Run read route. | |
| Z | Run drive route. | Underneath W |
| QB | Homerun: R Key: pre-snap: FS<br>Progression: 1. Y<br>2. Z/W<br><br>Outlet: | |

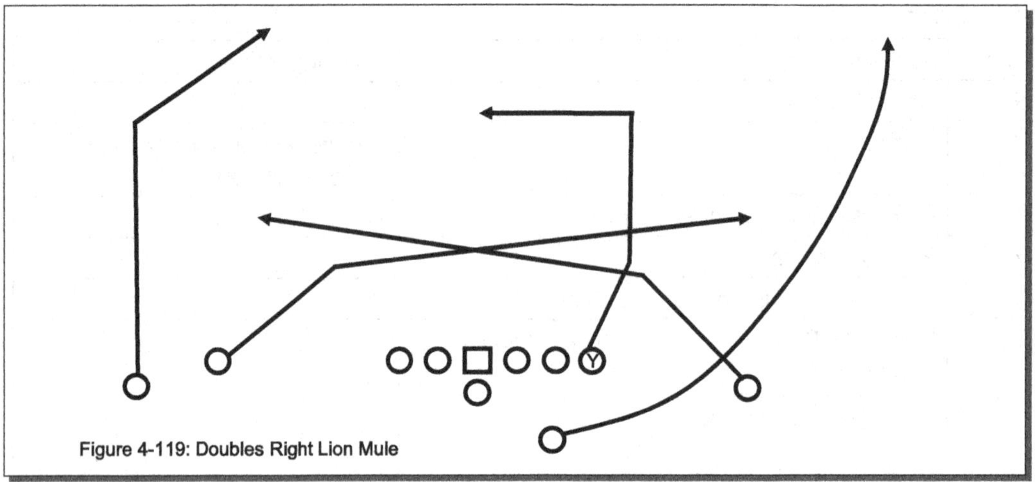

Figure 4-119: Doubles Right Lion Mule

**Play: Doubles Right: Ram Mule**

| Pos: | Assignment: | Coaching Points: |
|---|---|---|
| R | Run rail route. | |
| W | Run mesh route. | Over top of Z |
| X | Square corner up and run 12-yd post. | |
| Y | Run read route. | |
| Z | Run mesh route. | Underneath W |
| QB | Homerun: R Key: pre-snap: FS<br>Progression: 1. Y<br>2. Z /W<br><br>Outlet: R | Be alert to no flat player to strongside for Y. |

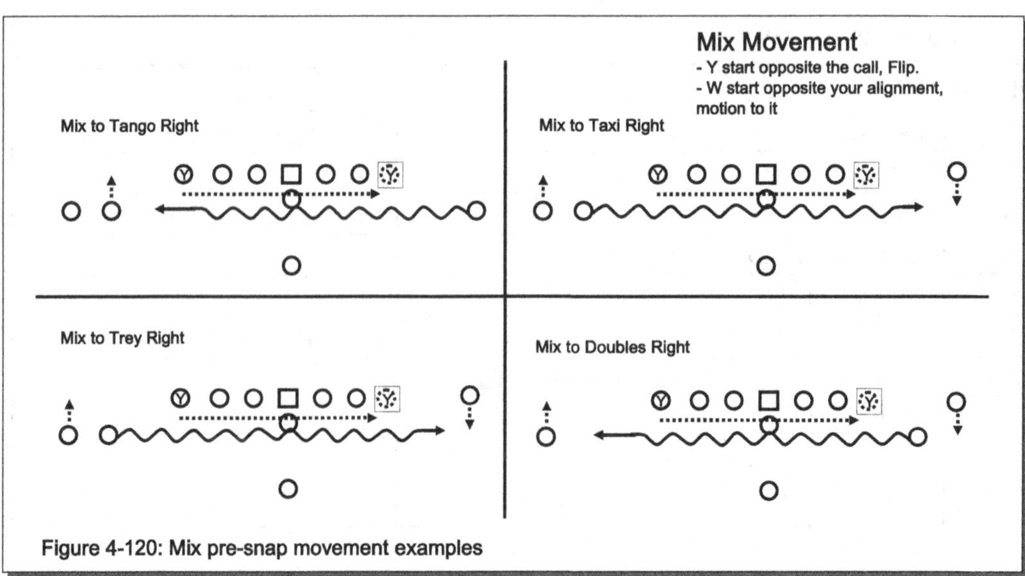

Figure 4-120: Mix pre-snap movement examples

We say, "the guy coming from the boundary is over the top" because we feel like he gets there quicker, and we don't want them to hesitate, when they set the mesh. If one guy is wrong, which can happen when bullets are flying, we say, "just don't hesitate and run into each other." Ideally, their angle should be at a target of six yards over the opposite tight end, so the "mesh" ends up being 3-to-4 yards, right over the ball. We've found that it's worth it with the wider college hashmarks to teach it this way instead.

❑ Mesh Drill

We practice this with a "mesh drill." We've always said, "the guy coming from the *boundary* is on top, the guy coming from the *field* is on the bottom, and you want to get close enough to clap hands." When we practice this, we actually *make* them clap hands.

Then, we have dummies out there as the outside linebackers, in order to practice identifying man or zone coverage. The guys holding the dummies signal each other "1 is man, 2 is zone." If it's 1, they put the dummies down, the receivers clap hands and stay on the mesh, and both of them catch balls on the run. If it's 2, they keep the dummies up and move, so then the receivers hook up at the opposite tackle areas and "show their dukes."

❑ Idaho

Against "match" teams, we have Y run a "spot" route instead of a read route, like he does on "Dakota." We found it easier to just give the concept a new name, so we call that "Idaho" (Figure 4-121). He ended up coming over the ball on a 10-yard spot route, and if he didn't get it, he broke back down his stem. A lot of times, he ended up totally uncovered after the mesh cleared. If he went over the top, the Mike would ride him and come off, but when he went in at that angle, the Mike would turn him loose and the next match defender wouldn't be able to get to him.

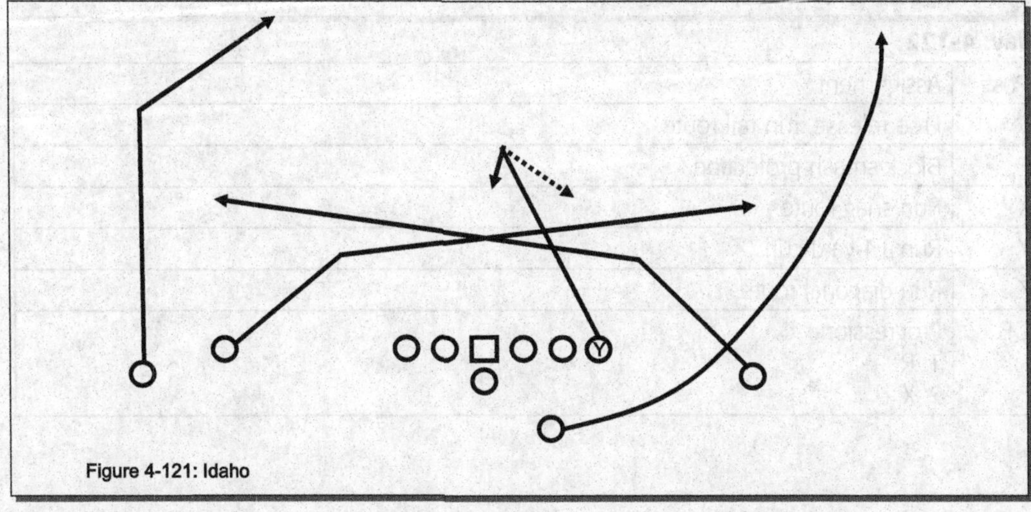

Figure 4-121: Idaho

What you tell the quarterback on the mesh concepts is "you need to have wide vision." You need to be able to understand that as they come on the mesh, you need to keep wide vision and see who comes open, to know who #1 is. Then, locate the tight end if the mesh isn't there. It's "peek for a touchdown, 1/1, 3." We always want to peek at that rail for a touchdown and then come back "1/1" for the mesh, and finally for "3" over the middle (even though on Idaho, we don't hit the rail route that much, because Y comes in on that angle and the Sam tends to just jump on the back).

❑ Smack Trojan

With the back to the singled side into the boundary, sometimes you can really hit that rail route for huge gains. That goes back to Reggie Bush with USC and the New Orleans Saints. One of their checks in 2-back, was "Smack Trojan." "Smack" meant the "Sam/ Mike" protection. The fullback had the Sam and the 4-down and Mike belonged to the offensive line. Then, the back had the rail route, with X on a snag (Figure 4-122).

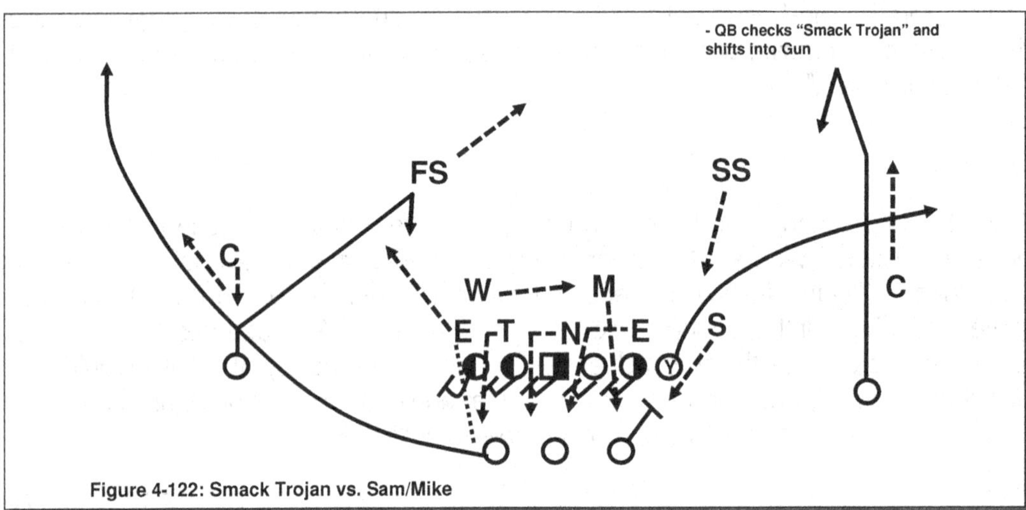

Figure 4-122: Smack Trojan vs. Sam/Mike

**Play: 4-122**

| Pos: | Assignment: |
|---|---|
| R | Free release, run rail route. |
| F | Block smash protection. |
| X | Run snag route. |
| Y | Run 14-yard curl. |
| Z | Run diagonal route. |
| QB | Progression:<br>1. R<br>2. X |

You're better off with it against 4-down, because that's a defensive end rather than a stand-up linebacker, for them, however, since nobody could ever cover Reggie Bush, it didn't matter if it was three or four down, it was their automatic 2-back check to field pressure. He would shift offset and they would just kill people with it. We have used that "smack" check and found it was good against the "Sam/Mike scrape," where you can get him running the rail route on a dropping defensive end. We did it at Louisville with Reggie Bonnafon, and it worked really well. Arguably, Reggie was not an "every down" back in the traditional sense, but he could do a *lot* of different things. I'm glad he got a chance in the league, I absolutely love that kid!

❑ Memphis

We ran "Memphis," which is "mesh-blue," out of "trey" sometimes, but we ran it more often out of "trips" (Figure 4-123). We can also tag "return" (Figure 4-124) or really any other "combo" out there, if we decide we want it, but our quarterbacks really *know* "blue." Memphis was pretty good at times, because some teams tried to read #2 or play us cover 2 out here to cheat the "blue" to Y (like on "silver" and "gold"), so then we'd just throw the mesh. We scored touchdowns on in the red zone when you get into "trips" and they bring the corner over, so you know that it's cover-zero. That's another great way to package a "2-play call" in the red zone: run Memphis but have an "alert" to an outside run, if they don't corner-over.

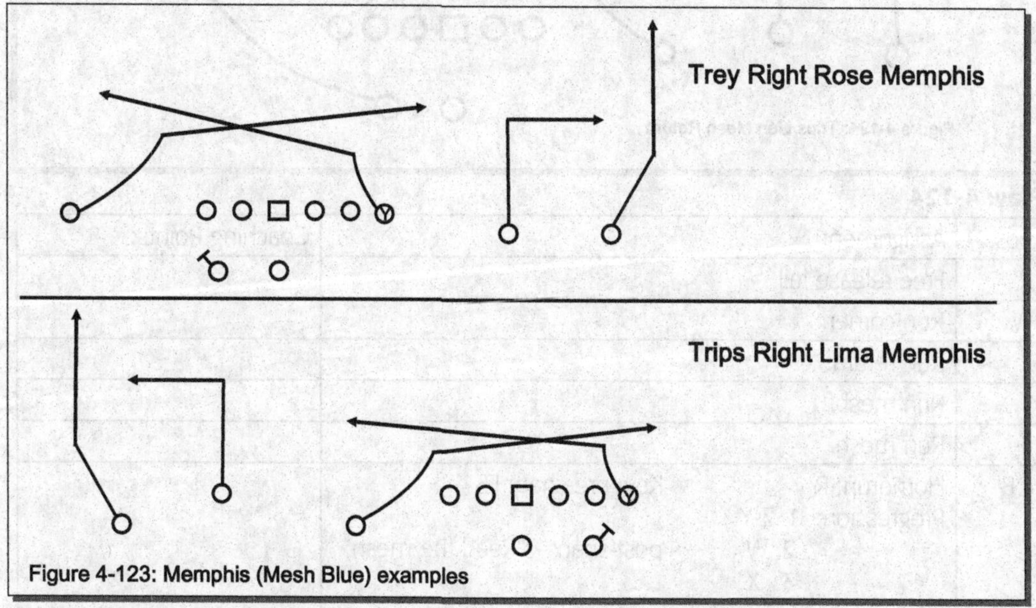

Figure 4-123: Memphis (Mesh Blue) examples

**Play: 4-123**

| Pos: | Assignment: |
|---|---|
| R | Block Lima protection. |
| W | Run 6-yd out. |
| X | Outside release go. |
| Y | Mesh route. |
| Z | Mesh route. |
| QB | Progression:<br>1. W/X<br>2. Z/Y |

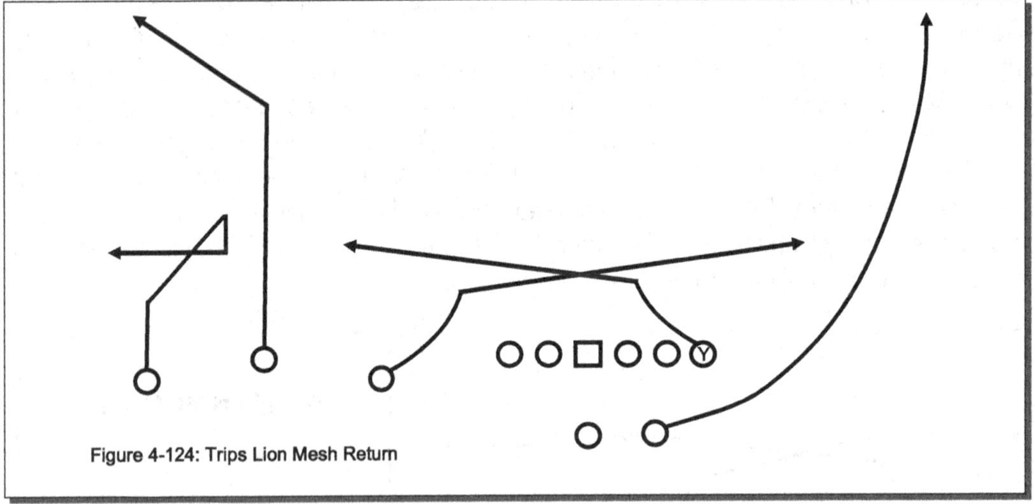


Figure 4-124: Trips Lion Mesh Return

**Play: 4-124**

| Pos: | Assignment: | Coaching Points: |
|---|---|---|
| R | Free release rail. | |
| W | Run corner. | |
| X | Run return. | |
| Y | Run mesh. | |
| Z | Run mesh. | |
| QB | Homerun: R Key: pre-snap: FS<br>Progression: 1. Z-Y<br>2. W post-snap – "Read the mesh"<br>3. X<br>Outlet: | |

❑ Red Zone "2-Play Call"

We give a one-word code name to any 2-play call we construct and always have a hand-signal for it. For example, let's say we're at the plus 10 going in. We get into "trips," and they bring the corner-over to go "man-zero," where much of the time it's a 1-linelinebacker look and they're going to double-edge blitz. There, we know it's a good look for "Lima Memphis," where we also have that fade available. The quarterback knows that he has to "beat the hugger," which in this instance is the Mike. Mike will see your back block and then come after you, so we always remind the quarterback "you have to beat the hugger."

If the corner stays home, that means there's two linebackers down in there, so now you package the mesh play with an outside run. We liked "red giant," which at that time was our code for "Q 38 boss." With the corner out there in support, the end is probably going to be a 7 or 8 technique, so you have them out-manned and the quarterback runs to the pylon behind the block of the running back (Figure 4-125). That's how you score in the red zone!

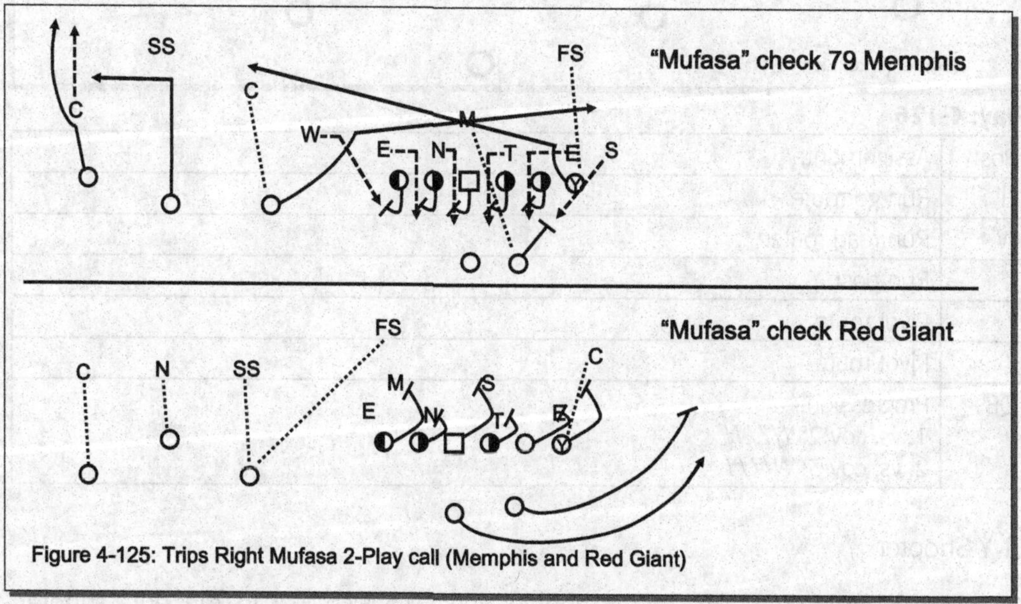

Figure 4-125: Trips Right Mufasa 2-Play call (Memphis and Red Giant)

We want to give all that a "one word" code name. That season, we called it "Mufasa." It's all you tell the quarterback: "Mufasa," and he gets them lined up in "trips right." He knows to go with what that corner is doing. "If that corner comes over in man, I'm calling the mesh. If he doesn't, I'm running it in myself." We just used another Lion King name because the other 2-play call in the package was "Simba" (with "zebra") and the players all just recognized what we were doing.

❑ Lion Pivot

We also carry "pivot," which is our code name for a "fake mesh" play. We like to set that up as "lion pivot" (Figure 4-126). Usually, the best "pivot" runner gets the ball, but sometimes the guy on the read route gets it, when they're playing him outside leverage. He pushes and snaps it, the pivot routes are covered, and then the middle opens right up.

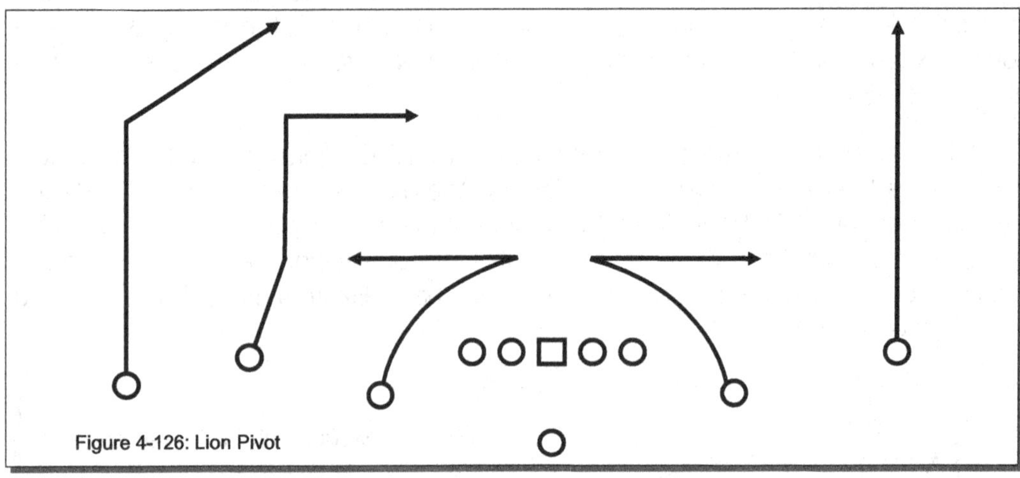

Figure 4-126: Lion Pivot

**Play: 4-126**

| Pos: | Assignment: |
|---|---|
| H | Run go route. |
| W | Run read route. |
| X | Run post. |
| Y | Pivot route. |
| Z | Pivot route. |
| QB | Progression:<br>1. vs. cov 2: Y/Z/W<br>2. vs. cov 3: W/Z/Y |

❑ Y Shooter

Against man-pressures, like a "6-1 double dog," we also like to run our "shooter" concept, usually with Y or Z. The mesh runner now gets two "picks" against man-coverage. We might be dating ourselves here, but my brother Paul and I named this after the movie Hoosiers, where the "Shooter" character said "we're gonna run the picket fence on em!" Alright, so here's "trips right, X half: 79, Y shooter" (Figure 4-127). Against man cover, the guy guarding the tight end now has to try to fight through both W and X. Then, what we do is say "if it's zone, X is hooking up over the opposite tackle, he's looking up over that tackle at six yards and Z is hooking up over the ball at 10 yards to create a "triangle" right there. And again, since it's a "miscellaneous" idea, we package this within the "9" category.

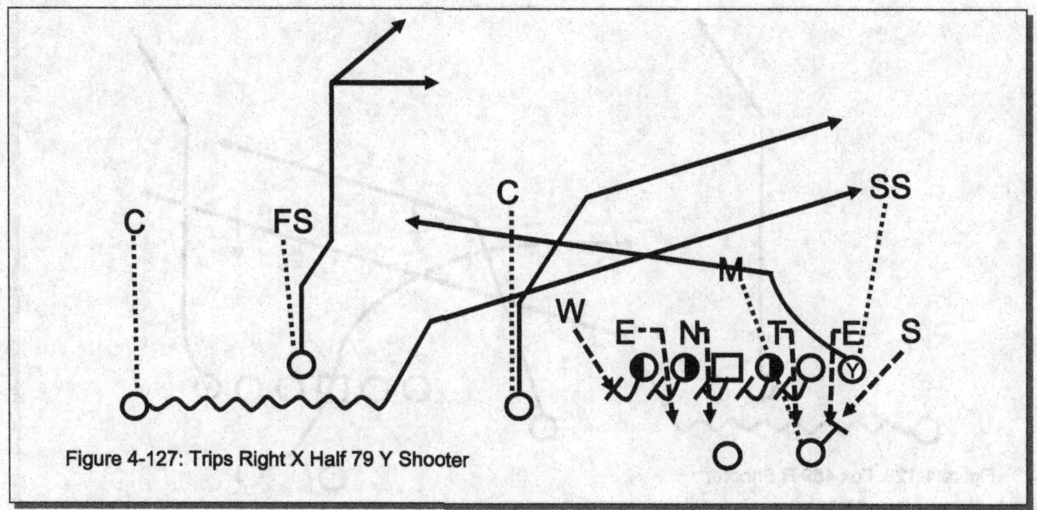

Figure 4-127: Trips Right X Half 79 Y Shooter

We like to build various ways to motion it down, so Z has the "rub" on the corner and then X is looking for a "rat" defender inside. On that "Y shooter," we used to run W on a corner route, but then changed it to a post, to get the corner's back turned, because there were a couple times a guy played through the corner route and made the tackle on Y, when it should have been a touchdown. This play requires drill work, if you want to execute it correctly, such as that "drift drill" for the quarterback, because he often has to "beat the hugger" (the Mike linebacker) and get the ball in there with some touch.

❑ R Shooter

Just like we did in our base shallow cross series, we can tag any eligible receiver as the "shooter" guy. With a versatile back like Reggie Bonnafon, we'd run "R shooter," for example, "gun star right: fox 489 R shooter" (Figure 4-128). We built this into a game plan against a boundary pressure team. In this case, our "picket fence" guys are coming. The low guy has the corner, high guy has the "rat," and the R comes out the backside, with the tight end on a corner route. It's really hard to defend this from man coverage.

❑ Z Shooter

We tend to put in one version of "shooter" for each weekly game plan, typically either Y, R, or Z shooter. I can remember one game where we scored two touchdowns on "Z shooter"—the first time, we lined up and went "doubles right snug, X half: 79 Z shooter" (Figure 4-129) and the very next drive we went "trips right bunch, Z mo: 79 Z shooter" (Figure 4-130). Like we keep saying, it's the same concept with different packaging, because with all our crossers, we like to have the ability to run them with a different formation, motion or shift. Some years, you'd say, "we're not good enough at tight end to call 'Y shooter,' so let's do it with Z." But if you have a Cole Hikutini or DJ Williams, the best version of it to run in the red zone is for the tight end!

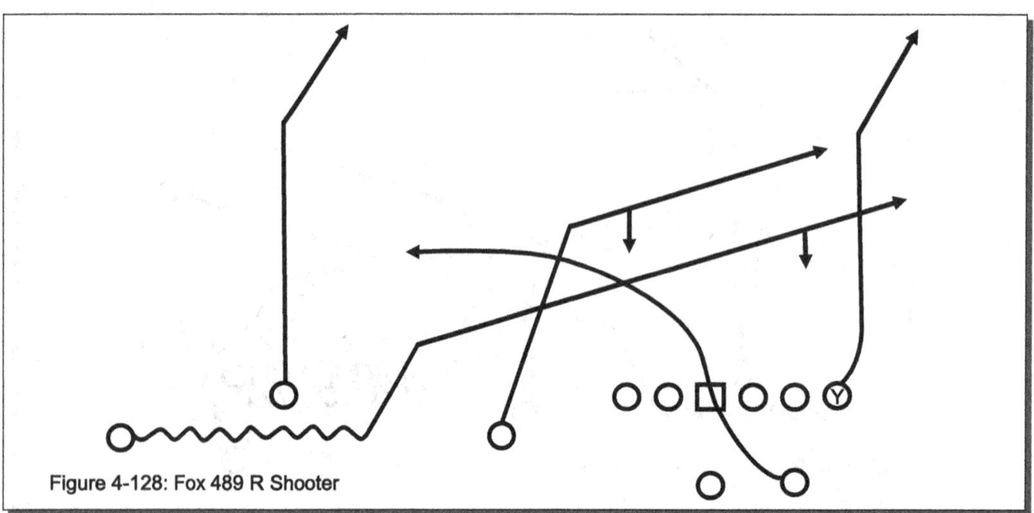

Figure 4-128: Fox 489 R Shooter

**Play: 4-128**

| Pos: | Assignment: | Coaching Points: |
|---|---|---|
| R | Free release. Run cross route. | |
| W | Run 12-yd post. | |
| X | Run 6-yd drag route. | vs. zone: sit down over ST at 6 yds |
| Y | Run 12-yd corner route. | |
| Z | Run 8-yd drag route. | vs. zone: sit down over C at 8 yds. |
| QB | Homerun: W<br>Progression: 1. W<br>2. R<br><br>Outlet: | vs. zone: R-Z-X |

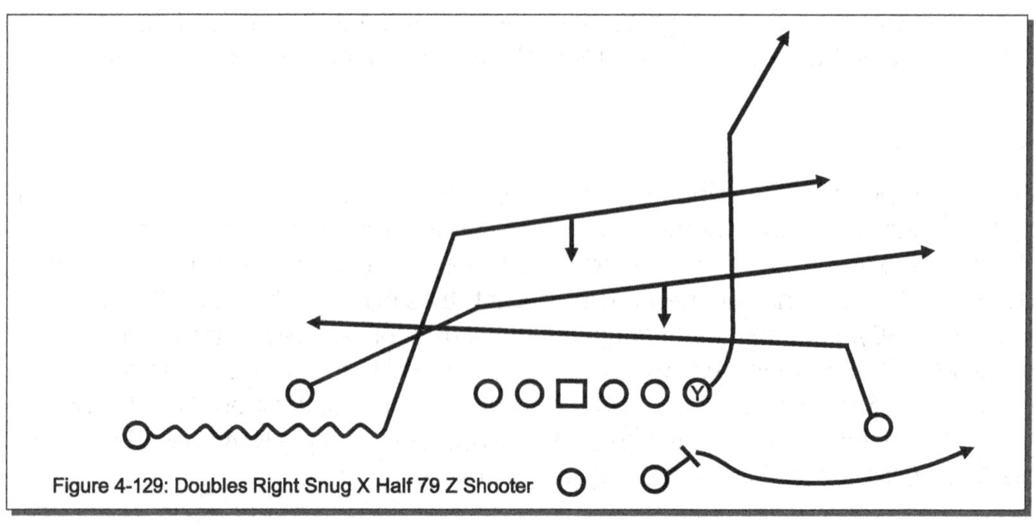

Figure 4-129: Doubles Right Snug X Half 79 Z Shooter

**Play: 4-129**

| Pos: | Assignment: | Coaching Points: |
|---|---|---|
| R | Check 70 protection. Run stretch route. | Catch the ball 2-3 yds from LOS. |
| W | Run crossing route on top of Z at 6 yds. Run through contact. | vs. zone: settle over center. |
| X | Run crossing route on top of Z at 8 yds. Run through contact. | vs. zone: settle over ST. |
| Y | Arc release to rub for Z then run corner route. | Alert CB technique over Z. |
| Z | Run drive route under W. you are responsible for the mesh. | |
| QB | Homerun: Y<br>Progression: 1. Y<br>2. Z<br>3. W/X<br><br>Outlet: R | vs. man: get the ball to Z<br>vs. press on Z: alert Y<br>vs. zone: W/X/Z |

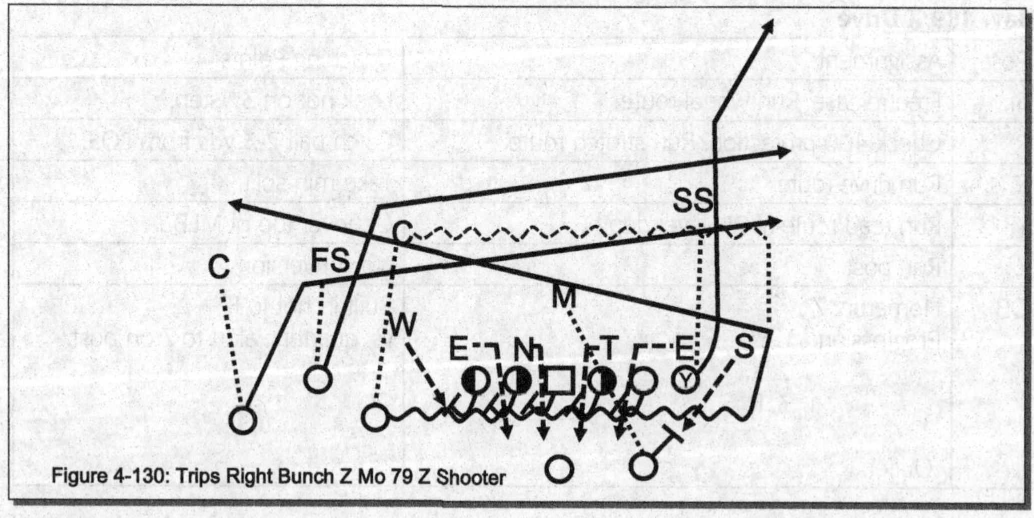

Figure 4-130: Trips Right Bunch Z Mo 79 Z Shooter

❑ X Drive & Flanker Drive

Out of 12 and 21 personnel, we also like "489 X drive" and "79 flanker drive" in our crosser series. When we first started running "489 X drive," we considered that a "buster beater," which goes back to Dick LeBeau. "2 buster" was from an under front, in which the Sam linebacker would take the first thing in the flat man, Mike would carry the vertical. If the corner got an inside release by the receiver, he would undercut it and play him man, but on an outside release, he would get hands on it and turn back inside to see who was coming. It was like a combination of man and zone out of cover 2. We would clear all those guys out and bring the X underneath, on something like "489 X drive" (Figure 4-131). Z has the post, T (or F) has the wheel route, and Y has the read route. X would catch the ball and run forever.

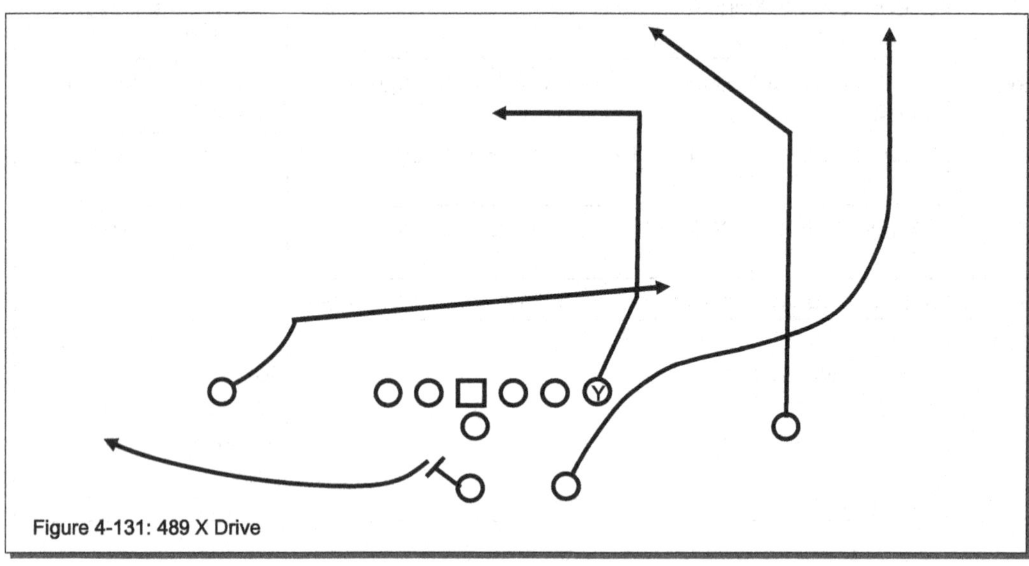

Figure 4-131: 489 X Drive

**Play: 489 X Drive**

| Pos: | Assignment: | Coaching Points: |
|---|---|---|
| F | Free release. Run wheel route. | Look hot on 3rd step. |
| R | Check 400 protection. Run stretch route. | Catch ball 2-3 yds from LOS. |
| X | Run drive route. | Take min split. |
| Y | Run read route at 2nd-level depth. | Get over top of MLB. |
| Z | Run post. | No conversion |
| QB | Homerun: Z<br>Progression: 1. Y<br>2. X<br>3. R<br><br>Outlet: R | Built-in hot to F.<br>vs. quarters: alert to Z on post. |

You could call it "487," like the basic crosser for X ("shark"), but we called it "489," because T (or W from 11 people, or F out of 21 people) ran that wheel route on this. If we said "7," he would tend to think that he has a "rub" corner instead and since we mainly run "X drive" and "flanker drive" out 12 and 21 personnel, we decided to just package it with the "9" category. If life is better from 11 personnel, we can still run "489 X drive" and we can certainly also use our "5" and "7" crossers as well.

We do that two different ways for Z, depending on what coverage we face. We'd first run "strong right: flow 79 flanker drive" (Figure 4-132). I always like "flow," if you know it's man-coverage, where you can also bring Z down in motion for the drive route.

F is running a corner route, Y runs a read route, and then the back has the "check down." When you call this play a lot, you'll even get some touchdowns to the running back: everything goes by, you check it down to him on the 20-yard line and since everyone on defense is chasing their guy in man coverage, he just runs it all the way in. By rule, X just has a go route, but if you have an X receiver who can win a 1-on-1 and a smart quarterback who can hand signal adjustments to him, you can allow them to take advantage of matchup opportunities on the backside as well.

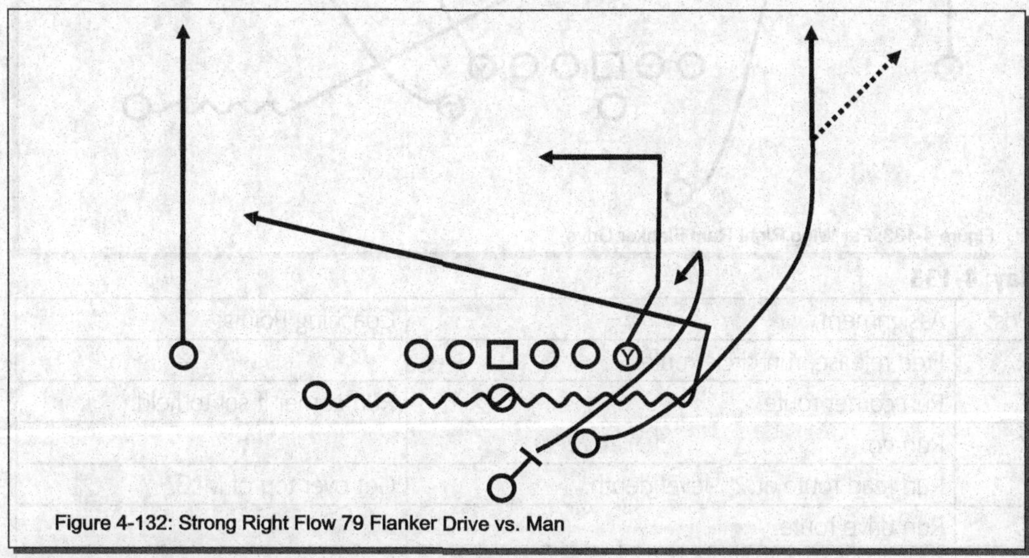

Figure 4-132: Strong Right Flow 79 Flanker Drive vs. Man

**Play: Strong Right: Flow 79 Flanker Drive vs. Man**

| Pos: | Assignment: | Coaching Points: |
|---|---|---|
| F | Free release. Run corner route. | Run corner if set to field. |
| R | Check 70 protection. Run 3x3 stop route. | |
| X | Run go. | |
| Y | Run read route at 2nd-level depth. | Get over top of MLB. |
| Z | Run drive route. | |
| QB | Homerun: F<br>Progression: 1. Z<br>2. Y<br>3. R<br>Outlet: | Key: pre-snap: FS<br>post-snap: strong ILB | |

However, when people started playing more quarters, we said "the Will is just sitting there, this play isn't ideal." So then, we put the back on the other side instead, Will has to carry it and now here comes the Z into the open space. When we run it like "far, wing right: ram flanker drive" (Figure 4-133), where the running back has the circle route to clear out the Will, it ends up very similar to that "ram trey right: W shallow."

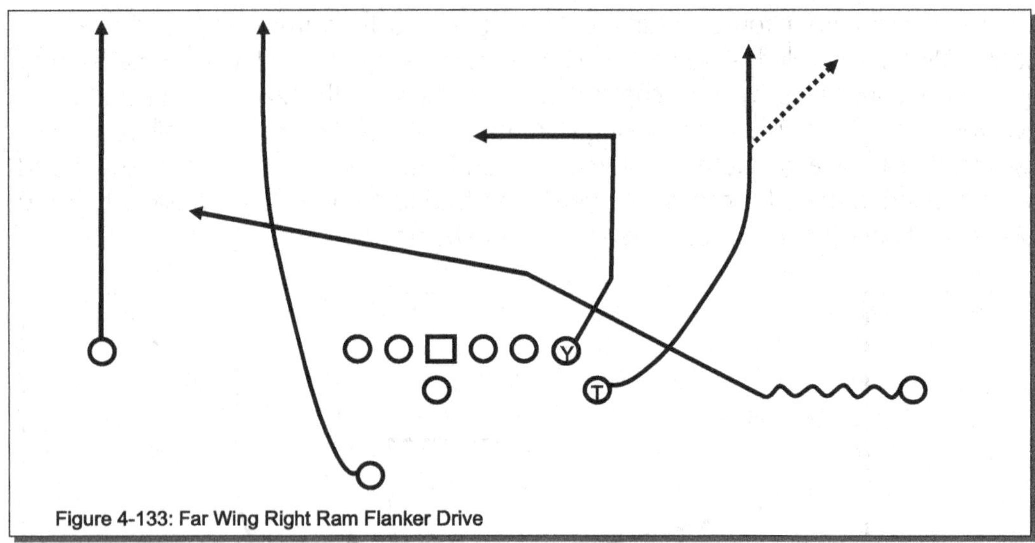

Figure 4-133: Far Wing Right Ram Flanker Drive

**Play: 4-133**

| Pos: | Assignment: | Coaching Points: |
|---|---|---|
| R | Free release, run circle route. | |
| T | Run corner route. | Run corner if set to field. |
| X | Run go. | |
| Y | Run read route at 2nd-level depth. | Get over top of MLB. |
| Z | Run drive route. | |
| QB | Homerun: R Key: pre-snap: FS<br>Progression: 1. Z<br>2. Y post-snap – weak ILB<br>3.<br><br>Outlet: | |

❑ Seahawk

This isn't necessarily a true crosser, but it's a good "3rd-&-medium" play that was useful on the hash, so its fits in the package. Out of a "trips" formation, we "bunch" the trips and go, "fox Lima Seahawk" (Figure 4-134). This is really good against teams that want to play man coverage in that situation, where a lot of teams will press the point, play him man, and play the outside receiver and inside receiver "in and out." We set the point of the bunch on the left hash. We like the "fox" protection on this, in order to get that linebacker out of the way for the rest of the route.

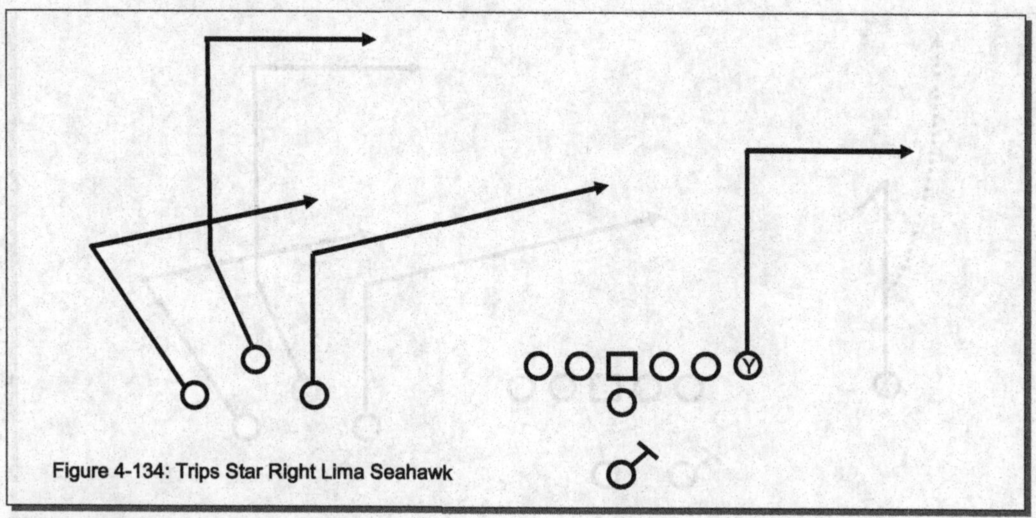


Figure 4-134: Trips Star Right Lima Seahawk

**Play: 4-134**

| Pos: | Assignment: |
|---|---|
| R | Block Lima protection. |
| W | Read route. |
| X | Expand 3 steps. Run slant. |
| Y | 6-yd out. |
| Z | 1-3 step slant. |
| QB | Progression: Alert Y with no flat defender.<br>1. Z-X<br>2. W |

The tight end has a 6-yard out (if it's a "gimme," you take it). The point receiver will expand and run a read route. The inside receiver would take a 1-step slant. The outside guy runs a 3-step "out-angle." This is really hard for the corner. When the outside guy starts outside, the corner deepens, and then you come back with that slant and the window really opens up.

We actually have two different ways to call that formation: it's a "trips right bunch," but we also started calling it "star right," which told the receivers it was a wider-aligned bunch. With experienced guys, they see the play and know exactly where to line up, so you don't have to carry another formation call. With inexperienced guys, we want to call "star," so they know where to line up. It's important to always assess "how much do they really understand about your offense" and "who's out there leading it?" If you have one guy who knows how to line up, he can tell the other two guys, especially in no-huddle situations. But for this play to work, they have got to get the alignment correct. We can always mirror the concept and call "bunch right: rose Seahawk, Z hitch" (Figure 4-135), but we usually liked to carry it with the "trips bunch" instead, so we could package it with "R shooter" and things like that.

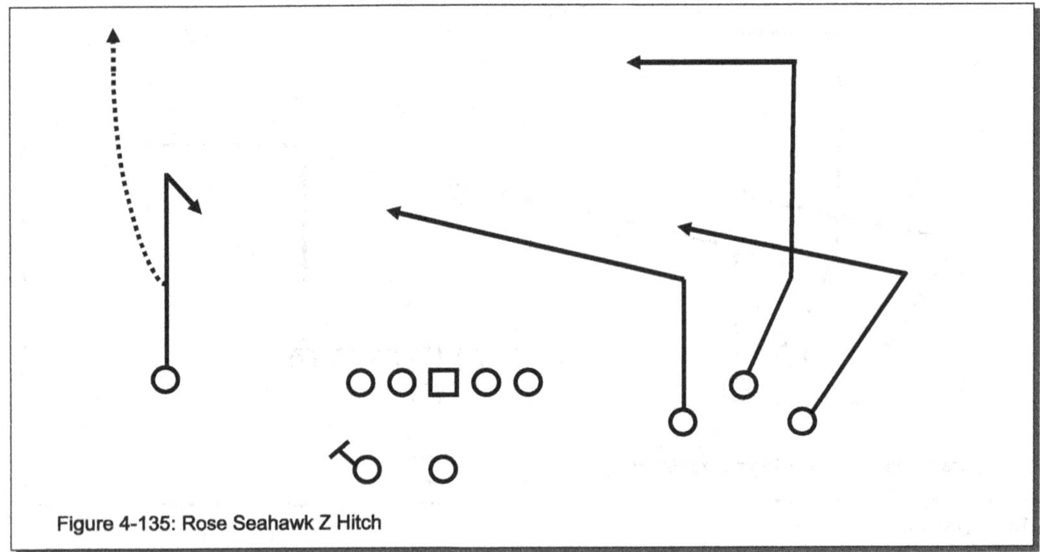
Figure 4-135: Rose Seahawk Z Hitch

**Play: 4-135**

| Pos: | Assignment: |
|---|---|
| R | Block rose protection. |
| W | 1-3 step slant. |
| X | Expand 3 steps. Run slant. |
| Y | Run read route. |
| Z | Run hitch. Normal conversion. |
| QB | Progression:<br>1. Z<br>2. W to X |

# Final Thoughts About Dropback Passing

These crossers can go on forever and they have really been our signature play in the dropback passing game. To be a great dropback passing team, it takes efficient planning, so you can be well coordinated, and it takes a lot of hard work and commitment to execute it right. We believe the way to do that is to think in *concepts*. Work the heck out of your basic concepts and then really focus on the ones where every eligible receiver is getting the ball. Use personnel, formations, shifts, and motions to package them, so teams can't force you out of your best plays. Use audibles, hand-signals, alerts, and "2-play calls" to take advantage of the vulnerabilities in each defense you face. Be willing to adapt to new ideas that can be better for your players, even if that means changing a name of a play. And when the game is on the line, take care of your quarterback, create your best matchups, and feed the studs!

# Chapter 5
## Philosophy of Empty

Empty is going to be called in every game. While the specific package may vary, depending on what personnel group we put into the game plan, we will utilize empty in every game we play. Against a defense that doesn't like to substitute personnel—in other words, on 1st or 2nd down they're going to try to keep their base defense in—we're going to run five wide receivers out there. We'll put the best group of five wide receivers on the field, have clearly-defined ways to protect the defensive pressures, and try to really work mismatches on the linebackers. If they're going to try to match personnel and utilize nickel-and-dime people, then we're going to disperse to empty out of either "regular" (21), "thunder" (12), or "spread" (20) personnel. We'll still have the ability to run the entire empty package and get our receivers into a mismatch against linebackers, but, in this instance, if we catch them in dime personnel, we can also use tempo the next play so they can't substitute, then line up in a run formation and pound the ball right at them.

We practice all of it and always carry the entire package. In some games, it becomes a major part of our offense and in some games, it's maybe as few as three or four plays, but it's always going to be available for us. Like we say, when you can throw the ball and get big plays when you *want* to—and in this case, that would be utilizing empty on 1st and 2nd down—then when you *have* to throw, it's available for you.

The following is how we like to label these guys: the inside guy to the boundary is "Y," the outside guy into the boundary, we started calling "H," because we line up a variety of different types of guys there. The inside guy to the field is "Z," #2 is "W," and the outside guy is "X" (Figure 5-1). It started life from "speed trips" and the history of that started out way back with Jack Elway and Dennis Erickson. We first started going "trips right Roy" and at that time, we called it "Y hitch" or "Y up" (Figure 5-2), which told the running back to go in motion toward the Y and run either an "up" or a "hitch." Then, when people started blitzing with the motion (they would just check to it and blitz us), we said "let's just line him up out there" and called that "shift right" (see Figure 5-1). Then if they stay in base coverage, we'll just put five wide receivers out there and detach #2 into the boundary. So, that's the history of the package and how it was built.

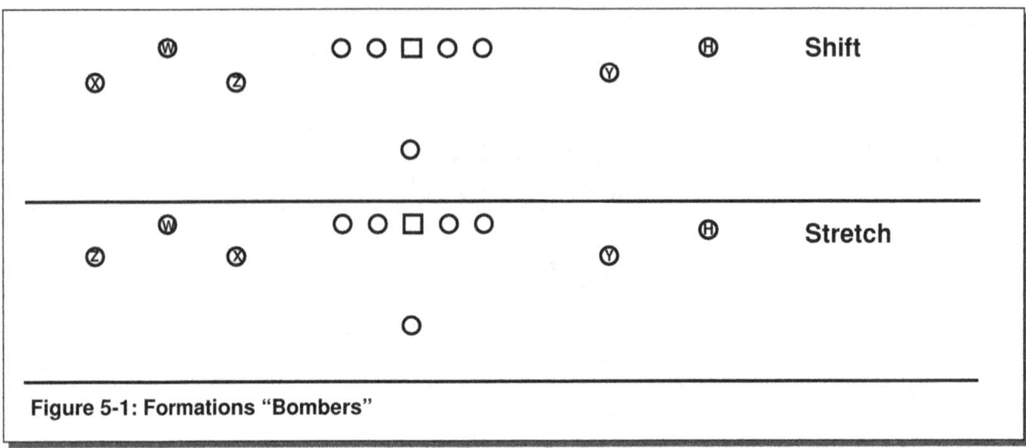

Figure 5-1: Formations "Bombers"

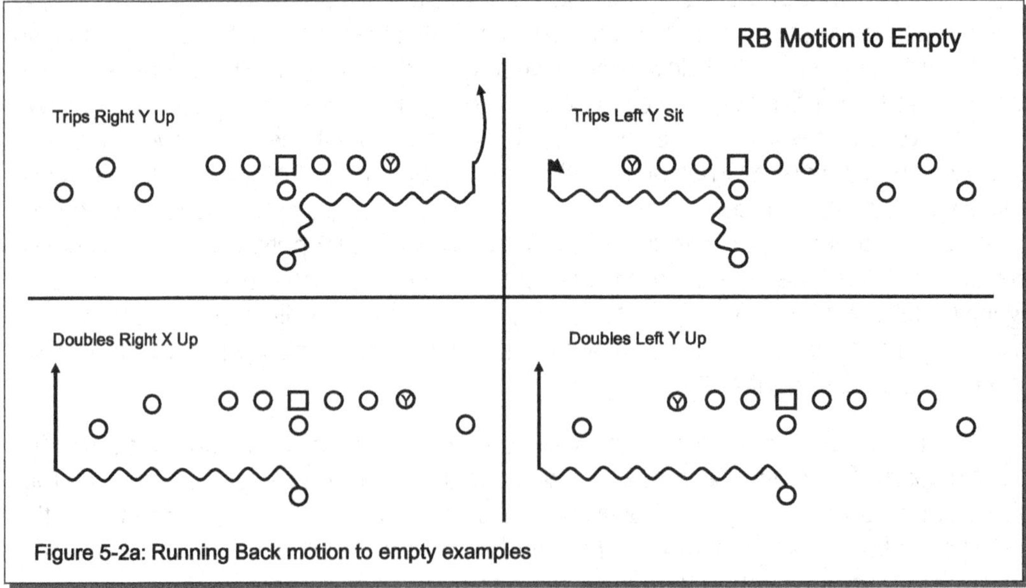

Figure 5-2a: Running Back motion to empty examples

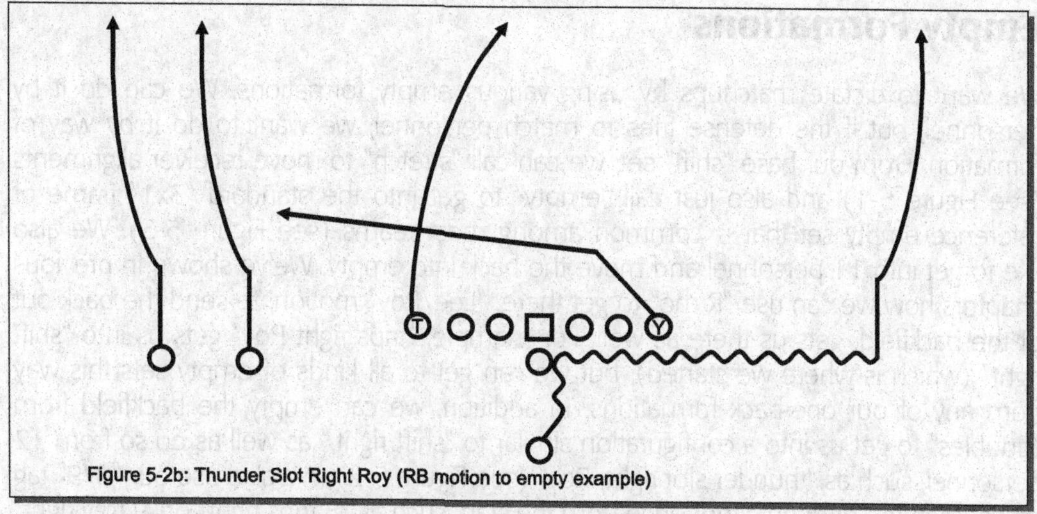

Figure 5-2b: Thunder Slot Right Roy (RB motion to empty example)

Z was intended to be the guy you couldn't cover. You might line another receiver up at H, so that anytime he's got a 1-on-1, you run hitch-fade or double-slant. As such, you know he is catching a lot of balls in this. For example, when Michael Bush was a true freshman, we'd put Michael there to give him some "sugar" and get him the ball. In order to see him reach his potential as a running back, we had to show him we were going to get him the ball (and as he developed his running back skills, he went on to a career in the NFL).

I believe most teams think of empty as a 3x1 (our "trey" or "taxi"), with an extra body out there in the boundary slot (Figure 5-3). We sometimes do that as well, but thinking of it first from our "trips" has seemed to make our empty package unique. We also believe our players retain the learning better this way, since it carries over from the quick game and the dropback packages.

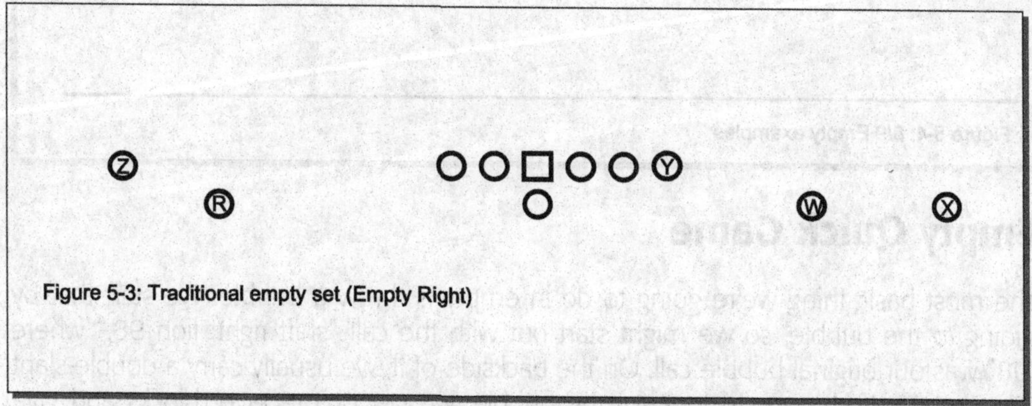

Figure 5-3: Traditional empty set (Empty Right)

## Empty Formations

We want to dictate matchups by using various empty formations. We can do it by personnel, but if the defense tries to match personnel, we want to do it by way of formation. From our base "shift" set, we can call "stretch" to move receiver alignments (see Figure 5-1) and also just call "empty" to get into the standard "3x1" frame of reference empty set that is common among most teams (see Figure 5-3). We also like to get into 11 personnel and move the back into empty. We've shown in previous chapters how we can use "R mo" to get there. "Lee/Roy" motion, to send the back out of the backfield, gets us there as well. For example, "trips right Roy" gets us into "shift right" (which is where we started), but we can get to all kinds of empty sets this way from any of our one-back formations. In addition, we can empty the backfield from "doubles" to get us into a configuration similar to "shift right," as well as do so from 12 personnel, such as "thunder slot right, Roy" (see Figure 5-2). We also use our "8/9" tag to just align the back on either edge from the start, such as "8 trips right" or "9 trey right" (Figure 5-4). This can get as specific as we want, from any of our one-back formations, depending on who we want into the boundary and to the field. Then, in each weekly game plan, we tend to package a new one or use a different variety of them, depending on the personnel grouping we think gives us the best advantage, where we want to dictate the matchups, and which of the following routes we want to use.

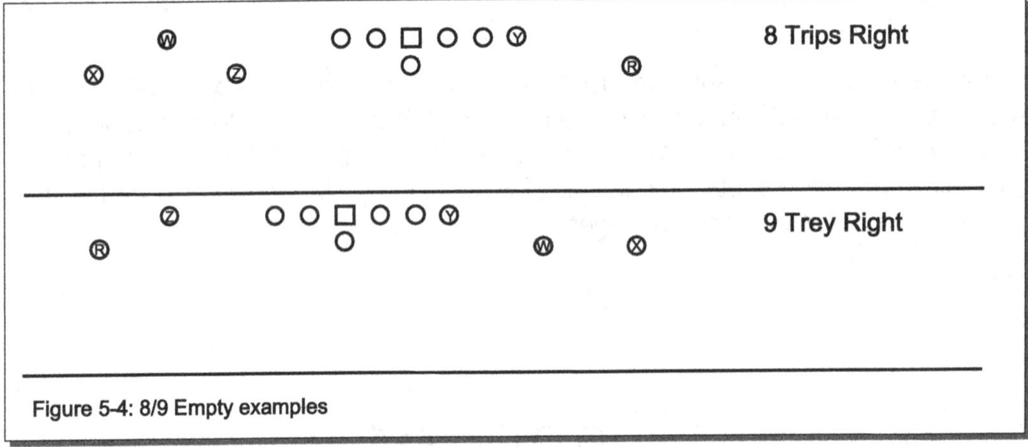

Figure 5-4: 8/9 Empty examples

## Empty Quick Game

The most basic thing we're going to do in empty is throw a bubble. We start that by sliding *to* the bubble, so we might start out with the call "shift right: lion 98," where "98" was our original bubble call. On the backside of it, we usually carry a double-slant (Figure 5-5). If it's a good look for the bubble, we get two receiver blocks and give #3 the ball when Mike is trying to cheat. You force the d-line to run to the sideline, which is a reason to run bubble: to try to make the pass rushers turn and run and wear themselves out. But if teams bring pressures or do things we can't block up, you have to be able to throw the double-slant and get the ball out. For example, when there's a blitz from off the ball on that edge toward the screen and they're dropping the safety over to it, the bubble doesn't tend to get a lot of yardage, so that's when you come back to the double-slant. Furthermore, we can certainly get into our entire variety of other bubble tags (which we cover next, in the screen game chapter).

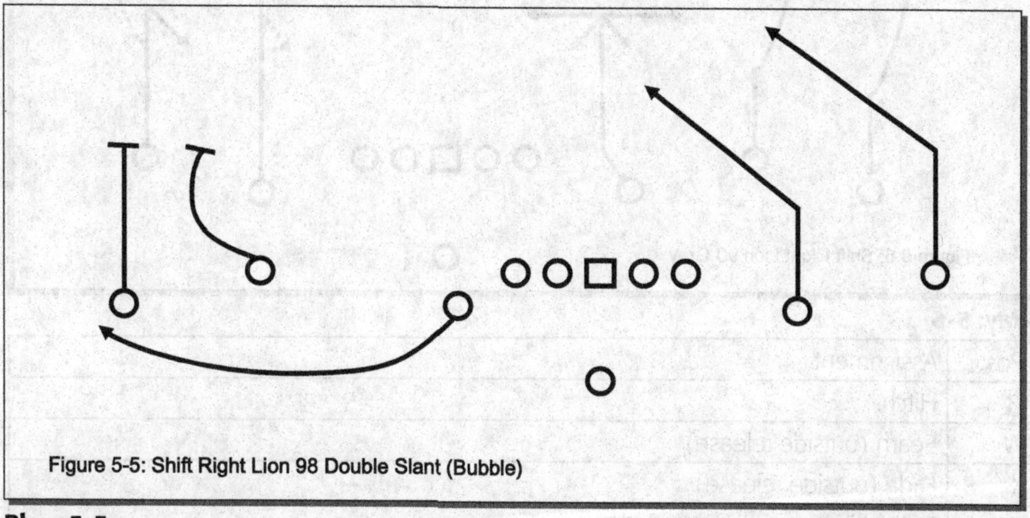
Figure 5-5: Shift Right Lion 98 Double Slant (Bubble)

**Play: 5-5**

| Pos: | Assignment: |
|---|---|
| H | Run 3-step slant. |
| W | Arc release & block for bubble. |
| X | Block for bubble. |
| Y | Run 1-3 step slant. |
| Z | Run bubble. Sprint to #'s after catch. |
| QB | Progression:<br>1. Y to H<br>2. Z |

From there, we carry over what we have already installed. Starting with the quick game in any empty set, we need the ability to run "90 grey" (Figure 5-6), where the "90" (hitch) would be to the 2-receiver side and the "grey" (option route to #3) would be to the 3-receiver side. If we're running the 6 to 8-yard option route (where the receiver can "break in, hook in, or break out") and we get split safeties vs. empty, the first thing the quarterback and #3 receiver should think is "take it over the top for a touchdown." We emphasize again that we need *great* get-off to get over the top for a touchdown. If Mike gets high, or if we get "2 zebra" (2 Tampa), then #3 can chase the Mike, turn around, and catch the ball. On the two-receiver side, we can decide whether you want "hitch-fade" or the "stab" *call* or *signal*. If we like the call "90 grey, alert: stab," and we get a free safety covering him, we will try to throw the touchdown on the "stab" (Figure 5-7).

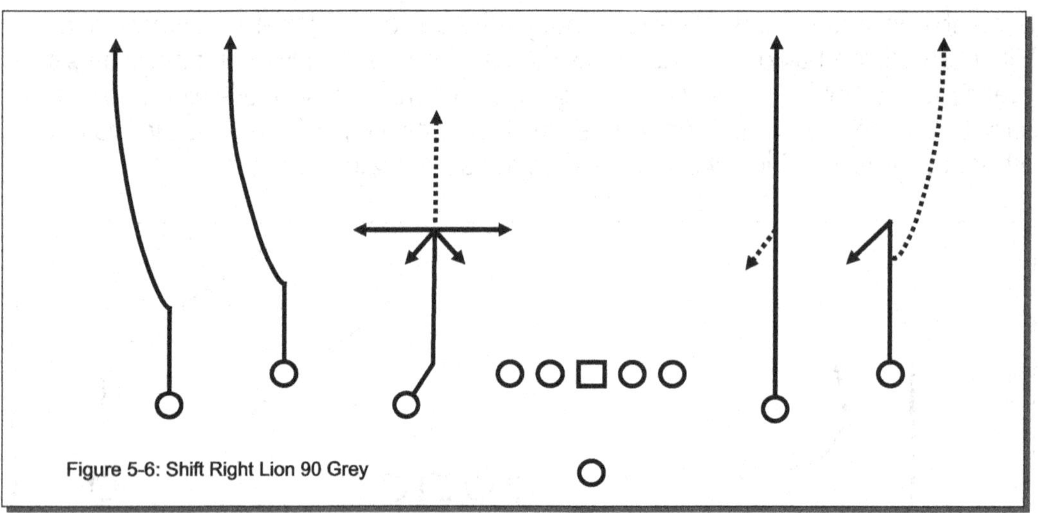
Figure 5-6: Shift Right Lion 90 Grey

**Play: 5-6**

| Pos: | Assignment: |
|---|---|
| H | Hitch. |
| W | Seam (outside release) |
| X | Fade (outside release) |
| Y | Seam-hitch |
| Z | 6-yd option |
| QB | Progression:<br>1. H<br>2. Z |

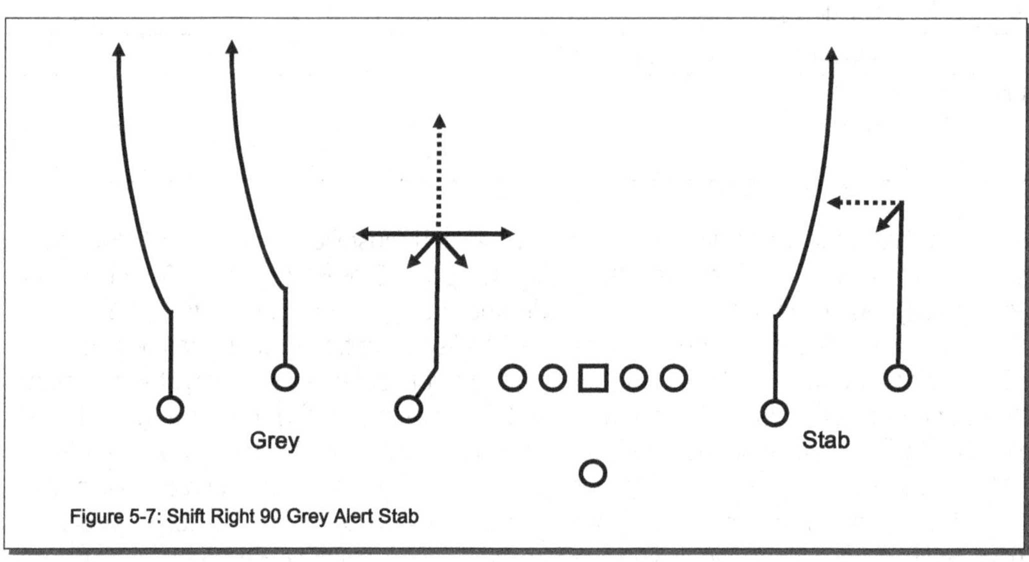

Figure 5-7: Shift Right 90 Grey Alert Stab

Next, we install "94" with options on both sides, just like we did in the original quick game installation (Figure 5-8). We have the "protect-seam" and "protect-fade" with the inside-option by #3 against split safeties, he really tries to get over the top if he can. The boundary option guy is really looking for single-high to take it over the top. We re-emphasize that he's really not going to take it through for a touchdown vs. cover 2, because the safety is sitting right over the top of him. But let's say the safety is working away from him and that's a Will linebacker over him instead, then he can take the seam route through for a touchdown. That's the *mindset* for a big play. What you're trying to do in empty is distort zone coverage, which forces them to play "man within the zone," and that opens up big plays for you. That opens up both the middle and the second level.

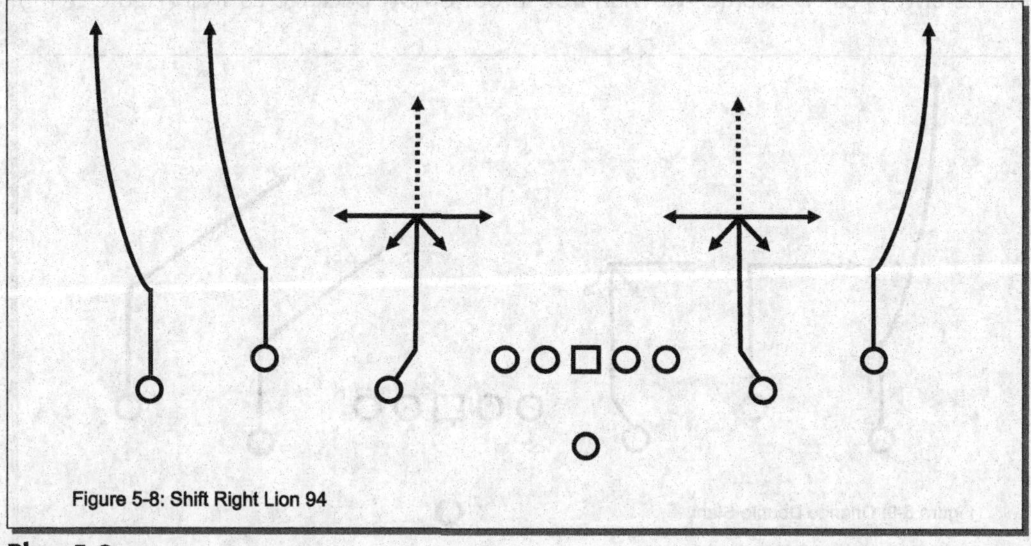

Figure 5-8: Shift Right Lion 94

**Play: 5-8**

| Pos: | Assignment: |
|---|---|
| H | Fade (outside release) |
| W | Seam (outside release) |
| X | Fade |
| Y | 6-yd option route |
| Z | 6-yd option route |
| QB | Progression:<br>1. Z<br>2. Y<br>Alert W on seam or H on fade. |

Like we said in the quick game discussion, I don't think "94" is the best call in the world against "man-free with a rat." So, that's again when you carry the *alert* to check to things like "Seattle" or "stab" or "Orlando / double-slant." I always want to have *alerts* from empty against "cover 1 rat," so we always carry a section in our game plan that says "man-free" and has a list of at least three quick game passes and three dropbacks, which enables us to defeat "man-free with the rat."

We like "shift lion (ram): Orlando/double-slant" against that (Figure 5-9). In this instance, we've got the "Orlando" route to the field and then the "rat beater" is the double-slant. The quarterback understands that "if I've got zone, I'm reading the Orlando side; if I get man-free, I'm reading the double-slant side." Like we say, "Oakland" is also a good call to the field, because you get a lot of off-coverage to the field (Figure 5-10), and we always carry "Seattle" vs. man-free in our empty package as well (Figure 5-11).

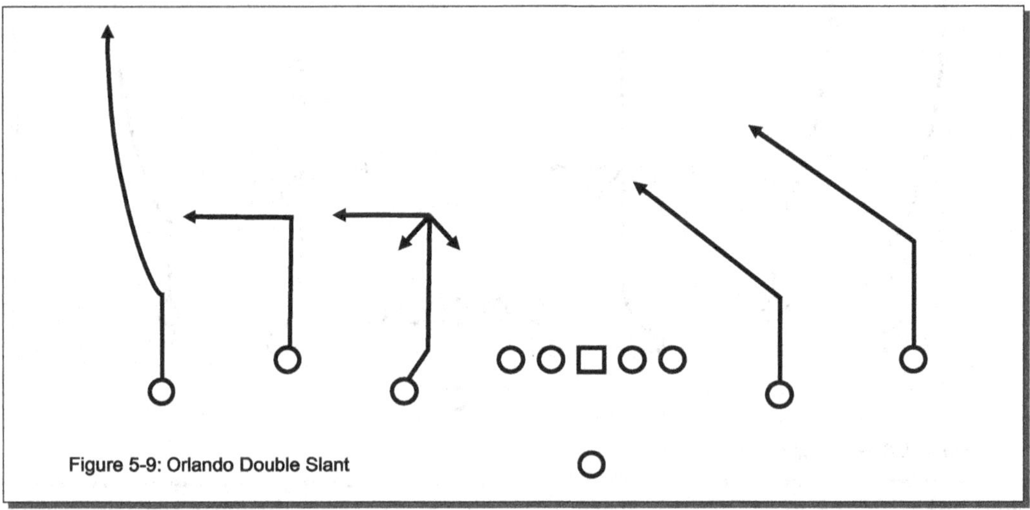
Figure 5-9: Orlando Double Slant

**Play: 5-9**

| Pos: | Assignment: |
|---|---|
| H | 3-step slant. |
| W | 6-yd out. |
| X | Fade (outside release). |
| Y | 1-3 step slant. |
| Z | 6-yd hook. |
| QB | Progression: Key middle linebacker<br>1. W, Z<br>2. Y, H |

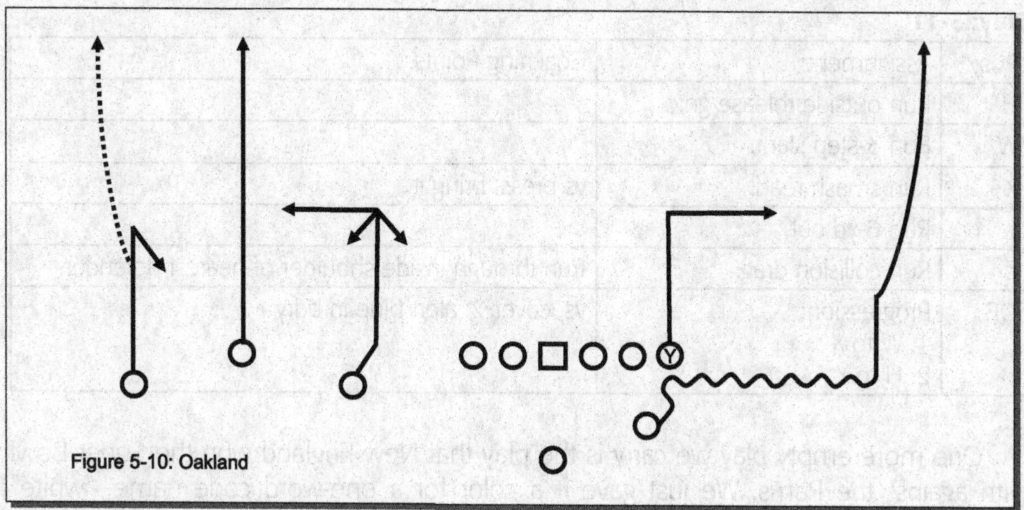

Figure 5-10: Oakland

**Play: 5-10**

| Pos: | Assignment: |
|---|---|
| R | Go route. |
| W | Seam. |
| X | Hitch. |
| Y | Blue route. |
| Z | Hook route. |
| QB | Progression:<br>1. X to Z<br>2. R to Y |

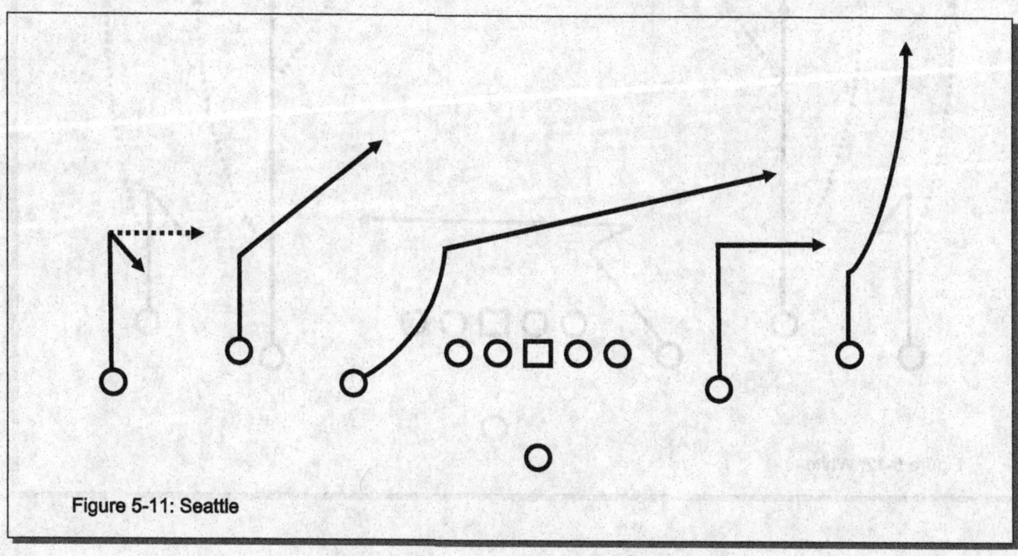
Figure 5-11: Seattle

**Play: 5-11**

| Pos: | Assignment: | Coaching Points: |
|---|---|---|
| H | Run outside release go. | |
| W | Run 3-step slant. | |
| X | Run smash read. | vs press: bring it. |
| Y | Run 6-yd out. | |
| Z | Run collision drag. | Run through inside shoulder of nearest defender. |
| QB | Progression:<br>1. W to X<br>2. H to Y | vs. cover 2: alert blue in bdry |

One more empty play we carry is the play that New England won the Super Bowl with against the Rams. We just gave it a color for a one-word code name–"white" (Figure 5-12). That would be "double-stab, Z jerk," where the #1 receivers have hitches, the #2 receivers to both sides have seam or stab routes (depending on zone or man), and the #3 guy has the "jerk" route, which means "he wants to go get the Mike linebacker, sit, act like he's breaking back out and then 'jerk' across his face." If we want to give that receiver the freedom to run a full-option route at the Mike and get open, then we can tag it a "jig" route instead of the "jerk." Now, he has the freedom to go either in or out. That all just depends on what we want to do and how we want to name it. That's what New England really won the Super Bowl with, which sometimes they did it from "21" and also out of "12" twice, using motion to set up their receiver releases and matchups.

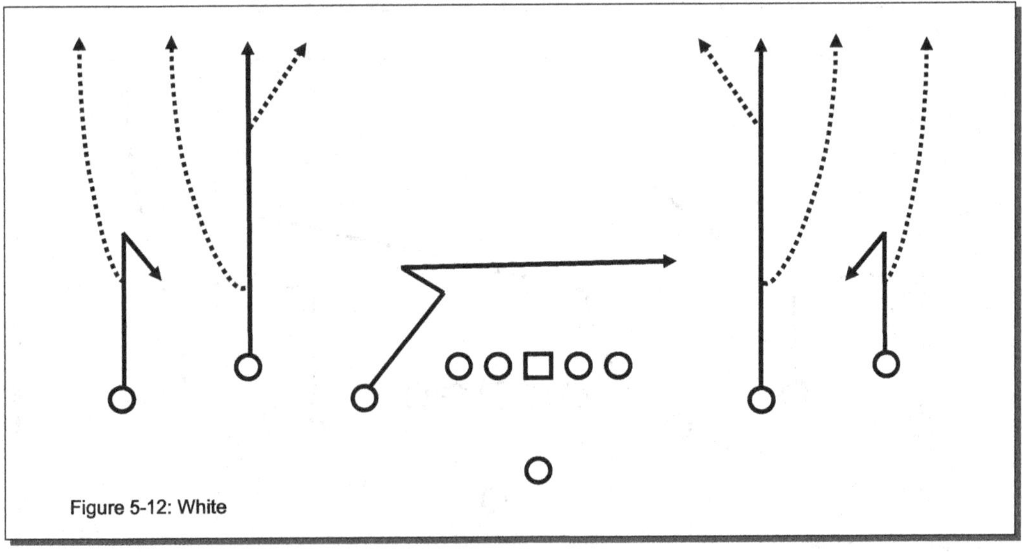

Figure 5-12: White

**Play: 5-12**

| Pos: | Assignment: | Coaching Points: |
|---|---|---|
| H | Run halt route. | vs. jam corner: convert fade |
| W | Run seam read. | vs. cov 11: run stab |
| X | Run halt route. | vs. jam corner: covert fade |
| Y | Run seam read. | vs. cov 11: run stab |
| Z | Run collision drag. | Run through inside shoulder of nearest defender. |
| QB | Progression:<br>vs. single high:<br>1. H/X to Y/W<br>2. Z<br>vs. 2 high:<br>1. Y to H<br>2. Z | |

❑ Empty Dropback

Most of this has already been put in, and since empty is usually the formation you get to in the last part of your installation, there's not a lot of new teaching. Rather, it's a lot of review of your foundation passes. It can look like a lot on paper, but the concepts have already been incorporated, so the players really do retain it. The basic thinking is, if you go across the board H, Y, Z, W, X, it's back to "FTS." How do I get the ball to each of those guys? We'll show you some things we do for each position.

❑ H Grab, H Laker

The first thing we look at when we talk about "H" is the ability to go "shift ram (lion): H grab." The 3-receiver side runs the 3x1 all-go: Z takes the middle, W is down the seam, and X is on a go route. Then, Y has the read route and H has the grab route. The "grab" concept went in the first day with the curls, so players already know it. It's a great 2-high play, no matter what the coverage is underneath. A lot of times, teams will play what we call "diamond" coverage to it, which is a cover 2 into the boundary, a "trio" coverage to Z and W, and man-up on the X. This play is good against that as well (Figure 5-13).

The next thing that we do is go "H Laker." We've already installed this route day-one as well. The quarterback is going to look at that 2-deep safety. If he gets width, he's got the chance to take Z right down the middle on the 3x1 all-go. If not, then he's got the "Laker" route, which is H on an in-cut and Y on the pivot-option, just like we installed it with the curl package. It's also a really good play and works consistently well. These two concepts of "grab" and "Laker" always kind of go together, hand in hand and the receivers always pick them up really quickly (Figure 5-14).

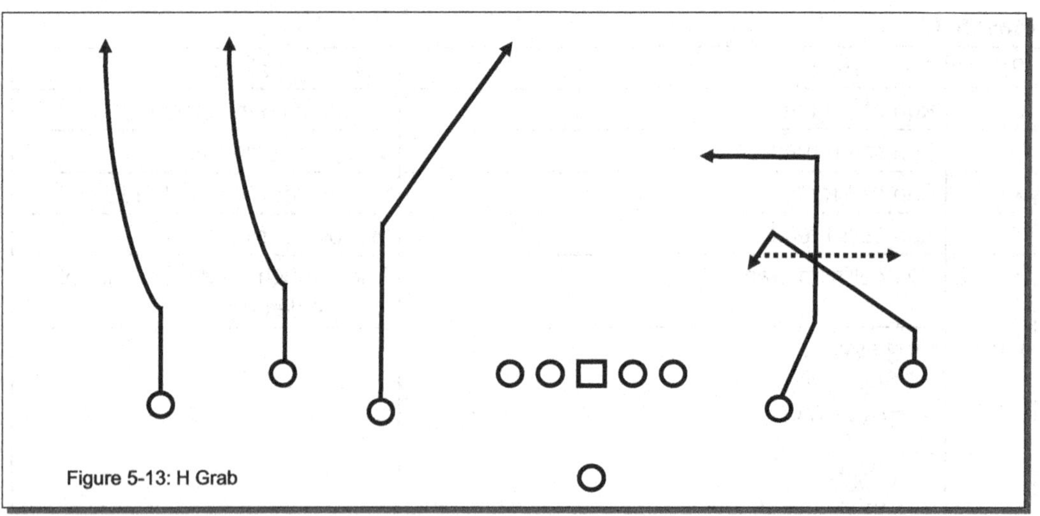
Figure 5-13: H Grab

**Play: H Grab**

| Pos: | Assignment: |
|---|---|
| H | Run grab route. |
| W | Run seam. |
| X | Fade (outside release) |
| Y | Run return route. |
| Z | Run seam down middle of the field. |
| QB | Progression:<br>Linebacker<br>1. W, Z<br>2. Y, H<br>3. Y |

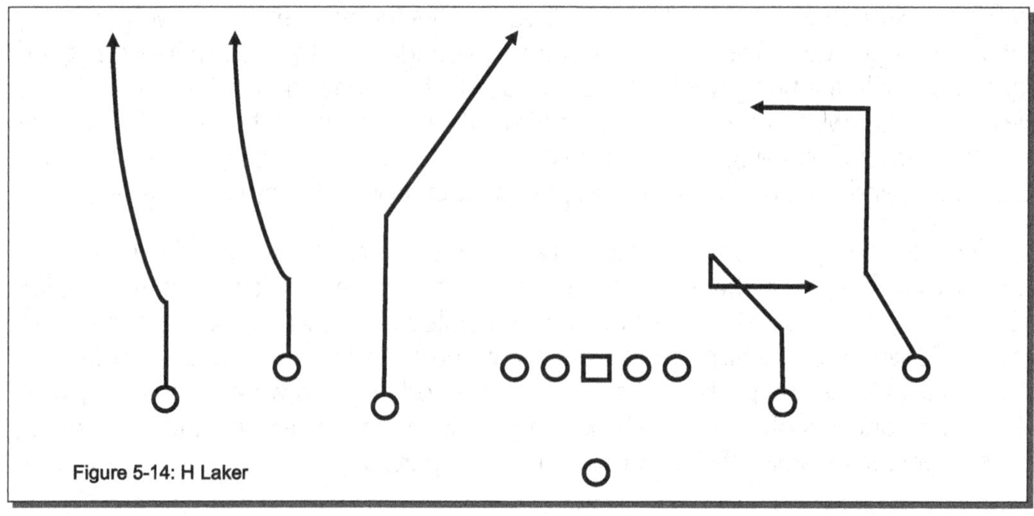
Figure 5-14: H Laker

**Play: H Laker**

| Pos: | Assignment: |
|---|---|
| H | Run 4-5 in-cut. |
| W | Run seam. |
| X | Run go (outside release). |
| Y | Run read route. |
| Z | Run seam down middle of the field. |
| QB | Progression:<br>Linebacker<br>1. W, Z<br>2. Y, H<br>3. Y |

❑ Y Patriot

The next thing we do in empty is call "ram (lion): Y patriot." This is built off our "double-seam" action, so Z has the seam route to the opposite hash, W has a seam route 2-yards outside his hash, and both X and H have "caddy" or "fall offs" that convert to go routes vs. jam corners. Then, Y has a "ditch" route, so the "Patriot" tag means he's the crosser (Figure 5-15).

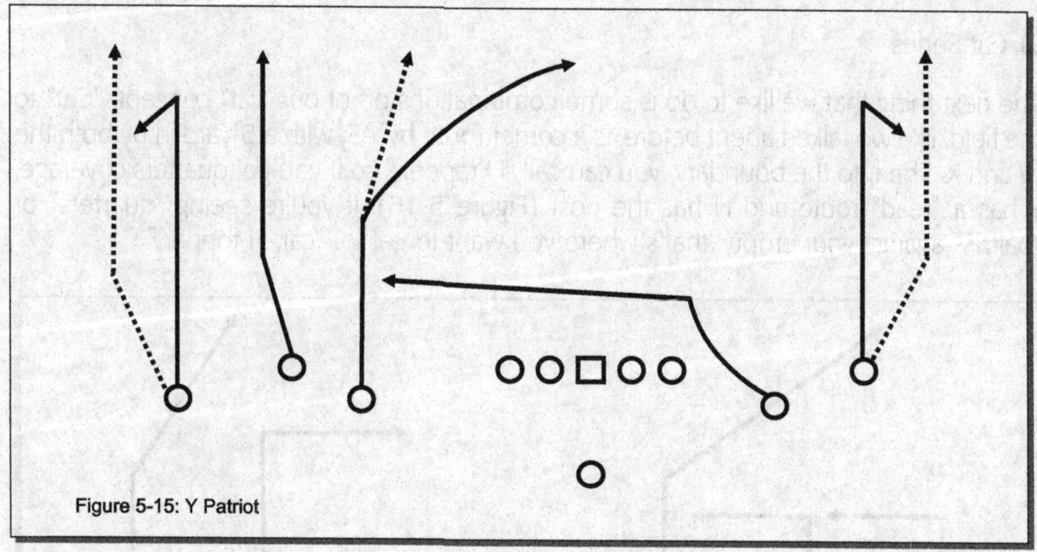

Figure 5-15: Y Patriot

**Play: Y Patriot**

| Pos: | Assignment: |
|---|---|
| H | Run titan route. |
| W | Run seam (ready to slip release). |
| X | Run titan route. |
| Y | Run ditch route. |
| Z | Take middle vs. cov 2. |
| QB | Progression:<br>vs. 1 high: key FS<br>vs. 2 high: pick a side (key safety on hash)<br>1. W-Z-Y |

You can vary it, similar to how we tag the crossers: you can call "Z Patriot," and you can call "W Patriot" and get some different looks off the double-seams. The most effective one throughout the years however, has been the "Y Patriot," with Z coming across on the 3x1 all-go concept. So, against a single-high safety, your progression is "Z/W to Y" on the crosser. If it's 2-high safeties, your progression is "Z to H to checkdown to Y" on the crosser. If it is "2 Tampa," you're then thinking "W to X to the field, with Y replacing it coming across." So, it's a good call vs. all coverages, with the exception of maybe "cover 11 man."

❑ Cat Series

The next thing that we like to do is some combinations off of our "cat" concept. "Cat" to the field, like we talked about before, is a corner route by #3, with a 5-yard in by both the W and X. Then, to the boundary, you can call "H topper," so if you get quarters coverage, Y has a "read" route and H has the post (Figure 5-16). If you're seeing "quarters" or "palms" against your empty, that's where you want to get to: "cat, H topper."

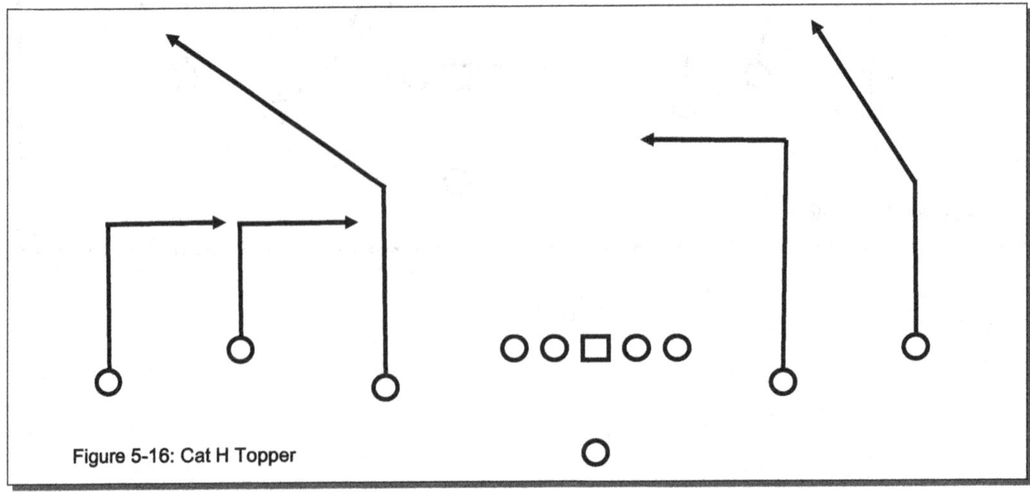

Figure 5-16: Cat H Topper

**Play: 5-16**

| Pos: | Assignment: |
|---|---|
| H | Run topper. |
| W | 5-yd under |
| X | 5-yd under |
| Y | Run read route at 2nd level. |
| Z | Run corner route. |
| QB | Progression:<br>1. H<br>2. Z |

You can call "cat, H blade," where you've got the "cat" route to the field, but now Y and H might switch alignments (put Y on the ball, with H off the ball), so Y runs the corner route and H stems down in behind him. He wants to get separation four yards behind him, push it to 12 yards, and run the post route. We're trying to affect that safety covering the Y and bring the H behind him to the post for a touchdown. The players will remember the idea, because we already installed it with the "1" category (Figure 5-17).

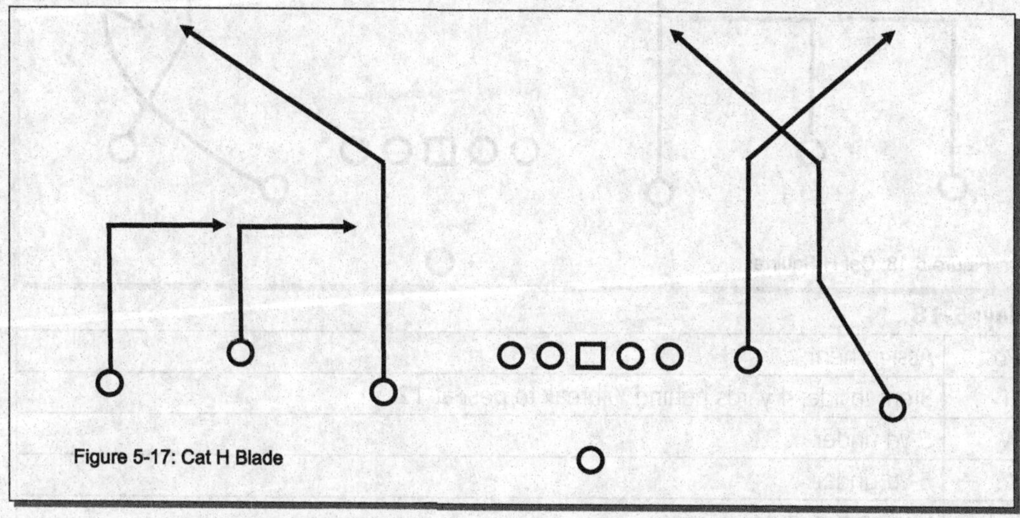
Figure 5-17: Cat H Blade

And then you can run "cat" with H or Y "squirrel," where you get that double-move, corner-post on a safety, when the linebacker is allowing you free access. On that play, you've got to make sure that you get off the ball and get free access to that safety, so that the linebacker doesn't knock you off your route (Figures 5-18 and 19). The key, in this instance, is great *get-off*.

**Play: Cat, H Blade**

| Pos: | Assignment: |
|---|---|
| H | Run 7-3 post. vs. Jam corner: convert fade. |
| W | 5-yd under |
| X | 5-yd under |
| Y | Run post. |
| Z | Run corner route. |
| QB | Progression:<br>vs. 2 high:<br>1. Y to H<br>vs. single high:<br>1. Z<br>2. W to X |

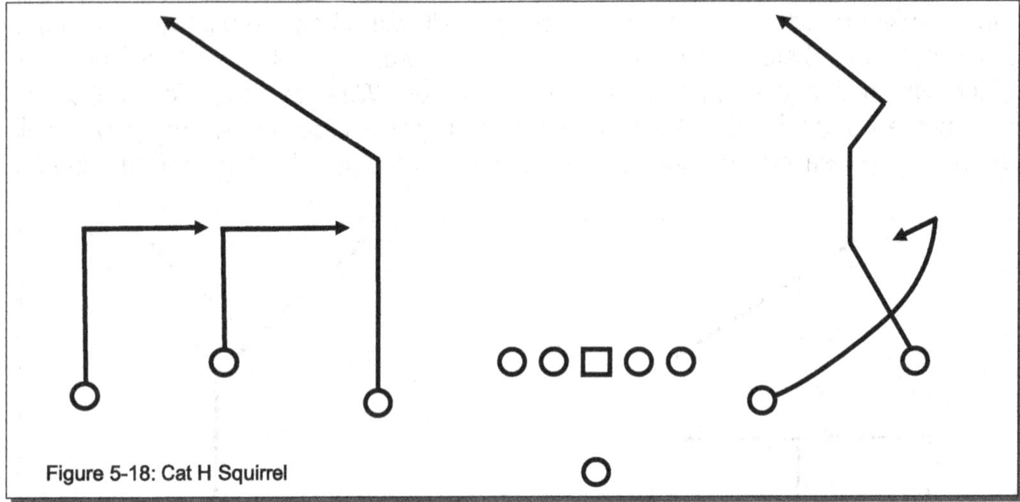

Figure 5-18: Cat H Squirrel

**Play: 5-18**

| Pos: | Assignment: |
|---|---|
| H | Stem inside, 4 yards behind Y, break to post at 12. |
| W | 5-yd under |
| X | 5-yd under |
| Y | Run corner route. |
| Z | Run corner route. |
| QB | Progression:<br>vs. 1 high: key FS<br>vs. 2 high: Pick a side (key safety on hash)<br>1. H – Y<br>2. Z – W - X |

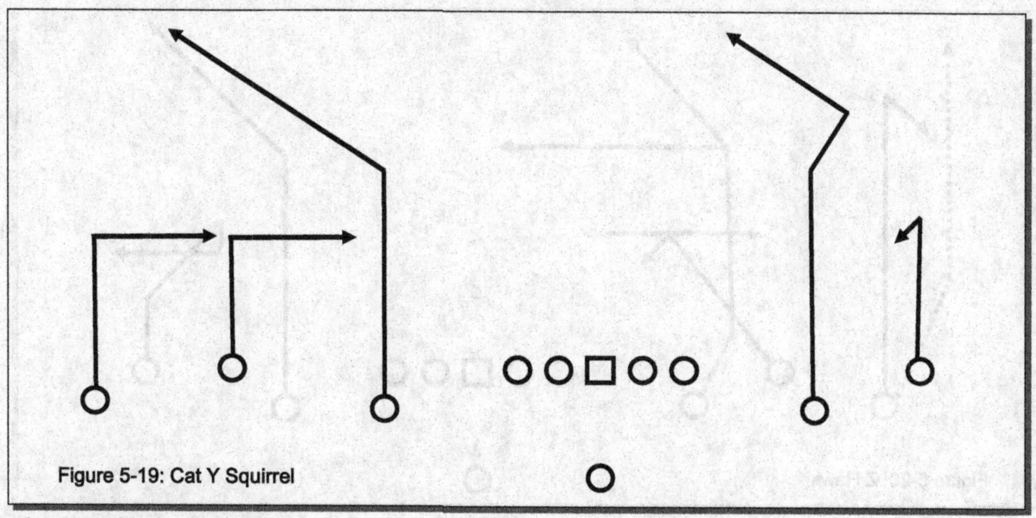

Figure 5-19: Cat Y Squirrel

**Play: 5-19**

| Pos: | Assignment: |
|---|---|
| H | Run 8-yd stop. |
| W | 5-yd under |
| X | 5-yd under |
| Z | Run corner route. |
| Y | Run squirrel route. |
| QB | Progression:<br>1. Y<br>2. Z |

❑ Z Hawk, Zipper

To feed the Z receiver, the first thing that we're going to call is "Z hawk." On "hawk," you have a "return" into the boundary, which makes it a play that carries over nicely in the red and "tight red zone." Z runs a "read route," where he wants to *expand*, and then push vertical. Then, W runs that "snag-option" that he has on "eagle," but we gave this a new name, because X is actually the in-cut receiver on "trey right: 480 eagle." In this instance, X has a post, but when you get down in the red zone, it becomes a "double-dig" for you and sometimes you'll get X on the back of the numbers, along the backline of the end zone in the "tight red zone." It's a good play, and we've had a lot of success in every place I've ever been with that "hawk" call (Figure 5-20).

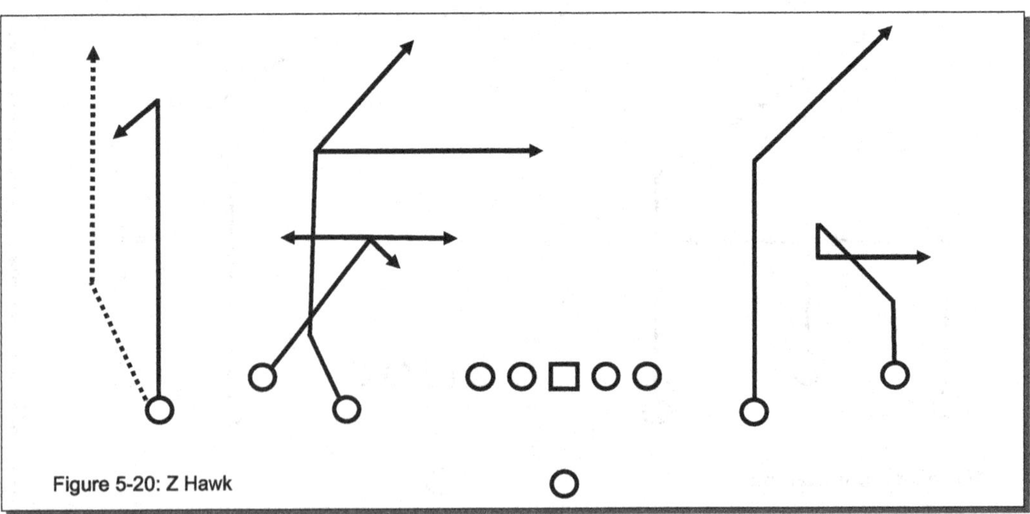

Figure 5-20: Z Hawk

**Play: Hawk**

| Pos: | Assignment: |
|---|---|
| H | Run return route. |
| W | Snag option at 6-yd depth. |
| X | Run caddy. Vs jam corner: convert fade. |
| Y | Run corner route. |
| Z | Run expand-read route. |
| QB | Progression:<br>1. Z – homerun: Y post (snap weak LB)<br>2. W – pre-snap: safeties<br>3. H |

Another thing we really like to do is called "zipper." On this call, we're running a "topper route" between Z and W, so when people are using "trio" coverage (when they want to play that 3-on-2 over Z and W), Z is going to get great get-off and snap the route. Most of time, the safety's going to lean to Z, saying that the linebacker needs help and then W is going to run a post over the top of that. Y runs a corner route, so he can occupy the backside safety, while H runs a drive route, so the quarterback has a place to check the ball down. X on the outside of that has a comeback, so there's a place to go if the quarterback has to scramble (Figure 5-21).

## Sinker/ Y Jerk

The next thing that we like is to include some double-moves. We start out with "sinker, Y jerk," since we've already put sinker in (Figure 5-22). On "sinker," Z runs the "hook-go," W runs a stab, and X runs a "locked halt" route outside. Y now has the "jerk" route, so he's going to come in, attack that linebacker, go back outside, and then "jerk" across his face. H has a "semi" into the boundary, which converts vs. cover 2.

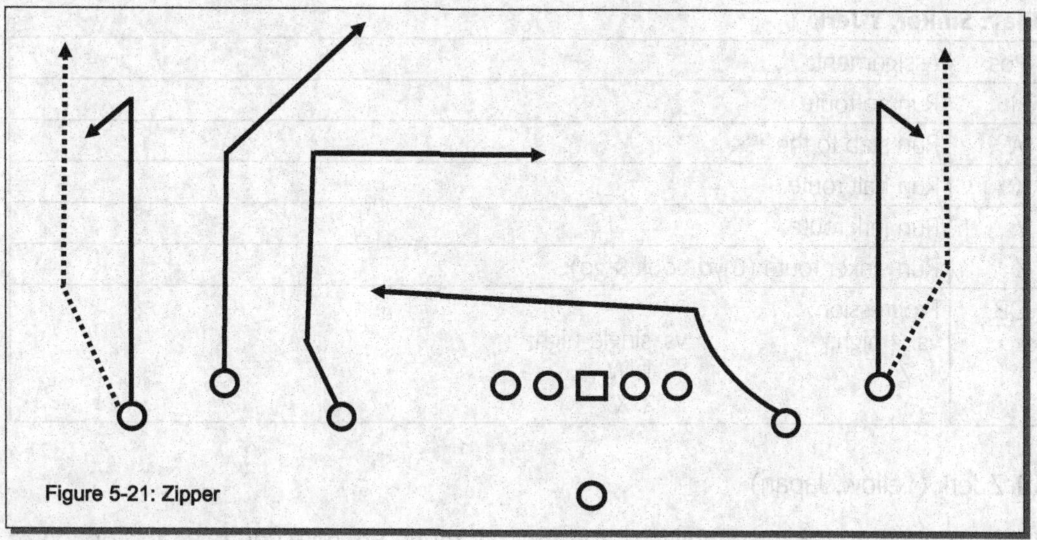

Figure 5-21: Zipper

**Play: 5-21**

| Pos: | Assignment: |
|---|---|
| H | Run semi route. |
| W | Run post route. |
| X | Run semi route. |
| Y | Run ditch route. |
| Z | Run read route at 2nd-level depth. |
| QB | Progression:<br>1. Z<br>2. Y<br>3. H |

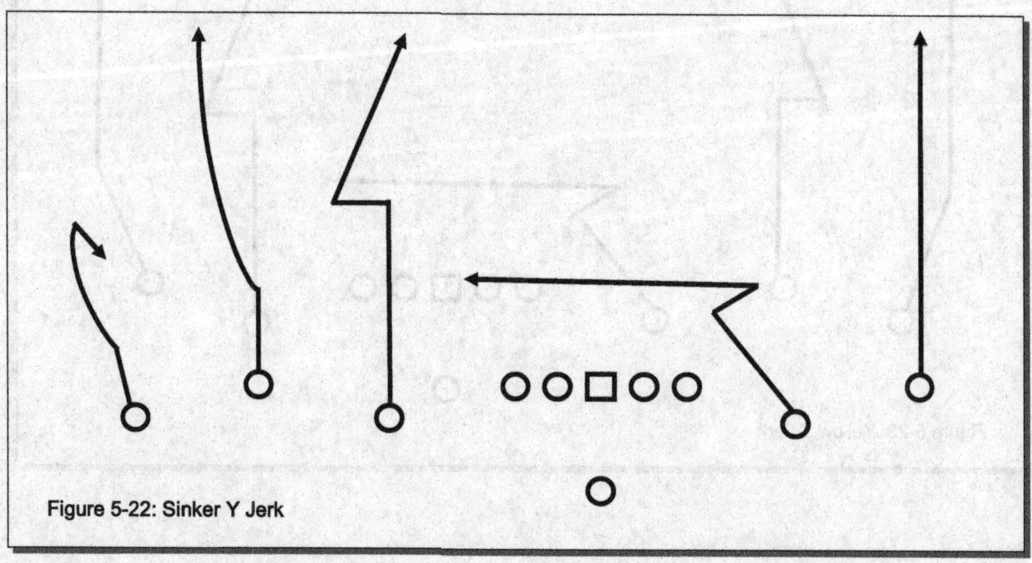

Figure 5-22: Sinker Y Jerk

**Play: Sinker, Y Jerk**

| Pos: | Assignment: |
|---|---|
| H | Run go route. |
| W | Run stab to the #'s. |
| X | Run halt route. |
| Y | Run jerk route. |
| Z | Run sinker route (6-yd hook & go). |
| QB | Progression:<br>vs. 2 high: vs. single high:<br>1. Z 1. W<br>2. Y 2. X |

❑ Z Jerk (Yellow, Japan)

We also want to give Z the ability to run the jerk route. So, now you have the option of running it two different ways. One, we call "yellow, Z jerk." On this call, both Y and W are running "sinker" routes, where they're going to drive up the field to six yards, break out like it's a "blue," and then come back inside on the "out-go" or "sinker" route. Both outside receivers are "locked go" and then Z is going to run the "jerk route," where he comes inside, gets on the Mike, goes back outside, and then crosses his face again (Figure 5-23). Over the years, there have been times when it's just opened up like the Red Sea for Z. There, he has to sit it down, put his "dukes up," catch the ball, and go North and South. So, if the jerk route is called and it just opens up, you abort the double-move and just stay open.

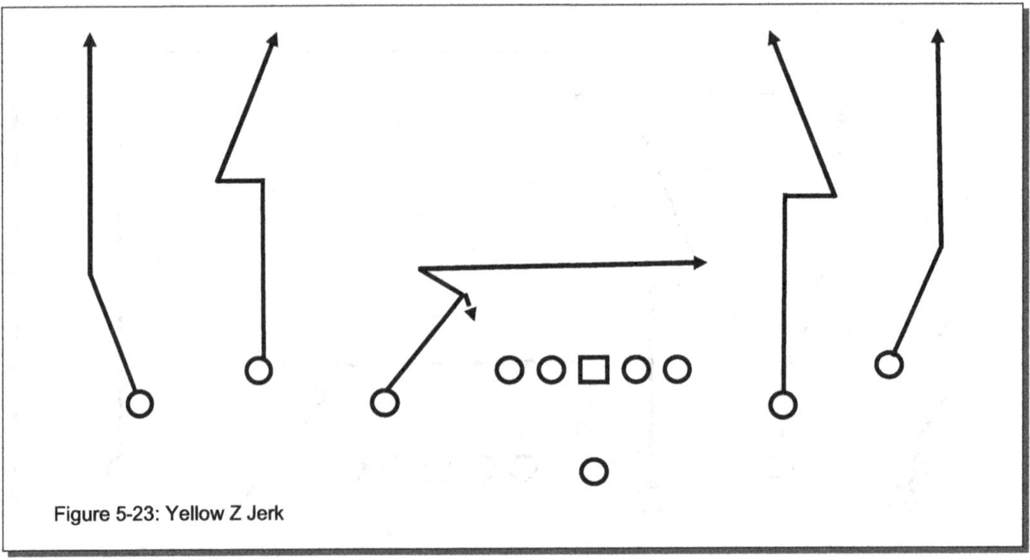

Figure 5-23: Yellow Z Jerk

**Play: 5-23**

| Pos: | Assignment: |
|---|---|
| H | Outside release go. |
| W | Run 6-yd hook & go. |
| X | Outside release go. |
| Y | Run 6-yd hook & go. |
| Z | Run jerk route. |
| QB | Progression:<br>1. Y to H or W to X<br>2. Z |

The thing that's worked well recently is to call "Japan, Z jerk." Now, you're going to have the "6 route" to the field, so W has the corner and X has the return. Z is going to stay with his "jerk route" on the linebacker. Y then runs a post for a touchdown. He's got the chance to get on the safety and snap a post for a touchdown. H is going to cut his split, and run a 6-yard out, and if he doesn't get the ball right away, he runs a late wheel down the sideline (Figure 5-24). It's good for the quarterback. Most of time the quarterback's base progression vs. 2 high is thinking "Y for a touchdown." One of the things we have done a little bit to tweak it is "if I get single-high, Y runs a seam. That's a bit of variation vs. different people. But that *package* has worked really well for us.

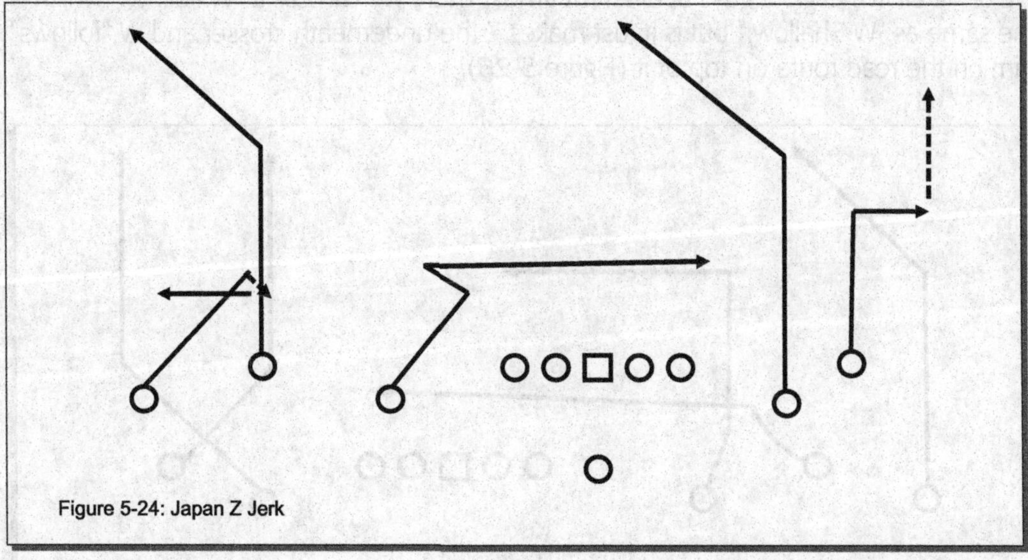

Figure 5-24: Japan Z Jerk

**Play: Japan, Z Jerk**

| Pos: | Assignment: |
|---|---|
| H | 6-yd out; late wheel up sideline |
| W | Corner route |
| X | Return route |
| Y | Post route |
| Z | Jerk route |
| QB | Progression: "think Y for a TD"<br>(Alert W)<br>1. Y<br>2. Z<br>3. H (late) |

❑ W Shallow, W Follow

We want to get the ball to the W. We come back to plays we already have in, such as "W shallow." In empty, we like to run a "cougar" or switch route into the boundary. The quarterback needs to give it a chance to win. H stems inside to Y's alignment and gets vertical. Y comes off of his rear end and gets vertical down the sideline. Z has the read route, W has the "shallow" route, X has a comeback out there to the field (see Figure 5-25). This has worked really well for us. Again, we know it's a good play, because we've hit all five eligible guys at different times. Then, we can call it "W Follow," which is the same as "W Shallow," but is it just makes Z the underneath crosser and W "follows" him on the read route on top of it (Figure 5-26).

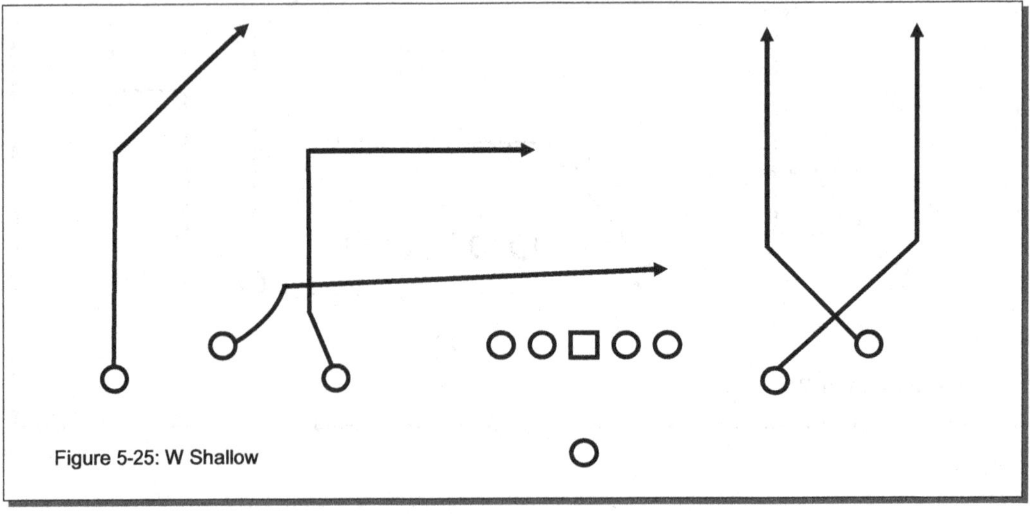

Figure 5-25: W Shallow

**Play: 5-25**

| Pos: | Assignment: |
|---|---|
| H | Run switch release seam route. |
| W | Run ditch route. |
| X | Run post. |
| Y | Run switch release go route. |
| Z | Run read route at 2nd level depth. |
| QB | Progression:<br>1. H to Y<br>2. Z to W |

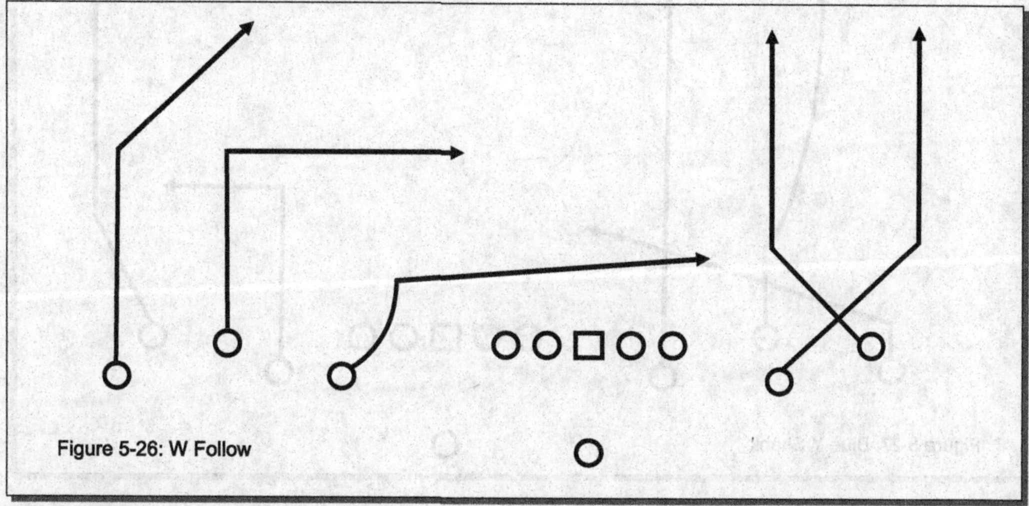

Figure 5-26: W Follow

**Play: 5-26**

| Pos: | Assignment: |
|---|---|
| H | Run switch release seam route. |
| W | 12-yard in-cut. |
| X | Run post. |
| Y | Run switch release go route. |
| Z | Run ditch route. |
| QB | Progression:<br>1. H to Y<br>2. Z to W |

❑ Blue Y/ Shank

So X doesn't feel completely left out in this formation, we can call "Blue Y, Shank." This is one of the things that we use in order to attack the "trio" coverage, which I think you're going to see a lot of in this empty formation. In this call, we have "blue" into the boundary, which is a fade and 6-yard out." "Shank" to the field gives Z a "go" down the middle, and W a stab route (that fade to the numbers). Then, X runs a 1-step slant and comes underneath it (Figure 5-27). This particular concept is also a really good RPO out of "trips" vs. that "trio" coverage. The "shank" route against the "trio" is almost impossible to defend, especially if they commit numbers to the run (which we will illustrate later, in the RPO chapter).

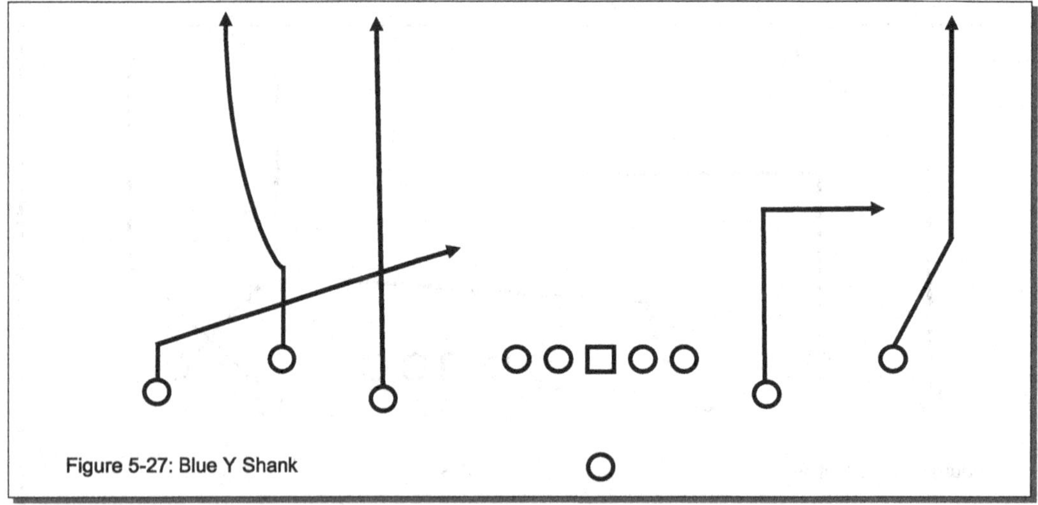

Figure 5-27: Blue Y Shank

❑ Falcon (Duck, Cougar)

We like to call "falcon/duck." "Falcon," the same as before, gets #3 down the middle and #2 on the pivot-option. Concurrently, X reduces his split to run the in-cut. The players all know that combination of Falcon. Then, "duck" into the boundary is the "diagonal/curl," so if you were to get single-high or "3 buzz," you have the ability to throw that "d-curl" into the boundary. As such, the receiver on the diagonal runs at less than full speed, so that the routes time up. It's been pretty easy for players to translate their comprehension of our "combo" philosophy to the empty game (Figure 5-28).

We like to run "falcon/cougar." That's pretty good, because you get Z down the middle and then you've got the "cougar" (switch route), with all of the options available over there. The thing about "cougar" is you can run the switch for a touchdown, you can stop on the sideline, and you can run in-cuts off the switch, just all those "run n shoot"-style options (Figure 5-29).

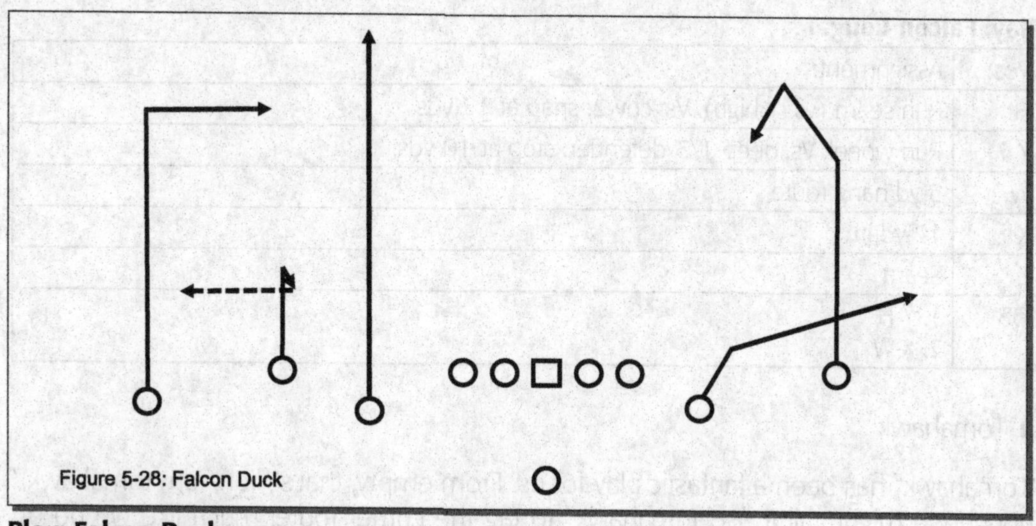
Figure 5-28: Falcon Duck

**Play: Falcon Duck**

| Pos: | Assignment: |
|---|---|
| H | Run 5-4 curl at 14 yds. |
| W | Run snag, then slide out. |
| X | Run 14-yd in-cut. |
| Y | Run choke release diagonal. |
| Z | Run read route at 2nd-level depth. |
| QB | 1. Z-X<br>2. W<br>1 High: H-Y |

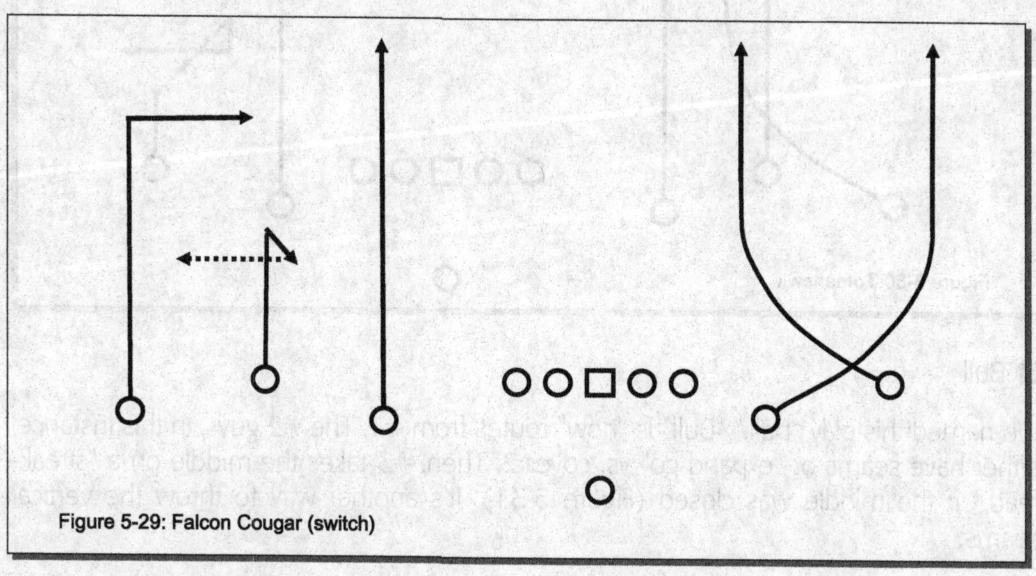
Figure 5-29: Falcon Cougar (switch)

**Play: Falcon Cougar**

| Pos: | Assignment: |
|---|---|
| H | Run seam (vs. 1 high). Vs. cov 2: snap at 12 yds. |
| Y | Run wheel. Vs. deep 1/3 defender: stop at 10 yds. |
| W | 5-yd hang route. |
| X | 12-yd in. |
| Z | Seam |
| QB | 1. Y-H<br>2. X-W |

❑ Tomahawk

"Tomahawk" has been a fantastic play for us. From empty, that's "lion/ram tomahawk," though we might call it "86 tomahawk" to tag the corner route, much like we do on "71C tiger." This is a nice red zone play, in that "fringe" area of long field goal range, where you have enough room for that seam route to develop (e.g., the 30-yard line). On this, you'd be amazed how often the seam route really comes open. It's not an easy throw, though. Quarterbacks need to practice it, so they don't hold it too long and overthrow it. They have to throw it before the receiver's open (Figure 5-30).

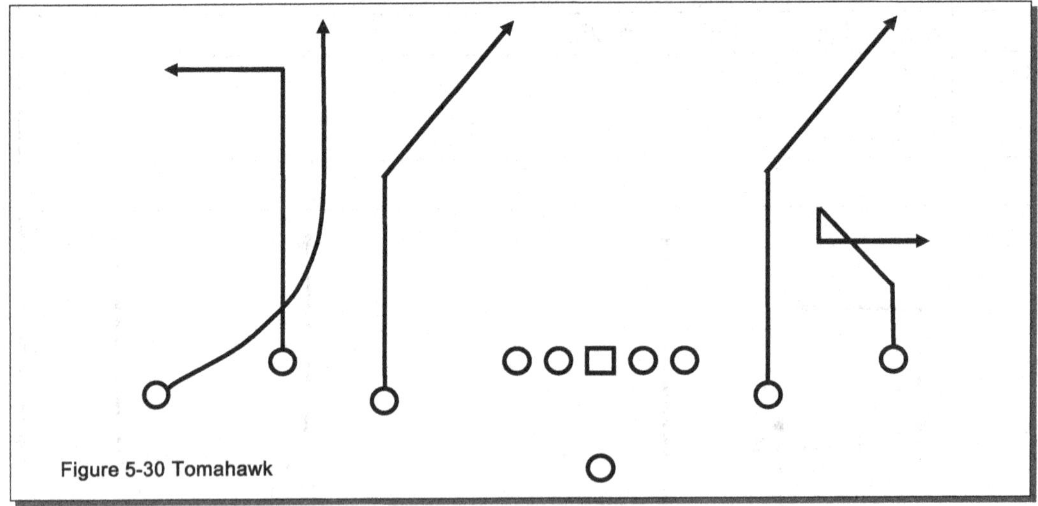
Figure 5-30 Tomahawk

❑ Bull

We named this play "bull." "Bull" is "now" routes from #1. The #2 guys, in this instance, either have seams or "expand go" vs. cover 2. Then, #3 takes the middle on a "streak-read," if the middle was closed (Figure 5-31). It's another way to throw the vertical seams.

**Play: 5-30**

| Pos: | Assignment: |
|---|---|
| H | Run return. |
| W | Run 18-yd out route. |
| X | Run delay seam. |
| Y | Run corner route. |
| Z | Run post. |
| QB | |

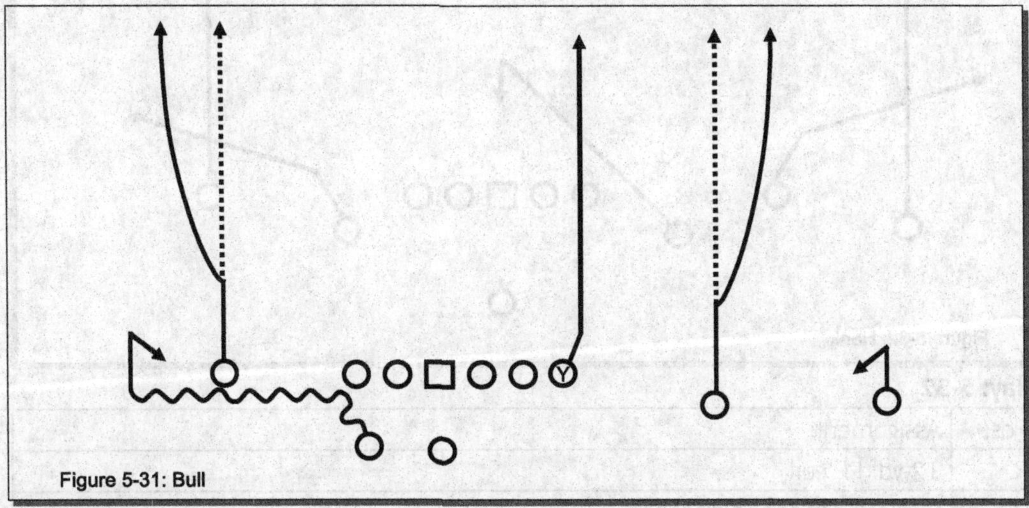

Figure 5-31: Bull

**Play: Bull**

| Pos: | Assignment: |
|---|---|
| R | 1-step now route |
| W | vs. 1 high: seam<br>vs. cov 2/cov 11: fade to #'s |
| X | 1-step now route |
| Y | Seam down middle of field |
| Z | vs. 1 high: seam<br>vs. cov 2: fade to #'s |
| QB | Progression:<br><u>vs. 1 high:</u> alert Z; 1. Y/W; 2. R/X<br><u>vs 2 high:</u> alert Z; 1. Z; 2. Y/W |

❑ Cover 11 (Shooter, Holster, Keno)

We always carry some calls for man coverage. Over the years, our best call for it has been "Hank," where it's the "look," with curls to both sides. We talked about that already (Figure 5-32). We have what we call "Z Shooter." Y and H will set the "picket fence" and Z will come off of them. We've talked about that already as well (Figure 5-33).

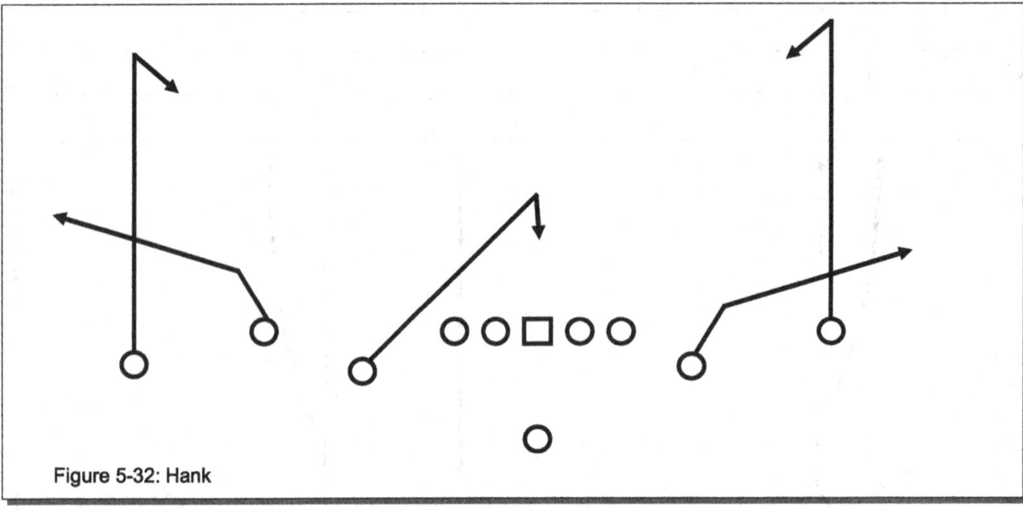

Figure 5-32: Hank

**Play: 5-32**

| Pos: | Assignment: |
|---|---|
| R | 12-yd PP curl |
| W | Run golf cart speed diagonal. |
| X | 12-yd PP curl |
| Y | Diagonal route |
| Z | Run look route over ball. |
| QB | Progression:<br>1. Z 1. Z<br>2. H 2. X<br>3. Y 3. W<br>Key: secondary rotation |

We have a version of that we call "Holster," where Y would give you the "rub" corner, Z and W would give you the "picket fence," and H would come underneath that. Again, if it's zone coverage, they spot up and get open in the zone. It's a "shooter" idea, but the one-word name for "H" seemed to stick with the players better (Figure 5-34).

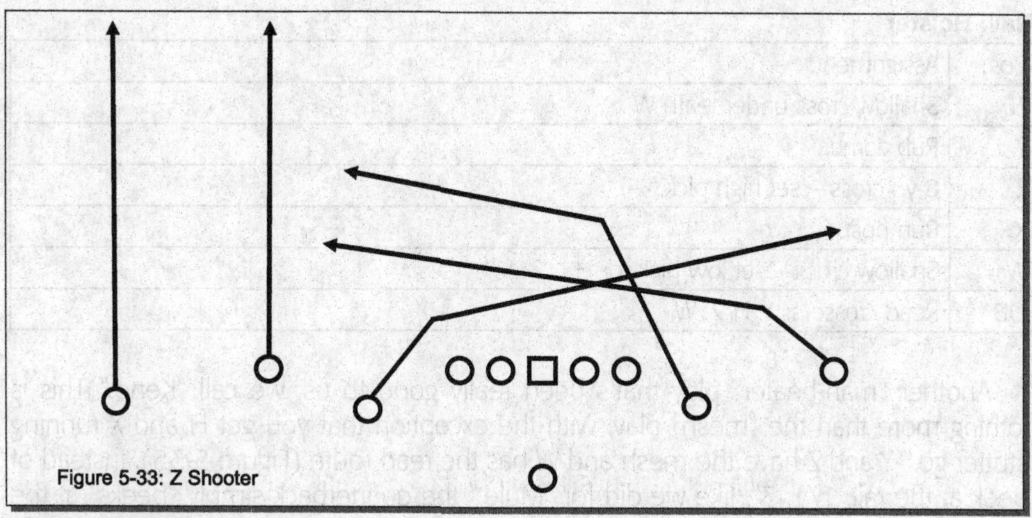

Figure 5-33: Z Shooter

**Play: Z Shooter**

| Pos: | Assignment: |
|---|---|
| H | Run shallow cross. Rub man on Z. |
| W | Run seam (most outside release). |
| X | Run outside release go. |
| Y | Run 8-yd crossing route. Pick the hole player. |
| Z | Run shallow cross underneath H. |
| QB | Progression:<br>Read the mesh Z to H. |

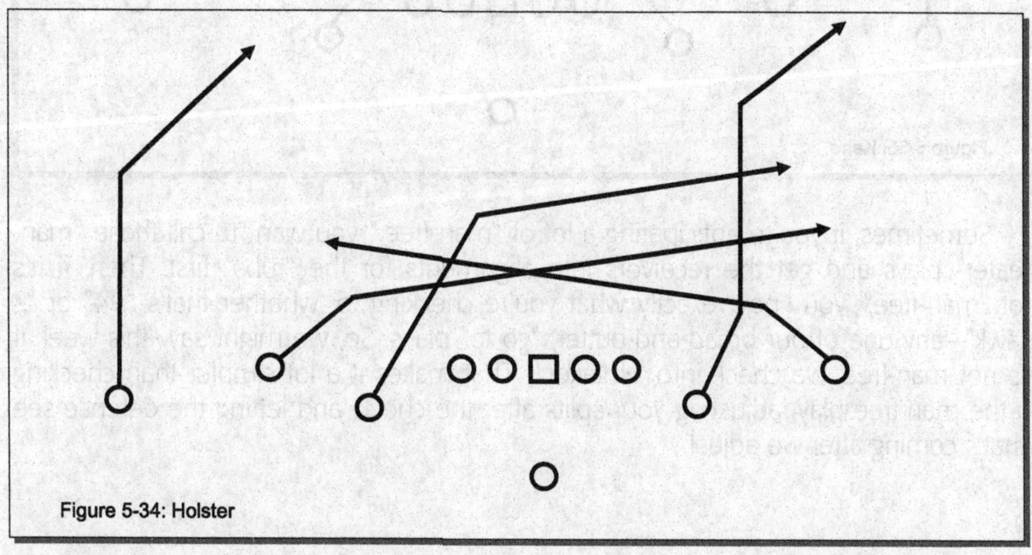

Figure 5-34: Holster

**Play: Holster**

| Pos: | Assignment: |
|---|---|
| H | Shallow cross underneath W |
| Y | Rub corner. |
| Z | 8-yd cross – set high pick. |
| X | Run post. |
| W | Shallow cross – set low pick for H. |
| QB | Read crossers: 1. H 2. W |

Another "man-beater" play that's been really good to us, we call "Keno." This is nothing more than the "mesh" play, with the exception that you get H and X running "stutter-go." Y and Z have the mesh and W has the read route (Figure 5-35). Instead of "peek at the rail, 1/1, 3", like we did for "Mule," the quarterback simply "peeks" at the double-moves on this, thinking "wide-to-narrow" vision.

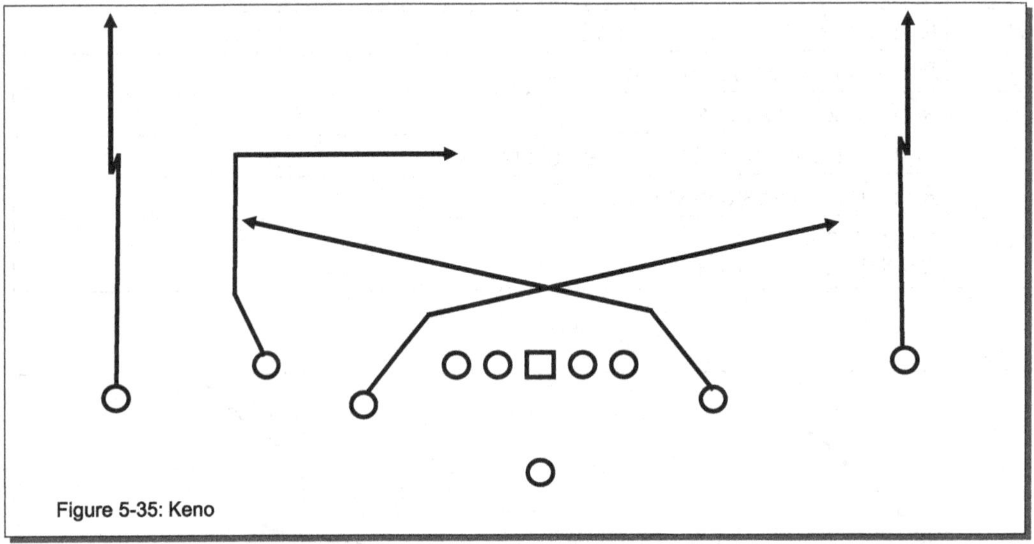
Figure 5-35: Keno

Sometimes, if you're anticipating a lot of "man-free," you want to call those "man-beater" plays and get the receivers into alignments for the "rubs" first. Then, if it's not "man-free," you know exactly what you're checking to, whether that's "94" or "Z Hawk"—any one of our bread-and-butter, "go to" plays. So, we might say "this week if it's not man-free, we check into 'H Laker.'" That makes it a lot simpler than checking *to* the man-free play, adjusting your splits after the check, and letting the defense see what's coming after we adjust.

**Play: Keno**

| Pos: | Assignment: |
|---|---|
| H | Run stutter go. |
| W | Run 12-yd in-cut. |
| X | Run stutter go. |
| Y | Run shallow cross. |
| Z | Run shallow cross. |
| QB | Homerun: H/X<br>Key: FS<br>Progression:<br>1. Z – Y 2. W |

# Final Thoughts About Empty

We have an entire catalog of empty plays, but what we covered in this chapter is enough to give you a good idea of what we're trying to accomplish. We are able to carry dozens of plays, because again, we want to think in terms of *concepts* and *packages*. The players have already been introduced to these ideas earlier in the installation, so they're really able to retain the plays, understand why we call them, and execute them.

| | **SPECIAL PLAYS** |
|---|---|
| (POSSE) G card flip 4/5 devil | (BANDIT) RT/LT W hald twister |
| (TH) TH SLT/WG SLT T fly odd even ninja | (REG) RT 542/543 flea flicker |
| (ACE) 5 POSSE Y half 12 LB cut | (ACE) top RT/LT close W fly burn 39/38 RT/LT tuba |
| (TH) rock T fly pitch 8/9 force | (ACE) taxi RT/LT even/odd reggie |
| (TH) tango 13/11 cut | (TH) TH RT/LT 239/238 juice |
| (Deuce) 5 WK storm even ninja | (ACE/POSSE) taxi/posse Hollywood |
| (ACE) 5 taxi top bow 24/5 "O" key | (TH) G tango RT/LT waggle LRT/RT tarzan |
| (TH) G storm R MO O/E bronco | |
| (TH) S storm T MO odd ninja | **NAKEDS** |
| (POSSE) S posse bow devil choice | BLAZE 16/17 LT/RT X dragon – WG T-fly |
| (TH) S king RT/LT odd noah | BLAZE 13/12 RT/LT T sail – WK storm/storm |
| (REG) RT/LT 36 39 boss | BURN 38/39 LT/RT T snk - rock |
| (TH) rock RT/LT bazooka 88/99 | BURN 39/38 RT/LT tube – rock T-fly |
| (TH) 5 WG SLT bow 24/25 "O" key | BLAZE 23/22 RT/LT "C" – WG SLT |
| (ACE) S top vow 27/26 OR shot top odd skull key | BLAZE 13/12 RT/LT tunnel - tango |
| (DEUCE) S WK storm even demon | BLAZE 39/38 RT/LT tunnel – TH Z fly |
| G storm RT/LT even cruise | BLAZE 38/39 LT/RT Z wheel – tango WG SLT |
| | BLAZE 38/39 LT/RT boat – DOT/DOS W half |
| | BLAZE 23/22 RT/LT Z dragon – DBLS |
| (ACE) taxi rose lime Oakland X hitch | BLAZE 33/32 RT/LT "Q"/dwarf/sail – top/taxi |
| (POSSE) S posse bow ram/lion grey swipe | BLAZE 32/33 LT/RT W wheel - trps |
| (TH) S WG SLT RT scat 79 snapper Houston | BURN 39/38 RT/LT tuba – top close |
| (BOMB) shift lion Seattle stab | |
| (ACE) G taxi RT Z half sara Raider X hitch (lion w half) | |
| (ACE) G trips O/E dart bench | **GET IT TO 18** |
| (DEUCE) G 6/7 RT/LT ram/lion Oakland swipe | (TH) WG SLT SCAT 79 snapper Z OPT - Houston |
| | (ACE) flood ram grey/orange/Oakland swipe |
| | (ACE) trps lima orange grey – 94 Y |
| (ACE) 5 dot RT/LT 80 | (ACE) taxi lee ram sinker X jerk |
| (ROCKET/POSSE) over/posse 489 cross – rose lime cross | (TH) storm close 73 Bill – (ace) dbls 483 Bill |
| (TH) 5 TH close 81 "C" X blade | (ACE) dbls 73 poker – scat 73 Miami/cub |
| (ACE) 5 trey 70 W wheel | (ACE) flood/taxi 480 Y chop – 489 Y captain 483 R patriot |
| (TH) 5 WG T ZIP 73 Bill | (TH) WG SLT scat 489 tuna |
| (ACE) 5 trps bow 79 dolphin | (ACE) flood RT FLASH LT green |
| (ACE) dbls 71 mayday X post | (TH) rock burn 39 RT T SNK – burn 38 T tube (T fly) |
| (ACE) G taxi Y fly scat 75 exxon | (ACE) top blaze 33 RT W sail |
| (TH) 5 TH close R 73 Bill | (REG) STR SLT RT 140 Y shake |
| (ACE) 5 trps RT/LT bow 71 "C" falcon | (TH) tango RT waggle LT tarzan – TH 239 juice |
| (ACE) G dbls into 489 jaws Z post | (ACE) taxi 79 bear X semi/hitch |
| | (ACE) S dot RT close Y fly KN 7 moses |
| | |
| (REG) WK storm close pepper 41 X squirrel | |
| (REG) RT/LT Z half 142/143 badger | |
| (ACE) G limo W back Louie/Roger X "V" | |
| (ACE) 5 flood flash LT/RT green | |
| (TH) rock T fly burn 39/8 RT T tube | |
| (ACE) DOS W half blaze 38/39 LT/RT boat | |
| (TH) tango RT/LT blaze 13/12 tunnel | |
| (ACE) tango RT/LT waggle LT/RT tarzan | |

# Chapter 6
## Screens

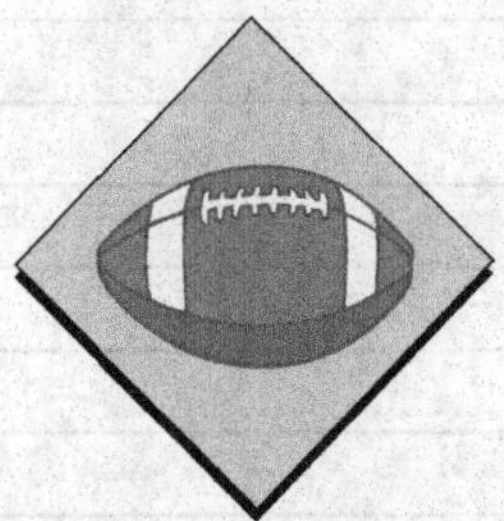

You run screens for a few reasons. The first is to try to do something to slow down the pass rush or take advantage of the pass rush. The second is to throw the ball out wide and make the defensive linemen run sideline to sideline and wear themselves out. The third is to have a "blitz beater," in which you can throw something like a jailbreak screen to a wide receiver, where you need one block and you have a chance to go for a touchdown. Some years we've been great at screens, some years we've emphasized other things, but it's always going to be a part of our offense. We use a variety of them: bubble screens, forms of fast screens, slow screens, slip screens, and bluff screens. This chapter takes a look at them.

## Bubble Screens

Bubble screens are the simplest way to start. We don't major in these like some teams do, but we certainly use them. If we call "bubble," the throw is to the innermost receiver (Figure 6-1). On the "field bubble" out of gun, the receiver goes "3 blind," so he's "1, 2, and then on the third step he looks for the ball," so we get width. On a "boundary bubble" he steps forward with one step and then backpedals slowly (Figure 6-2).

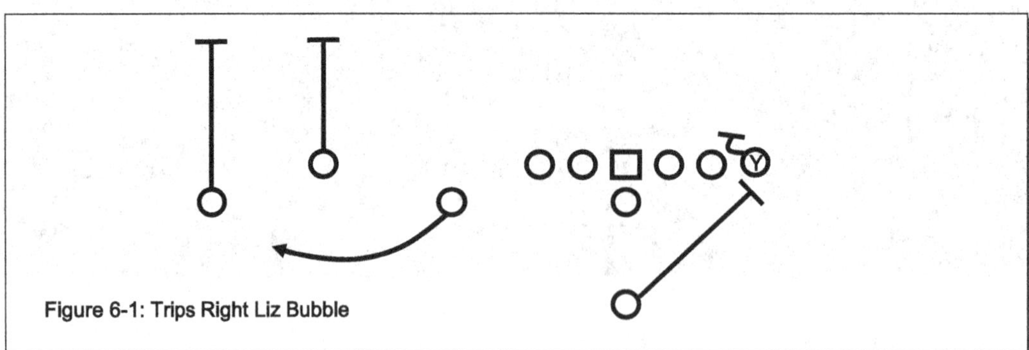

Figure 6-1: Trips Right Liz Bubble

**Play: 6-1**

| Pos: | Assignment: |
|---|---|
| R | Block quick Liz protection. |
| W | Block #2 – MDM. |
| X | Block #1. |
| Y | Block quick Liz protection. |
| Z | Bubble |
| QB | Progression:<br>1. Z |

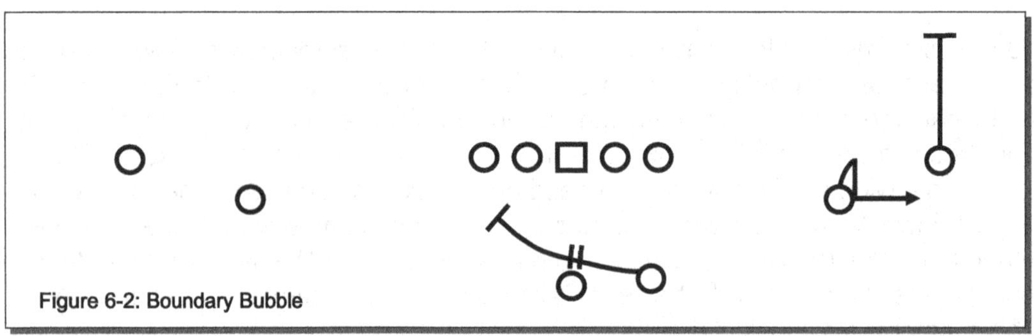
Figure 6-2: Boundary Bubble

As we said with empty game, we'd usually start by sending the protection *at* the bubble screen, such as "trips right: Liz bubble" (see Figure 6-1). We might have the back cross the formation with our "fox" tag, such as "fox, Lima bubble" (Figure 6-3). We can also use our "quick" tag to have the o-line cut the guys up front and slow down their pursuit. This could be "*quick* Liz bubble" for example.

Another version of the bubble screen is what we call "soap," where we either run an "arrow 'route down the line of scrimmage or we slip a tight end or a wide receiver from the opposite side of the formation to the arrow route (Figure 6-4). The "key" is to the outside receiver (Figure 6-5). On this, the aiming point to get the block is you want to be three yards deep over the alignment of the outside receiver. "Tac" is to a 3-receiver side, where we'd cross-block it (Figure 6-6). On that, an "alley" call puts the

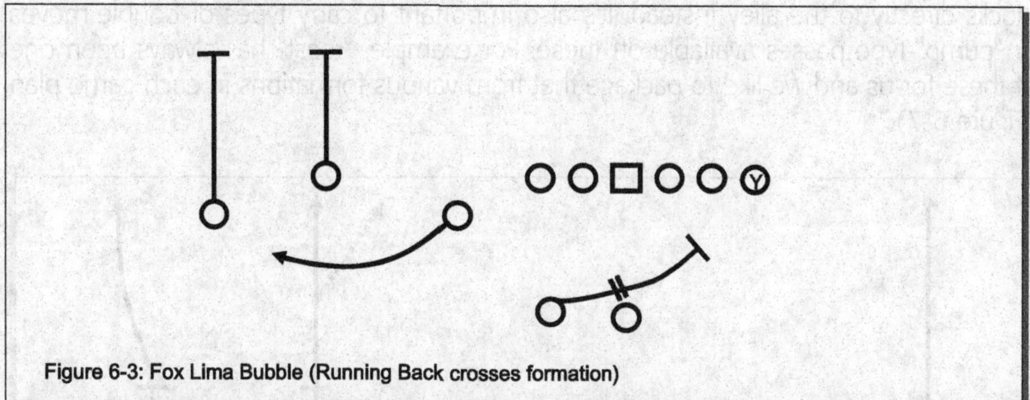


Figure 6-3: Fox Lima Bubble (Running Back crosses formation)

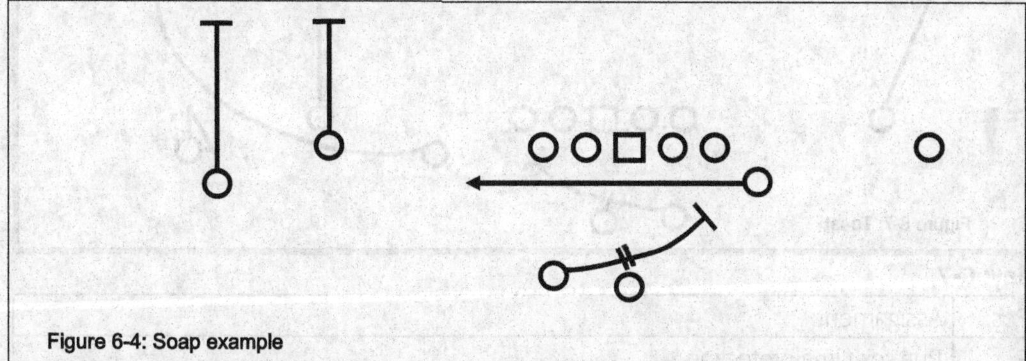

Figure 6-4: Soap example

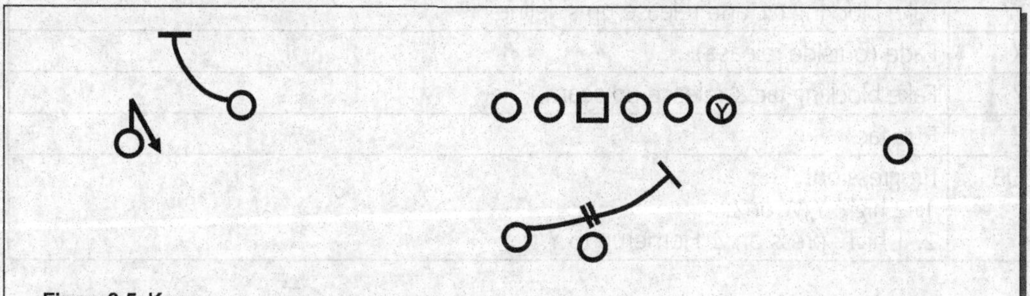

Figure 6-5: Key

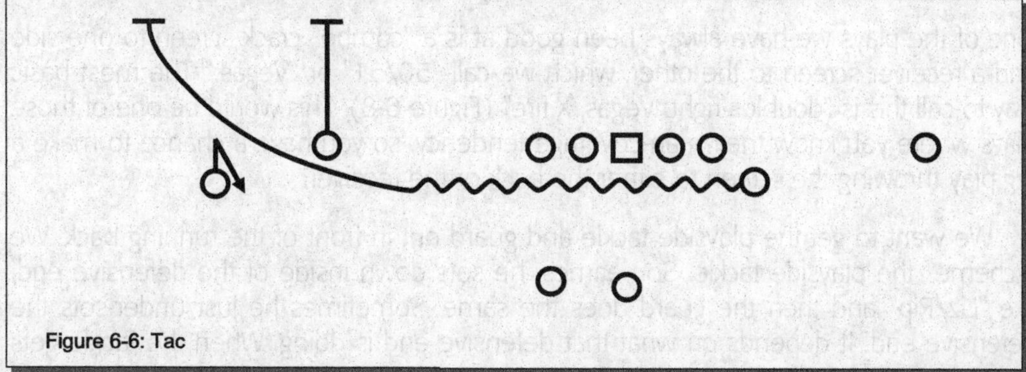

Figure 6-6: Tac

blocks directly to the alley instead. It's also important to carry types of double-moves or "pump"-type passes available off these. For example, "toast" has always been one of these for us and we like to package that from various formations in each game plan (Figure 6-7).

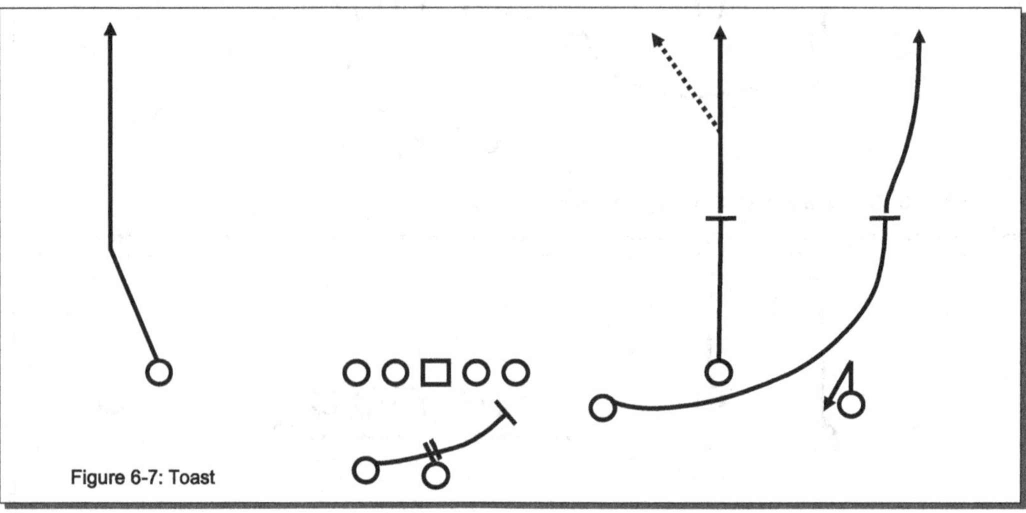
Figure 6-7: Toast

**Play: 6-7**

| Pos: | Assignment: |
|---|---|
| R | Run fox Lima protection. |
| W | Fake blocking tac and release up sideline. |
| X | Fade (outside release) |
| Y | Fake blocking tac & release up seam. |
| Z | Run tac. |
| QB | Progression:<br>1. 2 high: Y/W or Z.<br>2. 1 high: press on Z. Homerun to Y. |

## 50/51 Vegas

One of the plays we have always been good at is a "combo" crack screen to one side and a receiver screen to the other, which we call "50/51" or "Vegas." The most basic way to call this is "doubles right: Vegas, X fire" (Figure 6-8). This would be one of those plays where you know their man-coverage tendency, so you have a chance to make a big play throwing the screen to either the back or the receiver.

We want to get the playside tackle and guard out in front of the running back. We "scheme" the playside tackle. Sometimes, he sets down inside of the defensive end, like "Liz/Rip" and then the guard does the same. Sometimes he just under-sets the defensive end. It depends on what that defensive end is doing. When the tackle gets

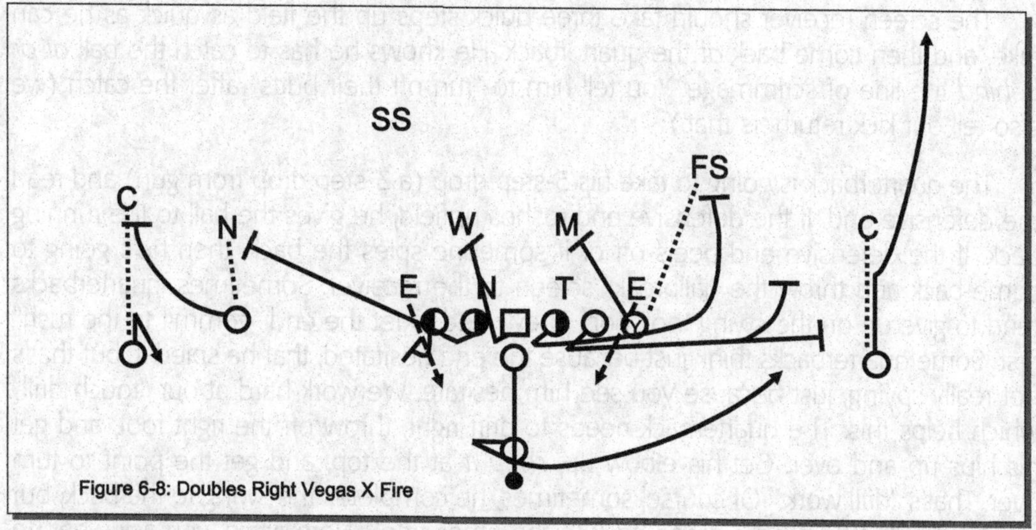

Figure 6-8: Doubles Right Vegas X Fire

out, he does what we call "run over the down marker." As he starts out to the flat, he needs to run over the down marker, and then if the corner is not there, he turns upfield. When you get a cloud corner that's going to come flying up, you have to stay as flat as you can to that down marker or he will run under you; then, it's easy to adjust *up field*. The guard is going to set inside slightly and then redirect the defensive tackle. We say, "set, redirect, go." There is no "count" for those guys. The guard is going to come off of the crackback block and block the alley. Sometimes, the tackle doesn't get out—often because he got bull-rushed and tied up—so, then the guard has to replace him. If the tackle gets held up of if somebody gets spied, the guard has got to replace him and "run over the down marker."

The "crack" receiver to that side should "step to the near hip of the defensive end." So, he comes down at that near hip as that defensive end goes to rush, and he does *not* let the linebacker come underneath him. He can no longer try to knock him out, so in reality he's got to learn that "I can put a shot on him, then separate, and then re-block him." If he just tries to put a shot on him and block him the whole time, we're going to get a holding penalty.

The backside tackle is going to set, and if the guy is in a "speed rush," he's just going to take him up the field. If the guy tries to bull rush him, then he's going to "butt him and cut him." The backside guard and center will have a "Lou/Ray" set, so they both set slightly to the left or right. They don't want to set together and block the guy on the line of scrimmage. The guard wants to set out and the center wants to set over. They then declare where the defensive tackle is going to rush: A or B gap. They are also "set, redirect, go." This is a "man blocking" scheme to that side: the guard has the man over the nearest receiver. The center's man is the Mike linebacker. Linemen, at first, make the mistake of going where he's at instead of where he's *going to be*.

The screen receiver should take three quick steps up the field as quick as he can take, and then come back *at* the quarterback. He knows he has to catch the ball *at or behind* the line of scrimmage. You tell him to "run off their butts" after the catch (we also tell our kick returners that.)

The quarterback is going to take his 5-step drop (a 3-step drop from gun) and read the defensive end. If the defensive end rushes upfield, he gives the ball to the running back. If the defensive end peels off or if someone spies the back, then he's going to come back and throw the "jailbreak" screen to the receiver. Sometimes, quarterbacks tend to give up on the swing too soon. They need to let the end "commit to the rush" first. Some quarterbacks think just because the end hesitated, that he spied it, but that's not really spying, just because you see him hesitate. We work hard at our "touch drill" which helps this. The quarterback needs to drift right, throw off the right foot, and get his hips up and over. Get his elbow up, *snap it* at the top, and get the point to turn over. That's "drill work." Of course, sometimes, he completes the swing to the back, but you say "look if he'd have come back to the other side!" Here again, you ask what he saw and, sometimes, you live with his decision. Then, you should come back and just call a straight "spark" screen to that side later in the game (see Figure 6-13).

It's been best, over the years, to call this to the hand of the quarterback, which would be "50" for a righty. If you're under the center, you really don't call this play to your left, but in "shot" (pistol), we have done it. In years past, we've tried to have him back straight out, but found that he doesn't get enough depth and it ends up being a lateral. From under the center, we really only call "50" for a right-handed passer.

One of the things you always have to know going into a game is "do they have a designated screen stopper?" In other words, are they sometimes rushing three guys and one guy is just sitting there playing screen or draw? If so, then you need to be able to "spy block" him, where that lineman doesn't go out with the screen, or you trap down on him with the guard and the center gets out and replaces him. (I always thought that it would be a disgrace to be the defensive lineman designated as the "screen stopper." Does that mean he's lousy at rushing the passer?) But anyways, there are a lot of games where the nose doesn't really rush the passer and instead plays the screen and it's something you need to account for in the game plan.

## Vegas Packages

This call is "50," which is out of "trips right" (Figure 6-9). In "trips," we have the ability to change up the tight end and tackle. The tight end might make a "Louie" call and then the tight end will arc for the corner. The arc block is supposed to be flat down the line of scrimmage, get no depth on a 3-step arc: "open, crossover, plant." I bet I've coached that more than anything in my entire life with tight ends. The tackle now knows he's going inside to block the Sam linebacker. You make this call according to how they coach the corner and whether the tackle can get the corner blocked or not.

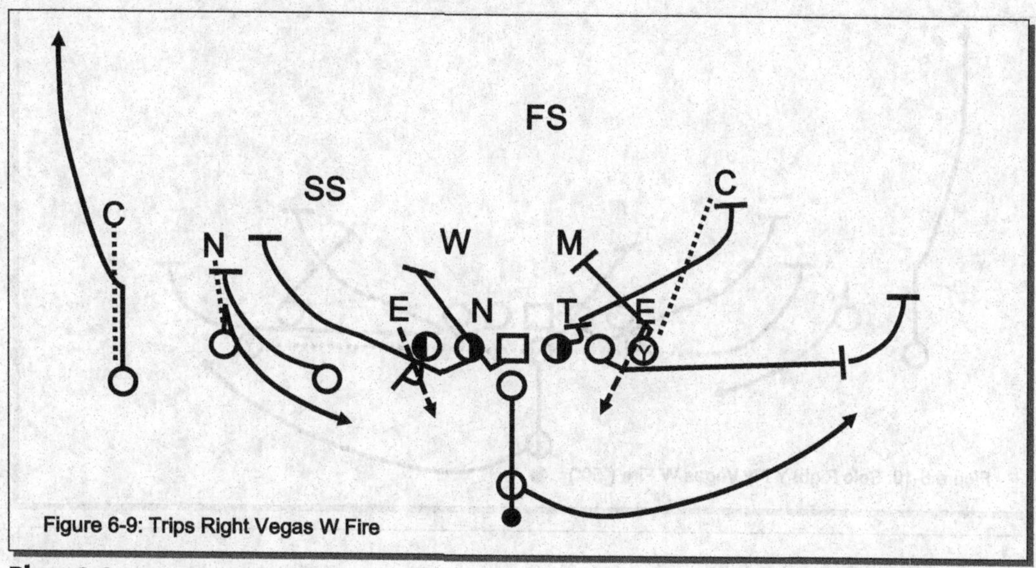

Figure 6-9: Trips Right Vegas W Fire

**Play: 6-9**

| Pos: | Assignment: |
|---|---|
| W | Take one step and run middle screen, losing two yards from the LOS. Throttle down # to half-speed toward the middle. Ball will come in 1st open window. |
| X | Run corner off. Must outside release. |
| Z | Block #2 defender to your side. |
| QB | Take a quick 5-step drop. Read EMLOS playside. If he rushes, throw to R. If he spies R, throw to W on the middle screen |

I think that if you can run it off motion and you can run it off of different formations, you have a much better chance to make yards on it. If you put the motion across, it is also a way to disguise the splits. This is "solo right, Y fly: 50" (Figure 6-10). This is part of the "solo formation package" we've introduced in previous chapters. This is another way good way to run something like "Z drive" (from the dropback chapter) by disguising splits. That's what we're doing here is trying to disguise Z's split for the jailbreak screen.

In years when we are a great "12 personnel team," we package it as "thunder left, T mo: 50" (Figure 6-11). I also like it this way as "tango right, T float: 50" (Figure 6-12). In some games, that can be better than sending the guy across in motion, depending on man vs. zone coverage or how they are bumping their under coverage. You always want to understand how the defense is being taught and build your packages to take advantage of their coverage rules.

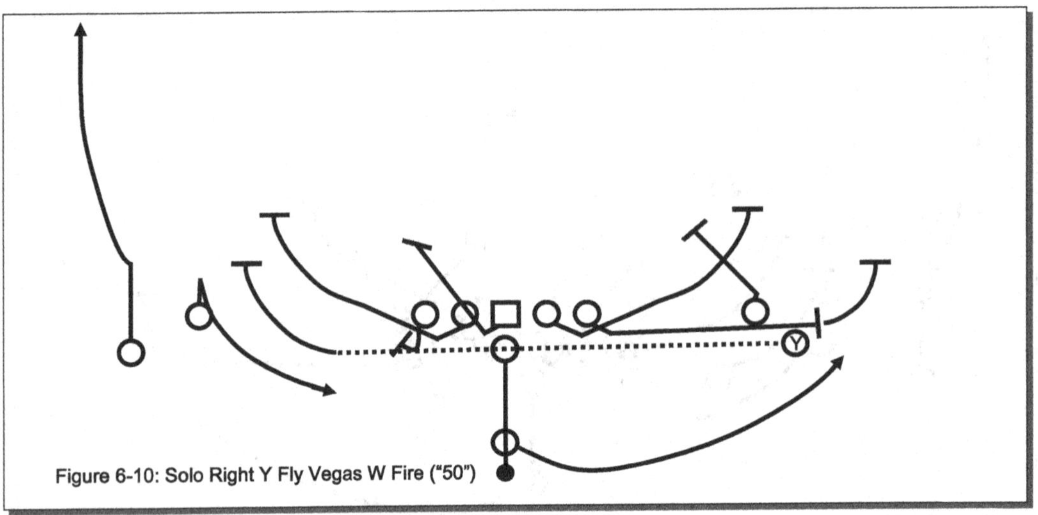


Figure 6-10: Solo Right Y Fly Vegas W Fire ("50")

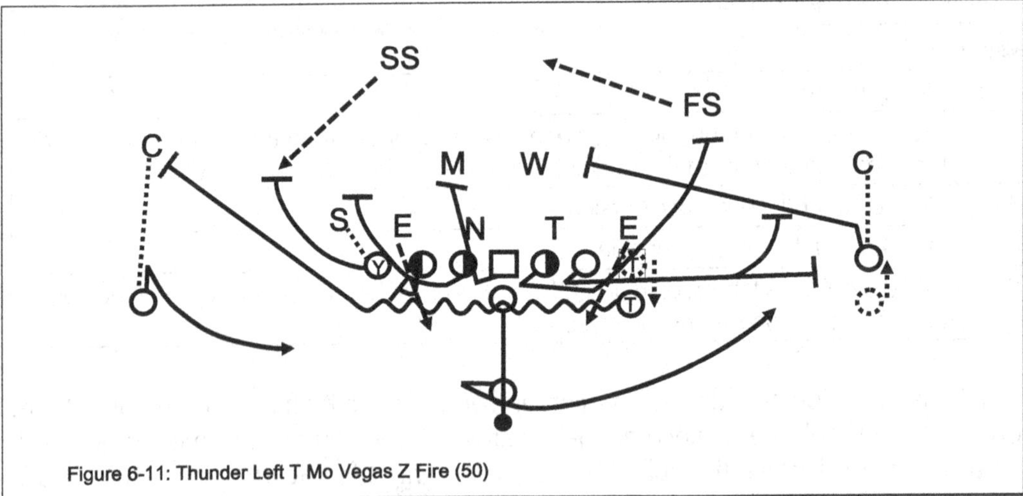


Figure 6-11: Thunder Left T Mo Vegas Z Fire (50)

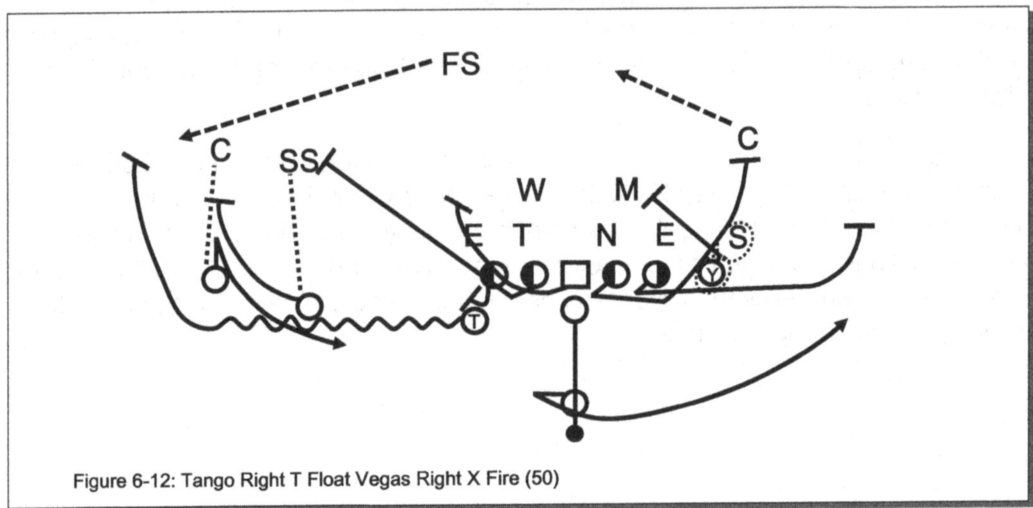


Figure 6-12: Tango Right T Float Vegas Right X Fire (50)

## Spark

We can simply call the receiver "jailbreak" screen to one side. On "spark right," both tackles' job is to "set, butt, and cut." The tight end blocks the man over Z, the guard blocks the man over the tight end, the center has the Mike linebacker, and the weak guard has the Will linebacker, unless there's a "spy" call (Figure 6-13). The line is still "set, redirect, go." We allow the linemen to cut on this, but *only* if it's his guy and not anyone else's.

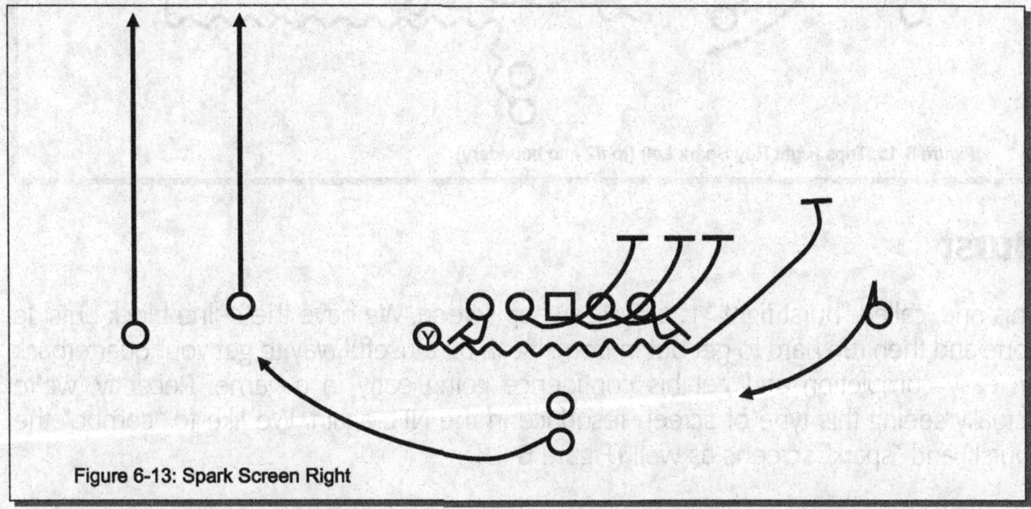

Figure 6-13: Spark Screen Right

We sometimes tag a bubble off the other side of it (Figure 6-14). We will call it into the boundary, as well as, to the #2 receiver (Figure 6-15). We give quarterbacks a lot of responsibility to make audibles but on this, we prefer to stay with the side called and not allow the quarterback to flip this over to the other side of the field.

Figure 6-14: Spark Screen Right with Bubble example

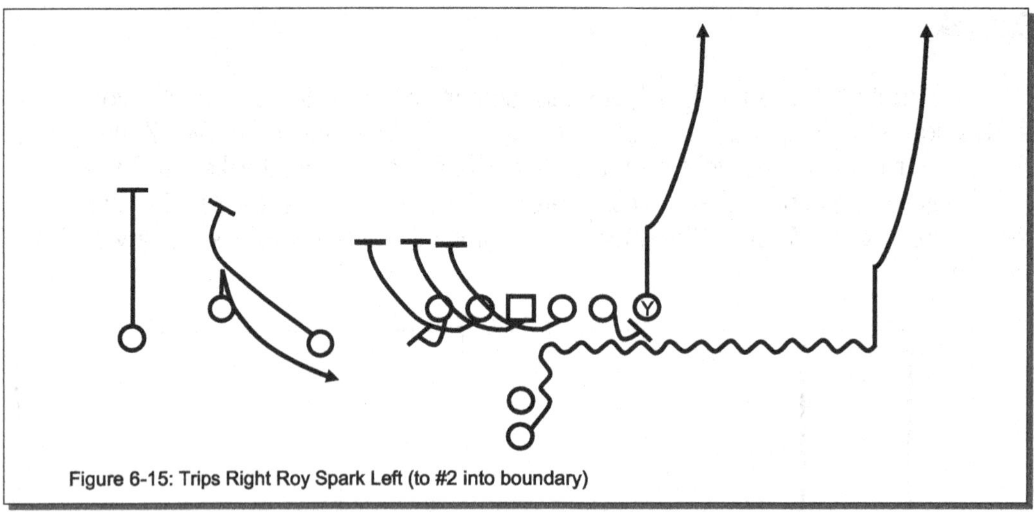


Figure 6-15: Trips Right Roy Spark Left (to #2 into boundary)

## Burst

This one, called "burst right," is a basic sweep screen. We have the o-line block outside zone and then run hard to get out in front. It can be a useful way to get your quarterback an easy completion and get his confidence going early in a game. Recently, we're actually seeing this type of screen resurface in the NFL again. We like to "combo" the "burst" and "spark" screens as well (Figure 6-16).

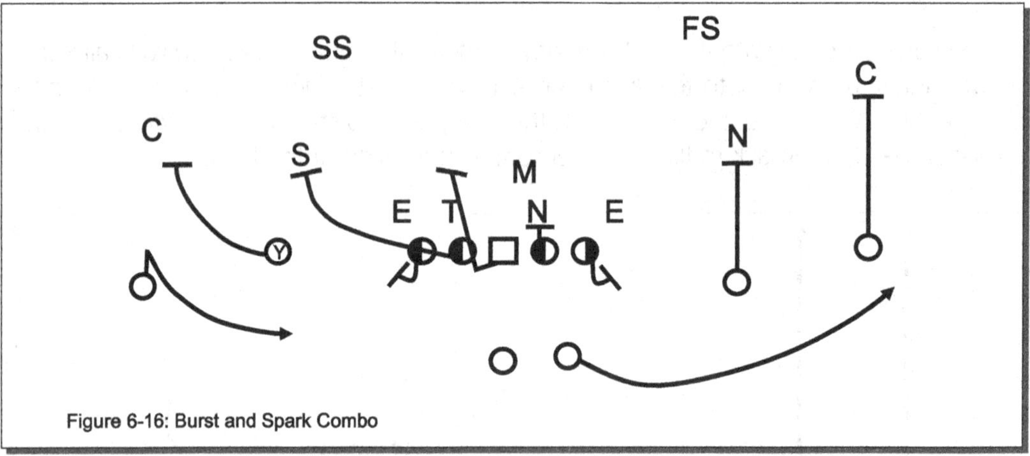


Figure 6-16: Burst and Spark Combo

## Turret Screen

Another fast screen "combo" we like is something we call "turret." There's our "tac" to one side and an outlet to the running back on the opposite side. If they don't run a defender across with the motion, you want to throw the "tac," because you have them outnumbered. If they run a defender over with motion, it means they're chasing him in man coverage. In this instance, the quarterback should pump, allow the singled receiver on the backside time to come down inside and take his coverage defender with him, and then find the running back sneaking across the formation, where the numbers advantage now is. It's another useful "combo" type of screen (Figure 6-17).

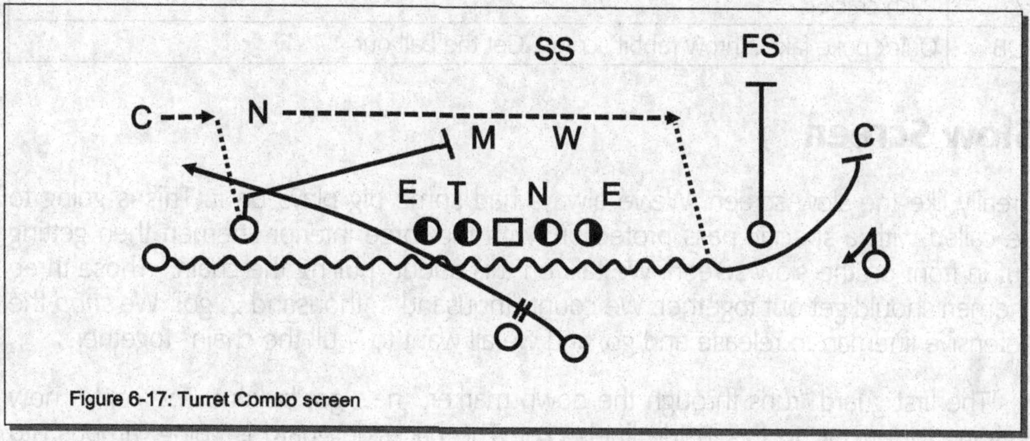

Figure 6-17: Turret Combo screen

## Rabbit/Lizard

We like to use our "rabbit/lizard" screen to protect our run plays. On this, the backside tackle steps down inside, and then retraces for the apex defender over the backside receiver. This is good from zone blocking schemes, but it sets up well from "power O" schemes as well (Figure 6-18). We typically set this up for the slot receiver in a 2x2 set or to the solo receiver on the backside of a 3x1 set, depending on what a game plan calls for.

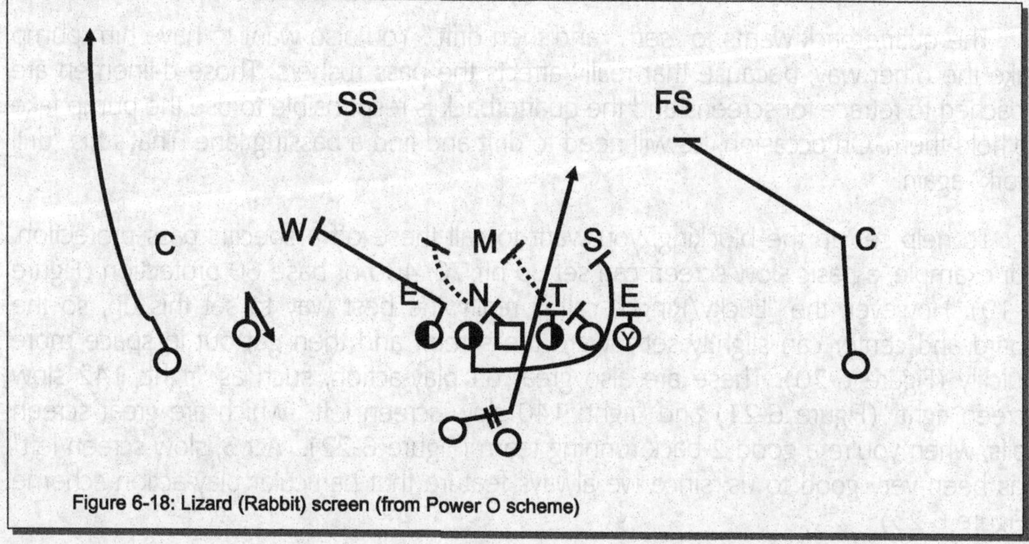

Figure 6-18: Lizard (Rabbit) screen (from Power O scheme)

**Play: 6-18**

| Pos: | Assignment: |
|---|---|
| W | Run rabbit screen. Get vertical immediately after catch. |
| X | Quick technique |
| Z | Push crack. |
| QB | Quick poke fake. Throw rabbit screen. Get the ball out. |

## Slow Screen

I really like the slow screen. We've always had some big plays on it. This is going to be called with a specific pass protection, with the three interior linemen then getting out in front on the slow screen. We talk on this about "pulling the chain." Those three linemen should get out together. We count "thousand 1, thousand 2, go!" We *snap* the defensive lineman to release and go, and we all want to "pull the chain" together.

The first guard "runs through the down marker," he's got kickout. The center now is going to turn up to the inside linebacker. The backside guard is going "ambush to trap." What that means, ideally, is he would get inside between the guard's kickout and the center's block and "trap the alley." What he does is "thousand 1, thousand 2, go!" I *snap* and go, and as I'm running to the hip of the center, my eyes are back here looking for a "spy" guy or a defensive end peeling back. If nobody shows, then I go "trap the alley." In other words, what the "ambush" means is that he's going to ambush any spy.

The running back can run this screen from any alignment. The back is going to set four yards deep on the inside leg of the guard, and "he doesn't leave till the guard leaves." Running backs always want to outrun the guard out there and the proper timing for a slow screen is something they need to really get a feel for.

The quarterback wants to "*set*... and then drift." You also want to have him pump fake the other way, because that really affects the pass rushers. Those d-linemen are coached to retrace for screens and the quarterback is responsible to use the pump fake to hold them. On occasion, he will need to drift and find a passing lane. That's his "drill work" again.

To help set up the blocking, you want to call these off a specific pass protection. For example, a basic slow screen can set up off 70, 400 or base 60 protection (Figure 6-19). However, the "Lucky/Ringo" call is really the best way to set this up, so the guard and center can slightly set toward the screen and then get out in space more quickly (Figure 6-20). These are also great off play-action, such as "right: 142 slow screen right" (Figure 6-21) and "right: 140 slow screen left," which are great screen calls, when you're a good 2-back running team (Figure 6-22). "Act 3, slow screen left" has been very good to us, since we always feature that particular play-action scheme (Figure 6-23).

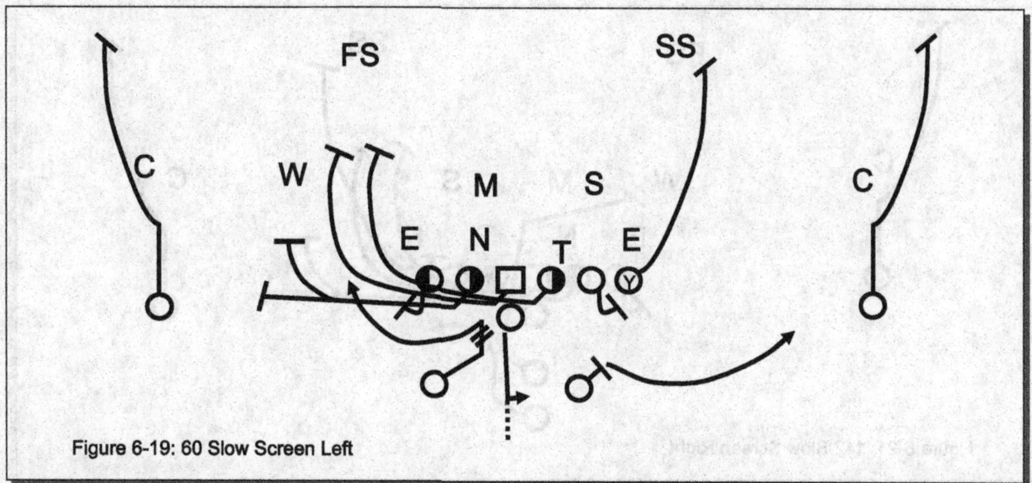

Figure 6-19: 60 Slow Screen Left

**Play: 6-19**

| Pos: | Assignment: |
|---|---|
| X | Outside release and block deep 1/3 to deep 1/2. |
| Z | Outside release and block deep 1/3 to deep 1/2. |
| F | Run stretch route. |
| QB | Pump to backside before throwing screen. |

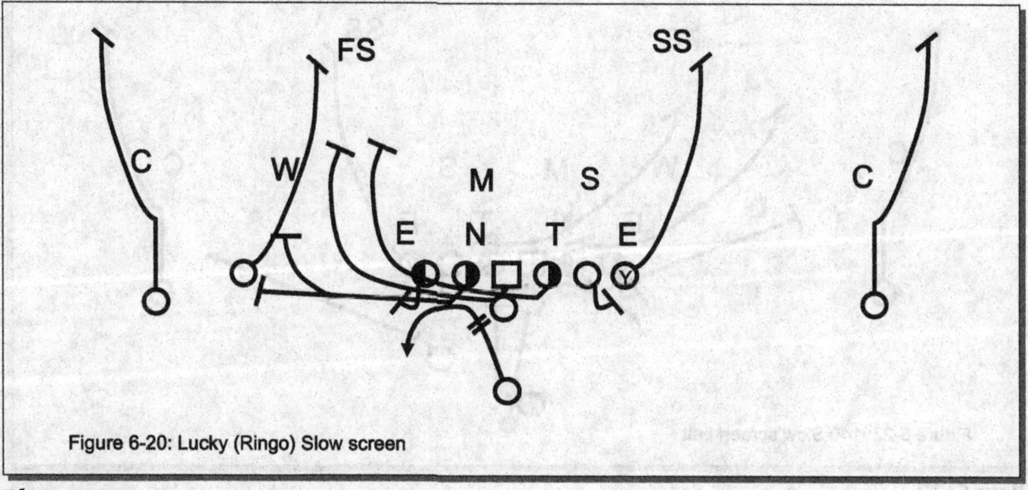

Figure 6-20: Lucky (Ringo) Slow screen

**Play: 6-20**

| Pos: | Assignment: |
|---|---|
| W | Outside release. Block deep 1/2 to deep 1/3. |
| X | Outside release. Block deep 1/2 to deep 1/3. |
| Z | Outside release. Block deep 1/2 to deep 1/3. |
| QB | Take long 5-step drop. Set, drift, draw the rush, and find a throwing lane. |

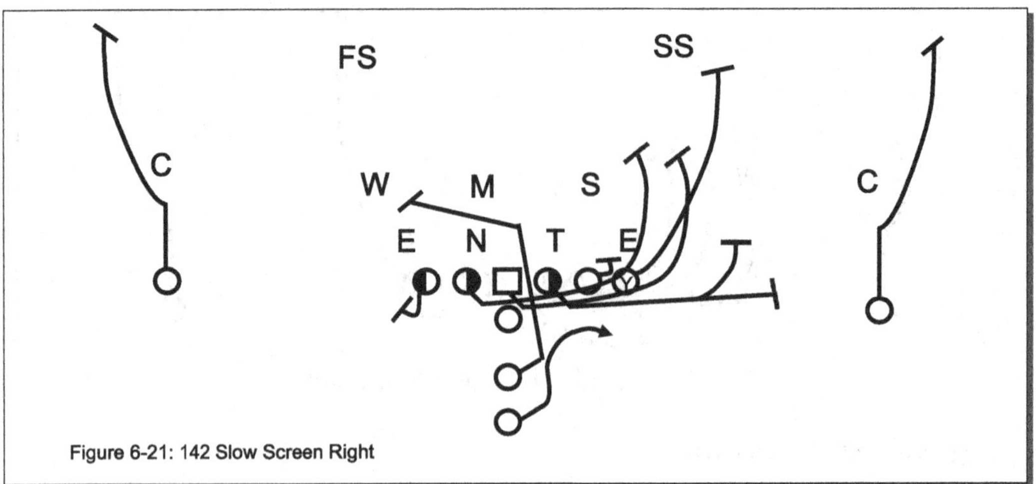

Figure 6-21: 142 Slow Screen Right

**Play: 6-21**

| Pos: | Assignment: |
|---|---|
| X | Outside release. Block deep 1/2 to deep 1/3. |
| Z | Outside release. Block deep 1/2 to deep 1/3. |
| QB | Take 5-step play-action drop. Set, drift, draw the rush, and find a throwing lane to complete pass to R. |

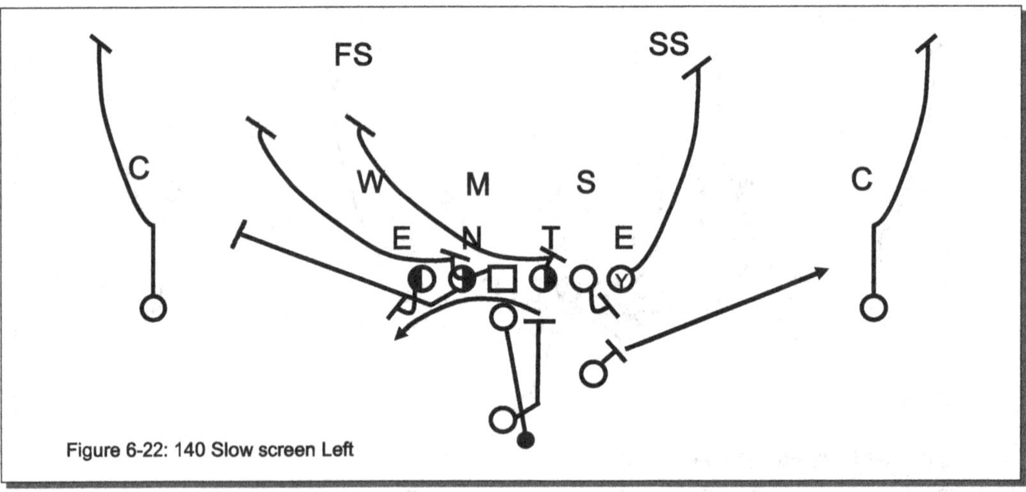

Figure 6-22: 140 Slow screen Left

**Play: 6-22**

| Pos: | Assignment: |
|---|---|
| X | Outside release and block deep 1/3 to deep 1/2. |
| Z | Outside release and block deep 1/3 to deep 1/2. |
| F | Block 140 protection. Run arrow route. |
| QB | Act 4 fake 5 steps. Pump to strongside before throwing screen. |

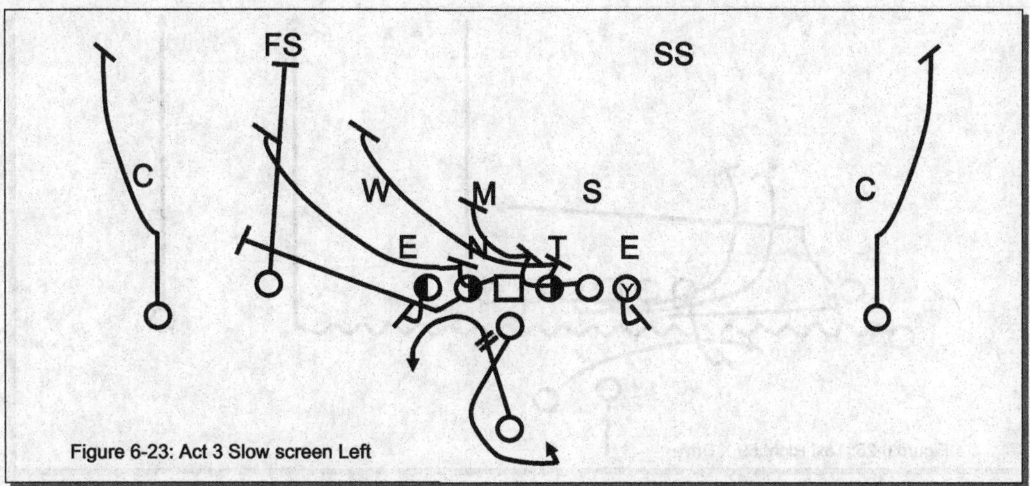

Figure 6-23: Act 3 Slow screen Left

**Play: 6-23**

| Pos: | Assignment: |
|---|---|
| W | Outside release. Block 2nd-level deep 1/3 to deep 1/2. |
| X | Outside release. Block deep 1/3 to deep 1/2. |
| Z | Outside release. Block deep 1/2 to deep 1/3. |
| QB | Step play-action. Act 3 drop – throw slow screen to R. |

We use the term "58/59" to tag it off specific downfield patterns. For example, this is "trips left: 59 Y drag, slow screen left" (Figure 6-24). We can call that same concept off "X drive" as well (Figure 6-25). These are really good, because they take the defenders' vision off the running back and the quarterback. You also get some natural picks, when you have guys running across their faces. This gives you an idea of how to think in terms of building slow screen packages off your best protections and pass routes.

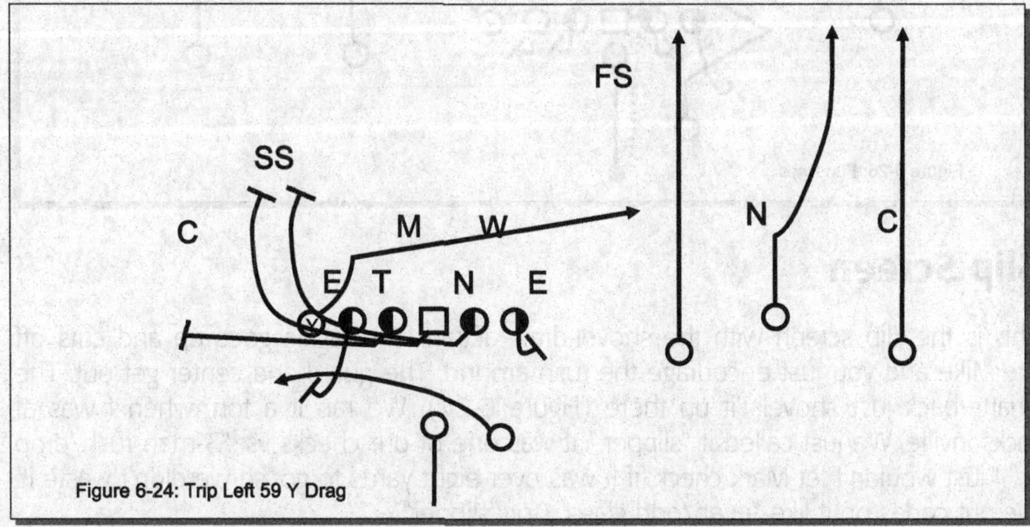

Figure 6-24: Trip Left 59 Y Drag

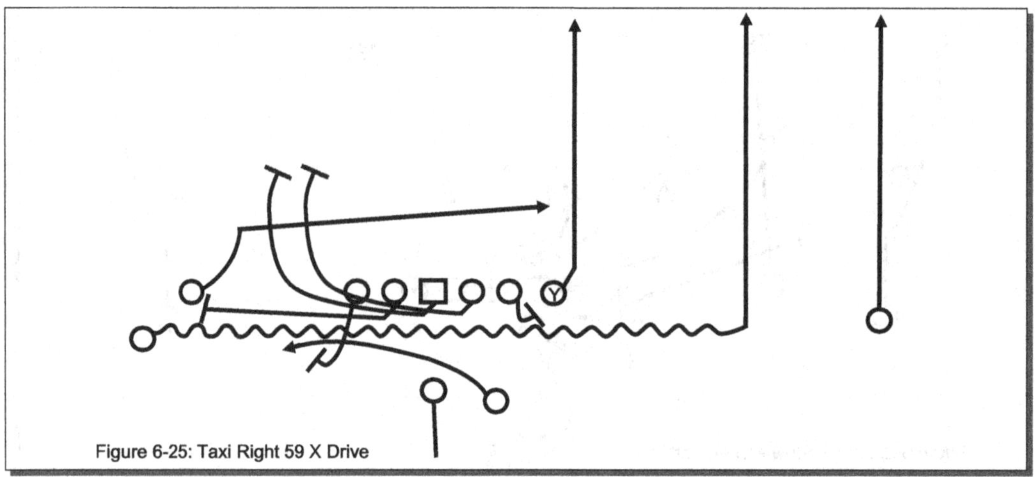

Figure 6-25: Taxi Right 59 X Drive

If you develop into a really good slow screen team, there are also ways to protect the slow screen itself. For example, we called this one "fun pass," as a way to set up the slow screen, get the linebackers flying out there to the sideline, and then release the running back over the middle, as the defenders pursue over the top of the screen blocking (Figure 6-26). We got really good at this in Jacksonville, when we were a really effective screen team in those years.

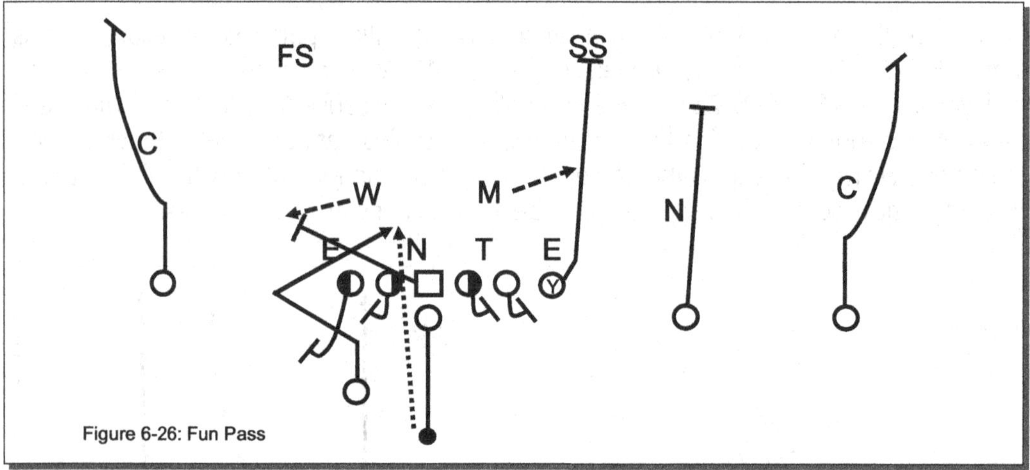

Figure 6-26: Fun Pass

## Slip Screen

This is the slip screen with the shovel-draw action. The tackle goes up and cuts off the Mike and you just encourage the rush around. The guard and center get out. The quarterback just shovels it up there (Figure 6-27). We ran it a ton, when I was at Jacksonville. We just called it "slipper." It was one of our checks vs. "3-man rush/drop 8." I just wouldn't let Mark check, if it was over eight yards to go, so we didn't waste it. We put codes on it like "even/odd glass" (for "slipper").

**Play: 6-26**

| Pos: | Assignment: |
|---|---|
| Z/W | Outside release, block deep 1/3 or 1/2. Look outside for corner or double safety with Y. |
| Y | Outside release, block safety. |
| FST | Fan EMLOS. |
| FSG | Block man on. Fake screen down LOS if uncovered. |
| C | Block man on. Fake screen down LOS if uncovered. |
| BSG | Block backside. Create space for the back. |
| BST | Fan backside. |
| X | Outside release, for deep 1/3 or 1/2. Vs cover 2, outside release for safety. |
| Q | Drop, pump screen, drift and find the back. |
| R | Chip off of protection, execute screen, release over middle as defenders pursue. |

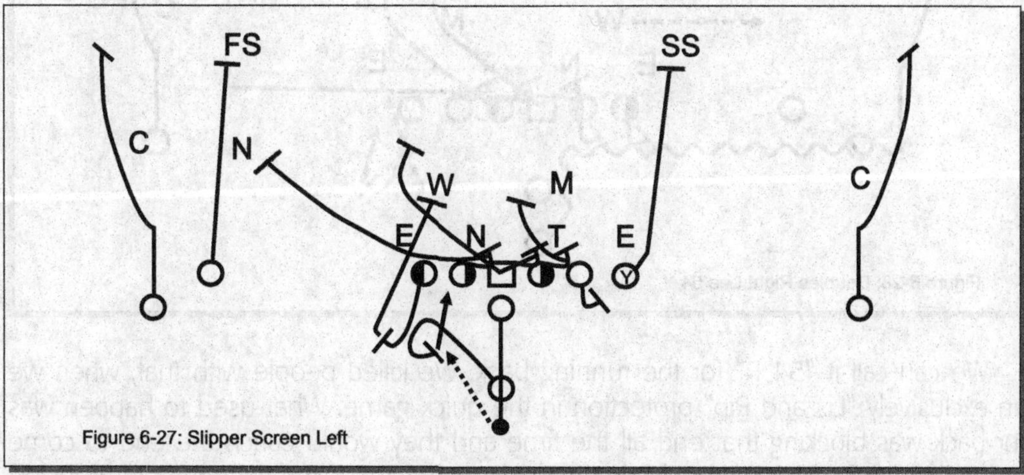

Figure 6-27: Slipper Screen Left

We were so good at this with the Jaguars. Tony Boselli would come out and "boom!" that defensive end would go flying and he'd go get the Mike. Tony just hit the guy so hard, the back didn't even have to worry about the defensive end. On the other side, you had Leon Searcy and the defensive guys would just go flying everywhere. That was fun!

## 54/55 Bluff Screen

This call is "54/55 Y," the bluff screen to the tight end. For the O-line, the playside is blocking it like "Vegas." They're going to slightly set inside. The tight end is going to set and redirect the defensive end. He wants to set firm on the line of scrimmage and not get too deep. If he is an outside rusher, he will punch with his inside hand, release, and spin back at the quarterback. He tries to over-set, he invites the defensive end inside, and then he'll punch with his outside hand instead and work away from the quarterback.

The tackle's got the "down marker." The guard gets the Sam linebacker. The center's now got the "ambush." Because you've got tackle, guard, and center "pulling the chain," so the third guy out has the ambush. The tight end needs to catch the ball and then set up his blocks. We like to package this one as "doubles right Lee: 54 Y" (Figure 6-28).

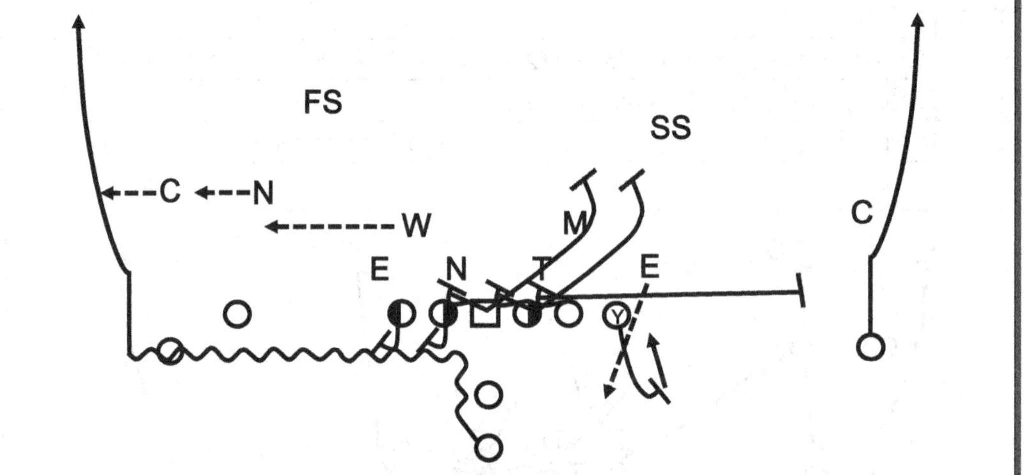

Figure 6-28: Doubles Right Lee 54 Y

We can call it "54 R" for the running back. We killed people with that, when we ran exclusively "Liz and Rip" protection in the quick game. What used to happen was our back was blocking that end all the time and they would coach the end to come underneath him. The back would do the same technique as the tight end did on "54Y" and we'd get big gains (Figure 6-29). But the following is something that can happen as your packages evolve: we put in the "Lima/ Rose" for quick game (see Chapter 2), because it gave Stefan LeFors more running lanes, when the route wasn't open, but then that killed our crack screen. That led us to evolve to other running back screens instead.

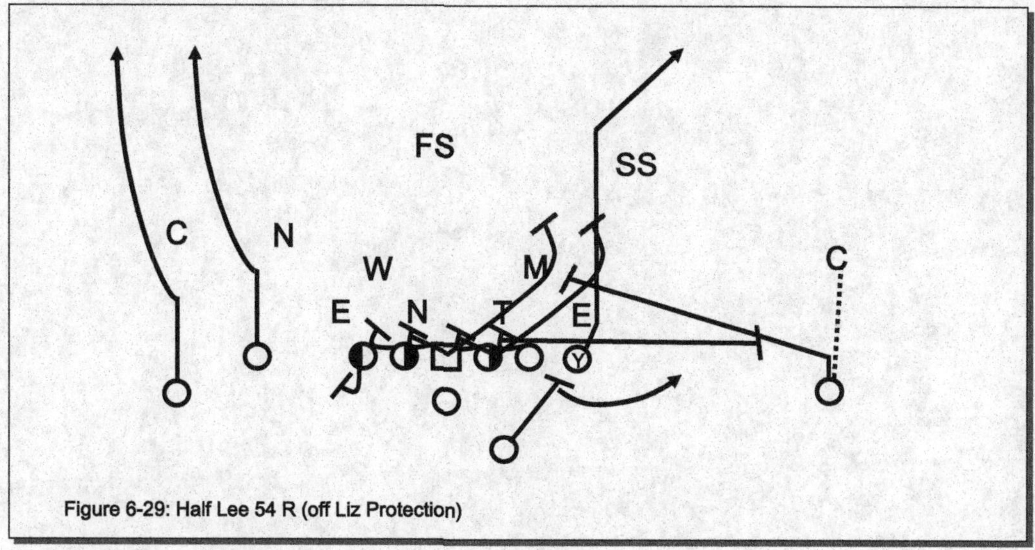

Figure 6-29: Half Lee 54 R (off Liz Protection)

## Final Thoughts About Screens

A good screen package has always been a part of what we believe in and as we've seen, we like to use a lot of them. Again, we use screens to slow the pass rush, to wear out defenders, and to defeat the blitz. As you can see, there are a number of productive ways to get that done and those detailed in this chapter are just a few of our favorite examples. Like the other concepts we've introduced, we always want to have the flexibility to package screens in a way that lets us dictate matchups to the defense. And whether that's to the back, to a wideout, or to a tight end, screens are another effective way to "feeds the studs."

# Chapter 7

## Play-Action, Bootlegs, and Nakeds

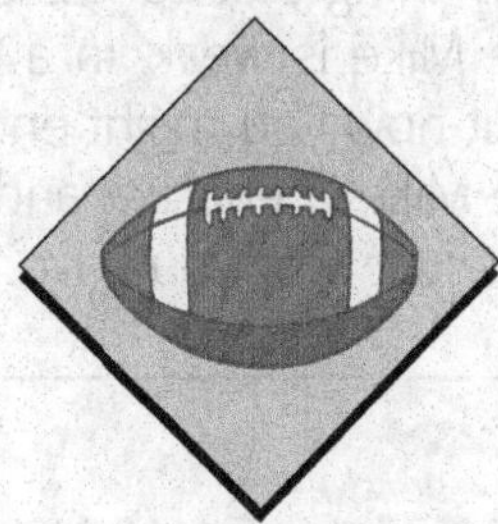

In order to be a formidable offense, you really need to invest in play-action passing, to enhance your ability to be aggressive and go for big plays. Our play-action game is always going to be set up off of what runs we're good at executing and with the utilization of our personnel groupings. We want to take some shots down the field and put some pressure on safeties. We are going after mostly safeties, you also have a chance to get after the corners a little bit and shouldn't be afraid to throw some "go" routes as well.

There were years where we'd throw play-action "go" routes once a quarter, and we were really good at them, as kind of a carryover from when I was in the NFL. In Jacksonville, Tom Coughlin liked to throw the "go" route once a quarter, saying that "three things could happen, two of which were good: completion, defensive pass interference, or incomplete. Coach Coughlin believed in taking shots down the field off play-action and that's something that has affected me throughout my coaching career.

Another thing that we try to do in our play-action game is to get these protections to correlate to the dropback protections that we've already learned. For example, we can drop straight back with the play-fake (100 series), we can move the launch-point with what we call "Act" (Act 3/Act 4), or we can run a variety of bootlegs, nakeds (300 series), and waggles. As you'll continue to see, many of the route concepts themselves carry directly over to play-action protection. We have had a lot of success with our play-action game over the years, we take pride in it, and we really strive to be the "best bootleg team in America."

## 100 Series: Dropback Play-Action

Our first play-action protection is what we call our "100" series. On this, the line is going to work *away* from the numbers of the playcall. If we say "142," the line knows that the point is going left, we're calling "hot left," and they would say "we have the 4-down plus the Will." The fullback has the Mike, and the tailback has the Sam, after faking the "42" isolation run. The two of them have to also be able to handle "Mike/strong safety" or "Sam/strong safety," so they have to be able to get "2 out of the 3" to the callside (Figure 7-1). If we were to say "143" protection, the o-line would have the "4 down plus the Sam," the fullback would have the Mike, and the tailback would have the Will after faking "43." The only thing that comes up on that, sometimes, is when you call "142" protection and the Mike is weak, in a true "over" front. The o-line still has the "4 down plus the Will," but now you might end up with "split flow," where the fullback has to go weak to get the Mike linebacker and you no longer get the isolation fake on the play-action pass. That's just how you have to do it.

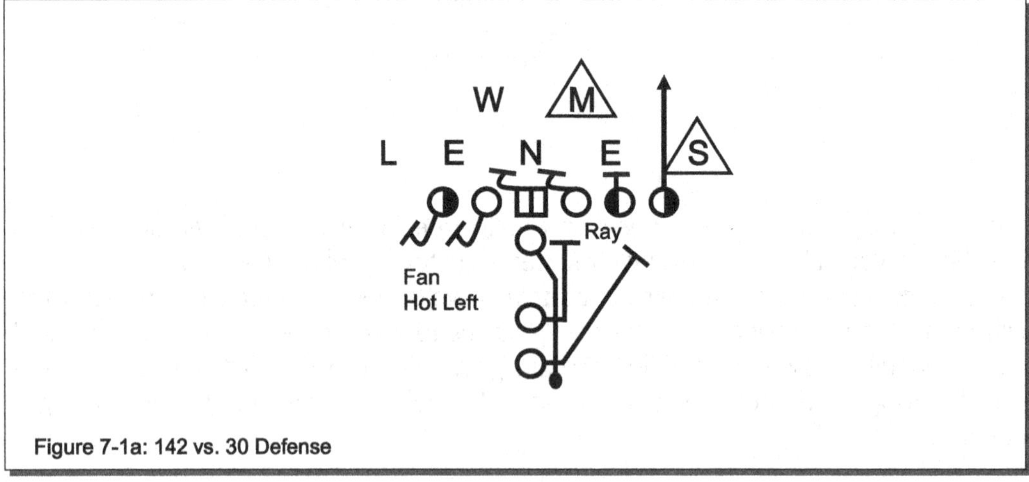

Figure 7-1a: 142 vs. 30 Defense

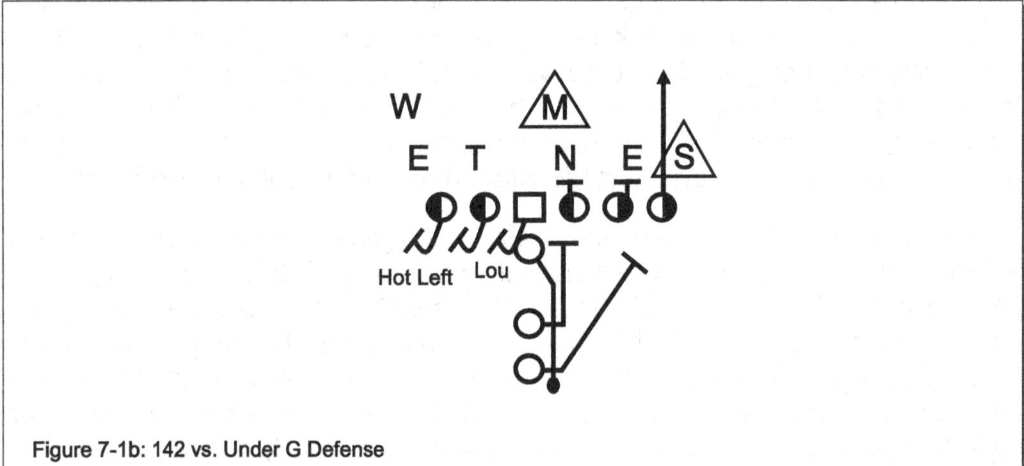

Figure 7-1b: 142 vs. Under G Defense

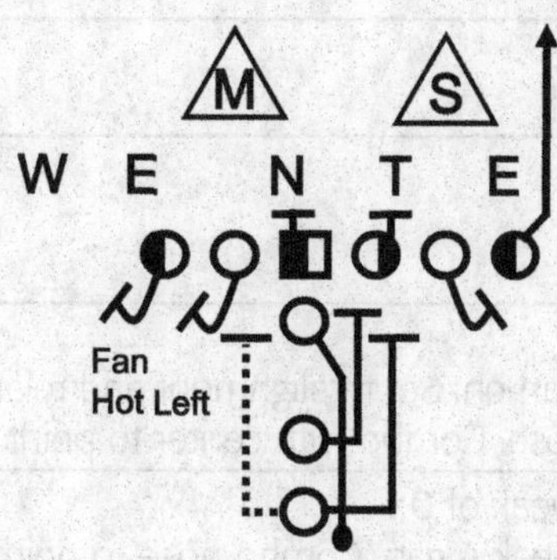


Figure 7-1c: 142 vs. Over Defense

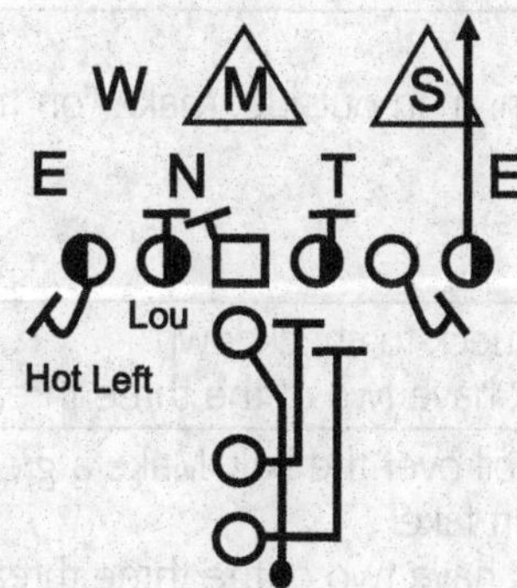


Figure 7-1d: 142 vs. College 4-3 Defense

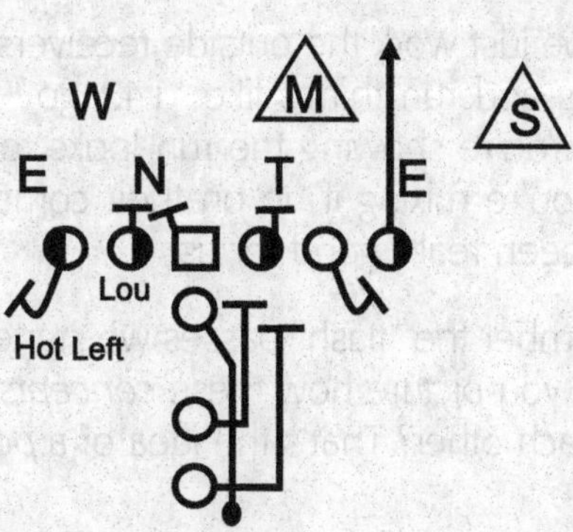


Figure 7-1e: 142 vs. 4-2 Defense

**Play: 7-1**

| Pos: | Rules: |
|---|---|
| Y | Free release. Run route:<br>1. Give ST a "white" call. |
| ST | 1st Man-on or outside:<br>1.Block man-on.<br>2.No help. |
| SG | 1st man-on or inside:<br>1.vs. covered: block man-on. Set to alignment and relationship.<br>2.vs. uncovered: set nose. Combo with center to point LB. |
| C | Weak A gap to 1st LB weak of 0:<br>1.vs. 30: set nose to weak A gap. Combo nose to point LB with RG<br>2.vs. uncovered: ID point LB, make "hot call to quickside. Make "fan" call based on point LB's alignment and LT call. |
| WG | B gap:<br>1.Gap set: alert to help WT in B gap.<br>2.vs. on call: make "fan" call. |
| WT | C gap:<br>1.Hot tackle vs. man-on, man-outside: make "on" call. No threat: no call. Alert to "fan" call from inside.<br>2.Zone all line games.<br>3.Alert cowboy. |
| F | 1.Use lead footwork. Check to checkdown.<br>2.vs. SS threat: F and R have two of the three threats (Mike, Sam, SS). |
| R | 1.Use lead footwork. Roll over the ball. Make a great fake. Run checkdown.<br>2.vs. Sam on LOS: abort fake.<br>3.vs. SS threat: F and R have two of the three threats (Mike, Sam, SS).<br><br>140/1: Check Mike to release. |

❑ 142 Go (Comeback, Caddy)

There will be times we just work the outside receivers on nothing more than basic "60 protection"-type plays and run things like "142 go," "deep 142 comeback," or "142 caddy" (Figure 7-2). You're showing the run looks to get the defense into single-high coverage and then you're mixing it up on their corners. That is pretty straight-forward stuff but has always been really good for us.

> (Note: Remember the "flash" passes we started with in the quick game chapter? Can you picture how these *concepts* are similar and continue to build on each other? That's the idea of a *package*.)

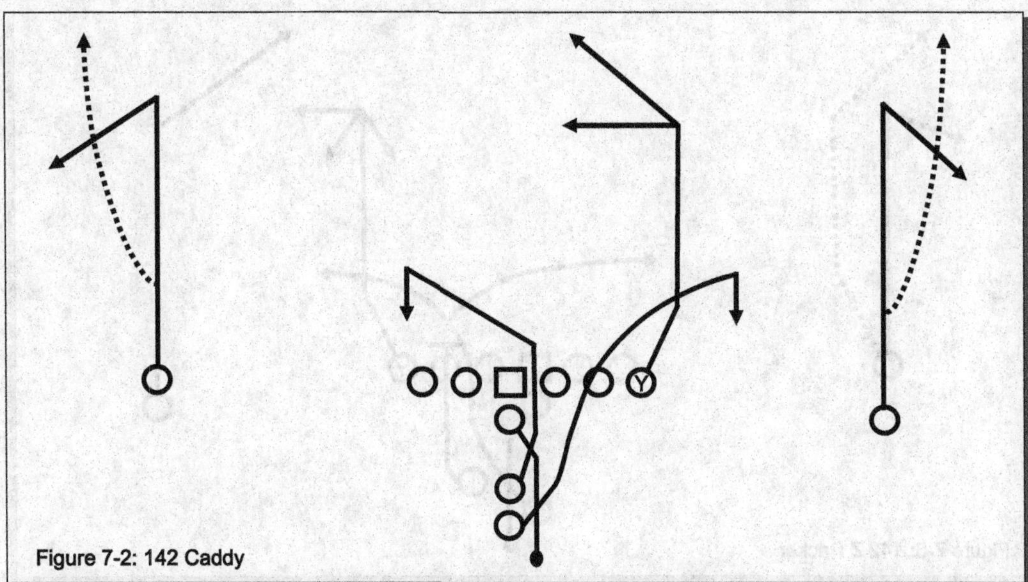

Figure 7-2: 142 Caddy

**Play: 7-2**

| Pos: | Assignment: |
|---|---|
| F | Check 142 protection. Run checkdown between center and OG at 3-5 yds depth. |
| R | Check 142 protection. Run checkdown. |
| X | Run caddy. Normal conversions |
| Y | Run streak read. |
| Z | Run caddy. Normal conversions |
| QB | Coaching points: Quick 5-step play-action.<br>Progression read away from secondary rotation.<br><br>Progression: 1. X/Z 2. Y 3. F/R<br>vs. cover 2: 1. Y 2. Z 3. R |

❑ 142 Z Packer

When we are a good lead draw/isolation team, we like to set up our play-action off of that. We can run "right 142 Z packer," which is really a "quarters beater," where you're running a hook route for Y, with a Z post over the top (where Z takes a "post-split"), and your boundary receiver is running that "circus" route (either a corner vs. 2-high or 15-yard comeback vs. 1-high). You're faking "42"; the tailback is coming out to the flat after the fake, and the fullback is going backside B-gap, hooking up and finding a window (Figure 7-3). It's been very successful as a way to get big plays down the field.

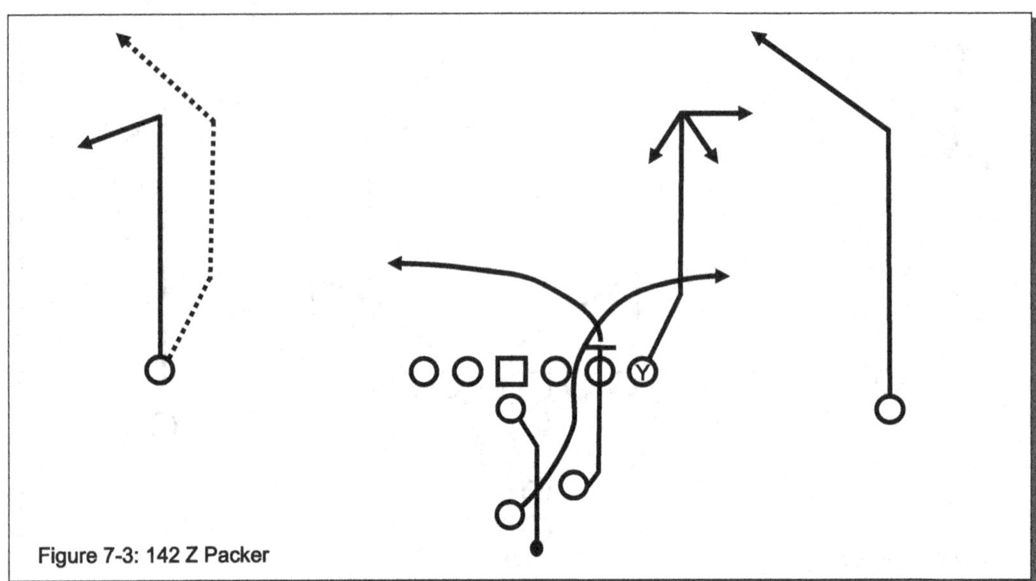


Figure 7-3: 142 Z Packer

**Play: 7-3**

| Pos: | Assignment: |
|---|---|
| F | Check 142 protection. Run drag. |
| R | Run play fake. Check 142 protection. Run diagonal. |
| X | Run circus. |
| Y | Run 10-yd hook. Hook in or break out. |
| Z | Run 9-step post route (no conversions). |
| QB | Coaching points: 5-step play-action.<br>vs quarters: alert z on post.<br><br>Progression: 1. Y 2. Z 3. R 4. F<br>vs. 1 high: work circus. |

❑ 140 X Dagger

The next concept we like to throw is "X dagger." To us, "dagger," means that we have a double-post away from a deep cross and as you'll see shortly, we can set that concept up several ways. In 21 personnel, we'd change the protection just a little bit by calling "right: 140 X dagger" (all "140" and "142" do is change the responsibility of the fullback and the tailback). As a result, the fullback has the Sam linebacker and the tailback has the Mike, so the fullback can get out in the flat very quickly (Figure 7-4). If the tight end is attached, he would just run a post through the middle-safety. If he is in a detached position, or if we set this up from "spread" people (20 personnel), then he would run a "dagger-post," where he stems it down for four steps, pushes up for five steps, and then crosses the formation. The concept stays the same and like we did with the crossers, we coach the details of the routes, so the timing and spacing stay the same as well.

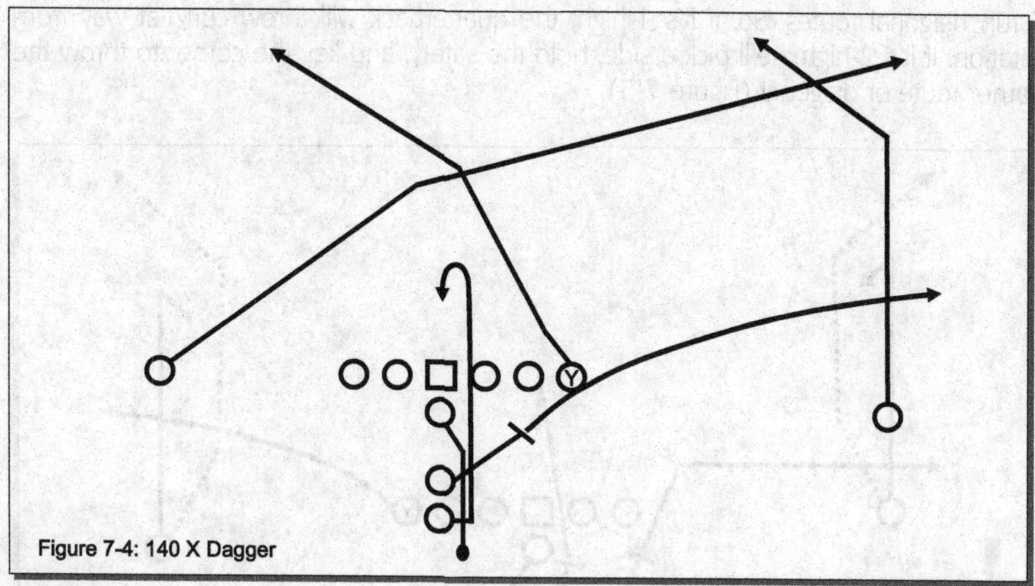

Figure 7-4: 140 X Dagger

**Play: 7-4**

| Pos: | Assignment: |
|---|---|
| F | Check 140 protection. Run diagonal. |
| R | Run play fake. Check 140 protection. Run checkdown over the ball. |
| X | Run dagger route to 22 yds at the opposite #'s |
| Y | Run over post at 10 yards. Cross the face of the FS. |
| Z | Run sail post. |
| QB | Coaching points: Controlled 7-step play-action.<br><br>Progression: 1. Z 2. X 3. F 4. R |

The quarterback would make the fake, and then locate the safety. He wants to think post first: "set your feet to throw the post." I think it's important for him to think of the big play first, and then "readjust his feet to throw the deep-over." Something else that happened a lot on this play is that fullback would end up wide open in the flat. The quarterback shouldn't be afraid to just give him the ball *right now*.

❑ Cobra

"Right: deep 141 (140) cobra" is another concept we like, though we really did more of that in the NFL than at the college level. It's also another example of how we like to use a post-snap option route combination. This is a weakside, play-action fake, where the O-line has the 4-down plus the Sam, the fullback has the Will, and the tailback has the Mike. On this, the Z and X would run the "cobra" route, which is a 16-yard point-to-point curl against free-access that converts to a corner route vs. a jam corner. Y and

F run diagonal routes. So, if it's 1-high, the quarterback will throw curl/flat way from rotation. If it's 2-high, he'll pick a side, hold the safety, and key the corner to throw the corner route or diagonal (Figure 7-5).

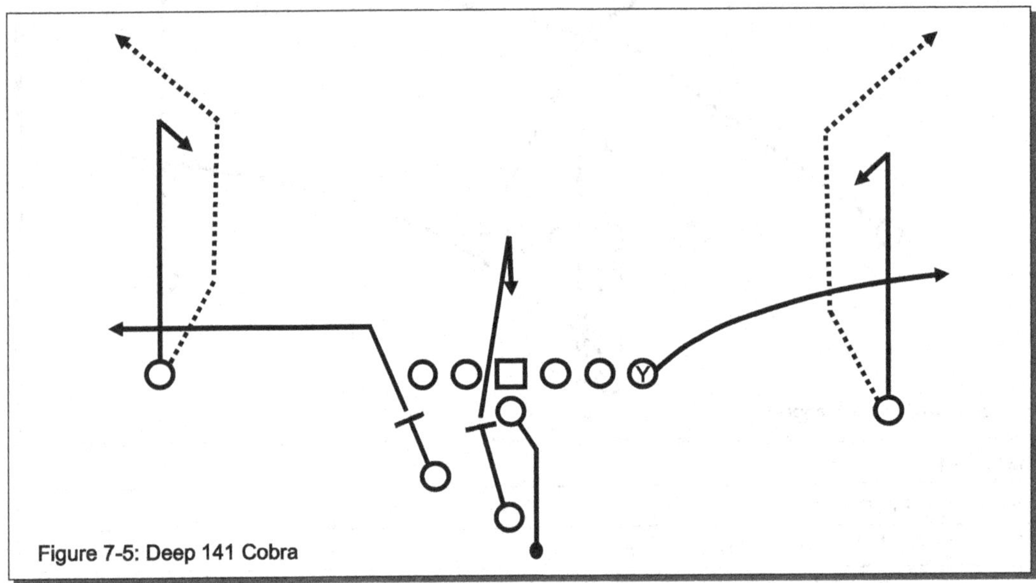

Figure 7-5: Deep 141 Cobra

(Note: "Deep" tells the tackles the quarterback is taking a 7-step drop, because it's now a deeper 16-yard curl route or corner route.)

❑ Slot 140

You can build a package of these ideas from a "slot" formation, for example, "slot right: 140 China/Y cop" (Figure 7-6). If your tight end is really talented, this is a great way to feature him. "Slot right: 140 Y corner, X dipper" is another one we like from that slot formation package (Figure 7-7). There are dozens of ways to set up the 100 series, but these are the first ones we like to install, and they have always been consistently good for us.

## Act 3 and Act 4

We like to run what we call "act 3 and act 4" protection. This is really just a form of "solid" protection, with some quarterback movement. The O-line has a run fake and comes off the ball on the double-teams before they choke it down, but it's really the same concept as "solid" protection. The line has the "4-down plus the Mike," the running back has the Will, and the tight end has the Sam linebacker (Figure 7-8). "Act

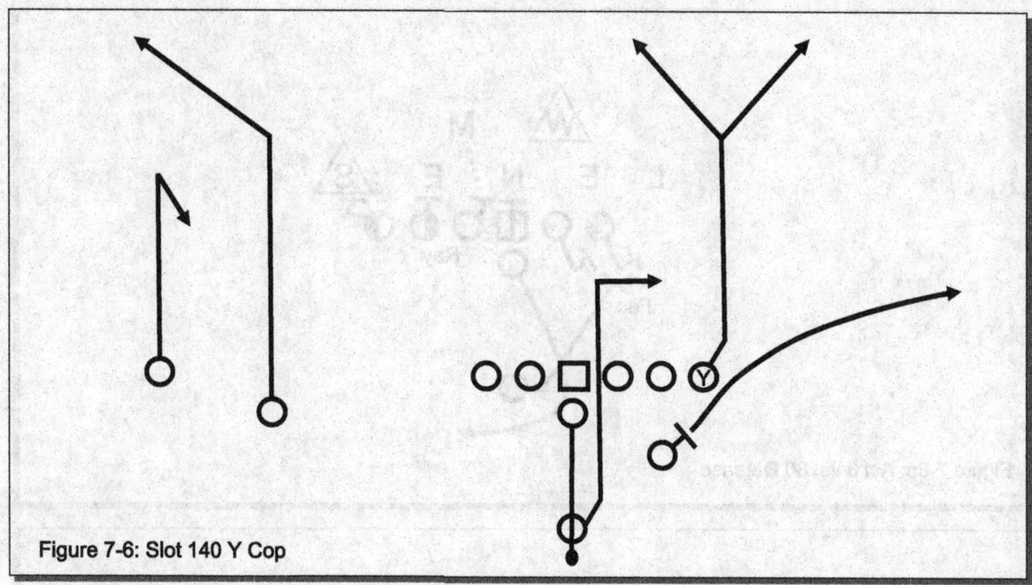

Figure 7-6: Slot 140 Y Cop

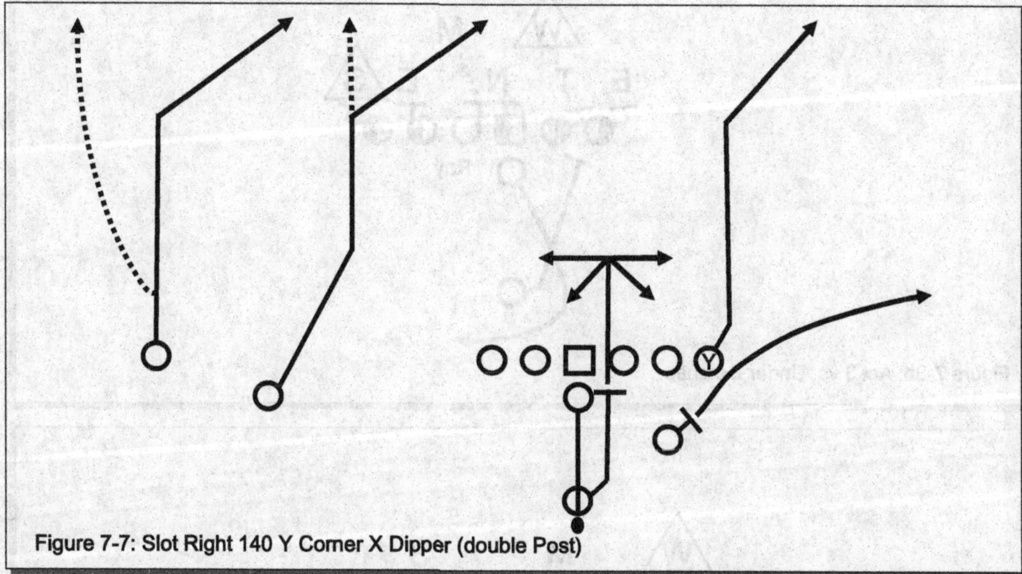

Figure 7-7: Slot Right 140 Y Corner X Dipper (double Post)

3" and "act 4," are where you're moving the quarterback, making a good weakside mid-zone fake with the "solid" protection, and trying to buy yourself time to work the ball down the field. On "act 3," the quarterback is going to start back, like he's "naked," but then set up right behind the center. He is going to extend his open hand a little more and hand fake to the back, and then hide the ball in his stomach with what we call a "third-hand" technique, so the seams are there when he grabs the ball.

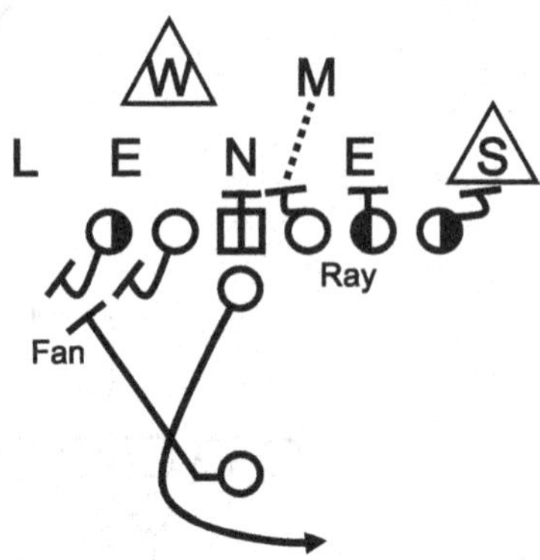


Figure 7-8a: Act 3 vs. 30 Defense

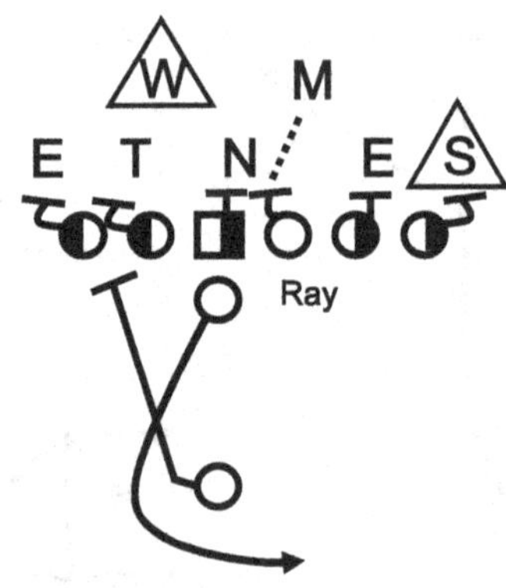


Figure 7-8b: Act 3 vs. Under Defense

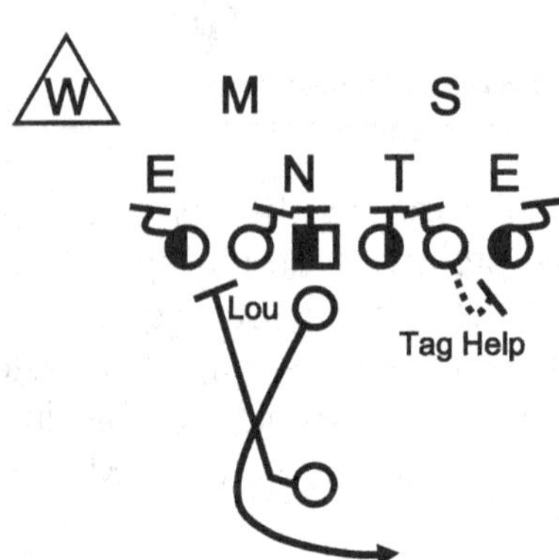


Figure 7-8c: Act 3 vs. Over Defense

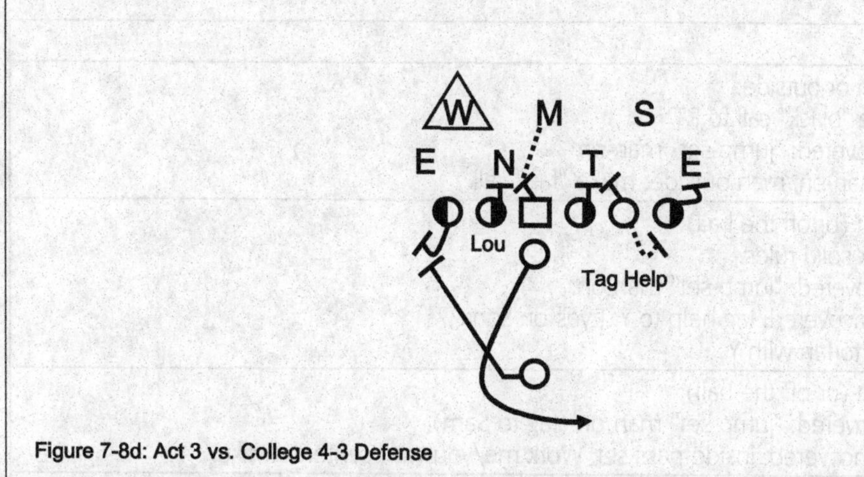

Figure 7-8d: Act 3 vs. College 4-3 Defense

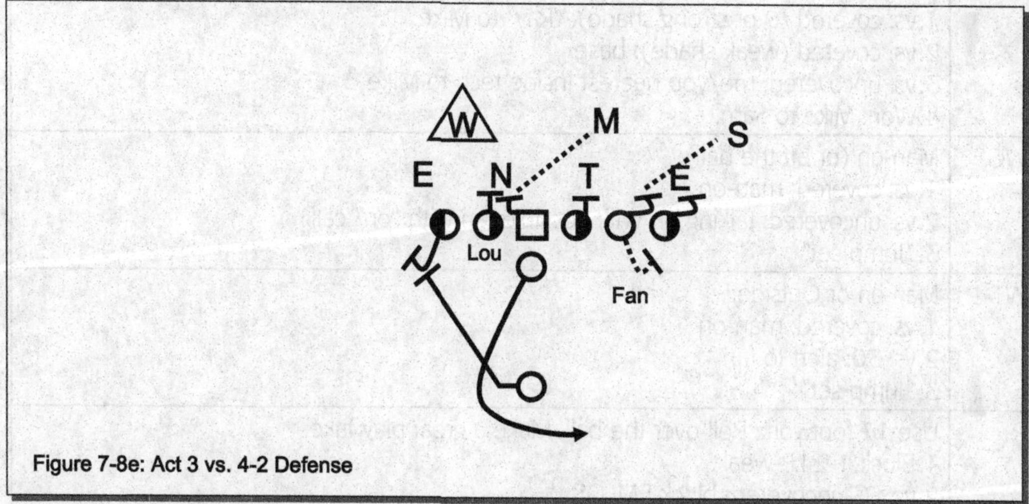

Figure 7-8e: Act 3 vs. 4-2 Defense

That's also how we make the play-action game correlate with the base protections and put them in the *same way*. When we're putting the "70" protection in, we're going to install the "100" play-action at the same time. When we put "400" in, we're going to put in "100 weak," so the thought process is the same for the o-line, the running backs, and the quarterback.

**Play: 7-8**

| Pos: | Rules: |
|---|---|
| Y | Man-on or outside:<br>1. Make "black" call to RT<br>2. vs. covered: "jump-set" man-on<br>3. vs. man-on, man-outside: make "fan" call. |
| ST | Man-on (or off the ball):<br>1. Block solid rules.<br>2. vs. covered: "jump-set" man-on.<br>3. vs. uncovered: tag help to Y. Eyes on Sam.<br>4. Alert to fan with Y |
| SG | Man-on (or off the ball):<br>1. vs. covered: "jump-set" man on (tag to Sam).<br>2. vs. uncovered: inside pass set. Work me/you with center to Mike. |
| C | Solid rules. Declare point as Mike or middle of 3:<br>1. vs. covered (0 or strong shade): "Ray" to Mike.<br>2. vs. covered (weak shade): base.<br>3. vs. uncovered: me/you nearest inside tech to Mike<br>4. Work Mike to Sam. |
| WG | Man-on (or off the ball):<br>1. vs. covered: man-on<br>2. vs. uncovered: talking on Will; possible fan with "on" call<br>3. "Jump-set" |
| WT | Man-on or Outside:<br>1. vs. covered: man-on<br>2. vs. 30: alert to fan<br>3. "Jump-set" |
| R | Use 17 footwork. Roll over the ball. Make a great play fake:<br>1. Block 1-2 LB weak.<br>2. vs. LG uncovered: block EMLOS.<br>3. vs. no threat: run route. |

❑ Act 3 Dagger

We have a good package with the dagger concept, and it works really well from the "act" series. The first way to do that off this protection would be "doubles right: act 3, Z dagger" (Figure 7-9). You've got the double-post from the field and then you've got the deep-over by Z. Then, the running back is going to run a "17 track" (or "16 track") at the inside leg of the tackle. The tackle counts on him, knowing that he's going to be there, so he can be aggressive when he "up-kicks" the defensive end and gets into him. If the defensive end wants to come inside, the back is going to be there to hit him and put him back on the tackle, before he runs his route to the flat and attacks the coverage.

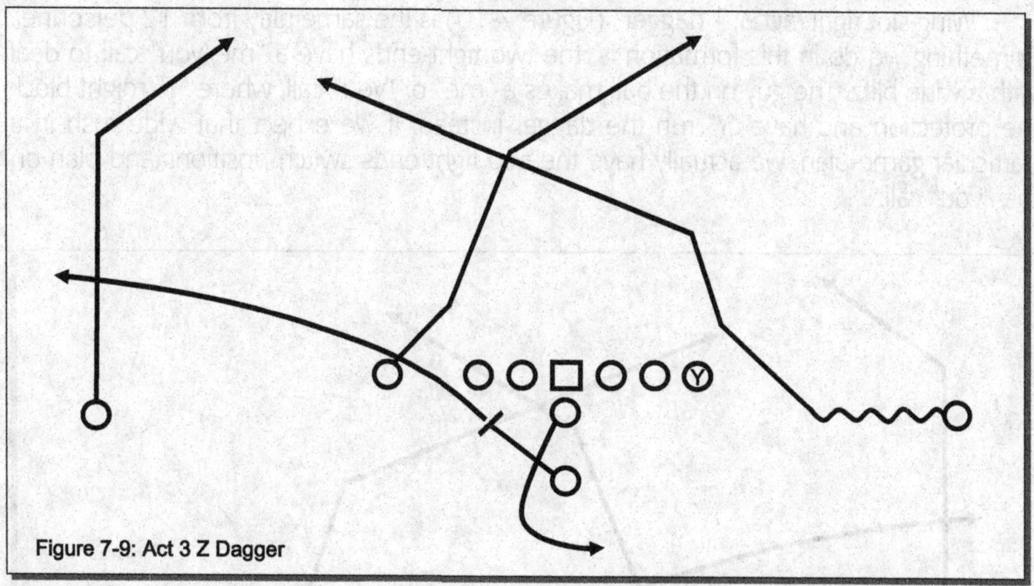

Figure 7-9: Act 3 Z Dagger

**Play: 7-9**

| Pos: | Assignment: |
|---|---|
| R | Run play fake. Check act 3 protection. Run diagonal. |
| T | Run dagger route to 22 yds on the opposite #'s. |
| X | Run 9-step post. |
| Y | Block act protection. Make "black" call to playside tackle. |
| Z | Run 4-5 over post. |
| QB | Coaching points: 7-step play-action. Make a good fake.<br><br>Progression: 1. X 2. Z 3. R |

You usually get a double-team between the center and the weak guard and a double team between the strong guard and strong tackle. Then, the strong tackle will get back out and help the tight end. On this play, it's really important that the strong tackle understands that the tight end has a lot of different responsibilities and pass protection is not something he works on all the time. The strong tackle must get back out there and help to allow the quarterback to make throws down the field.

Quarterbacks need to work at that dagger throw, so we're going to practice it and we say, "get them the ball between the college hash and the numbers." We also want to throw it against defenders or at least with tackling dummies out there, so the quarterbacks can get the feel for the touch that is needed. That helps a lot and is more effective than just trying to throw it on air. You actually get a lot of receptions for running backs on this as well and it's important to spend time with the quarterback, working all the way through the progression to the checkdown, so you can get big plays on it, no matter where the ball is thrown.

"Wing-slot right: act 3, T dagger" (Figure 7-10) is the same play from 12 personnel. Something we do in this formation is, the two tight-ends have a "me/you" call to deal with a wide blitz. The guy on the ball makes a "me" or "you" call, where "T" might block the protection and have "Y" run the dagger instead. If we expect that wide rush in a particular game-plan, we actually have the two tight ends switch positions and plan on the "you" call.

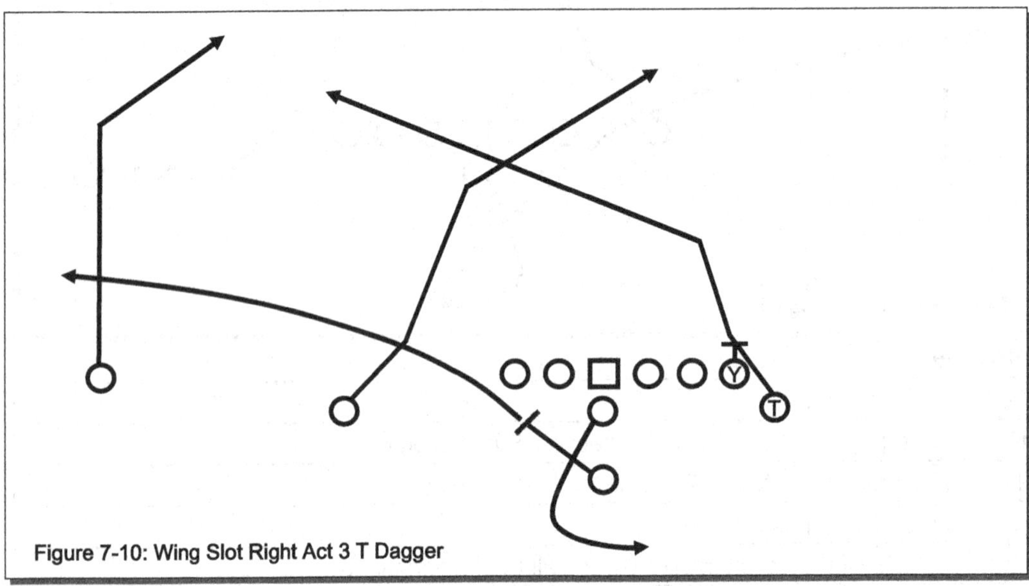

Figure 7-10: Wing Slot Right Act 3 T Dagger

**Play: 7-10**

| Pos: | Assignment: |
|---|---|
| R | Run play fake. Check act 3 protection. Run diagonal. |
| W | Run 10-yd over post. |
| X | Run post route. |
| Y | Block act protection. Make "black" call to playside tackle. |
| Z | Run dagger route to 22 yds on the opposite #'s. |
| QB | Coaching points: 7-step play-action. Make a good fake.<br><br>Progression: 1. X 2. T 3. R |

(Note: We actually got that from the Colts, when Peyton Manning played there. They did it on both "load" and "act" from wing-slot and it really does help the blocking angles).

We can package the dagger concept a number of ways and we can always adjust the protection a bit by game plan for example, "taxi right, Y peel: knock 9, X dagger" (Figure 7-11). We did it this way, when we faced a kamikaze blitz team. We weren't going to let them force us out of our stuff, but we didn't want to get the quarterback hit, either. We wouldn't package it like that against everyone, but we did it with that team, because they just brought everyone. We can also call either "trey right: act 3, W over" (Figure 7-12) or "wing right: act 3, T over" (Figure 7-13) to give the route to an inside receiver. We want to have the versatility to get whoever we want on that route and you get there by thinking in *concepts* and *packages*.

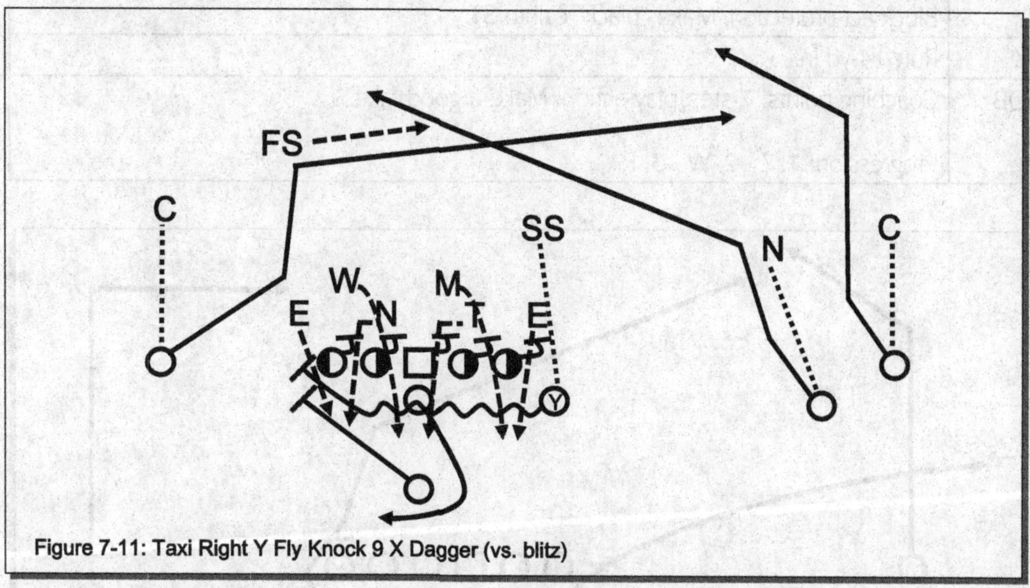

Figure 7-11: Taxi Right Y Fly Knock 9 X Dagger (vs. blitz)

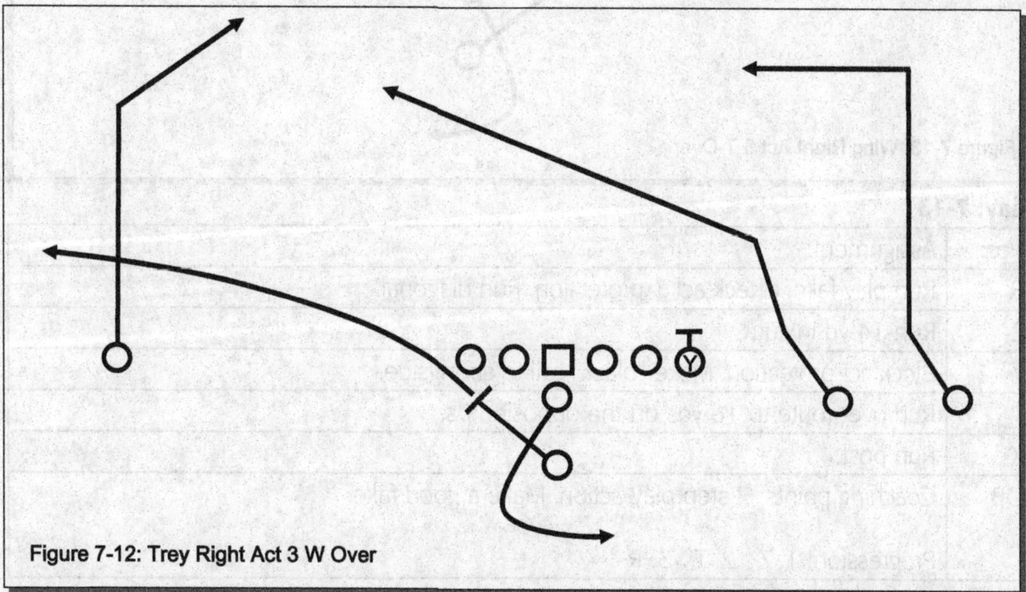

Figure 7-12: Trey Right Act 3 W Over

**Play: 7-12**

| Pos: | Assignment: |
|---|---|
| R | Run play fake. Check act 3 protection. Run diagonal. |
| W | Run over route to 16 yds on the opposite #'s. |
| Z | Run sail post. Step on CB's toes. |
| Y | Block act protection. Make "black" call to ST. |
| X | Run 14-yd in. |
| QB | Coaching points: 7-step play-action. Make a good fake.<br><br>Progression: 1. Z 2. W 3. R |

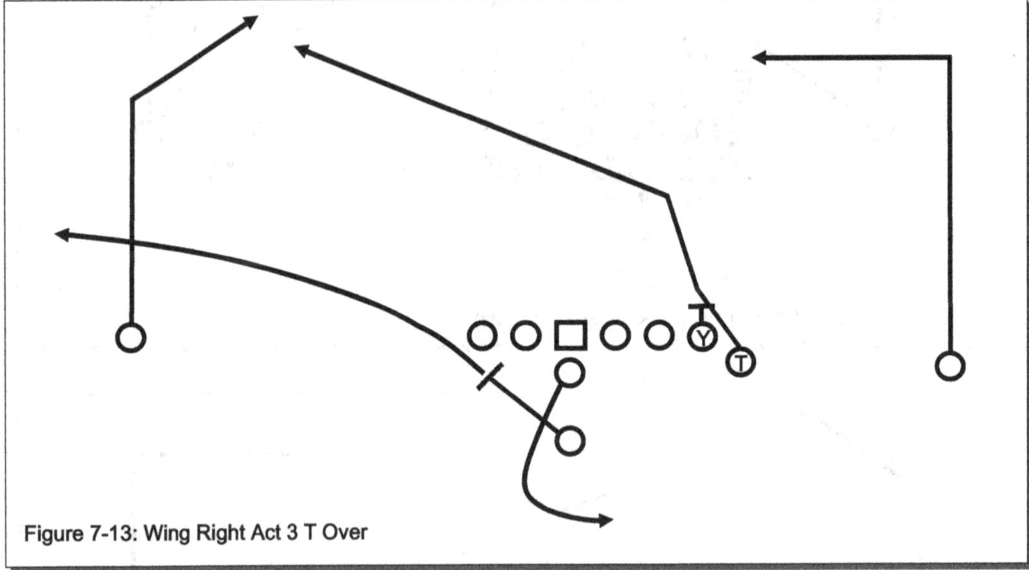


Figure 7-13: Wing Right Act 3 T Over

**Play: 7-13**

| Pos: | Assignment: |
|---|---|
| R | Run play fake. Check act 3 protection. Run diagonal. |
| Z | Run 14-yd in cut. |
| Y | Block act protection. Make "black" call to strongside. |
| T | Run over route to 16 yds on the opposite #'s. |
| X | Run post. |
| QB | Coaching points: 7-step play-action. Make a good fake.<br><br>Progression: 1. Z 2. T 3. R |

❑ Act 3 Diamond (and Sail)

The next thing we like is what we call "act 3 (act 4) diamond." This gives us the ability to have a "5-3 sail route" vs. quarters or middle-closed coverage (meaning 5-step stem, 3-steps to the post, and then back out to the sideline). Then if it's true cover 2, it converts to a "2-on-1" ball, with a seam and a go route. The #2 receiver is thinking "sail," when he sees the play. As he lines up, he's still thinking "sail" if it's a 2-high look. As he comes off the ball, if that safety gets width and it becomes true cover 2, he then takes the middle. Z has the "circus" on the backside, with the same reads and rules. This is something that has been very good to us and the conversions work really well (Figure 7-14). If we want to simplify it, we just call "sail" and remove the conversions. Once again, the tailback makes a good fake and leaks out to the flat (Figure 7-15).

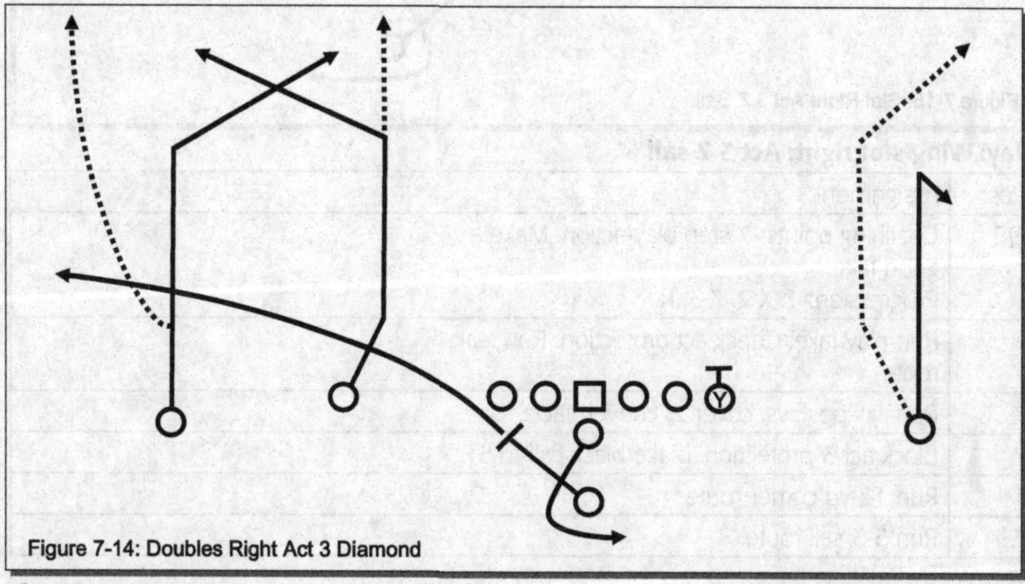

Figure 7-14: Doubles Right Act 3 Diamond

**Play: 7-14**

| Pos: | Assignment: |
|---|---|
| R | Run play fake. Check act 3 protection. Run diagonal. |
| Z | Run sail route. vs. cover 2: Stem in, push up, and snap post. |
| X | Run sail post. vs. cover 2: convert fade. |
| Y | Block act protection. Make "black" call to ST. |
| Z | Run circus. |
| QB | Coaching points: 7-step play-action. Make a good fake.<br><br>Progression: 1. X 2. W 3. R<br>vs. cover 2: 1. W 2. X 3. R |

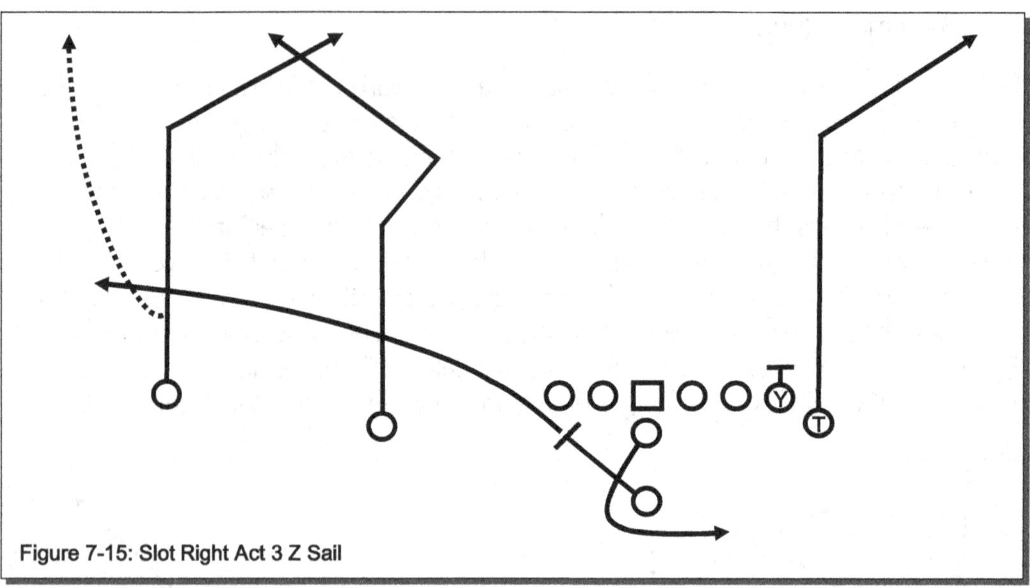
Figure 7-15: Slot Right Act 3 Z Sail

**Play: Wing slot right: Act 3 Z sail**

| Pos: | Assignment: |
|---|---|
| QB | Coaching points: 7-step play-action. Make a good fake.<br>Progression: 1. X 2. Z 3. R |
| R | Run play fake. Check act protection. Run leak route. |
| X | Run sail post. vs. cover 2: convert fade. |
| Y | Block act 3 protection. Make black call to ST. |
| T | Run 12-yd corner route. |
| Z | Run 5-3 sail route. |

❑ Act 3 Squirrel

Once we started running the "zone-read," people started playing the safeties in man coverage to let the linebackers play the run. That looks like quarters coverage, but it's what we called "zero-combo" (really a combination of man and zone). Then, the "squirrel" route became really good to us. It's a type of double-move on the safety, where you show him "sail," and then you give him the "squirrel." It's something that's been very effective for us and has created a lot of big plays.

We can set this a number of ways from a number of different formations, just like we did with the dagger concept. If we are starting from 2x2, we would call "doubles right: act 3, W squirrel" (Figure 7-16). On this, the W is going to run a "corner-post" route. So again, "eight steps, three to the corner, back across the face of the safety to the post." The X receiver is going to run an 8-yard stop ("gain-hitch") on the sideline. The running back has to understand that on this concept, the flat is occupied, so he just runs a "check-through," stops on his way to the flat, and tries to get open vs. zone coverage. The backside receiver has the "circus route" to go get that safety against 2-high, but against single-high coverage, he needs to expect the ball, because that's where the quarterback has to go against single-high.

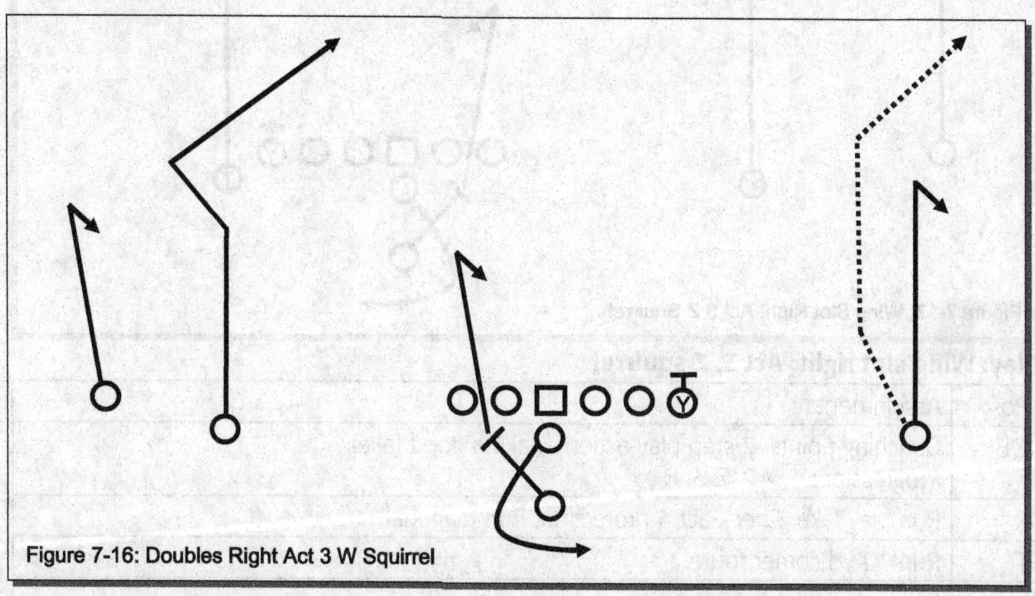

Figure 7-16: Doubles Right Act 3 W Squirrel

**Play: Doubles right: Act 3, W squirrel**

| Pos: | Assignment: |
|---|---|
| R | Act 3 protection. Check down. |
| W | Run squirrel route. |
| X | Run stop route, 8 yds. |
| Y | Block act protection. |
| Z | Run circus. |
| QB | Vs. 2-high: W-X-R; vs. single-high: Z-R |

As we said, we can dial this up for whichever receiver we want. The concept works well from the wing slot for Z (Figure 7-17). When we had DeVantae Parker at X, we opened the Florida State game in 2014 with "tango right: act 3, X squirrel" (Figure 7-18), in order to get X on that safety. When we call "tango," W goes to #3, X goes to #2, and Z plays #1, so it was a formation adjustment that in this case, gave us the ability to let X run that route.

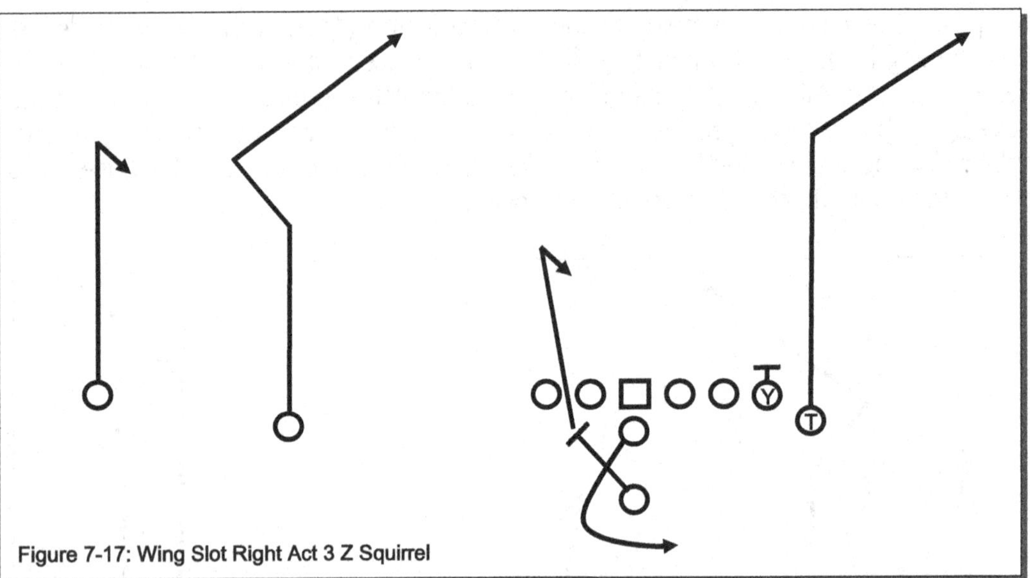

Figure 7-17: Wing Slot Right Act 3 Z Squirrel

**Play: Wing slot right: Act 3, Z squirrel**

| Pos: | Assignment: |
|---|---|
| QB | Coaching points: 7-step play-action. Make a good fake.<br>Progression: 1. X 2. Z 3. R |
| R | Run play fake. Check act 3 protection. Run diagonal. |
| T | Run 12-yd corner route. |
| X | Run stop route, 8-10 yds. |
| Y | Block act protection. Make "black" call to ST> |
| Z | Run squirrel route. |

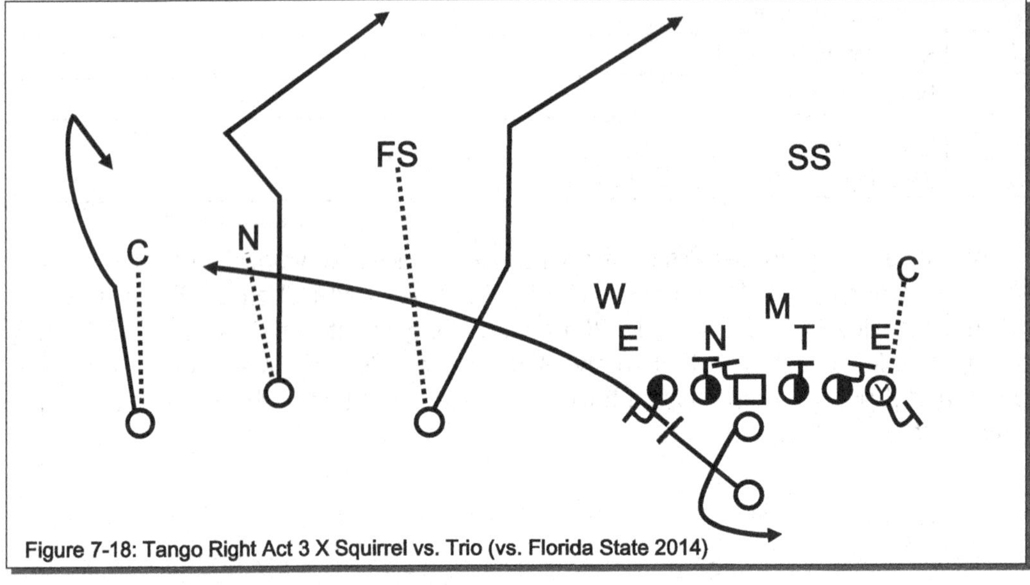

Figure 7-18: Tango Right Act 3 X Squirrel vs. Trio (vs. Florida State 2014)

## Load 2 (Slant Load 2)

What we call "load 2" is another way to really firm up the protection unit (Figure 7-19). If you want to add more nuance for the quarterback, the "load 2" call would give him a fake draw and then if you call "slant load 2," the back takes a jab-step, comes back to help the tight end on the double, and the quarterback does a reverse-pivot. When I was at Jacksonville, we called out the quarterback's technique on run plays like "ride 36/37" or "ride 34/35," but if we wanted the quarterback to reverse pivot, we called "slant" as a term to get the quarterback to reverse-pivot. We started calling "slant load 3" to get that throwback action, but in those years, we never did "slant load 2" (just "load 2" off a draw fake), since Mark Brunell was a lefty. A little history on how the package developed.

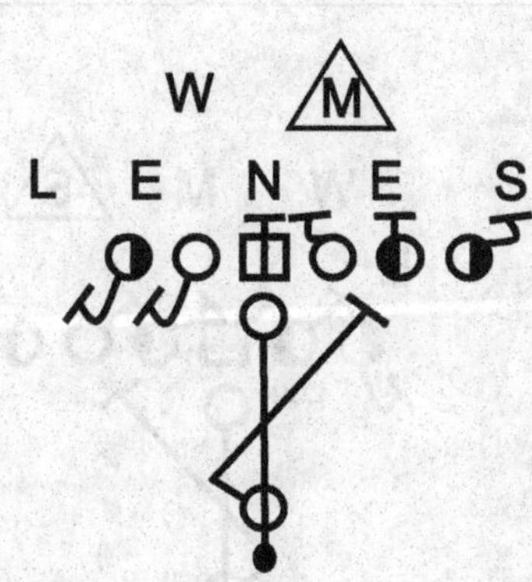


Figure 7-19a: Load 2 (Slant Load 2) vs. 30 Defense

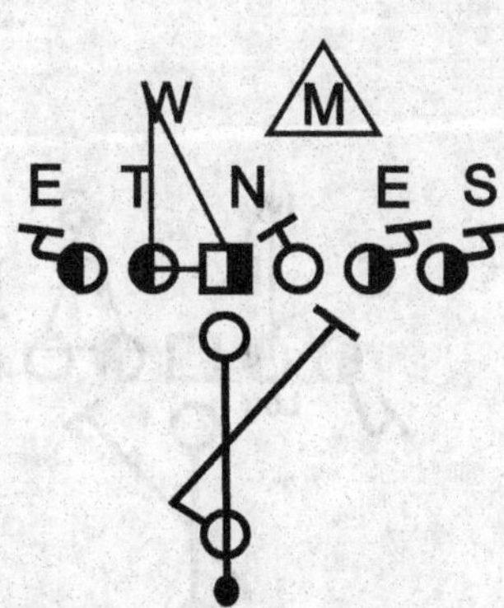


Figure 7-19b: Load 2 (Slant Load 2) vs. Under Defense

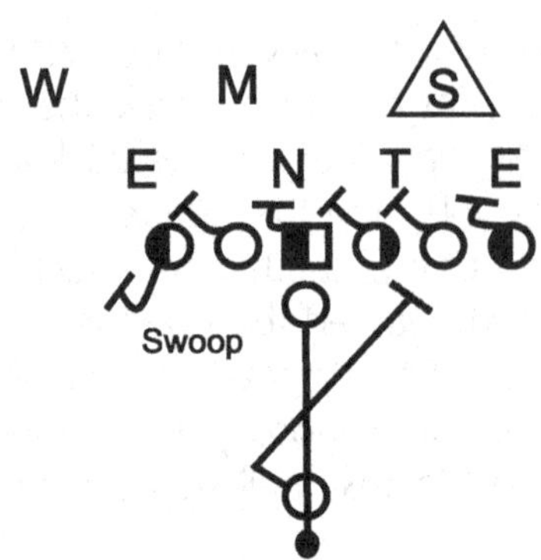


Figure 7-19c: Load 2 (Slant Load 2) vs. Over Defense

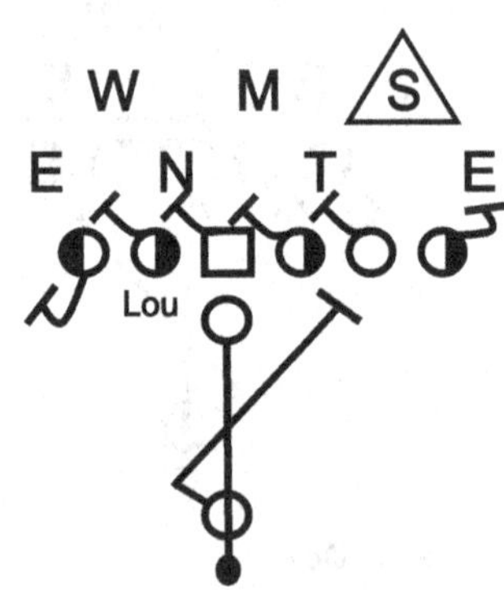


Figure 7-19d: Load 2 (Slant Load 2) vs. College 4-3 Defense

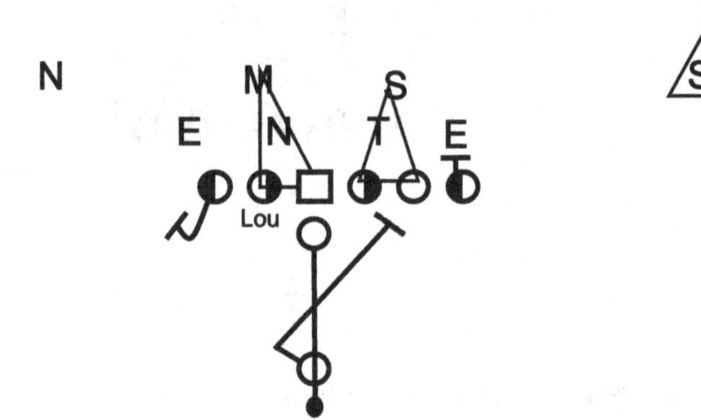


Figure 7-19e: Load 2 (Slant Load 2) vs. 4-2 Defense

**Play: 7-19**

| Pos: | Rules: |
|---|---|
| Y | Man-on:<br>1.vs. Man-on, man-outside: cannot fan. |
| ST | Man-on. B gap to 1st LB inside:<br>1.vs. covered: block man-on.<br>2.vs. uncovered: tag with SG.<br>3.Alert swoop call. Block Liz/Rip protection. |
| SG | Strong A gap:<br>1.vs. uncovered: set A gap. Key nose.<br>2.vs. covered with ST covered: block man-on.<br>3.vs, covered with ST uncovered: tag with ST to strong A gap. |
| C | Weak A gap:<br>1.Set back and get to guard's level. Block weak A gap.<br>2.vs. over front with on call: make "swoop" call.<br>3.Make "hot" call to weakside. |
| WG | Weak B gap:<br>1.Set B gap. Alert fan call. |
| WT | C gap:<br>1.Set for C gap defender.<br>2.vs. man-on, man-outside: fan. |
| R | Key: 1st LB from uncovered guard or tackle:<br>1.Help Y.<br>2.Release on route.<br><br>Slant lead: counter footwork. |

All of the concepts we've discussed—go, caddy, comeback, packer, dagger, dipper, cop, etc.—are compatible with "load 2/3." You can *picture* this as similar to 140, except that you lose the 2nd checkdown. The *concepts* are the same though. The 140 and load packages allow us to throw the ball down the field and win one-on-one matchups. For example, "doubles right: load 2, X packer (Figure 7-20) or "taxi right: load 2, Z packer" (Figure 7-21) are the same concepts as running it from 140 protection, but the W now has the hook route, as opposed to the Y. "Wing slot right: load 2, T corner/X dipper" (Figure 7-22) and "wing slot right: load 2, China/T cop" (Figure 7-23) are the same concept as they were from "slot right: 140." The "act" concepts work with "load" protection as well. For example, "W squirrel" works from load 2 the same as act 3 (Figure 7-24). You develop *packages* by thinking in *concepts*.

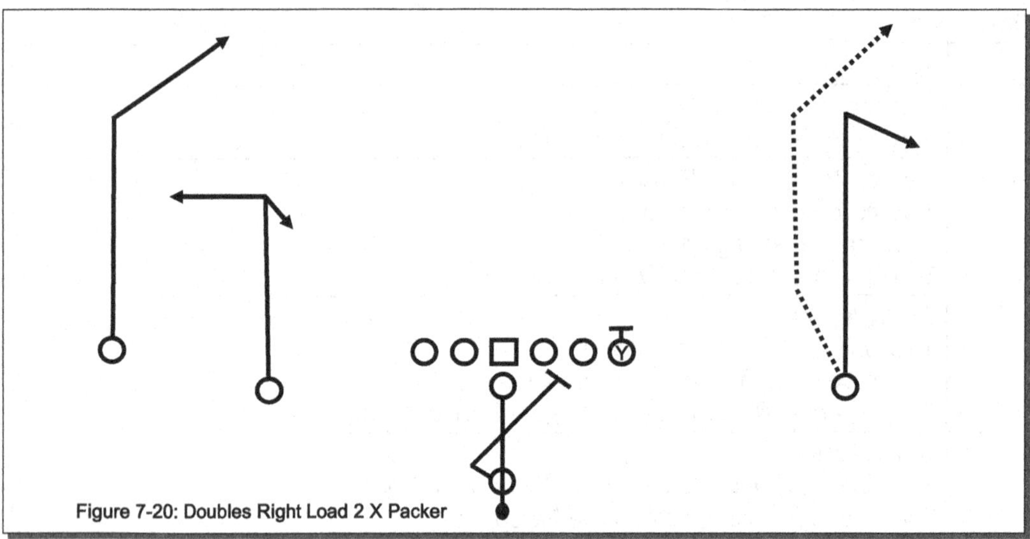

Figure 7-20: Doubles Right Load 2 X Packer

**Play: 7-20**

| Pos: | Assignment: |
|---|---|
| R | Run play fake. Execute load 2 protection. |
| X | Run post. |
| Y | Black |
| W | Run 10-yd hook. Hook in or break out. |
| Z | Run circus. |
| QB | Coaching points: 5-step play-action.<br>vs. quarters: alert X on post<br><br>Progression: 1. X 2. W<br>vs. 1 high: work circus. |

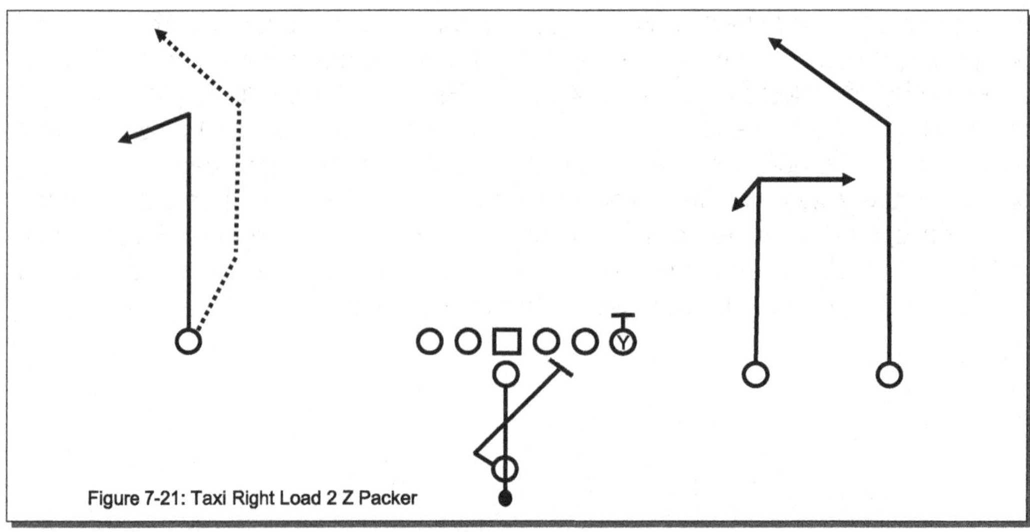

Figure 7-21: Taxi Right Load 2 Z Packer

**Play: 7-21**

| Pos: | Assignment: |
|---|---|
| R | Run play fake. Execute load 2 protection. |
| X | Run circus. |
| Y | Block load protection. Make "black" call to strongside. |
| W | Run 10-yd hook. Hook in or break out. |
| Z | Run 9-step post. |
| QB | Coaching points: 5-step play-action.<br>vs. quarters: alert Z on post<br><br>Progression: 1. Z 2. W 3. X<br>vs. 1 high: work circus. |

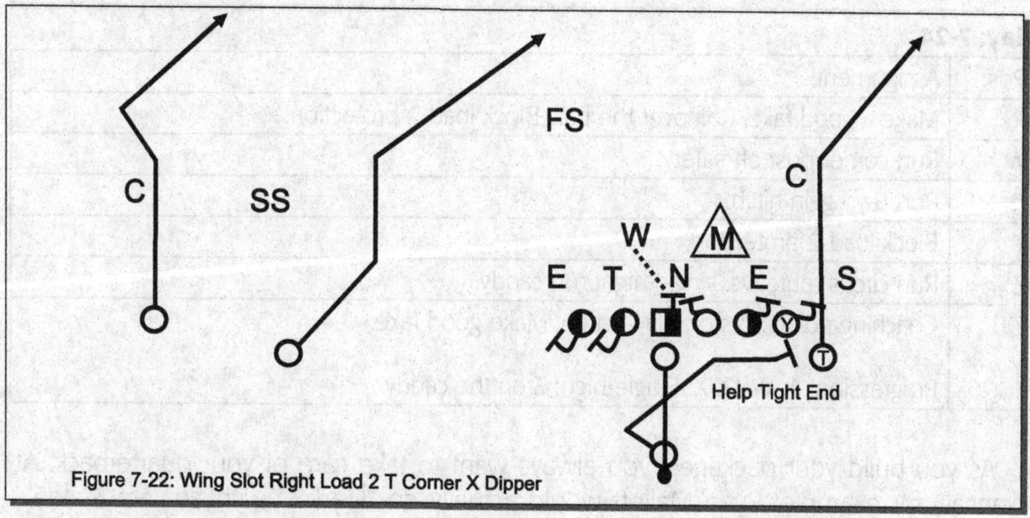

Figure 7-22: Wing Slot Right Load 2 T Corner X Dipper

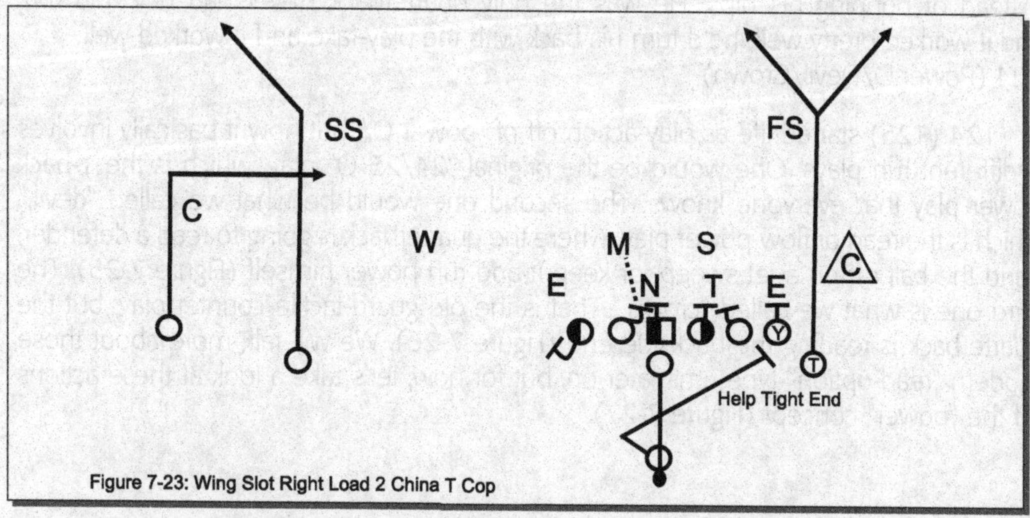

Figure 7-23: Wing Slot Right Load 2 China T Cop

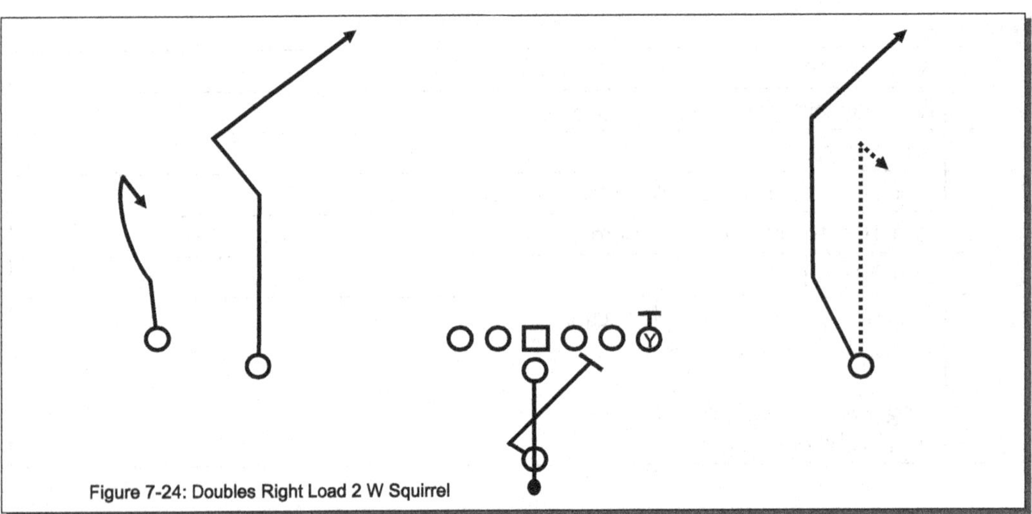
Figure 7-24: Doubles Right Load 2 W Squirrel

**Play: 7-24**

| Pos: | Assignment: |
|---|---|
| R | Make a good fake. Roll over the ball. Block load 2 protection. |
| W | Run corner post off safety. |
| X | Run 8-yd gain hitch. |
| Y | Block load 2 protection. |
| Z | Run circus route. vs. single high: run caddy. |
| QB | Coaching points: 7-step play-action. Make good fake.<br><br>Progression: 1. W 2. X Single-high: Z on the caddy. |

As you build your packages, you always want to take care of your quarterback. At Arkansas, for example, Ryan Mallett would actually do "load 3" with an "act 3" look, instead of popping his hips. He was the only quarterback I ever had who did that and it worked pretty well; he'd turn his back with the play-fake and it worked well.

124 (Power O/Devil/Crown)

124 (125) started life as play-action off of "power O," but now it basically involves 3 different run plays. One would be the original "24/25 O" play, which is the 1-back power play that everyone knows. The second one would be what we called "devil," which is the read or flow-power play, where the quarterback is going to read a defender, hand the ball off on a jet sweep, or keep it and run power himself (Figure 7-25). The third one is what we called "crown." That is the old guard-tackle counter play, but the quarterback is reading the backside end (Figure 7-26). We will talk more about those modern "read-option" type runs later on, but for now, let's take a look at these actions off the "power" concept (Figure 7-27).

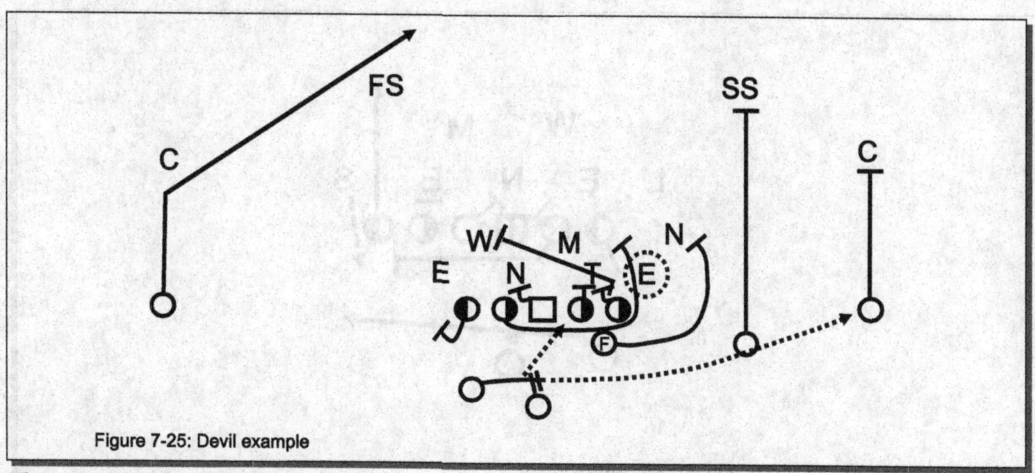

Figure 7-25: Devil example

**Play: 7-25**

| Pos: | Assignment: |
|---|---|
| W | Bypass. |
| X | Crossfield technique. |
| Z | Quick technique. |
| QB | Ride jet sweep and read EMLOS. If he closes, hand jet sweep to RB. If he stays upfield, run QB power. |

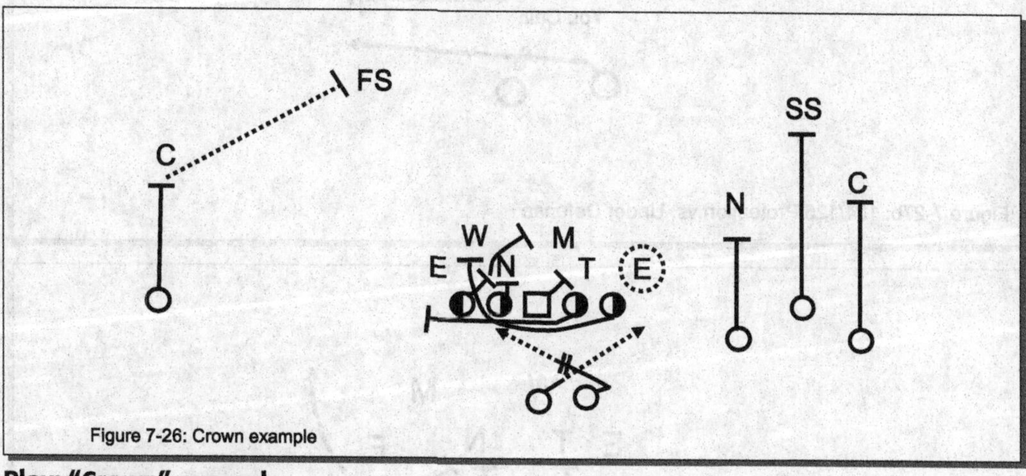

Figure 7-26: Crown example

**Play: "Crown" example**

| Pos: | Assignment: |
|---|---|
| QB | Lateral hop step to the call side. Must give six o'clock to the RB. Get your eyes to DE immediately. |
| W | Quick technique |
| X | Quick technique |
| Z | Quick technique |

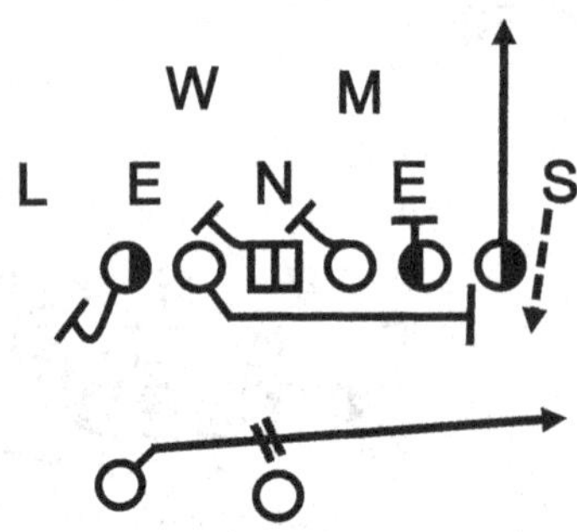

Figure 7-27a: 124/125 Protection vs. 30 Defense

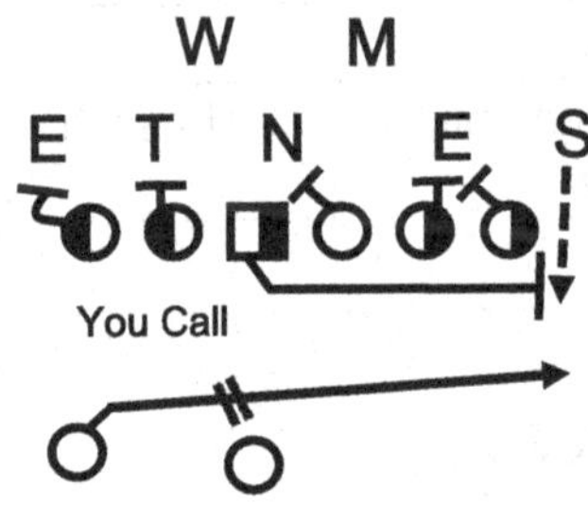

Figure 7-27b: 124/125 Protection vs. Under Defense

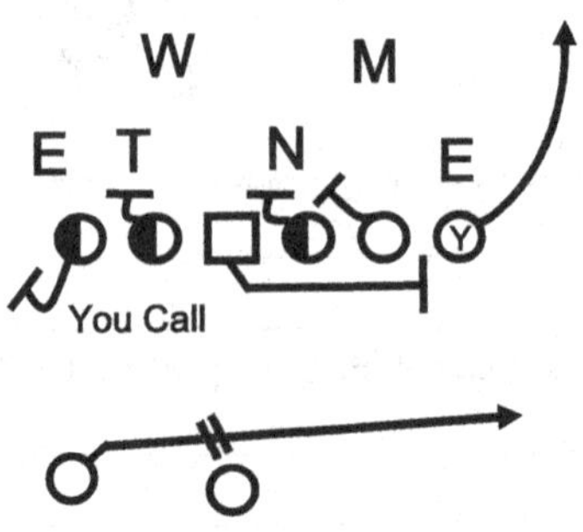

Figure 7-27c: 124/125 Protection vs. Over Defense

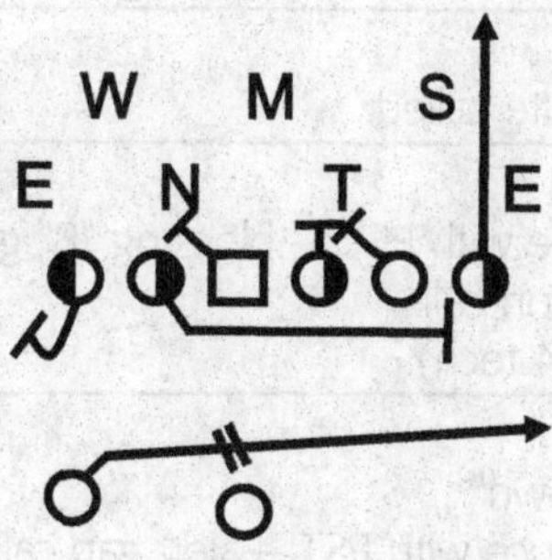

Figure 7-27d: 124/125 Protection vs. College 4-3 Defense

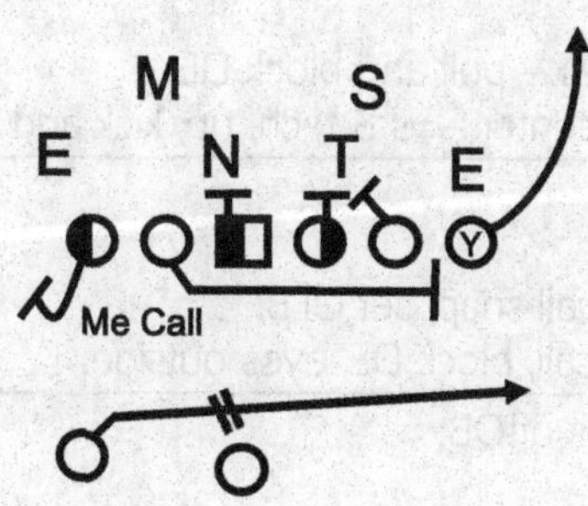

Figure 7-27e: 124/125 Protection vs. 4-2 Defense

## 20 Personnel

❑ 124 Alley

We tend to start this out of 20 personnel, where you would go "gun spread right" and your first play is "124/125 alley" (Figure 7-28). "124 alley" is really "double-seam," but with the "switch" by the two inside receivers. The slot receiver is going to slightly stem down inside. Most of the time someone's going to be playing him on an apex alignment, so he steps down like he's going to block that defender, pushes up over the top, and runs his seam to the opposite hash. Then, if you're in 20 personnel, the fullback comes out of the backfield and runs the seam down the near hash, hence the term "alley." It started out as a true four-verticals, but we ended up changing it to the boundary guy running a "caddy" and converting to a go route vs. a cloud corner. To the field, the outlet is the stretch route to the back to whom you fake.

**Play: 7-27**

| Pos: | Rules: |
|---|---|
| Y | 124-125 – (white):<br>Free release – run route called. |
| PST | B-gap:<br>1.(2-3) tech set deuce with PSG – blocking "B" gap defender.<br>2.Collect man-on vs "on call."<br>3.3 down – up kick (4 tech). |
| PSG | A-gap:<br>1.("zero"- tech) – "down"<br>2.(2-3 tech) – set deuce with PST – alert gap call from center.<br>3.Alert A gap run through to BSLB. |
| C | Backside A gap/pull:<br>1.Me/you call from BSG tell who will pull and block DE.<br>2."Me" call – BSG will pull. Center will block back on shade, 1, 2 tech.<br>3."You" call – center will pull and block DE.<br>4.3 down – spade vs "on" call. |
| BSG | Me/you call:<br>"Me call" (zero, 1, 2) – pull and block DE<br>(3) – "You call" to center – vs 3 tech, up, kick and block (3 tech). |
| BST | Backside DE:<br>1.Snap set DE<br>2.3 down vs. "on" call snap, set OLB.<br>3.3 down no "on" call, block DE, eyes outside. |
| R | Flat path across toes of QB:<br><br>Flash fake with QB, run stretch route – block DE if he gets up the field – hot off of $4^{th}$ rusher to your side |

There are two things that have to be handled in the protection. Number one, is to "sight adjust" off of 1-away from the call. So, if you're in "spread right," you run "124" and you're getting pressure from the left, X needs to sight adjust to slant or hitch (the same rules apply). And then if they bring outside pressure *to* the side of the call, our decision became to throw hot to the back that you fake to, as opposed to trying to tell him to block somebody off of the fake.

(Note: If we are under the center, then the back just has to make a fake off the traditional power run, and he is not part of the route. That is the only difference. We don't do it as much under the center.)

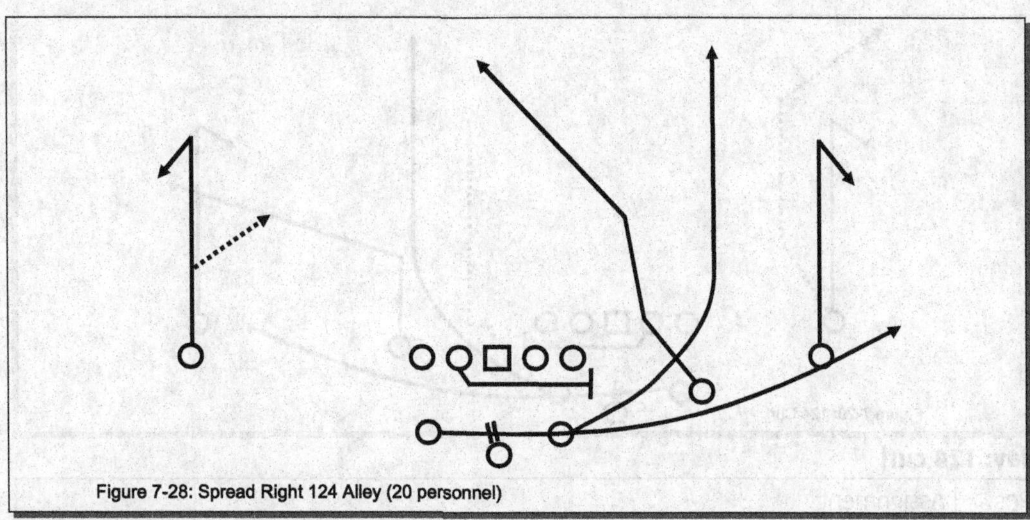
Figure 7-28: Spread Right 124 Alley (20 personnel)

**Play: 7-28**

| Pos: | Assignment: |
|---|---|
| R | Use counter footwork. Roll over the ball. Make a great fake. Alert to help WG with outside support. After protection is secure, run stretch. |
| X | Run caddy. Sit vs FS slant vs. cowboy, hitch |
| W | Run fence post. |
| Y | Run seam. |
| Z | Run caddy. |
| QB | Coaching points: 7-step play-action. |

❑ 124 Curl & Scout ("Cruise the Box")

As you're running that "crown" play, the fullback "cruises the box" and most of the time blocks the Mike linebacker. So, we wanted to give him a chance to take that same path as if he's going to "cruise the box" and then take it vertical, right down the middle. We carry two favorite plays where he could do that. One we called "124 curl" (Figure 7-29). The difference was that the Z receiver ran a 14-yard, "point-to-point" curl. We started W off on a diagonal but we ended up turning it into a wheel because you have the back replacing him with that stretch route. On the backside again, you still have the "caddy," with the necessary "sight" adjustment.

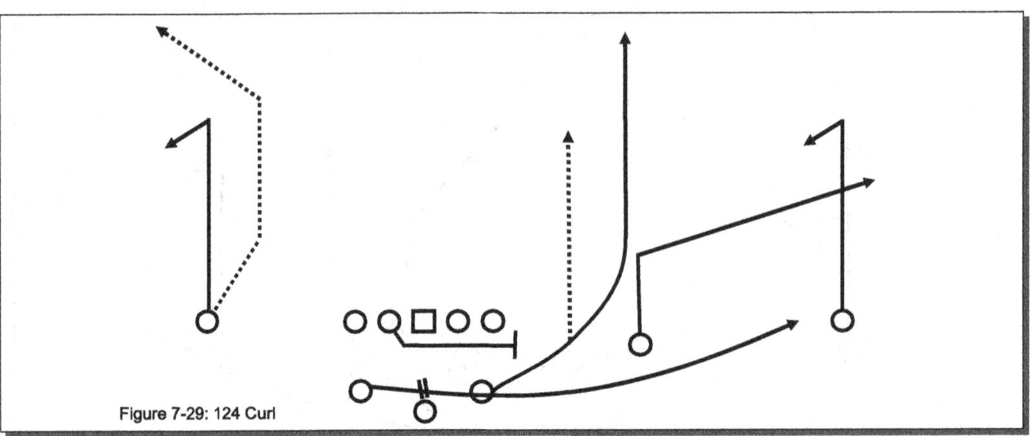
Figure 7-29: 124 Curl

**Play: 124 curl**

| Pos: | Assignment: |
|---|---|
| R | Use counter footwork. Roll over the ball. Make a great fake. Alert to help WG with outside support. After protection is secure, run diagonal. |
| F | Run circle route. |
| X | Run circus. |
| W | Run diagonal. |
| Z | Run 14-yd PP. Curl. |
| QB | |

The other way to get the fullback down the seam (or 2nd tailback, extra tight end—whoever has the ability to open his hips and pivot to make catches) is to call "124 scout (Figure 7-30). which gives you the "deeper blue read" to the field, with the seam route down the middle. On the backside, we ran "caddy" on it and we had to again be able to "sight adjust." While we didn't like exactly how it drew up on paper, you're still running your back on a "stretch" route after the fake. He would get the ball as the receiver was wide and be able to cut back up inside to get positive yards for you.

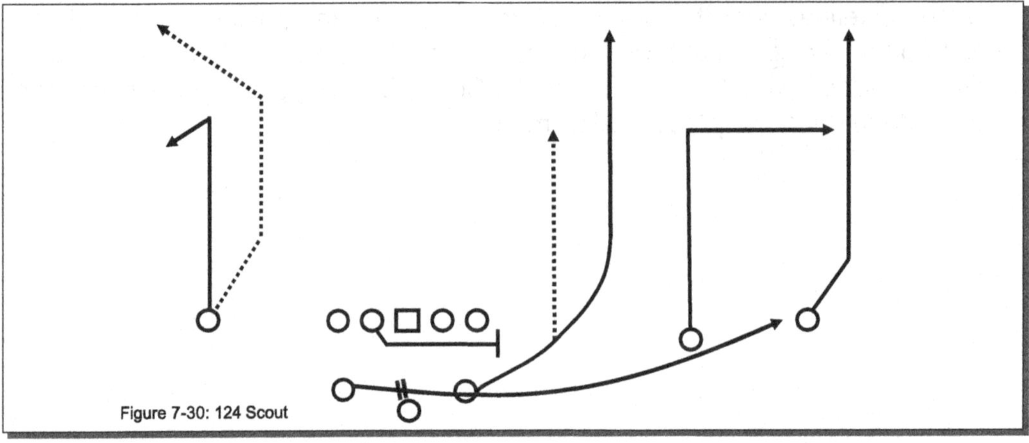
Figure 7-30: 124 Scout

**Play: 124 scout (gun)**

| Pos: | Assignment: |
|---|---|
| R | Use counter footwork. Roll over the ball. Make a great fake. Alert to help WG with outside support. After protection is secure, run diagonal. |
| F | Run circle route. |
| X | Run circus. |
| W | Run 10-yd out. |
| Z | Run go. Must outside release. |
| QB | |

(Note: Here again, we want everyone thinking in *concepts*. You can see how "scout" also works with the traditional power O from under center in Figure 7-31).

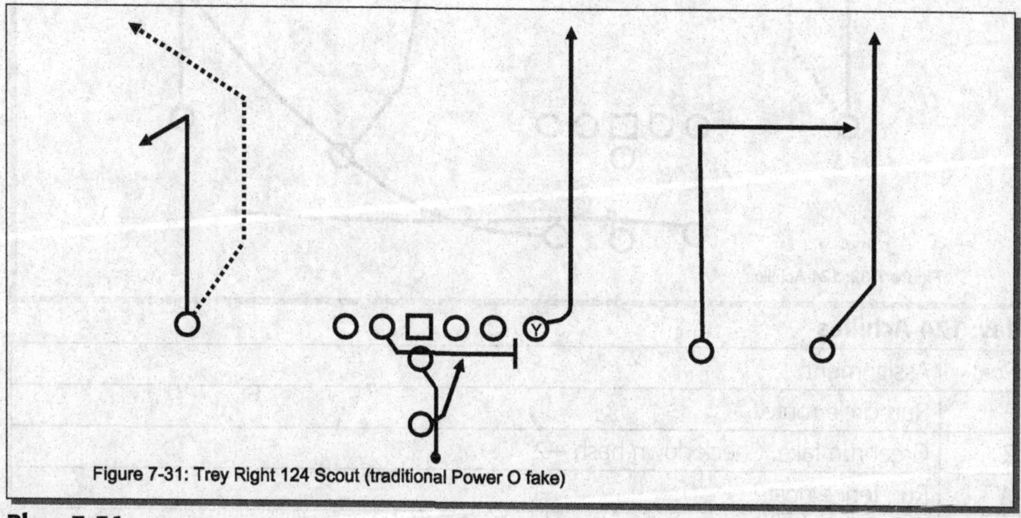


Figure 7-31: Trey Right 124 Scout (traditional Power O fake)

**Play: 7-31**

| Pos: | Assignment: |
|---|---|
| R | Use counter footwork. Roll over the ball. Make a great fake. Alert to help WG with outside support. |
| X | Run outside release go. |
| W | Run 10-yd out. |
| Y | Run seam. |
| Z | Run circus. |
| QB | Coaching points: 7-step play-action.<br>Reverse pivot. Make a good fake.<br><br>Progression: 1. X 2. W 3. Y |

❑ 124 Achilles & Hector

A good play to go for it deep as an "into" the boundary play, we called "124 Achilles." On "Achilles," the fullback is going to run a "rail" route down the outside of the numbers. The tailback makes a great fake and then checks down, two yards outside the hash. Then, the slot is going to run a "fence post," Z has a post, and X has as a "circus" route on the backside (Figure 7-32). You want to leave it as a "circus," because if you do get single-high, you have the ability to throw that "caddy" conversion and again there's the possibility of X having to "sight-adjust."

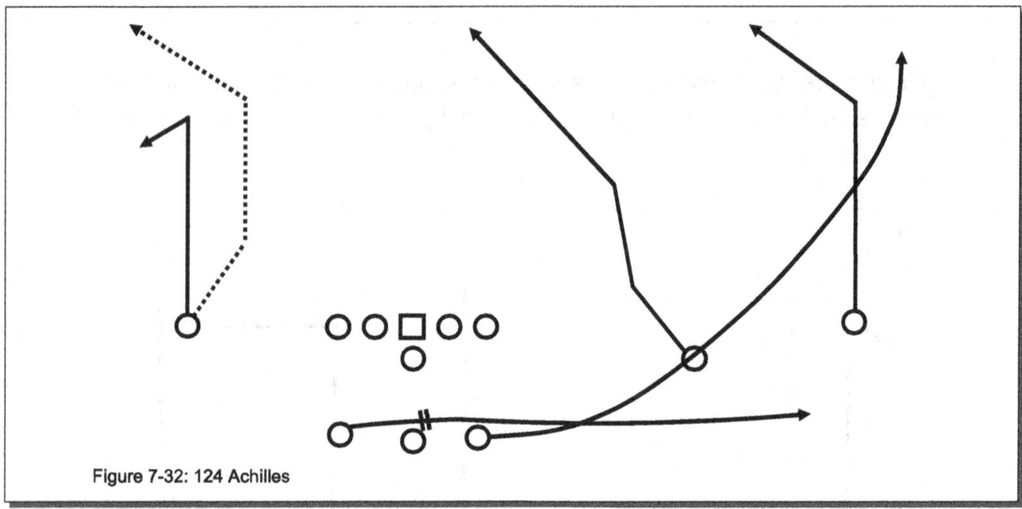

Figure 7-32: 124 Achilles

**Play: 124 Achilles**

| Pos: | Assignment: |
|---|---|
| F | Run circle route. |
| R | Great run fake. Check down hash +2 |
| W | Run fence post. |
| X | Run circus route.<br>1.High-caddy<br>2.High-4-5-1 corner |
| Z | Run post route. |
| QB | W-Z-F (outlet is R) |

My brother Paul likes to run this concept as "533 Right, Achilles" (Figure 7-33). The "500 series" keeps the tight end in on play-action, so this way he stayed in and blocked, and the back replaced the tight end's route. Sometimes, the back leaking out late can open up the wheel route, when the corner jumps the back late. Then, we called it "Hector," if we wanted to run the concept from something like "thunder slot" (Figure 7-34).

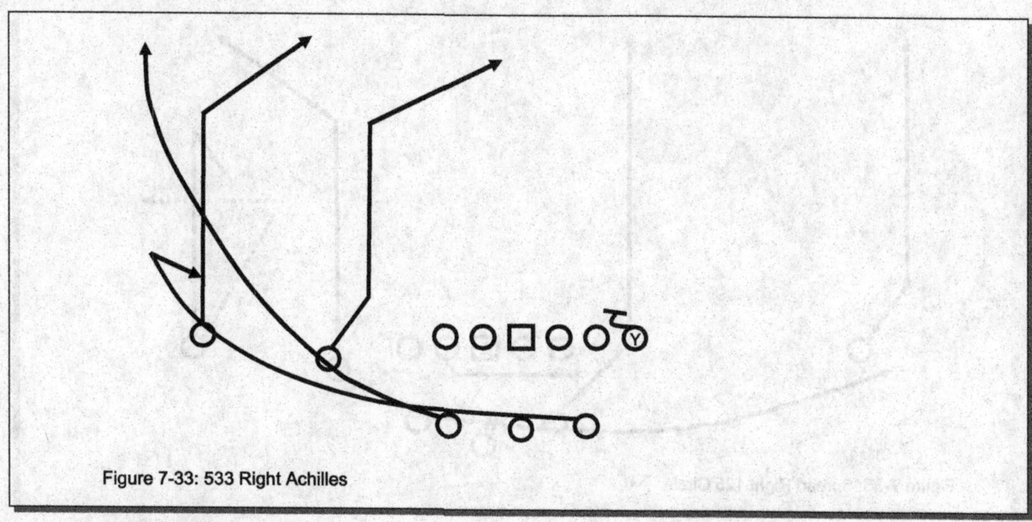


Figure 7-33: 533 Right Achilles

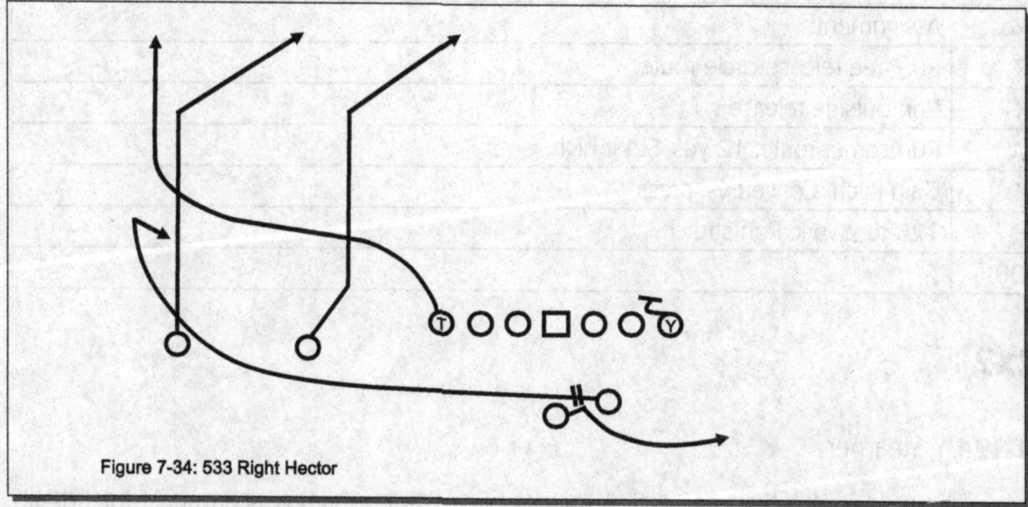


Figure 7-34: 533 Right Hector

❑ 125 Circle

The play we liked the best in this package was what we called "125 circle" (Figure 7-35). So, now the "R" is running the circle route, much like he does on "ram, W shallow." He wants to get outside the linebacker and pop his head as soon as he clears linebacker depth. This correlated really well to our read-counter play, because that's what R was doing, when you run "read-counter": he had that alley right there. You try to "look at the guy in the eyes and run right by him." X has an outside release go route. On the backside, we ended up running "China," so we had a "gain-hitch" (which converted to a "return" vs. press) and the W had a corner route.

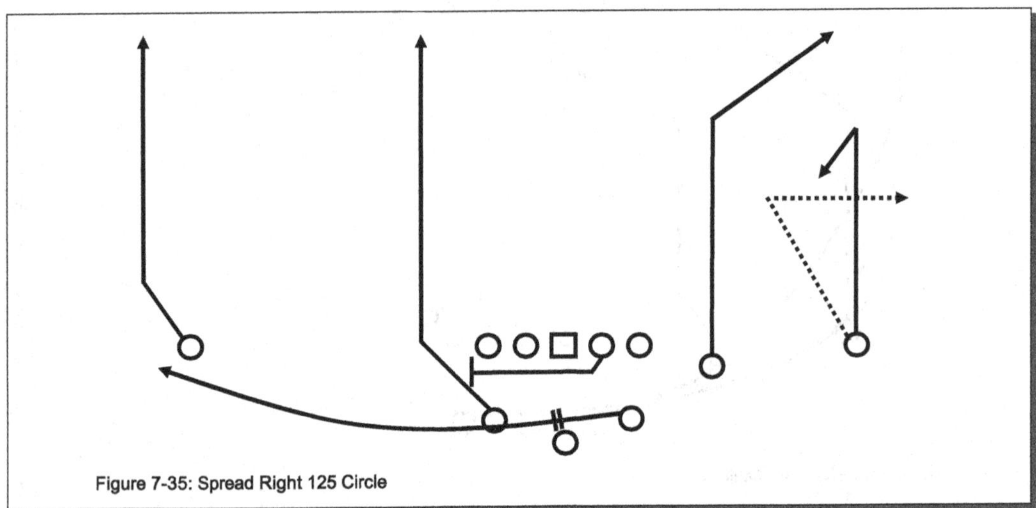

Figure 7-35: Spread Right 125 Circle

**Play: Spread right: 125 circle**

| Pos: | Assignment: |
|---|---|
| R | Run free release circle route. |
| X | Run outside release go. |
| W | Run corner route. 12 yds. Set it high. |
| Z | Gain hitch. Convert vs. press. |
| F | 125 footwork. Run stretch. |
| QB | |

## 2x2

❑ 124 Y Steamer

"Y steamer" is an effective play-action concept from 2x2, which was a part of the "devil" package. On this, we have the "steamer" concept to the side of the fake and the read route/under route on the backside. The W receiver has to be alert to pressure from his side and convert his route to a slant (Figure 7-36).

❑ 125 Green

We like the "green" concept. It carries over from our quick game installation and works nicely as a play-action pass from this 125 action, within the "devil" package. We would tend to call this off 125 and often hit the seam up the right hash (Figure 7-37).

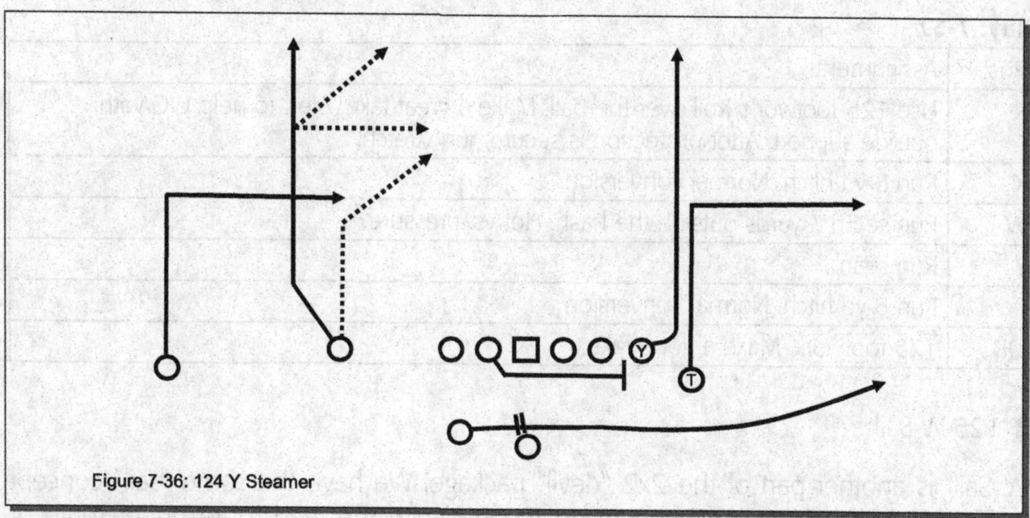

Figure 7-36: 124 Y Steamer

**Play: 7-36**

| Pos: | Assignment: |
|---|---|
| R | Use 124 footwork. Roll over the ball. Make a great fake. Alert to help WG with outside support. After protection is secure, run stretch. |
| X | Run 5-yd under. |
| Z | Run seam vs. 1 high. vs. 2 high run read route. vs hot slant. |
| Y | Run seam on your alignment. |
| T | Run speed out. |
| QB | 124 footwork. Make a good fake. |

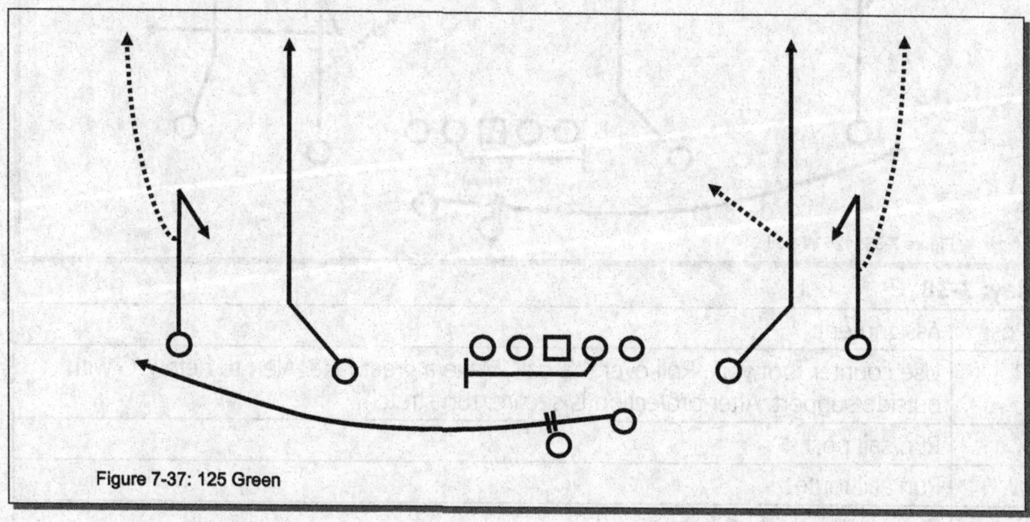
Figure 7-37: 125 Green

**Play: 7-37**

| Pos: | Assignment: |
|---|---|
| R | Use 125 footwork. Roll over the ball. Make a great fake. Alert to help WG with outside support. After protection is secure, run stretch. |
| X | Run 8-yd hitch. Normal conversion. |
| W | Run seam 3 yards outside the hash. Hot vs. pressure. |
| Y | Run seam. |
| Z | Run 8-yd hitch. Normal conversion |
| QB | 125 footwork. Make a good fake. |

❑ 125 W Sail

"W Sail" is another part of the 2x2 "devil" package. We have the same "sail" concept to the side of the fake and we could package it with the read route/under route or something like "Laker" on the backside. The W receiver has the same sail-route rules we talked about before, and since we will have already installed the play within the context of "act 3," the learning carries over and the players can execute this efficiently. We tended to call this concept from 125, rather than 124 (Figure 7-38).

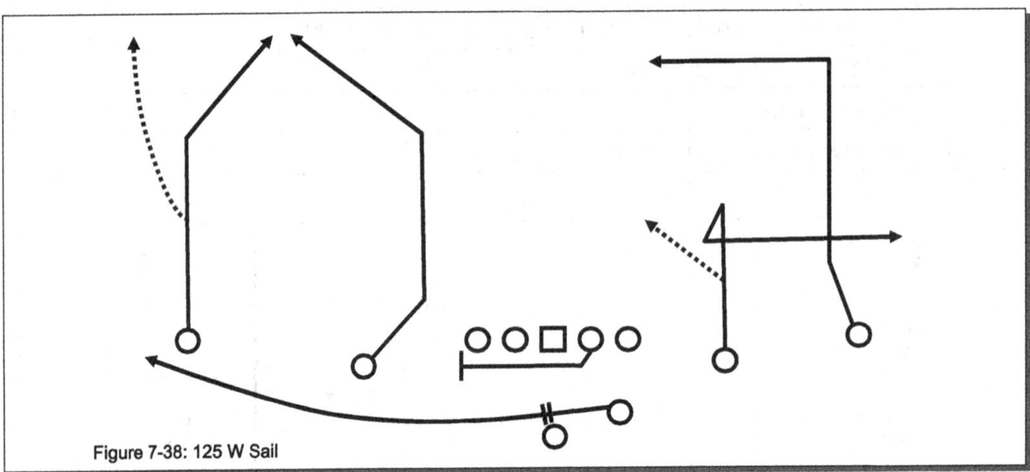

Figure 7-38: 125 W Sail

**Play: 7-38**

| Pos: | Assignment: |
|---|---|
| R | Use counter footwork. Roll over the ball. Make a great fake. Alert to help WG with outside support. After protection is secure, run stretch. |
| X | Run sail post. |
| W | Run sail route. |
| Y | Run pivot – slant vs. hot. |
| Z | Run in cut. |
| QB | 125 footwork. Make a good fake. 1. X 2. W 3. R vs. 4Q: 1. Z 2. Y |

❑ 125 Z Dream

When we get to a 2x2 set, one of the newer plays that we carried over from our dropback game which worked out really well was "125 Z dream." On this, we set the tight end into the boundary and ran "snag" to the field, with the fake away from him. Then, the tight end ran the corner route and Z stemmed down inside and went right up to seam, just inside of Y's alignment. It was consistently a really good play (Figure 7-39).

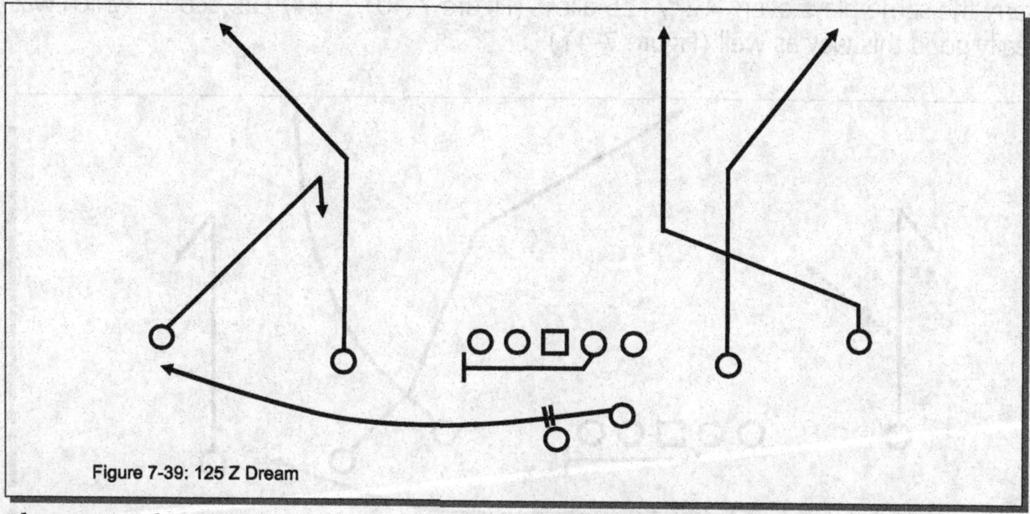
Figure 7-39: 125 Z Dream

**Play: 125 Z dream**

| Pos: | Assignment: |
|---|---|
| R | Use counter footwork. Roll over the ball. Make a great fake. Alert to help WG with outside support. After protection is secure, run stretch. |
| X | Run snag. |
| W | Run corner route 12 yds. |
| Y | Run corner route 12 yds. |
| Z | Run dream route 2-yd O/S hash. |
| QB | Vs. 2-high: Y-Z; vs. single-high: X-W-R |

You have to make sure the protection is right and then you need to have a "built-in" to Z off of that, if some pressure comes that way. There, his "drive-seam" route becomes a "snag," and he pops his eyes to look for the ball. That was really the only major coaching point you had to handle differently on that route.

## 3x1

❑ Alley, Scout

We also liked these a lot out of 3x1 or out of 11 personnel, either out of "flood" or "top" formation, depending on whether you wanted the tight end detached or attached. This way, it looks a little bit more like traditional 1-back power. We had the ability to carry the same plays over: "124/125 alley" (Figure 7-40), "124/125 scout," which was really good this way as well (Figure 7-41).

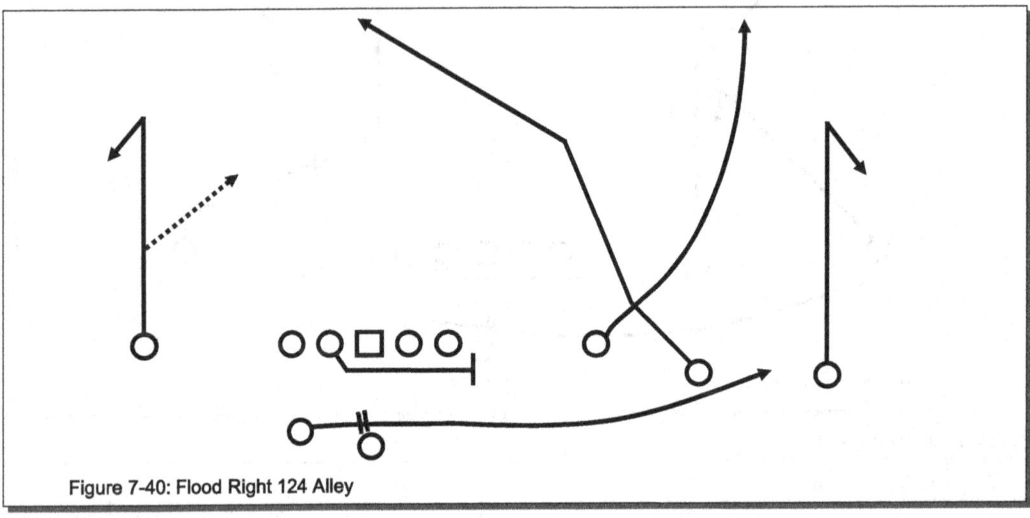

Figure 7-40: Flood Right 124 Alley

**Play: 7-40**

| Pos: | Assignment: |
|---|---|
| R | Use counter footwork. Roll over the ball. Make a great fake. Alert to help WG with outside support. After protection is secure, run stretch. |
| X | Run caddy. Sit vs FS: slant. vs. cowboy: hitch. |
| W | Run fence post. |
| Y | Run rail. |
| Z | Run caddy. |
| QB | Coaching points: 7-step play-action. Reverse pivot. Make a good fake.<br>1. W 2. Y 3. R Alert: 1-on-1 into the boundary |

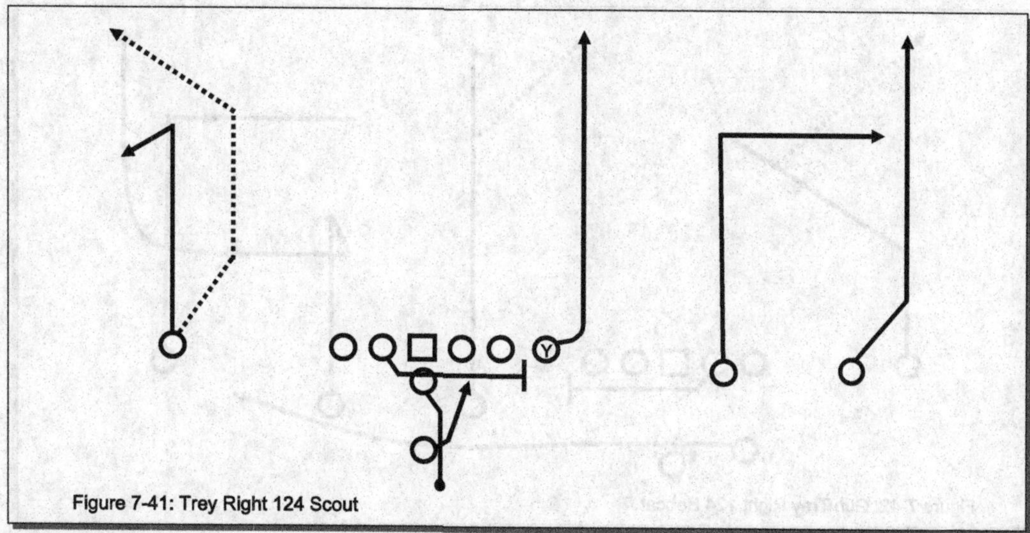

Figure 7-41: Trey Right 124 Scout

**Play: 7-41**

| Pos: | Assignment: |
|---|---|
| R | Use counter footwork. Roll over the ball. Make a great fake. Alert to help WG with outside support. After protection is secure, run diagonal. |
| X | Run outside release go. |
| W | Run 10-yd out. |
| Y | Run seam. |
| Z | Run circus. |
| QB | Coaching points: 7-step play-action. Reverse pivot. Make a good fake.<br><br>Progression: 1. X 2. W 3. Y |

❑ 124 Bobcat

We liked a play that we called "124 bobcat." On this, we're running a form of "falcon" to the field. Y would take the middle. If the middle is open, he'd stay right down it; if the middle was closed, he'd snap it across the face of the free safety. You have a "point-to-point" in-cut by X and your slot runs that pivot route, except that when he comes out of it, he then wheels down the sideline. (That was why we renamed it "bobcat." Sometimes, there wasn't anybody left in coverage out there.) Then, the back is the checkdown on the stretch route. We started out by saying "let's go ahead and run the sight-adjust for Z." Z runs a "slant to win," and if he doesn't get the ball, then he converts back outside to a corner route. Then, if it was a cloud coverage over there, he opens it up for Y down the middle (Figure 7-42). It looks like a lot on paper, but again the players are carrying over techniques they have already learned, so we are always able to install new ideas like this pretty easily.

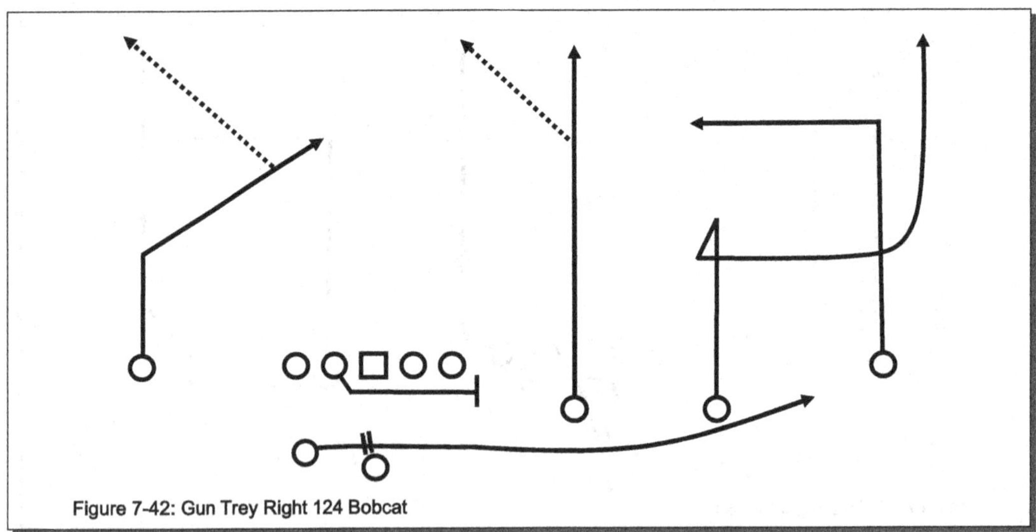
Figure 7-42: Gun Trey Right 124 Bobcat

**Play: Gun trey right: 124 bobcat**

| Pos: | Assignment: |
|---|---|
| R | 124 footwork. Run stretch. |
| X | Run 14-yd in-cut. |
| W | Run 5-yd hook then wheel. |
| Y | Run seam. |
| Z | Run slant to win. If you don't get ball, convert to corner route. |
| QB | Alert: Y down the middle. 1. X 2. W 3. R |

❑ 124 Bagel

We carried a fun play we called "124 bagel." This was a 3x1 "into" play, as part of a tempo package that we put together of "trey into" or "taxi into," where one of the run plays was 1-back power, on which you often add the "key" (or other bubble screen), where the quarterback can throw the ball right now to the wide receiver, if there's numbers. On this, what we were doing was building the action off the look of the 1-back power RPO, with a Z "key" (Figure 7-43). W releases as if he's going to block the corner, and then runs down the sideline. Y is on a seam. It's a really good tempo play. You have a chance to hit Y right now, popping him the ball on the seam. You also have an opportunity to hit W with the fake bubble screen.

> (Note: We have a play that we call "toast," where the back fakes the block and goes down the sideline. That's why we ended up naming this "bagel," so it would correlate to "toast" within the package.)

On the backside, we again carry the "circus" route, where we're influencing the backside safety or converting vs. 1-high. It's an "into" play, as well as and it's a "tempo

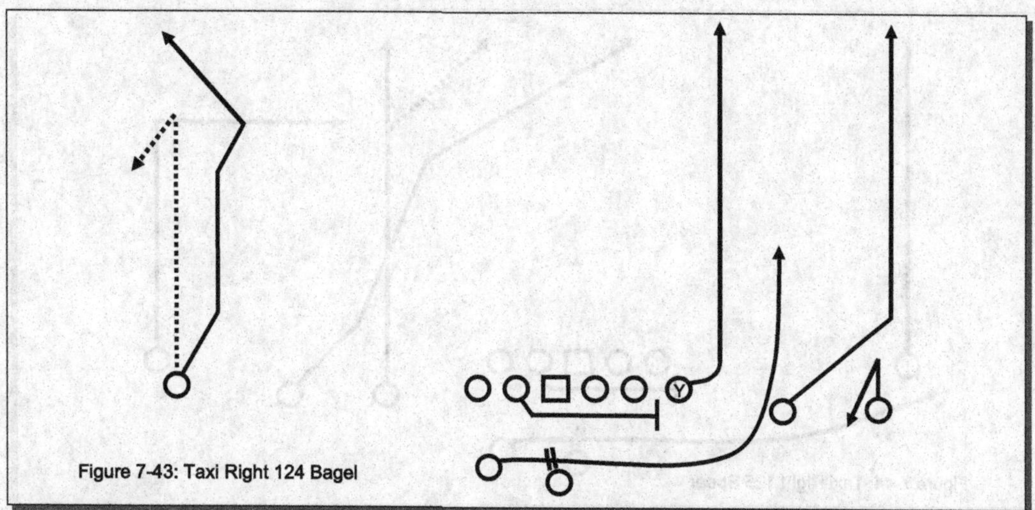

Figure 7-43: Taxi Right 124 Bagel

**Play: 7-43**

| Pos: | Assignment: |
|---|---|
| R | Use counter footwork. Roll over the ball. Make a great fake. Alert to help WG with outside support. After protection is secure, run alley route. |
| X | Run circus. |
| W | Choke release, fake block, and run go. |
| Y | Run arch seam. Stay tight. |
| Z | Run now. |
| QB | Progression:<br>1.Y or W to X<br>2.Outlet R |

play," as part of a "tempo-into" package, where these types of plays don't sit there or "stand alone" by themselves. Rather, they are *packaged* with the runs that we think are really good for us in any given season.

❑ 125 Spear

To fake the run weak (away from the 3x1), we had "125 spear," where the Y has the seam down the middle, and then W is going to stem down inside, push up, and run a deep cross or "spear" route. X has a "go" route, so he's got to climb and run right over the top of any off-corner. Behind the spear route for W is an in-cut by the Z, and the back runs the stretch (Figure 7-44). It's a really a good way to run something like "W over," while occupying a "trio" safety, with Y running right down the middle. It's a very difficult play to defend and very good against "quarters" or "quarter-quarter-half," when they're running that "trio" (3 over 2) to the 3-receiver side. It's a kind of "trio beater," where W gets open.

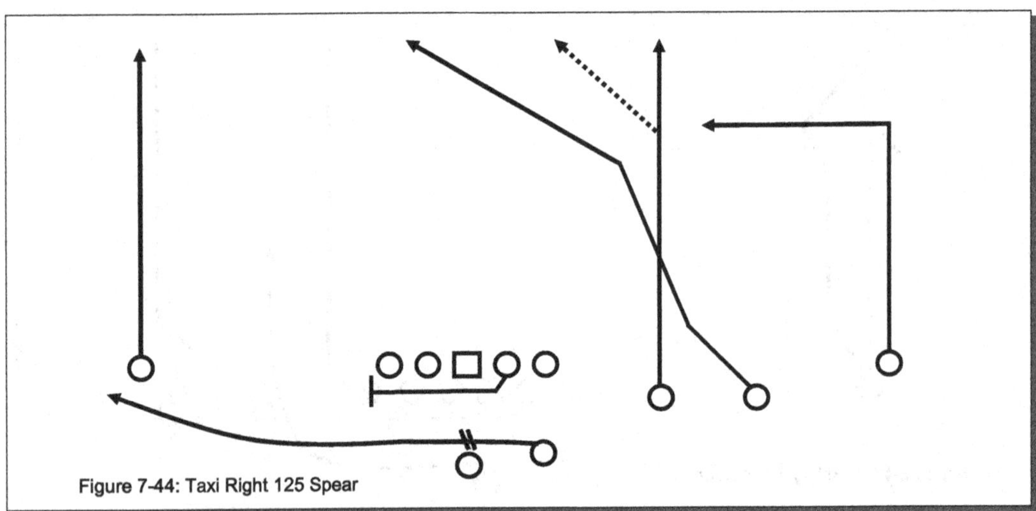
Figure 7-44: Taxi Right 125 Spear

**Play: Gun taxi right: 125 spear**

| Pos: | Assignment: |
|---|---|
| R | 125 footwork. Run stretch. |
| X | Run fade. Outside release. |
| W | Run spear 18-22 yds. |
| Y | Run seam. |
| Z | Run 14-yd in-cut. |
| QB | |

# Trips

❑ 524 Green

When we move on to the "trips" formation, the first thing we like is the ability to say "okay, we're going to protect the quarterback," we won't send the tight end out. We have the ability to call "524" and "525" to throw deep crossers and things like that, where the "500" series is play-action with the tight end staying home in protection.

We get into gun and first run "524 green" (Figure 7-45) which is where you have two seams. A seam by the Z receiver, where he's going to snap it across the single-high safety's face or take the middle vs. cover 2, and a seam by the W receiver, where he's going to get the cleanest release and be two yards outside the hash, pop his eyes, look for the ball, and then run a locked-hitch on the outside. The timing of when you get the ball to #3 (the Z receiver) on that is really what's important. It's not a deep throw, it's a 12-to-15 yard throw that hits him right on the helmet.

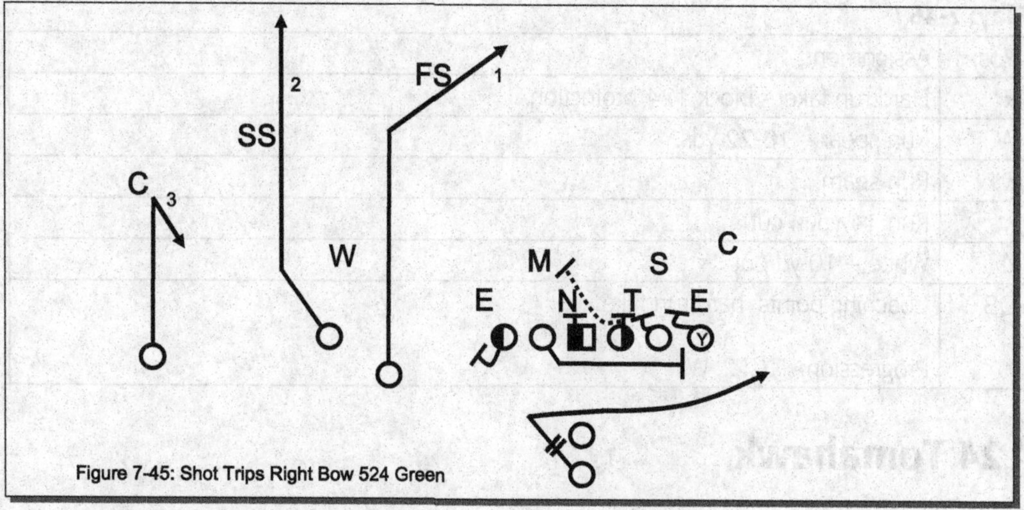

Figure 7-45: Shot Trips Right Bow 524 Green

(Note: The #1 receiver needs to run a clean route and trust the play, because sometimes we've called this, looked downfield, and then thrown the hitch really late out into the flat, caught the ball, and run for 20 yards, because the corner is working way back inside to #2.)

❑ 124 Spear

We carry over the "spear" plays in this formation. When you run "124 spear" out of the "trips" formation (Figure 7-46), the fake is strong to the tight end side. The tight end runs the 10-yard out, Z has the middle, and W has the spear route again right behind it. When you're getting single-high, this is a great way to affect that boundary corner and get a deep route over the top of him for a chunk play.

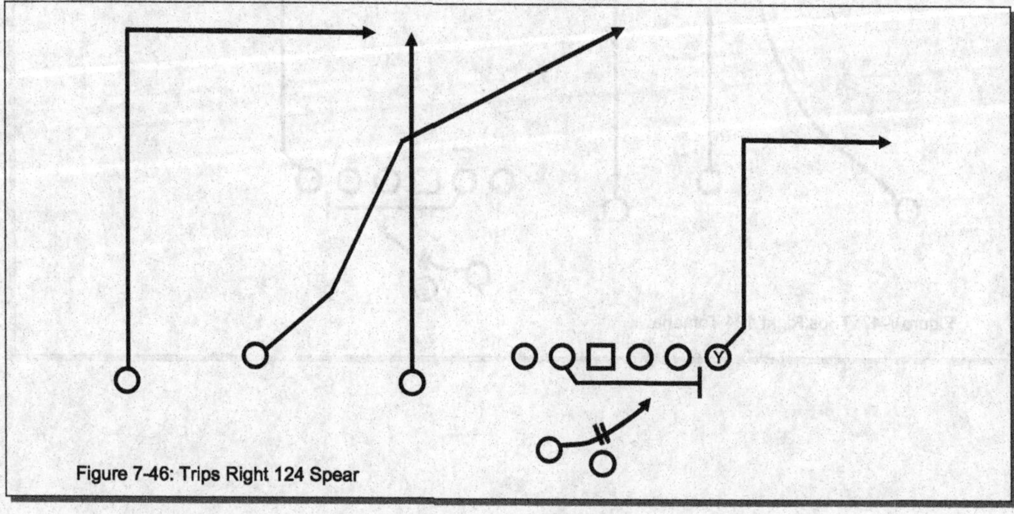

Figure 7-46: Trips Right 124 Spear

**Play: 7-46**

| Pos: | Assignment: |
|---|---|
| R | Hard run fake – block 124 protection. |
| W | Run spear – 18-22 yds. |
| Z | Run seam. |
| X | Run 14-yd in cut. |
| Y | White – 10-yd out |
| QB | Coaching points: hard run fake.<br><br>Progression: 1. Z 2. W |

## 124 Tomahawk

One last play that we like out of the "trips" formation off of the 124/125 package was the "tomahawk" concept. (We will have already installed tomahawk, so like most of these concepts, it isn't something new to the players.) Y is going to run the 10-yard out, and Z is going to take the middle. W is going to run down the seam to a depth of 15-to-17 yards and roll out of it to a deep-out. X is going to run a delay-seam down behind W and then up the hash. When W breaks outside, the corner has to honor it, so you have a chance to get X open in the seam (Figure 7-47). This is great around the 25-yard line, right on the edge of field goal range.

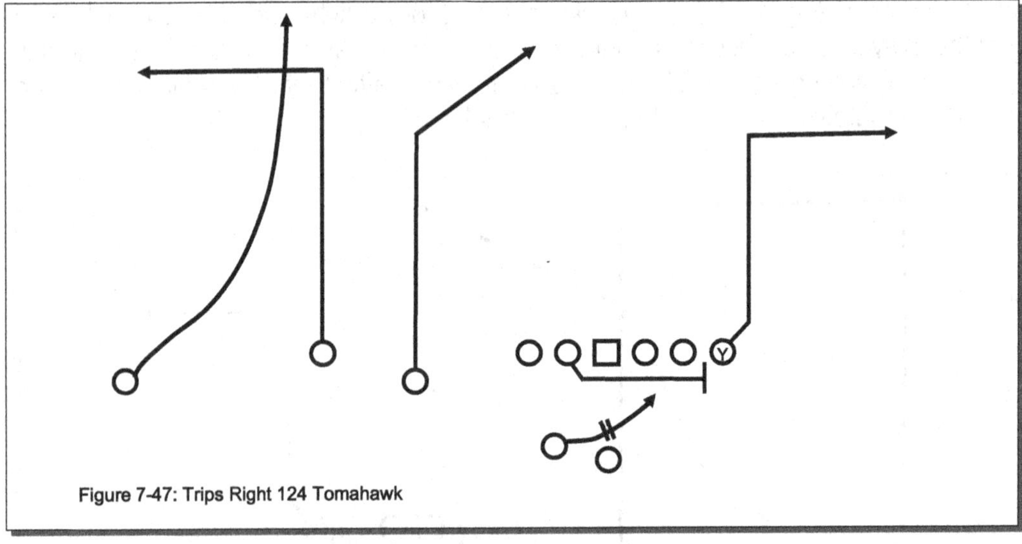

Figure 7-47: Trips Right 124 Tomahawk

**Play: 7-47**

| Pos: | Assignment: |
|---|---|
| R | Hard run fake – block 124 protection. |
| W | Run speed out – 15-17 yards deep |
| Z | Run post. |
| X | Run delay seam route. |
| Y | White – 10-yd out. |
| QB | Coaching points: hard run fake.<br><br>Progression: 1. Z 2. W Alert: Y with no flat defender. |

## Final Thoughts About 100 Series

These can go on for as far as your creativity takes you and your staff, but the main thing about play-action is that you want to be aggressive and you want to take shots down the field. It's a great way to get big plays. However, your quarterback has to give you the freedom to call them, knowing that he's going to get you out of a bad look vs. pressure and get into the right play. Once again, he needs to understand the appropriate alerts to get out of a play-action call when pressure shows up (often times, that's the corresponding run play or a run play the other direction, but, as a coach, you need to be clear with him about what you want done).

## 300 Series: Nakeds & Bootlegs

We take a lot of pride in our bootleg and naked game. We probably spend more time coaching nakeds than anybody else. With all the no-huddle and "run-pass option" that are popular today, teams seem to have gotten away from bootlegs, but it's still and will always be great football. We really believe in it, and to be a great bootleg team requires the time on task. You can really protect your best running plays and then get a lot of big plays down the field from the passes off them.

The timing of when you call these is important. One of the things you always look at when you're breaking down films is if you get guys who are reaching for that tackle's hip. When I start to see that—on film or during the game—then I'm going to run a bunch of "naked." We really do want to be the "best bootleg team in America" and we work hard to make that happen!

❑ Ball Handling Technique

First, some coaching points about ball handling. When we teach the running back the ball fake, we say "roll over the ball, rock the baby, and then run to the sideline if you don't get tackled, and then pump your outside arm." That's why I don't like the quarterback to stick the ball out there, just an empty hand. The quarterback slides the ball straight up and down to his stomach, which is another big part of this: as the quarterback, I go "hand and head in the hole" and the ball is secured in my "third hand." My "elbow is in," so that defensive end can't see the ball.

When we practice it, I actually stand right there, making sure they're hiding the ball. Then, when the quarterback fakes with his right hand, he reaches out and then slides his left hand back into his stomach with the ball, making that fake with "hand and head in the hole," elbow in so that defensive end can't see it and the strings are right there when he comes out of the fake. Right as I come out of it, I can grab the strings. A lot of people want to just "put the ball outside and back in," but the problem is that the ball can get knocked loose and also the quarterback's other arm just drops down and gives it away that it's not a handoff.

❑ Naked QB Drill

This is a drill that we do for naked and sprintout with the quarterback. What you do is you move, you get your shoulders square, you throw the ball, and you follow the ball. Typically, a righty will throw off his *right* foot, with the *left* foot out. Then, when you move to your left, you do the same thing: throw off your *right* foot, *left* foot out, and follow the ball.

But when there's big guys chasing you, you're sometimes not able to square your shoulders and do that. To practice that, we take the quarterbacks and put them 10-yards apart, and they run across the field on the line. Then, they're going to stay running on that line but throw the ball off their right foot. And I want to *hit the helmet* with the ball. Then, coming back across the field, we will put them 15 yards apart, because on those nakeds, the crosser is always somewhere between 10-and-15 yards away. This really helps the quarterbacks to deliver the ball accurately, even if they can't get their feet perfectly set.

Like we said earlier, with a natural thrower, his feet don't have to be set. Some other guys just can't make that "fade away jump shot," but I think that's the question about "can you teach a guy touch?" It's here with the "naked drill," with our "fade drill," and with what we do in our warm-up progression that can really help.

❑ Naked Sled Drill

If you want to be really good at nakeds, you should also do the "naked sled drill." We take the O-line, they offset, and then they all hit the sled. We have either a receiver or tight end run a "late shoot," another receiver or tight end running the drag, the quarterback making the fake, and the running back "rolling over the ball, 'rocking the baby,' and then running to the sideline if you don't get attacked." So, we coach every position on all those things. The day we put naked in, we're for sure going to run that "quarterback drill" and "naked sled drill," and then we install the naked, with the *teaching progression* of the play. The following takes a look at some of them.

## Base Naked

We use the term "bootleg" if we're pulling guards and say "naked" if nobody is pulling. Then from there, we'll have additional terms to code various routes and packages. Regardless of the way it's called, the offensive line needs to fire off with "low hats," sell the corresponding run play, and then recoil into protection. We don't believe you can just have the o-line turn and run like they're elephants on parade and expect to fool anyone that way, it takes a lot of work to do this effectively!

The first concept we install is what we call "base naked." This started out as the "300 series," where we called this "339 right," but we now also use the code word "blaze." We'd it "blaze 39 right/38 left" or "blaze 33 right/32 left."

> (Note: The difference between "blaze 38/39" and "blaze 32/33" is that the playside guard pulls to the backside on "blaze 33," so it's what we call "bootleg," as opposed to "naked.")

The foundation routes would be what we call a "late shoot," a drag, a comeback, and a backside post. To the side of the bootleg, we want to run a "late shoot" with that tight end. He drives down on the defensive end, and then releases late to a target of four yards at the sideline. Ideally, we catch that defensive end in an inside leverage, so we can slam down on him, secure the edge for the quarterback to break contain, and then shoot out late to the flat. This could be "thunder right: blaze 39 right" or something like "wing right, T fly: blaze 38 left" (Figure 7-48). Either way, it's the same "base naked" concept and the quarterback should always read it: "late-shoot, drag, comeback, run."

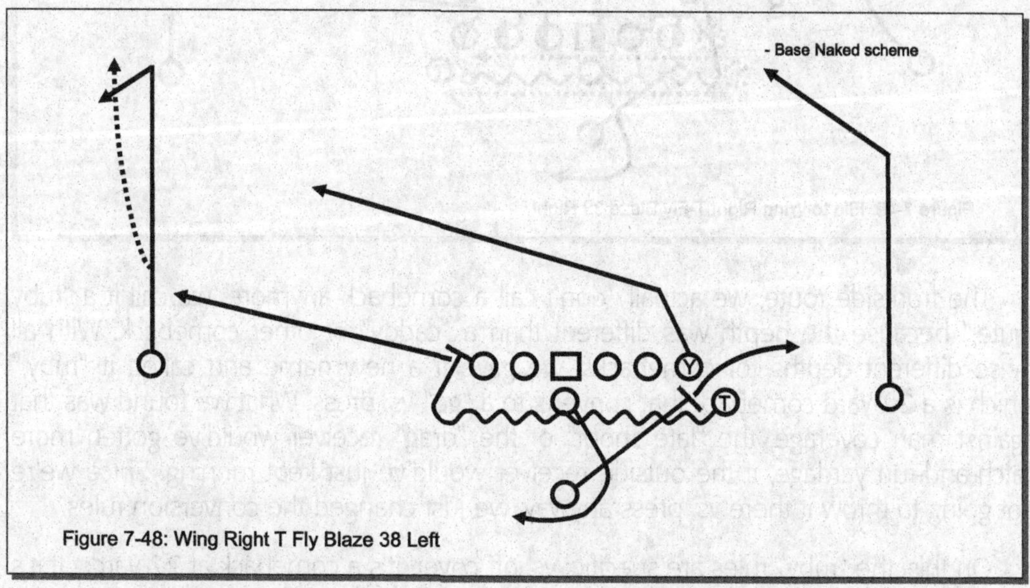

Figure 7-48: Wing Right T Fly Blaze 38 Left

**Play: Trips right, T fly: blaze 38 left ("base naked")**

| Pos: | Assignment: |
|---|---|
| QB | |
| Y | Run drag 10-12 yds. |
| X | Run ruby route 22 yds. |
| R | Good fake. Roll over the ball. |
| Z | Run post. |
| T | Run late shoot. |

When you create a game plan though, you often need to package the "base naked" concept in specific ways, in order to get the defensive end into an alignment that gives us the best leverage to run this. For example, in one game, we went "flip to wing right, T fly: blaze 39 right" (Figure 7-49) and we had to do all that to "make him an 8 technique." We knew they'd shift their front to that particular motion, so that's how we packaged it. We refuse to let the defense take us out of what we want to do!

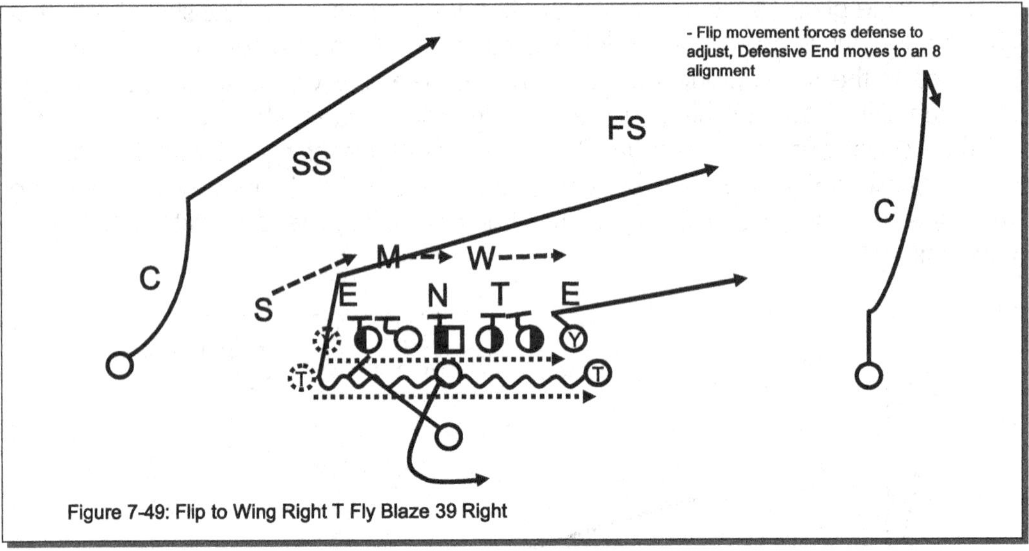

Figure 7-49: Flip to Wing Right T Fly Blaze 39 Right

The frontside route, we actually don't call a comeback anymore, we call it a "ruby route," because the depth was different than a "caddy" or other comeback. With all these different depths for comebacks, we gave it a new name and called it "ruby," which is a 22-yard comeback that converts to a "go" vs. press. What we found was that against man coverage, the "late shoot" or the "drag" receiver would've gotten more catch-and-run yardage, if the outside receiver would've just kept running. Since we're not going to throw it there vs. press anyway, we just changed the conversion rules.

On this, the "ruby" rules are specific: vs. off cover, it's a comeback at 22 yards. If it's a jam corner, he widens on the sideline, throttles down, and just kind of sits there at

15 yards. Then vs. press, he runs a "go." So, it's a "ruby route" (for "read comeback") to include all those rules and to get him at the precise depth needed to maximize spacing and create room for yardage after the catch.

The "drag" route needs to take a "release angle," and adjust to the near hip of the inside linebacker. Then, he needs to be "12-yards at the opposite hash." We used to say "10-yards at the opposite tight end," but sometimes he'd get too shallow. The word choice again for that route is "release at the near hip of the near inside linebacker," because the ball fake will cause that linebacker to step up. We want him to start on that angle (not run upfield) and then come across. Then, if we're doing a good job at all with our fake, the linebacker is going to step up and disappear. If there's a "quarters" safety and he jumps the "late shoot," the drag runner can take it over the top. But if he runs a good route, he's going right at that hip and then he gets to 10-or-12 yards, where he catches it near the opposite hash.

## Quarterback Technique and Responsibility on Nakeds

The quarterback needs to get his head around quickly after the fake. If it's a naked to the right (for a right-handed quarterback) and the d-end shows up in your face, what you want to do is back away and throw it to the "late shoot." What this means is, that after the fake and that guy shows up, I want to "back away" from him to get some separation, so I can either go over the top or sidearm it. I want to keep running in the same direction I started.

If it's a naked to the left and he shows up right away, I want to just "pop my feet and the throw the drag." Then, if he's not open, throw it at his feet. If you try to "back away," while going to the left, you can't get the ball out of your hand and you might also end up taking an awkward hit.

It's imperative that the quarterback understands when to get us out of a bad look. If they blitz into it, you can't just run a bootleg into pressure, which will get yourself killed. The quarterback has to understand to change the play. Usually, it's the corresponding run play going the other direction, away from that pressure, but you can plan other runs, depending on what you're best at or what a particular game plan calls for. When you can trust the quarterback with that, you can really dial these up and build up a great package of them!

## Sneak

The second naked concept we like to install is called "sneak." The route spacing is the same, but in this instance we want to "sneak" the flat receiver across from the other side of the formation. This can again be your second tight end, but this is also effective with a second back, if you have a fullback with good hands. We also want to introduce these off our various other run schemes besides outside zone, so the players are constantly thinking in *concepts*.

For example, we might script "strong right: burn 38 left, F sneak," where "burn" (rather than "blaze") is the code word for a toss fake (Figure 7-50). The fullback would then "sneak" to the opposite flat and the other routes remain the same as "base naked." In 12 personnel, we might draw this up as "shot wing right: blaze 12 left, T sneak" off our pistol "read-option" look (Figure 7-51). Different run fake, but the same *concept*. If you challenge the players like this from the outset, they really do comprehend things more quickly and thoroughly, which allows you to carry more offense.

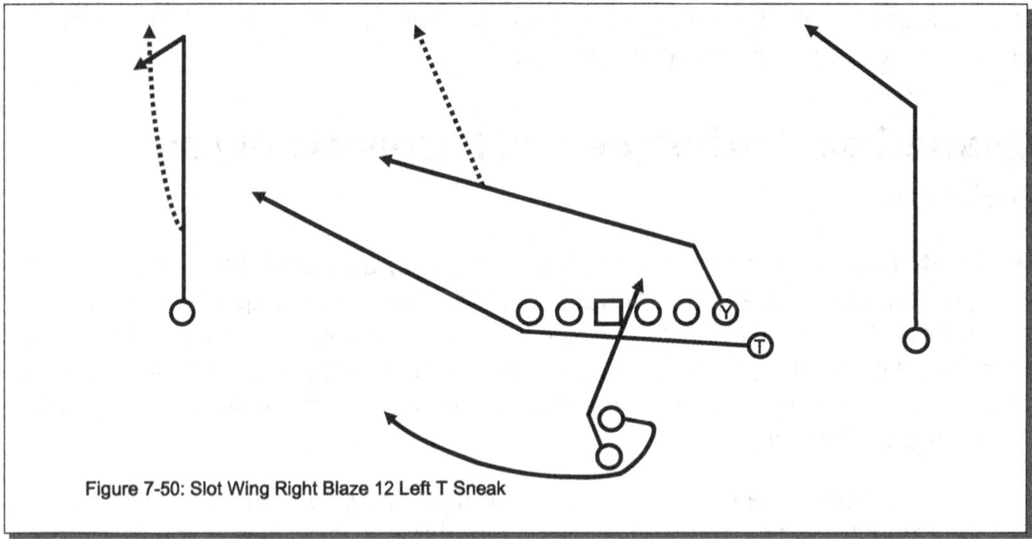

Figure 7-50: Slot Wing Right Blaze 12 Left T Sneak

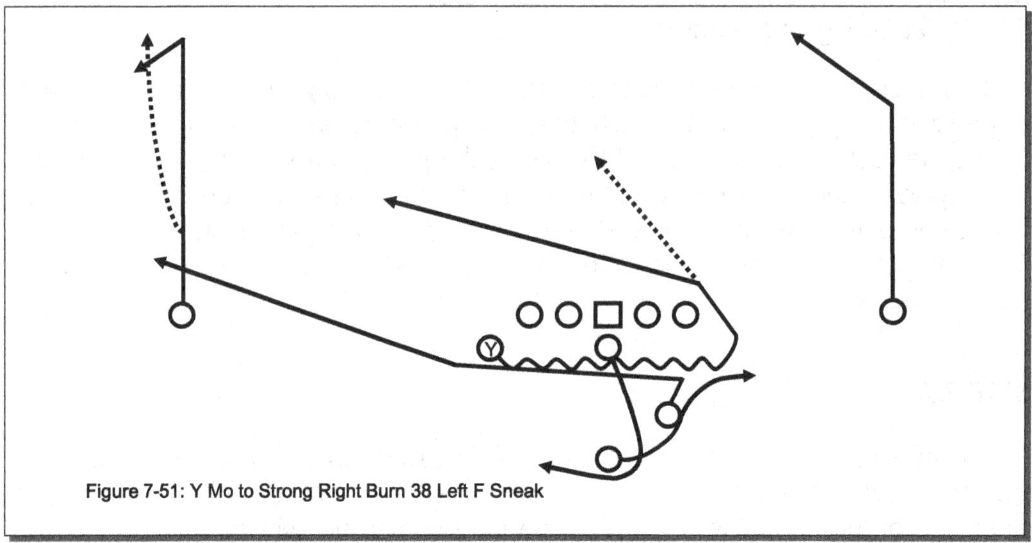

Figure 7-51: Y Mo to Strong Right Burn 38 Left F Sneak

**Play: Strong right: burn 38 left, F sneak**

| Pos: | Assignment: |
|---|---|
| Z | Run post. |
| X | Run ruby route 22 yds. |
| Y | Run drag 10-12 yds. |
| R | Burn 38 fake. |
| F | Run sneak route. |

# Y Delay

The third naked concept we like to install is called "Y delay." We first set this up toward the 3x1, instead of 2x2. On this, #1 has a post, #2 knows to run a wheel route and the #3 has the "late shoot." Now, the singled receiver runs the "drag" rather than backside post and he also has to know he can't take it over the top on "Y delay," because we have a post route working on the frontside over there. That really takes "drill work" to get the receivers to understand all the spacing.

"Wing right: blaze 39 right, Y delay" (Figure 7-52) has always been a part of what we do. We will also script shifts and motions, such as "*flip* to wing right" (Figure 7-53). We might change the run action to something like "blaze 23 right, Y delay," off our "K22/23" tackle-pull run. There, the quarterback and running back know they run "F" footwork, where the quarterback will "reverse pivot."

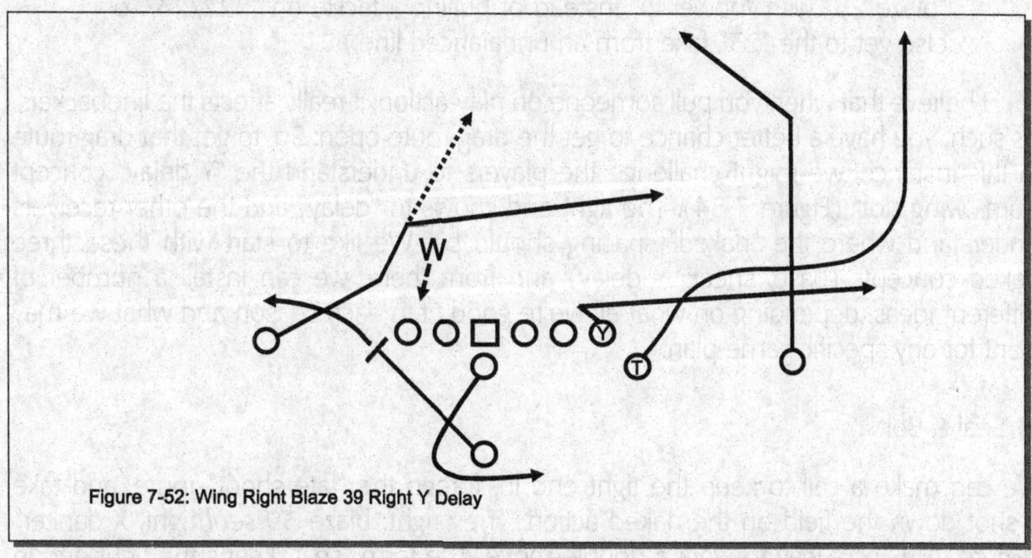

Figure 7-52: Wing Right Blaze 39 Right Y Delay

**Play: Wing right: blaze 39 right, Y delay**

| Pos: | Assignment: |
|---|---|
| QB | Peek at wheel – 1. late shoot 2. crosser 3. run |
| Y | Run late shoot. |
| X | Drag |
| R | Blaze 39 roll over the ball and carry out fake. |
| Z | Run post. |
| T | Run wheel route. |

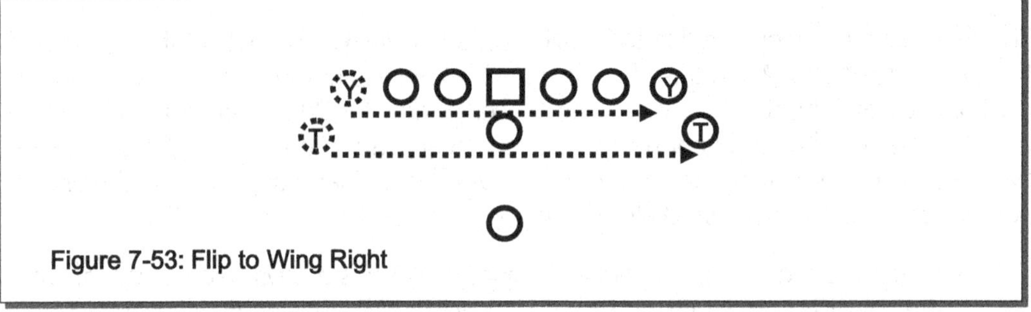

Figure 7-53: Flip to Wing Right

(Note: Anytime the quarterback "reverse-pivots," it's a better fake on nakeds. The pulling parts really affect the linebackers as well. If a defense covers up that tackle though, it's better to game plan these off "blaze 25" with "power O" instead of pulling a tackle on "K22/23," or else get to the "23" fake from an unbalanced line.)

I believe that when you pull someone on play-action, it really affects the linebackers. As such, you have a better chance to get the drag route open. So, to get that drag route in this instance, we might challenge the players to understand the "Y delay" concept from "wing slot" (Figure 7-54). The tight end knows to "delay" and the other receivers understand where the "naked" spacing should be. We like to start with these three naked concepts (base, sneak, Y delay) and from there, we can install a number of different ideas, depending on what all we're good at in each season and what we may want for any specific game plan.

❑ Seal & Bolt

We can make a call to keep the tight end in, forego the "late shoot" route, and take a shot down the field on the naked action. "Trey right: blaze 39 *seal* right, X dancer" (Figure 7-55) is a way to work a double-move. The term "seal" keeps the tight end in and provides more protection to work the ball deep downfield. We can modify this for a tight end who can really run, such as "wing right: seal 37 right, dog" (Figure 7-56). On this, the T replaces the seal responsibility, so Y can run the drag and go route.

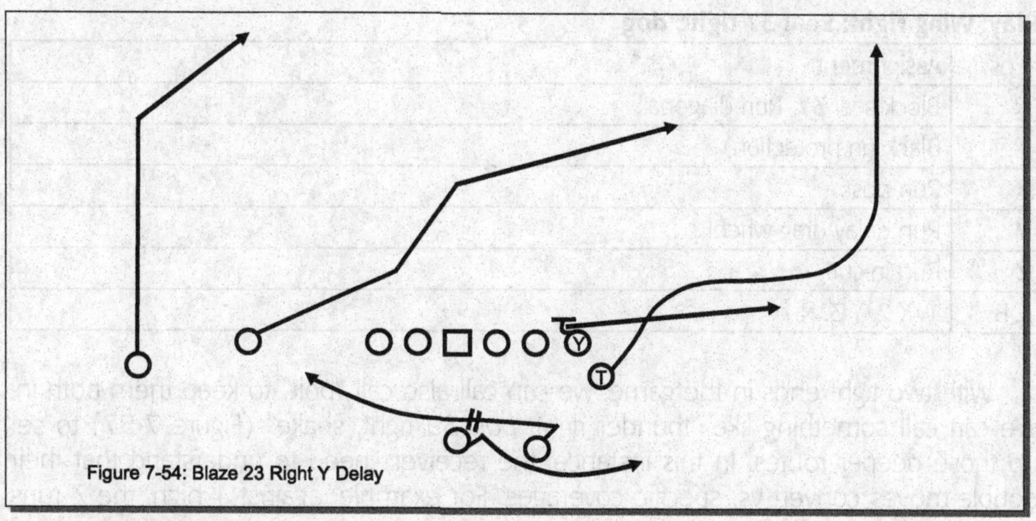

Figure 7-54: Blaze 23 Right Y Delay

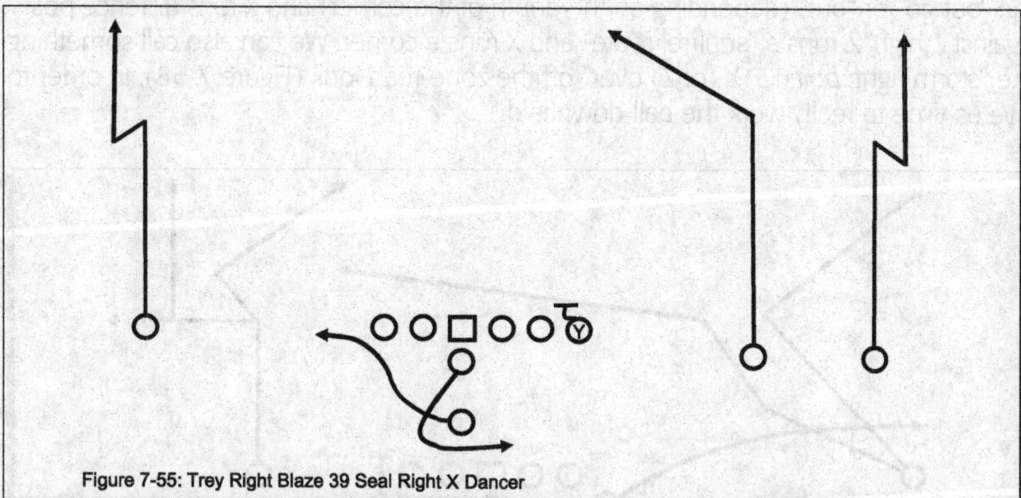

Figure 7-55: Trey Right Blaze 39 Seal Right X Dancer

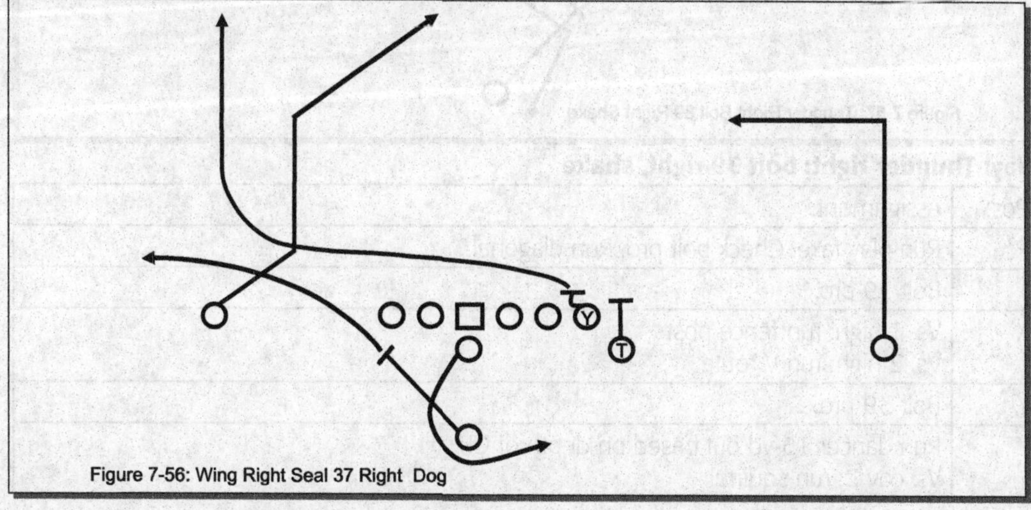

Figure 7-56: Wing Right Seal 37 Right Dog

**Play: Wing right: Seal 37 right, dog**

| Pos: | Assignment: |
|---|---|
| R | Block seal 37. Run diagonal. |
| T | Black (in protection) |
| X | Run post. |
| Y | Run delay drag wheel |
| Z | Run in-cut. |
| QB | 1. X 2. Y 3. R |

With two tight ends in the game, we can call also call "bolt" to keep them both in. We can call something like "thunder right: *bolt* 39 right, shake" (Figure 7-57) to set up those deeper routes. In this instance, the receivers need to understand that their double-moves convert vs. specific coverages. For example, against 1 high, the Z runs the "out-go" or "out" (depending on the depth of the corner) and X runs a "fence post." Against Z high, Z runs a "squirrel route" and X runs a corner. We can also call something like "storm right: *bolt* 13, X (or Z) over" off the zone-read look (Figure 7-58), in order to give us time to really work the ball downfield.

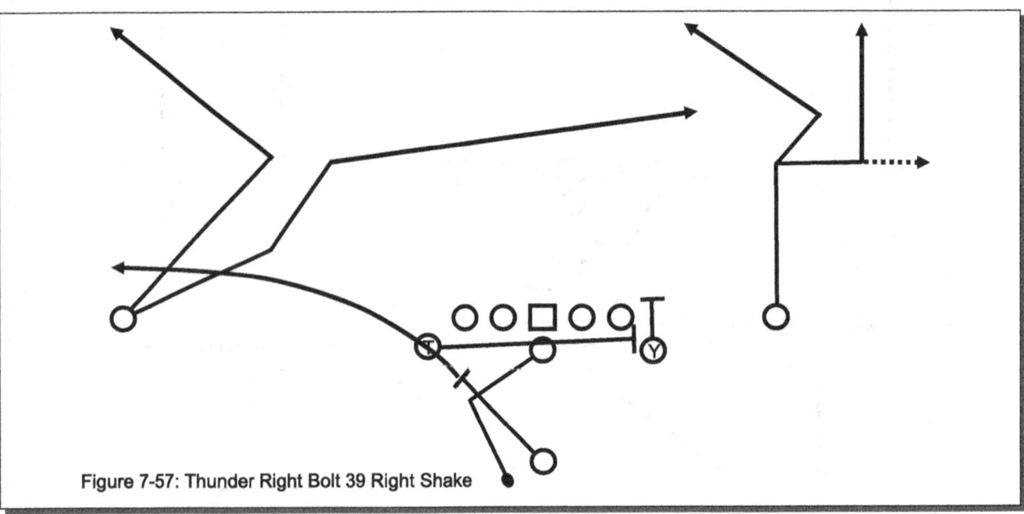

Figure 7-57: Thunder Right Bolt 39 Right Shake

**Play: Thunder right: bolt 39 right, shake**

| Pos: | Assignment: |
|---|---|
| R | Run play fake. Check bolt pro. Run diagonal. |
| T | Bolt 39 pro. |
| X | Vs. 1 high: run fence post.<br>Vs. 2 high: run V route. |
| Y | Bolt 39 pro. |
| Z | Run dancer 15-yd out based on depth of CB.<br>Vs. cov 2: run squirrel |

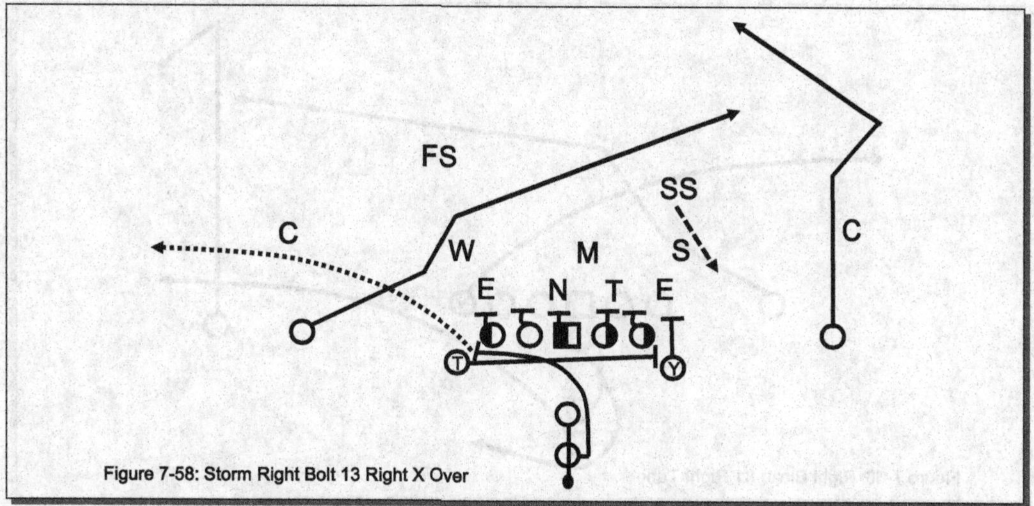

Figure 7-58: Storm Right Bolt 13 Right X Over

## Tube

This is called "tube." In the days people would play more "under, corner over, zone tilt," we did this to cause the Mike problems in that defense. This would be "doubles right, W peel: blaze 39 right, W *tube*" (Figure 7-59). We emphasize *W tube* when we call the play. "Tube" was a way to run a crosser with a "sneak" route. X now has the crosser. It's a sneak, a late shoot, a crosser, and the ruby route. You can do it with a 2nd tight end or if you have a versatile fullback. It's also great from 2-back, when people tend to run that "under tilt" defense. We've even done it off a fullback fake to sneak the tailback to the flat on "right: blaze 31 right, *tube*" (Figure 7-60).

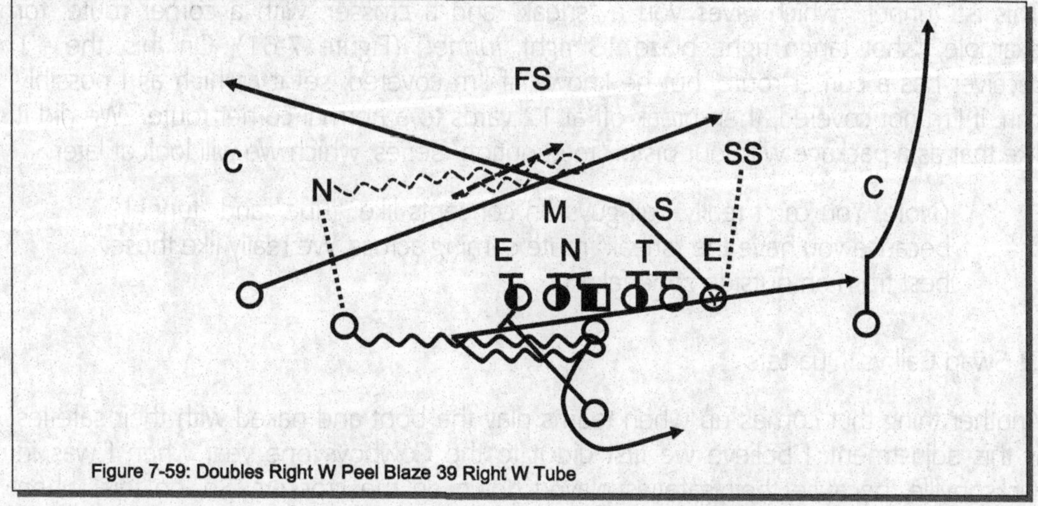

Figure 7-59: Doubles Right W Peel Blaze 39 Right W Tube

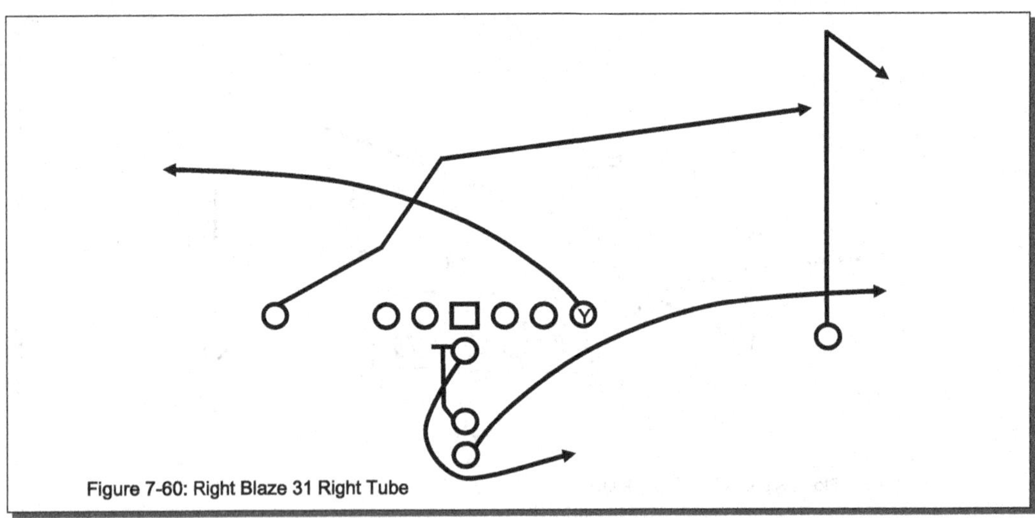

Figure 7-60: Right Blaze 31 Right Tube

**Play: Right: blaze 31 right, tube**

| Pos: | Assignment: |
|---|---|
| QB | |
| X | Run drag 10-12 yds. |
| Y | Run tube. Aim for defender's upfield shoulder. |
| Z | Run ruby route 22 yds. |
| R | Run free release diagonal. |
| F | 331 protection. Roll over the ball. |

❑ Tunnel

This is "tunnel," which gives you a "sneak" and a crosser, with a corner route, for example, "shot tango right: blaze 13 right, *tunnel*" (Figure 7-61). On this, the #1 receiver has a corner route, but he knows "if I'm covered, set it as high as I possibly can. If I'm not covered, then break off at 12 yards to a normal corner route." We did it like that as a package with our pistol "read-option" series, which we will look at later.

> (Note: You can't really pull guys on concepts like "tube" and "tunnel," because you have the "sneak" route coming across. We really like those best from an outside zone fake.)

❑ Swap Call vs. Quarters

Another thing that comes up when teams play the boot and naked with their safeties is this adjustment. I believe we first did it to the Cowboys one year when I was in Jacksonville, because their safeties played down on the crossers. So, on this, when you add motion on something like "thunder left, Z half: blaze 39 right *swap*," it gives the inside guy the post and the outside guy the crosser. If they're playing quarters, the safety isn't able to cover the crosser (Figure 7-62).

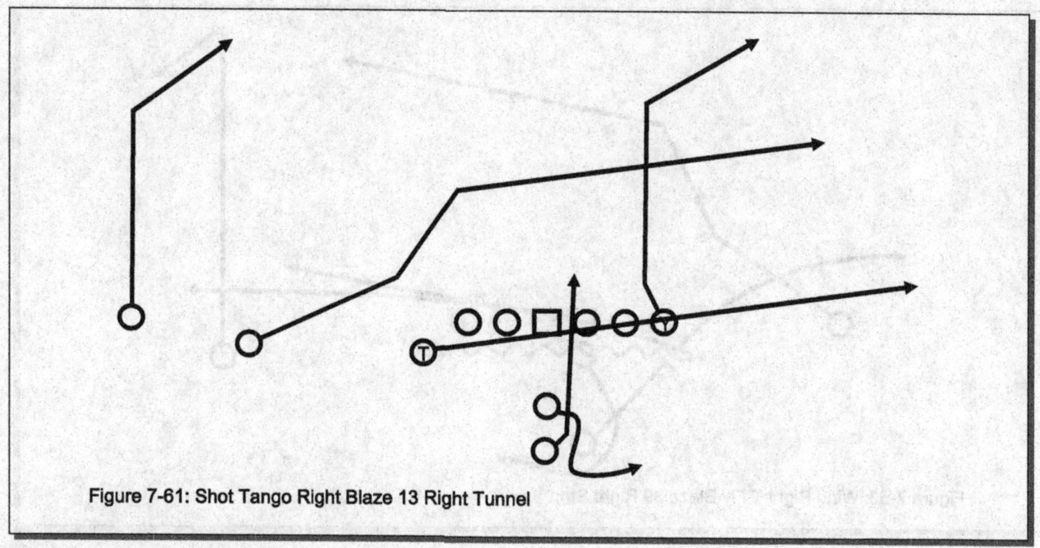

Figure 7-61: Shot Tango Right Blaze 13 Right Tunnel

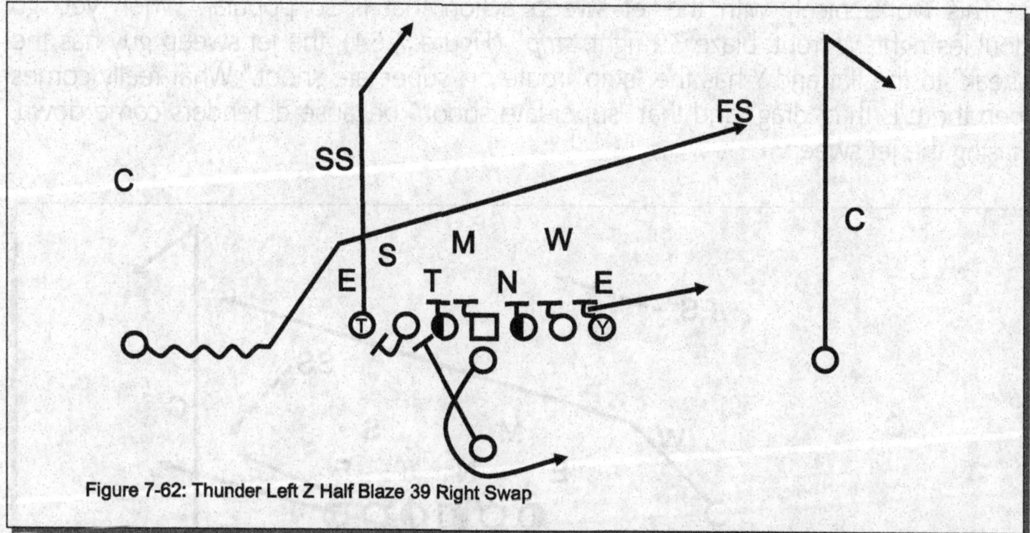

Figure 7-62: Thunder Left Z Half Blaze 39 Right Swap

At that time, we just said "whenever we motion, we're switching up who's running the crosser and who's running the post." We had really smart receivers in Jacksonville during those years, so it always worked like that. More recently, we just made it a "swap" call against quarters, which gave the route conversions more clarity for the receivers.

❑ Strip

This is "strip." The first way to do this is "wing right, T fly: blaze 39 right, *strip*" (Figure 7-63). T has the "sneak" route, and then the "strip" route from Y is a 5-step "super-late shoot." The "drag" route comes from X.

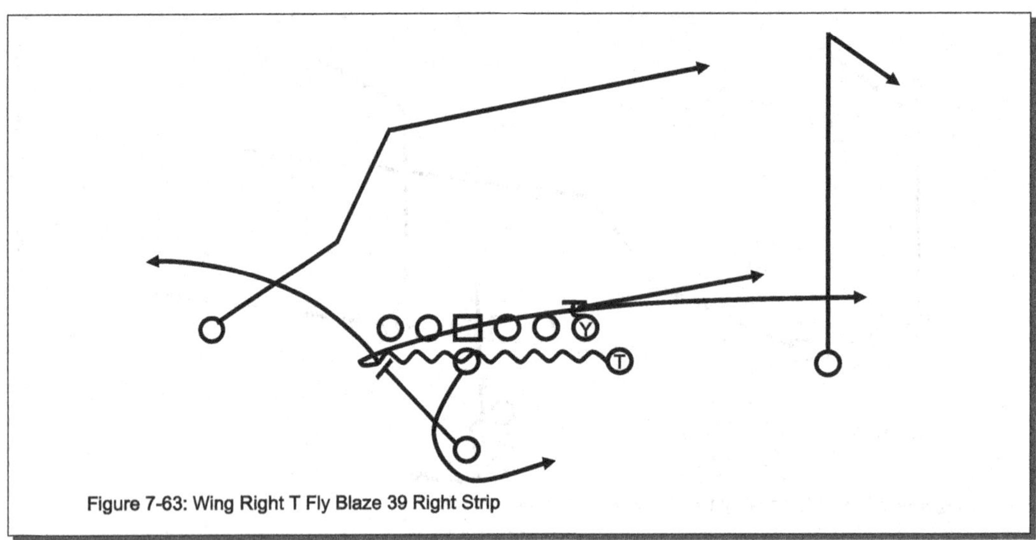

Figure 7-63: Wing Right T Fly Blaze 39 Right Strip

This works nicely with the jet sweep action that is so popular. When you go "doubles right, W front: blaze 39 right, *strip*" (Figure 7-64), the jet sweep guy has the "sneak" to the flat and Y has the "strip" route or "super-late shoot." What really comes open there is that "drag" and that "super-late shoot," because defenders come down, chasing the jet sweep.

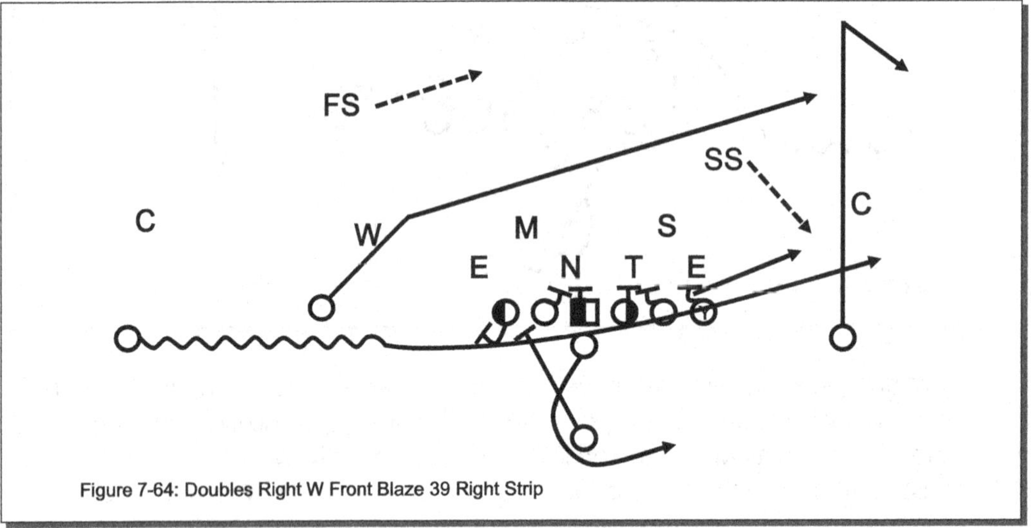

Figure 7-64: Doubles Right W Front Blaze 39 Right Strip

❑ Dragon

We call this "dragon." It is good in the red zone, where there isn't room for the "ruby" route. So, in the red zone, what you might do is "thunder right: blaze 16 left, X dragon" (Figure 7-65). Our "16/17" run is one of our favorite run schemes, so we always want to game plan ways to protect it. "Dragon" tells X to "run a drag through whoever has the late shoot in man." You can set a "combo" of these ideas up, such as "dot right, Y fly: *burn* 39 right, Y *sneak*, Z *dragon*" (Figure 7-66). On this, you have the toss fake and the "Y sneak" route along with the "dragon" concept.

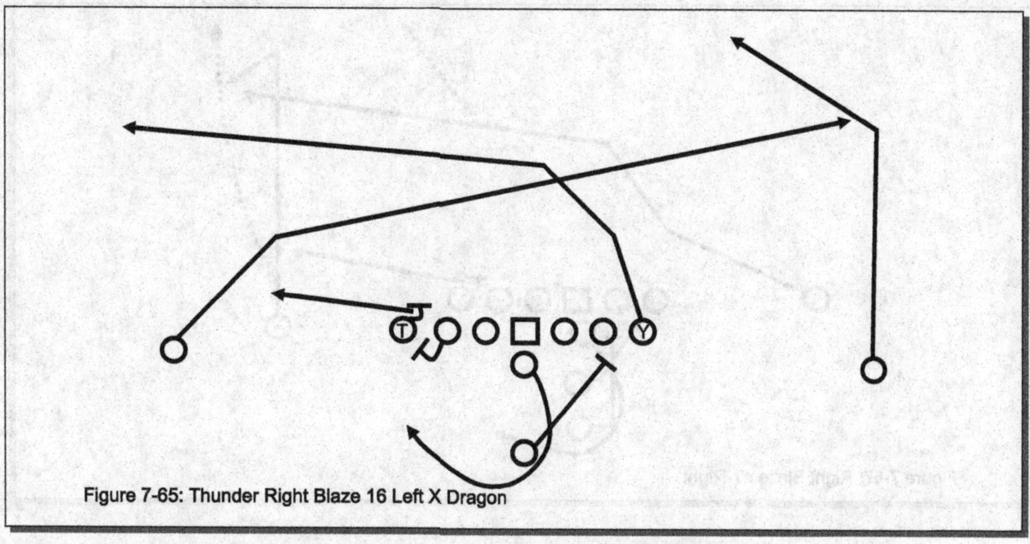

Figure 7-65: Thunder Right Blaze 16 Left X Dragon

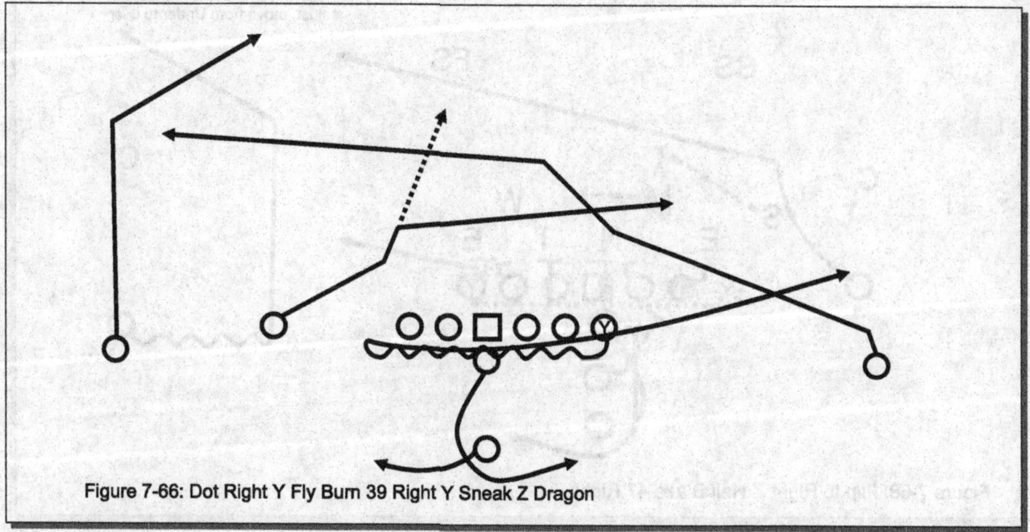

Figure 7-66: Dot Right Y Fly Burn 39 Right Y Sneak Z Dragon

## 2-Back Nakeds

In years where we run more 2-back offense, we can call it off "47/46," where the quarterback reverse-pivots. When he turns his back with the fake, it really helps sell the fake on something like "right: blaze 47 right" (Figure 7-67). On this, X runs the depth of the drag and Y runs a late shoot. One way we've packaged this was "*flip* to right: blaze 47 right" to take a team from "under" to "over." Since it's not as clean to run a "late shoot" off of a walked-up "under Sam" linebacker, we "flipped" them over and then that took their front from "under" to "over," which gave us a cleaner edge for the naked (Figure 7-68).

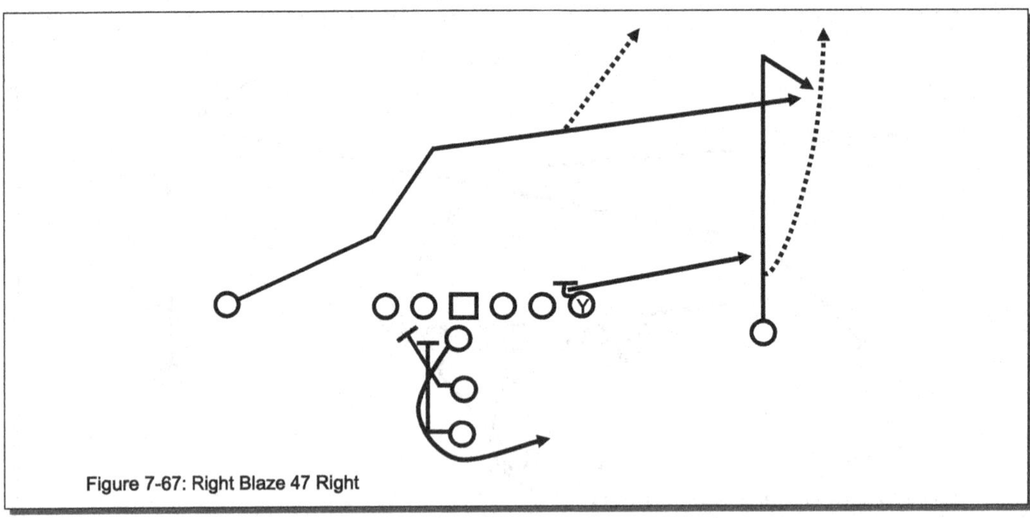

Figure 7-67: Right Blaze 47 Right

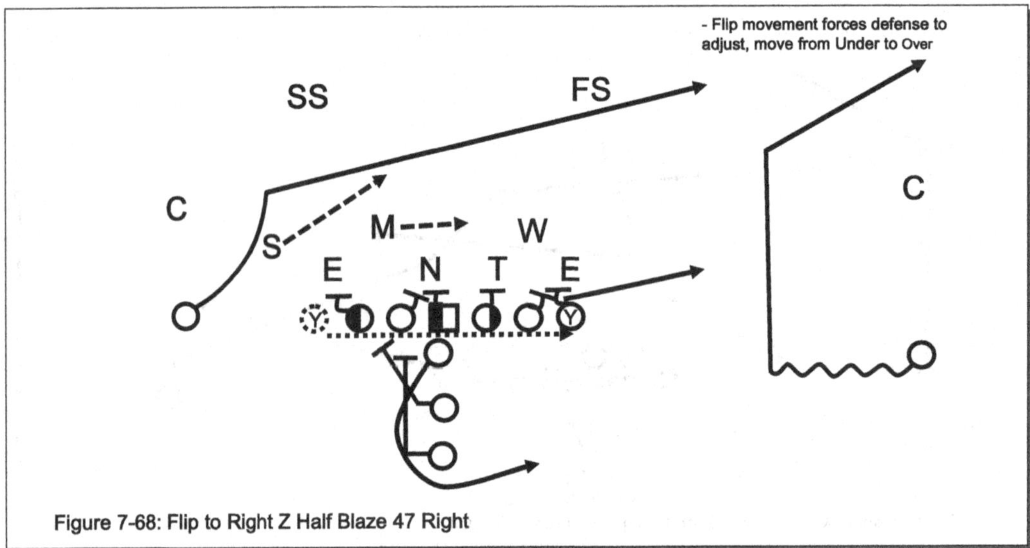

Figure 7-68: Flip to Right Z Half Blaze 47 Right

## Short-Yardage Nakeds

In our short-yardage package, we carry things like "right, Z fly tight: blaze 42 left" (Figure 7-69), where we block that backside end. Z would go to the flat, Y would run the "drag," X runs a Ruby, and the fullback and tailback would block the edge.

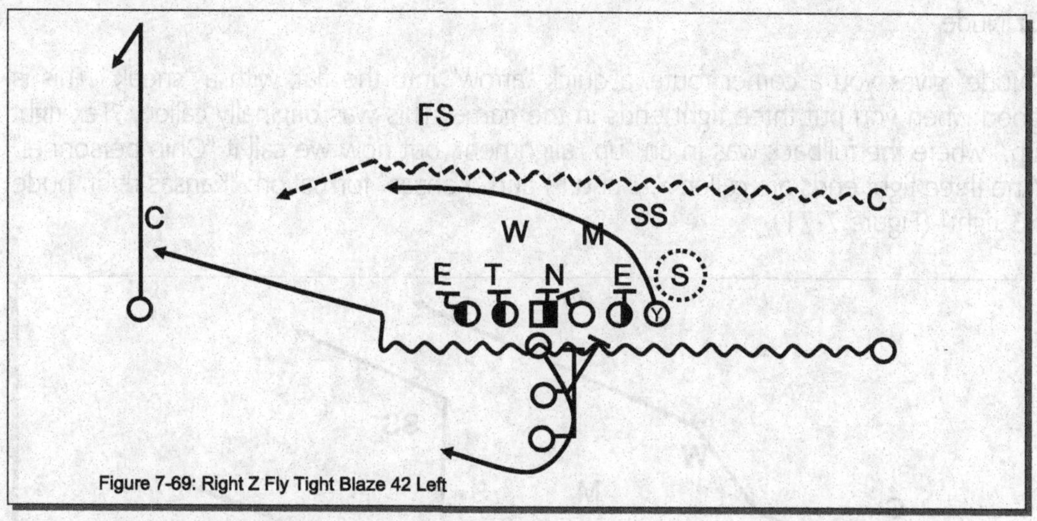

Figure 7-69: Right Z Fly Tight Blaze 42 Left

Note: "Tub" is what we call the "holdoff" short-yardage, inside zone run with the fullback as a free-hitter. "32 tub" with the "fly tight" motion is inside zone, with the fullback as a free-hitter (Figure 7-70). Then the hold-off receiver frees up the tackle to climb vs. over-fronts, whether that's the "T" in 22 personnel or the Z receiver in 21 personnel. We package these nakeds off of that as we've shown in this instance.

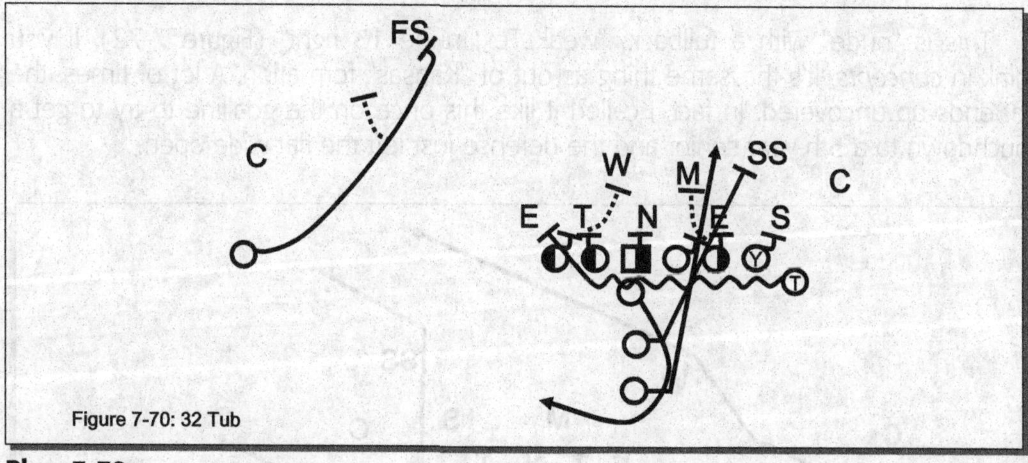

Figure 7-70: 32 Tub

**Play: 7-70**

| Pos: | Assignment: |
|---|---|
| X | Crossfield technique. |
| QB | Open, crossover, reach. It is very important to get the ball to the running back as quickly and as deep as possible. Boot out after handoff. |

❑ Nude

"Nude" gives you a corner route, a quick "arrow" into the flat, with a "sneak." This is good when you put three tight ends in the game. This was originally called, "Tex right up," where the fullback was in an "up" alignment, but now we call it "Ohio personnel" (the three tight ends are called Y, T and F) and "Kansas" formation: "Kansas right: nude 13 right" (Figure 7-71).

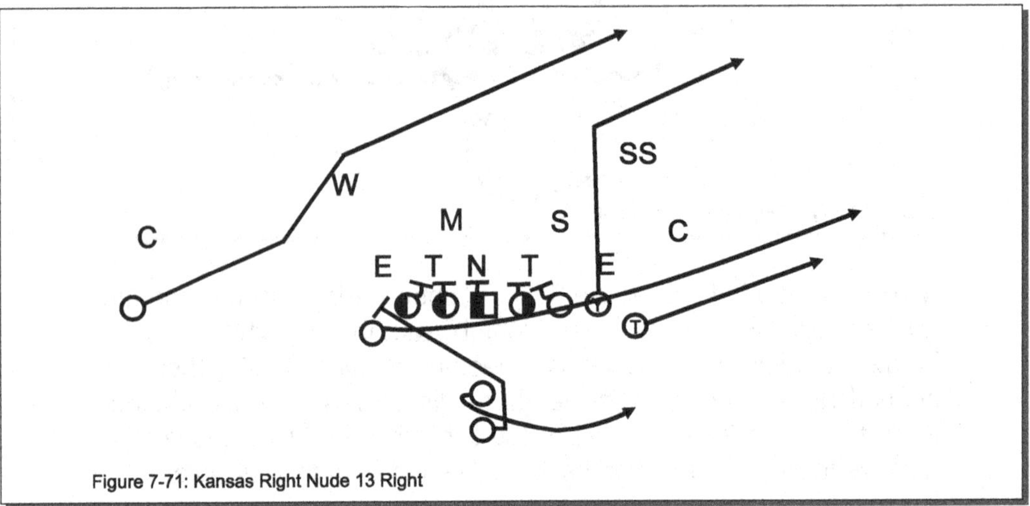

Figure 7-71: Kansas Right Nude 13 Right

This is "nude" with a fullback: "weak Tex: nude 13 right" (Figure 7-72). If you think in *concepts*, it's the same thing as out of "Kansas" formation. A lot of times, the flat ends up uncovered. In fact, I called it like this once on the goalline to try to get a touchdown to a 5th-year senior and the defense just left the flat wide open.

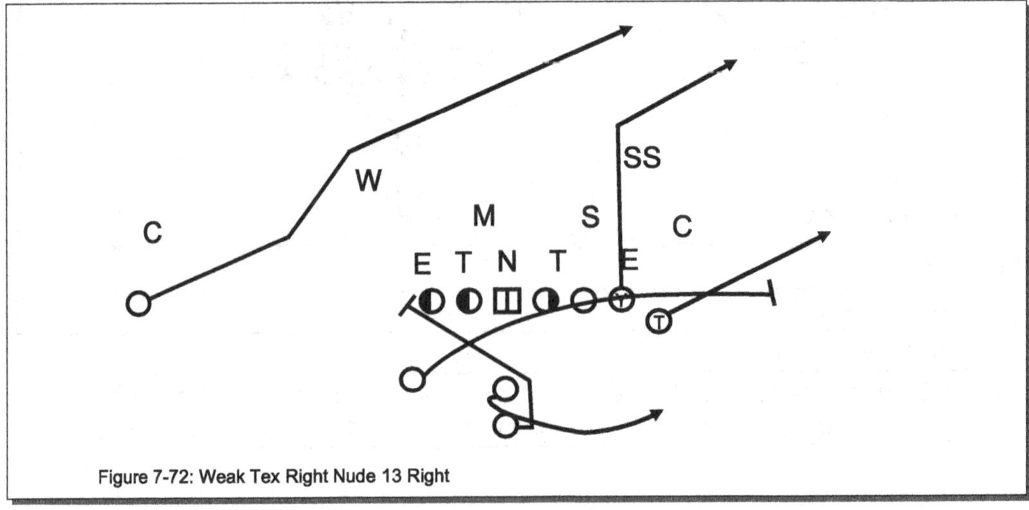

Figure 7-72: Weak Tex Right Nude 13 Right

## Goalline Nakeds

The key with goalline defense is "where's the adjuster?" You're trying to set the "adjuster," and then shift in order to get them outmanned. If we tag it "blaze corner" with big guys in the game, the pair of tight ends do the "me/you" call for who runs the corner route. On "blaze 23 right C" ("C means corner," from the "1" concept category), you've got a corner, and a late shoot, but here "C" tells them "you guys scheme up who's going to get the quarterback turned." We always do this from our heavy sets. This was called "Indian right move" from our "muscle" personnel (Figure 7-73).

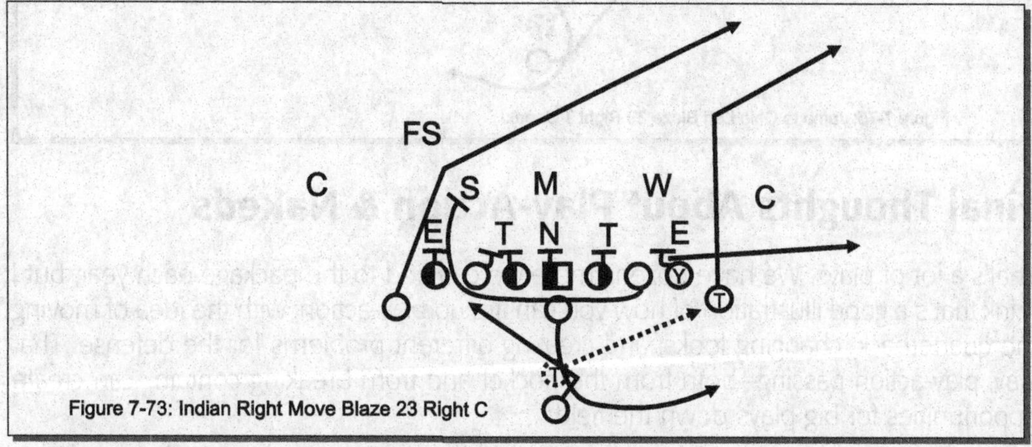

Figure 7-73: Indian Right Move Blaze 23 Right C

Unbalanced sets are effective in short yardage, such as "flip to lightning left: blaze 33 right," with a tackle over (Figure 7-74). Since this is such a short edge, it gives the quarterback a little protection. If you don't want to pull the guard, you can just go "jump to Ohio left: blaze 39 right, T sneak" (Figure 7-75). Goalline nakeds and bootlegs are always packaged with the idea of "where's the adjuster?"

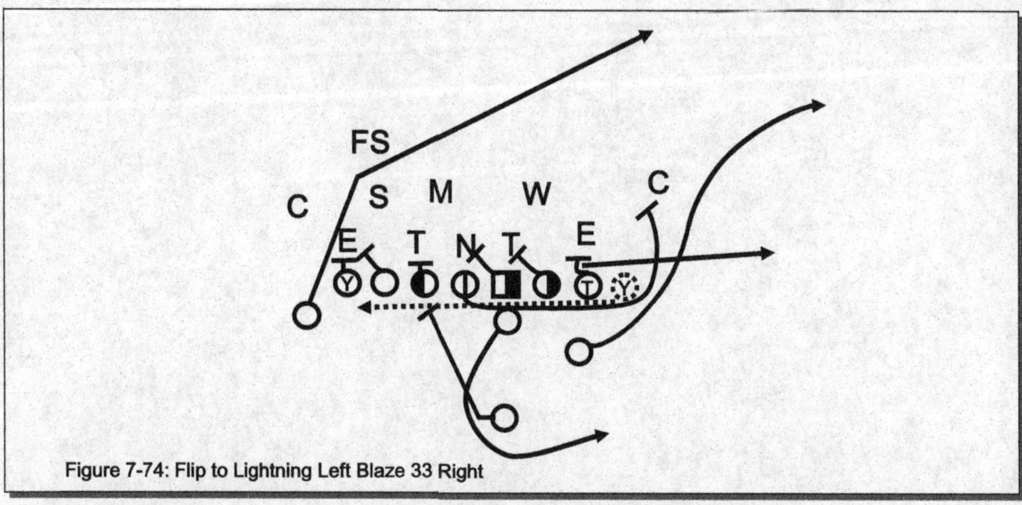

Figure 7-74: Flip to Lightning Left Blaze 33 Right

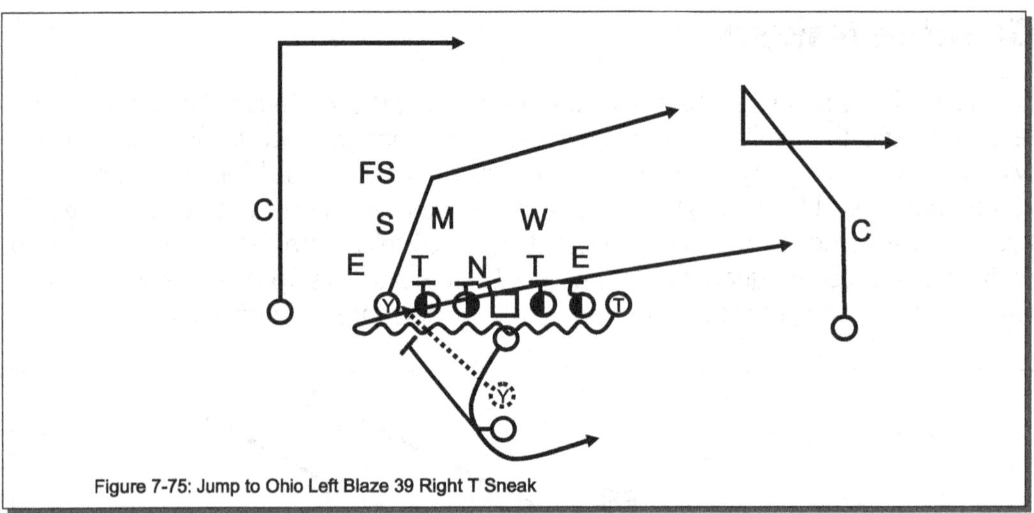

Figure 7-75: Jump to Ohio Left Blaze 39 Right T Sneak

## Final Thoughts About Play-Action & Nakeds

That's a lot of plays. We have dozens more we can add to the package each year, but I think that's a good illustration of how you can fire up play-action, with the idea of moving the quarterback, changing looks, and creating different problems for the defense. That way, play-action passing—both from the pocket and from breaking contain—can create opportunities for big plays down the field.

You want to build your play-action passing off your best run plays, with your best personnel groupings. You also want to take into account what your quarterback does well and play to his strengths. And as with all things offense, you want to create ways to get the ball to your best players!

# Chapter 8
# The Age of RPO

The "run/pass options"—what people are calling "RPOs"—are a popular way nowadays to defeat the blitz and put pressure on the run-fit players. That's where we call a run play, but if they pressure us or if run support is extremely aggressive, we have an option to throw the ball instead. I've probably heard more questions about this topic lately than anything else in football.

Run/pass options have become synonymous with fast tempo, which puts pressure on the defense and allows the quarterback to only have to focus on one or two defenders. When the Eagles won the Super Bowl, they did a lot of that with their quarterback. Those plays suited him really well and it allowed them to have success against New England's complex defensive schemes by simplifying the reads. Again, offense is always going to be about what the quarterback can and can't do, so your ability as a coach to understand that is critically important. The run/pass options can be another tool for getting that done.

One drawback is that sometimes a quarterback has to beat that free guy coming, which isn't fun. You can also just tell the back to block it and then it turns into quick game. There, we're running the RPO and I know the edge player is coming unblocked, so I just point him out to the running back. The back knows he's blocking him, and now we're throwing quick game, with the line blocking the run play (Figure 8-1). Of course, the "non-enforcement" of rules has also allowed for those kinds of RPOs, where you see inside zone with a slant-route throw, and a guard is seven yards down field.

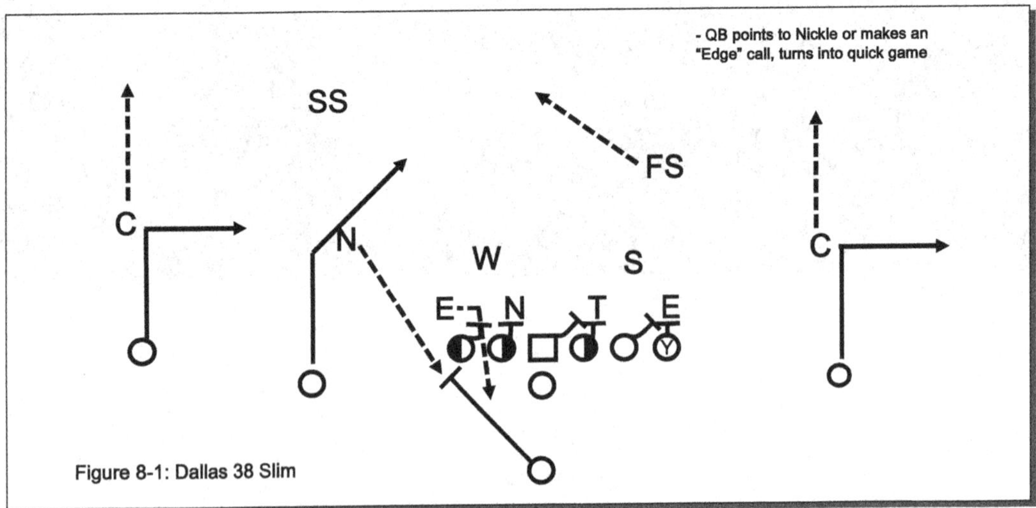

Figure 8-1: Dallas 38 Slim

We look at the RPO game a few different ways. The origins of these have existed for longer than people realize, and they really started life as just a bubble screen as an outlet for defeating pressure. In addition to those origins, we package them according to which level of defender we want to manipulate (what we call first, second, third level) and we also define a category, in which the quarterback is running with the ball after the "keeper" read but still has the option to throw on the run, much like a triple-option. So roughly speaking, we carry five categories of run/pass options.

What you really need to come to grips with on RPOs is what runs you're going to do it off of. How do you know what runs you're going to use? I think that's going to be about what you believe in, what your players can execute, and what any given game plan might call for. We've done these off all our favorite runs (down/stretch, inside-zone, outside-zone, draws, and power O). My belief, however, is the back should come *to you* as a quarterback from the same side as the pass-option that you're wanting to execute. I am aware that some teams have success with the back opposite the RPO read. On the other hand, if we want to read it "run to pass," we've found that our quarterbacks protect the football and make cleaner decisions, if we set the back to the same side as the read.

## RPO Origins

Before people started calling them "RPOs," we first thought of these as a way to defeat pressure, with just a bubble screen tagged off a basic run play. Sometimes, it was about if they're bringing pressure into where we're running the ball. Now, we're throwing one of the bubble series to beat it (Figure 8-2). The bubble screen serves as the simplest way to neutralize that, and we now consider this our first RPO concept category.

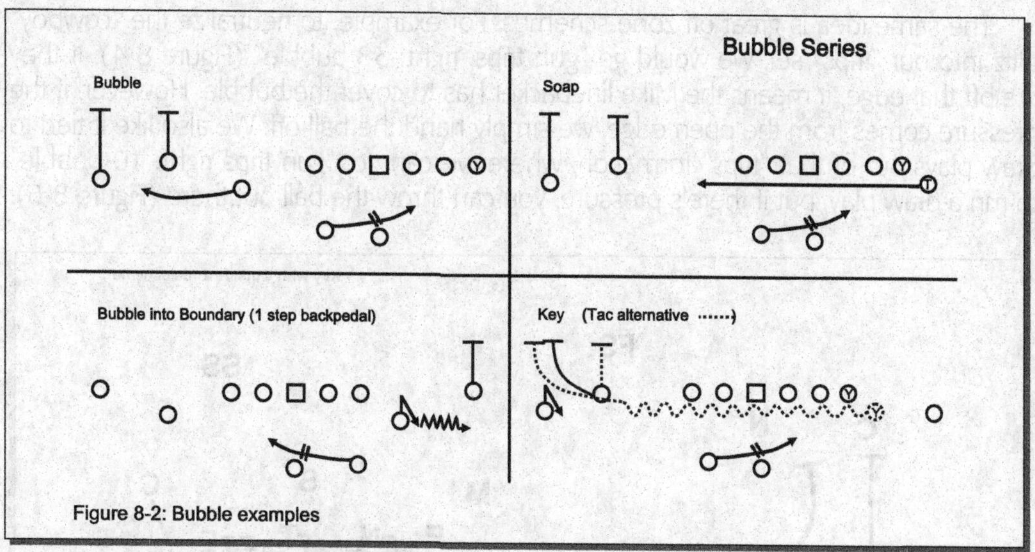

Figure 8-2: Bubble examples

The following is an early example of that from our years at Arkansas. We had a player named Joe Adams who could really run after the catch, so this was called "wing pair right: 16 key" (Figure 8-3). You had the Z and the W in the game and X came out, so we called it "pair personnel." That's an easy bubble screen throw, tagged onto our best run play. If we're getting pressure off the side of the run play, or if we're getting an apex player who's cheating in off the "pair," where you can just block 1-on-1, then we have a great chance to throw the bubble. That's pretty straightforward stuff, it's teachable and it's a high-percentage concept to execute.

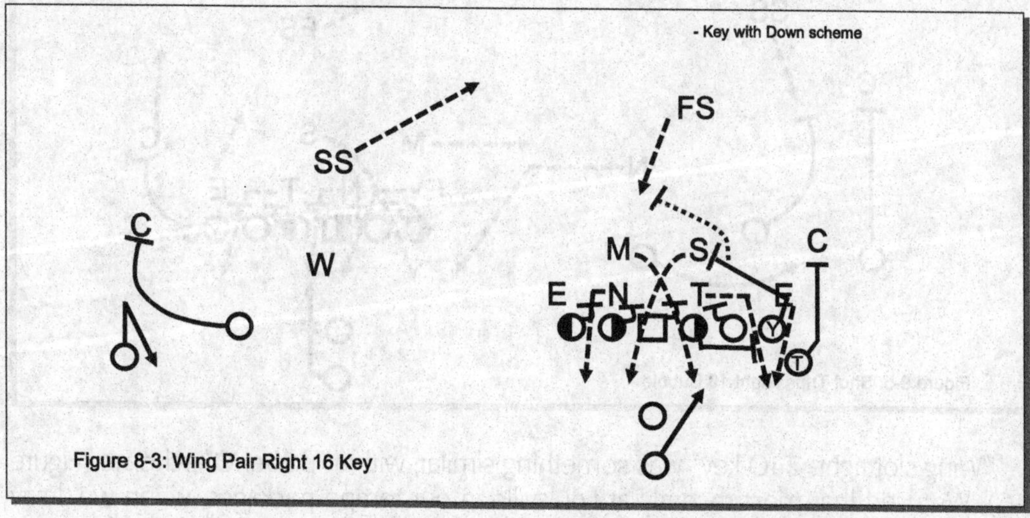

Figure 8-3: Wing Pair Right 16 Key

The same idea is great off zone schemes. For example, to neutralize the "cowboy" blitz into our "trips" set, we would go "gun trips, right: 38 bubble" (Figure 8-4). If they fire off that edge, it means the Mike linebacker has to cover the bubble. However, if the pressure comes from the open edge, we simply hand the ball off. We also like it tied to draw plays out of that "trips" formation, where we can go, "gun trips right: 10 bubble" to run a draw play, but if there's pressure, you can throw the ball out there (Figure 8-5).

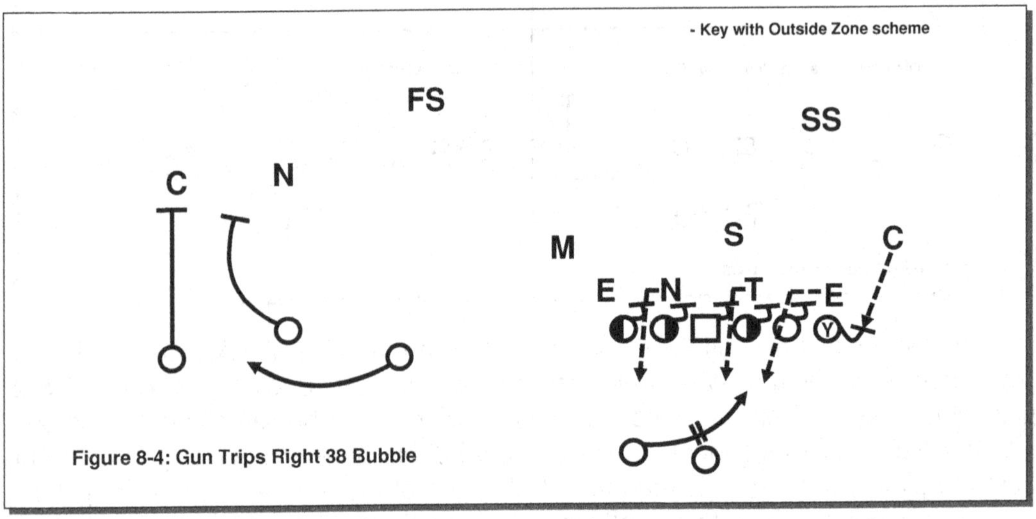

- Key with Outside Zone scheme

Figure 8-4: Gun Trips Right 38 Bubble

- Bubble with Draw scheme

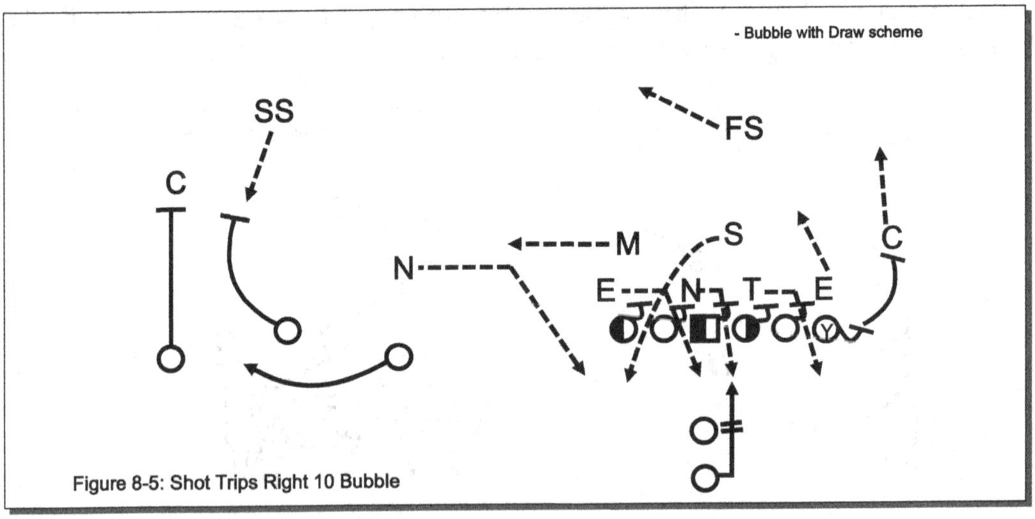

Figure 8-5: Shot Trips Right 10 Bubble

"Wing slot right: 240 key" was something similar, with a "power O" scheme (Figure 8-6). We used that most recently at Louisville in our tempo packages, when we'd say "don't worry about them, just worry about us. If they're not lined up, they're not lined up. If you think you want to fire that 'key' out there, fire it out there." We'd use the RPO like that in a fast-tempo context. Doing that actually gave us the chance to beat Clemson in 2016, because they were just standing there, and they wouldn't get lined up. We said "here's what we're going to do in the second half: we're just going to go fast. We're not going to do any '2-play calls,' we're going to utilize the RPOs, and we're going to call our base plays—what we do best—and *you guys* are going to go make plays and we'll get back in this game." We came back and fought within a yard of beating the national champion. So, that "blitz-beater" category was the original way we used the run/pass option concepts and it'll always be good football.

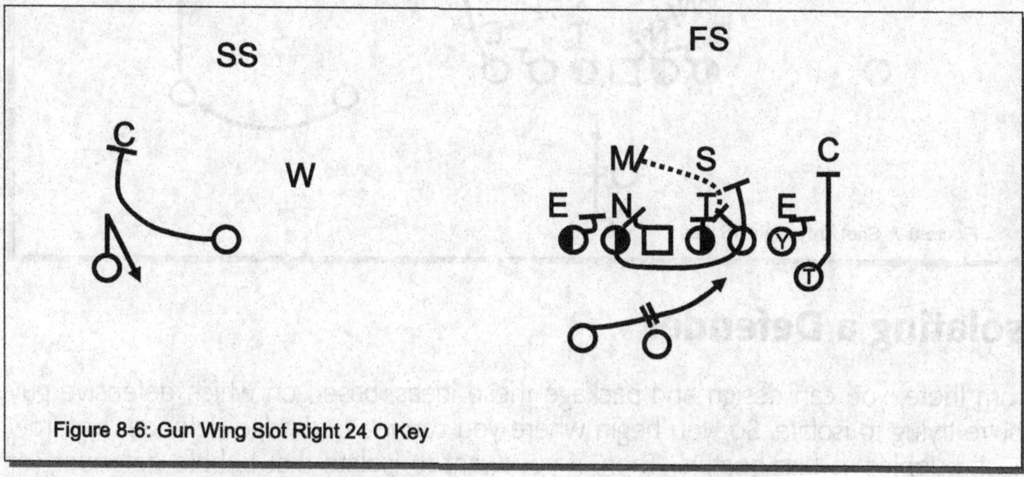


Figure 8-6: Gun Wing Slot Right 24 O Key

## Defining the Runs

The initial priority is to categorize what run concepts we want to utilize. Once the runs are established, I know the routes I like with them. The simplest way to start is just tagging the bubble to those base runs. On our bubble screen series, we never feel like we need to block the end or "lock" the end with a tackle, because the ball comes out so quickly, especially when you're utilizing fast tempo. However, once we started adding other pass concepts, what we were trying to do first was define the runs.

Besides the basic down, zone, draw, and power schemes, we have the ability to run it off other things, though some schemes and pass tags require us to deal with the backside end differently. For example, if we want to use a pass-option on "13," where the quarterback is stepping back and opening up, we found that we still want to block that edge or he's right on top of the quarterback. We ended up adding the term "15/14," which tells that backside tackle to "lock" and just read the linebacker instead (Figure 8-7). You can also make a call before the play called, so it's "bob 13," or "bob 25O," where "bob" tells the backside tackle to block their end. These are good off of "power O with a lock" and "outside or mid-zone with the lock." The most streamlined ways we found to package the runs are if you start them off of inside-zone (where you can add a "lock" or a "cut" backside), you tag them off draw plays, you do them off of "power O" with a "lock," or you do them off outside zone (with a "lock" or "cut"). Then, we do have a few stand-alone downfield concepts that we like to throw on the run, with a "read-option" of the defensive end.

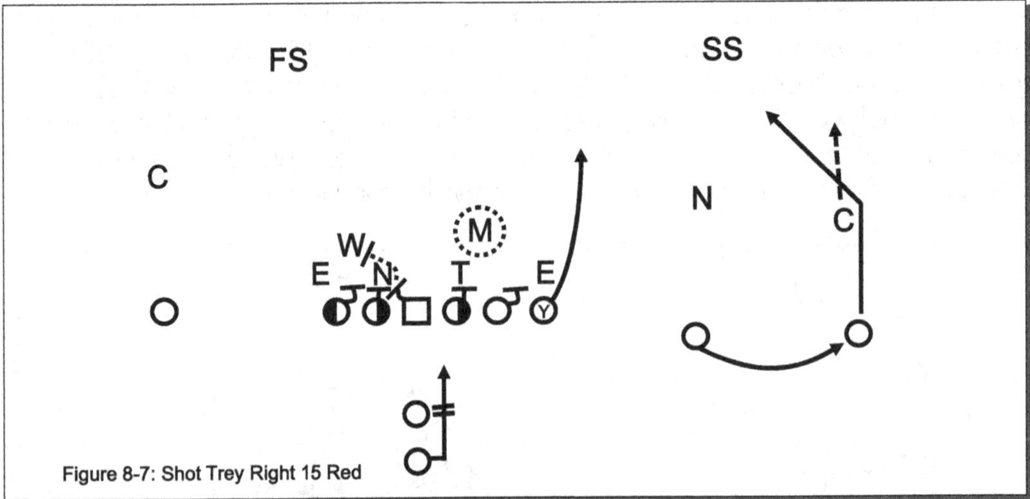

Figure 8-7: Shot Trey Right 15 Red

## Isolating a Defender

From there, you can design and package these ideas, based on which defensive guy you're trying to isolate. So, you begin where you can read an edge defender to throw those bubbles as blitz-beaters. Then, if you want to isolate that bubble defender (or force defender), you can "lock" the backside tackle and expose the linebacker, or you can "cut" the end by bringing a blocker across the formation, or you build something from two-tights that allows you to block up the entire front and get to those force guys for your run/pass read. You can isolate an inside linebacker by building your run/pass option off draw schemes (where it often become a "pass/run" option instead). Then, you can also isolate a drop-down support safety and get your outside receiver isolated in single coverage. We have the original "bubble as blitz-beater" package, but then we started referring to those as the three "levels" of defenders to read. In addition, we also packaged another category, in which the quarterback has a read-option run, but also has a pass-option element available, where he can throw late on the run. Given that we've already introduced the "blitz-beater" origins, let's take a look at some of these other concept categories.

## First Level

We define a "first-level" run-pass option as a read of a down lineman. As we said in the previous chapter, we've never majored in the true "midline" stuff, though we have had some success with reading those "4is" that are popular today in 3-4 defenses. We however, have a lot of ways to package a run-pass option off a defensive end or contain player. While the "now" or bubble series we just described is the most economical way to get that done, there are a number of other routes that are worth exploring.

We can build those like "dot right, Y fly: 32 tac" (Figure 8-8) or "dot left: 33 Reno (read), soap" (Figure 8-9). This is also compatible with our foundation "hitch" ideas, such as "trey right: 32 read, Z hitch," or "gun doubles right: 32 read, Houston" (Figure 8-10). We also started adding a "gimme" on the frontside of these, such as "doubles right: Dallas, 32 read, key" (Figure 8-11), where the quarterback can take that frontside "gimme" *right now*, if it's free-access, using all the same teaching from the quick game installation. Then, if Z is pressed, he follows his "Dallas" rules and converts, and the quarterback reads out the first-level RPO to the "key" side.

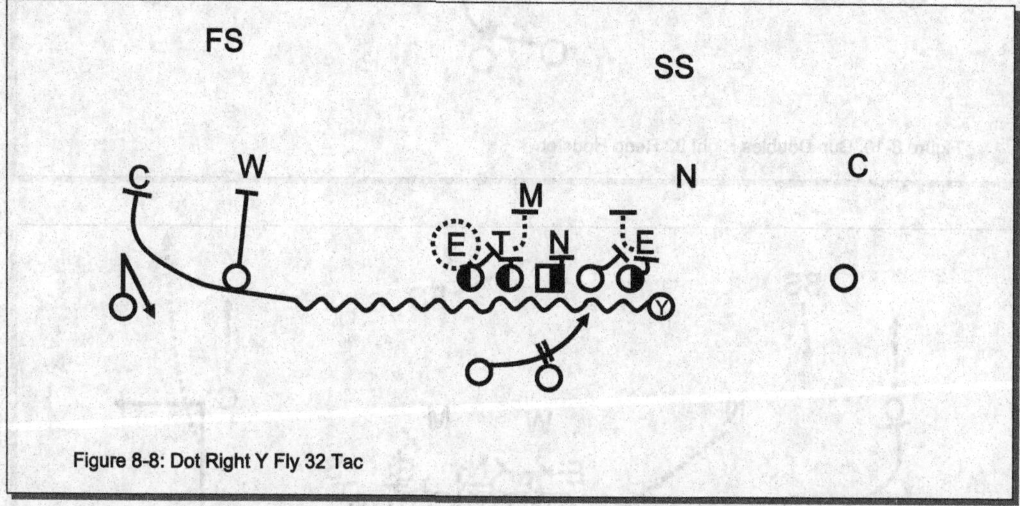

Figure 8-8: Dot Right Y Fly 32 Tac

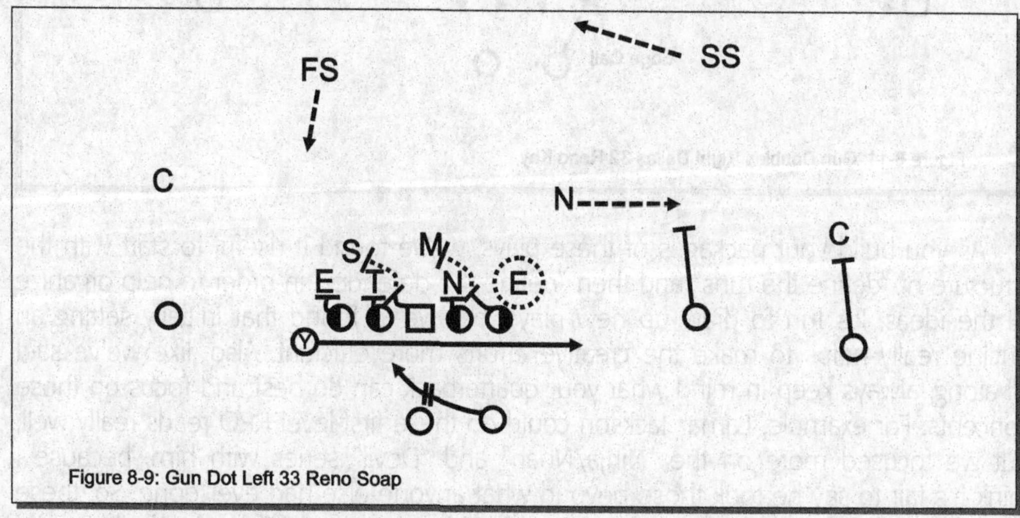

Figure 8-9: Gun Dot Left 33 Reno Soap

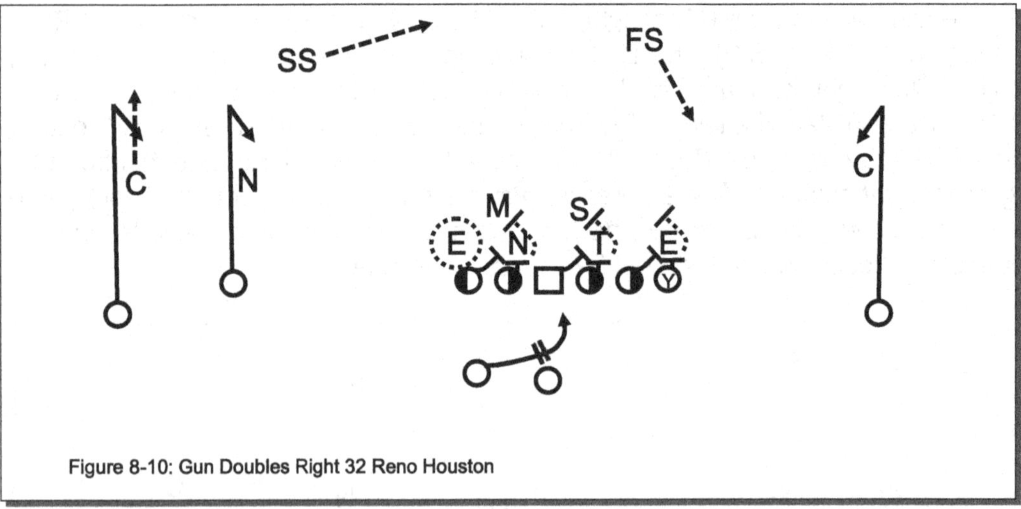


Figure 8-10: Gun Doubles Right 32 Reno Houston

Figure 8-11: Gun Doubles Right Dallas 32 Reno Key

As you build your packages of these plays, we've found it useful to start with the structure of "define the runs" and then "define the defender" in order to help organize all the ideas. It's fun to draw up new plays, but we've found that initially setting an outline really helps to make the creative efforts more efficient. Also, like we've said all along, always keep in mind what your quarterback can do best and focus on those concepts. For example, Lamar Jackson could do these first-level RPO reads really well, but we focused more on the "Ninja/Noah" and "Devil" series with him, because I think it's fair to say he took those beyond what anyone else had ever done. So, these first-level concepts are great, and reasonably simple to teach, if you've built a solid foundation of run game and quick game from which to work. From there, if we want to option a linebacker or force defender, instead of the end, we package those next and call that "level two."

## Second Level

The second level of RPO is where we are reading something at the linebacker level. Whether that's an inside linebacker or an outside nickel defender, we will package different types of run plays (such as down/stretch, inside-zone, gap, draw and outside-zone) and from there, stack on the pass concepts that are best suited to attack the defender we have isolated. We can achieve this in a few different ways. For example, isolating an inside linebacker happens naturally off draw actions. We can also get to it by adding a "lock" tag to block the defensive end and leave that corresponding linebacker for the read. We can also achieve the same thing by adding a "cut" tag to bring a blocker across.

To me, the second level is "we're zeroed in on one guy." If he's coming to support run, then we're replacing him with the throw. The only deal on this is that you have to carry an "edge" call. So, if I'm reading that outside linebacker and now all of a sudden, he's on the edge coming, I've got to be able to tell my back to just block him and turn it into quick game, so I don't lose my quarterback. So, the thinking in this instance is a little different than the original idea of using the pass-option explicitly to beat blitz. That's different, and if we're getting more of that, it takes us back to that original category.

## 2nd-Level Draw

We mentioned how a "draw RPO" started out as "trips right: 10/11 bubble." From there, "Oscar" is a really good route. We want to run "Oscar" out of 3x1, with a stop route, a bubble, and a go route. If my throw is there, I take it, and if not, I hand it off. That's "shot flood right: 11 Oscar" (Figure 8-12). This is a "pass/run option" off that inside linebacker. "Shot flood right: 11 red" became another one that was good for us (Figure 8-13). On this, we wanted to set the draw away from the read for the sake of spacing and so the back doesn't knock the ball out of the quarterback's hands.

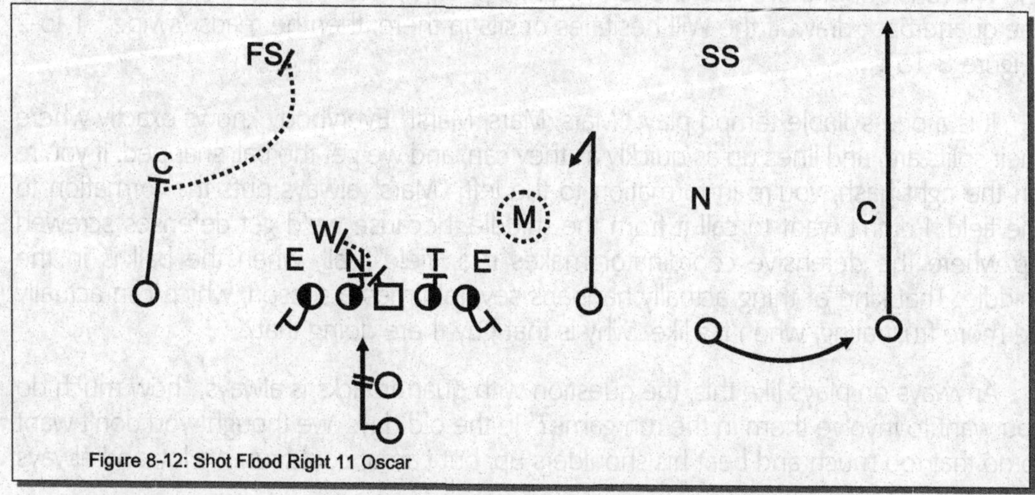

Figure 8-12: Shot Flood Right 11 Oscar

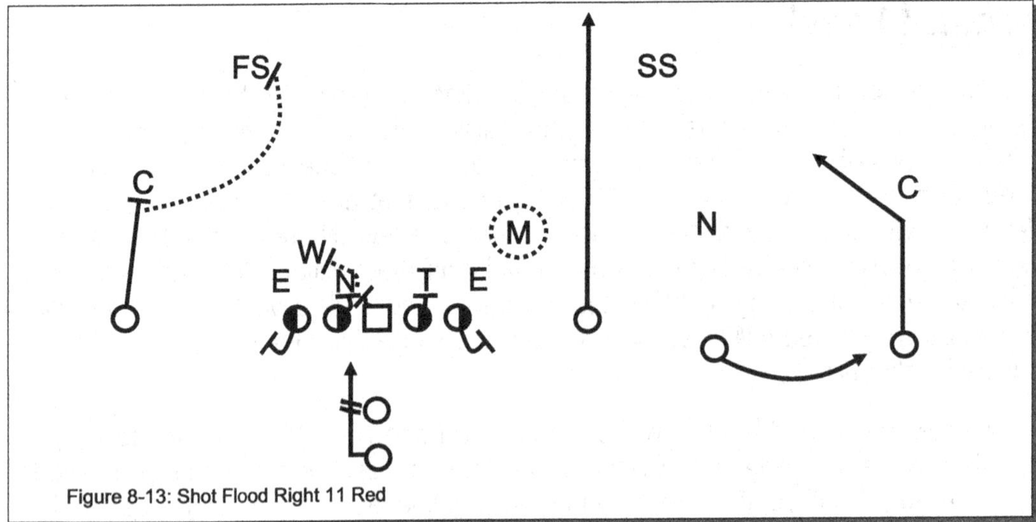

Figure 8-13: Shot Flood Right 11 Red

❑ Mars

With a quarterback who can run, you'll want to install what we called "Mars." On Mars, #3 widens his split and we run the Oscar concept to that side. It works better with the back offset, so if you've got a 1-linelinebacker look, then the offensive line is responsible for that linebacker. The line scheme is to "get that Will blocked on a quarterback draw." Backside, we ran "swipe" (slant/stretch).

The quarterback takes a "3-quick" drop and keys the Mike. If the Mike runs and gets underneath #3, he *lets him finish his route*. Then, once he finishes his route, he plants his right foot in the ground and runs the quarterback draw (Figure 8-14). Now, if it's a 2-linelinebacker look, the o-line has to set the point to the Mike linebacker instead. So now, the o-line is handling the "4-down plus the Mike" and the quarterback is going to key the Will linebacker. Quick 3-step drop, and he now looks at the Will linebacker. If the Will runs out of there with the running back, he puts his foot in the ground and runs the quarterback draw. If the Will hesitates or sits in there, then he reads "swipe," 1-to-2 (Figure 8-15).

It is a one-syllable tempo play: "Mars, Mars, Mars!" Everybody knows exactly where their splits are, and lines up as quickly as they can, and we get the ball snapped. If you're on the right hash, you're in formation to the left. "Mars" always puts the formation to the field. I didn't want to call it from the middle, because we'd get defenses screwed up where the defensive coordinator makes it a "field" call, when the ball is in the middle. That kind of thing actually happens several times a season, which can actually be more frustrating, when it's like "why is that guy there doing that?"

Anyways on plays like this, the question with quarterbacks is always, "how much do you want to involve them in the run game?" In the old days, we thought you don't want to do that too much and beat his shoulders up, but Lamar could run it a lot, and always

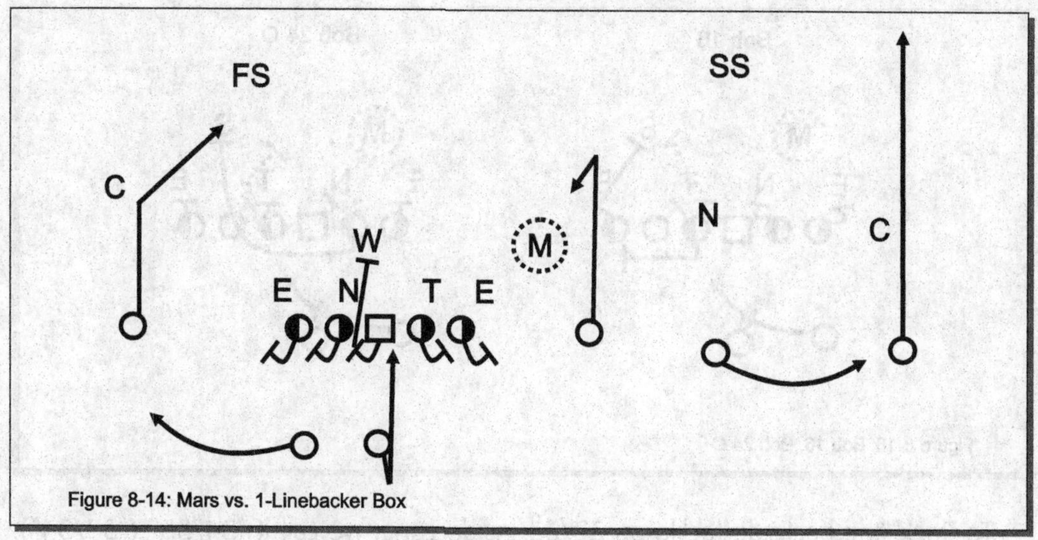

Figure 8-14: Mars vs. 1-Linebacker Box

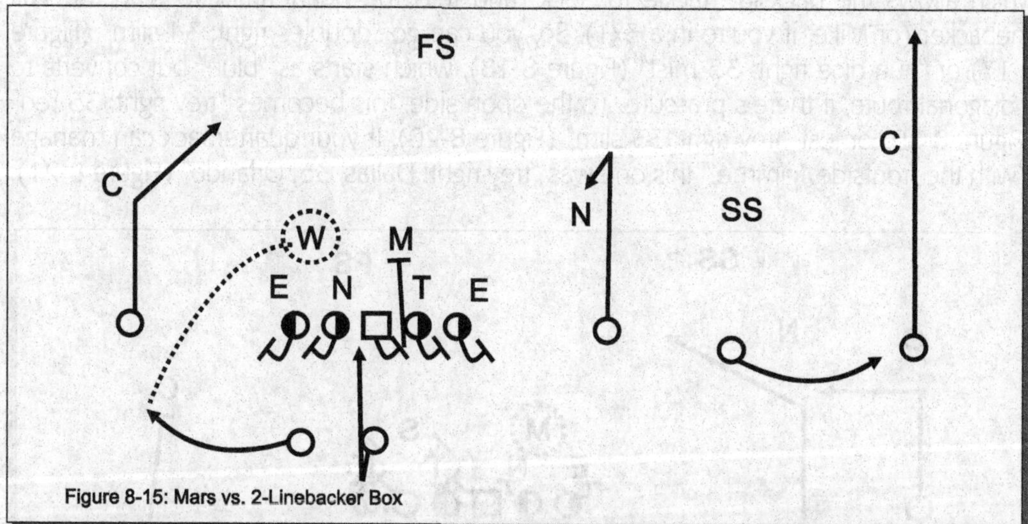

Figure 8-15: Mars vs. 2-Linebacker Box

protect himself from hits, and he still could make all the throws. We'd see it every day in practice, so we gave him the freedom. "FTS": we were "feeding the stud!"

❑ Level-2 "Lock"

You can also take all the basic runs, use a code-word to have the tackle "lock" the end, and read the linebacker instead. We have done that with "16/17," you can do it with "power O" (Figure 8-16). On the other hand, I actually don't think you need to add it to every single run play you have. With these, I think less is better. Looking at the following examples can be helpful.

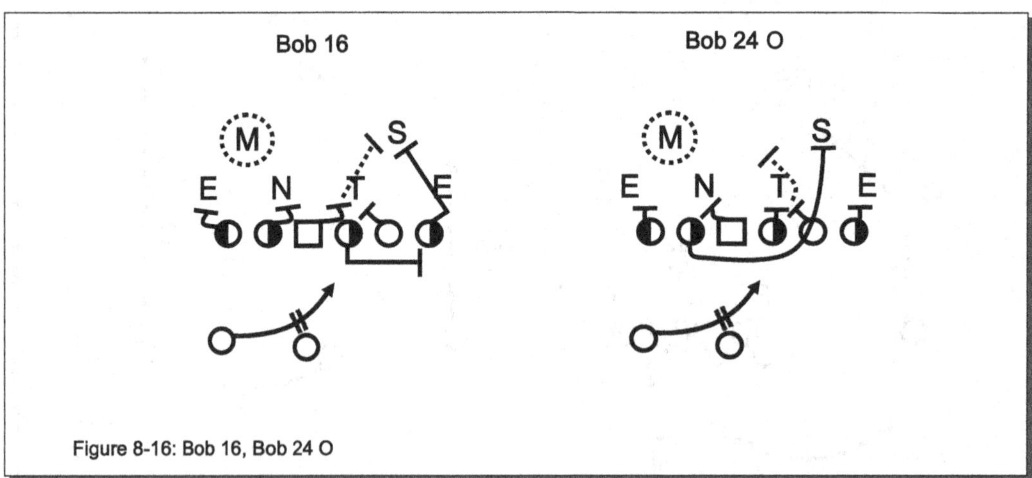

Figure 8-16: Bob 16, Bob 24 O

To "lock" the backside tackle on 32/33 inside zone, we call it "34/35" ("35/34"), which allows the backside tackle to "lock" and tells the quarterback to read the Will linebacker (or Mike, if you're in a 3x1). So, you can go "doubles right: 34 slim" (Figure 8-17) or "gun dice right: 35 mist" (Figure 8-18), which starts as "blue" but converts to a diagonal route, if there's pressure. To the open side, this becomes "trey right: 35 red" (Figure 8-19) or just "trey right: 33 slim" (Figure 8-20). If your quarterback can manage it with the frontside "gimme," this one was "trey right: Dallas, 35, Orlando" (Figure 8-21).

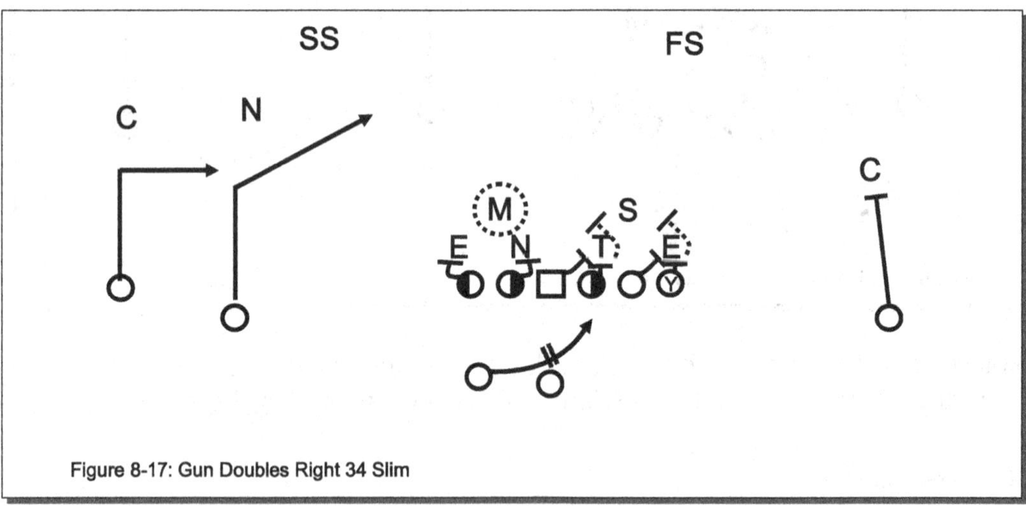

Figure 8-17: Gun Doubles Right 34 Slim

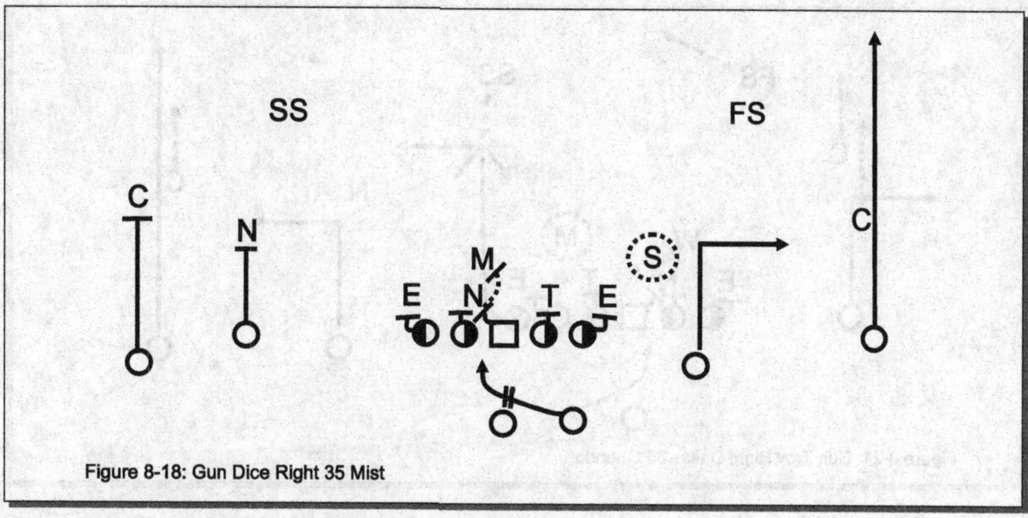

Figure 8-18: Gun Dice Right 35 Mist

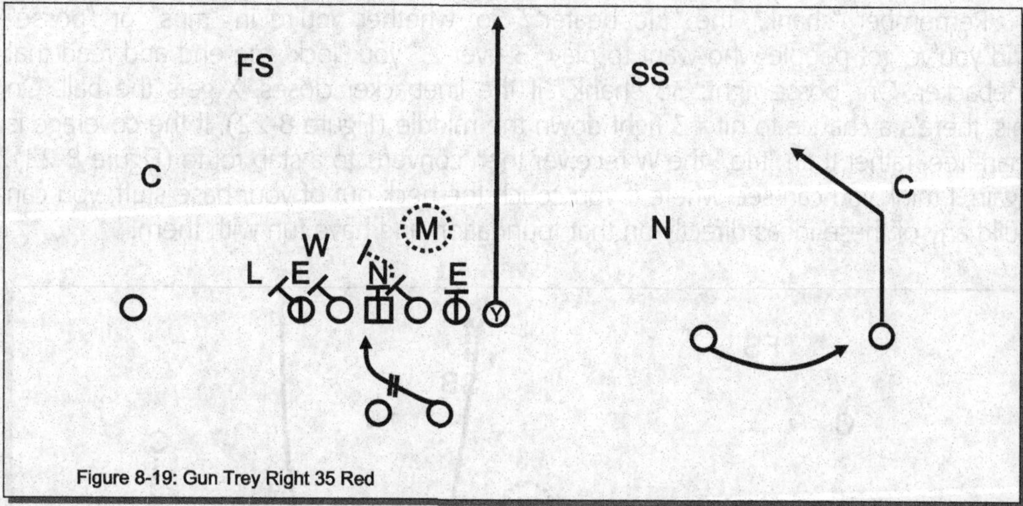

Figure 8-19: Gun Trey Right 35 Red

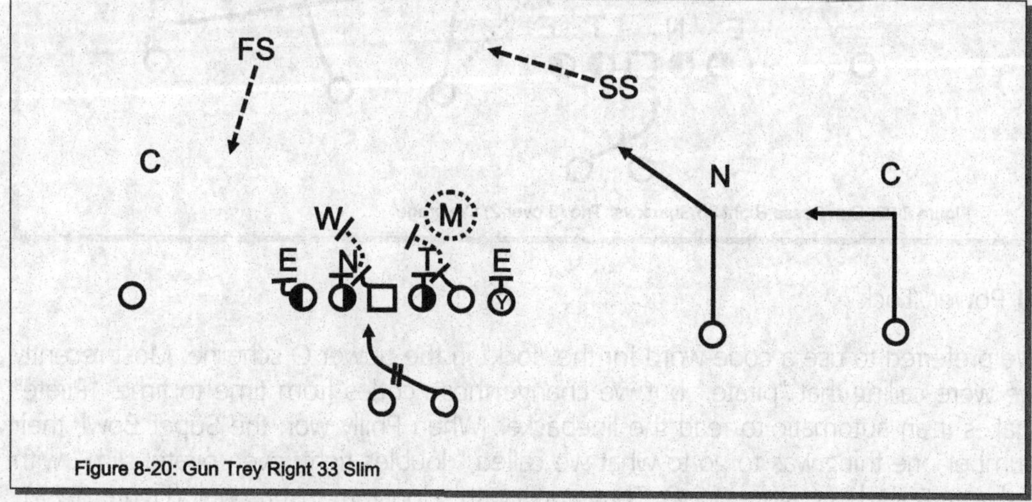

Figure 8-20: Gun Trey Right 33 Slim

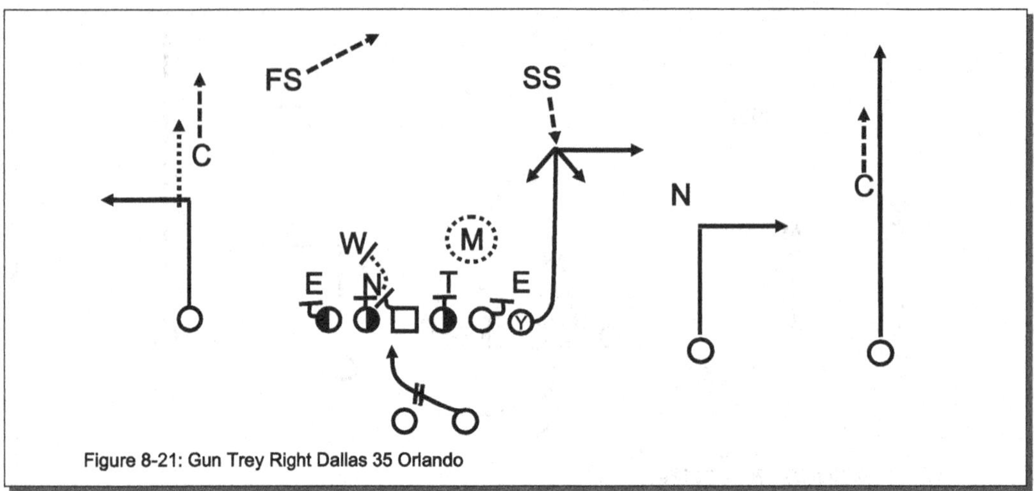

Figure 8-21: Gun Trey Right Dallas 35 Orlando

Remember "shank," the "trio beater"? So, whether you're in "trips" or "posse" and you've got people who want to play "3-over-2," you "lock" the end and read that linebacker. On "posse right: 35 shank," if the linebacker closes, X gets the ball. On this, there's a chance to hit #3 right down the middle (Figure 8-22). If the coverage is man-free, rather than "trio," the W receiver then converts to a stab route (Figure 8-23). Again, I think you can see where if you coach the heck out of your base stuff, you can build any of these ideas directly on that foundation and have fun with them!

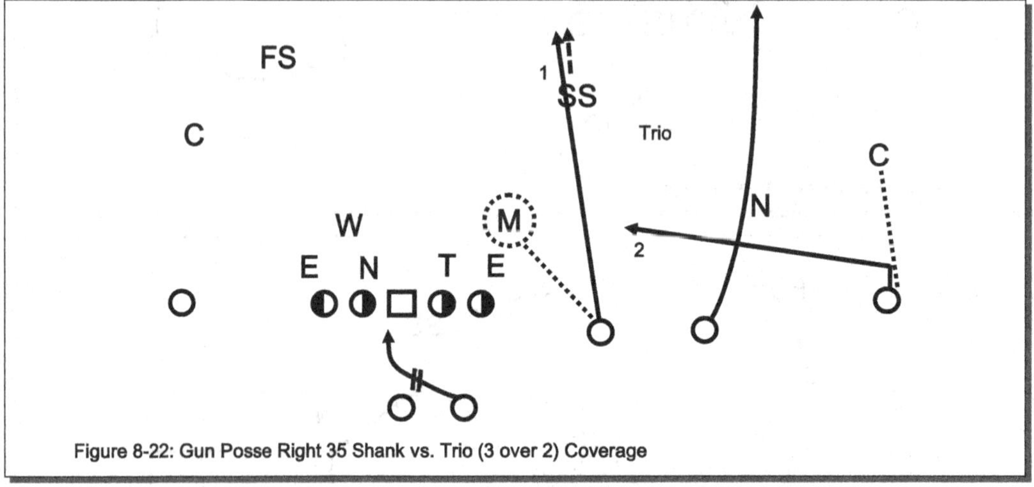

Figure 8-22: Gun Posse Right 35 Shank vs. Trio (3 over 2) Coverage

❑ Power "Lock"

We preferred to use a code-word for the "lock" in the power O scheme. Most recently we were calling that "pirate," but we change those codes from time to time. "Pirate" makes it an automatic to read the linebacker. When Philly won the Super Bowl, their number one thing was to go to what we called "doubles right: even pirate, slim," with a slant a 5-yard in (Figure 8-24). That works with "Houston" just as well (Figure 8-25).

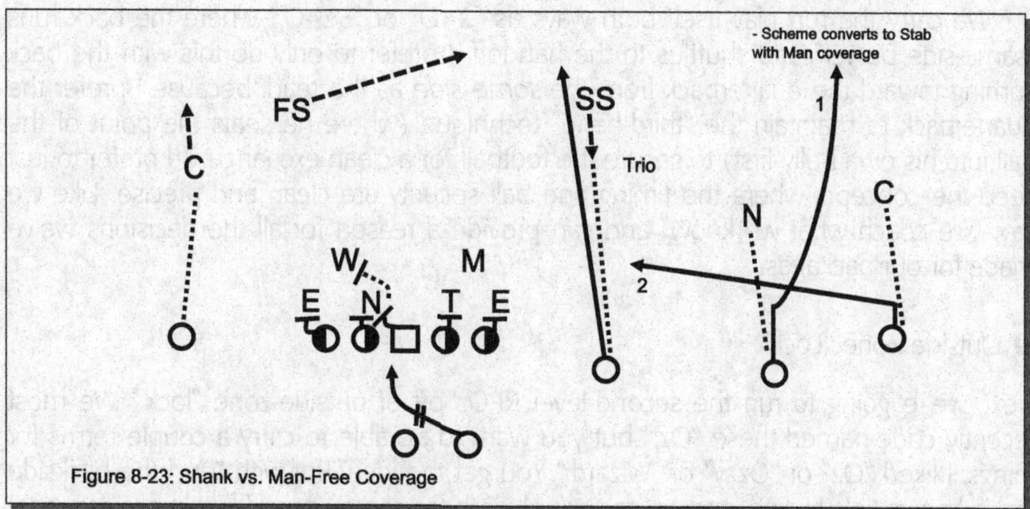


Figure 8-23: Shank vs. Man-Free Coverage

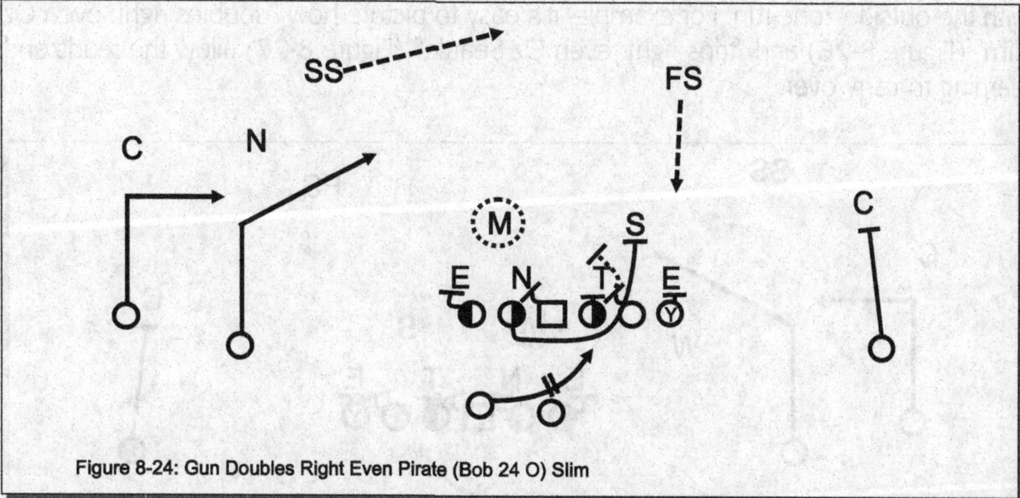


Figure 8-24: Gun Doubles Right Even Pirate (Bob 24 O) Slim

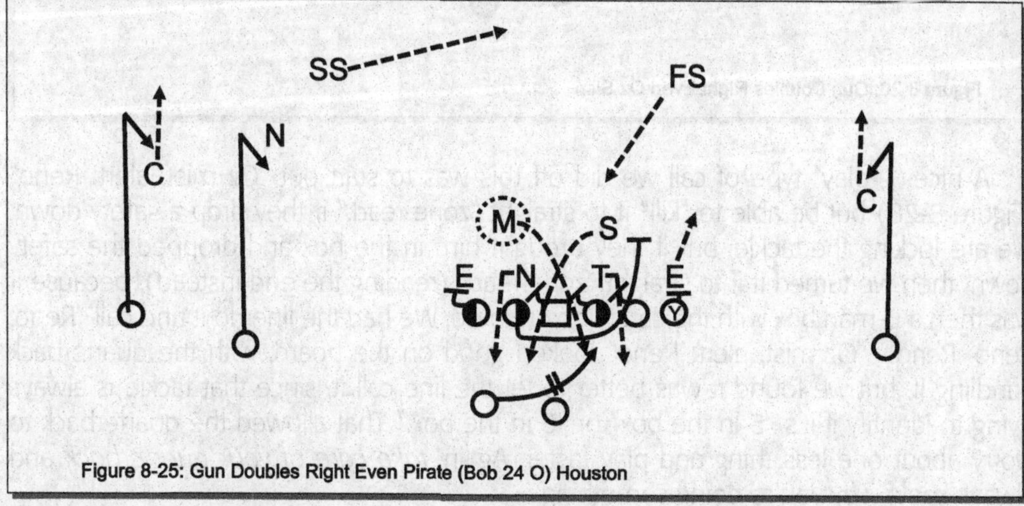


Figure 8-25: Gun Doubles Right Even Pirate (Bob 24 O) Houston

We carry the run play itself both ways as "240" or "S240," where the back runs "same-side power" and shuffles to the handoff. I prefer to only do this with the back coming toward the quarterback from the *same side* as the read, because I prefer the quarterback to maintain the "third-hand" technique (where he seats the point of the ball into his own belly first) to secure the football for a clean exchange. I'd prefer to just keep the concepts where the timing and ball security are clean and precise. Like we say, "we coach what we know" and can provide a reason for all the decisions we've made for our packages.

❑ Outside Zone "Lock"

Next, we're going to run the second-level RPOs off of outside-zone "lock." We most recently code-named these "Oz," but you want to be able to carry a couple terms for things. I liked "Oz" or "Ozzy" or "Wizard." You get the idea. But with "Oz," the backside tackle knows he's locked, and we can run all of these same second-level pass-concepts with the outside zone run. For example, it's easy to picture how "doubles right: even Oz slim" (Figure 8-26) and "trips right: even Oz Seattle" (Figure 8-27) allow the reads and learning to carry over.

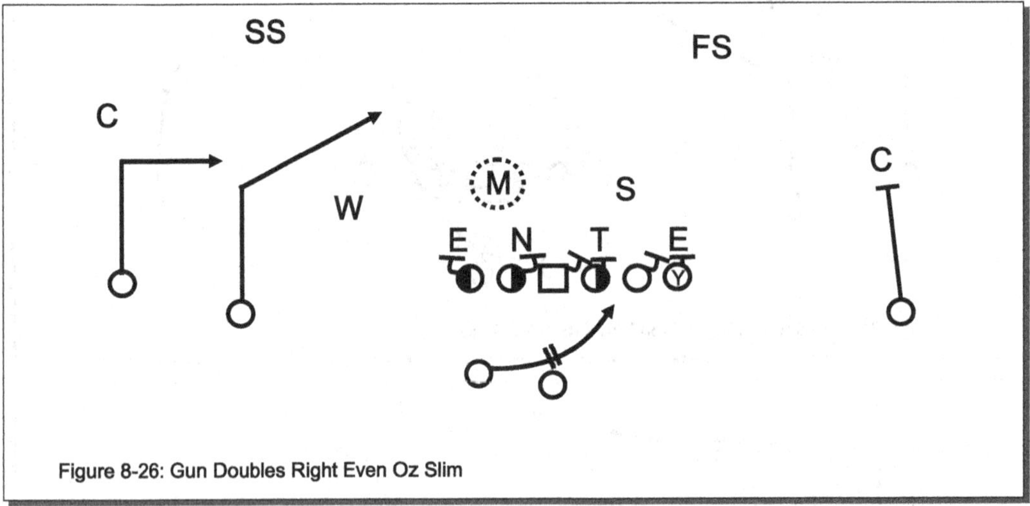

Figure 8-26: Gun Doubles Right Even Oz Slim

A nice "2-play" type of call we did off this was to start out "Oz mist, alert: Reno" (Figure 8-28) but be able to "kill" it to straight "zone-read," if they drop a safety down. We are locking the tackle, but if they brought him in the box and dropped the safety down, then we turned it into straight "zone-read" (reading the end instead), because it was then a 6-man box with the safety down there. We had the line do it and call "Reno, Reno, Reno!" "Oz mist, alert: Reno" looked good on the board, with the quarterback handling it, but we found it was better to let the line call it, since that tackle is always trying to identify if it's "5 in the box" or "6 in the box." That allowed the quarterback to worry about one less thing and play faster. Again, *take care of your quarterback* and always know *why* you're doing something.

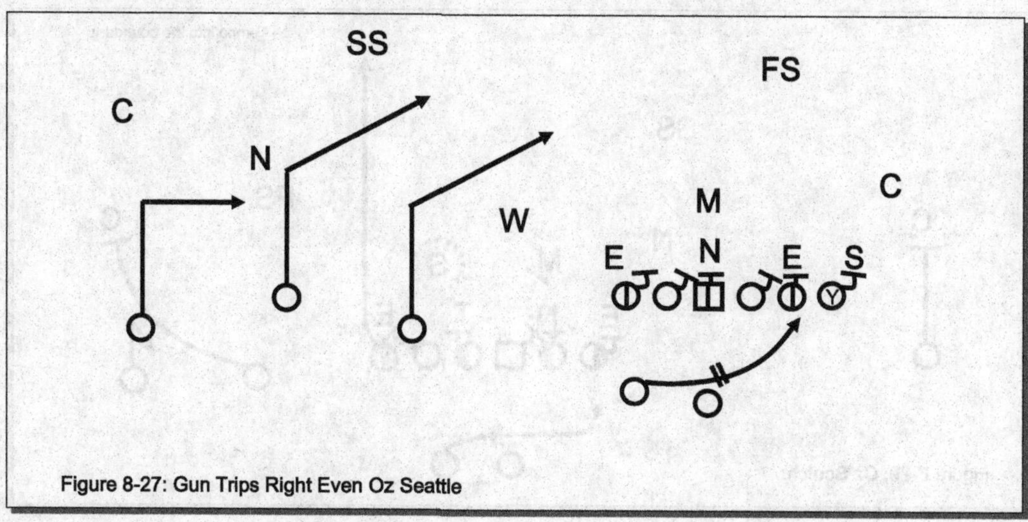

Figure 8-27: Gun Trips Right Even Oz Seattle

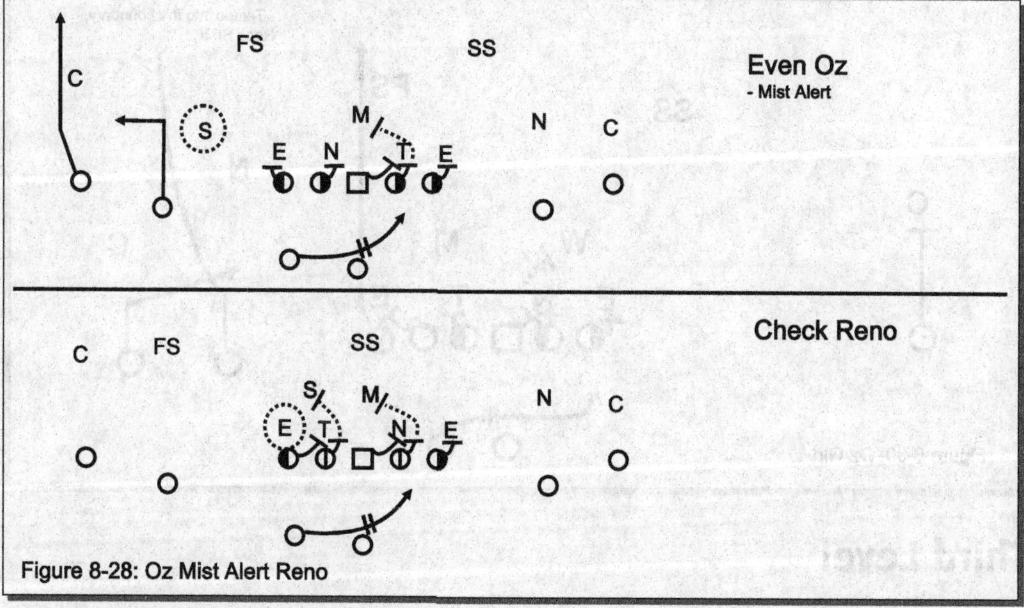

Figure 8-28: Oz Mist Alert Reno

"Scotch" and "gin" have also been good for us. These are both 3x1 "into the boundary" calls, where the tight end is the pass-option, with either a "key" (Figure 8-29) or a "stab" (Figure 8-30) outside of it. Quarterbacks tend to find this throw easier with "outside-zone lock," or "mid-zone lock," in which the back is taking a more horizontal path, as opposed to "inside-zone lock" where the quarterback is forced to ride the back vertically.

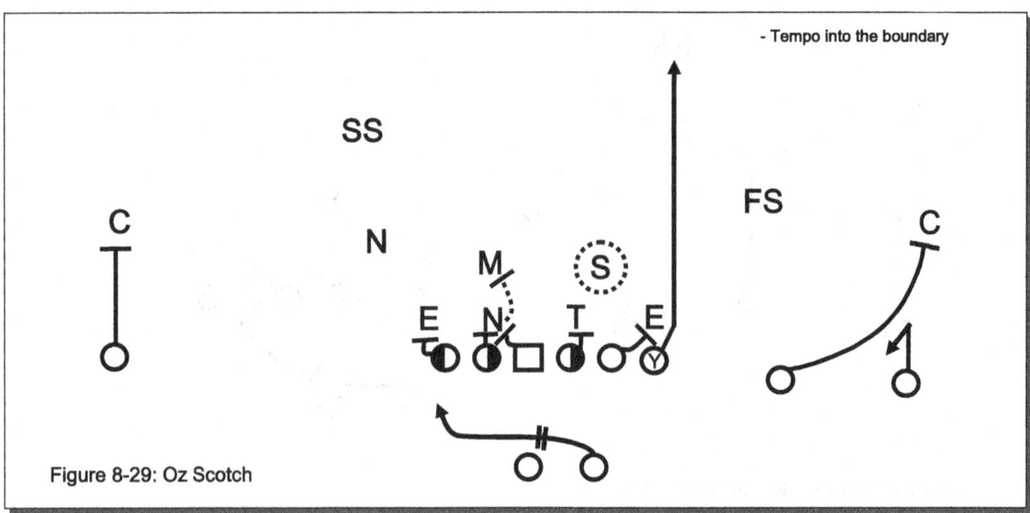

Figure 8-29: Oz Scotch

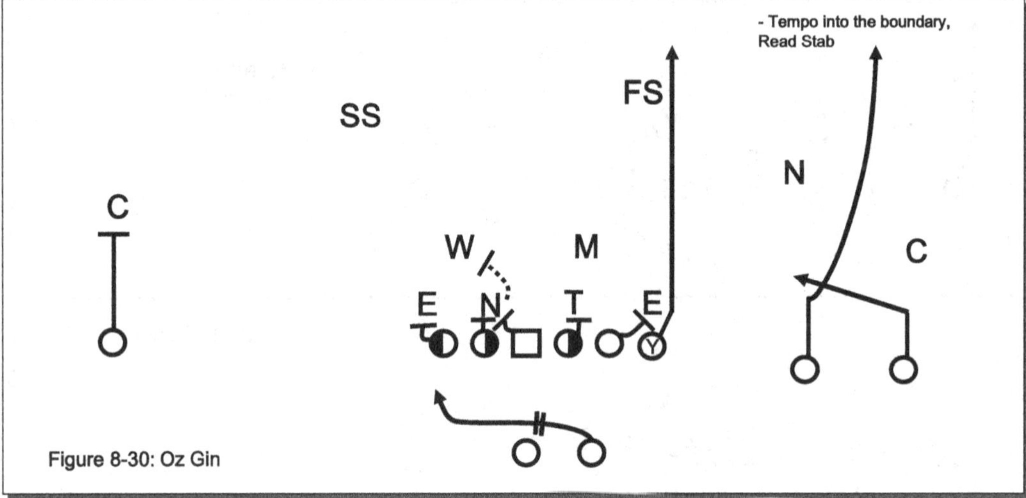

Figure 8-30: Oz Gin

## Third Level

We can read a "third-level" defender, where we're trying to take advantage of a defense bringing the bonus guy down in run support. Remember the "brown" route (5-step slant) from quick game? This is where that route fits nicely, because it times up well, when you're really trying to beat the safety. That's where you call "gun doubles right: S24O, brown," with the back on the same-side. Then, if that strong safety starts creeping down, you throw the deep slant to Z (Figure 8-31). Or go "gun trey right: north pirate, brown" (Figure 8-32) and run it from the other hash to the other side. Again, we prefer to set the back to the same side as the pass-option. Then if it's a single receiver side, "38 lock" or "outside zone" is great: "gun trey right: even Oz, brown" (Figure 8-33). Again, I want to define the runs first, and then decide on pass-options. For us, that "brown" route always goes to the boundary receiver.

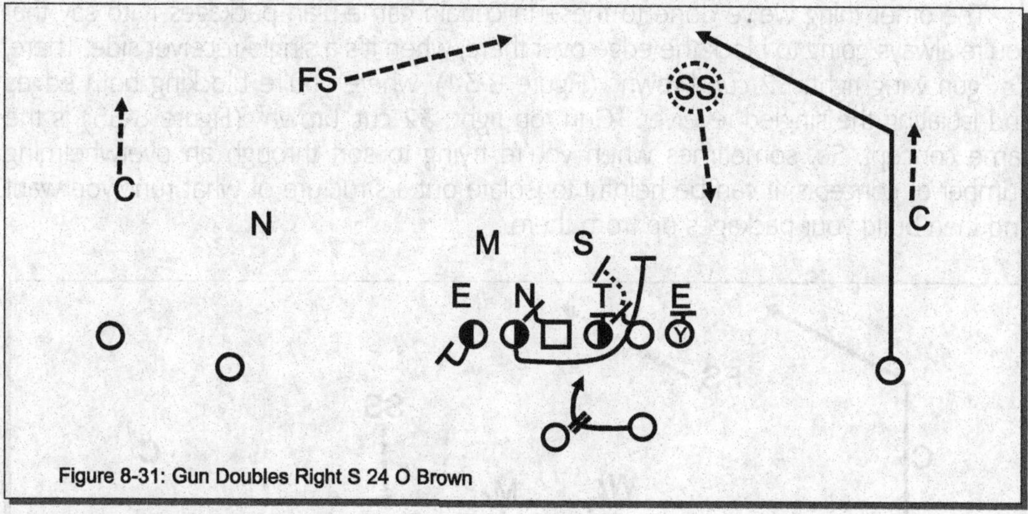

Figure 8-31: Gun Doubles Right S 24 O Brown

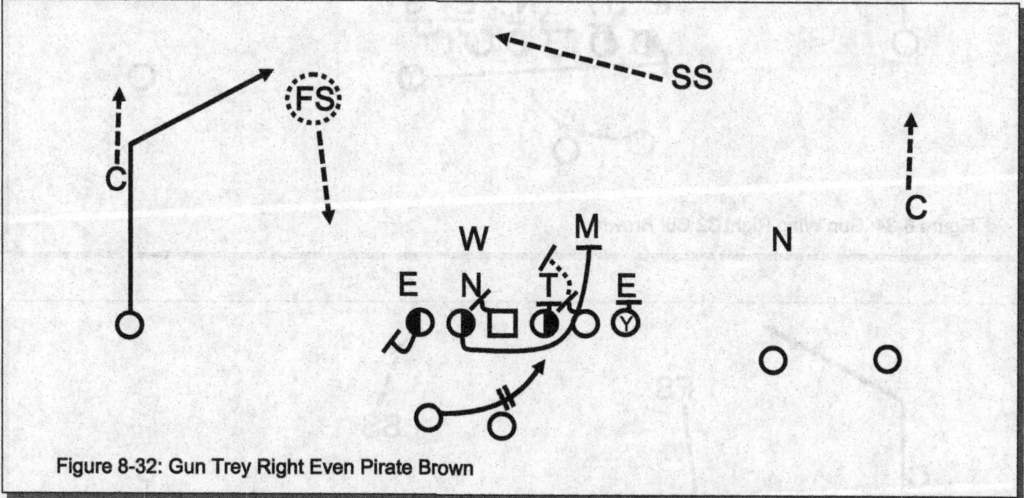

Figure 8-32: Gun Trey Right Even Pirate Brown

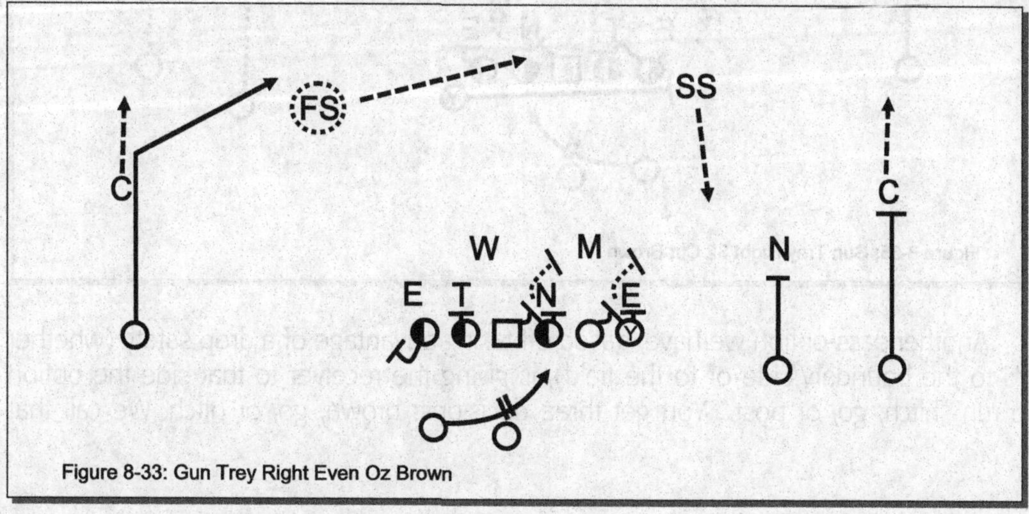

Figure 8-33: Gun Trey Right Even Oz Brown

The other thing we've done to these in certain game-plan packages is to say that you're always going to block the edge over there, when it's a single-receiver side. There, it's "gun wing right: 32 *cut*, brown" (Figure 8-34), where you're blocking both edges and isolating the singled receiver. "Gun top right: 32 cut, brown" (Figure 8-35) is the same concept. So, sometimes when you're trying to sort through an overwhelming number of concepts, it can be helpful to isolate out a structure of what runs you want and then build your packages up from there.

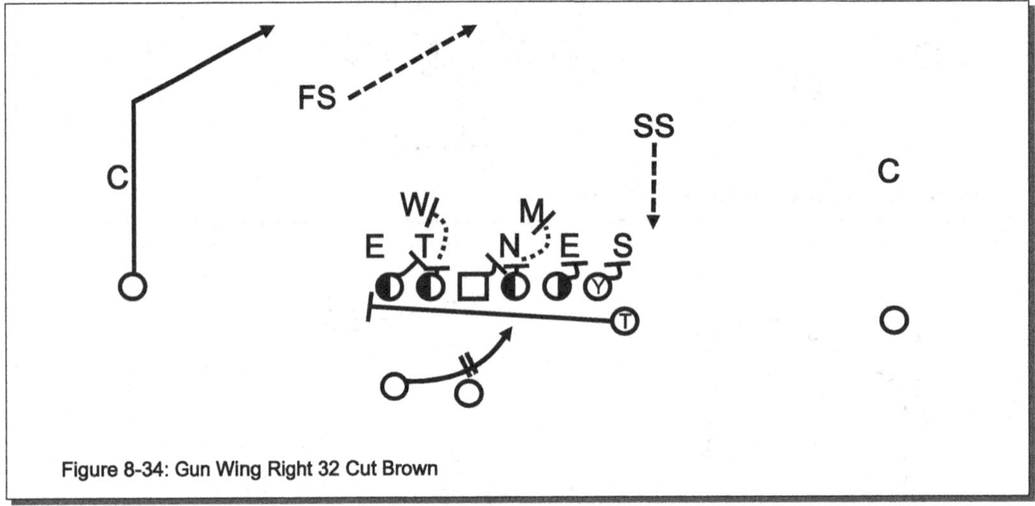

Figure 8-34: Gun Wing Right 32 Cut Brown

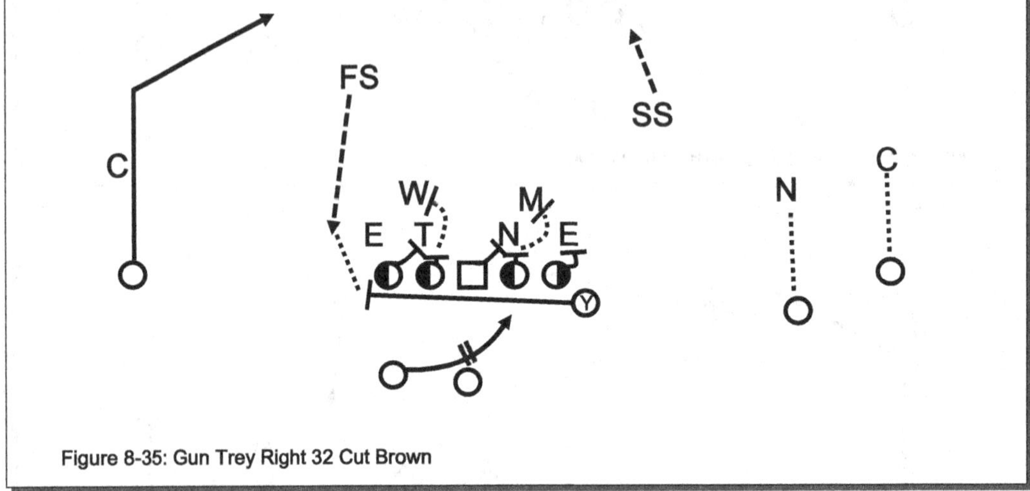

Figure 8-35: Gun Trey Right 32 Cut Brown

Another pass-option we have, based off taking advantage of a drop safety (whether it's to the boundary side or to the field), is giving the receiver to that side the option to run "hitch, go, or post." You get three decisions: brown, go, or hitch. We call that "mice," like "three blind mice" for three options (Figure 8-36). I like the timing better if the receiver is strict with the footwork, rather than letting the receiver make his decision seven or more steps downfield. On this, it's 5-step hitch, 5-step brown or just run a go: "three blind mice." So, we're talking "gun top right: 32 cut, Z mice," (Figure 8-37). "Thunder right: 32 mice" is where both receivers have the option route. The quarterback reads it away from the drop safety, or if they remain 2-deep, he hands the ball off (Figure 8-38).

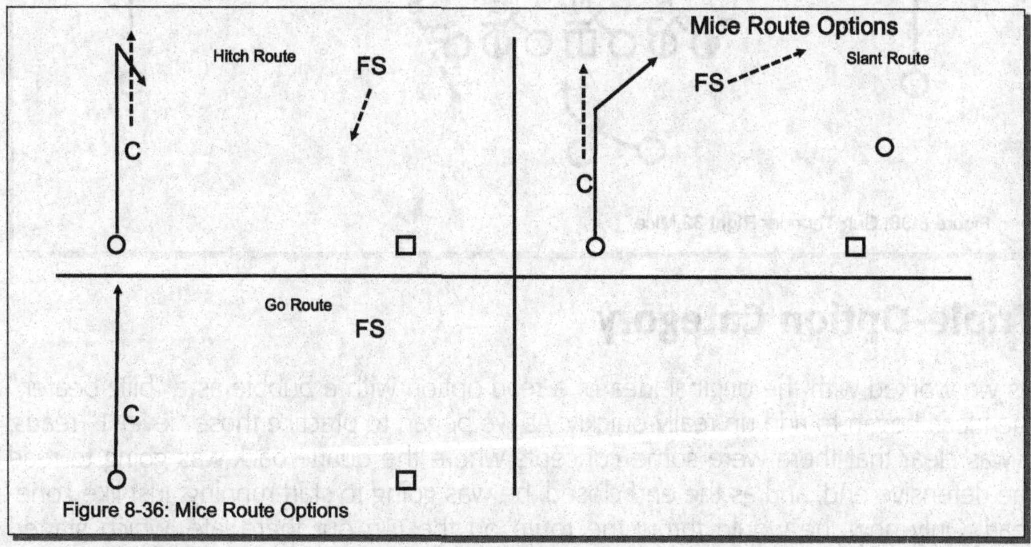

Figure 8-36: Mice Route Options

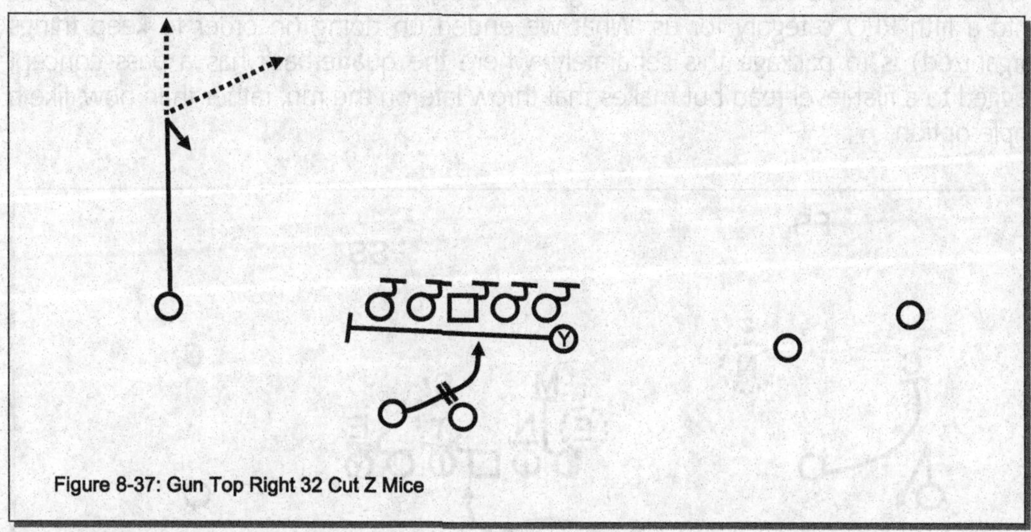

Figure 8-37: Gun Top Right 32 Cut Z Mice

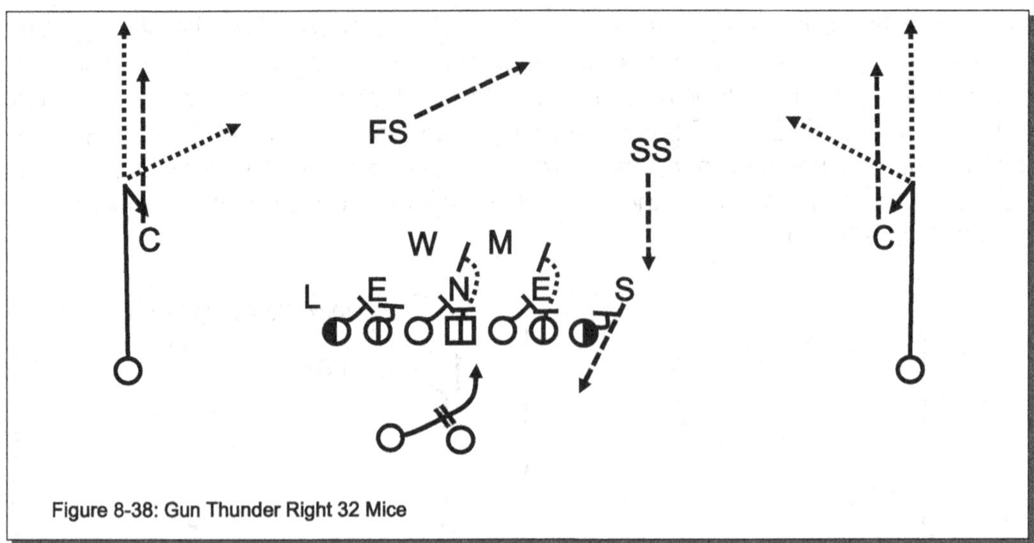


Figure 8-38: Gun Thunder Right 32 Mice

## Triple-Option Category

As we worked with the original idea of a read-option with a bubble as a "blitz-beater," the ideas began to add up really quickly. As we began to practice those "level-1" reads, it was clear that there were some concepts where the quarterback was going to read the defensive end, and as the end closed, he was going to start running, just like zone-read. Only now, he would throw the route on the run out there late, which started happening on the basic "gun double right: 32 read, key" (Figure 8-39). This developed into a fifth RPO category for us. What we ended up doing (in order to keep things organized) is to package this separately, where the quarterback has a pass concept tagged to a first-level read but makes that throw late on the run, rather than now, like a triple-option.

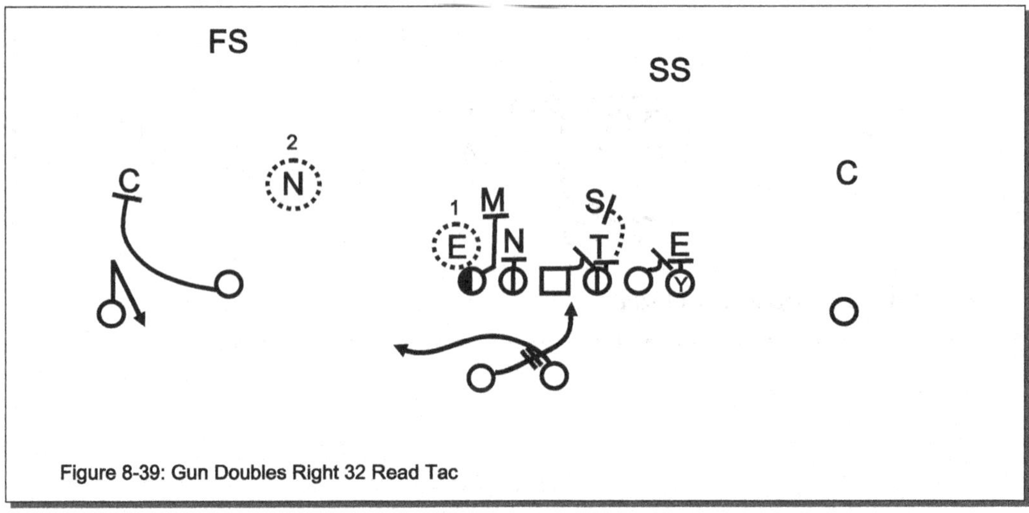


Figure 8-39: Gun Doubles Right 32 Read Tac

❑ Pepsi, Coke, Cage

We first started naming them Pepsi and Coke. These were good with Reggie Bonnafon at quarterback. Lamar Jackson excelled at the "double-cutters" (we will talk about those in the next chapter), but these "level-4 RPO" ideas really suited Reggie's skill set.

For example, Reggie threw a touchdown in the 2015 opener on "odd Reno, Pepsi" (Figure 8-40). We called that a "Pepsi" route, which is a 5-step slant (that converts vs. cover 2 to a fade) with a swing. He reads that defensive end, and then if he was keeping it, he had the option to throw that route late. In that game, he actually threw the ball late on the run and the receiver ran it right in.

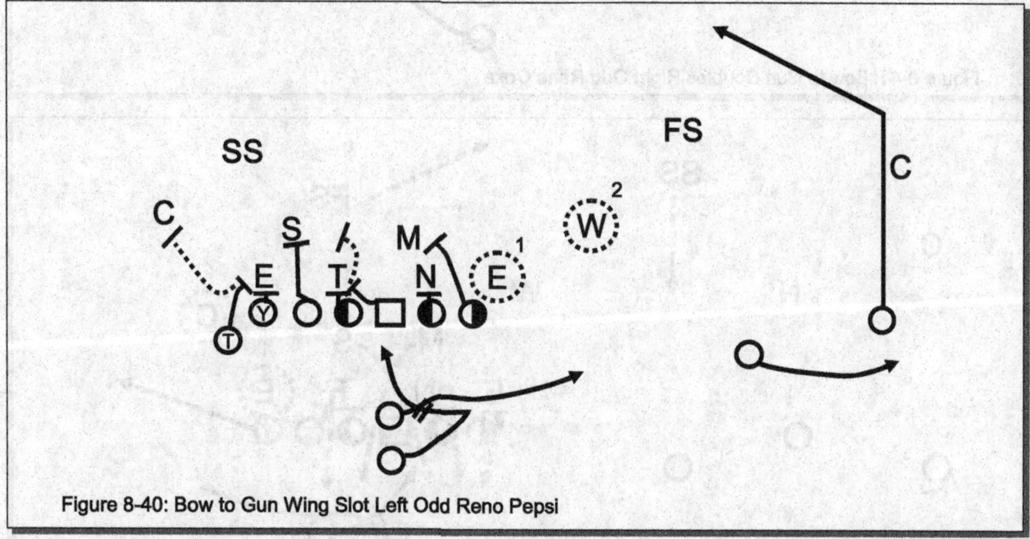

Figure 8-40: Bow to Gun Wing Slot Left Odd Reno Pepsi

"Gun doubles right: odd Reno, Coke" gives the tight end an arrow route and the outside receiver runs a "cage" route. On "cage," if you had a rolled-up corner, he would stalk and go (Figure 8-41). Out of "trips right: odd Reno, Coke" puts the tight end on an arrow to that side (Figure 8-42). The quarterback reads the defensive end and may end up throwing it to the tight end or keeping it and running the football himself. That's a similar effect to "Noah," or the arc block, with the Y releasing. "Gun Kansas right: even ninja Coke" is excellent in short yardage (Figure 8-43).

Another way we ran that when Reggie was a freshman was "shot dot left: odd ninja Pepsi" where we had the "cutter" coming across (Figure 8-44). One time he ran for a long gain, the next time he threw the swing route. "Shot top right: even ninja cage" also became part of this "Pepsi" or "triple-option" package (Figure 8-45). I'd really rather go "cut cage," so their guy is thinking about protecting his legs and he isn't trying to grab the quarterback. This allows your quarterback to attack the perimeter better. I felt like the quarterbacks were more comfortable with "cut" than they were with things like

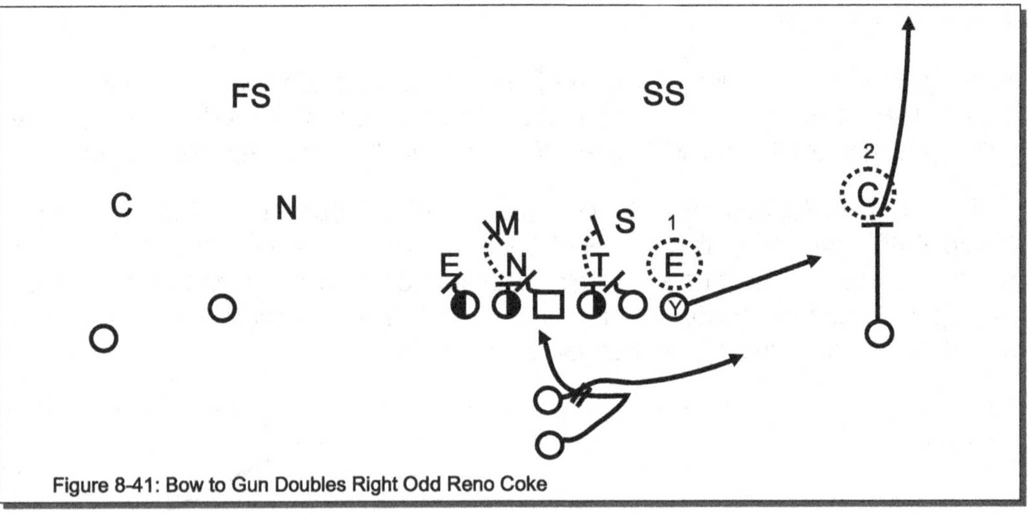

Figure 8-41: Bow to Gun Doubles Right Odd Reno Coke

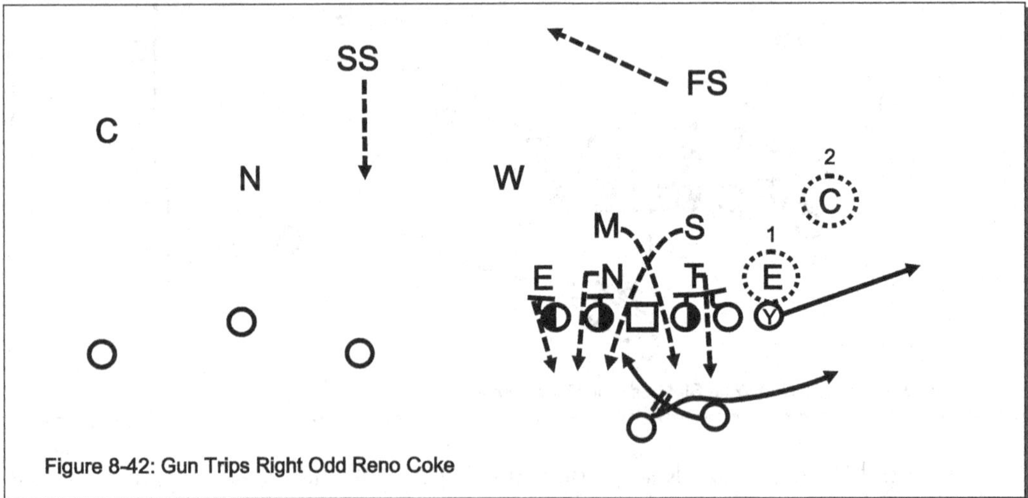

Figure 8-42: Gun Trips Right Odd Reno Coke

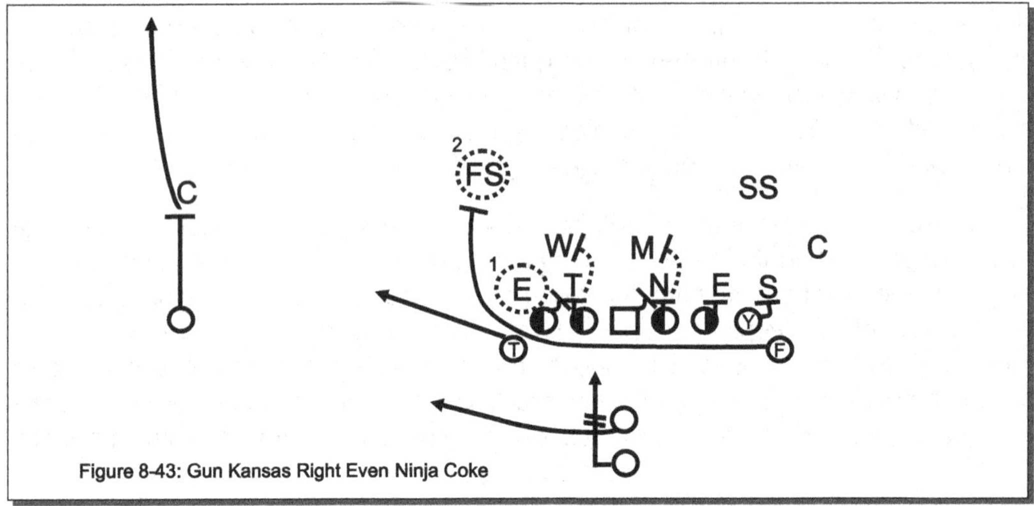

Figure 8-43: Gun Kansas Right Even Ninja Coke

"ninja cage," so we usually refined the package down to that. It's usually a quarterback keeper, unless the corner takes the quarterback and you throw it late to the single receiver. If you get press, throw the fade for a touchdown. It was a good 1st-and-10 call in the red zone.

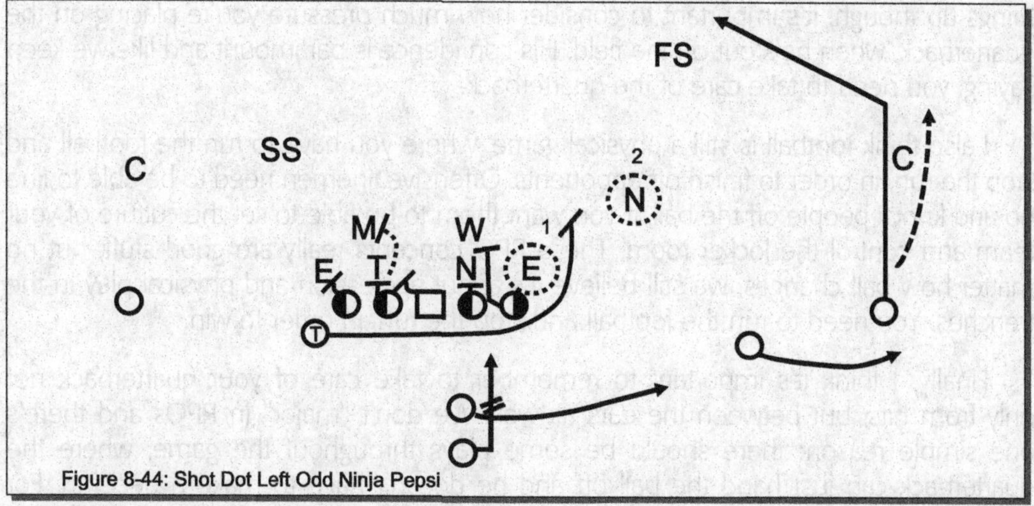

Figure 8-44: Shot Dot Left Odd Ninja Pepsi

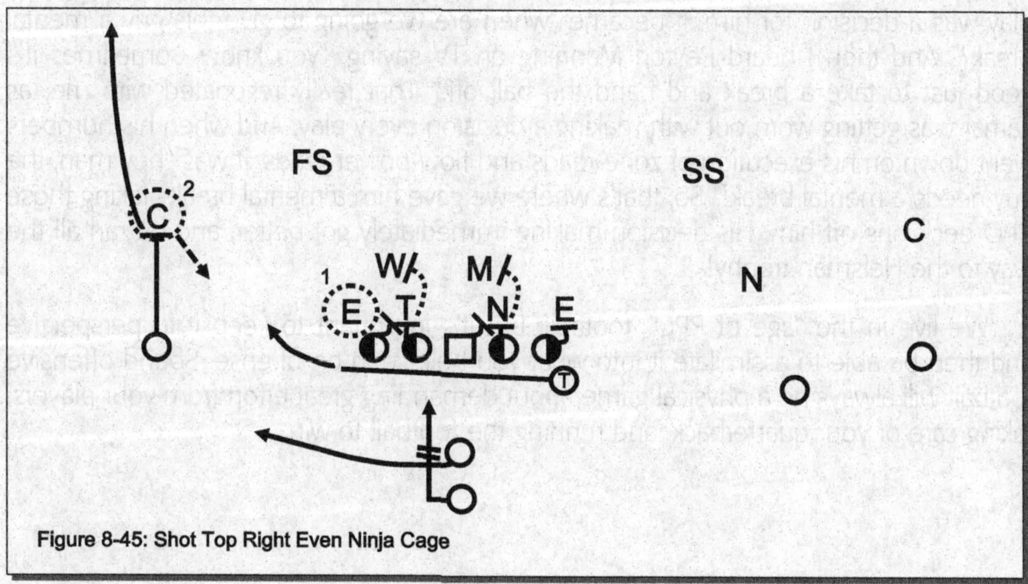

Figure 8-45: Shot Top Right Even Ninja Cage

## Final Thoughts Regarding Run/Pass Options

We frame the run/pass options into these five categories (blitz-beater, three levels of defenders for reads, triple-option). These ideas can be drawn up any number of ways and are basically only limited by a coach's imagination on paper. As you draw these things up though, it's important to consider how much pressure you're placing on the quarterback, when he's out on the field. His confidence is paramount and like we keep saying, you need to take care of the quarterback.

I also think football is still a physical game, where you have to run the football and stop the run, in order to finish off opponents. Offensive linemen need to be able to line up and knock people off the ball, if you want them to be able to set the culture of your team and control the locker room. These RPO concepts really are good stuff, but no matter how ball changes, we still believe it's about aggression and physical play in the trenches. You need to run the football and stop the run, in order to win.

Finally, I think it's important to remember to take care of your quarterback not only from hits, but between the ears as well. We don't "major" in RPOs and there's one simple reason: there should be some plays throughout the game, where the quarterback can just hand the ball off and he doesn't have to make a decision. For example, Lamar Jackson was doing so much read-option and dropback pass, so every play was a decision for him. It became "when are we going to give this guy a mental break?" And then I heard Peyton Manning on TV saying, "you know, sometimes it's good just to take a break and hand the ball off." That really resonated with me, as Lamar was getting worn out with making a decision every play. And when his numbers went down on his execution of zone-reads and flow-power reads, it was "hey man, the guy needs a mental break!" So, that's where we gave him a mental break–taking those RPO decisions off him. His decision-making immediately got better, and he ran all the way to the Heisman trophy!

We live in the "age of RPO" football, but it's important to keep it in perspective and then be able to assimilate it into what you believe in on offense. Sound offensive football will always be a physical game about demanding great effort from your players, taking care of your quarterback, and running the football to win.

# Chapter 9
## Option to the Heisman

I'd like to finish with some run game ideas, and I think it will be most useful to show you how we ran the football in the context of our "read-option" series. When you have a special player, it's important to be able to create packages that really maximize his talents. We did that most often with our zone schemes from pistol and with the power schemes from gun, each of which I'd like to describe for you now. When we got all 11 players firing together as a unit, Lamar Jackson ran the option all the way to the Heisman Trophy.

## Run Offense Basics

In our system, we always teach the run game to our players like we are in a right formation. Even numbers represent runs to the right, odd numbers denote runs to the left. When we list plays for our players, they also understand that if the even number comes first, it's a "closed-side" run (run toward the tight end side) and if we list the odd number first, then it's an "open-side" run (away from the tight end).

In our zone or "zone read" scheme from "shot," we use the numbers 12 and 13 (Figure 9-1). Therefore, the players know in our game plan that when we list (or call) "12/13," it's a closed-side blocking scheme and when we list (or call) "13/12," it's an open-side blocking scheme. This is a way to make sure the staff and players are always on the same page.

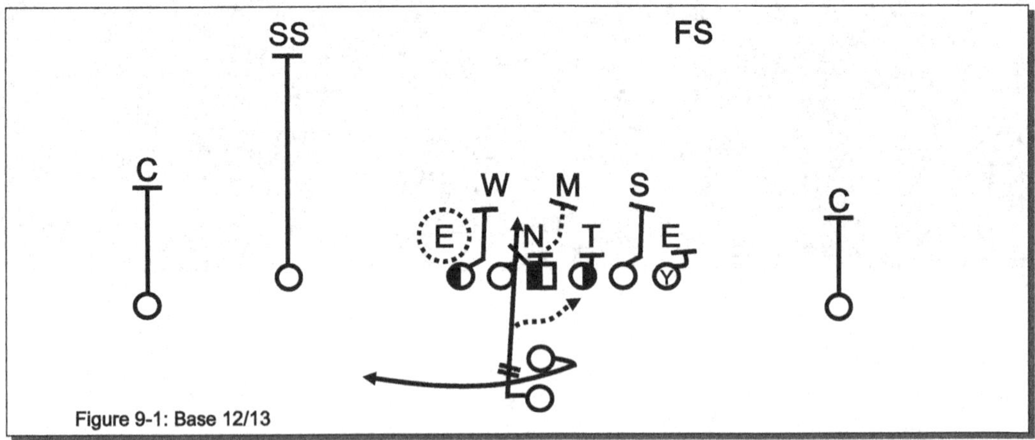

Figure 9-1: Base 12/13

**Play: 9-1**

| Pos: | Assignment: |
|---|---|
| W | Must anticipate QB keeping ball. Block outside number of alley defender. |
| X | Quick technique. |
| Y | Quick technique. |
| QB | Lateral hop step to the call side. Must give six o'clock to the RB. Get your eyes to DE immediately. |

## Pistol Origins and Installation

We like to run the "zone-read" schemes from "pistol" sets (what we call "shot," to save a syllable). This allows us to disguise the direction of the play, while also setting up some unique blocking schemes. In the origins, this scheme was first described in terms of "1-man, 2-man, and 3-man game." In sequence, that would be the base read-option, the "cut" block to hold off the open edge or the "slice" element to borrow a blocker from the backside for the keeper, and then the triple-option game. I don't necessarily think of the concept this way anymore, but it's the way we initially started installing the package. Before we take a look at how we categorize each level of the runs, let's first look at the fundamentals.

## O-Line Calls & Techniques

To run this scheme effectively, the offensive line must be able to identify fronts, make the correct calls and execute the blocks properly. The basic calls for us are "Ray/Lou," "tag," and "eat." The center always makes a "Ray/Lou" call to clarify which guard he's working toward and which linebacker they're working to. If he's covered, it's a "no" call, which then tells the guard to make a "tag" call to the tackle ("tag" means "tackle and guard"). If the center and guard are working together, the tackle would make an "eat" call to the tight end ("eat" means "end and tackle"), where they're pushing a 7 or 8 technique and getting movement to the linebacker level (Figure 9-2).

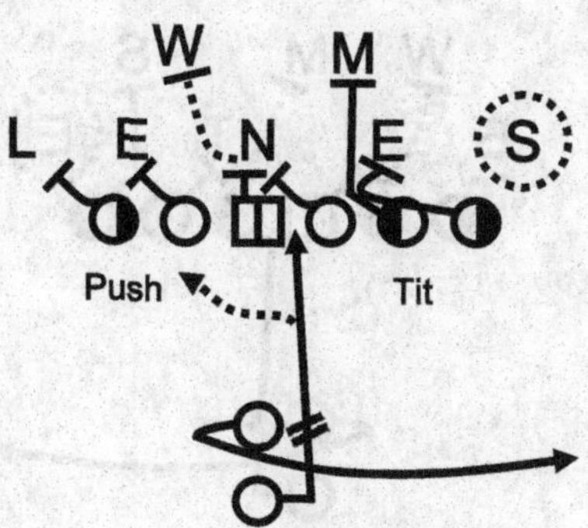


Figure 9-2a: Offensive Line Rules - 13/12 Noah vs. 30 Defense

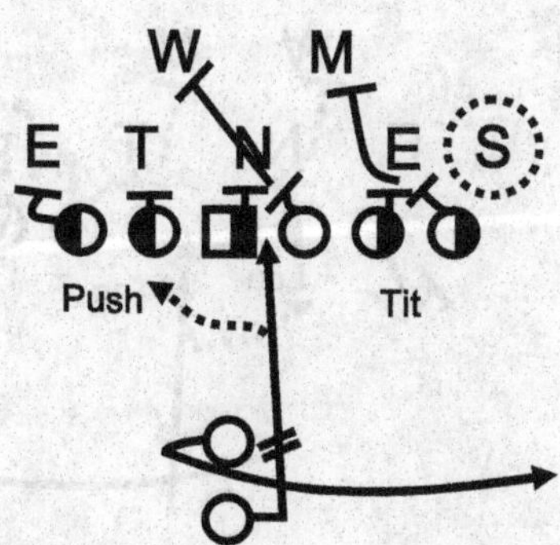


Figure 9-2b: Offensive Line Rules - 13/12 Noah vs. Under Defense

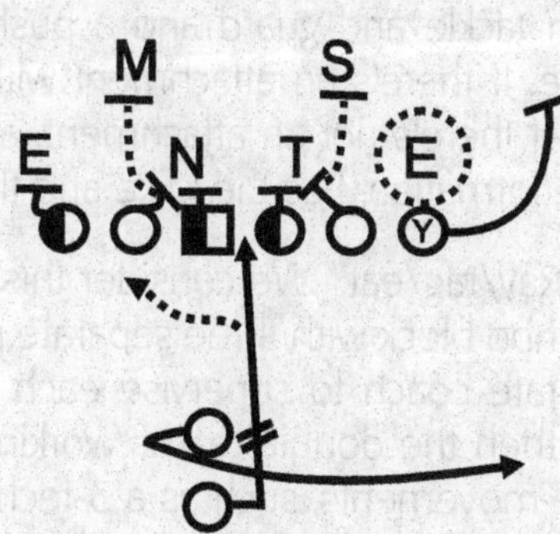


Figure 9-2c: Offensive Line Rules - 13/12 Noah vs. Over Defense

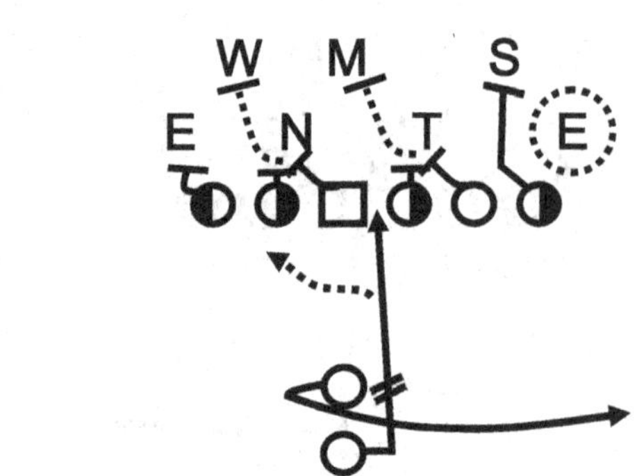


Figure 9-2d: Offensive Line Rules - 13/12 Noah vs. College 4-3 Defense

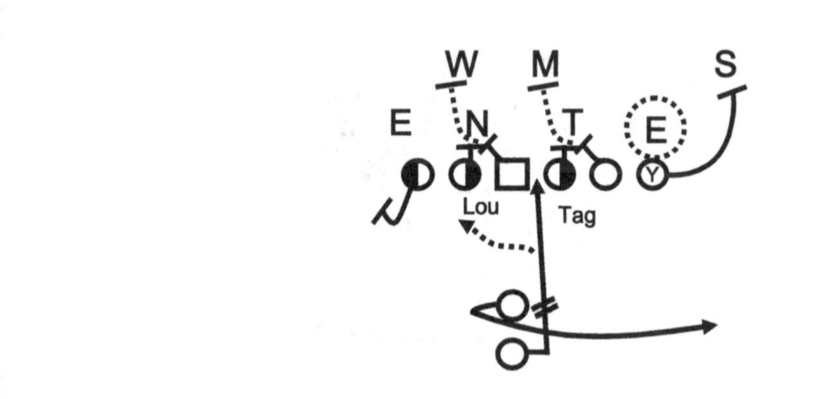


Figure 9-2e: Offensive Line Rules - 13/12 Noah vs. 4-2 Defense

The 3-4 front, especially with the "4I" techniques, will carry a "push" call, which means a frontside "fan" between tackle and guard and a push with the center and backside guard for the playside line. If there's an attachment with the backside tackle, the push is to the Mike linebacker. If there's not an attachment, a tight end "ice" blocker, coming from the other side of the formation, has the Mike and the backside tackle is "base."

Every day, we work "Ray/tag/eat." We consider this "E.D.D." or an "every day drill." Usually we work each combo block with three separate practice "pods" and sometimes, we'll even assign a separate coach to supervise each specific double-team. First, we work a base drive block, then the double-teams working to a linebacker, and then we progress to various D-line movements, such as a 3-technique becoming a 1-technique or a 7-technique playing out. The O-line must be able to handle various games, stunts, dogs, blitzes, and pressures. They need to work against all of that every day in practice, if you expect to be able to run this scheme effectively.

**Play: 9-2**

| Pos: | Rules: |
|---|---|
| Y | Arc to block alley:<br>1.Arc to block alley.<br>2.vs. man-on, man-outside: zone C gap. Make "hot" call.<br>3.vs. 9 tech: zone C gap, "empty" call.<br>4.vs. 7 or 8 tech: arc to SLB.<br>5.Orphan: arc past force in alley. Block next level. |
| ST | Area drive, B gap cylinder, tag:<br>1.vs. SG uncovered: zone B gap cylinder to backside LB. Alert fade/hook. You have LB.<br>2.Clamp back to DE with hot call. Scoop with TE.<br>3.vs. SG covered: zone B gap cylinder, (vs. 3 tech, alert to scoop.)(vs. 2 or 3 tech with wide LB: run 3 tech on and climb to LB.) |
| SG | Area drive, cut-off, tag:<br>1.vs. covered: cut-off, possible tag with ST to SLB. Alert alignment of SLB to degree of clamp. If SLB is wide, overtake 3 tech so ST can climb.<br>2.Tag with ST to MLB with empty call.<br>3.vs. uncovered: alert Ray call from center to point LB.<br>4.vs. uncovered (backside shade): cut-off. |
| C | Area drive, ray, clamp:<br>1.vs. covered (shade): "no" call, area drive.<br>2.vs. covered (0 tech): "Ray" call to backside LB, scoop.<br>3.vs. uncovered: Lou call to point. Alert to skin movement.<br>4.vs. 3-4 box: alert push call to full zone. Point LB is now WLB. |
| WG | Area drive, tag, Lou:<br>1.vs. covered: area drive DT. Lou with center to point LB.<br>2.vs. uncovered: tag with WT to WLB. (vs. shade: possible power to point LB).<br>3.Point LB changes to WLB with push call. |
| WT | Area drive, tag:<br>1.vs. covered: area drive DE. Possible tag with WG to WLB.<br>2.vs. uncovered: eat with TE to WLB. Alert WLB alignment. Possible fan/full call. |
| R | Take half of QB opposite the call. Press downhill. Aiming point is the inside hip of the callside guard. Press the vertical push until color shows in your window. Then, find the next vertical wall. |

## O-Line and Running Back Mechanics

A couple things do change from "shot" alignment, as opposed to offset gun. For the o-line, "shot" can create some gap control issues. It is still zone blocking, but the difference between pistol and traditional zone blocking is that linebackers are going to *fade*, so we tell the line to "block your cylinder." We don't let a guy go just because "he's not my guy." If he's "in my cylinder," I block him. You have to really coach that, and you even have to do it, when you're holding dummies and going against your own guys.

If you are running "32" from gun, and the back is coming across the formation, the linebackers are going to flow that way to get to their fits (Figure 9-3). But on "12" from shot, because the quarterback is now opening *opposite*, the linebackers are *fading* opposite of where the blocking is going (see Figure 9-1). They will fade even more, if we have any "cutters" involved. Therefore, when the running back gets the ball and cuts back, he needs to "hug the wall," so linebackers can't jump out of it. The running backs need to think, "I go opposite and then bend back to the call." We're trying to "set" the linebacker to the block and the back has to "hug the wall" for us to make that happen.

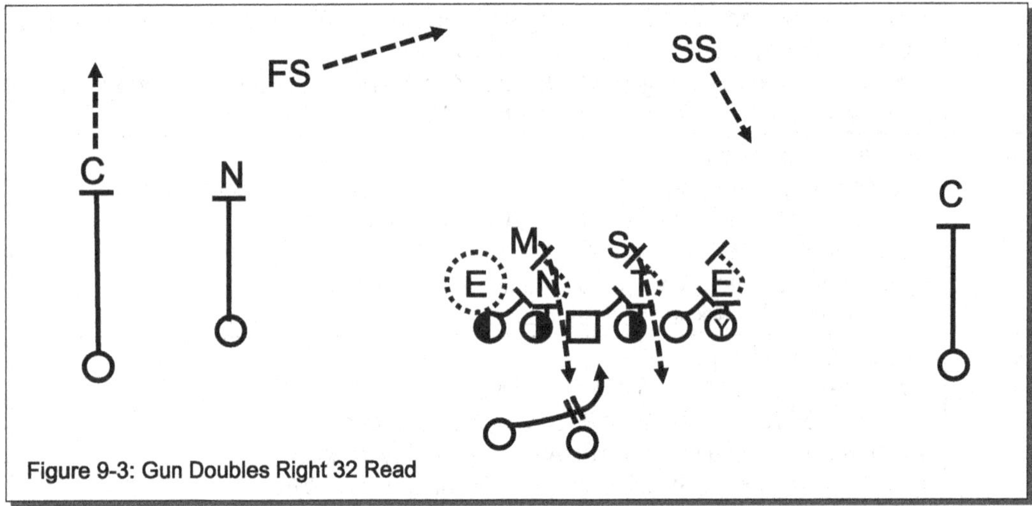

Figure 9-3: Gun Doubles Right 32 Read

The back reads the "A-gap to A-gap defender" but he needs to have an idea of whether that's a 1 or 3-technique. The quarterback needs to "give him the path," to the outside hip of the center. The quarterback has to pop laterally, get out of the way, and let the back take that path. If it's there, the back can hit it, especially to a 1-technique, because sometimes that open end plays the quarterback and it can pop right back outside. If it's clogged up, the back is going to bend back to where the point of attack is, and he understands that it's the same inside-zone blocking. In some sense, it's opposite of "gun 32," where you press the A-gap and can rollback; on "shot 12," you're pressing it, and then bending back *toward* the blockers.

## QB Mechanics and Mental Imaging

The read-option from "shot" (as opposed to offset gun) changes things slightly for the quarterback. The quarterback sets at a depth of 4 ½ yards. When he receives the football, he's going to pop laterally and at the same time, get his eyes to the read. He is going to extend the football just past his back hip, right at belly button level. Once the running back gets to the mesh, the quarterback will transfer his weight to his front foot and ride the back, while he makes a decision whether the "read" is taking the running back or quarterback. The quarterback *never* rides the back beyond his front hip.

The quarterback has to pop back and "give the back the A-gap," as he makes his read. The way we teach it to our quarterbacks is "I open opposite the call." Every guy, however, is going to think a little bit differently about how they picture it, so I always want to ask them. The goal in this instance is to establish how I *picture it in my mind*. One quarterback said "oh, I've always seen it as I put my butt to the hole." Ok, well keep thinking that way as long as you do it the right way! They may all verbalize something different, but as long as it's evident that the mental picture is correct, I try not to overcoach it.

By contrast, when we do something like "hitch" or "blue" in the quick passing game, the quarterback needs to use the *exact words* with the *exact emphasis* we teach. The rules for those particular plays are strictly defined, so we need all the players to be using the same words, in order to elicit the specific responses we want. With read-option ball though, we've found that you want to establish the *mental picture* first, and then allow the specific words to come after that. We actually teach the read-option runs to the quarterback similarly to how we coach the option-route series to the inside receivers. In other words, you need the quarterback to get the mental picture first, but if he demonstrates in practice that he can make good decisions and go make some plays, we then give him the freedom.

I think it's really about understanding that guys may learn it differently. You're going to do it the way we want you to, but how do you *say* that to yourself? How do you *picture* that in your mind? If we ask them and listen carefully to how they answer, there's actually been times where we've found "well hey, maybe that's a better way to think of it!"

## Receiver Blocking

With a quarterback who can run, you have a chance for a touchdown anytime you run this scheme, if all the receivers take pride in their blocking. The technique the receivers are taught on any of the option game is, "both sides are blocking like the play is coming to us," because we don't know who's carrying it. We use what we call "slow technique," which means they all need to exactly say:

- "Drive off the ball as hard as I can, I break down when he breaks down."
- "I get to the 'field area' (which is an arm's length apart)."
- "Punch, punch, mirror, mirror."
- "When he picks a side, I keep him there."

You have to time it correctly. Often times, if you just mirror him correctly, you can do a great job of blocking at receiver and never really "block" the guy. Then, you should "run off vs. press." You make it look like you're getting the ball. We've had guys who would jump and act like the ball was being thrown to them and who really took pride in it. If the receivers take pride in their role in the run game, you have a chance for a touchdown every time you run this scheme. That's what we mean by getting all 11 players to execute. Next, let's take a look at the schemes themselves.

## Category 1 (Base)

We organize the "12/13" run game the way we look at our RPO game, which means we categorize runs by how many players are involved in the option element. Category 1 would be what we call our "1-man game," where we hand the ball to the running back and block the zone play with no read. To the strong side, the play is called 12/13. To get the edge blocked, we either have to be in "thunder" formation to call "shot thunder right: 12" (Figure 9-4) or use a "cut" block by carrying "shot wing slot right: 12 *cut*" (Figure 9-5), where the "cut" blocker runs across the heels of the o-line and kicks out the defensive end.

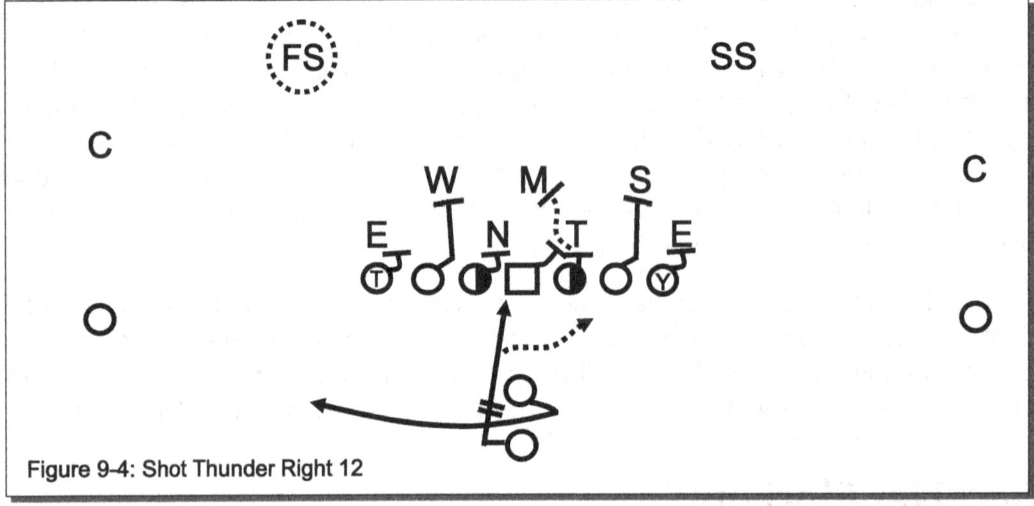

Figure 9-4: Shot Thunder Right 12

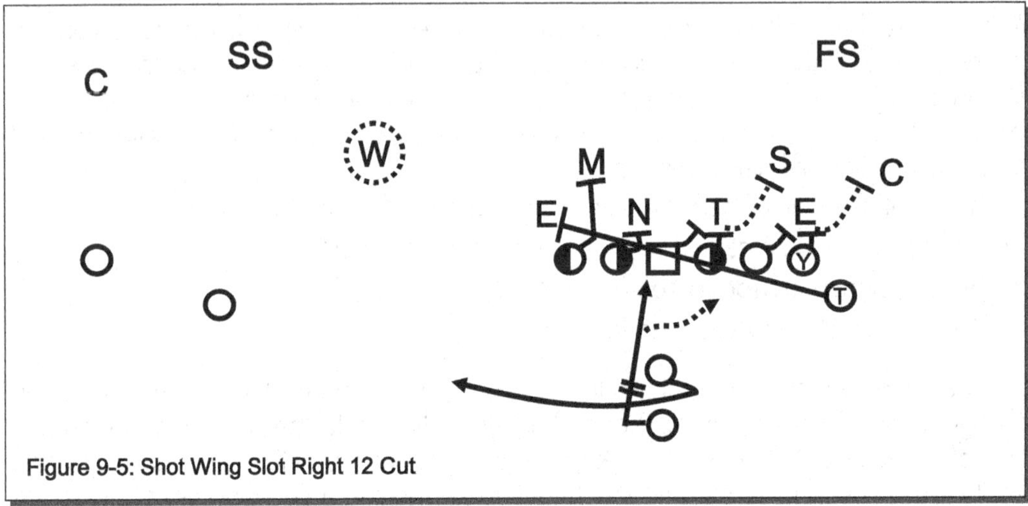

Figure 9-5: Shot Wing Slot Right 12 Cut

**Play: 9-5**

| Pos: | Assignment: |
|---|---|
| X | Slow technique.<br>vs. 1 high: man-on or run-off |
| Z | Slow technique.<br>vs. 1 high: man-on or run-off |
| QB | Lateral hop step to the callside. Must give six o'clock to the RB. Get your eyes to DE immediately. |

With the talent and ability of Lamar Jackson, this changed to where we allowed him to "read the alley" or as he verbalized it, "read the #4 defender." Lamar made a number of big plays doing that because of great ball handling and great fakes by our running backs, which caused the defensive secondary to hesitate and lose vision.

To the open side, it's called "13/12." On this, we have the tight end on the backside to block the defensive end and the quarterback again reads the alley (Figure 9-6). The quarterback must understand that if we are playing a 3-4 "I" defense, the offensive line has a "push" call. The quarterback then reads the Sam linebacker (Figure 9-7), which for the quarterback is still #4, so his reads stay consistent.

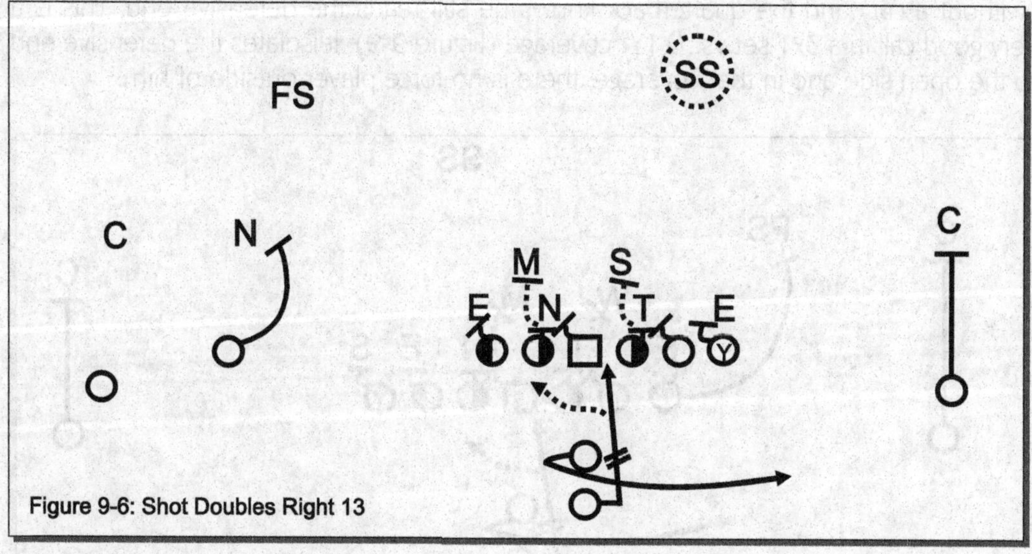

Figure 9-6: Shot Doubles Right 13

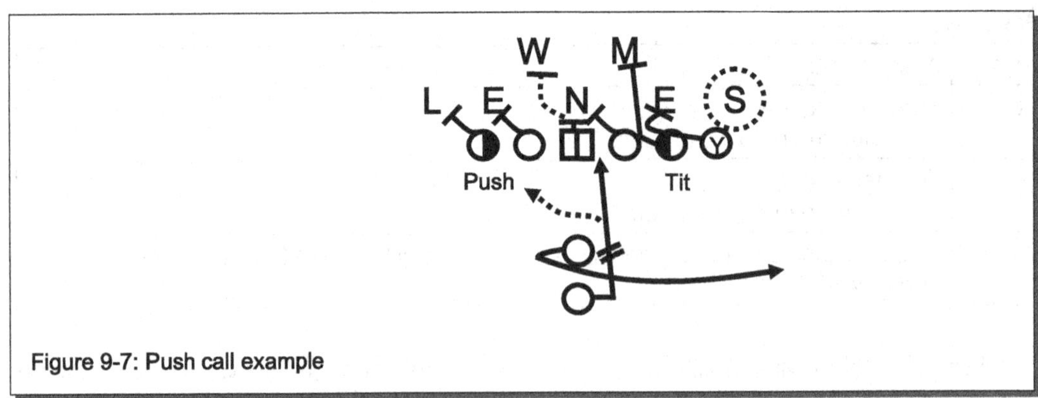

Figure 9-7: Push call example

## Category 2 (Read)

Category 2, or the "2-man game," introduces a called read for the quarterback, so we know either the quarterback or running back might carry the ball in this instance. The base play to the strongside is now called "shot thunder right: 12/13 Noah" (Figure 9-8), where we most recently used the code work "Noah" to indicate the arc block (like "Noah's Ark"). The "T" (second tight end) arc blocks the alley and the quarterback reads the defensive end. If there isn't a second tight end in the game, we just call "12/13" (without a *cut*) and the quarterback knows he still reads the defensive end. This is a very good call in a 3x1 set vs. "11Y" coverage (Figure 9-9). It isolates the defensive end to the open side and in that coverage, there is no force player outside of him.

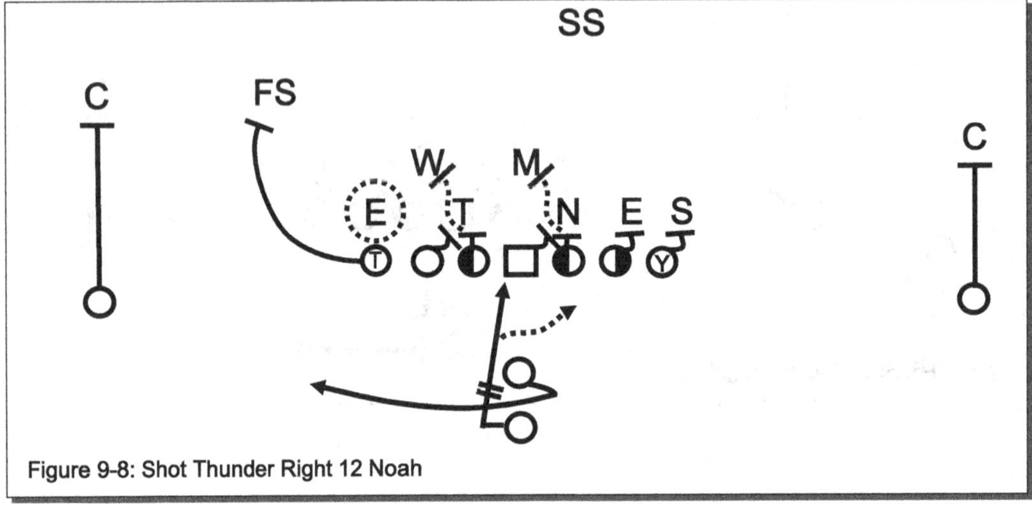

Figure 9-8: Shot Thunder Right 12 Noah

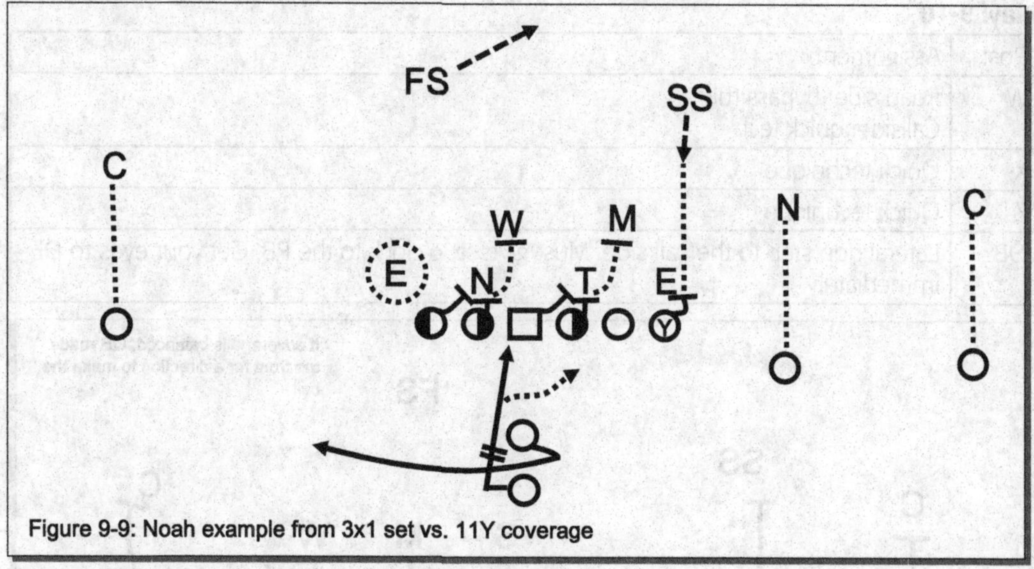

Figure 9-9: Noah example from 3x1 set vs. 11Y coverage

To the open side, we now use the same term for Y and call the play "13/12 Noah." The tight end (Y) has the arc block for the alley and the quarterback reads the defensive end (Figure 9-10). We added this to our "advantage run" category, where the huddle call (or no-huddle signal) would simply be "Noah *choice*." In this instance, "choice" means the quarterback is going to look at the defensive *front*, and then the *coverage* to decide which way to call the play. Let's say the play call is "thunder slot right: Noah *choice*." As the quarterback, if the *front* tells me one way and the coverage is balanced, I go with the *front* (Figure 9-11). If the front tells me one way (direction) and the *coverage* is rotated toward that weakness, then I go the opposite direction (Figure 9-12). If both the front and coverage are balanced, I base my direction on *personnel*, which means I call it toward my best blockers, or to a weakness in a defensive player. This has always been a great way to gain an advantage in "numbers" on a defense.

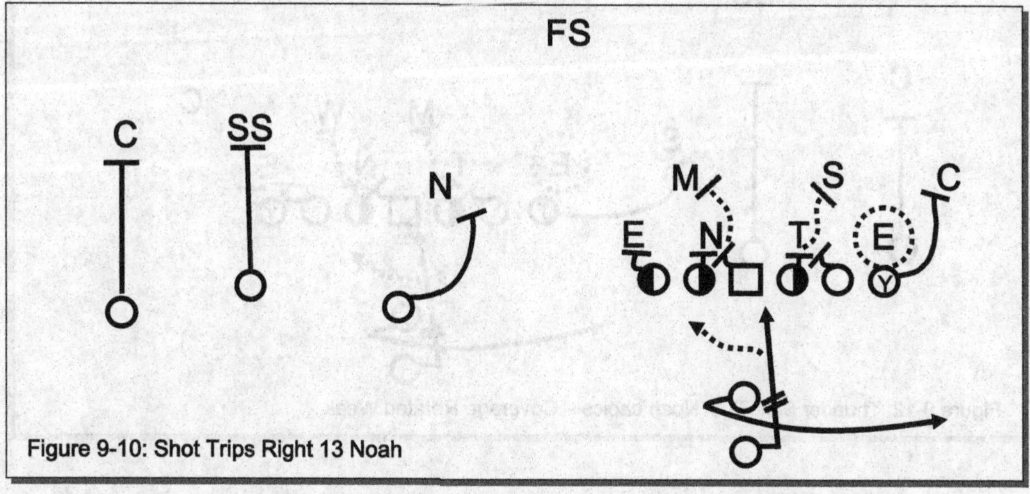

Figure 9-10: Shot Trips Right 13 Noah

**Play: 9-10**

| Pos: | Assignment: |
|---|---|
| W | Read side: bypass rule<br>Callside: quick tech |
| X | Quick technique |
| Z | Quick technique |
| QB | Lateral hop step to the call side. Must give six o'clock to the RB. Get your eyes to DE immediately. |

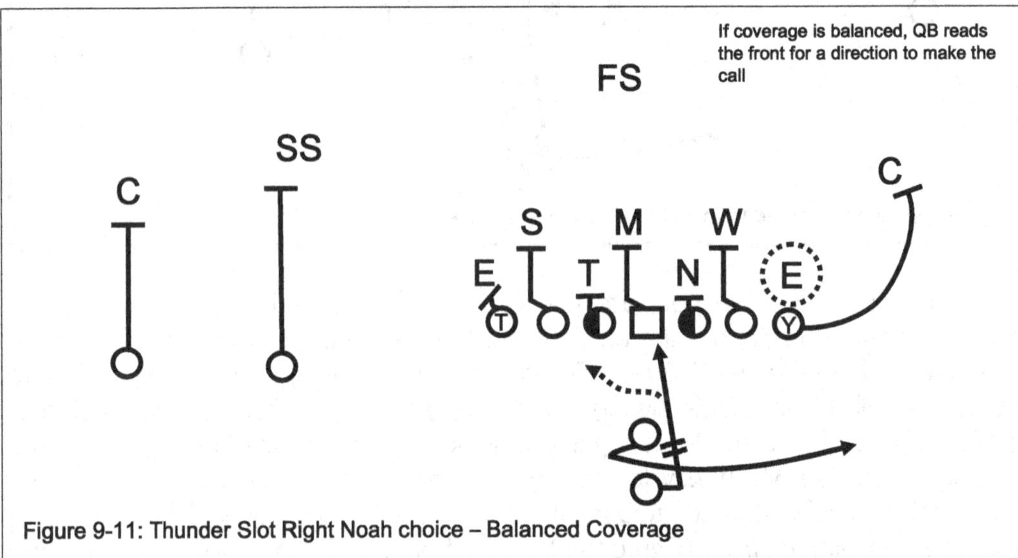


Figure 9-11: Thunder Slot Right Noah choice – Balanced Coverage

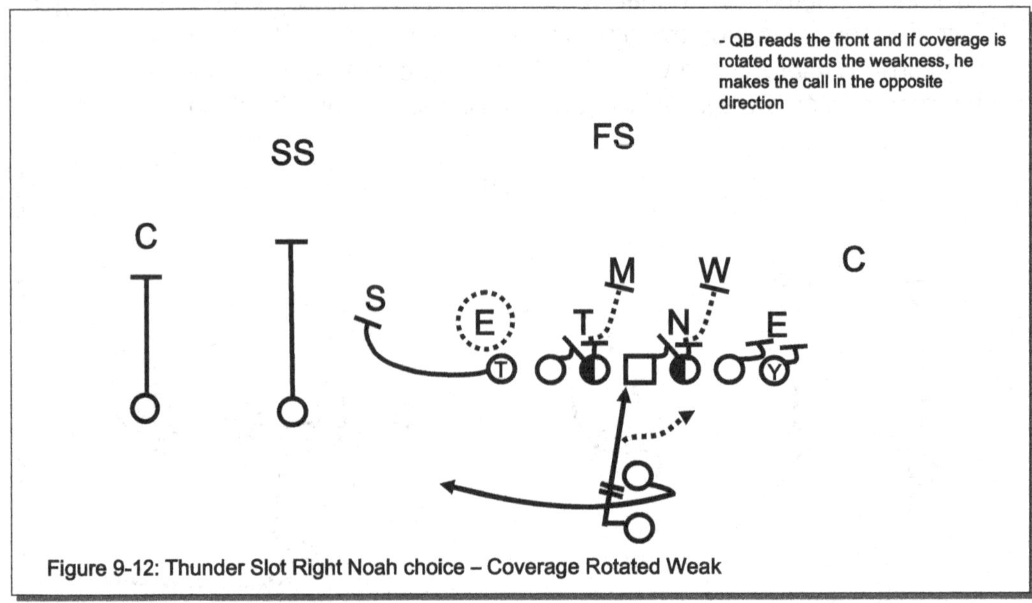


Figure 9-12: Thunder Slot Right Noah choice – Coverage Rotated Weak

(Note: Within this concept, we teach the quarterback to look at it in terms of which way he *himself* will potentially run the ball, rather than where he's sending the running back. This is different for him than the way we described traditional "zone choice" in Chapter 1, where he's handing it off from under center and only thinking of where the running back is going.)

## Category 3 (Slice)

Category 3 or the "3-man game" is where we involve a "slicer." The ideal way to set this up in a game plan is to run some *cut* plays at the defensive end first, before you call *slice* or add "front" motion with a receiver. The slicer distracts the end, so the quarterback can gain an advantage and get to the perimeter. However, it is very important that the quarterback reads it every time with no guessing.

One of our base plays and a good starting point is to call "shot top right: 12 *slice*" (Figure 9-13). When we *cut*, the tight end is coming across the heels of the offensive linemen to cut off the defensive end. However, we want the "slicer" to stay flatter and stay 1/2 a yard from the heels of the line. This allows him to read the defensive end and to either go around him or cut inside of him to get to his blocking assignment at the next level.

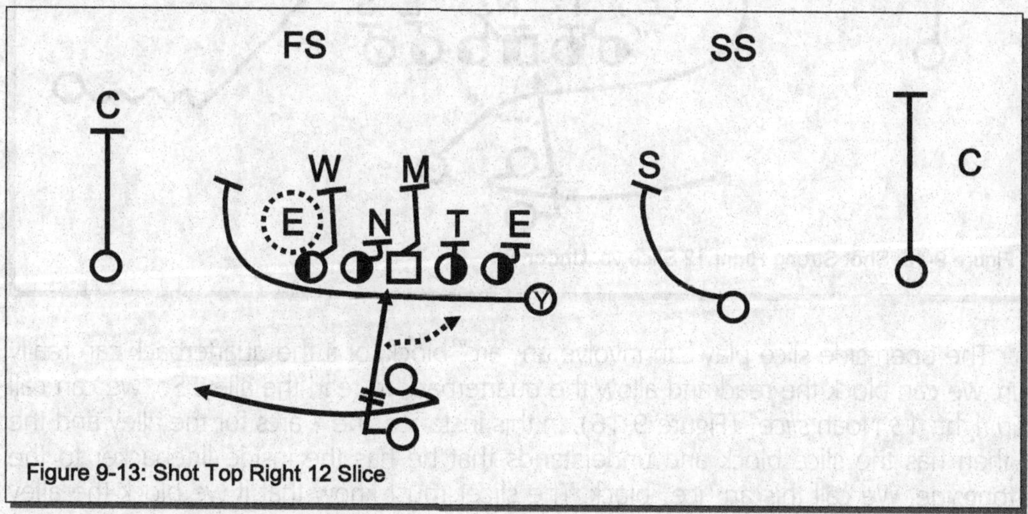

Figure 9-13: Shot Top Right 12 Slice

We also assign the slice block to wide receivers. To do so, we can call "shot limo right, W front: 12" (Figure 9-14). On this, we don't call "slice," because the W is the slicer by way of the motion call. We reserve the slice term for tight ends and fullbacks, instead. For example, in 21 personnel, this could be "shot strong right: 12 *slice*." This is a good call when the "strong" formation is getting a rotation by the defense to stop strongside runs, thus leaving the open side vulnerable to the *slice* action (Figure 9-15).

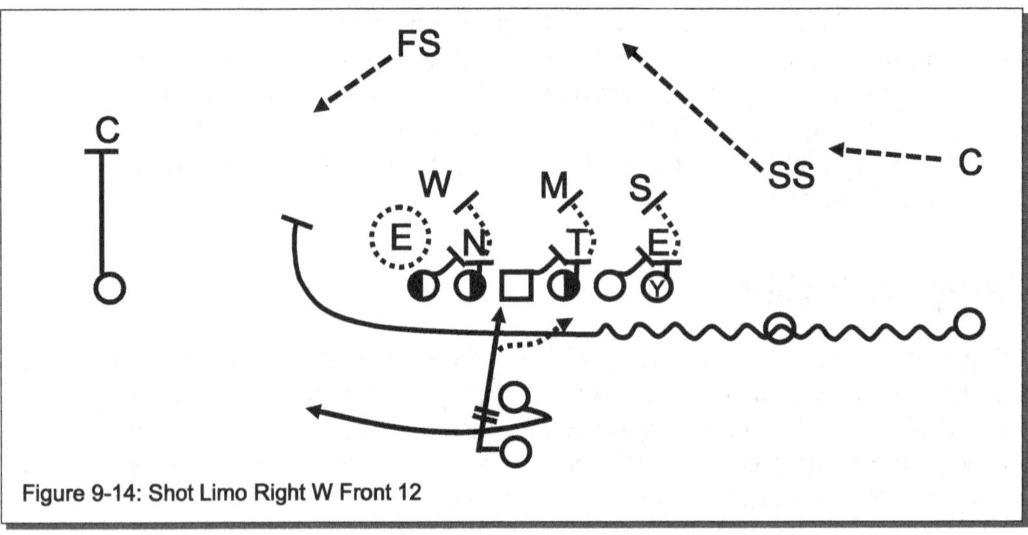

Figure 9-14: Shot Limo Right W Front 12

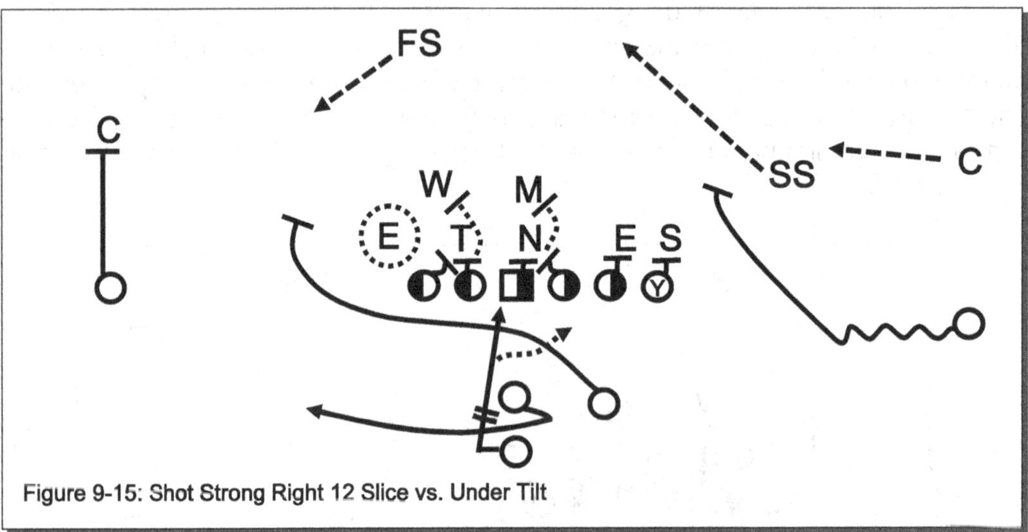

Figure 9-15: Shot Strong Right 12 Slice vs. Under Tilt

The open-side slice play can involve an "arc" block, or if the quarterback can really run, we can block the read and allow the quarterback to read the alley. So, we can call "tip right: 13 Noah *slice*" (Figure 9-16). In this instance, the Y arcs for the alley and the T then has the slice block and understands that he has the inside linebacker to the strongside. We call this an "ice" block. The slicer must know that if we block the alley (with an arc or another cutter), he has the "ice" (Figure 9-17). Another way to do that with some motion is to call "wing slot right, T fly: 13 Noah *slice*" (Figure 9-18). With a receiver, we'd call that "top right, W front: 12 *slice*" (Figure 9-19). This gives W the alley block and Y now has the "ice" technique. The slice players distract the eyes and distort the pursuit angles of defenders. This allows us to get the alley blocked for the quarterback to make big plays and causes adjustments by the secondary to allow the running back to pop big plays by creating poor pursuit angles.

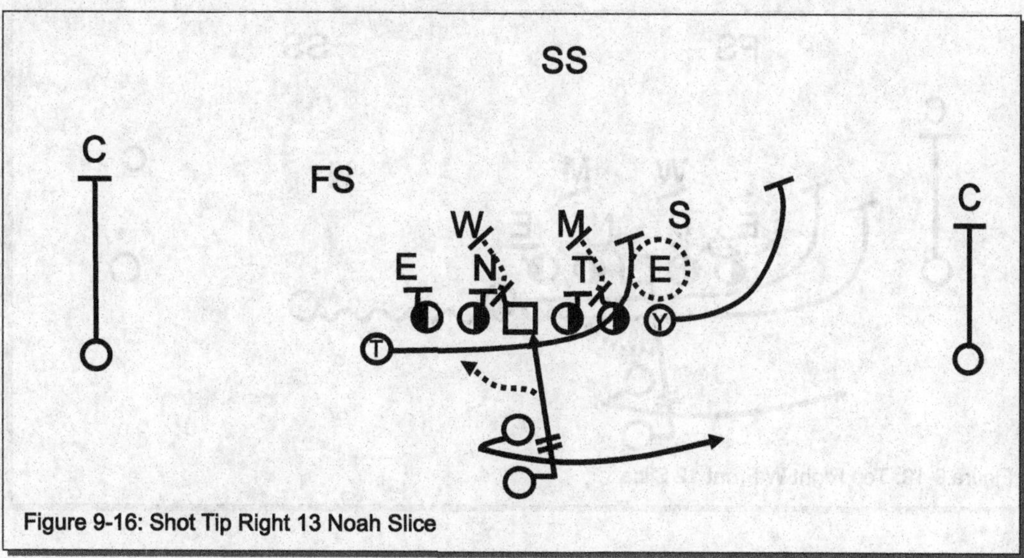

Figure 9-16: Shot Tip Right 13 Noah Slice

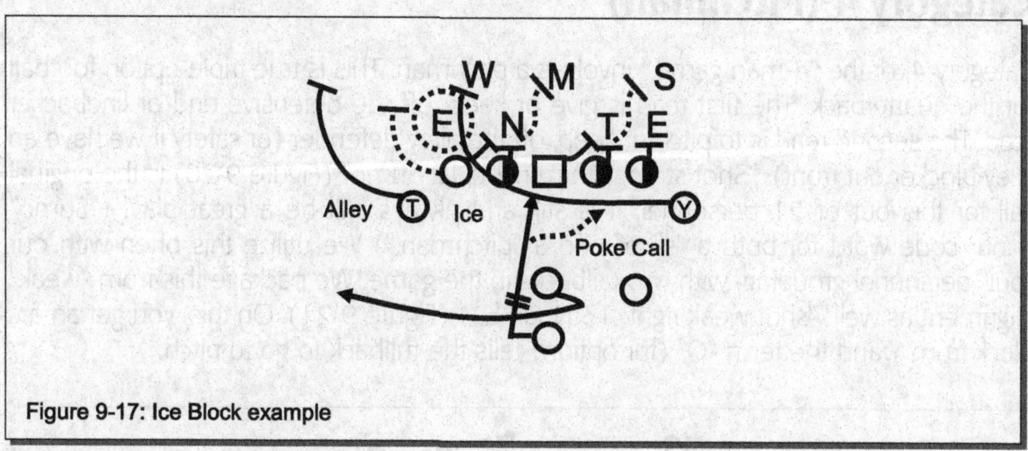

Figure 9-17: Ice Block example

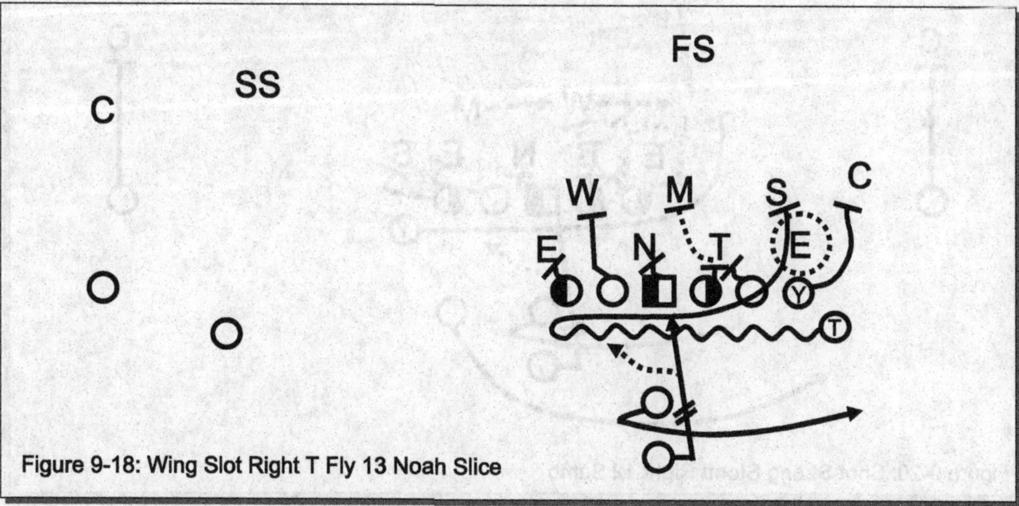

Figure 9-18: Wing Slot Right T Fly 13 Noah Slice

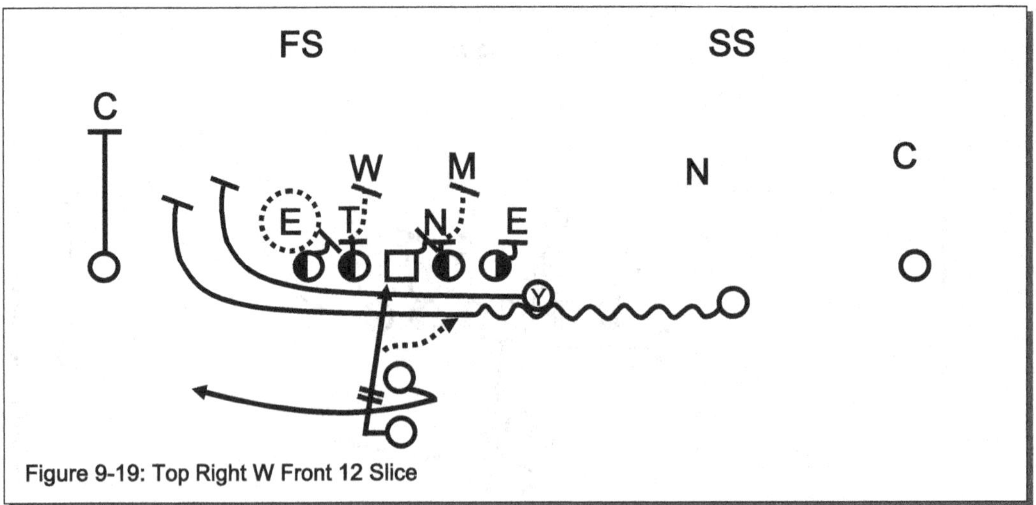

Figure 9-19: Top Right W Front 12 Slice

## Category 4 (Pitchman)

Category 4, or the "4-man game," involves a pitchman. This is true triple-option football for the quarterback. The first read is give or keep, off the defensive end or linebacker read. The second read is to pitch or keep, off the alley defender (or safety if we have an alley blocker out front). "Shot strong storm right: 12 Sumo" (Figure 9-20) is the original call for this out of 21 personnel. It is still and always will be a great play! ("Sumo" is our code word for both a "slice" and a "pitchman.") We utilize this often with our "out" personnel grouping, with two tailbacks in the game. We package this from "weak" alignment as well: "shot weak right: 13 Noah 'O'" (Figure 9-21). On this, you get an arc block from Y and the term "O" (for option) tells the fullback to go to pitch.

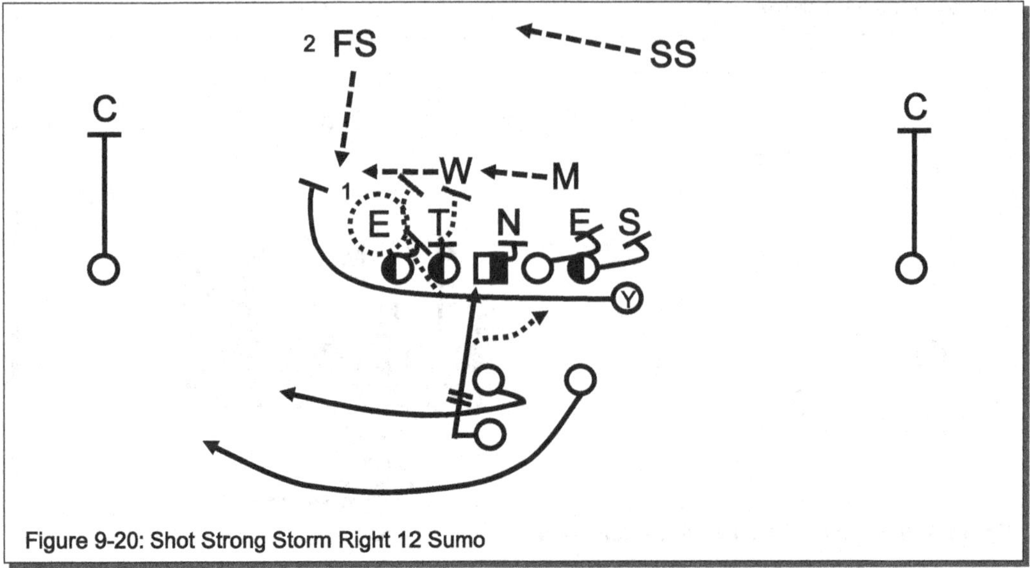

Figure 9-20: Shot Strong Storm Right 12 Sumo

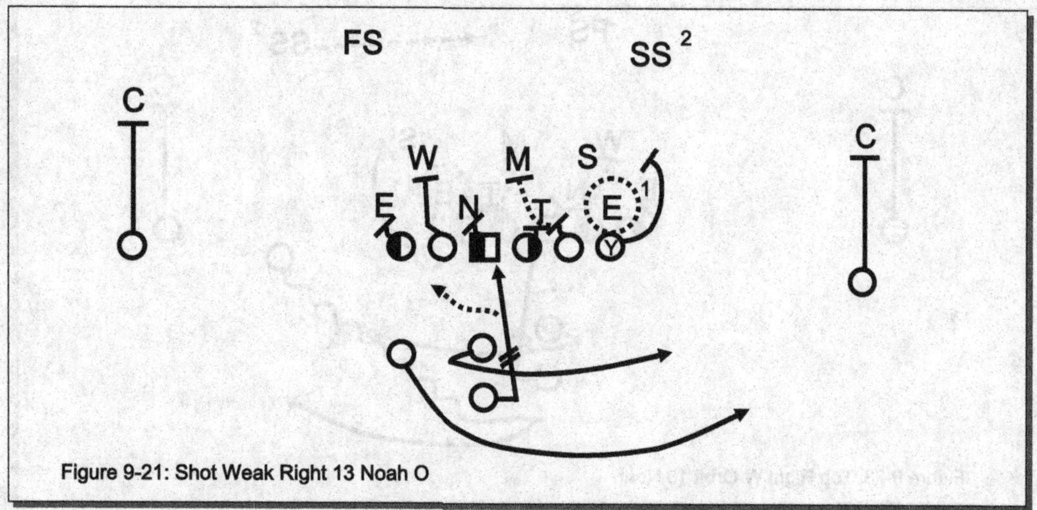

Figure 9-21: Shot Weak Right 13 Noah O

Those two calls translate seamlessly to 11 personnel. For example, "top right, W back: 13 *Sumo*" (Figure 9-22) makes the slot receiver the pitchman and Y now knows to *slice* from the "Sumo" call. We used the term "W orbit" to tell the slot receiver to run it the other way. For example, "top right, W *orbit*: 13 *Noah*" (Figure 9-23), where the term "orbit" is similar to the "O" tag in the 2-back package.

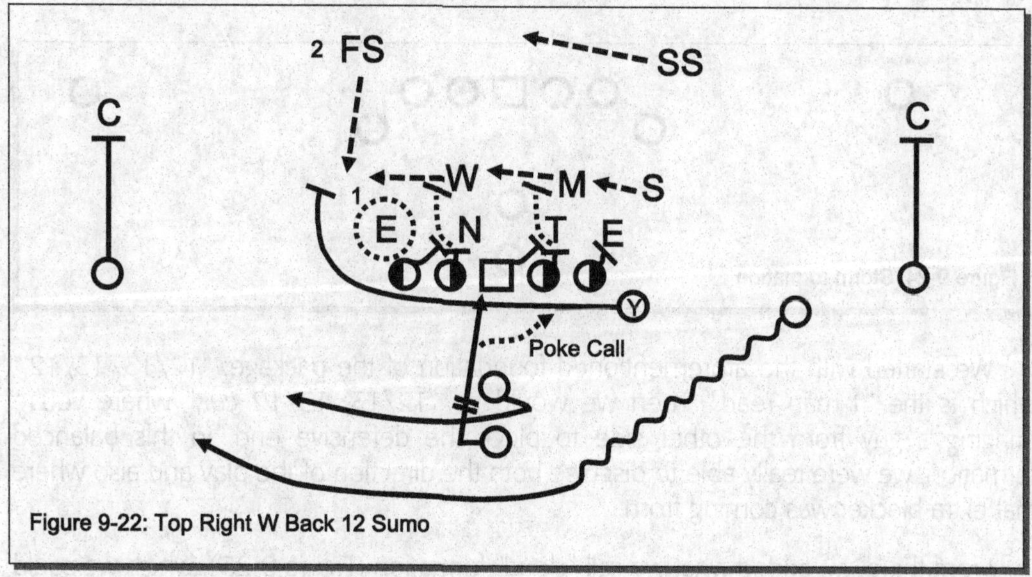

Figure 9-22: Top Right W Back 12 Sumo

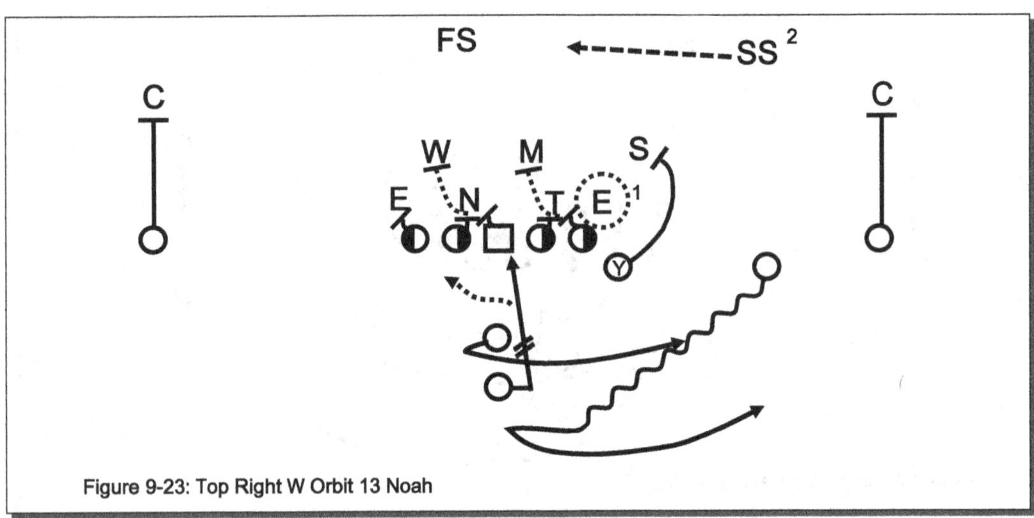

Figure 9-23: Top Right W Orbit 13 Noah

## Category 5 ("Storm" Package)

Something unique that we developed in the "shot" read-option game was to implement what we call "double-cutters." We really featured these from 12 personnel, in what we call our "storm" formation (Figure 9-24), which we named as a term to package with "thunder" formation.

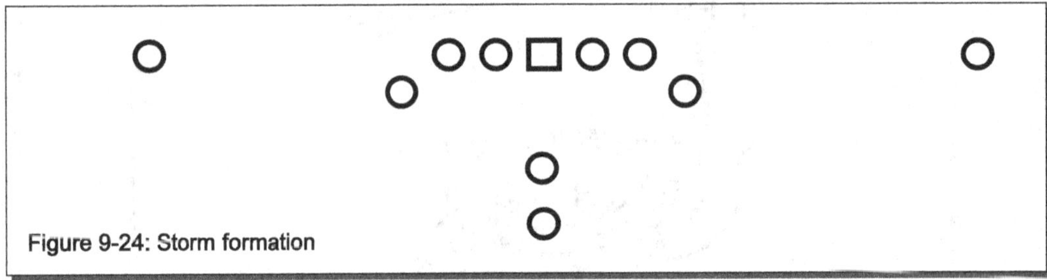
Figure 9-24: Storm formation

We started with the aforementioned foundation of the package: "12/13, 13/12," which is the "1-man read." Then we would go "12/13, 13/12 *cut*," where you're bringing a guy from the other side to block the defensive end. In this balanced formation, we were really able to disguise both the direction of the play and also where that extra blocker was coming from.

From there, we added what we call "cloud" formation (Figure 9-25), which we could get to from various shifts and motions, such as T mo or Y fly. This gave us the ability to add a second "slicer" or "cutter" in either direction. What you now do is block your inside zone rules, but you have the understanding that linebackers are going to "fade" even more with the "double-cutters," so it's critical that you "block the cylinders." You don't let a guy go, just because "he's not my guy." If he's "in my cylinder," I block him. That aspect became of critical importance as we developed the "double-cutter" series.

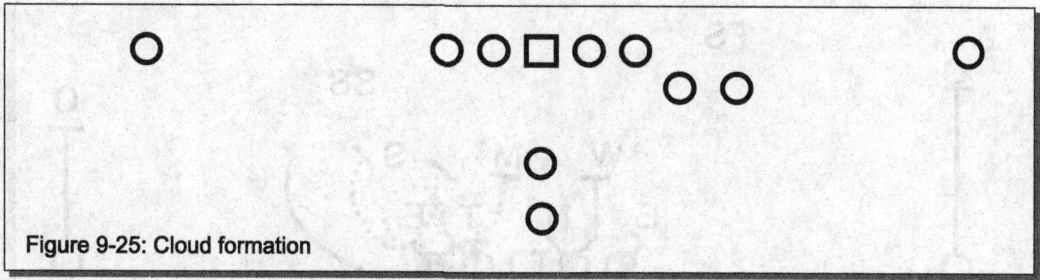
Figure 9-25: Cloud formation

We first implemented this in the spring of 2016. We started the concept out of "bone right," with the "arc" and "ice" coming from the backfield, in an inverted wishbone set (Figure 9-26). From there, it was really easy for the blocking backs to transition to 2x2 and we found that adjusting the blocking angles wasn't hard at all. They just moved up there to what we named "storm" formation, and it created a better package than having them back there in wishbone, because you now also have "4 quick" available for the passing game.

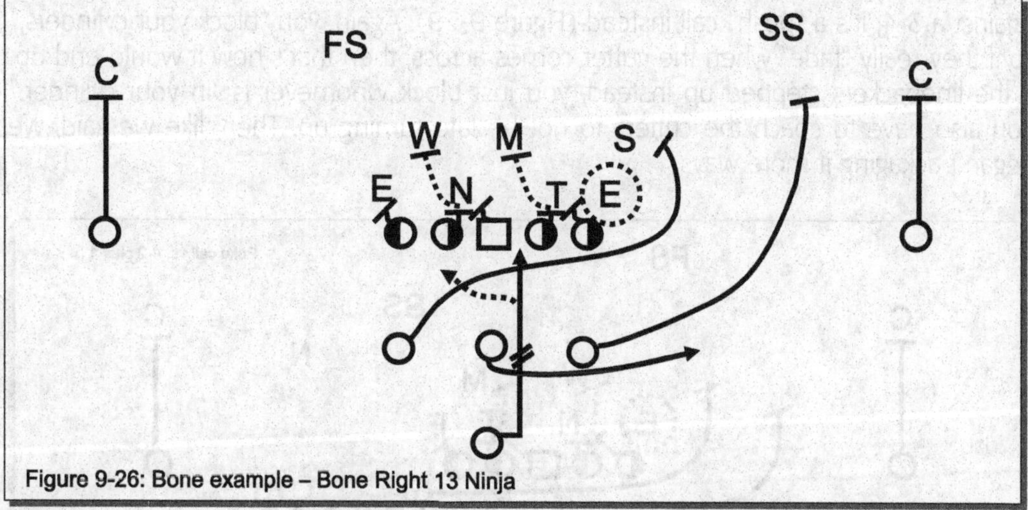

Figure 9-26: Bone example – Bone Right 13 Ninja

## Ninja

Let's look at the "double-slicers" first. This is "storm left, T mo: odd Ninja" (Figure 9-27). The players understood code words, so we just said, "we don't need to say 12 and 13 anymore, unless we just want the base play." We called the play "ninja" to give it a code-name similar to "cut" and "slice." The first time we called it in a game was up at Syracuse in 2016 and Lamar took it 80 yards untouched for a touchdown.

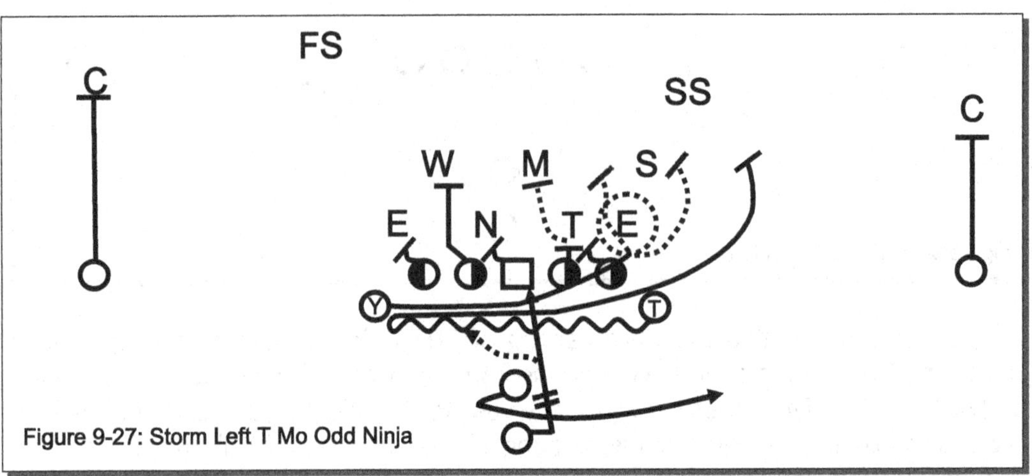

Figure 9-27: Storm Left T Mo Odd Ninja

This is primarily a 12 personnel concept, but we did break formation and add motion to it. This is "top right, T half: even ninja" against a basic 4-2 "plus one" defense (Figure 9-28). Numbers-wise with this play, the center should make a "poke" call. Against a 3-4, it's a "push" call instead (Figure 9-29). Again, you "block your cylinders," so if they really "fade" when the cutter comes across, then that's how it would end up. If the linebackers stepped up instead, you just block whomever is "in your cylinder." You also have to coach the cutters to not be late turning up. Then, like we said, we began packaging it more ways.

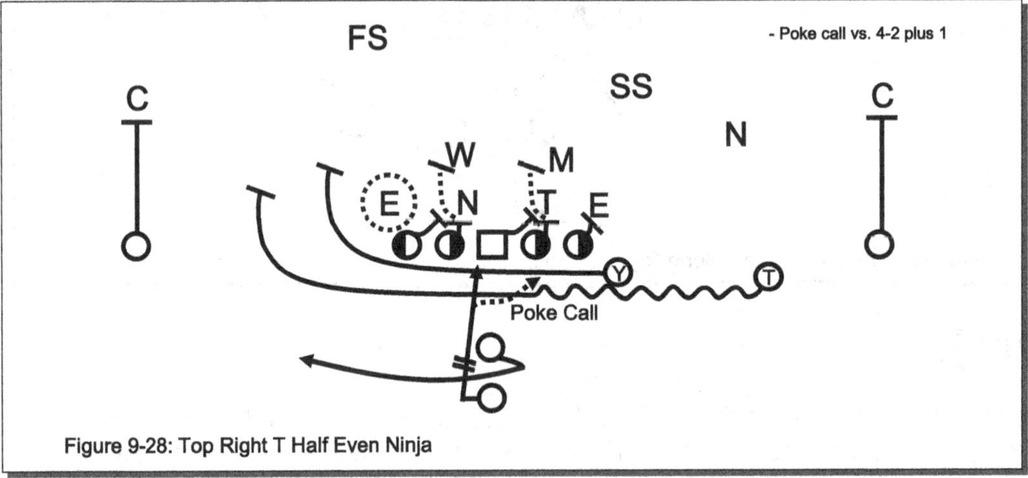

Figure 9-28: Top Right T Half Even Ninja

As our players got good at this, we found another way that we like to do this is to go "top right, W front: even *Ninja*" (Figure 9-30) and snap the ball, when the motion guy is at the tackle from that "jet sweep" motion that is trendy today. On this, the slot receiver has the alley block and Y now has the "ice" block. This is an 11 personnel formation, but we would also do it with 12 personnel, because Cole Hikutini as a tight end could run all the slot routes really well.

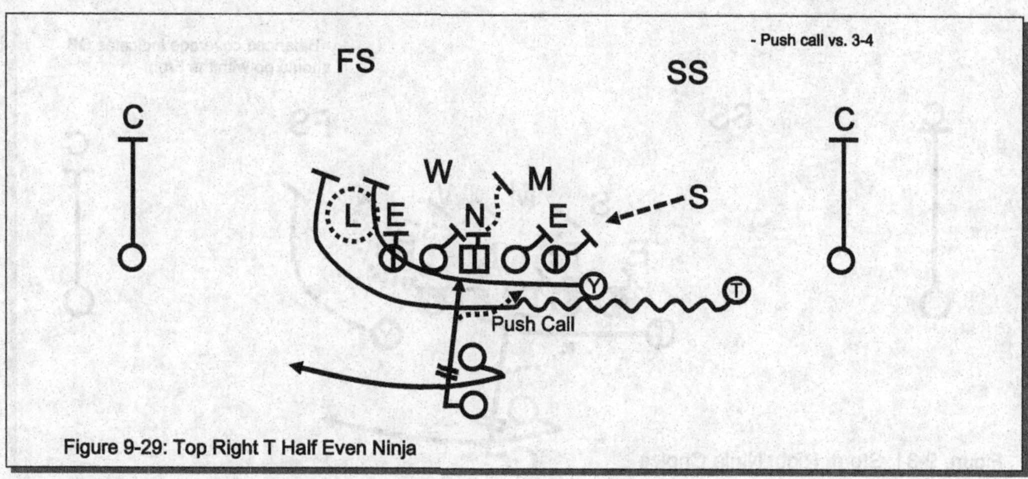

Figure 9-29: Top Right T Half Even Ninja

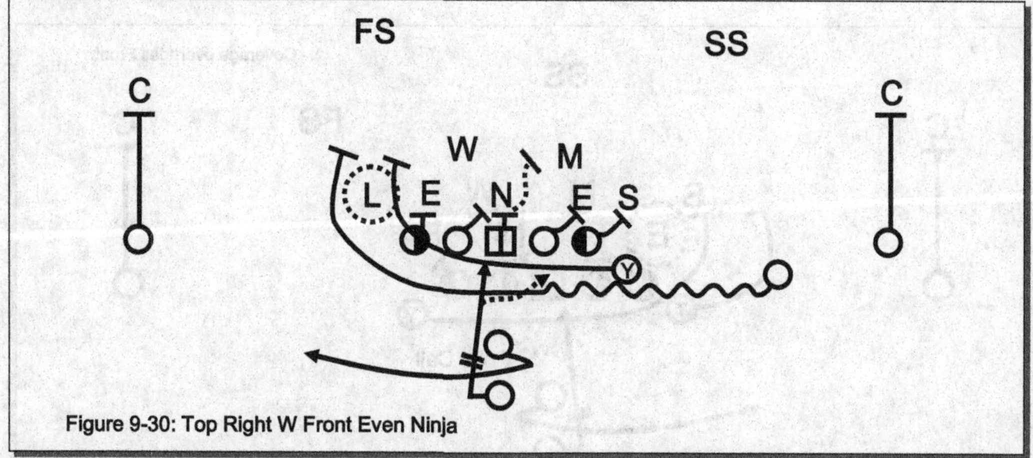

Figure 9-30: Top Right W Front Even Ninja

## Ninja Choice

This is "storm right: Ninja choice." The quarterback again looks for "front, coverage, personnel." If the *front* tells me one way and the coverage is balanced, I go with the *front* (Figure 9-31). Again, the quarterback needs to be aware of a free-access tackle. If the front tells me one way (direction), but the *coverage* is rotated toward that weakness, then I go the opposite direction (Figure 9-32). If both the front and coverage are balanced, I base my direction on *personnel*, which means I call it toward my best blockers, or to a weakness in a defensive player.

That is better than saying "go to the 1-technique." Normally, if you're running "inside-zone choice," you would want to run 32 *to* the 1-technique (Figure 9-33). But when you're running "ninja choice," you want to call 13 ("odd ninja"), because the tackle has free access to the linebacker and therefore it makes the read cleaner (see Figure 9-31). *That* takes a lot of coaching! There was a lot of work to really do this well and the coaches really deserve a lot of credit.

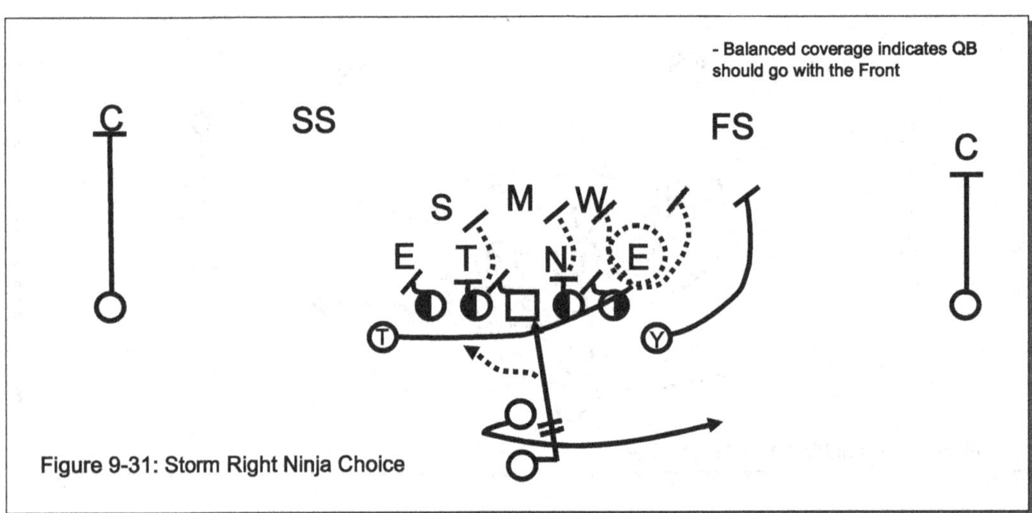

Figure 9-31: Storm Right Ninja Choice

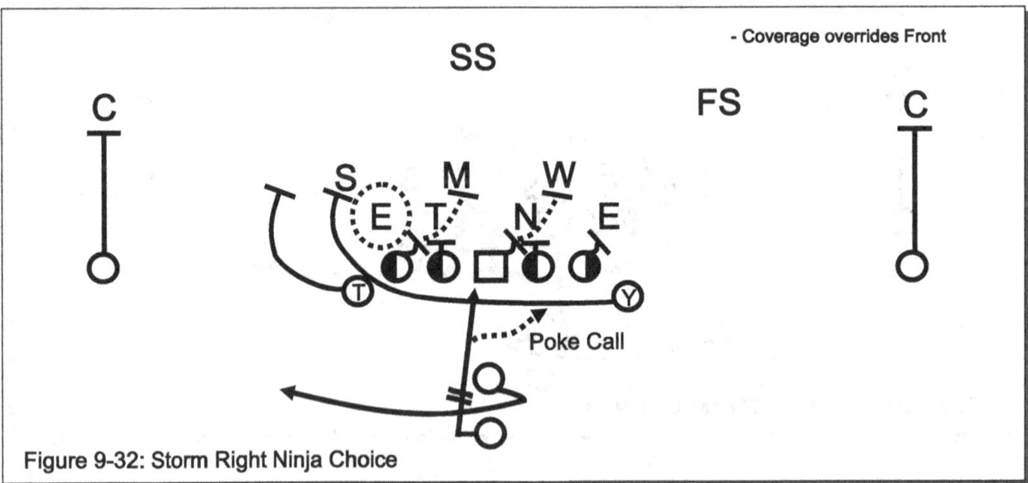

Figure 9-32: Storm Right Ninja Choice

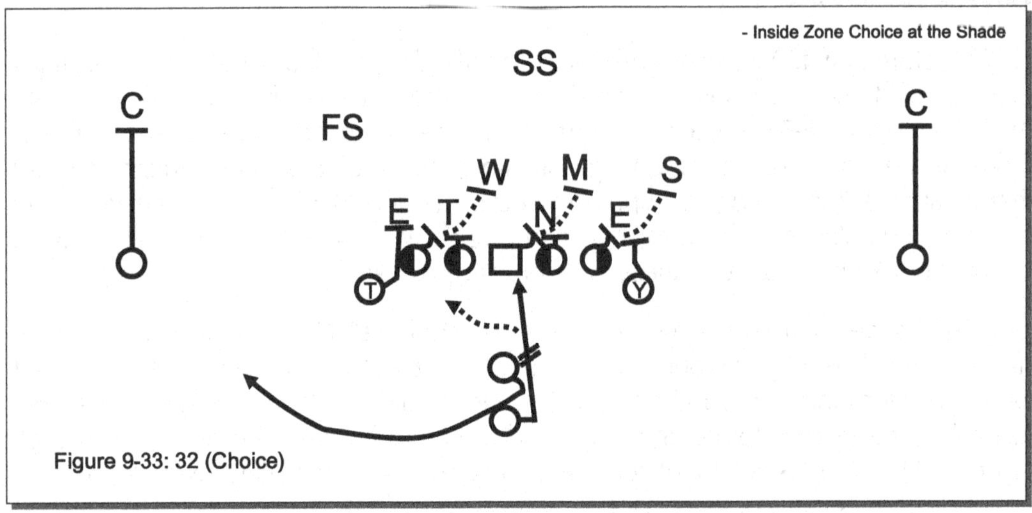

Figure 9-33: 32 (Choice)

## Noah

This is the second part of it, with the double-"arc" blocks, for example, "storm right, T mo: odd Noah" against the "4I's" (Figure 9-34). On this, you're getting "double-arc'ers." This is a "push" call against those "4I's," where Y tells the tackle, "I'm gone, I'm gone, I'm gone!" So, then the tackle knows I need to "push" to the outside linebacker. Then, we can add the jet motion again: "dot right, W front: odd Noah" (Figure 9-35). The tight end understands that he has the "cruise the box" rule, because we want him matched on a linebacker and the receiver with the second arc block matched on a safety instead. It's a "poke" call for the o-line but again, they know to block the cylinders. You need to be able to draw it up like that, 11 personnel and 12 personnel, because sometimes it's just as good out of three wides, if you can dictate personnel changes to the defense.

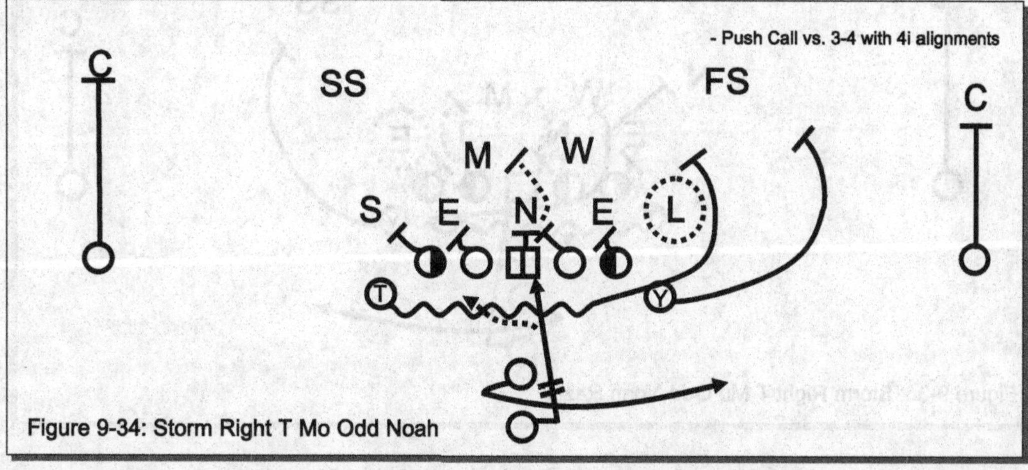

Figure 9-34: Storm Right T Mo Odd Noah

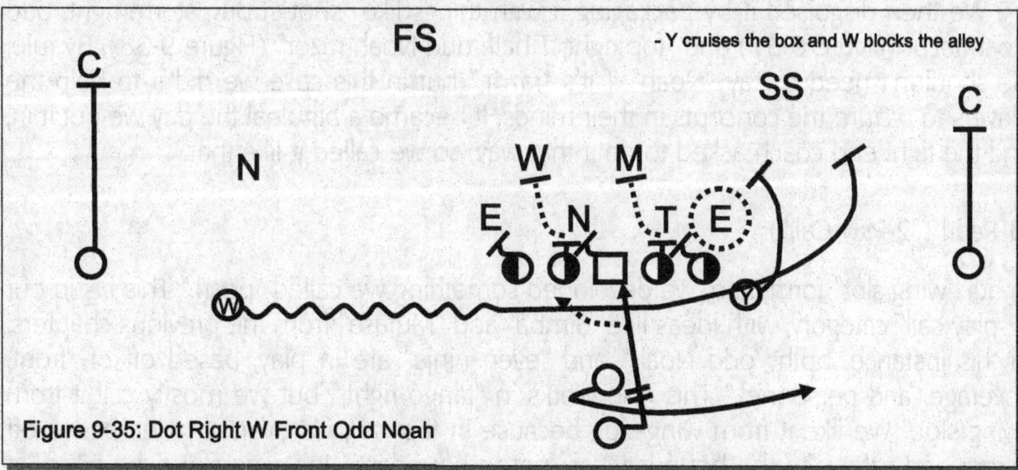

Figure 9-35: Dot Right W Front Odd Noah

## Razor

This was the third concept in the "storm" package. We wanted to use a code word similar to "cutter" (like "ninja"), so we called it "razor." This was "storm right, T mo: odd Noah razor" (Figure 9-36). Y had the "arc" block and the code-word "razor" tells T to slice back to where he came from and insert in either the B or C gap. That really creates problems for linebackers. This can generate numerous big plays for the running back, because he now has a lead blocker. The quarterback can also get big runs, because the pursuit of linebackers slows down, when they "fade" with the "razor" blocking. Again, the quarterback needs to read it out, trust the read, and react to what he sees.

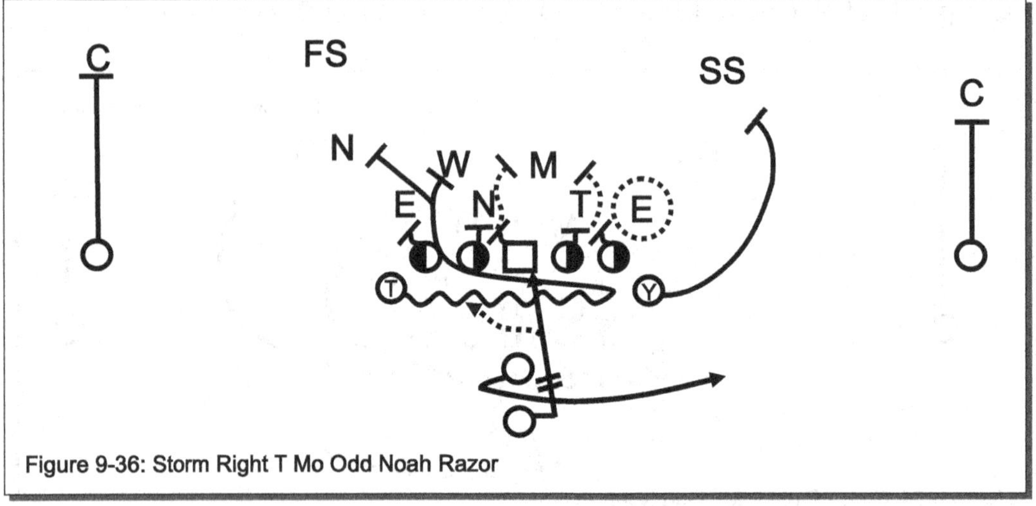

Figure 9-36: Storm Right T Mo Odd Noah Razor

We then disguised it by packaging it with things like "shot strong storm right, odd Noah razor (Figure 9-37) and "top right, T half: odd Noah razor" (Figure 9-38). By rule, we shouldn't need to say "Noah" if it's "razor," but in this case we did it to help the players to *picture* the concepts in their minds. It became a big deal the day we put it in, and the tight end coach asked to do it that way, so we called it like that.

❑ Pearl ("2-Play Call")

In our "wing slot" formation, we developed something we called "pearl." This fits in our "2-play call" category, with ideas like "Simba" and "Mufasa" from the previous chapters. In this instance, both "odd Noah" and "even ninja" are in play, based off of "front, coverage, and personnel." This also works in "tango right," but we mostly call it from "wing slot." We like it from wing-slot, because in that set, it's even simpler, based off corner and safety "to the boundary" or "not to boundary." In "wing slot right: pearl," if the safety is not there and it's just one defender into the boundary, the quarterback is calling "odd Noah," for the "double-arc'ers" (Figure 9-39). But if the corner and safety *are* there to the boundary, he's calling "even ninja" (Figure 9-40).

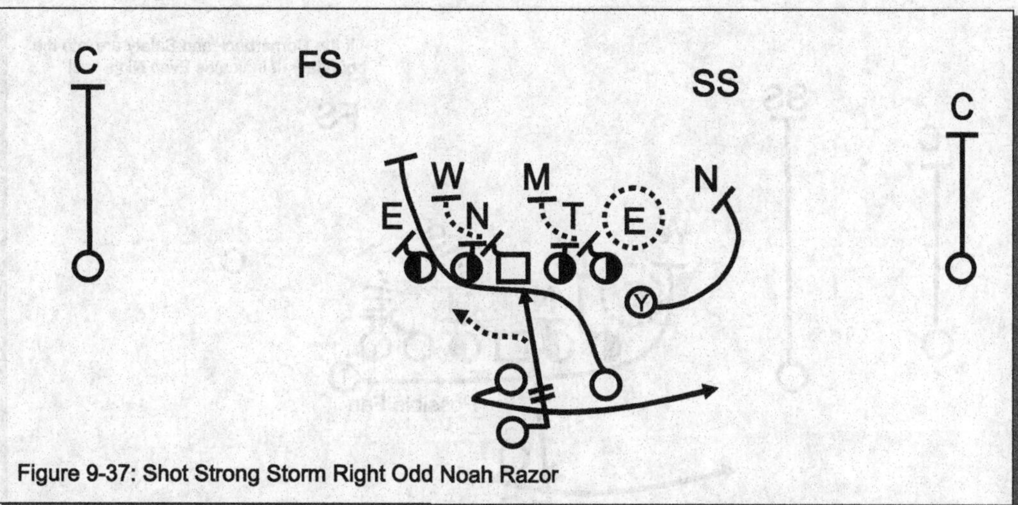

Figure 9-37: Shot Strong Storm Right Odd Noah Razor

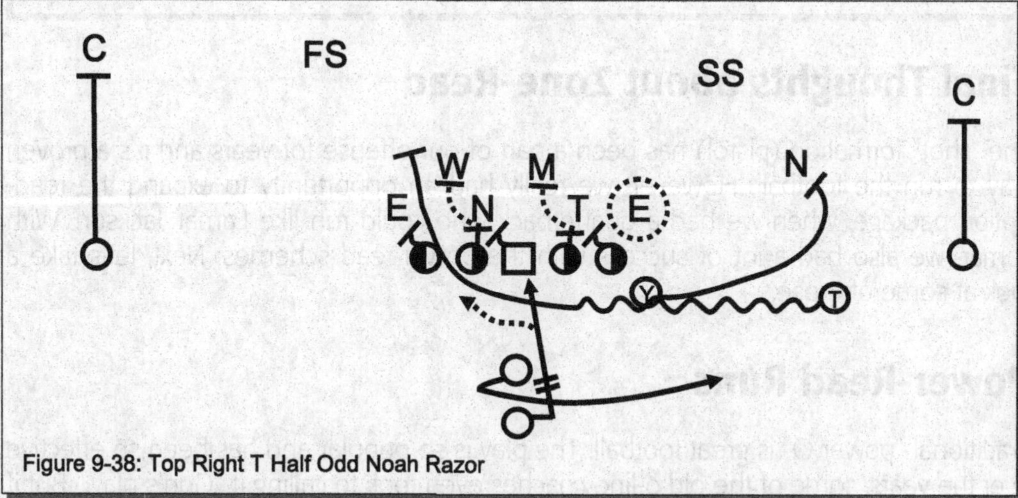

Figure 9-38: Top Right T Half Odd Noah Razor

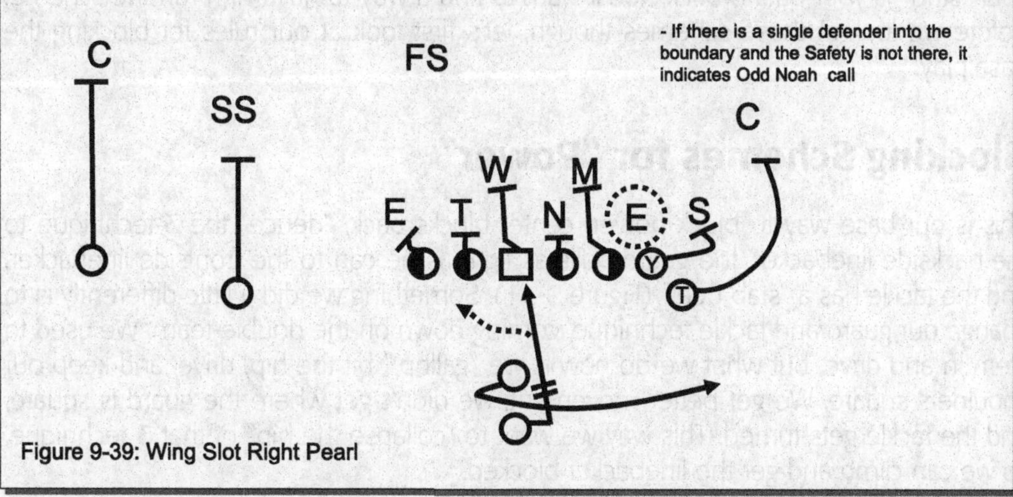

Figure 9-39: Wing Slot Right Pearl

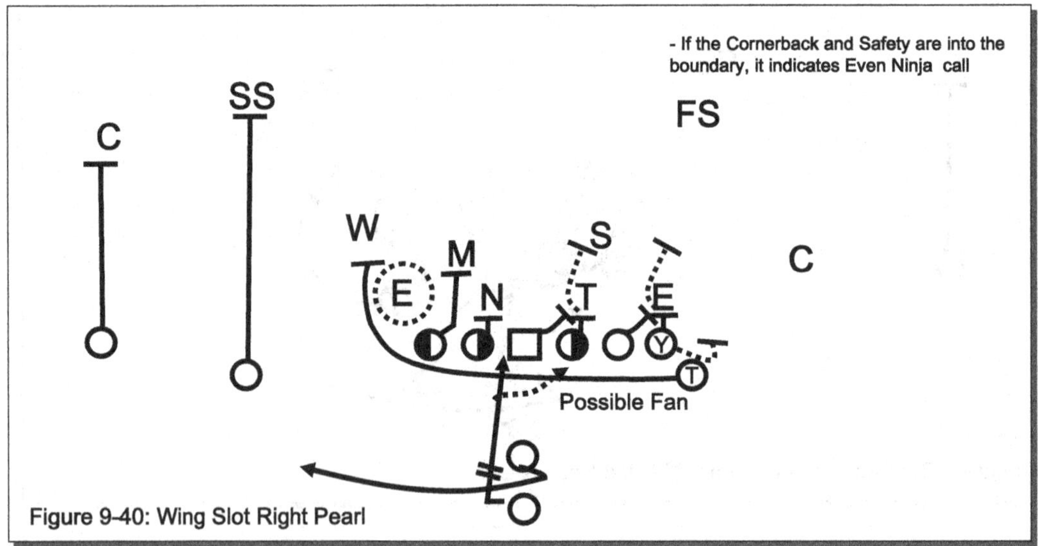

Figure 9-40: Wing Slot Right Pearl

## Final Thoughts about Zone-Read

The "shot" formation (pistol) has been a part of our offense for years and it's a proven way to run the football. However, we really had an opportunity to expand the read-option package, when we had a quarterback who could run like Lamar Jackson. With Lamar, we also had a lot of success with the power-read schemes. Next, let's take a look at some of those.

## Power-Read Runs

Traditional "power O" is great football. The play is so popular and has been so effective over the years, some of the old o-line coaches even took to calling it "God's play." But if your "stud" is your quarterback, you'll want to find a way to have him run the scheme. Before we look at those schemes though, let's first look at our rules for blocking the base play.

## Blocking Schemes for "Power"

This is our base way to block power: center blocks back, "deuce" the 3-technique to the backside linebacker, the guard pulls as tight as he can to the frontside linebacker, and the tackle has a "stab-peel" (Figure 9-41). Something we did a little differently is to change our guard and tackle technique, coming down on the double-team. We used to stem in and drive, but what we do now is we "gallop," hit the hip, drive, and keep our shoulders square. We get better movement, we didn't get where the guard is square, and the tackle gets turned. This way we want to "collapse the hip" of that 3 technique, so we can climb and get the linebacker blocked.

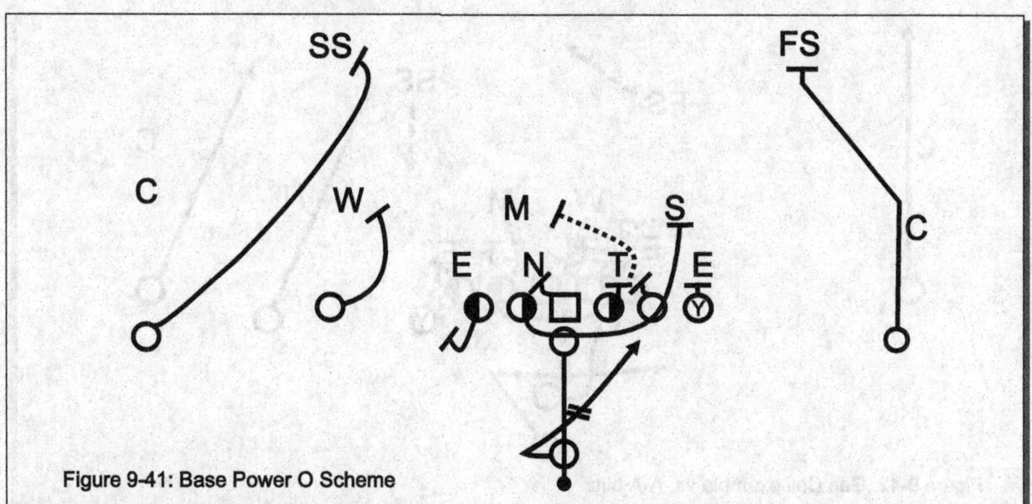

Figure 9-41: Base Power O Scheme

**Play: 9-41**

| Pos: | Assignment: |
|---|---|
| W | Crossfield technique |
| X | Crossfield technique |
| Z | Push crack |
| QB | Reverse out. Step at 6 o'clock. Get the ball to R as quickly and as deep as possible. |

We tell the running back—or the quarterback, if he's the ballcarrier—to "hug the wall" that's built. That's the same thing the back needs to do, when he cuts back on "12/13", is to "hug the wall," so linebackers can't jump out of it. Once again, we're trying to set the linebacker up to the block.

The line has to make the correct *calls*. We want to be able to use the "choice" call (particularly with the quarterback read-run) and the line has to make the correct calls in order to make the blocking happen. That way, you can call it from "front, coverage, and personnel" instead of just going at the 3 technique and allowing defenses to dictate to you. For us to dictate to the defense instead, they have to all make the calls.

Versus a 4-man front, if we're getting some type of pressure, then the center will make a "gap" call, so that if they're running an "A/A" blitz, we get it all blocked (Figure 9-42). Another blitz we saw frequently was something we named "nail." The center makes a "gap" call to get that blocked up (Figure 9-43). On a "gap" call, the center and playside guard must block the A-gap defender. The backside tackle is still going to "stab-peel," but now the playside tackle has to come down to block that 3-technique. If the 3 "cages" outside, the playside tackle stays with him and takes him out.

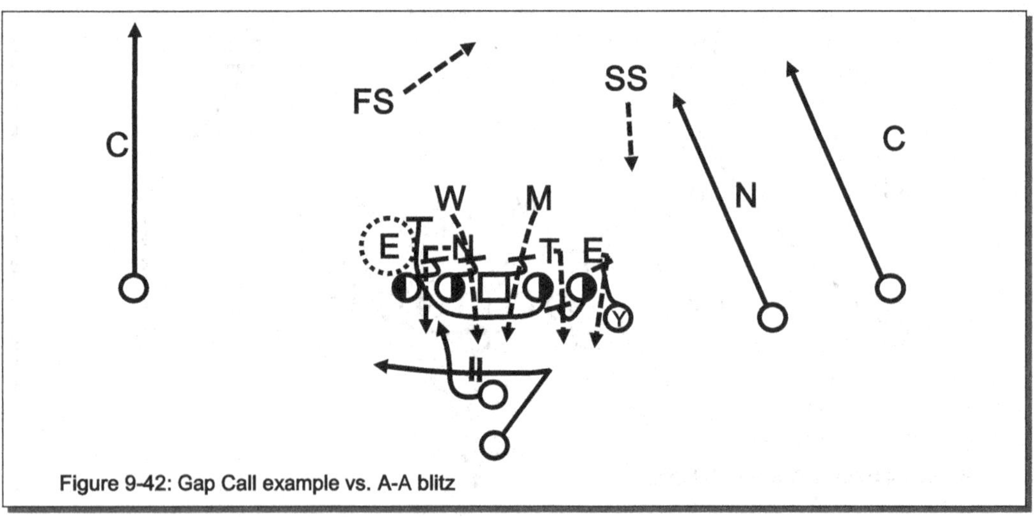


Figure 9-42: Gap Call example vs. A-A blitz

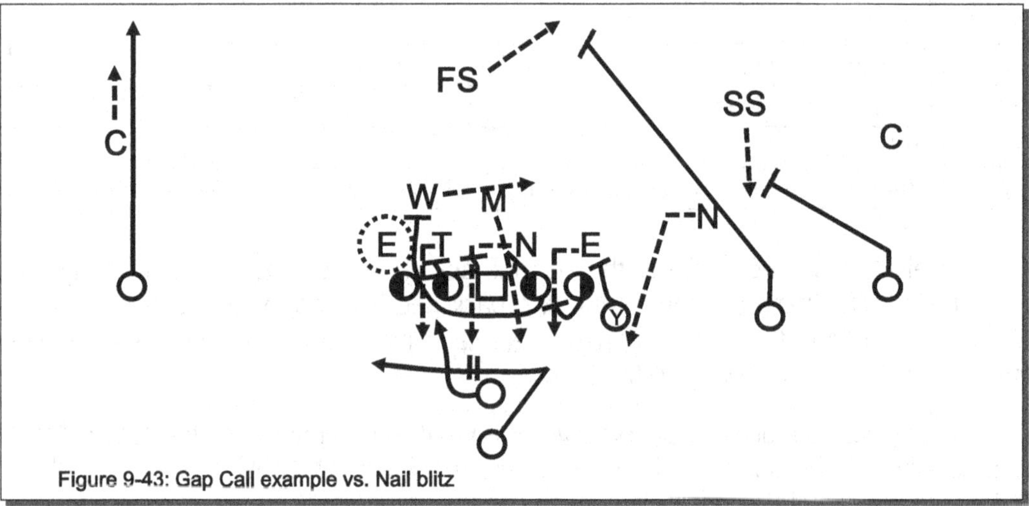


Figure 9-43: Gap Call example vs. Nail blitz

In "zone-read," the line knows to "block your cylinder," but when we make a "gap" call on power schemes, it's "I stay on my man" instead. If that was "zone-read," I'm going to let that go and "stay on my cylinder," but in this instance, I need to stick with him. As he steps down and that defender "cages," I have to go with him. That then opens up the gap for the quarterback to carry the ball downhill.

> (Note: Remember in Chapter 1 how we said a great offense can defeat the blitz with the run game? This is where Lamar Jackson got several big plays on the quarterback power-read.)

If it's a 3-4 and there is an overhang with the threat of the edge defender coming, then we make a call to make the center go back. The tackle calls "hang" first. The center listens for the tackle, "hang, hang, hang!" Then, the center will say, "spade!"

The center would "post the nose" and go back to the "4I" and then the tackle would "stab-peel" the 4I, back to the blitzer on the backside (Figure 9-44). So, we get a "hang" call that tells us to "spade." It takes a lot of work for the center to get good at posting the nose and getting all the way back to a "4I." Your line really needs to practice against all the possible fronts and games in order to be effective.

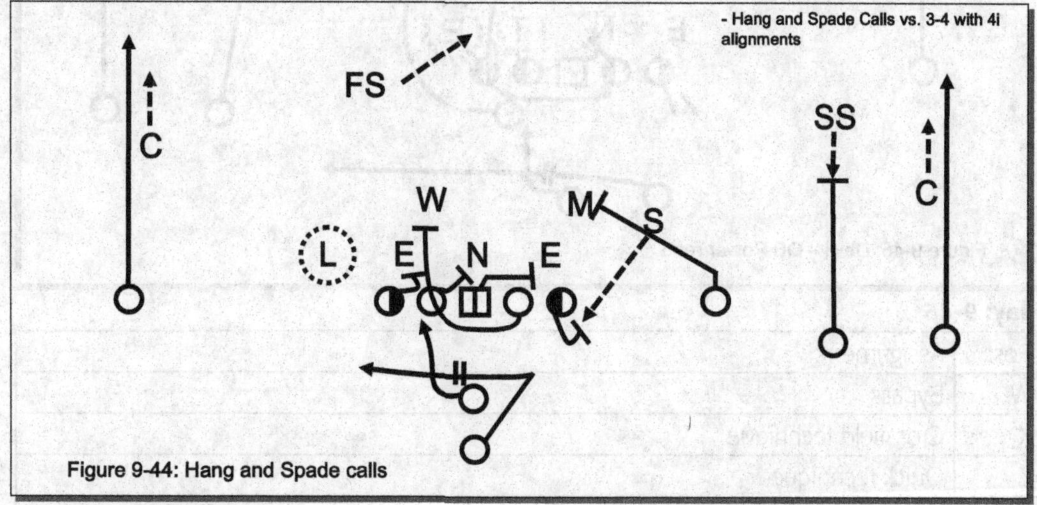

Figure 9-44: Hang and Spade calls

(Note: The quarterback has to allow the line to make their calls. Often times, a young quarterback will try to snap the ball, while they were making calls. The quarterback has to understand what the line is doing, let them make their calls, and time the cadence accordingly, especially when making a check: "one even G"—*pause* for a second to hear the line make their calls—then say it again "one even G… set, hut!")

## Devil

When we ran "quarterback power" with the running back on the sweep-read, we gave the play the code-name "devil" (Figure 9-45). The quarterback should think "I receive the snap, I take one short step in the direction of the play, and then a hop to read it." With a short step as opposed to a second hop, the ball isn't bouncing around, which allows the quarterback to read it more cleanly and make the right decision to hand it off or run with it. We have the back run "right over the top of the quarterback's toes." We give the back a specific track on outside zone from gun, but on this we just told him to run around the edge.

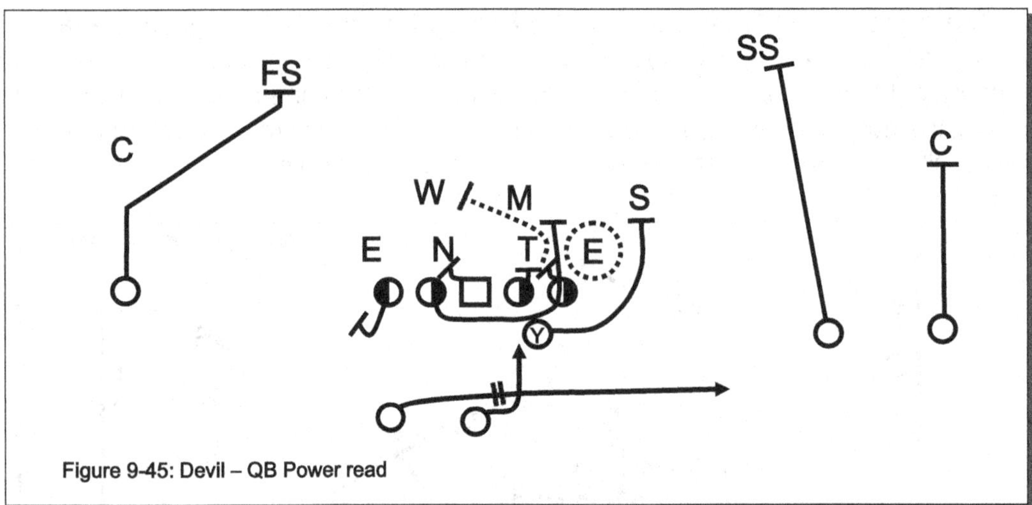

Figure 9-45: Devil – QB Power read

**Play: 9-45**

| Pos: | Assignment: |
|---|---|
| W | Bypass |
| X | Crossfield technique |
| Z | Quick technique |
| QB | Ride jet sweep and read EMLOS. If he closes, hand jet sweep to RB. If he stays upfield, run QB power. |

Again, it's the nuances of the line coaching and making sure their calls are right that allows the quarterback to set the play according to "front, coverage, and personnel," as opposed to just "run it at the 3-technique." If we trust the line to make the appropriate adjustments, we can give the "choice" to the quarterback and really free up our playcalling. The teaching is more front-loaded to install it this way, but we believe it's necessary to do it this way, in order to get the players to study hard and digest all the concepts. When we got it all clicking, I think it's fair to say we ran the play better than anyone else.

❑ Devil Packages

"Devil choice" was probably our best "tempo" play with Lamar Jackson. We liked to start in "shot" and then "bow" the back, where the quarterback would make the call and move the back right or left (Figure 9-46). Once again, the quarterback is choosing the direction of the play, based on "front, coverage, and personnel" and going off the secondary coverage or a free-access tackle. If you wanted to use the entire numbered system, this play would be called "24/25 devil," but when you're going fast no-huddle, it's easier to just call a one-syllable code-word. This was also a blitz check for us; Lamar liked it and really got good at it.

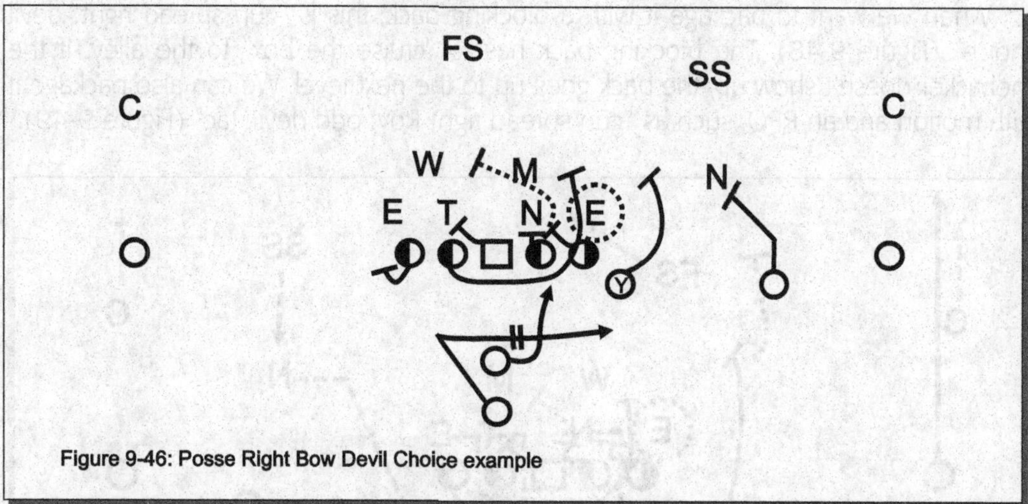

Figure 9-46: Posse Right Bow Devil Choice example

We called our "tempo" 4-wides package "rocket." On the sideline you yell "rocket, rocket, rocket!" The o-line sets up right now and the receivers run out there and get set on the right and left sides, so we can go at maximum pace. We like to flip-flop our linemen for our run game, but in this instance we always went to the right/left alignment, so we could go faster. All it really did was challenge me on how to call the passing game, because our 70s and 400s then became one-directional.

Since both of our slot receivers could run with the football, we wanted to get them involved in this package out of four-wides. So, we have "rocket right whip: even devil" (Figure 9-47). Then, if we wanted Y to come in the backfield in motion instead, we called "yank." In practice, we would bring those receivers down there once a week to what we call the "thunder period" and work the motion and hand the ball to them.

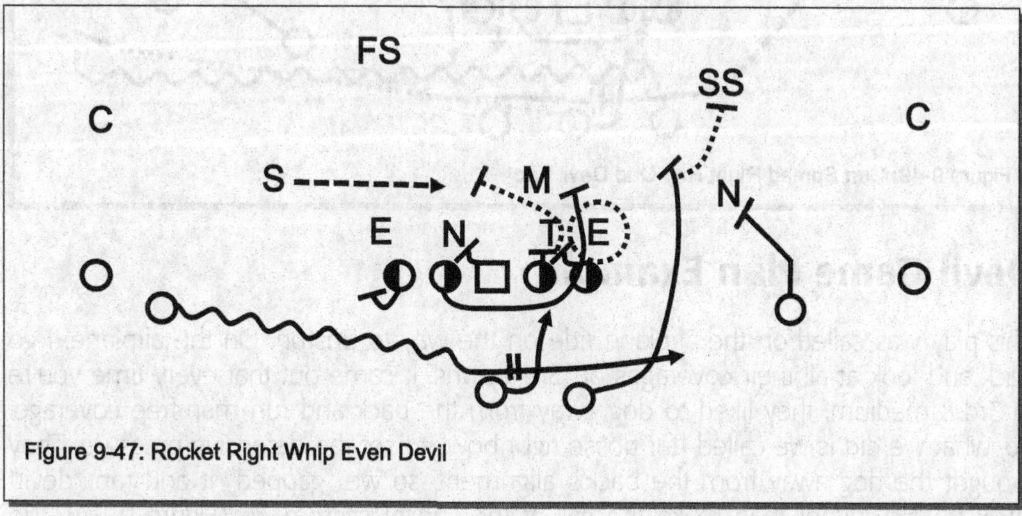

Figure 9-47: Rocket Right Whip Even Devil

When we want to package it with a blocking back, this is "gun spread right: devil choice" (Figure 9-48). The blocking back has to "cruise the box" to the alley. If the linebacker doesn't show up, the back goes up to the next level. We can also package it with motion and an RPO, such as "gun spread right Roy: odd devil, tac" (Figure 9-49).

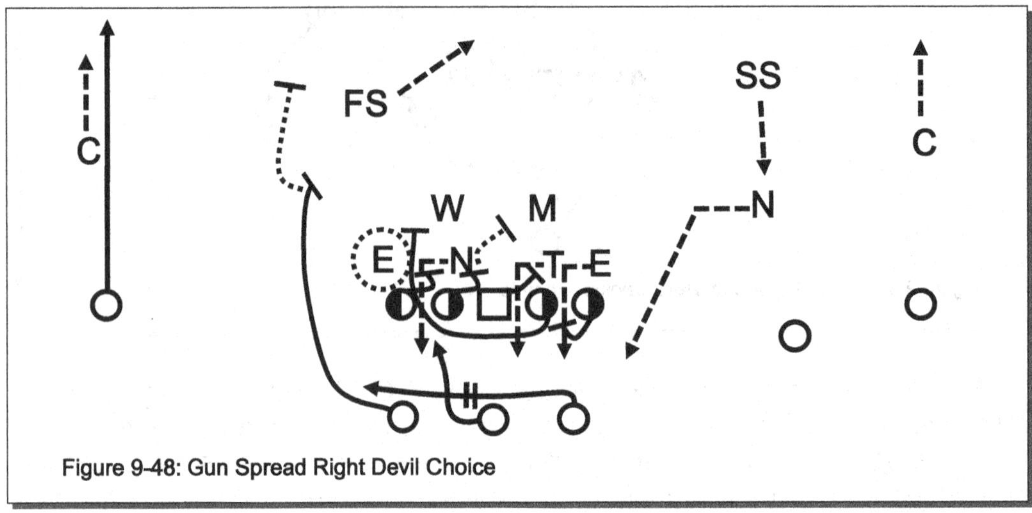

Figure 9-48: Gun Spread Right Devil Choice

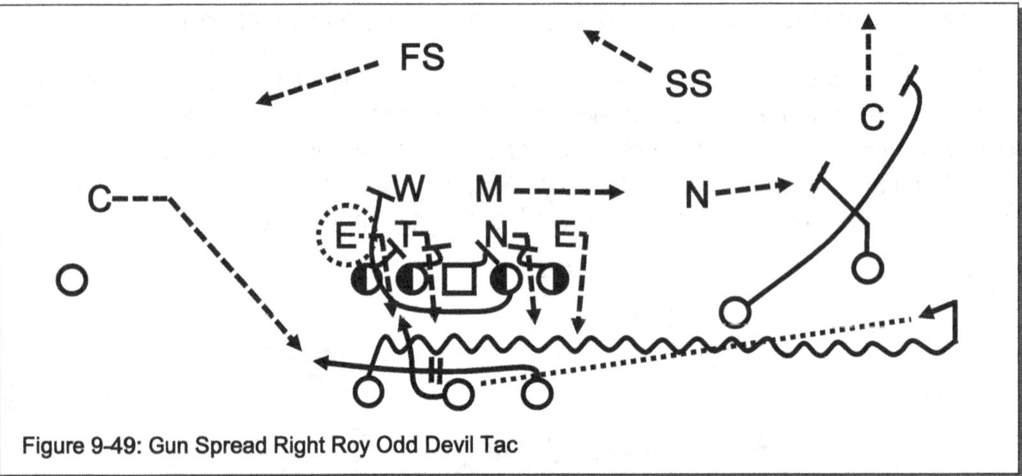

Figure 9-49: Gun Spread Right Roy Odd Devil Tac

## Devil Game Plan Example

This play was called on the airplane ride on the way to Boston. On the airplane, I go back and look at all their coverages on 3rd downs. It came out that every time you're in 3rd-&-medium, they liked to dog away from the back and run man-free coverage. So, what we did is we called "far posse right bow" to set the defensive pressure. They brought the dog away from the back's alignment, so we "gapped" it and ran "devil" away from it, rather than make the call at the line of scrimmage (Figure 9-50). We made the decision that this would be the first 3rd-&-medium call of the game and it ended up being the third play of the game. So, when you talk about calling plays, this was actually called on the airplane ride there. We knew they were going to blitz away from the back, so we did it this way, as opposed to starting in a "shot" alignment.

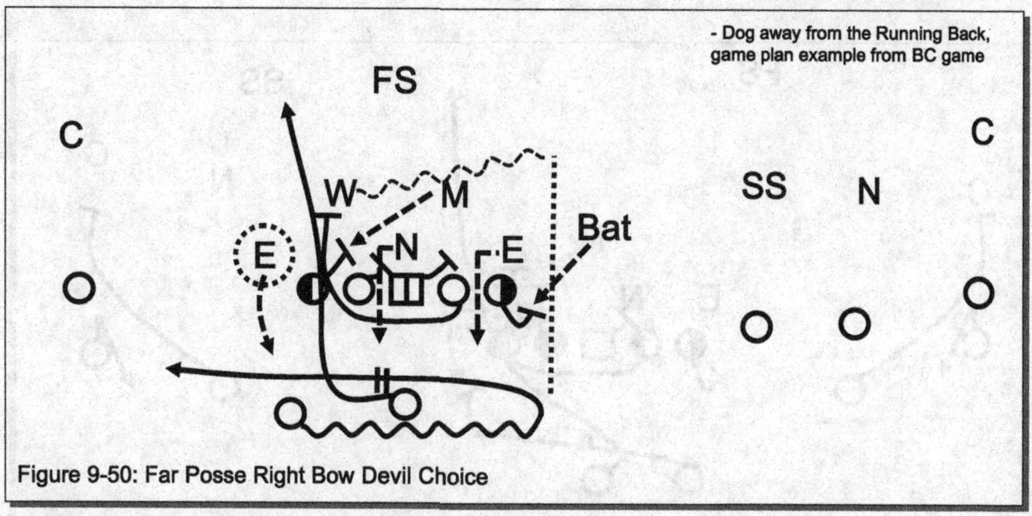

Figure 9-50: Far Posse Right Bow Devil Choice

## Kick

This is a play we put in, because teams started to send the defensive end away from the back on a "mesh-charge," which means he is trying to run at the mesh point, hit both guys, and confuse the quarterback. We call this "even kick" and instead of possibly handling the ball on a sweep, the running back is going to come across and just kick that end out, making the play a quarterback counter with no read (Figure 9-51).

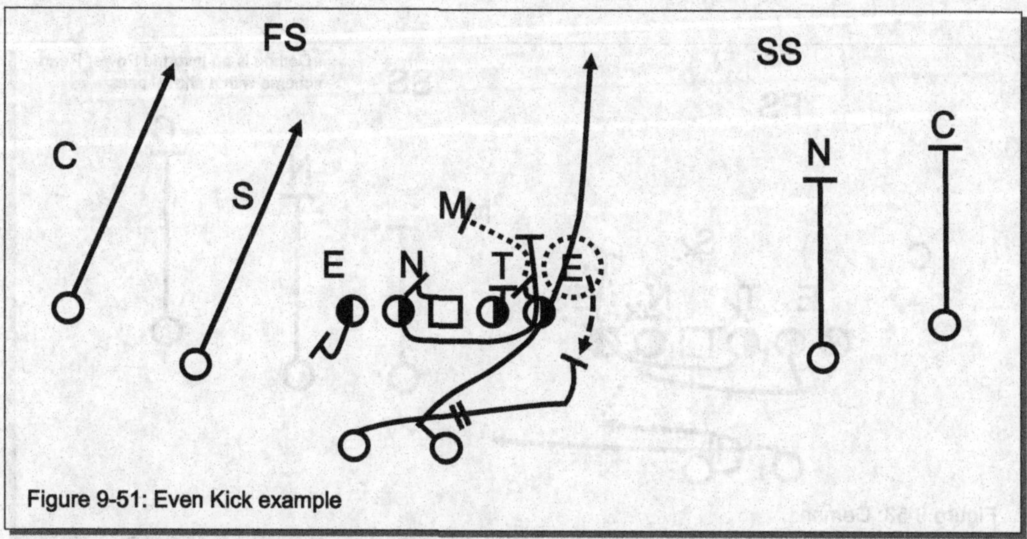

Figure 9-51: Even Kick example

When we started doing this, I had people ask me if it was to take some pressure off Lamar's decision making but that wasn't really it: it's about defeating the "mesh-charge." Then, when you call it that way, it's a great place to add an RPO with these "double-keys" outside, so he can fire that "key," if the force defender is cheating, or if the corner is sitting deeper that six yards (Figure 9-52).

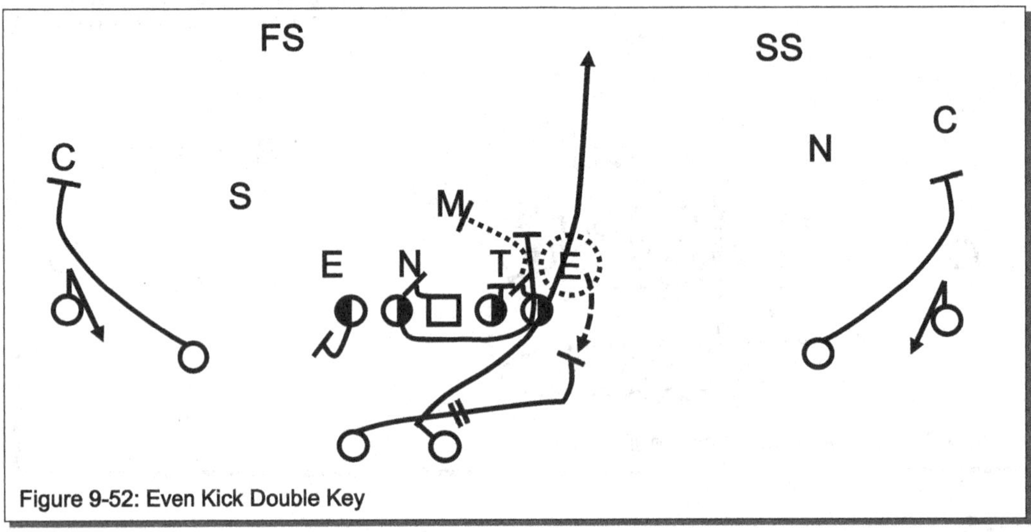

Figure 9-52: Even Kick Double Key

❑ Demon

"Demon" is the shovel pass, but it's the same blocking scheme. You categorize shovel pass—whether it's with screens and draws or whether it's part of the power of package—depending on how you use it. We carry it as part of "power" package, because it was another effective call vs. teams who tried to "mesh-charge" the quarterback's read on "devil." Our favorite way to do it is like this: (Figure 9-53).

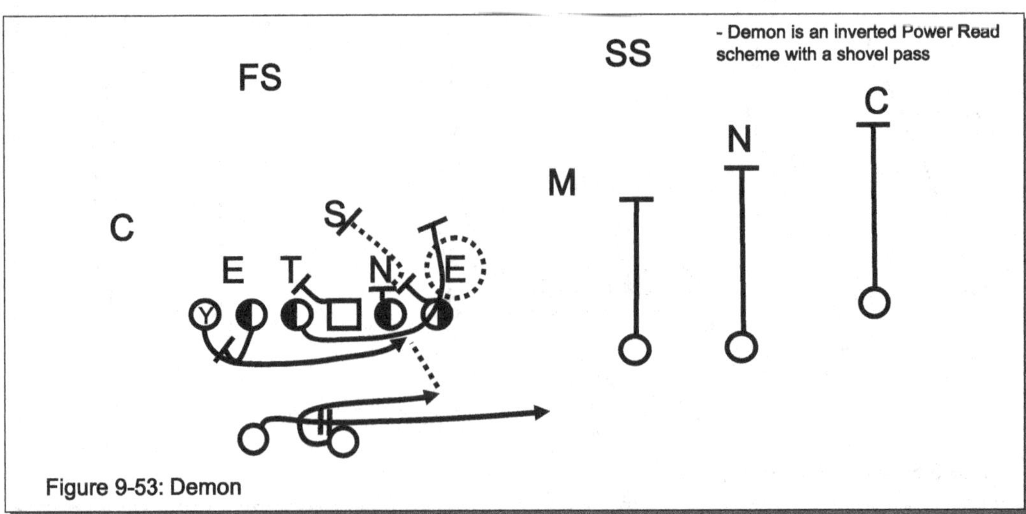

Figure 9-53: Demon

**Play: 9-53**

| Pos: | Assignment: |
|---|---|
| X | Crossfield technique away. Slow technique to you |
| Z | Crossfield technique away. Slow technique to you |
| QB | Mesh with RB and read DE. If DE closes, give to RB. If DE works upfield or slow-plays pitch, inside shovel to the TE. |

You lose the numbers of the quarterback as a run threat, but you ride the back across like "devil" and then can shovel it to the tight end coming underneath, as the defensive end commits to charging the mesh point. We gave it the name "demon," since the line is blocking "devil" and the code-words are similar. You do have to work with your T or Y to get vertical and not drift sideways after the catch. You want to coach them exactly the same at "hugging the wall." You'll also want to package it multiple ways, such as "6 dot right bow: odd demon" (Figure 9-54).

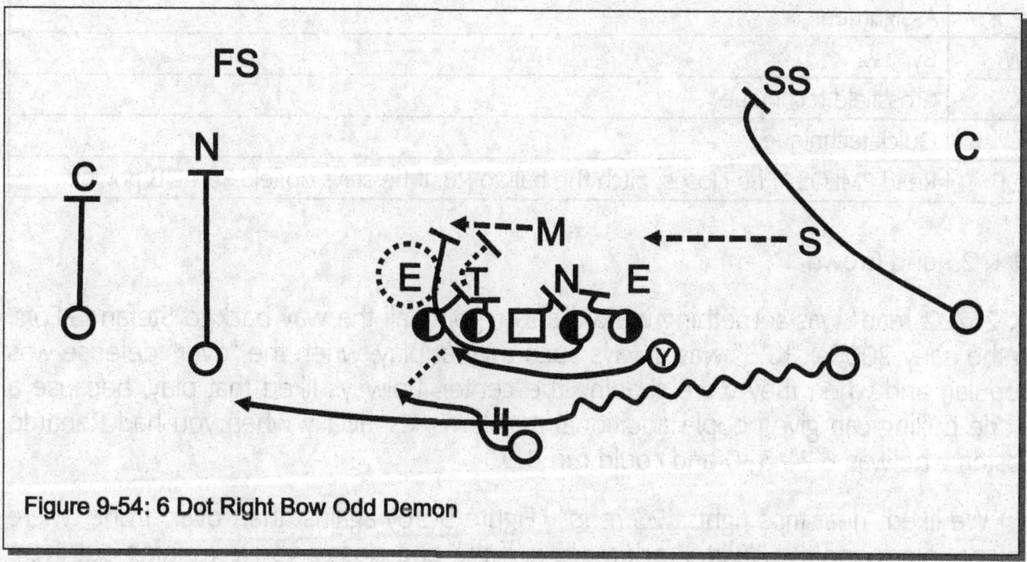

Figure 9-54: 6 Dot Right Bow Odd Demon

❑ Satan

"Satan" is where you can pitch it instead. You get the ball, you take that step and hop, and then you pitch it or run back up inside (Figure 9-55). I think that if you can do that to the same side of the back, it can create problems with the thought of the defensive "mesh charge." We think of this as a *package* with "devil," when they want to "mesh charge," along with "kick" and "demon." Our players clearly understood the code-words for these and they fit together as an effective modern "power" package.

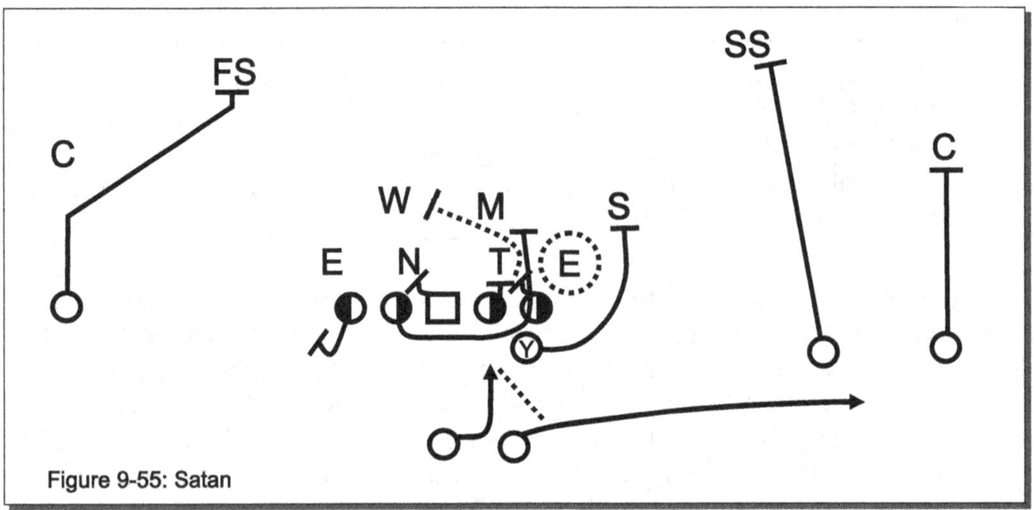

Figure 9-55: Satan

**Play: 9-55**

| Pos: | Assignment: |
|---|---|
| W | Bypass |
| X | Crossfield technique |
| Z | Quick technique |
| QB | Read EMLOS. If he closes, pitch the ball to RB. If he stays upfield, run QB power. |

❑ K 23 and Crown

"K 23/22 read" was something we did a ton, going all the way back to Stefan LeFors, in the early 2000s. "K23" was always such a great play, when the "over" defense was popular, and when they were shading the center. I always liked that play, because a tackle pulling can give people additional problems, especially when you had Renardo Foster, who was 6'7", 320 and could run 4.9."

We liked "near trips right: K23 *read*" (Figure 9-56) against that "over" front, where you arc block and the quarterback reads it. If the end closes, you're running out there behind that arc block and can go all the way. We ran it one year against Miami into the trips, where we went "far trips right: K22 *read*" (Figure 9-57). The strong guard would reach the 3-technique and then "power-arm" it. The tight end and tackle "schemed" for the defensive end and the corner. Then, that tackle pulled around, up in the A-gap, and the center had the backside linebacker from the double-team. Their defensive end was not going to let the quarterback run the ball, so Lionel Gates rushed for over 100 yards that day.

We also tag it with "race." You still read that end, but they switched responsibilities and the back "races" to the edge instead. If we call "gun top right: *race* K23" (Figure 9-58) against a 4-down look and that end chases the quarterback, he hands the ball off. If the end runs up the field, we run the quarterback counter.

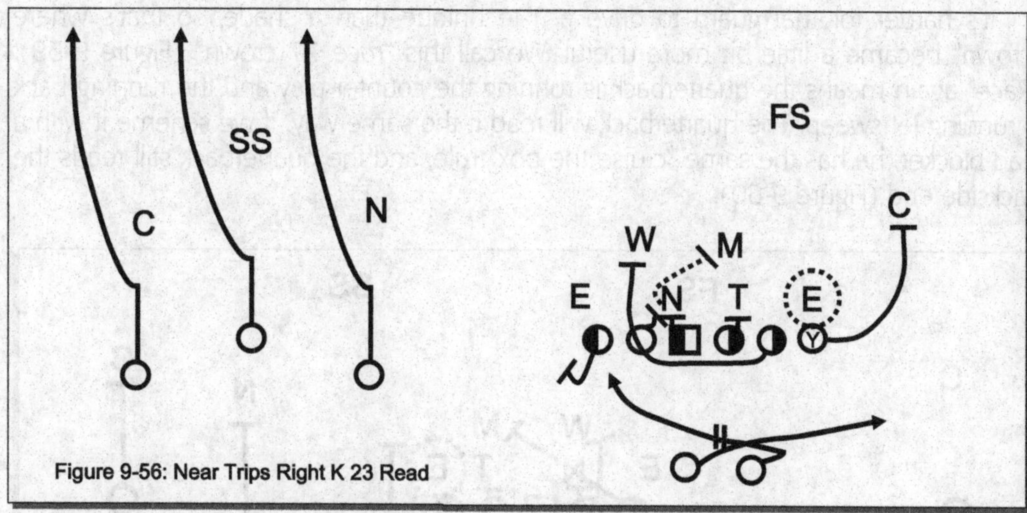

Figure 9-56: Near Trips Right K 23 Read

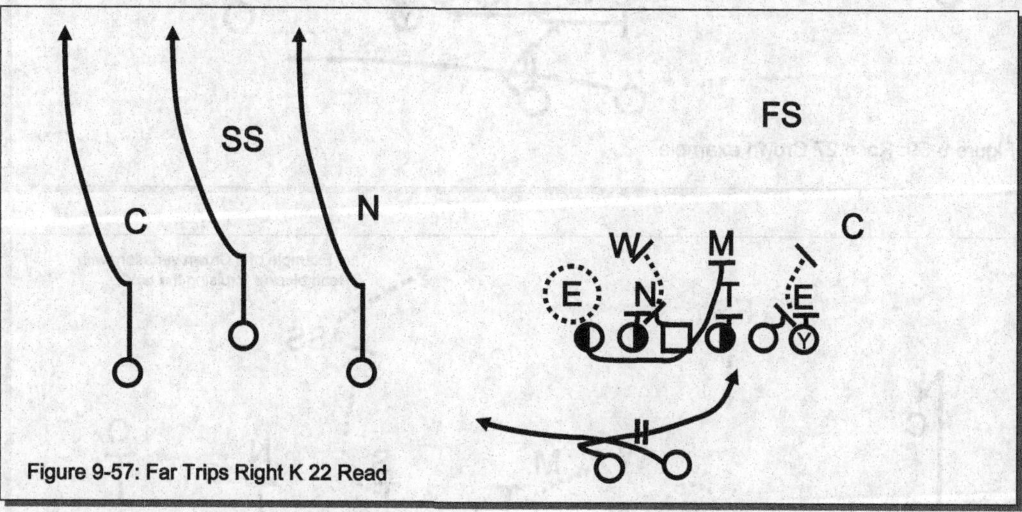

Figure 9-57: Far Trips Right K 22 Read

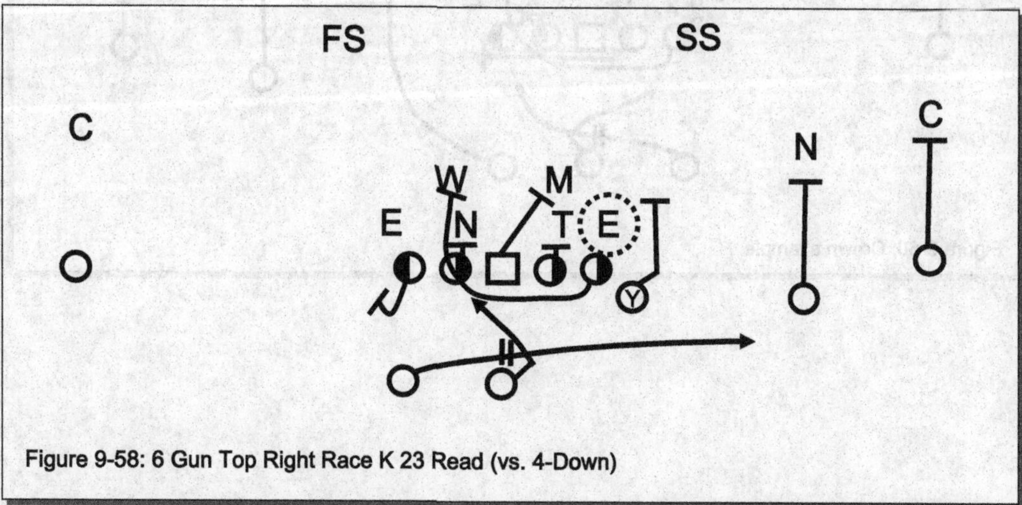

Figure 9-58: 6 Gun Top Right Race K 23 Read (vs. 4-Down)

It's harder for that guard to drive a 1-technique than a shade, so that's where "crown" became a little bit more useful. We call this "*race* 27 crown" (Figure 9-59). "Race" again means the quarterback is running the counter play and the running back is running jet sweep. The quarterback will read it the same way. If we scheme it with a lead blocker, he has the same "cruise the box" rule, and the quarterback still reads the backside end (Figure 9-60).

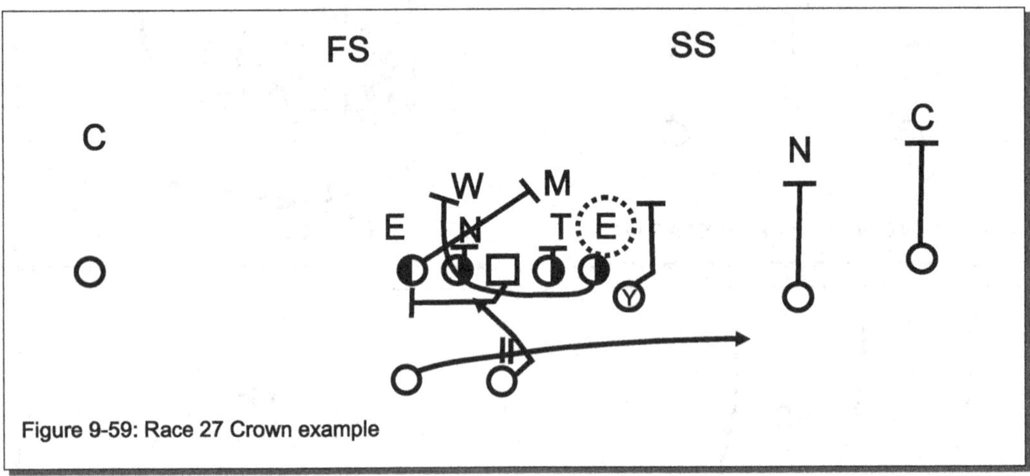

Figure 9-59: Race 27 Crown example

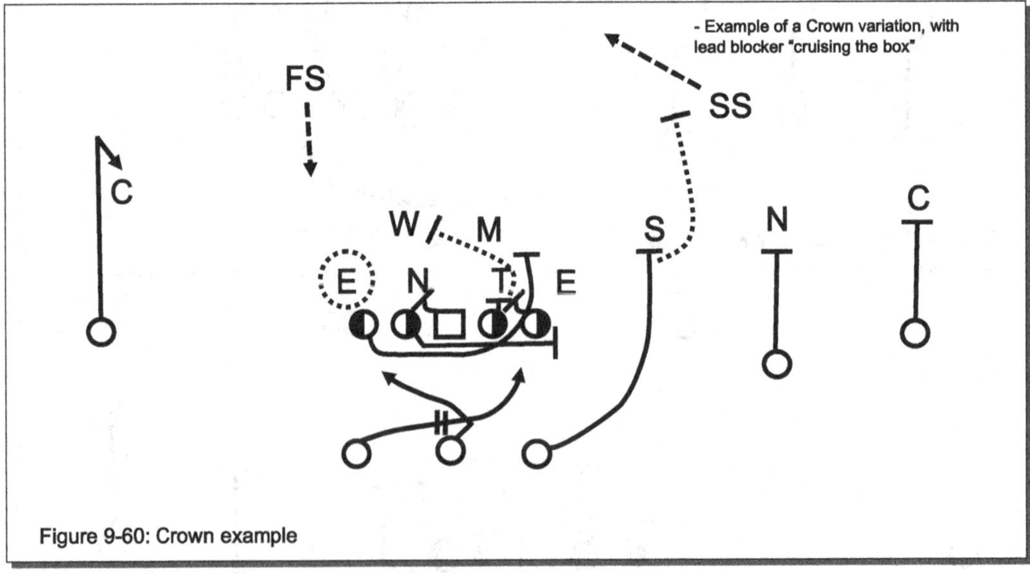

Figure 9-60: Crown example

## Final Thoughts

That's a lot of plays to feature the quarterback on read-option runs. This gives you an idea of the kinds of things we did, in order to set up a special player and showcase his running skills. It's always fun to create new ideas in football and you do that by paying attention to what your players can do well and finding ways to accent those strengths. However, regardless of the Xs and Os you want to draw up, we believe it's always important to "coach what you know."

We know we believe in taking care of the quarterback. We believe in "feeding the studs" and doing that with personnel, formations, and shifting. We believe in defeating the blitz, particularly with the run game, because you must run the football to win. We believe in effort and finish. We believe you get that done with fundamentally sound play. And maybe most importantly, you get the best out of great players by confronting them, demanding their best mental and physical effort, and then coaching them hard on all the little details within everything they do, inside the Xs and Os.

# APPENDIX A

## Football Players and Psychology Concepts With Dr. Joe

Coach Petrino has asked me to expound upon some psychology material that can apply to football. In this appendix, I'd like to share a few ideas and concepts that I think can be helpful to players and parents, but I believe will most useful for coaches, in particular. Hopefully there's an idea or two in this appendix that you can add to your mental skills toolbox!

## Psychology and Sports

Psychology is not new to football, dating as least as far back as coaches Pop Warner and Bob Zuppke during the 1920s. It's virtually omnipresent around sports today and the research deals with just about everything we can think of. Psychologists love collecting data and measurements. There have been studies about athletes on things like risk tolerance, personality traits, cognition, and leadership behaviors; I even found one recently about icing the kicker!

Psychologists have studied all kinds of other things related to sports, such as differences between men and women and various cultural differences. There are numerous mental toughness and motivational training systems available and interventions exist for things like stress management, performance anxiety, optimism when in a slump, and controlling the psychology of blame. Psychologists recently even worked with competitive marksmen to help them lower their heart rates before shooting! There is a lot of material out there, for sure.

For this appendix, I selected some ideas to share that might be a little different, but I believe you can find really useful. First, I'd like to show you two systems that measure psychological "types" and "traits": the *Myers-Briggs Type Indicator* (based on Carl Jung's work) and the *Five-Factor Model* (or "Big 5"). Then, I'd like to talk about the psychoanalytic perspective, which when applied to football, really just means we can learn a lot about a football player by paying attention to his relationship with his mom and dad. I'd then like to conclude with a few thoughts on non-verbal communication, aptitude tests, and social issues. I've listed some reference materials at the end, for individuals interested in additional reading. Let's take a look:

## Myers-Briggs Type Indicator

The Myers-Briggs Type Indicator is based on the original work of psychoanalyst Carl Jung. Jung wrote about what he called the "attitudes" of *extroversion* and *introversion*, along with other "functions" he called *intuition, sensation, thinking* and *feeling*. Everyone has natural preferences in each of those areas that affect our mental makeup. Myers and Briggs added to that what they called *perceiving* and *judging*, which measure how we each tend to interact with the outer world. The questionnaire categorizes each of these eight traits according to "dichotomies," which just means "one or the other." They are organized this way:

- Extroversion (E) / Introversion (I)
- Intuition (N) / Sensation (S)
- Thinking (T) / Feeling (F)
- Perceiving (P) / Judging (J)

For example, some people are *extroverts* (E) and thrive when they're around others. Some folks are *introverts* (I) and really need some space in order to recharge and reboot. Some people tend toward *intuition* (N), which means they are natural concept learners, while others toward *sensation* (S), making them step-by-step sequential learners, grounded in the sensory environment. Some people make decisions through *thinking* (T) where they are task-oriented and tough-minded and others decide by way of *feeling* (F), where they are relationship-oriented. Finally, people who tend toward *perceiving* (P) thrive when they are free to react and improvise in the moment, and those who tend toward *judging* (J) prefer to plan things ahead, with closure in mind. This particular instrument identifies a person's individual preference on each of these four pairs of traits, and then puts you into one of 16 psychological "types," denoted by an acronym.

Therefore, from a coaching standpoint, if you know an athlete is an extroverted concept thinker, who is task-oriented and likes to improvise in social situations (what this system would call an "ENTP type"), you'll have some tools to better understand how he's "wired" and to what he will and won't respond. By contrast, another individual might be an introverted step-by-step learner, who thrives on interpersonal relationships and who likes structured plans in social situations (what's called an "ISFJ type"). If you know those kinds of tendencies for each of your players, you can get a better sense of what's going on between their respective ears.

In addition, you'll have some practical answers for how your athletes will interact with each other and how they'll react in various situations. As everyone knows, each football team is made up of a variety of different personalities. This is a useful tool to sort some of that out. Then, if you know the "wiring" of your most influential players, you can keep that in mind as you build your team identity, whether that has to do with tactical strategies, certain teaching approaches, group activities, or whatever else you are planning and implementing. At the college level, this can also be useful in recruiting, if you know what specific kind of guys you're looking for, in order to fit your team philosophy and your own disposition as a coach.

If you're interested in this system, you might start with Jon and Jeremy Niednagel at www.braintypes.com. Jon calls his method "Brain Type" and he has developed a way to identify both mental and physical (what we call "kinesthetic") tendencies among athletes, according to typology. Jon and his son Jeremy are as devoted and genuine as any people you'll ever meet in sports! Their work actually inspired me to explore what I did in my doctoral dissertation and like the old saying goes, it's important to "give credit where it's due." Jon and Jeremy have really tailored their system specifically for working with athletes, so I'd encourage you to check out their material.

Roughly speaking, Jon has discovered that numerous successful ball players are "wired" similarly to each other. For example, great quarterbacks like Joe Montana, Dan Marino, and Peyton Manning are all similar to each other when evaluated within this system. Individuals who share their specific mental makeup will tend to process various social situations similarly and they'll also react similarly during competition, particularly under stress, when their instincts take over. By contrast, smooth striders, such as Jerry Rice and Marshall Faulk, are "wired" differently than the aforementioned quarterbacks but in this system, they are actually very similar to each other in terms of physical and mental tendencies. Furthermore, certain great coaches have a different mental makeup than those particular great athletes. For example, Vince Lombardi and Bill Belichick are more mentally similar to each other than they are to any of the aforementioned athletes, when understood within this system. It's fascinating and fun stuff!

## Five-Factor Model

Another useful system is the Five-Factor Model or "Big 5," which was developed by psychologists Robert McCrae and Paul Costa. In this model, the traits are each measured on a "spectrum" (such as a 1-10 scale), instead of an either/or "dichotomy." A person's individual traits can then be measured relative to averages in the general population. The five "factors" are as follows:

- Openness to Experience
- Conscientiousness
- Extroversion
- Agreeableness
- Neuroticism

*Openness* pertains to how people respond to new experiences. Highly open people enjoy new ideas and often respond positively to things they discover from new contexts. However, folks lower in openness will tend to prefer to stay within what's familiar.

*Conscientiousness* refers to impulse control, dutifulness, and reliability. As this pertains to ball players, mental toughness corresponds to this trait, when guys are self-motivated to put in the extra hard work. By contrast, individuals with lower conscientiousness usually need extrinsic supervision in order to keep them on task.

*Extroversion* on this model is measured along a scale. Some individuals, particularly those who are close to the middle of the distribution, prefer to frame extroversion/introversion this way. This trait can also be understood in terms of "breadth vs. depth," when relating to others in a social context.

*Agreeableness* is a measure of a person's cooperativeness and concern for the well-being of others. Agreeable people are sometimes thought of as more optimistic. However, this trait can sometimes be counterintuitive in a sports context, because disagreeable guys are often the most natural competitors.

*Neuroticism* is a person's susceptibility to negative emotion. While you obviously want individuals on your team who can control their emotions and are "Joe Cool" under pressure, there are certainly natural worriers who can still be successful athletes. This is especially the case when they have some tools and techniques available to help manage their mental game.

These are the original five "traits." The most useful "Big 5" resource I've found has been designed at the University of Toronto by clinical psychologist Dr. Jordan Peterson: www.understandmyself.com. This version of the test provides a personalized breakdown of your tendencies, along each of these domains, relative to the general population. Dr. Peterson is now famous as a popular author and lecturer, but he's been a devoted psychology researcher for many years. On his version, the five original "factors" are further divided into two "aspects" of each:

- *Aesthetic* and *intellectual* aspects of openness to experience
- *Industriousness* and *orderliness* aspects of conscientiousness
- *Enthusiasm* and *assertiveness* aspects of extroversion
- *Politeness* and *compassion* aspects of agreeableness
- *Well-being* and *volatility* aspects of neuroticism

For example, *intellectually* open people genuinely enjoy studying and learning, where *aesthetically* open people enjoy the arts. We've all known individuals who like academia but who don't care much for music concerts or museums, and vice versa. And of course, some people genuinely enjoy both. When it comes to football players, this can indicate how recruited athletes with various levels of *openness* might respond to things like what type of offense you run and how much offense you want to carry, whether that's the service academy's triple-option or a modern multiple spread.

*Industrious* people thrive on hard work, where *orderly* people respect authority, structure, and tradition. Both are considered aspects of *conscientiousness* and can provide added insight about a person. For example, a football player might love to work hard when it comes to ball (*industriousness*) but not care too much about getting a haircut and dressing nicely (low *orderliness*). While *industriousness* alone won't necessarily make an athlete more physically talented, it's a trait that can clearly separate someone from others within a range of similar ability. *Orderly* guys are a joy to coach, because they respect authority, but that doesn't necessarily have anything to do with athletic ability. And of course, there are ball players with lower *conscientiousness* who can still contribute, but they're going to need a firm structure and some negative reinforcement in order to stay on task. They won't like getting chewed out to work harder, but if they're competitors, they'll respond to it.

*Enthusiastic* people respond to positive emotions from others, while *assertive* people take initiative. Both are aspects of *extroversion*. For example, some people will speak up and go ask for what they want but won't react very much to emotional expression from others. Others may be happy and fun-loving but tend to avoid confrontation. You can see how this adds some nuance to the concept of *extroversion/introversion* and how various individuals on a team may display these traits in different ways. This can be helpful to understand, in the effort to communicate with and to motivate your players.

*Compassionate* people are empathetic toward others and *politeness* refers to an individual's ability to regulate his own disagreeable impulses. Both are aspects of *agreeableness,* which, in general, can make an individual a personable, team player but it doesn't necessarily mean he has the capacity to be a tough competitor. Perhaps ironically, it's often the *disagreeable* athletes who have a natural killer instinct. Every coach should have an idea of how he prefers to handle this particular trait with regard to himself and the players on his roster, on behalf of his team culture.

Individuals high in *well-being* tend to bounce back quickly from setbacks, where as people low in *volatility* are stable in their moods and emotional regulation. Both are aspects of *neuroticism*. Low *well-being* means a player may have trouble shaking off a bad play, a bad game, or a breakup with his girlfriend. Similarly, high *volatility* may make a guy susceptible to angry outbursts and losing his cool when he's frustrated. This isn't necessarily informative about a person's athletic ability, but it certainly can predict how an individual may react under pressure. Sport-psych interventions can really help players work through some of these challenges and to play consistently at their highest levels.

These are practical and useful things to know about yourself and your players. I think the traits are all visible in context, when you know how to identify and look for them. We're all unique and different from each other, but with an awareness of these individual traits, it's possible to work through weaknesses and accent strengths. Various athletes can have differences between the ears, just like they all wear different helmet, jersey, and shoe sizes. There are a lot of effective ways to organize a team philosophy but if you know what you're looking for, you can use these psychology instruments to better understand what makes each player "tick" and then employ that information to help galvanize your team.

## Examples of Traits

The following are some practical examples of aforementioned traits, including some anecdotes from throughout this book:

Coach Petrino himself is actually a good example of *openness to experience*. His offensive creativity, playcalling ability, and tactical adaptability can be understood in part because of this particular trait. Openness—both *intellectual* and *aesthetic*—lends a person to be constantly curious about new ideas. As we've seen throughout this book, there's been no shortage of creative ideas in Coach Petrino's offenses. For example, few coaches could or would successfully transform from a pro-style power running/dropback passing offense into an attack featuring the read-option at a no-huddle tempo in order to adjust to the unique skills of his quarterbacks and maintain a competitive advantage. By his own admission, some of his most creative ideas—the option route concepts, numerous dropback concepts, such as "Japan," the "Ninja/Noah", and read-option concepts, etc.—came to fruition as a result of paying attention to players and constantly trying out new things. Coach Petrino took an immediate interest in my doctoral thesis. As such, he is quite curious about all kinds of topics with regard to psychology and human behavior, which makes for fun conversations. He also told me recently that he genuinely enjoyed studying calculus in both high school and college. Frankly, he might be the only football guy I know who would say that!

Based on Coach Petrino's storytelling, Mark Brunell displayed a rare level of *conscientiousness*. The description in Chapter 1 of Mark's meticulous note-taking, his efforts to put his teammates first during practice, and his respect for the traditions of ball indicates both high *industriousness* and *orderliness*. Conscientious people are the intrinsically driven, hard workers. They do the right thing, even when no one is looking. They'll stay after practice to take extra reps, because they want to get it right. They'll sacrifice selfish interests for the good of the team. They're the individuals you want to lead your program!

Based on Coach Petrino's accounts, Lamar Jackson demonstrated especially high *enthusiasm,* which is an aspect of *extroversion*. His ability to be an energetic leader, such as running all the way to the end zone on every single carry in practice, and always happily sharing his success with teammates, can be understood as a function of this specific trait. Previously, traditional coaches called this a "high motor." We all know how valuable it is to the team culture to have a team leader who can energize practice during the dog days of camp or elevate the whole team late in a big game. Interestingly, the term *enthusiasm* is derived from the Latin word *entheos*, which roughly translated has a spiritual meaning: "to release God from within you." Lamar is a remarkable athlete and person, but his *enthusiasm,* in particular, sure makes him a joy to watch play!

*Agreeable* people can be both *compassionate* and *polite*. In general, these are pro-social qualities, because agreeable folks look out for others and they genuinely care about people. However—and this is perhaps ironic—people low in agreeableness tend to be the natural competitors. They don't want to cooperate with you; they want to *beat* you. The old saying "that guy would trample his grandmother to win a game" is a good example of how disagreeableness and ruthless competitiveness can occupy the same space within a person's mental makeup. By contrast, agreeable players are often great teammates, but they sometimes have to learn that it's ok to finish off an opponent. The saying "it's ok to knock him down, just help him up afterward" might resonate with them. On the other hand, ruthlessly competitive athletes sometimes need to understand that there are times when it's necessary to "love up" teammates and that the team needs everyone to work together in order to win. If they understand why it's important, they can learn to regulate disagreeable impulses. As an example, Tony Dungy and Mike Ditka are both legendary coaches, but I think it's fair to say they were polar opposites in how they went about this particular trait among their players. The key is to find what approach works best for you!

According to Coach Petrino's stories, Jake Plummer displayed the trait of low *neuroticism*, which means low *volatility* and high *well-being*. In Chapter 1, Coach said "Jake didn't worry or let things bother him." Players like Jake, who are high in *well-being,* bounce back quickly from setbacks. Individuals like him, who are low in *volatility,* are the consummate pressure players who can control their nerves when others get worked up. In other words, they don't have big mood swings and they stay cool when the game is on the line. However, other players with higher levels of *neuroticism* can still be effective, if they have some mental tools in place to help anticipate their responses to pressure and manage their emotions within competition. We all know stories about great players who had weird superstitions and all kinds of nervous habits, but who still managed to get all of that under control in order to play well. (Note: individuals like that can really benefit from sport-psych interventions.)

Psychologists can accurately measure all these traits. I also think good coaches really do have instincts for all these characteristics, which is why these formal descriptions of them make sense in context. If a player and coach understand what some of these traits are, it then becomes a more efficient process to confront and work on weaknesses, while at the same time accent strengths. This information can also be useful in the effort to put coaches and players together who are the most compatible with each other. We all know that there are a variety of different personalities who can all be successful in football. The best chance for success is when individuals can understand how and why to work together with each other and then come together as a team.

## Psychoanalysis

The psychoanalytic perspective takes a little more work to unpack. The conventional terms like *Id, Ego, Persona* and *Shadow* can seem a little strange, but from a practical standpoint, all of that refers to the process of understanding who we each truly are and what the influence of mom and dad is. For all of us, our individual traits, behaviors, motives, and beliefs are impacted tremendously by how we were each raised. To that end, some of these concepts from the psychoanalysts can really be helpful when applied to football players. I think this can be especially useful for coaches in particular.

## Integration and Individuation

In terms of understanding oneself, Coach Petrino is actually talking psychoanalysis when he says a quarterback should "respond to adversity according to his personality." Psychoanalyst Carl Jung wrote that if we try to act outside of ourselves, we become poorly *integrated*. Jung described a *Persona* as a mask or false-front we want others to see. Jung then described the *Shadow* as all the other parts of us we might be trying to hide from people. *Individuation* means putting all that together authentically; to examine yourself and be real about who you are. If you can sort out who you genuinely are, you can then act and react according to your true *Self.*

For example, with regard to the aforementioned trait of *extroversion*: if a football player is naturally *enthusiastic* and *assertive*, that's how he needs to carry himself, in order to be at his best. He'll be genuine that way. Furthermore, he will play better the more he spends time around teammates and coaches. However, if a player has a natural preference for *introversion*, he'll be at his best, when he can maintain room to get into his own headspace. If he isn't either a "trash talker" or "cheerleader" by nature, it can just distract from his concentration to try to act that way. So, whether a player has a personality like Shannon Sharpe or more like Barry Sanders, he'll be at his best when he can *integrate* who he truly is into his game. It's in this way, a player can get himself "in the zone," which is what psychologists call *flow*. I think you can see from this example of integrating *extroversion* how some of that comes together. Each of the other aforementioned traits we looked at can be understood and then *integrated* in this same way, in order to make oneself authentic as an individual.

## The Influence of Mom & Dad

The psychoanalytic literature gives us some understanding of the influence our parents have on us. Sigmund Freud and Carl Jung, two founders of psychoanalysis, wrote extensively about how a person's parents affect their psychological development. Freud used terms like "narcissistic" and "obsessive" to describe the balance of these parental relationships, where Jung referred to them as "complexes." All of us display various *defense mechanisms,* whenever some of that stuff comes to the surface. What that means, is simply that a positive or negative relationship with their mom or dad is going to have a profound effect on a person's mental makeup and behavior. As ball coaches, if we take the time to understand a player's relationship with his parents, we can understand him better as an individual.

Ideally, if a football player has a sturdy father who is a positive influence in his life, he will tend to respect authority and take systematically to coaching. Most of the time, you'll be able to coach him hard and he will respond positively to it. You can usually expect what you're teaching to be reinforced at home. As any coach will tell you, it's ideal for your team dynamic, if your quarterback has this kind of relationship with his father. However, this isn't always the case and it's not always the player's fault, if he has an unbalanced relationship with dad that might be interfering with his game.

For example, a harsh father can disrupt a young man's mental balance. In some cases, cruelty from a father can be the result of a desire to project his own sports aspirations onto his son. A dad like this is obviously tough on his son but he may also project hostility onto the coaching staff, due to his own internalized frustrations. Sometimes, a player with an unbalanced relationship with his father may need an "open set of ears" from a coach he trusts. As a rule, it'll typically be on his terms and you may be surprised by the timing of when he'll need to talk to you. What's also interesting is that a dad who behaves this way may sometimes release some of his irrational resentment for the staff, if a coach takes the time to just sit calmly and listen to him. Obviously, that isn't fun. It's often surprising, however, how effective it can be if a coach will stay calm and give an upset father the time to try to talk through his own emotions. This can then help improve his interactions with his son, which will then help the young man's game.

By contrast, a passive father (or even an absentee father) may have a different kind of impact on a young man. Young men in this situation may look for mentorship from other adult men and may place a coach on a "pedestal" that he didn't necessarily ask for. When someone says, "a coach is like a father to his players," it can be more than a metaphor in cases like this. A young man in this situation may sometimes have difficulty with masculine responsibility. He may get sensitive or respond poorly to criticism, even when it's constructive. He may need more "maintenance," in order to focus himself and play hard. This can make more sense, when you take the time to understand his home life.

Similarly, there can be insight found in understanding a football player's relationship with his mother. Ideally, he will have a balanced mother who loves her son unconditionally, and who challenges him to grow, while still affording him the space to do so. If mom supports her son, while allowing him to have his own learning experiences about overcoming adversity, he can develop into a balanced adult who can build healthy, productive relationships with others. Unfortunately, this isn't always the case in today's culture. In reality, it may not be the young man's fault, if he's out of balance with his mom.

For example, a strict, controlling mother may never have given her son the space to develop his own sense of identity. A "helicopter mom," who shelters her son, doesn't allow him to face any challenges or overcome any adversity, so he never gets to fully develop his own masculine confidence. If a player feels like he's being "de-balled" by his mom, the lack of balance can render him passive or sometimes produce a *Persona* (false front) to mask his insecurity. He will often have unproductive interactions and poorly developed relationships with other women, due to his frustration with his own mother. He may need to be taught exactly *how* to work hard and *why* it is so important to do so, for both the benefit of the team and for his own future life outcomes. A coach may, indeed, be the first adult male to ever point this out to him.

By contrast, a mother who is needy may unconsciously attempt to control her son by "spoiling" him. Here again, the young man doesn't get a chance to experience the value of effort and persistence, so he never develops his own masculine identity. He may lack self-discipline and struggle with his own intrinsic drive, an attribute that some coaches refer to as a "weak motor." The value of hard work seems obvious to a coach, but a young man in this situation can have a sense of entitlement, if he's simply never been exposed to opportunities to see a sustained effort investment pay off. Because he's out of balance, he may be completely passive or, he may compensate by projecting a *persona* of hardness that masks a fragile sense of self underneath it. This is sometimes the case when he has a young single mom, where she's unconsciously compensating for her frustrations with other men by how she raises her son.

A young man with this kind of home life, who acts out in response to constructive criticism, can benefit from private conversations to help him understand why he's feeling certain emotions. He may need to recognize and understand how teammates simply don't feel things as intensely as he does. It may also take time for him to understand both *why* and *how* to respect male authority, especially in instances where he's simply never worked through a productive interaction with a balanced male figure. In the most unfortunate of these instances, you, as a coach, will have to decide where you draw the line regarding these kinds of behaviors and exactly when they become detrimental to the team's culture. (We all know the infamous stories of tremendously gifted players who became volatile like this, to the point of rupturing an entire locker room.)

There are a number of such behaviors you might observe, that may not be under the player's conscious control. As a coach, you may be able to gain some insight and help him to become the best version of himself by paying attention to what's going on at home. If you watch carefully, when it comes to the parents, you can get a better sense of what makes a person "tick." Then, when a player trusts you, it's possible to help him to identify and then to work through some of these challenges, in order to play at his best.

It can be truly rewarding to help a young man overcome this kind of adversity. When a young man can learn to confront these kinds of imbalances and then *integrate* himself, he will not only play at his best, but he can then become deeply generous and altruistic in his various relationships with others. Psychoanalyst Carl Jung referred to this quality as a "finely differentiated *Eros*." I, myself, was very fortunate to have coaches who took the time to help me like this at crucial times in my life, from junior high all the way through college ball. Coach John Rosene (at my alma mater Knox College) did this for me and not only got me to play at my best but he was literally the reason I didn't drop out of school. Special coaches truly do understand the mental game!

## Non-Verbal Cues

If you want to better understand a player's non-verbal communication, American psychologist Paul Ekman's work regarding what he calls "micro-expressions," can be handy. Since most individuals' interactions truly are non-verbal, it's advantageous for coaches to understand various facial and body language cues, in the interest of communicating productively with athletes and helping them to play at their best. Emotions like happiness, curiosity, pride, fear, anger, contempt, disgust, and so on can be identified through involuntary facial cues.

For example, you can observe fear in the widening and tension around the eyes, eyelids, and mouth (Figure A-1), as well as, by a tightening of the neck and throat area. Rage shows up between and under the eyes (Figure A-2) and often with clenched fists. Contempt is displayed by a twitch of one side of the mouth, when a person is "put off" by something (Figure A-3). Depression can be observed in weak eye focus, and drooping around the mouth (Figure A-4), as well as in a person's posture and walk.

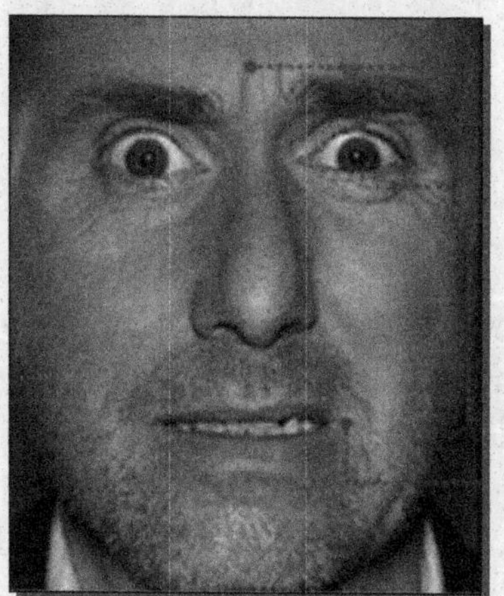

Figure A-1.

**Fear**

1. Eyebrows raised and pulled together
2. Raised upper eyelids
3. Tensed lower eyelids
4. Lips slightly stretched horizontally back to ears

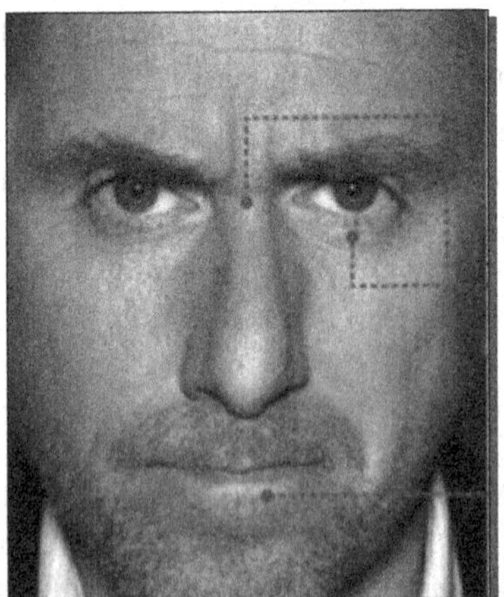

Figure A-2.

**Anger**

1. Eyebrows down and together
2. Eyes glare
3. Narrowing of the lips

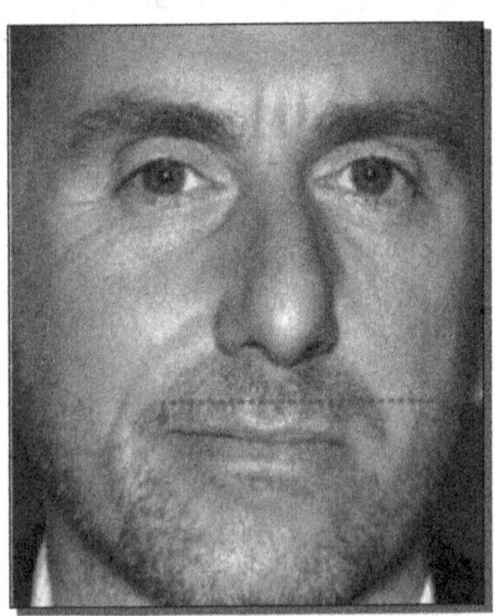

Figure A-3.

**Contempt**

1. Lip corner tightened and raised on only one side of face

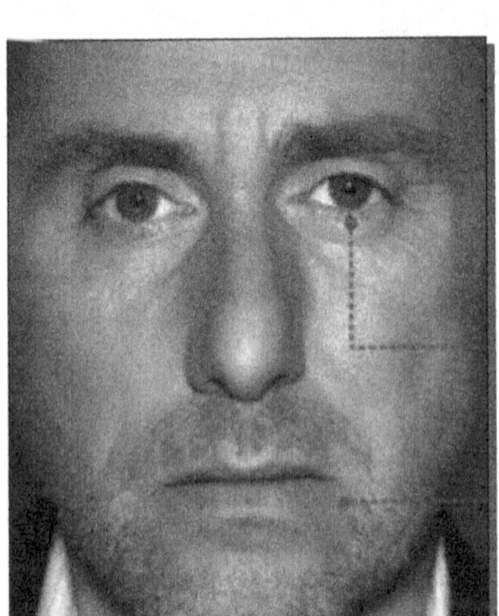

Figure A-4.

**Sadness**

1. Drooping upper eyelids
2. Losing focus in eyes
3. Slight pulling down of lip corners

Interestingly, these cues and many others can sometimes tell us when people are trying to deceive us. However, it's most useful to pay attention to micro-expressions for the purpose of identifying the specific emotions that are being displayed in context. You can check out Dr. Ekman's site www.PaulEkman.com for a useful primer on these and many other non-verbal signals.

## Mental Testing & Spatial Ability

There are different types of mental aptitudes that can be measured, and coaches should be careful about getting caught up in the wrong metrics. In particular, what psychologists call *verbal* ability and *spatial* ability aren't necessarily the same thing. Spatial ability is the aptitude for seeing patterns and shapes develop. Engineers, architects, and computer programmers need this ability. So do mechanics and plumbers. It's important to recognize that this aptitude doesn't always coincide with the ability to talk through the task itself and individuals who are really good at these tasks may not talk much about how they actually do them.

A word of caution as this pertains to football skills: there are certainly successful athletes who love to talk to the media about their game, but the skills required to read and react on the field aren't necessarily the same as being able to talk about it. (John Madden has a colorful anecdote about this very premise in his book "One Knee Equals Two Feet," where he tells a story about coaching linebackers in the NFL. In his own inimitable manner, coach Madden explains that the best linebackers couldn't really explain to him what they did!)

We, as coaches, sometimes inadvertently assess a player's potential by listening to him talk or by seeing his score on a reading comprehension test, rather than watching closely how he executes the necessary skills. This factor is particularly true at the quarterback position. For example, we can see throughout the examples in this book that Coach Petrino's quarterbacks are constantly asked to develop a clear mental image or "picture" of offensive concepts and various defensive strategies. This is an emphasis on the *spatial* aspects of the position. In addition, we can also see that the words Coach Petrino uses for playcalls are chosen specifically for what mental image they elicit, not just because they sound good. Words *do* matter for ball players, but terminology should be chosen in the interest of developing *spatial* acuity.

When we, as coaches, evaluate a player's skill set, it's sort of like the old cliché about going out on a date: don't listen to what a girl says, pay attention to what she does in order to get your cues. In other words, don't get too distracted by how well a player talks or how he scores on an academic aptitude test. Watch the video and let the film talk!

## Social Issues

From a sociological standpoint, sport and society are more inter-related today than ever. We need more than ever to be able to communicate productively about issues surrounding race, politics, social class, and ball, if we want to really get to know the individuals on our teams. It's often sensitive and difficult to get to the heart of these issues and we can only have meaningful discussions, if we engage each other in good faith. Football teams are made up of athletes from all different backgrounds, and a team is not a team until the players really understand and care about each other. The previous and following various psychology resources can really help with the mission of getting past superficial differences and genuinely learning about each other as individuals.

## Selected Psychology Resources:

- A masterpiece of sports psych is Harvey Dorfman's *"Coaching the Mental Game."* Harvey called himself a "meat-and-potatoes" mental skills coach and his literature is really practical and useful to apply. I'd encourage anyone interested in sports psychology to check out that book.
- For the Myers-Briggs typology, the best resource is https://braintypes.com/. Jon and Jeremy Niednagel have been doing sports consulting since the 1980s and they're first-class individuals. Their method, which is called "Brain Type", is designed specifically for a sports context. They will do personal consulting for you if you reach out to them. (I've also listed two of Jon's books in the reference section.)
- The most useful version of the Five-Factor Model can be found at: https://www.understandmyself.com/. Dr. Jordan Peterson's version of the "Big 5" offers practical nuance about the traits, along with straightforward (refreshingly non-sugar coated) explanations for how you answer the questions. It's worth the money you invest!
- Dr. Michael MacCoby's work is a great resource for psychoanalysis in the workplace. His book *Strategic Intelligence* includes a useful self-report inventory. He uses the terms "visionary," "exacting," "caring," and "adaptive" to describe the various personality styles that can manifest themselves in an organizational context. In his previous book *Narcissistic Leaders*, Dr. MacCoby called these "erotic," "obsessive," and "narcissistic," according to the "libidinal styles" of Freud's original terminology, but it's the same concepts. I also really like the questionnaire he offers in the older book. However, the idea is that we all display aspects of our personalities which pertain to our relationships with mom and dad. Both books are a very helpful reference point for psychoanalysis in the workplace and the ideas can be useful when you put a coaching staff and a roster together.

The important factor, in this instance, though, is just to pay close attention to a player's relationship with his parents. Ask your guys to talk about mom and dad and watch them carefully as they respond. Watch for signs of emotion surrounding certain family topics and try to understand how it affects them. Then, use your coaching instincts to address the things you observe and to help your guys to integrate themselves in a balanced manner. I'm really fortunate that I had special coaches who took the time to do that for me!

For a primer about non-verbal cues, check out www.PaulEkman.com . There was also a television show called "Lie to Me" that Dr. Ekman consulted on, in order to make sure they got his techniques right. The show ran for three seasons, but the first season is the most scientifically accurate and demonstrates many of the techniques in an entertaining context.

- When it comes to sport and social issues, I recommend Dr. Harry Edwards' work. His doctoral dissertation, *The Sociology of Sport*, is hard to find today (as are some of his books), but there's online videos available of some of his lectures, including memoirs of what he contributed to Bill Walsh's great 49ers teams. Again, players from different backgrounds must learn to genuinely care about each other for a team to really become a team.

I listed more formal resources which may be useful to you, in your effort to master the mental game. Good luck!

– Joe Metzka, Ph.D.
Joemetzka@gmail.com

# APPENDIX B

## Summary of Dr. Joe's Dissertation

Our study was called *the relationship between personality type, statistical performance and position played among elite collegiate football players.* The research was conducted with the cooperation of two different top 25 FBS teams, across both the 2015 and 1016 seasons. Coach Petrino asked me to include a summary of it in this appendix. Initially, I'd like to describe what we did in formal academic terminology, and then offer some practical suggestions for players, coaches, and administrators, based on the findings of the study.

## Academic Summary of the Study

In formal academic terms, the following abstract details what we did in my doctoral dissertation. Our study examined the players from two large NCAA schools ($n = 206$) in order to explore relationships between year of athletic eligibility, position played, and statistical performance, on the number of snaps played in a season and the personality type, as measured by the Myers-Briggs Type Indicator. Data were collected from both 2015 and 2016 to assess the participants from across two consecutive seasons. Four psychological types were revealed to be the most common among these participants. They represented over two-thirds of the total sample ($n = 141$), with over half of those subjects reporting as introverts. This subset of the sample was used for hypothesis testing.

A Pearson chi-square test revealed statistically significant differences ($p = .015$) among the ISTP types at defensive back and linebacker ($2(6) = 15.791$, $p < .05$). A two-way factorial ANOVA was used to analyze the impact of 1) the personality type on snaps played in a season, when the year of eligibility was held constant; 2) the personality type on year of eligibility, when snaps played were held constant; and 3) the year of eligibility on snaps played when personality type was held constant ($p = < .05$). Significant main effects were found for the 2016 year of eligibility on snaps played ($p = .014$) and the personality type on 2016 snaps played ($p = .023$). However, only year of eligibility was found to be significantly impactful, when 2016 data were truncated to exclude players who did not play in games.

Tukey HSD tests revealed a statistically significant difference between year of eligibility and snaps played, when the 2016 year of eligibility was held constant and when psychological type and 2016 snaps played were considered together. When personality type and 2016 year of eligibility were considered together, no significant interactions were found. Significant differences were, however, found for year of eligibility alone on snaps played and for psychological type alone on snaps played for ISTP types and ESTP types relative to ESTJ types. On the other hand, only the year of eligibility was found to be significantly different, when 2016 data were truncated to exclude players who did not actually play in games.

Traditional football statistics from both the 2015 and 2016 seasons were subsequently explored, which revealed that the ESTP and ISTP types were among the most prolific in terms of rushing, receiving, and tackling statistics, particularly in 2016. This revelation coincided with the statistically significant differences found in the original research questions for the study. These findings led to recommendations for various interventions and suggestions for future research.

## Practical Findings

Ok, so what does all that stuff mean in football terms? We studied the players on these two FBS teams across both the 2015 and 2016 seasons. We found that the vast majority of the players on both of these teams identified as grounded, practical thinkers, and step-by-step, sequential learners. This suggests that coaches would do well to clarify concepts into a clear *teaching-sequence*, in order to connect most effectively with the majority of athletes on a team. This also means you'll want to check for concrete feedback, as well as an understanding of what all you're teaching, rather than just leaving it assumed.

Make your players repeat back what you're showing them during the game plan installation. Have them take quizzes over the playbook so they see concretely what they need to sort out. Make them talk through what they're seeing on film, and so on. Individuals with these traits won't really respond to theorizing, they just want to know what's next and to see concretely what is going to work. This reminder is especially important for coaches who, like John Madden said, like to sit up late at night with a pot of coffee and draw up a bunch of new plays.

Coaches should address players with these traits with stepwise, concrete information, rather than abstract ideas or speculation. Metaphors will be most effective when they appeal to these sensibilities (e.g., "be the hammer, not the nail," "beat your man to the punch"). Players with these traits respond well to language that appeals to task-orientation (e.g., "do your job") and sensory reference points (e.g., "see it before you do it"). To this end, there is little surprise that these kinds of phrases are used so often in football.

Coaches may also need to keep these types of individuals on task, in the event that they indulge in a tendency to seek new stimulation, before the current tasks are completed. Players with these traits may also find it more difficult to take *mental reps* in practice (watching another player at his position carry out an assignment in practice, while visualizing his own responsibility on the task). They may need to be taught explicitly *how* to do it and *why* it's so important for their progress to do so.

Classroom time for learning is a must, but these types of individuals really need to get on the field in order to demonstrate that they have their requisite skills together. This is an important reminder for coaches who are adept at learning conceptually, since most of the athletes we studied tended toward step-by-step, experiential processing. Because of this, some of the most talented players may actually have difficulty learning and verbally articulating new concepts in a classroom environment. Again, they ultimately need to get onto the field to show you they know what they're doing. To that end, an individual's task mastery should not be based solely on his ability to comprehend a new concept and verbally articulate that task. Get him on the field and then let the video talk!

## Defenders

We were somewhat surprised to find that over half of the athletes on these two FBS rosters self-reported as introverts, most of whom were defensive players. While this might seem counterintuitive among big college rosters, we theorized that it makes sense, since many defensive players are most effective when they are able to just zone-in, read, and react. Hall of Famer Ronnie Lott is a good example of a legendary defensive back who is believed to have this psychological type. Hall of Famers Jack Lambert and Charles Haley are front-seven defenders who are also believed to be this type. These individuals are great examples of the tremendous mental instincts and fierce physical toughness displayed by athletes with this psychological type (which is called "ISTP" in this particular psychology system).

## O-Line

We found some interesting data regarding the offensive line. The O-line at "University 1" had problems with sacks surrendered, particularly in 2016, even with a dual-threat QB. They did have some injury issues and substituted more players up front over the course of the two seasons, but interestingly, the five primary starters in 2016 self-reported as all different psychological types. By contrast, "University 2" was a pure dropback team and surrendered substantially fewer sacks, even with a virtual statue starting at quarterback. Four of their five O-line starters were able to stay healthy and stick together across both the 2015 and 2016 seasons. Interestingly, however, they also self-reported psychological traits which were much more similar to each other.

Given the checks and calls O-linemen are responsible for, we theorized that players with similar traits would have more efficient verbal and especially non-verbal communication, given their psychological similarities. We recommended that coaches seek likeminded offensive linemen (based on similar psychological type, particularly at G-C-G) and attempt, as best as possible, to keep the same starters in place, in order to encourage cohesion and seamless communication up front.

## Receivers, Backs, and Specialists

Many of our findings were consistent with Jon Niednagel's previous research at www.braintypes.com. A number of what Carl Jung called both extroverted and introverted "feeling" (relationship-oriented) types were found both at running back and especially at wide receiver among the players in our study. These types of athletes are smooth, graceful striders who seem to move and play effortlessly. Marvin Harrison is a good example from Jon's research of the "introverted-feeling" type. Stefon Diggs and Michael Thomas are current players, whom Jon and Jeremy have identified as this type. Jerry Rice and Marshall Faulk are great examples of the "extroverted-feeling" types. They all appear to fit naturally at receiver and running back.

The reports of the leading individual rushers from each team in our study indicate that they were "wired" similarly to how Jon has evaluated Jim Brown and Eric Dickerson ("extroverted-thinking" or "ESTP"). It seems clear, however, that other psychological types can also do well running with the ball. For example, the aforementioned "feeling" types can obviously be excellent runners as well.

We found that three of the four starting specialists at these schools were the "extroverted-intuition" ("ENTP") type, which Jon has indicated to be the most successful among kickers and punters. Special-teams players such as Adam Vinatieri or Morten Andersen are believed to be this type. All of these particular findings were consistent with Jon's original research.

## Quarterbacks

The traditional dropback passers at "University 2" put up some impressive passing numbers in the two seasons we studied. Their reports indicate that they shared psychological traits with how Jon has evaluated modern pure passers, such as Tom Brady and Drew Brees. Notably, they were natural concept-thinkers (*intuition*), as opposed to step-by-step learners (*sensation*), like the majority of other teammates were. Conversely, the successful dual-threat quarterbacks at "University 1" were wired more similarly to how Jon has evaluated classic "old-school" guys like Brett Favre or John Elway, in that they possess traits that are much more similar to the other successful position players on their team. These findings appear to suggest that the kind of offense you want to run can benefit from knowledge of psychological traits for the best specific fit at the quarterback position.

## Introverts

More than half of the players on these two teams self-reported as introverts. Therefore, despite the large rosters and emphasis on team play, coaches can benefit by affording introverted athletes adequate space to be alone and "recharge," like a mobile phone. Examples of this may include (but are certainly not limited to) solitary access to film study, quiet study groups, individual access to the weight room, or simply free time spent near their lockers.

Perhaps more importantly, non-verbal communication is critical when you're working with a natural introvert. To gauge a response and to verify what they're thinking, you'll usually have to watch them closely and then ask them outright. Introverts won't tend to initiate a conversation, especially around a bunch of extroverts. As a rule, you'll need to ask them explicitly what they're thinking or feeling. An example would be when you're privately speaking to introverted team leaders, while you're trying to gauge the collective state of the team at large.

## Underperforming Players

In instances where a player is underperforming, it is sometimes the case that his psychological type diverges from the most common types we found in our study and that he would respond to a varied approach. For example, we found fewer *feeling* types in this particular study, as opposed to *thinking* types. They'll tend to respond more favorably to relationship-oriented word choice, such as reminders to look out for teammates and messages about family. They can sometimes put a lot of pressure on themselves, especially when things aren't going well. Visceral confrontation won't tend to be as effective with them, especially when they're in a slump.

We also found substantially fewer *intuition* types, as opposed to *sensation* types, in this particular study. As natural concept thinkers, they'll tend to learn quickly in the classroom, but they may need cues to trust sensory information and to be mindful of the present moment. Reminders to "see it before you do it" and to "trust your preparation" may be useful, especially when their game is off. They can also benefit from an emphasis on physical reps in practice in order to re-establish a skill set, even though they think they already know the idea. (Incidentally, this was something my high school coach Bob Prout did for me. He would then remind me of the old football stereotype of the "dumb, smart kid." I loved playing for him!) These are just a couple examples of using psychology to calibrate coaching points to different types of players.

## Second and Third Year

We found that the most productive players in this study saw their snaps played really jump up in the second and third years they were enrolled at each school. This makes sense, since by then they'd have a chance to integrate into each coach's respective system. It also suggests that a new college coach probably needs until his second and possibly third year to see his own recruits make an impact, even if he's going after junior college transfers.

This jump up in snaps played was particularly vivid among players in their second year with each team, during the 2016 season. These findings also coincided with the bump in success both teams demonstrated on the field during the 2016 season, both in terms of win/loss record and also offensive statistics compiled. Based on the findings from this study, athletic programs should be mindful of this time frame as they evaluate a coach's performance.

## Conclusions

For a number of reasons, football teams can benefit by investing in psychological assessments. For example, this kind of information about players can help programs with recruiting; if a coach likes to really get after his players in practice, he's going to do better with guys who are wired for that kind of intensity. Psychology assessments can also help to identify learning preferences among players. In general, to accommodate the most common learning preferences and personality styles found among players in our study, a clear teaching sequence, with an emphasis on obtaining concrete feedback from players as they learn, is expected to be most effective.

This material can help to develop specific interventions to help each individual player with his mental game. These may be especially useful, when an athlete is wired differently than most of his teammates, or where he is a unique personality type among his position group (such as a starting d-back or o-lineman who is a different psychological type than the other starters in his position group).

In addition, psychological testing can provide a resource for looking beyond race and social class issues, when assessing athletes. In order to be successful, athletes and coaches need to interact productively with individuals from all kinds of different backgrounds. These issues seem to be as sensitive as ever today, especially within the context of sports. Psych profiles are an objective way to see each other both ethically and objectively, regardless of where we each come from.

While there's more that can be said, that's a practical summary of what we found. Players, coaches, and administrators can definitely benefit from understanding and incorporating psychology research into football. I'll be happy to send you a copy of the entire study or to talk to you more about the research. Good luck with the mental game!

Thanks again,

– Joe Metzka, Ph.D.

Joemetzka@gmail.com

# REFERENCES

Baum, S. (2009). *Lie to Me*. Fox Network. MiddKidd Productions. Los Angeles, CA: 20th Century Fox Television.

Csikzentmihalyi, M. (1990). *Flow: The psychology of optimal experience* (1st ed.). New York, NY: Harper & Row.

DeYoung, C., Quilty, L., & Peterson, J. B. (2007). Between facets and domains: 10 aspects of the Big Five. *Journal of Personality and Social Psychology, 93*(5), 880-896.

Dorfman, H., & Tosca, C. (2003). *Coaching the mental game: Leadership philosophies and strategies for peak performance in sports, and everyday life.* South Bend, IN: Taylor Trade.

Edwards, H. (1973). *The sociology of sport.* New York, NY: Dorsey Press.

Ekman, P., & Friesen, W. (1971). Constants across cultures in the face and emotion. *Journal of Personality and Social Psychology, 17*(2), 124-129.

Ekman, P., & Rosenberg, E. (1997). *What the face reveals: Basic and applied studies of spontaneous expression using the Facial Action Coding System (FACS).* London, United Kingdom: Oxford University Press.

Freud, A. (1936). *The ego and mechanisms of defence.* New York, NY: International Universities Press.

Freud, S. (1931). *Libidinal types.* The standard edition of the complete psychological works of Sigmund Freud, volume XXI (1927-1931): The future of an illusion, civilization and its discontents, and other works, 215-220.

Jung, C. (1946). *Psychological types or the psychology of individuation.* London, United Kingdom: Kegan, Paul, Trench, Trubner & Co.

Jung, C. (1969). *Collected works of C. G. Jung: Vol. 9 (part 2). Aion: Researches into the phenomenology of the self.* H. G. Baynes (Trans.). Revised by G. Adler & R. F. C. Hull. Princeton, NJ: Princeton University Press.

MacCoby, M. (2007). *Narcissistic leaders: Who succeeds and who fails.* Boston, MA: First Harvard Business School Press.

MacCoby, M. (2015). *Strategic intelligence; conceptual tools for leading change.* Oxford, United Kingdom: Oxford University Press.

Madden, J., & Anderson, D. (1986). *One knee equals two feet (and everything else you need to know about football)*. New York, NY: Villard Books.

McCrae, R., & Costa, P. (1990). *Personality in adulthood.* New York, NY: Guilford Press.

Metzka, J.C. (2018). *The relationship between personality type, statistical performance and position played among elite collegiate football players.* (Doctoral dissertation). Capella University, Minneapolis, MN.

Myers, I., McCaulley, M., Quenk, N., & Hammer, A. (1998). *Manual: A guide to the development and use of the Myers-Briggs Type Indicator.* Palo Alto, CA: Consulting Psychologist Press.

Myers, P., & Myers, K. (2015). *Myers-Briggs Type Indicator, Step 1 (Form M).*

Niednagel, J. (1997). *Your key to sports success.* Palo Alto, CA: Laguna Press.

Niednagel, J. (2016). *Brain type and parenting.* Palo Alto, CA: Laguna Press.

# ABOUT THE AUTHORS

**Coach Bobby Petrino** is renowned for his work with quarterbacks, for his play-calling, and for building winning teams with innovative, high scoring offenses. His offenses have led the Big East, the SEC, and the ACC statistically in multiple years, broken in excess of 100 various school records, and ranked in the top 3 nationally in passing offense, scoring offense and total offense in multiple seasons. He holds a career win/loss record of 119-56 in NCAA Division 1/FBS play, ranking him 8th in history.

Throughout his career, he has coached and developed Pro Bowl, Heisman Trophy, and Walter Payton Trophy-winning quarterbacks. A number of his college players have gone on to successful professional careers. Coach Petrino's unique and comprehensive approach to offensive football and to coaching the quarterback is now being shared for the first time in this book. An elite athlete in his own right, Bobby was a state champion high school quarterback, as well as an NAIA All-American at Carroll (Mt.) College. Bobby and his wife Becky have four children and six grandchildren.

**Dr. Joe Metzka** is a professor of psychology at McKendree University and O'Fallon Township High School, both in suburban St. Louis. Joe is a member of www.heterodoxacademy.com. He was a small school NCAA All-American at Knox (Il.) College, and has been inducted into the I.V.C. (Il.) high school sports hall of fame. Joe coached high school football for many years. Joe and his wife, Cherie, live in suburban St. Louis. He can be reached at Joemetzka@gmail.com.